Routledge Handbook of International Criminal Law

International criminal law has developed extraordinarily quickly over the last decade, with the creation of *ad hoc* tribunals for the former Yugoslavia and Rwanda, and the establishment of a permanent International Criminal Court. This book provides a timely and comprehensive survey of emerging and existing areas of international criminal law.

The *Handbook* features new, specially commissioned papers by a range of international and leading experts in the field. It contains reflections on the theoretical aspects and contemporary debates in international criminal law.

The book is split into four parts for ease of reference:

- **The Historical and Institutional Framework**—Sets international criminal law firmly in context with individual chapters on the important developments and key institutions which have been established.
- **The Crimes**—Identifies and analyses international crimes, including a chapter on aggression.
- **The Practice of International Tribunals**—Focuses on topics relating to the practice and procedure of international criminal law.
- **Key Issues in International Criminal Law**—Goes on to explore issues of importance such as universal jurisdiction, amnesties and international criminal law and human rights.

Providing easy access to up-to-date and authoritative articles covering all key aspects of international criminal law, this book is an essential reference work for students, scholars and practitioners working in the field.

William A. Schabas is director of the Irish Centre for Human Rights at the National University of Ireland, Galway, where he also holds the chair in human rights law.

Nadia Bernaz is Lecturer in Law at Middlesex University, London.

Routledge Handbook of International Criminal Law

Edited by William A. Schabas and Nadia Bernaz

Routledge
Taylor & Francis Group
LONDON AND NEW YORK

This edition published in paperback in 2013

First published 2011
by Routledge
2 Park Square, Milton Park, Abingdon, Oxon, OX14 4RN

Simultaneously published in the USA and Canada
by Routledge
711 Third Avenue, New York, NY 10017

Routledge is an imprint of the Taylor & Francis Group, an informa business

British Library Cataloguing in Publication Data
A catalogue record for this book is available from the British Library

Library of Congress Cataloging in Publication Data
Routledge handbook of international criminal law / edited by William Schabas and Nadia Bernaz.
p. cm.
ISBN 978-0-415-55203-5 (hbk) – ISBN 978-0-415-52450-6 (pbk) –
ISBN 978-0-203-83689-7 (ebk)
1. International criminal courts. 2. International offenses. I. Schabas, William, A. 1950- II. Bernaz, Nadia. III. Title: Handbook of international criminal law.
KZ6304.R68 2011.
345-dc22 2010022449

ISBN: 978-0-415-55203-5 (hbk)
ISBN: 978-0-415-52450-6 (pbk)
ISBN: 978-0-203-83689-7 (ebk)

Typeset in Bembo by
Taylor & Francis Books

Contents

Acknowledgements

The editors are grateful to Victoria J. Moore who reviewed most of the manuscript and made constructive suggestions. We remain responsible for all the errors that may be found in this book.

Contributors

Mohamed Elewa Badar is a Lecturer in Law and Deputy Director, Centre for International and Public Law, Brunel Law School, Brunel University, London. He is the author of *Mens Rea in International Criminal Law* (Oxford: Hart, December 2010).

Nadia Bernaz (PhD, Aix-Marseilles III, France) is Lecturer in Law at Middlesex University, London (UK) and Adjunct Lecturer of the Irish Centre for Human Rights (NUI Galway, Republic of Ireland). She is the author of *Le droit international et la peine de mort* (International Law and the Death Penalty, Paris: La Documentation française, 2008) and has written and presented papers on a wide range of subjects in international law and human rights law.

Neil Boister BA, LLB, LLM (Natal), PhD (Nottingham) joined the University of Canterbury (New Zealand) from the University of Nottingham at the beginning of 2003. He teaches and researches in criminal law, international criminal law and transnational criminal law. Together with Professor Robert Cryer of the University of Birmingham he is the co-author of *The Tokyo International Military Tribunal, A Reappraisal* (Oxford University Press, 2008) 382 pp and co-editor of *Documents on the Tokyo International Military Tribunal* (Oxford University Press, 2008) 1568 pp.

León Arturo Castellanos-Jankiewicz is Licenciado en Derecho (Universidad Anáhuac Mayab, Mexico), and holds a Master in International Law from the Graduate Institute of International and Development Studies in Geneva. He is currently a PhD candidate at the Amsterdam Centre for International Law.

Nancy Amoury Combs is the Cabell Professor of Law at William and Mary Law School. She earned her JD from the University of California at Berkeley School of Law and her PhD from Leiden University. She has published extensively on topics of international criminal law.

Robert Cryer is Professor of International and Criminal Law at the University of Birmingham. He is the author, *inter alia*, of *Prosecuting International Crimes* (Cambridge, 2005), *The Tokyo International Military Tribunal: A Reappraisal* (Oxford University Press, 2008)(with Neil Boister) and *An Introduction to International Criminal Law and Procedure* (Cambridge, 2nd ed, 2010)(with Håkan Friman, Darryl Robinson and Elizabeth Wilmshurst).

Anthony Cullen BA, MA, LLM, PhD is a Researcher on the joint British Red Cross and International Committee of the Red Cross (ICRC) project to update the collection of practice underlying the ICRC's Study on Customary International Humanitarian Law. He is also a

Research Fellow at the Lauterpacht Centre for International Law and a Visiting Fellow at Wolfson College, University of Cambridge. His book *The Concept of Non-International Armed Conflict in International Humanitarian Law* was published by Cambridge University Press in April 2010.

Shane Darcy LLM, PhD is a lecturer at the Irish Centre for Human Rights, National University of Ireland, Galway. He is the associate editor of *Criminal Law Forum* and the author of *Collective Responsibility and Accountability under International Law* (Transnational, 2007).

Margaux Day is a federal judicial clerk for Judge Solomon Oliver, Jr, Federal District Court for the Northern District of Ohio, and is an Adjunct Professor at Case Western Reserve University School of Law. She was a member of the 2008 Philip C. Jessup International Moot Court World Champion Team.

Fidelma Donlon was Deputy Registrar of the Bosnian War Crimes Chamber and former Head of the Criminal Institutions and Prosecutorial Reform Unit in the Office of the High Representative. She was advisor to the Special Court for Sierra Leone on its residual issues and its residual court and the British Institute for International and Comparative Law on the 'Armed Conflict and Transitional Justice Law as a Solution' EU project. She is a PhD candidate at the Irish Centre for Human Rights, National University of Ireland.

Margaret M. deGuzman is Assistant Professor of Law, Temple University Beasley School of Law. Professor deGuzman teaches and writes about international criminal law and was a legal advisor to the Senegal delegation at the Rome Conference on the International Criminal Court.

Fiona de Londras BCL, LLM, PhD (NUI) is a lecturer in the School of Law, University College Dublin, where she is also affiliated with the Institute of Criminology. She has published on terrorism and counter-terrorism in journals such as the *Oxford Journal of Legal Studies, Modern Law Review* and *Israel Law Review*.

Mohamed M. El Zeidy (PhD, National University of Ireland, Galway) is a Legal Officer at the Pre-Trial Division of the International Criminal Court. Prior to his current position, he served as a judge and senior public prosecutor in Egypt (1997–2007). He is widely published in international criminal law, the author of *The Principle of Complementarity in International Criminal Law* (Martinus Nijhoff, 2008) and co-editor of *The ICC and Complementarity from Theory to Practice* (Cambridge University Press, 2010).

Carla Ferstman is Director of REDRESS (www.redress.org).

Håkan Friman is Deputy Director-General at the Swedish Ministry of Justice, Division for Criminal Cases and International Judicial Cooperation. He is visiting Professor at University College London, Faculty of Laws, a Member of the Swedish ICC Delegation and the co-author of *An Introduction to International Criminal Law and Procedure* (Cambridge: Cambridge University Press, 2nd edn, 2010).

Paola Gaeta is full Professor at the Law Faculty of the University of Geneva, Adjunct Professor at the Graduate Institute of International and Development Studies and Director of the LLM Programme of the Geneva Academy of International Humanitarian Law and Human Rights.

Her publications include *The Rome Statute of the International Criminal Court* (ed. with A. Cassese and J. R. W. D. Jones), 2002, and *The UN Genocide Convention. A Commentary* (ed,). 2009.

Louise Mallinder is a lecturer at the Transitional Justice Institute, University of Ulster. She has published her doctoral thesis as *Amnesty, Human Rights and Political Transitions: Bridging the Peace and Justice Divide* (Hart Publishing, 2008) and this monograph was awarded the 2009 Hart SLSA Early Career Award and was jointly awarded the 2009 British Society of Criminology Book Prize. Before starting the lectureship in November 2009, Louise worked as a research fellow on a two-year AHRC-funded research project which investigated the impact of amnesty laws within Argentina, Bosnia-Herzegovina, South Africa, Uganda and Uruguay.

Thomas Margueritte is a PhD candidate at the Centre de Recherches Internationales et Communautaires of the Université Paul Cézanne (Aix Marseille III, France). His research interests are international criminal law, international humanitarian law and human rights. Prior to this, he was a fellow of the Court of Bosnia Herzegovina.

Guénaël Mettraux appears as counsel and consultant before international criminal jurisdictions. He is a guest Professor at the University of Leiden and at the Academy of Humanitarian Law (Geneva) and has published extensively, including three books published by *Oxford University Press*.

Joseph Powderly is Researcher in International Criminal and International Humanitarian Law at the TMC Asser Instituut, The Hague. He is a PhD candidate at the Irish Centre for Human Rights, and was awarded a Government of Ireland Postgraduate Scholarship in 2008. He is a contributor and co-editor with Dr Shane Darcy of *Judicial Creativity in International Criminal Tribunals*, which will be published by Oxford University Press in 2010.

Kimberly Prost is an *ad litem* judge at the ICTY. She was formerly Chief of the Legal Advisory Section UNODC, Head of Criminal Law Section Commonwealth Secretariat and Head of Canadian International Assistance Group. She was a member of the Canadian delegation for the negotiation of the Rome Statute and she is the author of several publications on the ICC, international criminal law and international cooperation in criminal matters.

Rémy Prouvèze is a researcher at the Centre d'Etudes et de Recherches Internationales et Communautaires (CERIC) in Aix-en-Provence (France). Specializing in public international law and international criminal law (publishing several papers in these fields), he was awarded a PhD for his study on *Immunity from Criminal Jurisdiction of State Authorities in International Law* at the *Université Paul Cézanne* in Aix-en-Provence in 2006.

Luc Reydams is an Associate Professional Specialist in the Department of Political Science at the University of Notre Dame. He is the author of *Universal Jurisdiction: International and Municipal Legal Perspectives* (Oxford: Oxford University Press, 2003) and the editor of the *Global Activism Reader* (forthcoming with Continuum Publishing).

Leila Nadya Sadat is the Henry H. Oberschelp Professor of Law and Director of the Whitney R. Harris World Law Institute at the Washington University School of Law (USA). The author of more than 50 articles and several books, and the recipient of several academic prizes, Professor

Sadat is well-known for her work in international criminal law and human rights. Professor Sadat holds leadership positions in several learned societies, has served as a Commissioner on the United States Commission for International Religious Freedom, and will serve as the Alexis de Tocqueville Distinguished Fulbright Chair (Paris, France) in Spring 2011.

William A. Schabas is director of the Irish Centre for Human Rights at the National University of Ireland, Galway, where he holds the chair in human rights law. He is also a Global Legal Scholar at the University of Warwick, in the United Kingdom, and honorary professor at the Chinese Academy of Social Sciences, in Beijing. He is the author of more than 20 books and 275 journal articles, on such subjects as the abolition of capital punishment, genocide and the international criminal tribunals. Professor Schabas was a member of the Sierra Leone Truth and Reconciliation Commission. He is the chairman of the Board of Trustees of the United Nations Voluntary Fund for Technical Cooperation in Human Rights. He is an Officer of the Order of Canada and a member of the Royal Irish Academy.

Michael P. Scharf is the John Deaver Drinko-Baker & Hostetler Professor of Law, and Director of the Frederick K. Cox International Law Center, at Case Western Reserve University School of Law. He is also Managing Director of the Public International Law & Policy Group, an NGO that provides pro bono legal assistance to governments and international tribunals related to prosecution of war crimes.

David Scheffer is the Mayer Brown/Robert A. Helman Professor of Law and Director of the Center for International Human Rights at Northwestern University School of Law, Chicago, Illinois. He was the US Ambassador at Large for War Crimes Issues from 1997 to 2001.

Nicolaos Strapatsas (LLB UQAM, LLM NUIG) is a doctoral Candidate at the Irish Centre for Human Rights (National University of Ireland, Galway) and a lecturer at the University of Quebec at Montreal. He also is the associate editor of *Criminal Law Forum*.

Eric Wiebelhaus-Brahm is currently a Senior Research Fellow at the International Human Rights Law Institute at DePaul University. His publications include *Truth Commissions and Transitional Societies: The Impact on Human Rights and Democracy* (Routledge, 2010).

Eric Wyler is Professor of International Law and has taught at the following Universities: Neuchâtel, Lausanne, Geneva, Paris II-Pantheon Assas and Paris I-Sorbonne (Visiting Professor). He currently is associated Professor at SciencesPo, Paris, Chargé d'enseignement at the Graduate Institute of International Studies (HEID), Geneva, and at the European Institute of the University of Geneva. He is the author of *L'illicite et la condition des personnes privées* (1995), *L'éthique du droit international* (1997, with Alain Papaux), *L'extranéité ou le dépassement de l'ordre juridique étatique* (1999, Wyler-Papaux, ed.).

Introduction

William A. Schabas and Nadia Bernaz

The chapter headings of this handbook provide a good indication of the meaning of the term 'international criminal law'. Nevertheless, it is not a simple matter to furnish a succinct definition. The French language distinguishes between *droit international pénal* and *droit pénal international*. The difference between the two terms seems to reside largely in the types of crimes they address. Thus, *droit pénal international* refers to a body of law governing relationships between states in the suppression of so-called ordinary crimes, such as murder and rape, as well as organized criminal activity when it takes on an international dimension. By contrast, *droit international pénal* is focussed on crimes that are international in nature, generally because of their cross-border or transnational dimensions. Piracy is the classic example.

But when today's lawyers and specialists talk of 'international criminal law', they are rarely talking about piracy. Rather, the focus is on crimes that are also, by and large, gross and systematic violations of human rights: genocide, crimes against humanity and war crimes. The acts underlying these offences, which are said to 'shock the conscience of humanity', have been perpetrated since the beginning of human society. However, their codification as international crimes is a recent phenomenon.

The first efforts at defining international war crimes were made at the Paris Peace Conference in 1919. There is a list in the report of the Commission on Responsibilities that includes murders, torture, rape and the murder (but not the taking) of hostages, as well as acts that today would not figure in a list of international crimes, such as destruction of fishing boats and poisoning of wells. The post-world war period was only a foretaste. The first really dynamic period began in the final months of the Second World War. It brought with it a recognition of three new categories of international crime: genocide, crimes against humanity and crimes against peace. The international military tribunals that sat at Nuremberg and Tokyo were the first truly international trials. But in the early 1950s, it all ground to a halt.

International criminal law went through its great renaissance in the 1990s. This exciting period is still continuing, and there is no end in sight. It has brought with it new institutions, most of them temporary, but also a permanent addition: the International Criminal Court. The definitions of crimes have been fine-tuned and refreshed. Moreover, the field has become more complex to the extent that it actively involves national justice systems. It is associated with a concept known as transitional justice, which views criminal accountability for atrocity as a necessary stage as states recover from conflict, and especially civil wars. The dynamism of international criminal law is in large part associated with growth and excitement in two cognate areas—international human rights law and international humanitarian law (the law of armed conflict).

Eminent scholars in this new discipline have contributed the chapters in this handbook. It is intended to provide readers with an accessible introduction to the field, and a guide to further research. It may serve as both a reference volume and a textbook and is divided into four parts.

Part I sets the scene by presenting past experiences—the Nuremberg and Tokyo Trials and a selection of domestic trials involving crimes committed during the Second World War—as well as contemporary institutions: the permanent International Criminal Court and temporary tribunals, purely international and hybrid. Part II presents the crimes, focusing on the 'core' crimes—genocide, crimes against humanity and war crimes—but also dedicating specific chapters to aggression, the crime of terrorism and other crimes such as drug trafficking and money laundering. Part III aims at portraying the practice of international tribunals and covers the issues of jurisdiction, admissibility, procedure and evidence. It also goes into the different modes of participation in crimes, defences and sentencing. Finally, Part III examines the key issues of state cooperation and transfers. In Part IV, the last of the book, the authors explore a selection of relevant issues in the field of international criminal law and, more largely, post-conflict justice: universal jurisdiction, immunities, truth commissions, state responsibility and international crimes, victims' rights, amnesties and a chapter on international criminal law and human rights.

Part I

Historical and institutional framework

1
Trial at Nuremberg

Guénaël Mettraux

The road to Nuremberg, in short

The Second World War witnessed the commission of crimes of unprecedented brutality and scale. The magnitude and cruelty of these events presented a challenge to the Allied leaders charged with determining the fate of those thought to be responsible for these crimes. Given their nature, it was agreed that they could not go unpunished. However, the choice of means and methods of punishment was far from self-evident. As one author pointed out, '[t]he "law" of an armistice or a treaty is, in the final analysis, the will of the victor'. Hence, the Allied Powers considered a whole range of political and executive responses that did not involve any legal or judicial elements.[1] However, neither retaliation nor brutal reprisal were capable of bringing a sense of justice to victims whilst at the same time helping to restore peace to the continent.[2] The view that eventually prevailed was that those suspected of committing these crimes should be subject to a judicial process that would investigate and pass judgment on their individual responsibility. Henry Stimson understood too well the symbolic value of giving the defendants rights and privileges associated with a genuine judicial process that they had denied so systematically to those who had opposed them: 'We gave to the Nazis what they had denied their own opponents—the protection of the Law'.[3] In that sense, what would become the Nuremberg Tribunal was not intended to be an instrument of vengeance, 'but the reverse'.[4]

The fact that the decision to subject the accused to a judicial process might have been motivated as much by laudable ideals of justice as by the lack of appeal of the alternatives[5] should not detract from the extraordinary advance that this decision represented:

> It is the virtue of the Nuremberg trial that it was conceived in hatred of war, and was nurtured by those starved of peace. To realize how grateful we should be for this birth, consider the alternative.[6]

In some ways, the decision to punish these crimes after a criminal trial was born of the failure to do so after the First World War, a bitter lesson not lost on the Allied Powers.[7] And so, the idea that the Nazi leaders should be put on trial grew ever more popular over the course of the war.[8] Already, on 25 October 1941, Churchill had announced that '[r]etribution for these crimes must henceforward take its place among the major purposes of the war'.[9] A few months later, representatives of nine occupied countries adopted the Declaration of St James Palace, which placed among the Allied's 'principal war aims' the following:

> the punishment, through the channel of organized justice, of those guilty and responsible for these crimes, whether they have ordered them, perpetrated them or in any way participated in them, [and to] determine in a spirit of international solidarity to see to it that (a) those guilty and responsible, whatever their nationality, are sought for, handed over to justice and judged, (b) that the sentences pronounced are carried out.

President Roosevelt of the United States echoed this Declaration, saying that those responsible for these crimes 'shall have to stand in courts of law . . . and answer for their acts'.[10] Shortly thereafter, on 7 October 1942, the United Nations War Crimes Commission was created to gather and collect information regarding the commission of and responsibility for these international crimes.[11] The push towards a judicial response to these atrocities continued to gain momentum and, on 30 October 1943, the leaders of the United States, the United Kingdom, and the USSR adopted a Statement on Atrocities, which formed part of the Moscow Declaration and provided as follows:

> At the time of granting any armistice to any government which may be set up in Germany, those German officers and men and members of the Nazi Party who have been responsible for or have taken a consenting part in the above atrocities, massacres and executions will be sent back to the countries in which their abominable deeds were done in order that they be judged and punished according to the laws of these liberated countries of free governments which will be erected therein. . . . The above declaration is without prejudice to the case of German criminals whose offenses have no particular geographical localization and who will be punished by joint decision of the government of the Allies.[12]

As the war was nearing its end, representatives of the same three great powers, plus France, sat down to negotiate the terms of what would eventually become the Charter of an international criminal tribunal based in Nuremberg, Germany. These negotiations were not without their problems, as differences of views as to the purpose of the trial and the procedures to be applied led to lengthy and sometimes quite acrimonious exchanges between the four sets of negotiators.[13] What the delegates faced, Justice Robert H. Jackson is recorded as saying, was 'the legal equivalent of drafting the Ten Commandments'.[14] But on 8 August 1945, the governments of the four negotiating powers eventually signed the London Agreement, which provided for the creation of an International Military Tribunal for the trial of war criminals 'whose offences have no particular geographical location whether they may be accused individually or in their capacity as members of organizations or groups or in both capacities'.[15] With this agreement, the four Signatories had given life to an *ad hoc*, military, and international criminal tribunal, which was to apply a mostly new set of rules and principles to exceptional events.[16] The constitution, jurisdiction, and functions of the Tribunal were set out in the Charter of the Tribunal, which was annexed to the Agreement.[17]

The adoption of the London Agreement was itself quite a feat of politics and diplomacy as it would prove to be one of the last significant international agreements of that era between a group of countries that would soon become opponents in the Cold War. From a legal perspective, too, the adoption of the Agreement and the Charter was a commendable achievement.[18] That achievement was the creation of a genuinely international body of criminal law capable of universal application that brought together several different legal traditions. 'The significance of the international character of the Nuremberg and Tokyo tribunals', Nuremberg Prosecutor Telford Taylor noted, 'was a recognition of the inadequacy of single-nation courts for authoritative interpretations of international law, and the necessity of establishing an international jurisdiction and working acceptable international procedures if international penal law was to develop at all satisfactorily'.[19] However, as he himself noted, the international character of that process was also one of its main weaknesses, as it amplified the legal 'exceptionalism' of the Nuremberg Tribunal and its successors:

> The shortcoming of the tribunals was that, although international, they were unilateral; they were constituted by the victor nations and had jurisdiction only over the vanquished, and this circumstance has remained a negative factor in subsequent evaluation of the trials.[20]

Some, indeed, decried what they saw as victor's justice—political vengeance under the cloak of justice.[21] Victory, however, in its military form, was a condition of justice.[22] What could be criticized is not the manner in which justice was delivered at Nuremberg, which most agree was fair, but the fact that the mandate of the judicial institution that was tasked to deliver justice was so openly selective and one-sided.

The Nuremberg Charter and Nuremberg Tribunal

Whilst some claimed that the Charter of the Nuremberg Tribunal merely codified existing principles, others were more forthcoming in acknowledging that, in fact, a great deal of it was new law. Before the Charter had even been adopted, Glueck had acknowledged the need for the law to grow to meet the demands of the day:

> In a relatively undeveloped and plastic field of law it is but following an historical process to blend 'political' with legal concepts in stimulating the growth of standards and principles. Much of the law of nations has its roots in custom. Custom must have a beginning; and customary usages of States in the matter of national and personal liability for resort to prohibited methods of warfare and to wholesale criminalism have not been petrified for all time. 'International Law was not crystallized in the seventeenth century, but is a living and expanding code'.[23]

The defeat of Germany, the destruction of Europe, the anger of the world, and the irrelevance to which international law had been reduced by the war all provided fuel for a decisive and 'rare legislative moment'.[24] If there was no law to punish these crimes, it was the general view that law should be made. And so it was.

The Charter, a short document of 30 articles, does not abandon altogether the principle of *nullum crimen sine lege*, but rejects its literal application, maintaining this principle only in 'the spirit or the idea conveyed by it'.[25] Thus, despite protestations that crimes listed in the Charter were existing criminal prohibitions prior to that time, this document created new categories of international crimes: namely, 'crimes against humanity' and 'crimes against peace', in addition to existing ones ('war crimes').[26] The Charter also put to rest defenses which, until then, had arguably formed part of the accepted standards of international law, such as the defense of 'superior orders' and official immunity for 'acts of state'.[27] The Charter may thus be said to have adopted as *law* what, for a while, had been in a state of hesitancy. The Charter of the Tribunal was at once a codification of and a contribution to international law.

The Charter did not just add or remove pieces from existing international law. It also marked a paradigm shift in the international legal—and, arguably, political—universe. First, the Charter pierced through the concept of state sovereignty and inflicted much damage to the idea of absolute sovereignty under the law. As already noted, the Charter literally retired vibrant legal symbols of the idea of state sovereignty—namely, the doctrine of 'acts of state'—and caused official immunities to shrink, including those granted to heads of state.[28] By criminalizing breaches of law committed against a state's own citizens under the label of 'crimes against humanity' and setting penal limits to the permissible use of military force through 'crimes against peace', the Charter reached deep into the sovereign territory of states.

Second, and no less significantly, the Charter recognized individuals as subjects of international law, with consequent rights and obligations. Article 6 of the Charter expressly provided that '[l]eaders, organizers, instigators and accomplices participating in the formulation or execution of a common plan or conspiracy to commit any of [the crimes listed in the Charter] are responsible for all acts performed by any persons in execution of such plan'. Liability was, therefore, individual and penal in character and arose directly from international law. As for rights of individuals, they were perhaps more insidiously implanted into the Charter. In *The Subjects of the Law of Nations*, Professor Lauterpacht noted the following about the new concept of 'crimes against humanity':

> Thus upon analysis, the enactment of crimes against humanity in an international instrument signifies the acknowledgement of fundamental rights of the individual recognised by international law. It is possible that this result did not occur to the authors of the Charter nor, perhaps, to the Tribunal which applied it. Yet, unless the Charter is conceived as an *ad hoc* piece of vindictive legislation enacted by the victor against the vanquished, this is its inevitable and logical result. In terms of law, to the conception of crimes against humanity there must correspond the notion of fundamental human rights recognised by international law and, as a further result, of an international status of the individual whose rights have thus been recognised.[29]

The Charter also contained innovations of a procedural sort. It provided a set of rules and procedural principles for the prosecution and trial of international crimes before an international criminal tribunal.[30] This rather scanty regime was later fleshed out by a set of rules of procedure and evidence, which the Tribunal adopted in accordance with its powers under Article 13 of the Charter.[31] However, the actual conduct of the proceedings and most of the evidential decisions were left almost exclusively to the discretion of the Judges, which effectively resulted in a combination of features and practices from the common law and civil law traditions.[32] Rulings did not always remain consistent throughout the proceedings, but the concern of the Judges was, first and foremost, to ensure fairness rather than to create a theoretically satisfactory regime of procedural and evidential rules and principles.

The Bench consisted of four Judges and four alternates, one for each nation represented.[33] Lord Lawrence, of the United Kingdom, was chosen by his colleagues to preside over the case, which he did with great skill and diplomacy. Prosecutors, too, came from the four original Signatories of the London Agreement. Prior to trial, they divided among themselves the responsibility of presenting the Prosecution's case, although ultimate control over the case was and remained to a very large extent in the hands of the American prosecution team.[34] As for the defendants, they were all represented by German counsel, whose ability varied greatly, but whose commitment to the defense of their clients no doubt contributed to the perception that these proceedings were fair and judicial in nature.

The indictment and the trial

An indictment was filed on 20 October 1945 against 24 defendants. Charges under Count 1 (Common Plan or Conspiracy) were brought against all of the defendants; charges under Count 2 (Crimes against Peace) against 16 of them; charges under Count 3 (War Crimes) against 18; and charges under Count 4 (Crimes against Humanity) against 18 of them.[35] A number of groups and organizations were also charged with being 'criminal groups or organizations', pursuant to Article 9 of the Charter.[36]

The defendants effectively represented a 'sample' of the criminality of the Nazi regime and its affiliates. Some, like Fritzsche, were selected in large part because others—in his case, Goebbels—were dead or unavailable. Bormann, who could not be located and who was probably already dead at the time, was tried *in absentia*. Because of his mental state, it was considered that Gustav Krupp, who had been indicted as a symbol of the contribution of German industrialism to the Nazi regime, could not be tried *in absentia*, and his case was therefore separated from those of the other defendants.[37] Robert Ley committed suicide before the trial started, so that only 21 of the 24 original indictees were tried in their presence by the Nuremberg Tribunal and one (Bormann) in his absence.

The trial commenced on 20–21 November 1945 with the memorable opening speech delivered by Chief US Prosecutor Robert H. Jackson, who was on leave from the US Supreme Court. His words set the tone of the entire enterprise, a tone of 'melancholy grandeur' as Jackson described it,[38] dispassionate but fully conscious of the historical significance of the process:

> The privilege of opening the first trial in history for crimes against the peace of the world imposes a grave responsibility. The wrongs which we seek to condemn and punish have been so calculated, so malignant and so devastating, that civilisation cannot tolerate their being ignored, because it cannot survive their being repeated. That four great nations, flushed with victory and stung with injury, stay the hands of vengeance and voluntarily submit their captive enemies to the judgment of the law, is one of the most significant tributes that Power ever has paid to Reason.
>
> This Tribunal, while it is novel and experimental, is not the product of abstract speculations nor is it created to vindicate legalistic theories. This inquest represents the practical effort of four of the most mighty of nations, with the support of seventeen more, to utilize International Law to meet the greatest menace of our times—aggressive war . . . Merely as individuals [the prisoner's] fate is of little consequence to the world. What makes this inquest significant is that these prisoners represent sinister influences that will lurk in the world long after their bodies have returned to dust.[39]

The trial was conducted, simultaneously, in four languages: English, French, Russian, and German. Both sides called witnesses and produced a large amount of evidential material. Because he thought that the record would be less impeachable in that way, Jackson had decided that the Prosecution case would primarily consist of documents—of which 90 percent or so had come from the Nazis' own archives—rather than witnesses.[40] The record of the trial eventually bulked up to 17,000 pages of shorthand record from 403 open sessions, and the evidence included approximately 185,000 pages of 'prosecution document books', as well as many thousand pages of affidavits.[41] The actual presentation of the Prosecution and Defense cases took approximately eight months. In the words of a Nuremberg Prosecutor, the Nuremberg trial was 'the greatest murder trial of record, covering, in a conservative estimate, six or seven million homicides'.[42]

The trial of 22 Nazi leaders at Nuremberg could hardly be impeached for having lacked fairness. Instead, the trial has come to stand as a symbol of fairness and justice both because of the horrors of the crimes that were subject to that inquiry and because those who controlled the judicial process could so easily have decided to depart from those principles guaranteed in all democratic legal orders, and yet did not. As I have suggested somewhere else,

> [t]he Nuremberg trial now stands as proof of the proposition that an international criminal tribunal armed with the right tools and driven by a legitimate call for justice is capable of engineering a fair and impartial trial for those who have violated the most basic tenets of international law. The fairness of these proceedings explains that today the Nuremberg trial forms part of our collective memory both as the record of the great crimes committed by the defendants, but also, most importantly, as a symbol of justice.[43]

But for rare exceptions, the trial was described by witnesses as a rather boring affair—lengthy, technical and lacking the expected dramatic tension. One observer of the trial noted that '[t]here were no fanfares of victory at Nuremberg. It was a patient inquiry by a world that had just experienced the immensity of total war'.[44] That quality, however, and the 'product' that resulted from the trial might be the Tribunal's most enduring legacies. Here was a genuinely judicial review of facts that produced a detailed record of historical events and incidents spanning half a decade and a continent. In 10 or so months, 'five and a half days a week, six hours per day',[45] a small group of men and women, judges, prosecutors, and defense counsel, recreated in a German courtroom a miniature version of the war and its criminal artifacts, subjecting it to the acid test of the law and to the most robust of challenges from the defendants.

The Judgment

The Judgment of the Tribunal was rendered over two days on 30 September and 1 October 1946. The public gallery was full once again, and a great deal of anxiety was apparent among the defendants. Judges took turns reading the 200-page verdict.

The Tribunal was bound, the Judgment says, by the terms of the Charter. The law of the Charter existed for them to apply, not to question.[46] It was clear to the Judges, however, that they would have been criticized had they failed altogether to address the justice of the law that they were asked to apply to this group of men. A memorandum of 5 October 1945 was sent to Judge Biddle and Judge Parker advising them that '[t]he justice of the Agreement must be confronted in any event in determining what punishment—of those convicted—is just'.[47] That advice was duly followed, and the Judges subjected most, though not all, aspects of the Charter to a study of their consistency with existing international law and expressed the general view that the terms of that document were consistent therewith, whilst in some respects representing a permissible development of existing standards:

> The Charter is not an arbitrary exercise of power on the part of the victorious nations, but in the view of the Tribunal . . . it is the expression of international law existing at the time of its creation; and to that extent is itself a contribution to international law.

To the credit of the Tribunal, 'it did not evade in this manner the issue whether the Charter is derogatory from, or declaratory of, international customary law'.[48] In so doing, the Tribunal transformed the law applied to 22 men into a universal set of prohibitions capable of general and universal application.

The Judgment cannot, however, be regarded in purely neutral fashion, as it is, in some respects, a compromise and, in others, a progressive development of international law.

Compromise is particularly evident as regards the concept of common plan or conspiracy, with which the French judges, and to a lesser extent, the Russian ones, had difficulties. As a result of their concerns, the concept was interpreted narrowly and conservatively by the Tribunal. An equally narrow reading of the concept of 'criminal organizations' was adopted as the Judges feared that a more extensive interpretation might later result in the conviction of individuals for little more than their membership and the most remote of relationship to crimes committed by others. The generally cautious approach of the Tribunal limited the potential scope of application of these notions, but it also protected their integrity as criminal prohibitions.[49]

The Tribunal's jurisprudential conservatism had limits. In fact, much of law that the Judges applied had been new when it was first adopted in the London Agreement. The Judges' contribution to this new set of principles was to develop and articulate an argument, quite convincingly in some respects, that these standards had preexisted their Judgment. In a memorandum of 10 July 1946, Judge Biddle was strongly advised to provide intellectual muscle to the legal reasoning contained in the Judgment:

> It is essential to state the views of the Tribunal as to just what the international law *was*. It is not too cynical to point out that whether it was or was not before your honors spoke, from the period when you do so speak it *is* the law.[50]

The record of the discussion of the draft Judgment suggests that Judge Biddle was fully receptive to that advice:

> The General [Steer] asks why a discussion of the law is necessary and I [Francis Biddle] suggest why it is advisable to show this is not *ex post facto*.[51]

The Tribunal thus convinced itself and many others that crimes against humanity, crimes against peace, and the other standards laid down in the Charter did not constitute new law. In so doing, the Charter and the Judgment of the Tribunal solidified in law what, in many respects, had, until that time, constituted part of our moral, rather than legal, world. In that sense, Nuremberg may be said to have brought 'our law in balance with the universal moral judgment of mankind'.[52] As for the principle of legality, which defendants had said would prevent the Tribunal from taking such a course, the Judges treated it not as a limitation of sovereignty, but as a principle of justice. The question was thus, as Judge Biddle later explained, not whether it was *lawful* to try Goering and his colleagues, but whether it was *just* to do so.[53]

Where the Tribunal was perhaps most successful is in convincing the world that individuals could be criminally liable as a matter of international law, rejecting in passing the Defense arguments that international law only provided liability for states, not individuals. 'Crimes against international law', the Tribunals said, 'are committed by men, not by abstract entities, and only by punishing individuals who commit such crimes can the provisions of international law be enforced'.[54] The Tribunal added that the obligations that are binding upon individuals as a matter of international law are superior and must be given precedence over their national duties and obligations:

> Individuals have international duties which transcend the national obligations of obedience imposed by the individual state. He who violates the laws of war cannot obtain immunity while acting in pursuance of the authority of the state if the state in authorizing action moves outside its competence under international law.[55]

Commenting years after the Judgment, Telford Taylor observed that the Judgment of the Tribunal had contributed to an expansion of criminal liability, not just vertically, but also horizontally:

> The Nuremberg extensions of criminal liability were not only vertical but also horizontal. Generals and admirals were by no means the only defendants. Cabinet ministers and other civilian officials were a majority of those put to trial, and there were also a number of individuals who were 'private' in the sense that their criminal liability was not primarily charged on the basis of whatever government connections they may have had, but by reason of their responsibilities as directors of large industrial concerns where foreign 'slave' labor was extensively utilized under inhumane conditions.[56]

No less impressive was the Tribunal's effort to establish the facts that formed the background of the charges—those of a bloody war that had destroyed nations and an entire continent. In that sense, the Judgment of the Nuremberg Tribunal made an important, and perhaps a central, contribution to the historiography of the Second World War.[57]

At the end of the case, three of the accused—Schacht, Fritzsche, and von Papen—were acquitted of all charges. For those who were convicted, sentences ranged from a 10-year imprisonment for Doenitz to death by hanging for 12 of the defendants. The Soviet member of the Tribunal dissented with respect to the acquittal of Schacht, von Papen, Fritzsche and in relation to Hess insofar as he would have sentenced him to death.[58] But as his colleague Francis Biddle pointed out, the dissent of the Soviet member 'involved no disagreement with the majority Judgment on the fundamental principles of international law, but only over the inferences that should be drawn from conflicting evidence'.[59]

Before his sentence was carried out, and a day after his appeal for clemency to the Control Council had been rejected, Goering committed suicide by swallowing a cyanide capsule that had been smuggled into his cell, possibly by one of the guards. The other 11 defendants sentenced to death were executed and their ashes dispersed. Hess died in 1987 in the Spandau prison where he was detained and where, for some time, he had been the only occupant.

Conclusion—the legacy of a historical trial

It has been said in relation to the Nuremberg process that '[w]here hopes have been pitched unreasonably high, disappointment is apt to be equally exaggerated'.[60] To a limited extent, this statement contains a grain of truth in relation to Nuremberg. No code of international criminal law was ever drafted based on Nuremberg's lessons, despite suggestions it should be done in order to make the law of the Nuremberg trial truly universal. War crimes prosecutions were and remained for a long time one-sided, creating a sense of injustice and selectivity among many Germans and others. Some of the law that the Tribunal had sanctioned as forming part of the law common to all nations was not accepted as such, most evidently in the case of the prohibition of aggressive war. But most of what made up 'the law of Nuremberg' has stuck, and it now constitutes the core of what contemporary tribunals regard as being part of customary international law.

The principles laid down in the Judgment of the Nuremberg Tribunal did not fall by the wayside after they had been used against the Nazi leaders. They served as the basis for the thousands of subsequent prosecutions undertaken all over Europe in the aftermath of the war. On 11 December 1946, the United Nations General Assembly adopted Resolution 95(I), affirming the principles of international law recognized by the Charter and the Judgment of the Tribunal.[61]

These principles, as identified and presented by the International Law Commission, were never formally adopted—nor, as Professor Cassese rightly points out, rejected—by the General Assembly.[62] However, the resolution of the General Assembly indicated as follows:

> a recognition that judicial not political action had been taken, that Nuremberg did not signify an ephemerical [*sic*], opportunistic deviation from the established rules, but a permanent, irrevocable change, and that it was not a unilateral provision, but general law, binding the whole community, which had been applied.[63]

Furthermore, these principles continued to live on. They found a new home half a century later in new *ad hoc* international criminal tribunals created to deal with the situations of the former Yugoslavia, Rwanda, Sierra Leone, and other places. These and a number of national tribunals have applied not just the law but also the spirit of Nuremberg to new circumstances, thereby turning that trial and its jurisprudential legacy into a genuine precedent.[64]

More significant still may be the fact that Nuremberg happened at all. 'For the first time in history', Whitney Harris pointed out, 'the judicial process was brought to bear against those who had offended the conscience of humanity by committing acts of military aggression and related crimes'.[65] The Nuremberg trial thus brought a needed sense of justice and comfort to the millions who had suffered from the crimes of the Nazi regime:

> [E]vil unpunished deprives us of a sense of moral symmetry in life, and [to] punish evil has a healthy cathartic effect, confirming our belief in the ultimate triumph of good over evil. Nuremberg may have been flawed law, but it was satisfying justice.[66]

Nuremberg contributed significantly to eroding the idea that mass atrocities would necessarily go unpunished, and it set an important historical record of the crimes committed during the Second World War. 'The purpose of the Nuremberg trial', Jackson said after the trial, 'was not merely, or even principally, to convict the leaders of Nazi Germany and affix a punishment upon them commensurate with their guilt. Of far greater importance, it seemed to me from the outset, was the making of a record of the Hitler regime which would withstand the test of history'.[67] This it certainly succeeded in doing, and the trial itself has become a part of that history.

Finally, the Nuremberg proceedings provided both a general architecture and the philosophical underpinning for a new international penal legal order that is still being built. It was an attempt to 'replace the role of force by the rule of law'.[68] It was also a symbol of Man's resistance to its own inhumanity. While it might not have been the first root of international criminal law, Nuremberg might still be the most important and strongest of all its foundations.

Notes

1 S. Glueck, 'The Nuremberg Trial and Aggressive War', *Harvard Law Review*, 1945–1946, vol. 59, 396, reprinted in G. Mettraux (ed.), *Perspectives on the Nuremberg Trial*, Oxford: Oxford University Press, 2008, pp. 72, 74. It was the generally accepted view at the time that by right of *debellatio*, the victors could do with Germany as they pleased and that they were, therefore, permitted to create a judicial institution to try its leaders. See e.g. G. Schwarzenberger, 'The Judgment of Nuremberg', *Tulane Law Review*, 1947, vol. 21, 329, reprinted in Mettraux, *Perspectives on Nuremberg*, p. 167, at 169, 174–5.

2 For an account of the history of the making of the Nuremberg Tribunal, see generally G. J. Bass, *Stay the Hand of Vengeance—The Politics of War Crimes Tribunals*, Princeton: Princeton University Press, 2000. See also A. Tusa and J. Tusa, *The Nuremberg Trial*, New York: Atheneum, 1983, p. 24.

3 H. Stimson, 'The Nuremberg Trial, Landmark in Law', *Foreign Affairs*, January 1947, vol. 25, 179, reprinted in Mettraux, *Perspectives on Nuremberg*, p. 617.

4 F. Biddle, 'The Nuremberg Trial', *American Philosophical Society Proceedings*, August 1947, vol. 91, 294, reprinted in Mettraux, *Perspectives on Nuremberg*, p. 200, at 202.

5 G. Mettraux, 'Judicial Inheritance: The Value and Significance of the Nuremberg Trial to Contemporary War Crimes Tribunals', in Mettraux, *Perspectives on Nuremberg*, p. 599, at 602.

6 R. West, 'Foreword', in A. Neave, *Nuremberg—A Personal Record of the Trial of the Major Nazi War Criminals*, London: Hodder and Stoughton, 1978.

7 See e.g. Tusa and Tusa, *Nuremberg*, pp. 19, 29. After the trial, Justice Jackson observed that to expect the Germans to bring their leaders to justice was 'out of question': 'That was proved by the farcical experiment after World War I'. R. H. Jackson, 'Introduction', in Whitney R. Harris, *Tyranny on Trial—The Evidence at Nuremberg*, New York, Transaction Publishers, 1997, reprinted (in edited and redrafted fashion) in Mettraux, *Perspectives on Nuremberg*, p. 697, at 699.

8 See, generally, B. Smith, *The American Road to Nuremberg—The Documentary Record*, Stanford, CA: Hoover Press Publication, 1982. See also *Nuremberg: A History of US Military Government*, issued by the US Forces European Theater, 1946.

9 *US Department of State Bulletin*, vol. 5, 317, 1941.

10 R. Jackson, 'Nuremberg in Retrospect: Legal Answer to International Lawlessness', *American Bar Association Journal*, 1949, vol. 35, 813, reprinted in Mettraux, *Perspectives on Nuremberg*, p. 354, at 356.

11 *US Department of State Bulletin*, vol. 7, 797, 1942. See generally *History of the United Nations War Crimes Commission and the Development of Laws of War*, London: HMSO, 1948.

12 See *A Decade of American Foreign Policy: Basic Documents, 1941–49, Prepared at the Request of the Senate Committee on Foreign Relations by the Staff of the Committee and the Department of State*, Washington, DC: Government Printing Office, 1950; See also Mettraux, *Perspectives on Nuremberg*, Appendix 2, at 730.

13 See *Report of Robert H. Jackson to the International Conference on Military Trials*, London, 1945.

14 J. Persico, *Nuremberg—Infamy on Trial*, New York: Penguin Books, 1994, p. 32.

15 Reprinted in Mettraux, *Perspectives on Nuremberg*, Appendix 3, at 734. Nineteen other states later gave an indication of their adherence to the Agreement.

16 For a review of each specific characteristic of this institution, see, in particular, ibid., at 169 ff.

17 Ibid., Appendix 4, at 736.

18 See generally *Report of Robert H. Jackson to the International Conference on Military Trials*, London, 1945, pp. viii–x.

19 T. Taylor, *Nuremberg and Vietnam: An American Tragedy*, Chicago: Quadrangle Books, 1970, p. 82.

20 Ibid.

21 See e.g. Lord Hankey, *Politics, Trials and Errors*, Chicago: Henry Regnery Company, 1950.

22 See W. Maser, *Nuremberg: A Nation on Trial*, translated from the German by R. Barry, New York: Scribner, 1979, p. 277.

23 S. Glueck, *War Criminals—Their Prosecution & Punishment*, New York: Alfred A. Knopf, 1944, pp. 13–14 (footnote omitted) (quoting *In re Piracy Jure Gentium*, Jud. Com., House of Lords, A.C. (1934), 586, 592, per Viscount Sankey, L.C.).

24 Mettraux, *Judicial Inheritance*, in Mettraux, *Perspectives on Nuremberg*, p. 599, at 610.

25 S. Glaser, 'La Charte du Tribunal de Nuremberg et les Nouveaux Principes du Droit International', *Schweitzerische Zeitschrift fur Strafrecht/Revue Pénale Suisse* 1948, vol. 13, translated and reprinted in Mettraux, *Perspectives on Nuremberg*, p. 55, at 61.

26 See, respectively, Charter, Art. 6(c), (a). The Charter also provided two provisions pertaining to the criminalization of certain groups or organizations in Articles 9 and 10. These provisions were primarily intended to facilitate and expedite the subsequent proceedings of members of such groups and organizations.

27 See Charter, Art. 7, 8.

28 See e.g. S. Glaser, 'La Charte du Tribunal de Nuremberg et les Nouveaux Principes du Droit International', *Schweitzerische Zeitschrift fur Strafrecht/Revue Pénale Suisse*, 1948, vol. 13, translated and reprinted in Mettraux, *Perspectives on Nuremberg*, p. 55, at 55–6.

29 H. Lauterpacht, 'The Subjects of the Law of Nations', *Law Quarterly Review*, 1948, vol. 64, 97, at 104. See also H. Lauterpacht, *International Law and Human Rights*, London: Stevens & Sons, 1950, p. 36; G. Aldrich, 'Individuals as Subjects of International Humanitarian Law', in I. Makarczyk (ed.), *Theory of International Law at the Threshold of the 21st Century, Essays in Honour of Krysztof Skubszewski*, The Hague: Kluwer Law International, 1996, p. 851, at 853–5.

30 See generally Charter, Art. 17 ff. See also *Report of Robert H. Jackson to the International Conference on Military Trials*, London, 1945, pp. viii–x.

31 Rules of Procedure and Evidence of the International Military Tribunal, 29 October 1945.

32 See F. Biddle, 'The Nuremberg Trial', *American Philosophical Society Proceedings*, August 1947, vol. 91, 294, reprinted in Mettraux, *Perspectives on Nuremberg*, p. 200, at 202–3. See also Charter, Art. 19, which provides that '[t]he Tribunal shall not be bound by technical rules of evidence. It shall adopt and apply to the greatest possible extent expeditious and non-technical procedure, and shall admit any evidence which it deems to have probative value'.

33 See Charter Art. 2, which provides as follows: 'The Tribunal shall consist of four members, each with an alternate. One member and one alternate shall be appointed by each of the Signatories. The alternates shall, so far as they are able, be present at all sessions of the Tribunal. In case of illness of any member of the Tribunal or his incapacity or some other reason to fulfil his functions, his alternate shall take his place'.

34 See R. Conot, *Justice at Nuremberg*, New York: Carroll & Graf, 1983, p. 59.

35 *Indictment*, corrected version confirmed 7 June 1946, in *Trial of the Major War Criminals Before the International Military Tribunal, Nuremberg, 14 November 1945–1 October 1946*, vol. 1, Nuremberg: International Military Tribunal, 1947–1949, p. 27.

36 The groups indicted in such a way were the following: the Reichcabinet, the Leadership Corps of the Nazi Party, the SS and including the SD, the Gestapo, the SA, the General Staff and High Command of the German Armed Forces.

37 B. Smith, *Reaching Judgment at Nuremberg*, New York: Basic Books, 1967, p. 9.

38 J. Persico, *Nuremberg—Infamy on Trial*, New York: Penguin Books, 1994, p. 115.

39 IMT, *The Trial of German Major War Criminals by the International Military Tribunal Sitting at Nuremberg, Germany (Commencing 20th November 1945): Opening Speeches of the Chief Prosecutors for the United States of America, the French Republic, the United Kingdom of Great Britain and Northern Ireland and the Union of Soviet Socialist Republics*, London: HMSO, 1946.

40 See e.g. R. H. Jackson, 'Introduction', in W. R. Harris, *Tyranny on Trial—The Evidence at Nuremberg*, New York: Transaction Publishers, 1997, reprinted (in edited and redrafted fashion) in Mettraux, *Perspectives on Nuremberg*, p. 697, at 701–2. Only thirty-three witnesses were called by the Prosecution over the seventy-two days of the proceedings.

41 See W. Maser, *Nuremberg: A Nation on Trial*, translated from the German by R. Barry, New York: Scribner, 1979, p. 273.

42 T. Dodd, 'The Nuremberg Trials', *Journal of Criminal Law and Criminology*, January 1947, vol. 37, 357, reprinted in Mettraux, *Perspectives on Nuremberg*, p. 190.

43 Mettraux, *Judicial Inheritance*, p. 613. See also *Report of Judge Biddle to the President of the United States, Harry Truman*, 9 November 1946 (on file with author): 'It was interesting to feel—what all of us so keenly felt—the change in the point of view of the defendants and their lawyers as the trial progressed. At first, they were indifferent, skeptical, hostile. But very soon, as the Tribunal ruled on the merits of the motions that arose, frequently against the prosecution, and went to great pains to obtain witnesses and documents even remotely relevant to the defendants' case, this attitude changed: the defendants began to fight for their lives. And what had threatened to be a sounding board for propaganda or a stage for martyrdom, turned into a searching analysis of the years that felt Hitler's rise to power and his ultimate destruction—the objective reading of this terrible chapter of History. This change was in itself an instinctive tribute to our concept of Justice'.

44 A. Neave, *Nuremberg—A Personal Record of the Trial of the Major Nazi War Criminals*, London: Hodder and Stoughton, 1978, p. 351.

45 See note 42.

46 The Judgment provides that the provisions of the Charter 'are binding upon the Tribunal as the law to be applied to the case'. See generally Q. Wright, 'War Criminals', *American Journal of International Law*, 1945, vol. 39, 257.

47 *Memorandum for Judge Biddle and Judge Parker*, 5 October 1945 (on file with the author).

48 G. Schwarzenberger, 'The Judgment of Nuremberg', *Tulane Law Review*, 1947, vol. 21, 329, reprinted in Mettraux, *Perspectives on Nuremberg*, p. 167, at 176.

49 See, generally, B. Smith, *Reaching Judgment at Nuremberg*, New York: Basic Books, 1967, p. 304: 'By advancing a conservative and cautious interpretation of the law of the London Charter, the Court sharply limited the utility of such concepts as 'aggressive war' and 'crimes against humanity' in any future victors' trials. Of even greater importance was the Tribunal's achievement in virtually eliminating the collective guilt features by emasculating the conspiracy-common plan charge and the system for prosecuting members of organizations'.

50 *Memorandum signed JHR for Judge Biddle*, 10 July 1946 (on file with the author).
51 *Notes on draft Judgment*, 27 June 1946 to 26 September 1946 (on file with the author).
52 H. Stimson, 'The Nuremberg Trial, Landmark in Law', *Foreign Affairs*, January 1947, vol. 25, 179, reprinted in Mettraux, *Perspectives on Nuremberg*, p. 617, at 621.
53 F. Biddle, 'The Nuremberg Trial', *American Philosophical Society Proceedings*, August 1947, vol. 91, 294, reprinted in Mettraux, *Perspectives on Nuremberg*, p. 200, at 205.
54 *Judgment of the International Military Tribunal for the Trial of German Major War Criminals*, Nuremberg, 30 September and 1 October 1946, New York: William S. Hein & Co., 2001, p. 41.
55 IMT, *The Trial of German major War Criminals: Proceedings of the International Military Tribunal Sitting at Nuremberg, Germany, 20th November, 1945 to 1st December, 1945—Taken from the Official Transcript*. 21 vols, London: HMSO, 1946, Judgment of the International Military Tribunal, p. 223; also quoted in Furundžija (IT-98-17/1), Judgement, 10 December 1998, para. 155.
56 T. Taylor, *Nuremberg and Vietnam: An American Tragedy*, Chicago: Quadrangle Books, 1970, p. 83.
57 See, generally, D. Bloxham, *Genocide on Trial, War Crimes Trials and the Formation of History and Memory*, Oxford: Oxford University Press, 2001.
58 The Soviet member also dissented with respect to two of the organizations that had been charged pursuant to Article 9 of the Charter.
59 F. Biddle, 'The Nuremberg Trial', *American Philosophical Society Proceedings*, August 1947, vol. 91, 294, reprinted in Mettraux, *Perspectives on Nuremberg*, p. 200, at 212.
60 L. Kahn, *Nuremberg Trials*, New York: Ballantine Books, 1972, p. 11.
61 General Assembly Resolution 95(I), Affirmation of the Principles of International Law Recognised by the Charter of the Nürnberg Tribunal, 11 December 1946.
62 See A. Cassese, 'Affirmation of the Principles of International Law Recognized by the Charter of the Nürnberg Tribunal'. Available at: http://untreaty.un.org/cod/avl/pdf/ha/ga_95-I/ga_95-I_e.pdf (accessed 23 April 2010).
63 C. Pompe, *Aggressive War: An International Crime*, The Hague: Martinus Nijhoff, 1953, p. 317.
64 On the value and significance of Nuremberg to modern-day international criminal tribunals, see generally, Mettraux, *Judicial Inheritance*.
65 W. R. Harris, *Tyranny on Trial—The Evidence at Nuremberg*, New York: Transaction Publishers, 1997, p. 537.
66 J. Persico, *Nuremberg—Infamy on Trial*, New York: Penguin Books, 1994, p. 440.
67 W. R. Harris, 'Foreword', *Tyranny on Trial—The Evidence at Nuremberg*, New York: Transaction Publishers, 1997, p. vii.
68 W. R. Harris, *Tyranny on Trial—The Evidence at Nuremberg*, New York: Transaction Publishers, 1997, p. 496.

2
The Tokyo Trial

Neil Boister

Introduction

The Tokyo Trial was the 'other' big post-war trial sponsored by the Allied victors in World War II. The 28 accused were indicted on 29 April 1946 on 36 counts of crimes against peace, 16 of murder and only three counts of conventional war crimes.[1] More than two years and 50,000 pages of court record later, judgment was handed down on the 10 November 1948.[2] Twenty-five of the accused were convicted on 10 counts, finding each accused guilty on at least one count. Seven were sentenced to death, 16 to life, one to 20 years and one to seven years.

There are few today other than specialists who know much about this trial of Japan's war leaders.[3] Those who do know something generally share the view of the US historian Richard Minear that it was victor's justice of the worst kind.[4] Leading international criminal lawyer Professor Cherif Bassiouni's comment is typical:

> Tokyo . . . was a precedent that legal history can only consider with a view not to repeat it.[5]

This chapter investigates whether there are good reasons for taking account of the Tokyo Trial in the historical development of the institutional and normative framework of international criminal law. As Professor Bassiouni's comment suggests—such reasons might be entirely negative—they might serve solely as a guide to prevent the making of the same mistakes. Alternatively, there may be something positive—something that may be useful today in the revival of international criminal law.

Background

The Tokyo Trial was the Allied response to Japan's invasion of East and South East Asia and various states and colonial territories in the Pacific.[6] Building on the Cairo Declaration in which the Allies had labelled the Japanese war 'aggressive',[7] the Allied leaders—Stalin, Roosevelt and Churchill—had enunciated a clear intention to mete out 'stern justice' to 'war criminals' in a Declaration made at Potsdam in the ruins of the German Reich on 26 July 1945.[8] Japan and the nine Allied Powers that signed the Instrument of Surrender on 2 September 1945[9] undertook to 'carry out the provisions of the Potsdam Declaration in good faith' and to follow the orders of the Supreme Commander for the Allied Powers—General Douglas MacArthur—in giving effect to the Declaration.[10]

The purposes of the Tokyo Trial

The United States was the primary architect of the Tokyo Trial and it designed the trial to serve its purposes. Although the Japanese had committed atrocities, the US was motivated not by the need to respond to atrocities as it had been at Nuremberg but by memories of defeat at Japanese hands. General MacArthur had originally wanted to try only those responsible for the surprise attack on Pearl Harbour on 7 December 1941.[11] However, there were other grounds for denunciation, such as the brutalities meted out to prisoners of war by Japanese during the Bataan Death March in April 1942 in the Philippines. US propaganda had whipped up the idea of the treacherous Japanese and the US public wanted retribution. Once the notion of holding a trial like Nuremberg at Tokyo began to take hold, the United States' purposes in holding the trial expanded to include the education of the Japanese people about the aggressive nature of Japan's actions and the barbaric nature of its conduct of the war.[12] There is also evidence that one of its purposes was to remodel Japan so that Japan would cease to be a threat and its government would become favourable to US ends.[13]

The execution of these designs through an international military tribunal brought unanticipated complications. The US found that it had to make room at the trial for its Allies who had their own purposes. The Australians, for example, wanted to denounce the Emperor Hirohito and had labelled him 'War Criminal Number One'.[14] The USSR produced evidence of the Japanese bio-warfare programme and sought indictment of the leaders of this programme and of leaders of Japanese military activities against the USSR at Lake Khasan and Nomonhan.[15] The Chinese had, as we shall see, perhaps the strongest case for such a trial.

The legal basis of the trial

Much of the argument at Nuremberg was about the legality of imposing a criminal process on the accused when Germany had not agreed to that process and there was no general basis for it in international law. At Tokyo, however, that argument was largely avoided because of the consent of the State of Japan to war crimes trials in the Instrument of Surrender. The focus at Tokyo was instead upon the extent of the scope of that consent and whether the crimes tried fell outside of that scope.

One of General MacArthur's tasks as Supreme Commander for the Allied Powers[16] was the punishment of war criminals. Under instruction from his superiors in Washington[17] he established the Tokyo Tribunal by proclamation on 19 August 1946.[18] According to its Charter, which was heavily modelled on the Nuremberg Charter, the purpose of the Tribunal was the trial of 'major war criminals'. While the Proclamation required that each such criminal be charged with crimes against peace, the Charter also provided for the Tribunal's jurisdiction over war crimes and crimes against humanity. Initially only a unilateral US action, the proclamation of the Tribunal was sanctioned by the Allies' Far Eastern Committee (FEC),[19] which met in Washington, thus re-characterising it as an international action.[20]

The way in which the Tribunal was established avoided much of the controversy associated with Nuremberg. While Nuremberg was based on a treaty among the four major Allied Powers and imposed a process on Germany without German participation, Tokyo was based on a proclamation based on a treaty of surrender—the Instrument of Surrender—between the Allies on the one hand, and Japan on the other, which explicitly contemplated war crimes trials. Japan's signature of the Instrument of Surrender answered two fundamental complaints raised by the defence.

The first was that neither General MacArthur nor the Allies had a right to unilaterally proclaim such a tribunal for such trials.[21] The Instrument of Surrender indicated Japan's consent to the process.

The second was that Japan had not anticipated prosecution of its leaders for crimes against peace. The Potsdam Declaration did not clarify whether 'war criminals' included those responsible for making an illegal war. The majority's answer to this complaint was that when it signed the Instrument of Surrender, Japan understood that General MacArthur as Supreme Commander was going to prosecute war criminals for crimes against peace.[22] According to evidence given at the Tokyo Trial, when the Japanese Emperor Hirohito eventually gave his authority to surrender he said: 'I could not bear the sight of those responsible for the war being punished, but I think that now is the time to bear the unbearable'.[23] A more plausible explanation, however, of the roots of the authority to prosecute crimes against peace is that interpretive and decisive power in regard to the designation of war criminals vested in General MacArthur through Japan's consent to the terms of the Potsdam Declaration in signing the Instrument of Surrender, and he used those powers when proclaiming the Tribunal.[24]

The defence made various other *ad litem* challenges to the Tribunal and its Charter powers but these were simply batted away by the majority of the Tribunal, who noted both that they were bound by the Charter and their 'unqualified adherence' to the Nuremberg Judgment in regard to these issues.[25] This cursory response did not satisfy Judges Pal[26] and Röling,[27] who attacked the majority's reliance on the Charter and on Nuremberg. For them, the Tokyo Charter was simply a jurisdictional document which could be measured against positive international law, and they did so, and found it wanting.

A broad multinational trial

In contrast to Nuremberg, which was simply entitled the 'International Military Tribunal', the Tokyo Trial was designated in its Charter as the 'International Military Tribunal for the Far East', an unsubtle signifier of the orientalism of its creators. The fact that 11 nations were represented on the bench at Tokyo is another obvious difference with Nuremberg.

General MacArthur appointed the 11-member bench in February 1946, drawing on nominees from the USSR, UK, US, China, France, the Netherlands, Canada, Australia, New Zealand, India, and the Philippines.[28] Although the bench contained no neutral or Japanese members, it was far more cosmopolitan than Nuremberg in this regard (as it was in many other respects). But this broad representation of Allied interests proved to be part of the Tokyo Trial's undoing.

The judges were a diverse group. Lord Patrick, a Senator of the Scottish College of Justice, was joined at the centre of the majority by Edward Stuart MacDougall, a Puisne Judge of the Appeals Division in Quebec, and Erima Harvey Northcroft, a retired Supreme Court Judge from New Zealand. This nucleus, the most influential on the legal questions facing the Tribunal, was later supported by the US Judge Advocate General Myron C. Cramer, drafted back into judicial service when the first US appointment John P. Higgins, a Superior Court Judge from Massachusetts, resigned at the start of proceedings because of criticism of his qualities from the US Chief Prosecutor (his replacement prompted an unsuccessful challenge by the defence).[29] The other members of the majority included Ju-Ao Mei, a member of the Nationalist Yuan in China, Ivan Michyevich Zaryanov, a Major General of Justice from the USSR and Delfin Jaranilla, a Supreme Court Judge in the Philippines.

Three judges dissented in part or whole. Radhabinod Pal, member of the High Court of Calcutta, was a nationalist but anti-communist whose beliefs clearly influenced his renowned dissenting judgment. The youngest member of the bench, the Dutch nominee, Bernard V. A. Röling, had expertise in Indonesian law and revealed a strong grasp of public international law in his critique of the majority judgment. Henri Bernard was a former French colonial magistrate who had become chief prosecutor for the Free French. He proved to be a trenchant critic of the procedural aspects of the trial.

Perhaps the most complex figure at the trial was its Australian President, Sir William Flood Webb. A former Chief Justice of Queensland, Webb's control of the only microphone on the bench (a considerable design error) meant that all questions had to be put through him. Over-exposed at the fulcrum of the trial, he emerged as an authoritarian figure with a poor grip on a difficult and lengthy trial. The core of the majority—Patrick, Northcroft, and MacDougall—coalesced in response to what they considered to be Webb's poor draft judgment[30] on the legal issues and to his inability to control dissenters like Pal. Webb responded badly to their criticism and they grew to dislike him; Northcroft, for example, considered him 'stupid' and 'mean'.[31] The immediate result of their rejection of his draft judgment was delay in issuing reasons for rejection of the defence challenge to the legal basis of the trial until the end of the trial, which led to this challenge being reiterated at the end of the prosecution case and again on summation. The ultimate result was a split judgment.[32] The judgment of the majority, which was given in the name of the Tribunal, upheld most of the charges; although given in the name of the Tribunal, it was designed mainly by the three 'British' judges. Joined by two separate concurring opinions by Webb and Jaranilla, the majority judgment was supported by all except the dissenters Pal, Bernard, and Röling. Yet what this account of Webb's frailties fails to reveal is that he had serious doubts about the legality of the crimes against peace charges.[33] Moreover, the notion that it would have been possible to paste over the bitter divisions between, in particular, Pal and the majority through rapid action early on is probably unrealistic.

In order to ensure US control of the prosecution, a control the US had not had at Nuremberg where there had been four Allied prosecutors of equal status, General MacArthur through the Tokyo Charter designated a Chief Prosecutor, an American, to be assisted by Allied associate prosecutors.[34] The choice for the position, Joseph Keenan, was a former Deputy US Attorney General who had worked against organised crime in the US but was also a Democratic Party political fixer. Keenan wanted to make a strong impression at Tokyo but made a poor one. He was criticised for his overblown rhetoric, poor judgment, incompetence in court, poor organisation, and for abuse of alcohol leading to long absence.[35] Yet in spite of efforts to unseat him, he remained the Chief Prosecutor and head of the International Prosecution Section,[36] a US organisation, until the close of the trial. The British Prosecutor, Arthur (later Sir) Comyns-Carr, was considered the best of the associate prosecutors. Apart from the quality of its leader, the Tokyo prosecution suffered from many other ills: limited time to prepare a case based on superficial knowledge, an overly ambitious indictment covering too many offences over too long a period, and excessive reliance on documentary and affidavit evidence, all of which resulted in a lengthy and costly trial, and all of which remain enduring ills of international criminal trials.

The accused were initially represented by Japanese counsel.[37] Although unschooled in adversarial criminal trials, they included lawyers with a far better grasp of international law than any among the prosecution. These Japanese counsel were intent on examining the validity of the trial in positive international law. For example, when the prosecution made the bizarre argument (discussed below) that, because the war was unlawful, all actions taken in the war were unlawful and thus the accused were all guilty of murder, the leading Japanese counsel, Kenzo Takayanagi, a Harvard graduate, responded:

> You see the conjurer borrow an ordinary hat. He plants it on the table, and mutters some incantations over it. Then he lifts it up—and the table is swarming with little rabbits. There were no rabbits in the hat. He put them there . . . . The argument of the Prosecution, we venture to say, is exactly like that. It takes an ordinary hat, the nice, well-known, respectable hat of international law, covering states and nations. It places the hat on the table and intones over it some weird incantations among which we can catch the words, in a crescendo, 'unlawful', 'criminal', 'murder'. And then the hat is lifted, and immediately the Tribunal swarms with new-born little doctrines drawn from odds and ends of municipal law, to the extreme amazement of us all. Where the Prosecution got them is immaterial. They were surely not in our silk hat. The Prosecution put them there.[38]

Takayanagi's criticism is that international criminal law was being developed using domestic dogma drawn up into it for reasons of expedience by prosecutors unfamiliar with anything else in disregard of the formal requirements for the formation of international law. A prominent feature of the prosecution's methodology, it too remains a characteristic of international criminal law.

Concerns about the adversarial trial experience of the Japanese counsel led to the deployment of US-appointed lawyers to assist them in April 1946 after the trial had opened.[39] The US lawyers for the most part pursued the defence of their individual clients rather than an attack on the law. Their focus on the alleged procedural irregularities of the trial served to both slow the trial down and proved to be an irritant for those British Commonwealth judges unused to dealing with combative American litigation techniques in the polite terms *de rigeur* in US court rooms. At one stage when President Webb intervened to stop the taking of technical points, he commented that 'to those who do not truly understand it, it would appear as if the accused were being denied a fair trial'.[40] Judicial review was an obvious goal for the US defence counsel.

A selective trial

The Tokyo Tribunal was only one of a large number of post-war trials of Japanese personnel accused of war crimes. It differed, however, from those other trials because while they only dealt justice (some of it very rough) to Class B and C prisoners—the middle and junior ranks immediately responsible for war crimes such as maltreatment of POWs or crimes against humanity such as systematic murder of civilians—the Allies put 28 of Japan's leaders (categorised as Class A prisoners because of their alleged responsibility for crimes against peace) on trial before the Tokyo International Military Tribunal.

The selection of those to face trial was an incoherent process based on an incoherent policy.[41] The UN War Crimes Commission (UNWCC) had originally suggested a focus on particular roles in the preparation of an aggressive war, but under US influence this transformed into a policy that categorised the accused into one of the three classes outlined above—A, B, and C—insisting that for trial before the Tokyo Tribunal all prisoners had to be implicated in and indicted for Class A offences.[42] The UNWCC's idea reemerged in the particularisation of Class A offences as the planning, preparing, initiating and waging of aggressive war, or conspiring to do so.[43]

The Tokyo Trial was selective in that all of the accused were Japanese.[44] There was no mention at the trial of potential Allied culpability for war crimes through the use of nuclear weapons on civilians in Japan other than exclusion of defence evidence in this regard.[45] But the trial was also selective in that the accused were drawn primarily from among the Japanese leadership. In making the selection the prosecution relied heavily on the records of interrogation of the fairly large number of Class A prisoners held at Sugamo Prison in Tokyo and the personal diary of the Emperor Hirohito's closest advisor, the Privy Seal, Marquis Kido.[46]

The accused included individuals who had developed the ideology of Japanese military expansionism such a Shūmei Ōkawa, an intellectual and writer, the military officials who took the first steps in executing aggression in Manchuria such as General Seishiro Itagaki, who was active in the Manchurian Incident, commanders who had waged aggressive war in the field such as General Iwane Matsui, the commander at Nanking, civilian leaders such as former Prime Minister Kōki Hirota, in charge in 1936 when expansionist plans were adopted, military leaders including the demonised General Hideki Tōjō, in charge when the attacks on Pearl Harbour and other Pacific territories were made, civilian finance officials such as Naoki Hoshino, who had played a significant role in financial affairs in the puppet state of Manchukuo, and diplomats such as Ambassador Hiroshi Ōshima, who while ambassador in Berlin had been a key player in negotiation of the Axis alliance with Germany. The accused were a representative sample of Japanese leaders engaged at different levels of Japanese military expansionism from 1932 to 1945. Their selection meant that the trial was in effect a trial of Japan and its foreign policies during this period. The selection of those responsible for atrocities during this expansion, such as General Heitaro Kimura, commander in Burma in 1944, seemed to have been something of an afterthought and had to be linked to their participation in the waging of aggressive war. Kimura, for example, was Vice Minister of War in 1941–4.

While Nuremberg and Tokyo share the common characteristic that none of the victors were on trial, unlike at Nuremberg significant figures in the Japanese war-time leadership were not before the court at Tokyo.[47] Of these the most significant omission was the Emperor Hirohito. It has been suggested by Herbert Bix that the trial was at least in part a set-up by the Imperial household, Navy, and elements in US Intelligence to make the Army and in particular General Tōjō, who became the face of the accused, the scapegoat for Emperor Hirohito in respect of the starting of the war.[48] Hirohito, constitutional head of the Japanese state, was not indicted apparently at General MacArthur's insistence because of the risk of political unrest in occupied Japan.[49] At the time the prosecutors considered that his role had been mainly titular, but more recent evidence has revealed his involvement in decisions to go to war.[50] Although the majority judgment made no comment in this regard, two judges—Webb the Australian president, and Bernard, the French judge—were not convinced of his innocence and made this patent in their separate judgments.[51] The Emperor's closest advisor, the Privy Seal Marquis Koichi Kido, seems to have been chosen as a substitute for Hirohito. Many of the other Class A suspects detained at Sugamo who for reasons unknown never made it onto the final list, later went on to great things, such as Nobusuke Kishi, prime minister in 1957.[52]

The United States' immediate tactical goals also prevented the selection of certain accused. It emerged long after the trial that members of Unit 731, the Japanese biowarfare unit, which had inter alia dropped anthrax and cholera on Chinese cities and run vivisectional experiments on live human beings, were given exemption from prosecution in a secret deal with the US government in return for their knowledge.[53] Leaders of the industrial conglomerates like Mitsubishi, and those responsible for the 'comfort women' sex slavery programme, were also omitted from the list of those put on trial.[54]

An unfair trial

In order to function as a reference point for modern international criminal law the conduct of the Tokyo Trial is best viewed through the lens of fairness. Article 9 of the Tokyo Charter guaranteed a fair trial through a clear statement of charges in Japanese, the right to be charged and tried in Japanese, the right to counsel, the right to a defence and to examine witnesses, and the right to request the production of evidence.[55]

At the outset of the trial, allegations of preexisting bias were made against two of the judges—Webb, for his participation in the Australian War Crimes Commission investigations into atrocities in New Guinea where he had made recommendations, and Jaranilla, because he had participated in the Bataan Death March as a prisoner.[56] The Tribunal (sitting in Chambers without those challenged) avoided the merits of the complaint—which appeared overwhelmingly in favour of the defence in both cases—and fell back on the argument that it was not for it to unseat any appointment made by the Supreme Commander for the Allied Powers. Apart from not unseating their brethren when they should have, their reasons for not doing also signalled that the Tribunal did not believe it had an inherent power of reviewing the terms of its establishment in spite of the fact it was a judicial body.

The course of the proceedings revealed a more deep-seated actual bias on the part of President Webb (it was probably pervasive among the judges from former colonial powers and Australia and New Zealand) who would not admit to the historical parallels between Japanese and European imperialism; judgment revealed the negative of that bias—Judge Pal's pro-Japanese position.[57]

The indictment, which according to Article 9(a) of the Charter was supposed to consist of a 'plain, concise and adequate statement of each offence charged', was exceedingly long and complex.[58] It contained 56 separate offences and the combinations of allegations made against various accused resulted in the trial having to deal with over 700 individual charges. Together with the detailed appendices listing further factual particulars and rules allegedly breached, it made for an unwieldy mass of allegations that was sprung on the accused at a very late stage. The defence struggled to cope, which set the stage for a very long trial.

A number of additional factors compounded this trend towards length: primarily, the requirement of simultaneous oral translation and the translation of all documents into and from Japanese.[59] There were also so many issues before the court, that in spite of the provision in Article 12(a) of the Charter which required that the trial be confined to 'an expeditious hearing of the issues', the trial dragged. Trainin, who attended the proceedings, contrasted its immobility with the mobility of its participants:

> Against this motionless background of the trial proceedings, there is constant movement, a sort of perpetuum mobile of the various persons taking part. Defence lawyers, prosecutors and even judges alternatively come and go. The defendants have to stay put more or less, but two of them, evidently despairing of hearing the judgment in this world, have removed themselves to the next.[60]

The rules of procedure and evidence in the Tokyo Charter, following the Nuremberg model (which in turn followed the model used in US military commissions), were nontechnical in order to facilitate a speedy trial. They abandoned the common law exclusionary rules of evidence so as to facilitate the admission of a range of evidence inadmissible in a common law trial for whatever probative value it may have.[61] This built-in flexibility dismayed the US defence counsel who repeatedly challenged its various manifestations in the procedural rulings made by the Tribunal but without success.

The defence's dismay was compounded by the steady decline, under pressure from a prosecution pursuing the nontechnical approach to its benefit, of judicial control over what was considered as admissible evidence leading to the admission of excerpts of documents, documents without authentification and affidavits without the presence of the deponent, all rationalised by

President Webb in the name of haste.[62] Yet when the Tribunal reimposed the common law exclusionary rules such as the best evidence and opinion rules on the defence evidence, this was perversely also rationalised in the name of haste.[63] Apart from the glaring unfairness of doing so, it suggests that a completely nontechnical approach is not functional to a trial of crimes of such great historical magnitude because of the danger of the trial being swamped by the evidence. The exclusion of tu-quoque evidence such as Russian invasion of Finland and of evidence of the communist threat in China and the use of nuclear weapons supports condemnation of the trial as unfair; Pal did not hesitate to condemn it in his dissent.[64]

The defence also made a failed objection to the absence of judges from the tribunal.[65] Webb was absent for 22 days when the trial actually sat hearing defence evidence, ostensibly because he was needed on the Australian High Court. Pal was also absent for significant periods to visit his wife who was ill. The formal response of the Tribunal to defence complaint was that Article 4(c) of the Charter permitted absence while Article 4(b) only required a quorum of six of the 11 judges.

The process of the writing of the judgment itself also raised issues of fairness.[66] The split in the bench was a result of the original defence challenge to the legality of the trial. Judges Pal and Röling believed that the Tribunal could review the legality of the process by which it was founded. The majority response was formalistic reliance on the Charter. Webb fell out with the majority after they criticised the quality of his draft judgment, a split reinforced by a later dispute on the legality of the inchoate crime of conspiracy in international law. When it came to the development of the Tribunal's judgment—both in law and in fact—the dissentients were excluded from the process, leading to their bitter criticism of the majority. Bernard was particularly disparaging about the fact that the 11 judges had never met to discuss the findings of fact.[67] These findings were drafted by 'clerks' such as Captain Quentin Quentin-Baxter, the New Zealand barrister who assisted Northcroft, and Lt Colonel Harold E. Hastings, who assisted Cramer. They were accepted almost without alteration by the majority and form the basis of the judgment today.[68]

The most trenchant judicial critic of the procedure, Bernard wrote in his dissent that '[a] verdict reached by a Tribunal after a defective procedure cannot be a valid one'.[69] There was sufficient irregularity in the trial judged against the standards of the time to justify the conclusion that the procedure was defective and that it would not have withstood judicial scrutiny by a reviewing court.

A trial mainly of crimes against peace

While at Nuremberg crimes against peace were important, at Tokyo they were all-important; the first 36 of the 56 counts in the indictment charged such crimes. Article 5(a) of the Tokyo Charter described '[c]rimes against the peace' as

> the planning, preparation, initiation or waging of a declared or undeclared war of aggression, or a war in violation of international law, treaties, agreements or assurances, or participation in a common plan or conspiracy for the accomplishment of any of the foregoing; . . .

The only precedent for crimes against peace was Nuremberg. As noted above, the defence challenged *ad litem* the prosecution's interpretation of 'war criminals' in the Potsdam Declaration to include those responsible for crimes against peace. The defence's strongest legal objection was that while 'waging' an aggressive war may have been an international wrong—a wrong against a state—it was not a crime at the time Japan invaded Asia or the Pacific. The majority's response was simply to reaffirm the Nuremberg judgment in this regard, but they added rhetorically 'that aggression was a crime at international law long prior to the date of the Declaration of Potsdam'.[70] The defence was correct—the crime was created and applied after the fact—and in this respect the epithet 'victor's justice' fits. This ground for criticising the trial has played a significant role in delegitimising the Tokyo Trial to the point where the judgment has been rendered largely invisible in Japan.[71] The absence of judicial activity since Tokyo in regard to crimes against peace has not helped. This neglect has led to doubts about the validity of crimes against peace.

The detail of the charges for crimes against peace reveal that prosecution at Tokyo embraced the US position at Nuremberg that charging a grand conspiracy was a method of resolving the legality issues surrounding, in particular, crimes against peace and crimes by Axis leaders. Counts 1–4 charged the accused with involvement in conspiracies as 'leaders, organisers, instigators, or accomplices' to dominate East Asia and the Pacific and Indian Oceans or geographical subsets thereof. Count 5 alleged involvement with Germany and Italy in the Axis conspiracy for global domination. Counts 6–36 indicted the accused for the substantive offences, i.e. planning, preparing, initiating, or waging of these wars of aggression against various states threatened or invaded by Japan.

Once on trial, at least in respect of these charges, the accused generally did not defend their own actions by denying personal involvement in these crimes, but tried to defend the actions of the Japanese State by arguing that what had been done by Japan—invasion—was legal under international law as an exercise of self-defence to ensure its security against communism in China and later against Allied encroachment on their oil supplies, a rationalisation still familiar today.

In its judgment, the Tribunal approved of the conspiracy charge even though conspiracy had been de-emphasised in the Nuremberg judgment. In convicting the accused on count 1 for conspiring to dominate East Asia and the Pacific and Indian Oceans, the Tribunal held:

> These far reaching plans for waging wars of aggression and the prolonged and intricate preparation for and waging of these wars was not the work of one man. They were the work of many leaders acting in pursuance of a common plan for the achievement of a common object. That common object, that they should secure Japan's domination by preparing and waging wars of aggression, was a criminal object. Indeed no more grave crimes can be conceived of than a conspiracy to wage a war of aggression or the waging of a war of aggression, for the conspiracy threatens the security of the peoples of the world and the waging disrupts it. The probable result of such a conspiracy and the inevitable result of its execution is that death and suffering will be inflicted on countless human beings.[72]

The Tribunal then found it unnecessary to deal with counts 2–4, which it considered subsets of the conspiracy alleged in count 1.[73] It did not find count 5, the allegation of a grandiose conspiracy with Germany and Italy to dominate the world, had been proved.

The Tribunal relied on its findings on conspiracy to avoid making findings on planning and preparing (counts 6–17) aggressive war because of the overlap, and because of the overlap with waging, avoided making findings on initiating (counts 18–26).[74] Relying then on waging aggressive war, the majority found counts 27, 29, 31, 32, 33, 35, and 36 proved (waging aggressive war against China, the US, British Commonwealth, the Netherlands, France, the USSR, and Mongolian People's Republic).[75] The Tribunal's lengthy findings of fact to support the convictions of conspiring to and waging of aggressive war[76]—a lengthy judicial summary of the prosecution's version—has been heavily criticised for its untutored reductivity.[77]

The Tokyo Trial is studied by most students of international law only because of the great—in size, profundity, and repetition—dissenting judgment of the Indian Judge Radhabinod Pal.

For Pal the trial was a sham employment of legal process to satisfy the Allied thirst for revenge. His judgment is an object lesson in legal positivism. After taking as his premise that the Allies would not have disregarded existing international law when promulgating the Tokyo Charter which contained its substantive jurisdiction, he searched for the positive source of the rule that individuals could be held individually criminally responsible for aggression, and found none.[78] Pal overstates the case against the Kellogg–Briand Pact by suggesting that because it allowed those who exercise self-defence to decide when it is valid to do so, it was without value even as a vehicle of state responsibility.[79] But his rejection of international criminalisation of aggression through the Pact is correct.[80]

At a factual level, Pal debunked the prosecutor's theory, accepted uncritically by the majority judgment, that there had been a grand rolling conspiracy from 1928 to 1945, to which the accused all belonged, bent on the common goal of expansion of the Japanese empire in East Asia and the Pacific and Indian Oceans by force. Pal commented: 'The story has been pushed a little too far, perhaps, to give it a place in the Hitler series'.[81] Most historians today agree that such a conspiracy was largely a construct of order imposed on a chaotic history.[82]

However, Pal's apparently value-free analysis cannot disguise his respect for the accused as the leaders of an Asian state who had attempted to free Asia of the yoke of European colonialism. Pal's judgment can be read as a precursor to the great debate in international law about the rights of colonised peoples to lawfully pursue self-determination through the use of force.[83] However, Pal ignored the fact that the Japanese freed the Indo-Chinese, Malaysians, Indonesians, Timorese, Papuans, and so forth from the European imperial yoke, only to impose their own.

Judge Röling echoed many of Pal's concerns about the legal justifications of crimes against peace. He denied that they were part of international law prior to the end of the war but did not view the maxim *nullum crimen sine lege* as preventing the application of these crimes by victors in a just war in order to contain rather than punish a threat to the international order.[84]

A trial of peculiar evidence and unusual crimes

One of the more peculiar features of the Tokyo Trial included the leading of evidence of violation of international drug prohibition treaties by the Japanese through their involvement in regulated supply of opium in China in order to substantiate accusations of crimes against peace.[85] The majority found that profit from the traffic had been used to undermine the local populace and sustain Japan's military aggression.[86]

But the most bizarre feature of the trial, in legal terms at least, was contained in counts 37–52 of the indictment, whereby the prosecution laid charges of murder against the accused. The prosecution's theory was that as the war was in violation of international law this removed the justification of individual actions of killing performed by Japanese combatants during the war, rendering them open to charges of the domestic crime of murder, which charges could be attributed back to those who had ordered them, the accused.[87] Although not provided for in the Charter, these charges were motivated by a desire to avoid expost facto arguments about every charge laid before the tribunal and to label the accused as common criminals. Apart from the lack of authority in the Charter, the charges fallaciously confused the legality of going to war with the law about how a state's forces conduct themselves once at war—two entirely separate doctrinal schemes.[88] The majority avoided controversy by choosing not to decide these charges, as in its view the conduct the murder charges sought to punish was already adequately dealt with by the allegations of the illegality of aggressive war. Yet it opined: 'All killings in an unlawful war were condemned as unlawful killings'.[89] One of the casualties of these murder charges was, however, charges of crimes against humanity, for although provision was made in Article 5(c) of the

Charter for the Tribunal's jurisdiction over such charges, no such allegations were laid in order to make way for the murder charges.

But it was also a war crimes trial

Only counts 53–55 of the indictment charged conventional war crimes. They drew their authority from Article 5(b), which provided for the Tribunal's jurisdiction over violations of the laws and customs of war. Count 53 alleged a conspiracy to authorise and plan war crimes and to prevent effective repression of breaches of the law of war. It was dismissed by the majority judgment because conspiracy to commit war crimes was not provided for in Article 5 of the Charter.[90]

The principal war crimes charged became count 54, which charged the ordering, authorising and permitting of war crimes, and count 55, which alleged the deliberate and reckless disregard of the legal duty on the accused to take adequate steps to secure observance of and thus to prevent breaches of the applicable laws of war.

The primary legal difficulty with these counts was trying to identify which laws had actually bound the Japanese in their conduct of the war and their treatment of victims. The majority held that Japan was bound in its conduct of the war by the Hague Regulations as they were customary international law.[91] With respect to treatment of victims, the issue was more complex. Although Japan had not ratified the 1929 Geneva Prisoners of War Convention it had assured the Allies that it would apply it *mutatis mutandis*. The majority held that this meant first, that Japan had made a binding undertaking to apply the treaty provisions, and second, that no plausible interpretation of its reservation that it would only do so *mutatis mutandis* could conclude that it permitted the atrocities carried out by the Japanese.[92]

Although the majority did not attempt to summarise the findings of fact on the war crimes counts,[93] the record of the Tokyo Trial preserves much of the evidence in support of these counts, and reveals that the 'Rape of Nanking' was not the only massacre in China or elsewhere in Asia and the Pacific committed by Japanese soldiers against civilians and POWs. The conviction of the accused on count 54 for either giving the order for the commission of these offences or for wilfully permitting their commission is entirely defensible in international law.[94]

Their conviction on count 55 for failing to take steps to prevent the commission of these offences—effectively on the basis of command responsibility—is more controversial. Arguably, the majority went too far in attributing responsibility for an omission to establish an effective system to protect prisoners of war. Particularly questionable was their reliance on retention of cabinet membership by an accused once he became aware of the commission of atrocities as the basis for responsibility.[95] Röling's very pithy test for command responsibility for omissions is to be preferred: (i) Did they know or should they have known of the atrocious conduct of their subordinates? (ii) Were they under a duty and power to prevent the wrong? (iii) Did they fail to do so?[96] In contrast, Pal's dissent was at its weakest when dealing with the war crimes charges. It reflects an underlying predilection towards the innocence of the accused which strains against the evidence.[97]

Conviction, punishment, and immediate aftermath

On judgment in November 1948, the majority found all the accused guilty of at least one of the 10 counts it upheld.[98] It sentenced Doihara, Itagaki, Kimura, Matsui, Mutō, Hirota, and Tōjō, to death. It sentenced Araki, Hashimoto, Hata, Hiranuma, Hoshino, Kaya, Kido, Koiso, Minami, Oka, Ōshima, Sato, Shimada, Shiratori, Suzuki, and Umezu to life imprisonment. It sentenced Tōgō, to 20 years and Shigemitsu to seven years.[99] No reasons were given for individual sentences. However, it appeared that war crimes were punished with death, crimes against peace with life.[100]

Röling obviously took this view because he would have sentenced Oka, Sato, and Shimada to death because of their commission of war crimes, but Araki, Hashimoto, Hiranuma, Hoshino, Minami, Kaya, Ōshima, Shiratori, and Suzuki to life imprisonment for crimes against peace. However, he would have acquitted Hata, Hirota, Kido, and Shigemitsu for lack of evidence.[101] In his separate opinion, Webb refused to impose the death penalty because of the absence from the indictment of the Emperor.[102] Jaranilla, also in a separate judgment, felt that many of the penalties were not severe enough.[103] The procedural defects prevented Bernard from formulating a sentence.[104] Pal would have acquitted them all.[105]

Immediately following the trial General MacArthur reviewed all of the sentences in terms of the powers given to him under Article 17 of the Charter and confirmed them.[106] A challenge to the tribunal in the US Supreme Court failed when the Supreme Court held that the Tokyo Tribunal was outside domestic US jurisdiction.[107] The death sentences were executed on 23 December 1948. The Cold War and Japan's role as potential ally meant that, when the trial was over, it was the US which acted to bury it and to get the convicts paroled as quickly as possible. The last parolees were given an unconditional release less than 10 years after judgment, and some returned almost immediately to cabinet-level positions in the Japanese Government.[108]

A bungled trial?

Tokyo has endured significantly more criticism than Nuremberg, for good reason. The judges joined in this chorus of disapproval through the various dissents. Bernard, for example, found himself unable to formulate a verdict but was able to state that '[t]he most abominable crimes were committed on a large scale . . . [and] there is no doubt in my mind that certain defendants bear a large part of the responsibility for them . . .'.[109] The subtext is that he thought there was a case against the accused but the trial was bungled. If so, it was bungled in the conception of the trial as mainly one of crimes against peace because it was this conception that presented the opportunity for the making of poorly designed allegations of grand conspiracy and much that followed. We should be cautious, however, before condemning the trial in its entirety, because to do so would be to ignore the validity of convicting the accused for war crimes; the atrocities Japanese forces carried out called for an answer and the trial gave one.

A trial of as-yet unresolved conflicts

The allegations of crimes against peace may not have been as legally plausible as the war crimes charges but in 1945 condemnation of Japanese aggression was a political necessity. The trial of the leaders of the major Asian power by Western nations, many of them former colonial powers in the Far East who had lost their colonies through the actions of Japan, brought into sharp focus questions of Western imperialism not present at Nuremberg; Judge Pal answered these questions in his dissent. He did not, however, respond to the bitterness that many of the Asian victims of Japanese imperialism still harbour towards Japan in regard to its 'advance' across Asia. In this ongoing conflict, 'the Tokyo Trial view of history' has become a terrain of contest.[110] The range of attitudes within Japan to the trial and indeed to its war responsibility in China includes angry denial of responsibility by some. Japanese critics of the trial clearly venerate Pal. He is the only member of the Tokyo Tribunal who has a memorial built to him outside the Yasukuni Shrine in Tokyo. The Shrine is the resting place of the nearly 2.5 million deified Japanese who died fighting for the Emperor, including the seven accused who were executed at Tokyo. The more openly nationalist Japanese post-war prime ministers have both worshipped at the Shrine and venerated Pal. Grist for those who accuse Japan of revisionism in regard to its war responsibility one might think, but to do so is to construct the Japanese response to the trial as monolithic when in fact there are many different views of the trial within Japan, including plain ignorance.[111]

Conclusion

Although it is a common view in Japan that the trial was inevitable because Japan lost the war,[112] the trial was more than crude victor's justice. The Allies, for example, did not simply use the Tokyo Charter to direct that aggression was a crime and that Japan had committed aggression. The New Zealand Judge Northcroft made the obvious point that this 'would have made plausible the popular criticism that such trials are acts of vengeance or retribution visited by victorious nations upon the vanquished'.[113] This is an issue which is highly pertinent today as states parties to the Rome Statute argue about whether the Security Council must play a role in finding aggression has occurred before the International Criminal Court can exercise its jurisdiction over the crime.

The Tokyo Trial is worth rescuing from the wastelands of legal history not in order to thrust at the victor or vanquished, but because of its many parts, which arguably makes it more interesting and relevant today than Nuremberg. As soon as Nuremberg had laid the foundation of international criminal law, Tokyo began to rip it out. The Allies then tried to bury it, but because of the unresolved questions of justice in the historical period it dealt with, it keeps on being dug up. It is a clear antecedent to the modern international criminal tribunal, where identifying the villain and the victim is often more difficult than many assume.

Notes

1 The full Indictment, including appendices on particulars of charges and laws violated, is reproduced in Neil Boister and Robert Cryer (eds), *Documents on the Tokyo War Crimes Tribunal: Charter, Indictment and Judgments* (Oxford: OUP, 2008), p. 16 (hereinafter Boister and Cryer, *Documents*). The original transcript of the trial (hereinafter *Transcript*) and Judgment of the Tribunal (hereinafter *Judgment*) in the United States of America *et al.* versus Araki, Sadao *et al.*, is available at a number of locations, including the MacMillan Brown Archives, University of Canterbury, Christchurch, New Zealand. The comprehensive published edition of the trial documents is R. J. Pritchard (ed.) *The Tokyo Major War Crimes Trial: The Records of the International Military Tribunal for the Far East with an Authoritative Commentary and Comprehensive Guide* (Lewiston, Lampeter, Queenston: Edwin Mellen Press, 1998–2005, 124 vols).

2 See Boister and Cryer, *Documents*, pp. 71ff.

3 A selection of the main sources available in English include: Neil Boister and Robert Cryer, *The Tokyo International Military Tribunal: A Reappraisal* (Oxford: OUP, 2008) (hereinafter Boister and Cryer, *Reappraisal*); Madoka Futamura, *War Crimes Tribunals and Transitional Justice: The Tokyo Trial and the Nuremberg Legacy* (London and New York: Routledge, 2008); Solis Horwitz, 'The Tokyo Trial' (1950) 465 *International Conciliation* 471; Richard H. Minear, *Victor's Justice: The Tokyo War Crimes Trial* (Princeton: Princeton University Press, 1971); B. V. A. Röling and Antonio Cassesse, *The Tokyo Trials and Beyond: Reflections of a Peacemonger* (Cambridge: Polity Press, 1993); Yuma Totani, *The Tokyo War Crimes Trial: The Pursuit of Justice in the Wake of World War II* (Cambridge, MA and London: Harvard University Asia Center, 2008). Joseph B. Keenan and Brendan F. Brown, *Crimes Against International Law* (Washington: Public Affairs Press, 1951) was co-authored by the Chief Prosecutor and it shows. Arnold Brackman, *The Other Nuremberg: The Untold Story of the Tokyo War Crimes Trials* (New York: William Morrow, 1987) is a contemporary account by a journalist.

4 This opinion is present in the title and throughout the content of his book.

5 M. C. Bassiouni, 'Nuremberg Forty Years After', 1986 *Proceedings American Society of International Law*, p. 64.

6 A detailed historical examination of the stages and major events of the so-called 15-year war is beyond this chapter. See Boister and Cryer, *Reappraisal*, pp. 6–17 for a summary.

7 Cairo Declaration, 1 December 1943 (1944) reproduced in 38 *American Journal of International Law* (Special Supplement) 8, p. 11.

8 See Principle 10 of the Proclamation Defining Terms of Japanese Surrender, 26 July 1945, reproduced in Boister and Cryer, *Documents*, p. 1.
9 Reproduced in Boister and Cryer, *Documents*, p. 3.
10 *Judgment*, p. 48417, Annex A-2 of the Judgment, Boister and Cryer, *Documents*, p. 72.
11 Totani, *The Tokyo War Crimes Trial*, pp. 23–4.
12 Boister and Cryer, *Reappraisal*, p. 315; Totani, *The Tokyo War Crimes Trial*, p. 9.
13 Futumura, *War Crimes Trials and Transitional Justice,* p. 56, citing SWNCC 150/4/A (21 October 1945).
14 The 'No. 1 Australian List: Japanese Major War Criminals', is annexed to Memorandum from Department of External Affairs, Wellington, to NZ High Commission, London, 2 February 1946, File no. EA 106/3/22, Part 2, Archives New Zealand.
15 Boister and Cryer, *Reappraisal*, p. 63, p. 54.
16 The Allied Foreign Ministers had agreed at a conference held in Moscow on 26 December 1945 that SCAP shall issue orders for the implementation of the Terms of Surrender—see Transcript, p. 48418. They also established the Far Eastern Commission (FEC) to formulate policy for Japan's fulfilment of its obligations under the Instrument of Surrender and to review SCAP decisions—see Boister and Cryer, *Reappraisal*, p. 24.
17 The Proclamation was made under a directive from the State War Navy Coordinating Committee (SWNCC); see Boister and Cryer, *Reappraisal*, p. 22.
18 Special Proclamation—Establishment of an International Military Tribunal for the Far East, 19 January 1946, and Charter of the International Military Tribunal, 26 April 1946; see *Transcript*, pp. 48418–9, Boister and Cryer, *Documents*, pp. 5, 7; discussed at Boister and Cryer, *Reappraisal*, p. 25.
19 The Moscow Conference of Allied Foreign Ministers established the FEC to formulate policy for Japan's fulfilment of its obligations under the Instrument of Surrender and to review SCAP decisions—see Boister and Cryer, *Reappraisal*, p. 24.
20 The FEC's Policy on Apprehension, Trial and Punishment of War Criminals in the Far East, FEC 007/03, effectively ratified the SWNCC Directive to SCAP. See Boister and Cryer, *Reappraisal*, p. 26–31 for discussion.
21 The complaints were made *ad litem* by the defence in challenges to jurisdiction, see *Transcript*, 120ff. They were discussed by the Majority judgment at *Judgment*, pp. 48435. ff. Boister and Cryer, *Documents*, p. 79ff. For discussion see Boister and Cryer, *Reappraisal*, pp. 32. ff.
22 *Judgment*, p. 48440, Boister and Cryer, *Documents*, p. 81.
23 *Judgment*, pp. 48440–1, Boister and Cryer, *Documents*, p. 81.
24 Boister and Cryer, *Reappraisal*, p. 42.
25 Judgment, pp. 48436–7, Boister and Cryer, Documents, p. 79.
26 See International Military Tribunal for the far East, The United States of America and others versus Araki Sadao and others, Judgment of the Hon'ble Justice Pal, Member from India, pp. 32ff. Boister and Cryer, *Documents*, p. 809 at pp. 824ff.
27 See Opinion of the Member for the Netherlands (Mr. Justice Röling), Boister and Cryer, *Documents*, p. 679 at p. 680.
28 See Boister and Cryer, *Reappraisal*, pp. 80–3, Totani, *The Tokyo War Crimes Trial*, pp. 10–7.
29 *Transcript*, 2286; see Boister and Cryer, *Reappraisal*, pp. 93–4.
30 There are various iterations of this judgment in *The Papers of William Flood Webb*, Australian War Memorial, Canberra.
31 Northcroft to M. Myers, Wellington, 18 May 1947, File no. EA 106/3/22, Part 5, Archives New Zealand. Northcroft later gave extensive examples from the Record in support—Northcroft to the NZ Chief Justice, Sir Humphrey O'Leary, 18 March 1947, File no. EA 106/3/22, Part 5, Archives New Zealand.
32 See Boister and Cryer, *Reappraisal*, pp. 99–101.
33 Boister and Cryer, *Reappraisal*, pp. 130, 213.
34 Robert Donihi, 'War Crimes' (1992–1993) 66 *St. John's Law Review* 733, 741.
35 Minear, *Victor's Justice*, p. 211, Totani, *The Tokyo War Crimes Trial*, pp. 30–41; but *contra* Brackman, *The Other Nuremberg*, p. 55.
36 On the prosecutors see Boister and Cryer, *Reappraisal*, pp. 77–8.
37 See Boister and Cryer, *Reappraisal*, pp. 78–80.
38 *Transcript*, pp. 42200–1; quoted in Boister and Cryer, *Reappraisal*, pp. 163–4.
39 Boister and Cryer, *Reappraisal*, p. 79.
40 Letter From R. Quilliam to NZ Dept of External Affairs, 22 July 1946, File no. EA 106/3/22, Part 3, Archives New Zealand. Quilliam was the New Zealand Associate Prosecutor.

41 See Boister and Cryer, *Reappraisal*, pp. 50–4, Totani, *The Tokyo War Crimes Trial*, pp. 42–62.
42 Article 1 of the Tokyo Charter.
43 Article 5 of the Tokyo Charter.
44 The full list of accused is: General Sadao Araki; General Kenji Doihara, Colonel Kingoro Hashimoto; Field Marshal Shunroku Hata; Baron Kiichiro Hiranuma; Prime Minister Kōki Hirota; Naoki Hoshino; General Seishiro Itagaki; Okinori Kaya; Marquis Koichi Kido; General Heitaro Kimura; Prime Minister Kuniaki Koiso; General Iwane Matsui; Yōsuke Matsuoka; General Jiro Minami; General Akira Mutō; Admiral Osami Nagano; Admiral Takasumi Oka; Shūmei Ōkawa; Hiroshi Ōshima; General Kenryo Sato; Mamoru Shigemitsu; Admiral Shigetaro Shimada; Toshio Shiratori; General Teiichi Suzuki; Foreign Minister Shigenori Tōgō; General Hideki Tōjō; General Yoshijiro Umezu. For a synopsis of their records and the reasons for their selection see appendix E of the Indictment, see Boister and Cryer, *Documents*, p. 15 at p. 22. See also Totani, *The Tokyo War Crimes Trial*, pp. 63–72.
45 *Transcript*, p. 17662.
46 Boister and Cryer, *Reappraisal*, pp. 51–3.
47 See Boister and Cryer, *Reappraisal*, pp. 61–9.
48 Herbert P. Bix, *Hirohito and the Making of Modern Japan* (New York: Harper Collins, 2000), pp. 583ff.
49 See Boister and Cryer, *Reappraisal*, p. 67, Totani, *The Tokyo War Crimes Trial*, p. 57.
50 See Bix, *Hirohito*, p. 240,325. He considers the characterisation of the Emperor as a powerless constitutional monarch as gross misrepresentation (p. 583).
51 See Webb, USA and Others v. Araki and Others, Separate opinion of the President, p.18; Boister and Cryer, *Documents*, p. 638; Bernard, Dissenting Judgment of the Member from France of the International Military Tribunal for the Far East, p.19; Boister and Cryer, *Documents*, p. 675; See Boister and Cryer, *Reappraisal*, p. 68 for discussion.
52 John Dower, *Embracing Defeat* (1999), 562.
53 Boister and Cryer, *Reappraisal*, p. 63.
54 See Boister and Cryer, *Reappraisal*, pp. 62–4.
55 Ibid., pp. 85-8, for a discussion of the rights of the accused and the powers of the Tribunal under the Tokyo Charter.
56 Ibid., pp. 83–4.
57 Ibid., pp. 94–5.
58 See Boister and Cryer, *Documents*, pp. 16–70; discussed in Boister and Cryer, *Reappraisal*, 69–73.
59 See Boister and Cryer, *Reappraisal*, pp. 89–90.
60 A. Trainin, 'From Nuremberg to Tokyo' (1948) 12 *New Times* 11, p.13, cited in Boister and Cryer, *Reappraisal*, p. 97. Admiral Nagano and Foreign Minister Matsuoka died during the course of the trial.
61 Article 13 of the Tokyo Charter.
62 See Boister and Cryer, *Reappraisal*, pp. 104–10.
63 Ibid., pp. 111–4.
64 *Dissent*, pp. 321–48, Boister and Cryer, *Documents*, pp. 950–62; see Boister and Cryer, *Reappraisal*, p. 111.
65 Boister and Cryer, *Reappraisal*, pp. 96–6.
66 Ibid., pp. 98–101.
67 *Dissent*, pp. 19–20, Boister and Cryer, *Documents*, pp. 675–6.
68 Boister and Cryer, *Reappraisal*, p. 100.
69 *Dissent*, p. 20, Boister and Cryer, *Documents*, p. 676.
70 *Judgment*, pp. 48437–40, Boister and Cryer, *Documents*, pp. 80–1.
71 Futamura, *War Crimes Tribunals and Transitional Justice*, pp. 91–104.
72 *Judgment*, pp. 49768–9, Boister and Cryer, *Documents*, p. 596.
73 *Judgment*, pp. 49769–71, Boister and Cryer, *Documents*, pp. 596–7.
74 *Judgment*, pp. 48447–8, Boister and Cryer, *Documents*, pp. 84–5, 89.
75 *Judgment*, pp. 49582a–4, Boister and Cryer, *Documents*, pp. 527–8.
76 *Judgment*, pp. 48454–91, Boister and Cryer, *Documents*, pp. 86–530.
77 See, for example, Gordon Ireland, 'Uncommon Law in Martial Tokyo' (1950) 4 *Yearbook of World Affairs* p. 54 at p. 62. The historical value as a record is in the trial record itself rather than its judicial summary.
78 *Dissent*, pp. 39ff. Boister and Cryer, *Documents*, pp. 727ff.
79 *Dissent*, pp. 110–16ff. Boister and Cryer, *Documents*, pp. 856–9ff. see Boister and Cryer, *Reappraisal*, pp. 126–8.
80 Boister and Cryer, *Reappraisal*, pp. 131–2.

81 *Dissent*, p. 693, Boister and Cryer, *Documents*, p. 1143.
82 Including B. Curtis, *The Tokyo War Crimes Trial of Hiroshi Oshima* (Hattiesburg, MS: Unpublished Thesis, University of Southern Mississippi, 1975), p. 60; Marius B Jansen, *The Making of Modern Japan* (Cambridge, MA: The Belknap Press of Harvard University Press, 2000), p. 673; Minear, *Victor's Justice*, pp.129–34; Philip R. Piccigallo, *The Japanese on Trial : Allied War Crimes Operations in the East, 1945–1951* (Austin: University of Texas Press, 1979), p. 212; R.J. Pritchard, 'The International Military Tribunal for the Far East and the Allied National War Crimes trials in Asia' in M.C. Bassiouni (ed.), 3 *International Criminal Law* (2nd edn, Ardsley on Hudson: Transnational 1999) pp.109,119.
83 Elizabeth Kopelman, 'Ideology and International Law: The Dissent of the Indian Justice at the Tokyo War Crimes Trial' (1990–1991) 23 *New York University Journal of International Law and Politics* p. 373 at pp. 375–6.
84 *Opinion*, pp. 11–53, Boister and Cryer, *Documents*, pp. 684–704. See Boister and Cryer, *Reappraisal*, pp. 132–4.
85 See *Indictment*, Appendix A, Section 4, and *Transcript*, pp. 3892ff.
86 *Judgment*, p. 49280 and p. 49322, Boister and Cryer, *Documents*, p. 412 and p. 429. See also, Neil Boister, 'Punishing Japan's "Opium War-Making" in China: "Treaty" or "Core" International Crime?' in Gerry Simpson and Tim McCormack, *Rethinking the Tokyo War Crimes Tribunal* (Kluwer, forthcoming, 2010).
87 *Transcript*, pp. 39030–4. See Boister and Cryer, *Reappraisal*, 154–74.
88 Boister and Cryer, *Reappraisal*, p. 174.
89 *Judgment*, pp. 48452–3, Boister and Cryer, *Documents*, p. 86.
90 *Judgment*, p. 48451, Boister and Cryer, *Documents*, p. 85. See Boister and Cryer, *Reappraisal*, pp. 206–7.
91 Judgment, p. 48491, Boister and Cryer, *Documents*, pp. 181–2.
92 *Judgment*, pp. 49716–21, Boister and Cryer, *Documents*, pp. 577–9. For discussion, see Boister and Cryer, *Reappraisal*, pp. 183–8.
93 *Judgment*, pp. 49592, Boister and Cryer, *Documents*, p. 531.
94 Idem.
95 Judgment, pp. 48443–6, Boister and Cryer, *Documents*, p. 82–4. See Boister and Cryer, *Reappraisal*, pp. 231–2.
96 *Opinion*, pp. 54–61; Boister and Cryer, *Documents*, pp. 704–7.
97 See, for example, his discussion of killings of Allied air crews examined at pp. 1191ff. Boister and Cryer, *Documents*, pp. 11403ff. See Boister and Cryer, *Reappraisal*, pp. 195–6.
98 The individual verdicts begin *Judgment*, p. 49773, Boister and Cryer, *Documents*, p. 598.
99 The sentences are at *Judgment*, p. 49854, Boister and Cryer, *Documents*, p. 626. Two of the accused had died during the course of the trial and one placed under observation because of questions as to his fitness to stand trial.
100 See Boister and Cryer, *Reappraisal*, pp. 252–7.
101 *Opinion*, p. 178, Boister and Cryer, *Documents*, p. 775.
102 *Separate Opinion*, p. 20, Boister and Cryer, *Documents*, p. 639.
103 The Concurring Opinion of the Member for the Philippines (Delfin Jaranilla), p. 32, Boister and Cryer, *Documents*, p. 658.
104 *Dissent*, pp. 20–2, Boister and Cryer, *Documents*, pp. 676–7.
105 *Dissent*, p. 1226, Boister and Cryer, *Documents*, p. 1422.
106 Boister and Cryer, *Documents*, p. 70 for the review. See Boister and Cryer, *Reappraisal*, p. 261.
107 Hirota v MacArthur, 338 US 197, 198.
108 See Boister and Cryer, *Reappraisal*, pp. 264–9.
109 *Dissent*, p. 123, See Boister and Cryer, *Documents*, p. 679.
110 See John Dower, *Defeat: Japan in the Aftermath of World War II* (London, Norton, 1999), p. 474; Futamura, *War Crimes Tribunals*, p. 93.
111 See Futamura, *War Crimes Tribunals and Transitional Justice*, p. 99.
112 Ibid., p. 129.
113 Mr Justice EH Northcroft, *Memorandum for the Right Honourable the Prime Minister Upon the Tokyo Trials 1946–1948*, p. 14, File no. EA 106/3/22, part 9, Archives New Zealand.

3

The trials of Eichmann, Barbie and Finta

Joseph Powderly

Introduction

Between the immediate post–World War II judgments in Nuremberg and Tokyo and the establishment of the *ad hoc* International Criminal Tribunals for the former Yugoslavia and Rwanda, there was very little case law providing for the individual criminal responsibility of those accused of committing heinous international crimes. The cases which are discussed in this chapter—the trial of Adolf Eichmann in Israel, Klaus Barbie in France and Imre Finta in Canada—represent three of the most significant efforts by domestic courts to address the crimes committed in World War II. These prosecutions span decades, and the decisions and judgments which they gave rise to are notable for their contribution to the law on genocide, crimes against humanity, war crimes and universal jurisdiction. They have a broader import, however, as examples of the continuing efforts of the international community to bring an end to impunity, and the inextinguishable importance, even decades later, of pursuing criminal justice against those accused of committing international crimes. The discussion of each case will attempt to provide a brief overview of the charges and the most noteworthy judicial holdings which resulted from the legal process, as well as to provide some biographical context for the individuals charged. For reasons of economy, the cases will be examined both in chronological order and in a degree of depth relative to their significance, both domestic and international.

The trial of Adolf Eichmann

> Men still ask themselves, and they will certainly continue to ask in days to come: How could it have happened? How was it possible in the middle of the twentieth century? The judges at the Nuremberg Trials also asked themselves this question, examined its various aspects and arrived at interesting formulations; yet it would be difficult to claim that a full or satisfactory answer was given. I doubt whether in this trial we on our part will succeed in laying bare the roots of the evil. This task must remain the concern of historians, sociologists, authors and psychologists, who will try to explain to the world what happened to it. But we shall nevertheless endeavour, however briefly, to describe the background, in an attempt to explain what is perhaps altogether inexplicable by the standards of ordinary reason.[1]

While the hardly quantifiable crimes perpetrated in pursuit of the 'Final Solution' were a key component of numerous post–World War II criminal prosecutions arising in a variety of jurisdictional fora, they were rarely (if ever) the sole, explicit focus of proceedings. The Trial of the Major War Criminals at Nuremberg is naturally the most obvious example, with the Judgment of the Tribunal as well as a significant proportion of the documentary record consisting of an extensive examination of the machinery of the Holocaust. The evidence adduced in this respect was not limited to the elaborate bureaucratic paper trails that dominated the proceedings—reducing the courtroom to 'a citadel of boredom'[2]—but rather included the screening of the now iconic Signal Corps documentary, *Nazi Concentration Camps*. The film, which consisted of just over one hour of edited footage compiled by Allied military photographers documenting the liberation of a number of camps,[3] had a profound impact on the tenor of the proceedings, bringing to the fore that which literally could not be expressed in words.[4] While of limited (if practically irrefutable) evidentiary value, the film presented to the court on the afternoon of 29 November 1945 powerfully reminded all those present of the import and full potential horror of the evidentiary record that was unfolding before them. Explaining the context of the film, executive counsel to the American prosecutorial team Thomas Dodd stated:

> This is by no means the entire proof which the prosecution will offer with respect to the subject of concentration camps, but this film which we offer represents in a brief and unforgettable form an explanation of what the words 'concentration camp' imply . . . . We intend to prove that each and every one of these defendants knew of the existence of these concentration camps; that fear and terror and nameless horror of the concentration camps were instruments by which the defendants retained power and suppressed opposition to any of their policies.[5]

Having been screened in the Palace of Justice, *Nazi Concentration Camps* would not be readmitted into the evidentiary record of a case of truly international legal significance until the commencement of proceedings against Adolf Eichmann in April 1961. The true historical significance of the Eichmann prosecution, perhaps, lies in the fact that his trial 'was to be the first and, in certain respects, only trial of international significance that explicitly focused on the crimes of the Holocaust'.[6] As was dramatically—and, in the view of Lawrence Douglas, hyperbolically[7]—expressed by the Attorney-General of Israel, Gideon Hausner, in his opening statement before the District Court of Jerusalem, 'there was only one man who had been concerned almost entirely with the Jews, whose business had been their destruction, whose place in the establishment of the iniquitous regime had been limited to them. That was Adolf Eichmann'.[8]

Unsurprisingly, in the years since the final judgment of the Supreme Court of Israel (sitting as the Court of Criminal Appeal), there has been a wealth of literature focusing on the manifold, multidisciplinary issues contained in the proceedings and which continue to resonate today. The modest objective of this contribution is to highlight the issues arising from the case which are of ongoing relevance to the pursuit of international criminal justice.

The accused—biography, entry into custody and charges

At the conclusion of hostilities in Europe in May 1945, Eichmann held the rank of Lieutenant-Colonel or *Obersturmbannführer* in the Gestapo (*Geheime Staatspolizei*) or Secret State Police of the Third Reich. As such, his activities, or responsibilities if they can be so termed, were subsumed and directed under the auspices of the Reich Main Security Office (*Reichssicherheitshauptamt*) or RSHA, which was primarily concerned with the realization of the Final Solution.[9]

Between 1942 and 1945 Eichmann directed Section IV B(4) of the RSHA, the division responsible for 'Evacuations and Jews',[10] a somewhat euphemistic departmental heading which failed to fully express the fact that Eichmann was an important component in the Nazi infrastructure for the transportation of millions of European Jews to concentration/death camps in Eastern Europe. However, that being said, as a Lieutenant-Colonel he was not considered of sufficient seniority to warrant inclusion in either the indictment of the International Military Tribunal (IMT) at Nuremberg or any subsequent indictment under Control Council Law No. 10.

While Eichmann evaded prosecution under the Nuremberg process, the IMT was far from silent with respect to his involvement in the machinery of the Holocaust. In fact, Eichmann appears on several occasions in the transcripts of the main proceedings and is mentioned on three occasions in the IMT Final Judgment.[11] A number of witnesses testified as to his involvement in the destruction of European Jewry, most notably Captain (*Hauptsturmführer*) Dieter Wisliceny, who testified before the Tribunal on 3 January 1946. As the quoted passage below illustrates, Wisliceny's testimony was both incriminating and shocking:

> Lt. Col. Brookhart: When did you last see Eichmann?
> Wisliceny: I last saw Eichmann towards the end of February 1945 in Berlin. At that time he said that if the war were lost he would commit suicide.
> Lt. Col. Brookhart: Did he say anything at that time as to the number of Jews that had been killed?
> Wisliceny: Yes, he expressed this in a particularly cynical manner. He said he would leap laughing into the grave because the feeling that he had 5 million people on his conscience would be for him a source of extraordinary satisfaction.[12]

As these proceedings were taking place, Eichmann was working as a lumberjack in Lower Saxony under the assumed name of Otto Heninger. However, no doubt acutely aware of his new position in the conscience of the world community, in 1950, Eichmann successfully (but obviously fraudulently) obtained an International Committee of the Red Cross passport under the name Riccardo Klement, and made his way to the Axis refuge that was Argentina. He remained there until his abduction by agents of the state of Israel in May 1960. During his 10 or so years in Argentina, Eichmann, whose family joined him in 1952,[13] worked variously at a Mercedes-Benz manufacturing plant in Buenos Aires and—quite bizarrely—as a commercial rabbit farmer.[14]

Eichmann was abducted in Buenos Aires by Israeli agents on 11 May 1960, an act clearly in violation of Argentinean sovereignty, which unsurprisingly gave rise to a very real diplomatic incident between the two states culminating in the passing of a 'scolding' United Nations Security Council Resolution.[15] He was detained for 1 week, interrogated[16] and transported (via a commercial flight[17]) to Tel Aviv.[18] On 23 May, Israeli Prime Minister David Ben-Gurion informed the Knesset that, 'a short time ago one of the greatest of the Nazi war criminals, Adolf Eichmann ... was found by the Israeli security services'.[19] He commented further that he would 'shortly be placed on trial in Israel under the law for the trial of the Nazis and their collaborators'.[20]

The law Ben-Gurion was referring to was the Nazi and Nazi Collaborators (Punishment) Law, 1950. Eichmann was charged with 15 counts falling under three headings: (i) crimes against the Jewish people as defined under Section 1(a); (ii) crimes against humanity as defined under Section 1(b); and (iii) membership in a criminal enemy organization contrary to Section 3 of the law. The definitions of the offences under the law were broadly derived from existing instruments relevant to international criminal law. 'Crimes against the Jewish people', which on the face of it appears to be an entirely new and unique offence, is in fact a particularization of Article II of the Genocide Convention of 1948: '"crime against the Jewish people" means any of the following acts, committed with intent to destroy *the Jewish people* in whole or in part . . .'.[21] However, it did develop the definition somewhat to include a reference to cultural genocide: Section 1(b)(6) refers to 'destroying or desecrating Jewish religious or cultural assets or values'.[22] The definition of crimes against humanity under Section 1(b) of the law was closely modeled on Article 6(c) of the Charter of the IMT and Article 5(c) of Control Council Law No. 10, with a couple of exceptions: (i) it was not necessary to establish a nexus between the impugned acts and the armed conflict or other crimes committed under the law; and (ii) in terms of temporal jurisdiction, the law applied to acts committed during the entirety of the Nazi reign, i.e. stretching back to 1933.[23] The definition of war crimes under Section 1 was likewise derived from the Charter of the IMT and the Control Council Law, with the narrowing exception that it did not extend beyond the enumerated categories of conduct to other violations of the law and customs of war.[24] There are a host of issues which make the law somewhat irregular and apparently troubling from a human rights and rule of law perspective: namely, the law is retrospective, extra-territorial, has a flexible approach to the principle of double jeopardy or *ne bis in idem*, and carries the death penalty. These issues were raised by Eichmann and dealt with by both the District and the Supreme Court.

The proceedings—defence strategy

Eichmann was arraigned before the District Court of Jerusalem on 11 April 1961. However, given the enormous national and international interest in the case, the proceedings did not take place in their normal setting, but rather were housed in the Beit Ha'am community centre and theatre which had a capacity audience of over 1,000 persons. While Beit Ha'am was renovated to accommodate the requirements of a modern trial, the proceedings took on an essentially theatrical or dramatic context.[25] The theatrical spectacle of the proceedings was only enhanced by the presence of the accused, who, flanked by two court guards, sat stage left, housed in a bulletproof glass booth throughout the proceedings.[26] In response to each of the 15 charges, Eichmann stated rather ambiguously, 'Not guilty in the sense of the indictment'.[27] His lawyer, Dr. Robert Servatius,[28] chosen by Eichmann and paid for by the state of Israel, attempted to clarify any ambiguity by stating, 'Eichmann feels guilty before God, not before the law'.[29] Over the course of the 14 weeks of the trial, the courtroom rarely descended into the condition of a 'citadel of boredom', characteristic of the Nuremberg proceedings. This was due in large measure to the pedagogic role assumed by the prosecution. It soon became clear through the extensive use of witness testimony—which had been something of a rarity at Nuremberg—that the process was to be as much about the sharing of individual survivor memory as it was about a clinical prosecution of the accused. Witness upon witness poured forth their personal stories of loss and survival, the details or circumstances of which, on the majority of occasions, were of little specific evidentiary value.[30]

Eichmann's defence strategy was composed of a number of interweaving strands including, *inter alia*: (i) challenges to the compatibility of the 1950 Law and the proceedings in general with the principle of legality, or *nullem crimen sine lege*, i.e. its retrospective nature; (ii) the ability of the state of Israel to exercise jurisdiction over the alleged crimes given that they were not committed on its territory or against its citizens and which indeed were being prosecuted by a state that did not exist at the time of their commission; (iii) the impossibility for the three-judge bench of the District Court to remain impartial and ensure a fair trial; (iv) his illegal detention and transport into the custody of the state of Israel in violation of basic principles of public international law; (v) the conduct with which he was charged should be considered as acts of state; and (vi) irrespective of issues surrounding the legality of the proceedings, at a fundamental level he should be found not guilty on the charges as in all aspects of his conduct he had been merely faithfully and patriotically carrying out the orders of his superiors. Eichmann claimed repeatedly during the three weeks of his testimony that he was simply an 'official preparing timetables for the trains which carried the deportees to the East from their various countries',[31] that he was but a '"small cog" in the extermination machine'.[32]

Legal findings—their contribution to international law

The District Court found Eichmann guilty on all counts. However, it should be noted that with respect to counts 1–4 of the indictment relating to crimes against the Jewish people, the court ruled that he should be only found guilty of those acts committed after October 1941, the date on which they determined he became fully and explicitly aware of the plan to exterminate the Jews. He was sentenced to death by hanging. Eichmann appealed the conviction and sentence of the court on a number of grounds that had already been brought to the attention of court during the trial proceedings:[33] namely, the court's lack of jurisdiction, the inability of the bench to guarantee a fair and impartial process and the fact that he played only a minor role in the implementation of the final solution.

The legal challenges that Eichmann, or more accurately Servatius, made to the prosecuting law and process were based on questions of fundamental importance to the rule of law. It should be clear that they were not frivolous or deliberately disruptive, as is characteristic of a certain proportion of defence motions in contemporary international criminal trials. However, they were all ultimately unsuccessful.

Eichmann's argument that the 1950 Law constituted retroactive criminal punishment in violation of the principle of legality and other international legal principles was roundly rejected by both the District and Supreme Court. Building on the findings of the IMT, the District Court stated, '. . . all of the above mentioned crimes constituted crimes under the laws of all civilized nations, including the German people, before and after the Nazi régime . . . [a] law which enables the punishment of Nazis and their collaborators does not "conflict", by reason of its retroactive application, "with the rules of natural justice". . . on the contrary, it gives reality to the dictates of elementary justice'.[34] The Supreme Court commented further that in any event, the principle *nullum crimen sine lege* had not 'yet become a rule of customary international law'.[35]

At a fundamental level, the Eichmann trial and the law on which it was based was an expression of Israel's desire to exercise its right to *universal jurisdiction* over the crimes of the Holocaust:

> The abhorrent crimes defined in this law are not crimes under Israeli law alone. These crimes, which struck at the whole of mankind and shocked the conscience of nations, are grave offences against the law of nations itself (*delicta juris gentium*). Therefore, so far from international law negating or limiting the jurisdiction of countries with respect to such crimes, international law is, in the absence of an International Court, in need of the judicial and legislative organs of every country to give effect to its criminal interdictions and to bring the criminals to trial. The jurisdiction to try crimes under international law is *universal*.[36]

This finding was affirmed by the Supreme Court which stated:

> Not only do all of the crimes attributed to the appellant bear an international character, but their harmful and murderous effects were so embracing and widespread as to shake the

> international community to its very foundations. The State of Israel therefore was entitled, pursuant to the principle of universal jurisdiction and in the capacity of a guardian of international law and an agent for its enforcement, to try the appellant. That being the case, no importance attaches to the fact that the State of Israel did not exist when the offences were committed.[37]

As the Supreme Court asserted, it was of no significance that the state of Israel did not exist at the time, nor that the crimes were not committed on the territory of the (at that point) future state. The Supreme Court noted the judgment of the Permanent Court of International Justice in the *Lotus* case in concluding that, 'as yet no international accord exists on the question of the jurisdiction of a State to punish persons who are not its nationals for acts committed beyond its borders'.[38] Both courts however, insisted that there was a very real link between the victims of the crimes charged and the state.[39] Such an irrefutable link satisfied the protective principle relevant to jurisdiction under international law. While Eichmann may have asserted that there were 18 other states with a more concrete claim to jurisdiction, none of these states had objected to, or were unsupportive of the proceedings.[40]

The reliance of both courts on the doctrine of universal jurisdiction as the basis for the proceedings represents the true international legal legacy of the case. However, it is worth mentioning a number of issues which continue to be the source of significant debate. As noted above, the definition of 'crimes against the Jewish people' under the 1950 Law was closely derived from the Genocide Convention of 1948. If it was not obvious enough from the text, the District Court explicitly acknowledged that the provision was 'defined on the pattern of the crime of genocide',[41] as provided for in the Genocide Convention. With the prosecution's reliance on universal jurisdiction, certain questions had be asked as to the applicability of this principle to the crime of genocide. Eichmann argued that Article VI of the Genocide Convention specifically precluded the exercise of universal jurisdiction over acts of genocide, stating as it does that, '[p]ersons charged with genocide or any of the other acts enumerated under Article III shall be tried by a competent tribunal of the State in the territory of which the act was committed, or by such international penal tribunal as may have jurisdiction with respect to those Contracting Parties which shall have accepted its jurisdiction'.[42] The District Court disagreed. Citing General Assembly Resolution 96(1) and the Advisory Opinion of the International Court of Justice on the question of *Reservations to the Convention on Genocide*, it found rather that the absence of a provision establishing universal jurisdiction was a 'grave defect in the Convention', likely 'to weaken the joint effort for the prevention of the commission of this abhorrent crime'.[43] Furthermore, this defect could not result in the conclusion that universal jurisdiction could not be exercised over the crime of genocide.[44] This conclusion largely ignored the fact that, during the drafting of Article VI, the issue of universal jurisdiction was discussed at length and specifically rejected.[45] Whether this interpretation is compatible with the object and purpose of the Convention is in significant doubt; however, what is clear is that it is not in accordance with the ordinary meaning of Article VI.[46]

With respect to Eichmann's contention that his actions should be considered acts of state, the District Court determined that, '[i]t is true that under international law Germany bears not only moral, but also legal, responsibility for all the crimes that were committed as its own "acts of State", including the crimes attributed to the accused. But that responsibility does not detract one iota from the personal responsibility of the accused for his acts'.[47] On the related contention that the acts were merely carried out in obedience to the orders of his superiors, the Supreme Court noted that Section 8 of the 1950 Law specifically removed the applicability of this argument as a complete defence to the charges and could only be considered as possible grounds for mitigation of punishment. This provision was entirely compatible with Nuremberg Principles.[48]

Neither the District Court nor the Supreme Court attached any importance to the manner in which Eichmann was brought into the custody of the state. At the commencement of proceedings, Israeli-Argentinian relations had been restored following the passing of United Nations Security Council Resolution 138 noting the infringement of Argentinian sovereignty and the issuance of a joint communiqué declaring the matter resolved. Argentinian sovereignty was the victim not the accused; in this respect the District Court noted that, 'it is an established rule of law that a person being tried for an offence against the laws of a State may not oppose his trial by reason of the illegality of his arrest or of the means whereby he was brought within the jurisdiction of that State'.[49]

In supporting Eichmann's conviction by the District Court in its judgment of 29 May 1962, the Supreme Court also confirmed the sentence of death. Eichmann, as well as a number of diverse interest groups who opposed the proceedings from the start, pleaded to Itzhak Ben-Zvi, the President of Israel, for mercy.[50] On the evening of 31 May, Ben-Zvi formally rejected all pleas and Eichmann was hanged two hours later, his body was cremated and the ashes scattered in the Mediterranean. Eichmann remains the only person in Israeli history to be put to death on order of the state.[51] The legal legacy of the trial is vast and continues to be frequently cited in both domestic and international decisions relevant to international criminal law. However, perhaps more important is the didactic role that the proceedings have played in the preservation of Holocaust memory.

The trial of Klaus Barbie

As a member of the Allies and signatory of the IMT Charter, France played a central role in the Trial of the Major War Criminals at Nuremberg. Indeed, in this respect, it is worth noting the contribution of the primary French Judge at the IMT, Henri Donnedieu de Vabres, who was extremely outspoken on issues such as conspiracy, individual criminal responsibility and the principle of legality.[52] On the domestic plane, however, France's immediate post–World War II record with respect to the prosecution of international crimes, specifically crimes against humanity, left much to be desired until the prosecutions of Paul Touvier, Klaus Barbie and Maurice Papon in the 1970s, 1980s and 1990s.[53] The failure to pursue successful prosecutions was a consequence of statutory ambiguity as to the interpretation to be given to the applicable law, but also involved a certain political reluctance to potentially reopen the historical record with regard to the acts committed during the Vichy and colonial Algerian periods. Focusing on this issue of statutory ambiguity, the relevant piece of legislation in this respect is Law Number 64–1326 of 26 December 1964 ('1964 Law'), which in just one sentence aims to incorporate the Nuremberg conception of crimes against humanity into the domestic penal code:

> Crimes against humanity as defined in the Resolution of the United Nations of 13 February 1946, that took note of the definition of crimes against humanity as set forth in the Charter of international tribunal of 8 August 1945, are not subject to any statute of limitations by their nature.

The first opportunity to formulate an interpretation of the law, and thus to the scope of the meaning of crimes against humanity, did not arise until the *Touvier* case in 1975.[54] In this instance, the Criminal Chamber of the Court of Cassation stated that 'crimes against humanity are ordinary crimes committed under certain circumstances and for certain motives specified in the text that defines them'.[55] In 'defining' the offence in this way the Court was attempting to distinguish crimes against humanity from war crimes; however, the effect of the description of crimes against humanity as ordinary criminal acts was essentially to trivialize or 'banalize' their true character.[56] Furthermore, the decision failed in an elemental sense to clearly lay down the distinguishing characteristics of war crimes and crimes against humanity. It neglected to comment on whether the law was applicable to acts committed by French citizens and, crucially from a practical prosecutorial perspective, it did not resolve the question of whether the law's express abolition of the statute of limitations for crimes against humanity was of retroactive applicability, a process viewed with deep unease in the French legal tradition. When the question came before the Criminal Chamber of the Court of Cassation in October 1975, it was decided that the answer was dependent on the interpretation of Article 6 of the IMT Charter and Article 7 of the European Convention on Human Rights.

As the interpretation of international treaties was a matter for the executive branch, the question was referred to the Minister for Foreign Affairs, who did not issue a formal response until 15 July 1979—some four years later.[57] When it was finally issued, the interpretation was unpublished and sent only to the parties in the case, making it difficult for practitioners to be fully aware of the state of the applicable law.[58] The essential finding of the Minister, as noted by the Court of Cassation (Criminal Chamber) in Barbie, was as follows:

> [T]he only principle with regard to the statutory limitation of prosecution for crimes against humanity which is to be deducible from the text [of the IMT Charter] is that the prosecution of such crimes is not subject to statutory limitation . . . the prosecution of crimes against humanity is in accordance with the general principles of law recognized by civilized nations and, on this account, such crimes are not subject to the operation of the principle of the non-retroactivity of criminal laws.[59]

With ministerial confirmation that the 1964 Law was retroactively applicable, the prosecution of alleged instances of crimes against humanity committed during the Vichy period could recommence with the case against Klaus Barbie. During the course of the proceedings a number of fundamental legal questions were addressed: most significantly, the exact contours of the definition of crimes against humanity for the purposes of the 1964 Law.

The accused—biography, entry into custody and charges

Nicholas 'Klaus' Barbie was born in Bad Godesberg, on the German–French border, in October 1913. An enthusiastic participant in the Nazi Youth movement, at the conclusion of his secondary education he carried this verve into the SS (*Schutztaffeln*) and the Gestapo, which he joined in 1935. With the occupation of the Netherlands in May 1940, Barbie was appointed to Section IV of the security police (*Sicherheitsdienst*) and the Security Service of the SS ('the SD') in Amsterdam. His primary tasks were to weed out and destroy any Resistance forces and to identify Jews for deportation and execution.[60] In November 1942, he became head of the Gestapo in Lyons (holding the rank of Lieutenant or *Obersturmführer*) and was charged with complete suppression of the flourishing Resistance movement in the city. It is estimated that between November 1942 and August 1944—when Barbie was promoted to the rank of Captain (*Hauptsturmführer*) in the SS—over 4,000 individuals had been executed on his express orders and almost 8,000 deported to death camps.[61] Barbie's reliance on torture in gathering information both on Jewish families and on the activities of the Resistance earned him the moniker 'the Butcher of Lyons',[62] an alias revised years later by Alain Finkelkraut, who designated him the 'poor man's Eichmann'.[63] Heinous as these acts were, it was for the death of Resistance talisman Jean Moulin that Barbie was most notoriously remembered.[64]

By the end of 1944, Barbie had appeared on the United Nations List of War Criminals as War Criminal No. 239.[65] Barbie's post-war activities are narratively extraordinary, not to say embarrassing for a number of states. Between 1947 and 1951, Barbie was employed by the United States Counter Intelligence Corps (CIC) in West Germany and was actively engaged in searching for communists and Soviet agents despite the fact that the French authorities were very actively seeking his prosecution. The CIC protected Barbie during this time, concealed his activities from the French authorities and in 1951 provided him (and his family) with funds, false documentation and transit to Boliva. The full extent of American involvement in perpetuating Barbie's impunity was revealed in the 'Ryan Report' commissioned by the then United States Attorney General.[66] While Barbie remained elusive, in April 1952 and November 1954 he was charged and convicted *in absentia* for war crimes and sentenced to death by the *Tribunal Permanent des Forces Armées de Lyon*.

Barbie remained in Bolivia (and for certain periods in Peru) for more than 30 years, became a Bolivian citizen and a highly successful illegal arms trader or so-called Lord of War. He was a close confidant of successive Bolivian regimes and held the rank of honorary colonel in the Bolivian Army.[67] The French authorities became aware of Barbie's whereabouts during the 1960s and 1970s; however, due to the lack of an extradition agreement with Bolivia and the fact that Barbie had ingratiated himself with the Bolivian authorities, it was not possible to bring him into custody.[68] The situation changed in 1982 with the election of socialist President Sile Zuazo, who, with the sweetener of a generous aid package from the Mitterrand government, agreed to deport—not extradite—Barbie. On 5 February 1983, Barbie was expelled from Bolivia on the grounds that he had entered the country under a false name. He was flown to Cayenne in French Guiana, whereupon he was arrested, spirited to France and imprisoned in Montluc prison in Lyons, the very site of his past brutalities.[69] He was charged with 17 counts of crimes against humanity falling under the 1964 Law.[70]

The proceedings—defence strategy

Barbie was defended during the trial proceedings by Jacques Vergès,[71] a highly controversial French lawyer and veteran Marxist revolutionary, who transformed the proceedings into a public attack on French actions in Algeria and on his perception of Western Imperialism generally.[72] Leaving Vergès' politicization of the process to one side, Barbie's legal defence centered on two arguments: (i) he was the victim of an illegal extradition procedure and had been effectively kidnapped by the French authorities (in much the same way as Eichmann); and (ii) the proceedings were in violation of the principle of double jeopardy (*ne bis in idem*) as his activities during the period 1942–1944 had already been the subject of *in absentia* war crimes proceedings in 1952 and 1954, the convictions from which were statute barred as of November 1984 (citing the 20-year prescription rule for war crimes).

Barbie was in custody in Lyon for over four years before substantive proceedings against him commenced before the *Cour d'assises du Rhône* in May 1987 (these of course are distinguishable from proceedings addressing procedural and jurisdictional matters that had been ongoing since 1983). The 36 days of the trial dominated the French media; the Barbie trial was in effect to France what Eichmann had been to Israel,[73] in that the proceedings played an important role in the revival of Holocaust, Vichy and Resistance memory. Barbie, however, was not the willing participant that Eichmann had been. On the third day of the trial, Barbie addressed the court stating:

> Mr. Prosecutor, I would like to say that I am a Bolivian citizen and that if I am present here it is because I have been deported illegally . . . I place it fully in the hands of my lawyer to defend my honour in front of justice, despite the climate of vengeance [and] the lynching campaign set forth by the French media.[74]

Barbie's waiver of his right to be present throughout the proceedings was accepted by the court.

Legal findings—issues of relevance to international law

The *Cour d'assises du Rhône* found Barbie guilty of all charges and sentenced him to life imprisonment. During the course of the proceedings several core aspects of the 1964 Law were subject to creative, highly innovative judicial interpretation. This was primarily the case with respect to the enumeration of the applicable definition of crimes against humanity. Of particular concern was whether or not acts committed against members of the Resistance were to be considered war crimes, crimes against humanity or (in certain circumstances) both. If they were designated as war crimes only, Barbie's acts would be subject to the applicable statute of limitations, meaning, *inter alia*, that it would be not be possible to prosecute him for the death of Jean Moulin. A decision of the Indicting Chamber or *Chambre d'accusation* held just this on 4 October 1985.[75] Based on an interpretation of Article 6(c) of the IMT Charter, it was determined that the Resistance was to be considered an organized fighting force not part of the civilian population.[76] This interpretation, however, was overturned on appeal by the Court of Cassation, which stated that

> Neither the driving force which motivated the victims, nor their possible membership of the Resistance, excludes the possibility that the accused acted with the element of intent necessary for the commission of crimes against humanity. In pronouncing as it did and excluding from the category of crimes against humanity all the acts imputed to the accused committed against members or possible members of the Resistance, the *Chambre d'accusation* misconstrued the meaning and the scope of the provisions listed in these grounds of appeal.[77]

The crucial element distinguishing war crimes from crimes against humanity, therefore, was not the identity or status of the victim as such, but rather the specific intent and ideological motivation of the perpetrator. This was expressed in more detail in the unique definition of crimes against humanity forwarded by the Court of Cassation:

> The following acts constitute crimes against humanity within the meaning of Article 6(c) of the Charter of the Nuremberg International Military Tribunal annexed to the London Agreement of 8 August 1945, which are not subject to statutory limitation of the right of prosecution, even if they are crimes which can also be classified as war crimes within the meaning of Article 6(b) of the Charter: inhumane acts and persecution committed in a systematic manner in the name of a State practicing a policy of ideological hegemony, not only against persons by reason of their membership of a racial or religious community, but also against the opponents of that policy whatever the form of their opposition.[78]

This formulation of crimes against humanity does not have any basis in the text of Article 6(c). The bizarre implication of the requirement that the acts be committed in the name of a state in pursuit of ideological hegemony means that, in the absence of such an express policy, crimes against humanity cannot be committed. In addition, the Court of Cassation had, perhaps unconsciously, designated all those who lost their lives opposing Nazism, by whatever means, victims of crimes against humanity.[79]

Despite the weak foundations of the definition, the decision of the Court is noteworthy for the clear qualitative distinction it draws between war crimes and crimes against humanity:

> [I]n contrast to crimes against humanity, war crimes are directly connected with the existence of a situation of hostilities declared between the respective States to which the perpetrators and the victims of the acts in question belong. Following the termination of hostilities, it is necessary that the passage of time should be allowed to blur acts of brutality which may have been committed in the course of armed conflict, even if those acts constituted violations of the laws and customs of war or were not justified by military necessity, provided that those acts were not of such a nature as to deserve the qualification of crimes against humanity.[80]

In so doing, the Court effectively rejected its own characterisation of crimes against humanity as 'ordinary crimes' as laid down in the *Touvier* case.[81]

Addressing Barbie's contention that he was illegally brought before the court, the Court of Appeal of Lyons made perhaps an inadvertent, but valuable statement that continues to be cited, relating to the applicability of the principle of universal jurisdiction to crimes against humanity. It stated:

> [B]y reason of their nature, the crimes against humanity with which Barbie is indicted do not simply fall within the scope of French municipal criminal law, but are subject to an international criminal order to which notions of frontiers and extradition rules arising therefrom are completely foreign.[82]

This statement was modestly endorsed by the Court of Cassation, who added that there 'is no obstacle to the bringing of a prosecution against the accused on national territory provided that the rights of the defence are fully and freely ensured before both the examining magistrate and the trial court'.[83]

Barbie appealed the judgment and sentence of the *Cour d'assises du Rhône* on some 14 grounds, all of which were rejected by the Court. He thus became the first person in French legal history to be convicted of crimes against humanity. He died in his cell in Montluc prison on 25 September 1991.

The trial of Imre Finta

The absence from the Canadian Criminal Code of a jurisdictional basis for the prosecution of war crimes and crimes against humanity committed outside of the territory of Canada was finally addressed by way of a legislative amendment in 1987, which gave rise to Section 6(1.91).[84] It provided:

> [E]very person who, either before or after the coming into force of this subsection, commits an act or omission outside Canada that constitutes a war crime or a crime against humanity and that, if committed in Canada, would constitute an offence against the laws of Canada in force at the time of the act or omission shall be deemed to commit that act or omission in Canada at that time if . . . (a)(i) that person is a Canadian citizen or is employed by Canada

in a civilian or military capacity, (ii) that person is a citizen of, or is employed in a civilian or military capacity by, a state that is engaged in an armed conflict against Canada, or (iii) the victim of the act or omission is a Canadian citizen or a citizen of a state that is allied with Canada in an armed conflict.

The prosecution of Imre Finta within months of the entry into law of the amendment provided the Canadian criminal justice system with the initial opportunity to explore both the legislation's efficacy from a prosecutorial perspective and its compatibility with the Canadian Charter of Rights and Freedoms. The issues encountered throughout the process by the High Court of Justice, the Ontario Court of Appeal and the Supreme Court closely mirror those raised in the prosecutions of Eichmann and Barbie, insofar as all three prosecutions explored issues relating to the principle of legality (retroactivity), extraterritoriality (universal jurisdiction), and the interpretation of the definition of war crimes and crimes against humanity as derived from Article 6(b) and (c) of the IMT Charter.

The accused—biography, entry into custody and charges

Imre Finta was born in 1912 and, after studying law, he joined the Royal Hungarian Gendarmerie, an armed paramilitary police force. He rose through the ranks, ultimately being promoted to Captain, and in 1944, was transferred to Szeged as Division Commander of Gendarmerie Investigations.[85] Following the passing of the 'Baky decree' by the German-installed Hungarian government in April 1944 and the ghettoisation of the Hungarian Jews, Finta was responsible for the forcible detention of 8,617 Jews in the Szeged brickyards, their interrogation and eventual deportation.[86] After the war, Finta reportedly spent 18 months in an American POW camp in Germany; in 1951, he emigrated to Canada and opened a restaurant in Toronto.[87] He became a Canadian citizen in 1956.

In 1948, Finta was tried *in absentia* and convicted of 'crimes against the people' by a Hungarian court.[88] In 1970, a general amnesty was issued which covered Finta's conviction. Finta's wartime activities were brought to the attention of the Canadian authorities, in part, because of two civil libel suits launched by Finta in 1983 against the head of the Canadian Holocaust Remembrance Association and the television network CTV, both of whom had issued publications linking Finta to Nazi war crimes.[89] He was to drop both suits shortly after the commencement of the respective legal hearings, but shortly afterwards—and only three months after the adoption of the Canadian war crime provisions—Finta was indicted in Ontario and charged with unlawful confinement, robbery, kidnapping and manslaughter as crimes against humanity and war crimes under the Canadian Criminal Code.[90]

Proceedings—defence strategy

Finta was represented by Douglas Christie, who had also represented Ernst Zundel in his trial for Holocaust denial (during which he challenged the introduction of *Nazi Concentration Camps* on the grounds of hearsay since the unnamed narrators were not available for cross-examination,[91]) He launched a spirited (though not uncontroversial) defence on a number of legal grounds. Christie challenged the war crimes provisions of the Criminal Code as, *inter alia*, a violation of the guarantee of equality before the law as provided for in the Charter of Rights and Freedoms, on the basis that Finta's involvement in the deportation of Hungarian Jews to Auschwitz was similar to the deportation of Japanese citizens in Canada during World War II, yet the Criminal Code only covers acts or omissions performed by individuals outside Canada.[92] Christie also condemned the Criminal Code as unconstitutional on the basis that it amounted to retroactive criminal legislation. He argued that war crimes and crimes against humanity had not existed at the time relevant to the indictment, that the war crimes legislation violated the principle of extraterritoriality and that the evidence against Finta was of questionable value as it emanated from governments which were not regarded as free and democratic. During the jury trial itself, Christie chose not to call Finta to testify, at least in part 'to avoid potentially damaging cross-examination'.[93]

In July 1989, Judge Callaghan of the Supreme Court of Ontario issued a decision on the pre-trial motions which upheld the constitutionality of the war crimes provisions of the Canadian Criminal Code and dismissed the defence objections.[94] The decision stated that the effect of the war crimes provisions was *retrospective*, not retroactive; it 'did not transform a formerly innocent act into a criminal offence, but changed the legal consequences of an existing offence'.[95] Judge Callaghan rejected Christie's argument that war crimes and crimes against humanity were not recognized as criminal offences prior to 1945, and quoted the IMT judgment in support of the finding that war crimes and crimes against humanity were offences under international law or general principles of law recognized by the community of nations by 1939.[96] The argument that the Criminal Code was discriminatory and breached the equality provision of the Charter was also dismissed, on the basis that the treatment of Japanese citizens by the Canadian government, although unjust, was both distinguishable and 'dramatically different' from the treatment of Hungarian Jews.[97] Judge Callaghan also invoked the principle of universal jurisdiction in rejecting the defence argument that the Criminal Code provisions constituted an unjustifiable exercise of extraterritorial jurisdiction.[98]

Legal findings—issues of relevance to international criminal law

There are a range of issues of import to international justice arising from the proceedings; however, this section will briefly focus on just one that had a direct bearing on Finta's acquittal on all of the charges: the determination of the applicable *mens rea* or mental element for crimes against humanity. Supporting Presiding Judge Campbell's instructions to the jury with respect to this issue, Supreme Court Justice Cory writing with the majority stated that '[t]he requisite mental element of a war crime or a crime against humanity should be based on a subjective test'. However, he added that 'the mental element of crimes against humanity must involve awareness of the facts or circumstances which would bring the acts within the definition of a crime against humanity'.[99] These elements are relatively uncontroversial, but significant concerns arose from the inclusion of the following additional requirement:

> [T]he additional element is that the inhumane acts were based on discrimination against or the persecution of an identifiable group of people .... These elements must be established both in order for a Canadian court to have the jurisdiction to try the accused and in order to convict the accused of the offence.[100]

Thus, in order for an individual to be prosecuted for crimes against humanity, discriminatory or persecutory intent must be established. This finding was strongly criticized by Judge La Forest in his dissenting opinion, who held that 'there [was] no need for the jury to be concerned with the mental element in relation to war crimes and crimes against humanity beyond those comprised in the underlying domestic offence'.[101] The factual conditions required for war crimes and crimes against humanity, such as the existence of an armed conflict or presence of an occupying force, were relevant only in relation to jurisdiction over the offences and did not go to individual criminal responsibility.[102]

It is questionable whether the standard set by the majority was in conformity with customary international law at the time. Indeed, subsequent case law of the Yugoslavia Tribunal specifically rejected the requirement of proof of the presence of discriminatory intent for all crimes against humanity beyond that of the crime of persecution.[103]

Conclusion

Each of the cases discussed above highlights a number of challenges inherent in retrospective domestic prosecutions of international crimes. The apprehension and trial of Adolf Eichmann were legally problematic, but provided a vital pedagogical function for a young state still trying to comprehend the horrors of the Holocaust. The legacy of the Klaus Barbie trial encompasses both an attempt to expansively interpret the category of victims of crimes against humanity in World War II, and was a painful and politically sensitive examination of the previously suppressed crimes of Vichy France. The failed prosecution of Imre Finta arose as a result of Canada's commendable enthusiasm for vigorously pursuing justice for international crimes, but ultimately illustrated the pitfalls of attempting to create a workable definition for such crimes within domestic criminal law.

Each of these cases were pioneering in their own way; each made their own modest contribution to the evolution of international criminal law at a time when such case law was particularly sparse; and each, though initiated for essentially political reasons, managed to transcend the constraints of domestic jurisdiction to become a truly significant international precedent.

Notes

1 Attorney-General of the Government of Israel v. Adolf Eichmann, Criminal Case. 40/61, District Court of Jerusalem. Opening statement of Attorney-General Gideon Hausner, accessed originally at http://www.nizkor.org/hweb/people/e/eichmann-adolf/transcripts/Sessions/Session-006-007-008-01.html.

2 R. West, *A Train of Powder*, New York: Viking Press, 1955, p. 3.

3 Specifically, Buchenwald, Dachau, Nordhausen, Ohrdruf and Penig Concentration Camps.

4 For an in-depth discussion of the significance of the film in the context of the overall proceedings, see: L. Douglas, *The Memory of Judgment: Making Law and History in the Trials of the Holocaust*, New Haven, Yale University Press, 2001, pp. 11–37; and C. Delage, *La Vérité par l'image: De Nuremberg au process Milosevic*, Paris, Denoël, 2006, pp. 91–180.

5 Trial of the Major War Criminals before the International Military Tribunal, Nuremberg, Volume II, 14 November 1945—1 October 1946, proceedings of 29 November 1945 at 431–2.

6 Douglas, *The Memory of Judgment*, p. 97.

7 Ibid., p. 98.

8 Opening statement of Gideon Hausner, as quoted in Douglas, *The Memory of Judgment*, p. 98.

9 Douglas, *The Memory of Judgment*, p. 98, quoting from R. Hilberg, *The Destruction of European Jews*, New York, Harper & Row, 1961, p.185. The National Socialist administrative structure was extremely complex. For the purposes of its judgment, the District Court succinctly summarized the fundamental pillars: See, Attorney-General of the Government of Israel v. Adolf Eichmann, (District Court Judgment, 12 December 1961), 36 ILR 5 (1968), [hereinafter Eichmann District Court Judgment], pp. 85–6.

10 The statement of the District Court with respect to Eichmann's basic biographical information (to 1945) can be found at: Eichmann District Court Judgment, pp. 84–5 and 86–93. See also, M. Lippman, 'Genocide: The Trial of Adolf Eichmann and the Quest for Global Justice', *Buffalo Human Rights Law Review* 8, 2002, 45–121, at pp. 47–53.

11 Trial of the Major War Criminals before the International Military Tribunal, Nuremberg, Volume I, Official Documents, Judgment, pp. 250, 252 and 265. A number of secondary sources recount that during the drafting of the Final Judgment, American Judge Francis Biddle had to be reminded

of who exactly Eichmann was—e.g. D. Bloxham, *Genocide on Trial*, Oxford, Oxford University Press, 2001, p.107.

12 Trial of the Major War Criminals before the International Military Tribunal, Nuremberg, Volume IV, 17 December 1945—8 January 1946, proceedings, 3 January 1946, p. 371.

13 Arendt writes in this regard, 'He was still cautious, but he now wrote to his wife in his own handwriting and told her that "her children's uncle" was alive . . . in the summer of 1952 he had his wife and children join him'. H. Arendt, *Eichmann in Jerusalem: A Study in the Banality of Evil*, New York, Penguin, 1992 pp. 236–7.

14 The thought of Eichmann as a rabbit farmer throws forth bizarre images of a Jean de Florette bent on National Socialism.

15 See: Lippman, 'Genocide: The Trial of Adolf Eichmann', pp 54–64; D. Lasok, 'The Eichmann Trial: A Judicial Precedent', *International Affairs (Royal Institute of International Affairs)* 38, 1962, 485–93; R. Rein, 'The Eichmann Kidnapping: Its Effects on Argentine–Israeli Relations and the Local Jewish Community', *Jewish Social Studies* 7, 2001, 101–30.

16 A note verbale from the Embassy of Israel in Buenos Aires to the Ministry of Foreign Affairs and Religion of the Argentine Republic, included the text of a letter of consent submitted by Eichmann to his captors which stated, *inter alia*, that, 'I the undersigned, Adolf Eichmann, declare of my own free will, that since my true identity has been discovered, I realize that it is futile for me to attempt to go on evading justice . . .'. See, Letter Dated 21 June 1960 from the Permanent Representative of Israel to the President of the Security Council, United Nations Security Council, S/4342, (21 June 1960).

17 According to Hans Baade, Eichmann was transported on an El Al plane which had been used to transport the Israeli Security Minister Abba Eban to Buenos Aires on 20 May 1960—H. W. Baade, 'The Eichmann Trial: Some Legal Aspects', *Duke Law Journal* 1961, 400–20.

18 Question Relating to the Case of Adolf Eichmann, United Nations Security Council Resolution 138 (23 June 1960), UN. Doc. S/4349.

19 Statement of Prime Minster David Ben-Gurion to Knesset, 24 May 1960.

20 Ibid.

21 Nazi and Nazi Collaborators (Punishment) Law, 1950 (Law 5710/1950).

22 Ibid., s. I(a)(1).

23 Ibid., s. I(a)(2).

24 Ibid., s. I(a)(3).

25 Hannah Arendt commenting on the housing of the trial in the Beit Ha'am said that, '. . . Judge Landau [Presiding Judge of the District Court] . . . is doing his best, his very best, to prevent this trial from becoming a show trial under the influence of the prosecutor's love of showmanship. Among the reasons he cannot always succeed is the simple fact that the proceedings happen on a stage before an audience, with the usher's marvelous shout at the beginning of each session producing the effect of the rising curtain', Arendt, *Eichmann in Jerusalem*, p. 4.

26 Simon Wiesenthal suggested to Gideon Hausner that Eichmann should be forced to wear his uniform. Hausner rejected this suggestion since 'while emotionally right, it would give the whole event the theatrical aura of a show trial'. A. Levy, *Nazi Hunter: The Wiesenthal File*, Robinson, London, 2006, p.156.

27 Wiesenthal also proposed that he be forced to plead with respect to six million counts of murder. Ibid. pp. 156–7.

28 Servatius was a hugely experienced criminal lawyer and veteran of the Nuremberg trial, having defended Fritz Saukel. He also represented a number of defendants prosecuted under Control Council Law No. 10: namely, Karl Brandt and Paul Pleiger. According to Arendt, he contacted Eichmann's stepbrother in Linz to offer his services. Arendt, *Eichmann in Jerusalem*, p. 243. See also, 'Servatius, Robert', in A. Cassese (ed.), *The Oxford Companion to International Criminal Justice*, Oxford, Oxford University Press, 2009, pp. 512–3.

29 Quoted in Arendt, *Eichmann in Jerusalem*, p. 21.

30 See Douglas, *The Memory of Judgment*, pp. 91–182. In such instances, Servatius frequently waived recourse to cross-examination.

31 Eichmann District Court Judgment, p. 225.

32 Ibid., p. 226.

33 Indeed, the Supreme Court commented that, 'were it not for the grave outcome of the decision of the Court which constitutes the subject of the appeal, we would have seen no need whatever to give a reasoned opinion separately and in our language . . . since the conclusions of the District Court rest on solid foundations'. Attorney-General of the Government of Israel v. Adolf Eichmann (Supreme Court Judgment 29 May 1962) 36 ILR. 279 (1968) [hereinafter Eichmann Supreme Court Judgment].

34 Eichmann, District Court Judgment, p. 23. Affirmed by the Supreme Court at 36 ILR. 283.

35 Ibid., p. 283. See, L.C. Green, 'The Maxim Nullum Crimen Sine Lege and the Eichmann Trial', *British Yearbook of International Law* 28, 1962, 457–71.
36 Eichmann, District Court Judgment, p. 27.
37 Eichmann, Supreme Court Judgment, p. 304.
38 Ibid., p. 285.
39 Eichmann, District Court Judgment, p. 50.
40 Ibid., p. 53.
41 Ibid., p. 30.
42 Convention on the Prevention and Punishment of the Crime of Genocide, 78 UNTS 277 (1951), Art.VI.
43 Eichmann, District Court Judgment, p. 25.
44 Ibid.
45 W. A. Schabas, 'Judicial Activism and the Crime of Genocide', in S. Darcy & J. Powderly (eds), *Judicial Creativity at the International Criminal Tribunals*, Oxford, Oxford University Press, forthcoming 2010—Advance copy on file with author.
46 Ibid.
47 Eichmann, District Court Judgment, p. 48.
48 Eichmann, Supreme Court Judgment, pp. 255, 256
49 Eichmann, District Court Judgment, p. 59.
50 Servatius also made a last ditch attempt to have the West German Government demand Eichmann's extradition. See Arendt, *Eichmann in Jerusalem*, p. 250.
51 Even though the death penalty for murder was formally abolished in Israel by the 1954 Law for the Amendment of the Criminal Law (Modes of Punishment), it was retained for convictions under the 1950 Nazi and Nazi Collaborators Law. See Green, 'Nullum Crimen and the Eichmann Trial', p. 462.
52 See, A. Cassese, 'Donnedieu de Vabrès, Henri', in A. Cassese (ed.), *The Oxford Companion to International Criminal Justice*, Oxford, Oxford University Press, 2009, pp. 304–5.
53 This not to suggest that there were no prosecutions for war crimes in the post-war period, 'France, like many other countries tried enemy nationals and nonenemy nationals under different laws and in different courts'; however, '[n]o one was punished by a French court for "crimes against humanity", strictly speaking'—L. S. Wexler, 'The Interpretation of the Nuremberg Principles by the French Court of Cassation: From Touvier to Barbie and Back Again', *Columbia Journal of Transnational Law* 32, 1995, 289–380, pp. 317–8.
54 The *Touvier* case is highly significant in the context of the development of French law on war crimes and crimes against humanity—in April 1994 he became the first French citizen to be convicted of crimes against humanity. The procedural course of the case is extremely complex (spanning five decades, and variously involving trial and sentence to death *in absentia*, the enforcement of a statute of limitations, Presidential Pardon, reinvestigation, trial and sentence) and is mired in controversial political maneuvering. For a full discussion of the case, see L. S. Wexler, 'Reflections on the Trial of Vichy Collaborator Paul Touvier for Crimes Against Humanity in France', *Law & Social Inquiry* 20, 1995, 191–221; Touvier Case, 100 ILR 337 (1995); and V. Thalmann, 'Touvier', in A. Cassese (ed.), *The Oxford Companion to International Criminal Justice*, Oxford, Oxford University Press, 2009, pp. 956–8.
55 Judgment of 6 February 1975, Court of Cassation, Cass. Crim., 1975 D. S. Jur. 386. See also Touvier, France, Court of Appeal of Paris, 13 April 1992, 100 ILR 350 (1995).
56 Wexler, 'Touvier to Barbie and Back Again', p. 327.
57 As noted by Wexler, '[h]aving thus neatly shifted the problem from the courts to the executive branch, the interpretation of the 1964 law (not to mention the *Touvier* prosecution) was to stagnate for some time'—Wexler, 'Touvier to Barbie and Back Again', p. 331.
58 Wexler, 'Touvier to Barbie and Back Again', p. 331, fn. 188.
59 Barbie, France, Court of Cassation (Criminal Chamber), 26 January 1984, 78 ILR 125 (1988), pp. 131–2.
60 G. Binder, 'Representing Nazism: Advocacy and Identity at the Trial of Klaus Barbie', *The Yale Law Journal* 98, 1989, 1321–1383, p. 1325.
61 Binder, 'Representing Nazism', p. 1325.
62 Ibid.
63 A. Finkielkraut, *Remembering in Vain: The Klaus Barbie Trial and Crimes Against Humanity*, New York, Columbia University Press, 1992, p. 3.
64 Y. Beigbeder, *Judging War Crimes and Torture: French Justice and International Criminal Tribunals and Commissions (1940–2005)*, Leiden, Martinus Nijhoff Publishers, 2006, pp. 204–6.

65 N. R. Doman, 'Aftermath of Nuremberg: The Trial of Klaus Barbie', *University of Colorado Law Review* 60, 1989, 449, p. 450.
66 See: A. J. Goldberg, 'Klaus Barbie and the United States Government', *Harvard Civil Rights-Civil Liberties Law Review* 19, 1984, 1–14; and A. A. Ryan, Jr, 'Klaus Barbie and the United States Government: A Reply to Mr. Justice Goldberg', *Harvard Civil Rights-Civil Liberties Law Review* 20, 1985, 71–8.
67 Doman, 'The Trial of Klaus Barbie', p. 452.
68 The impetus for Barbie's prosecution was largely a result of the efforts of 'Nazi Hunters' Serge and Beate Klarsfeld, who traveled to Peru in 1971, publicly revealed Altmann's true identity and demanded his extradition and prosecution before a French court.
69 Doman, 'The Trial of Klaus Barbie', p. 454.
70 A. Reinhard, 'Barbie', in A. Cassese, *The Oxford Companion to International Criminal Justice*, Oxford, Oxford University Press, 2009, 597–601, p. 599.
71 Since Vergès did not have a right of audience before the Court of Cassation, Barbie was represented in appeal proceedings by Guy Lesourd and Benoit Baudin.
72 See Binder, 'Representing Nazism'.
73 For a critical account of the process, see Finkielkraut, *Remembering in Vain*.
74 Quote taken from Beigbeder, *Judging War Crimes and Torture*, p. 207.
75 Barbie, France, Court of Cassation (Criminal Chamber), 20 December 1985, 78 ILR 125 (1988) [hereinafter Court of Cassation summary of findings], p. 139.
76 Barbie, France, Court of Cassation summary of findings, p. 139.
77 Ibid., p. 140.
78 Ibid., p. 137.
79 Binder, 'Representing Nazism', p. 1337.
80 Barbie, France, Court of Cassation summary of findings, p. 136.
81 Touvier, France, Court of Appeal of Paris, 13 April 1992, 100 ILR 350 (1995).
82 Judgment of 8 July 1983, Indicting Chamber of the Court of Appeals of Lyon, 1983 JDI 782–783.
83 Barbie, France, Court of Cassation (Criminal Chamber), 6 October 1983, 78 ILR 130 (1988).
84 Section 6(1.91) became Section 7(3.71) and has been referred to as the 'Made in Canada Nuremberg Legislation'—see I. Cotler, 'Bringing Nazi War Criminals in Canada to Justice: A Case Study', *American Society of International Law Proceedings* 91 1997, 262–269, p. 262. It has since been replaced by the Crimes Against Humanity and War Crimes Act, S.C. 2000, c. 24.
85 R. v. Finta (No. 3), (Judgment of the Canadian Supreme Court, La Forest J., Dissenting Opinion, 24 March 1994), 104 ILR. 285 [hereinafter Finta, Supreme Court] La Forest dissent, pp. 293–4.
86 R. Braham, 'Canada and the Perpetrators of the Holocaust: The Case of *Regina v. Finta*', *Holocaust and Genocide Studies* 9 1995 293–317, p. 298.
87 Braham, 'Canada and the Perpetrators of the Holocaust', p. 312–3, fn. 13.
88 Finta, Supreme Court, la Forest dissent, pp. 293–4.
89 Braham, 'Canada and the Perpetrators of the Holocaust', p. 299.
90 Finta, Supreme Court, la Forest dissent, pp. 293–4.
91 See Douglas, *The Memory of Judgment*, p. 226.
92 D. Matas, 'Prosecution in Canada for Crimes Against Humanity' *New York Law School Journal of International and Comparative Law* 11 1990 347–56, p. 352.
93 Braham, 'Canada and the Perpetrators of the Holocaust', p. 304.
94 R v. Finta, Canada, High Court of Justice, 10 July 1989, 82 ILR (1990) 424.
95 Finta, Canada, High Court of Justice, p. 426. This finding was later supported by both the majority and dissenting judgments of the Supreme Court. See Finta, Supreme Court, pp. 306–8.
96 Finta, Canada, High Court of Justice, p. 439.
97 Ibid., p. 448.
98 Ibid., p. 444.
99 Finta, Supreme Court, Cory J., Opinion, pp. 360, 362.
100 Ibid., p. 358.
101 Finta, Supreme Court, la Forest dissent, p. 314.
102 Ibid., p. 316.
103 Tadić (IT-94-1-A), Appeals Chamber, 15 July 1999, paras. 283, 292 and 305; Blaškić (IT-95-14-T), Trial Chamber, 3 March 2000, paras. 244 and 260; Kordić *et al.* (IT-95-14/2-T), Trial Chamber, 26 February 2001, para. 186.

4

The *ad hoc* international criminal tribunals

Launching a new era of accountability

Michael P. Scharf[1] *and Margaux Day*[2]

The International Criminal Tribunal for the former Yugoslavia (ICTY) and the International Criminal Tribunal for Rwanda (ICTR) are *ad hoc* international criminal tribunals established by mandate from the Security Council of the United Nations. Each tribunal was established in response to particular atrocities and is limited to prosecuting perpetrators of particular international crimes.

International Criminal Tribunal for the former Yugoslavia

The ICTY is the first international war crimes tribunal established by the international community since the Nuremberg and Tokyo tribunals. The world began to learn of the atrocities occurring in the former Yugoslavia in the summer of 1992.

As detailed in the book *Balkan Justice*, one of the authors of this chapter, Scharf, then serving as Attorney Adviser for UN Affairs at the US Department of State, had the privilege of playing a behind-the-scenes role in the creation of the Yugoslavia Tribunal.[3] As recounted in that book, in 1992 some Permanent Members of the Security Council, most notably China, felt that the Council did not have legal authority to establish a modern-day Nuremberg-like tribunal; other Permanent Members, Britain and France, felt that the establishment of a tribunal would interfere with the peace process; and another Permanent Member, Russia, was generally opposed to any punitive measures against its ally, Serbia. Even the strongest proponent of the idea, the United States, initially saw the Tribunal and the indictments it would issue more as a public relations ploy than as an effective instrument of justice, believing it unlikely that a Security Council-created Tribunal would ever obtain custody of high-level perpetrators such as Slobodan Milosevic, President of Serbia, and Radavan Karadzic, President of the Bosnian Serb Republic.

While the Security Council did not initially embrace the idea of an international tribunal, in 1992 it did agree to establish, through Security Council Resolution 780, a Commission of Experts tasked with undertaking investigations, submitting a detailed report to the Council about the international crimes that were committed in the former Yugoslavia, and recommending next steps. Reflecting continuing ambivalence about the endeavor, the Council did not provide the Commission more than a token budget and staff. Yet, under the creative and energetic leadership of the Commission's Chair, M. Cherif Bassiouni, the Commission raised millions in voluntary donations; received, in kind, support of personnel, facilities, and computers, from several private sources; and ultimately submitted to the Security Council 3,300 pages of detailed information and analysis in April 1994, which the Commission concluded proved that genocide, crimes against humanity, and war crimes had been committed.[4]

The work of the 780 Commission fueled momentum for the establishment of the Yugoslavia Tribunal. The Europeans proposed that the Tribunal be established by treaty, like Nuremberg, while the United States favored the Tribunal's creation via a Chapter VII Security Council Resolution, which would ensure more expeditious establishment and universal application. The gulf was bridged through agreement on a three-step process. In the first step, on 22 February 1993, the Security Council determined that an international criminal tribunal should be established and invited states to submit proposals to the UN Office of Legal Affairs, which would draft a Statute.[5] In the second step, the Council decided to adopt the UN Office of Legal Affairs' proposed Statute without alteration, though several members of the Council issued "interpretive statements" in their explanations of vote on the Resolution in an effort to provide interpretive gloss on the provisions of the Statute.[6] In the third step, the Judges were authorized to adopt rules to govern the proceedings and operation of the Tribunal, based on proposals submitted by states and organizations. The most comprehensive proposal was submitted by the United States, resulting in the adoption of Rules that largely reflected the Anglo-American adversarial system as opposed to the Continental European inquisitorial system,[7] though a series of subsequent amendments over the years have incorporated more and more features of the inquisitorial system.

It took 14 months for the Security Council to agree on the first Prosecutor of the Yugoslavia Tribunal, eventually selecting South African jurist Richard Goldstone on 8 July 1994.[8] The election of judges went somewhat more smoothly, following 10 contentious rounds of voting over three days in September 1993.[9] At first, the Tribunal, which shared offices with an insurance company in The Hague, had little to do, since the only suspects in custody were low-level foot soldiers and camp guards. Even after the Dayton Accords brought a fragile peace to Bosnia in 1995 to be patrolled by 65,000 NATO troops, NATO declined to authorize its personnel to hunt for or apprehend indicted war criminals. This policy slowly changed in the late 1990s, while at the same time the international community used conditionality of economic assistance to induce the Croatian, Bosnian, and Serbian governments to surrender suspects to The Hague.[10]

Current statistics

As of December 2009, the ICTY has indicted 161 persons.[11] Thirty-six people are in custody at the UN ICTY Detention Unit. Two people are on provisional release until further notice. As for ongoing proceedings, there are currently 40 accused in 17 different cases, the most high profile of which is the trial of Radovan Karadzic. Thirteen accused are before the Appeals Chamber, 24 accused are currently at trial, one accused is at the pretrial stage, and two accused, including the most-wanted Bosnian Serb General Ratko Mladic, remain at large.

The ICTY has concluded proceedings for 121 accused in 86 cases. The Tribunal has acquitted 11 people in eight cases and sentenced 61 people in 49 different cases. Slobadon Milosevic stood trial for four years but died of natural causes before a judgment could be rendered. Some perpetrators have already served their sentences. Thirty-six people in 22 cases have had their indictments withdrawn or are deceased.

Jurisdiction of the ICTY

Article 1 of the ICTY Statute, entitled 'Competence of the International Tribunal', states that the Tribunal 'shall have the power to prosecute persons responsible for serious violations of international humanitarian law committed in the territory of the former Yugoslavia since 1991 in accordance with the provisions of the present Statute'.[12] The Statute goes on to state in Article 9 that '[t]he territorial jurisdiction of the International Tribunal shall extend to the territory of the former Socialist Federal Republic of Yugoslavia, including its land surface, airspace and territorial waters. The temporal jurisdiction of the International Tribunal shall extend to a period beginning on 1 January 1991'. Thus, the ICTY is limited in both temporal and territorial scope. It cannot prosecute accused for crimes occurring before 1 January 1991, and it cannot prosecute accused for crimes committed outside the territory of the former Socialist Federal Republic of Yugoslavia.

The Tribunal has jurisdiction over individual persons and not organizations, political parties, army units, administrative entities, states, or other legal subjects. Although the ICTY and national courts have concurrent jurisdiction over serious violations of international humanitarian law committed in the former Yugoslavia, the ICTY can claim primacy and may take over national investigations and proceedings at any stage if this proves to be in the interest of international justice. It can also refer its cases to competent national authorities in the former Yugoslavia. The Tribunal has authority to prosecute and try individuals for four categories of offences: grave breaches of the 1949 Geneva Conventions, violations of the laws or customs of war, genocide, and crimes against humanity. The ICTY has no authority to prosecute states for aggression or crimes against peace; these crimes are within the jurisdiction of the International Court of Justice.

Jurisdiction—the Tribunal's jurisprudence

Naturally, various Defendants have challenged the jurisdiction of the ICTY, so the Tribunal itself has had the opportunity to opine on and generally uphold its own jurisdiction over particular Defendants. In the Tribunal's first case, Dusko Tadic challenged the jurisdiction and lawfulness of the existence of the ICTY on three grounds before the Appeals Chamber: (1) illegal foundation of the ICTY; (2) wrongful primacy of the ICTY over national courts; and (3) lack of subject-matter jurisdiction.[13] The *Tadic* Appeals Chamber determined that it had the ability 'to determine its own jurisdiction,' which 'is a necessary component in the exercise of the judicial function'.[14] The Appeals Chamber decided that the threat to the peace in the former Yugoslavia justified the Security Council's invocation of Chapter VII of the United Nations Charter and that Article 41 of the Charter served as an appropriate legal basis for establishing an international criminal tribunal.[15] Thus, the Appeals Chamber found that the ICTY was 'established by law'.[16]

In the *Nikolic* case, the Trial Chamber addressed the argument that illegal arrest may deprive the Tribunal of jurisdiction.[17] The Defense challenged the principle of *male captus, bene detentus* (bad capture, good detention) and argued that the illegal arrest of Nikolic by unknown individuals should be attributable to the ICTY, consequently barring the Tribunal from exercising jurisdiction. Even if the arrest were not attributable to the Tribunal, the Defense argued that the illegal character of the arrest itself should bar the Tribunal from exercising jurisdiction. The court rejected this argument and opted to exercise jurisdiction in part because Nikolic's captors were not court or government officials.

The ICTY further determined that it is limited by the doctrine of *nullum crimen sine lege*. As the *Blaskic* Appeals Chamber determined, '[t]he jurisdiction *ratione materiae* of the International Tribunal is circumscribed by customary international law', so the 'Tribunal cannot impose criminal responsibility for acts which, prior to their being committed, did not entail such responsibility under customary international law'.[18] The Tribunal further explained that the principle of *nullum crimen sine lege* 'also prohibits a conviction entered in excess of the statutory or generally accepted parameters of the definition' of a crime.[19]

Application and interpretation of international law norms

The ICTY has had the opportunity to opine on various international law norms. In its determinations of substantive criminal law norms, the ICTY can rely on 'previous decisions of international tribunals'.[20] The primary sources on which the ICTY relies are other decisions of the ICTY and decisions of the Rwanda Tribunal, with an emphasis on Appeals Chamber decisions.[21] As a secondary source, the ICTY may be 'guided by the case-law of the Nuremberg and Tokyo Tribunals, the tribunals established under Allied Control Council Law No. 10, and the Tribunal for East Timor'.[22] Furthermore, the ICTY may apply customary international law, and it may apply treaty law, so long as the treaty '(i) was unquestionably binding on the parties at the time of the alleged offence; and (ii) was not in conflict with or derogating from peremptory norms of international law, as are most customary rules of international humanitarian law'.[23] When applying treaties, the ICTY recognized that it should interpret conventions in conformity with Articles 31 and 32 of the Vienna Convention on the Law of Treaties.[24]

The ICTY determined that the crimes covered by Articles 2, 3, 4, and 5 of the Tribunal's Statute reflect customary international law.[25] The *Blaskic* Appeals Chamber, quoting the *Hadzihasanovic* case, stated, in the context of a discussion of *nullum crimen sine lege*, that 'it has always been the approach of this Tribunal not to rely merely on a construction of the Statute to establish the applicable law on criminal responsibility, but to ascertain the state of customary law in force at the time the crimes were committed'.[26]

Crimes covered by the ICTY Statute

To be responsible for any of the listed crimes, the ICTY Statute requires that a person be individually responsible for a crime. Article 7(1) states, '[a] person who planned, instigated, ordered, committed or otherwise aided and abetted in the planning, preparation or execution of a crime referred to in articles 2 to 5 of the present Statute, shall be individually responsible for the crime'.[27] The *Simic, Tadic, and Zaric* Trial Chamber further emphasized that Article 7(1) does not require that an individual physically commit a crime; rather, criminal responsibility may be extended 'to those who participate in and contribute to the commission of a crime in various ways, when such participation is sufficiently connected to the crime, following principles of accomplice liability'.[28] Specifically, Article 7(1) covers both an individual who commits an unlawful act and that person's superior, who ordered or instigated the unlawful act but did not physically participate in it.[29]

Grave Breaches

In addition, the ICTY Statute limits the crimes over which it has jurisdiction to Grave Breaches of the Geneva Conventions, violations of the laws or customs of war, genocide, and crimes against humanity. Article 2 of the Statute provides that the ICTY has jurisdiction to prosecute accused for Grave Breaches of the Geneva Conventions of 1949.[30] These include (1) willful killing; (2) torture or inhuman treatment, including biological experiments; (3) willfully causing great suffering or serious injury to body or health; (4) extensive destruction and appropriation of property, not justified by military necessity and carried out unlawfully and wantonly; (5) compelling a prisoner of war or a civilian to serve in the forces of a hostile power; (6) willfully depriving a prisoner of war or a civilian of the rights of fair and regular trial; (7) unlawful deportation or transfer or unlawful confinement of a civilian; and (8) taking civilians as hostages.

In order for the ICTY to prosecute an accused for Grave Breaches of the Geneva Conventions under Article 2 of the Statute, 'the offence must be committed, *inter alia*: (i) in the context of an international armed conflict; and (ii) against persons or property defined as "protected" under the Geneva Conventions'.[31] The Trial Chamber in *Brdanin* found that four conditions must exist in order for the Tribunal to apply Article 2 of the Statute. These are the following: '(i) the existence of an armed conflict; (ii) the establishment of a nexus between the alleged crimes and the armed conflict; (iii) the armed conflict must be international in nature; and (iv) the victims of the alleged crimes must qualify as protected persons pursuant to the provisions of the 1949 Geneva Conventions'.[32] The *mens rea* required for Article 2 violations 'includes both guilty intent and recklessness which may be likened to serious criminal negligence'.[33]

War crimes

Article 3 of the ICTY Statute provides jurisdiction over violations of the laws or customs of war.[34] These violations include, but are not limited to the following: '(a) employment of poisonous weapons or other weapons calculated to cause unnecessary suffering; (b) wanton destruction of cities, towns or villages, or devastation not justified by military necessity; (c) attack, or bombardment, by whatever means, of undefended towns, villages, dwellings, or buildings; (d) seizure of, destruction or willful damage done to institutions dedicated to religion, charity and education, the arts and sciences, historic monuments and works of art and science; (e) plunder of public or private property'. Article 3 is considered to be a residual clause, covering serious violations of humanitarian law not included in other articles of the Statute.[35] The *Furundzija* Trial Chamber emphasized that Article 3 has a 'very broad scope', 'constitutes an "umbrella rule" ', and 'makes an open-ended reference to all international rules of humanitarian law'.[36] Article 3 of the ICTY Statute is considered to be customary international law.[37]

Four conditions must exist for the Tribunal to apply Article 3 of the Statute. First, the violation must infringe on a rule of international humanitarian law. Second, the rule must be customary in nature or, if it belongs to treaty law, the required conditions must be met. Third, the violation must be serious, and the breach must involve grave consequences for the victim. Fourth, the violation of the rule must entail individual criminal responsibility of the person breaching the rule.[38] These four requirements must be met regardless of whether the crime is expressly listed in Article 3.[39]

Genocide

Article 4 gives the ICTY jurisdiction over the crime of genocide.[40] Genocide is defined as 'any of the following acts committed with intent to destroy, in whole or in part, a national, ethnical, racial or religious group, as such: (a) killing members of the group; (b) causing serious bodily or mental harm to members of the group; (c) deliberately inflicting on the group conditions of life calculated to bring about its physical destruction in whole or in part; (d) imposing measures intended to prevent births within the group; [and] (e) forcibly transferring children of the group to another group'. In addition to genocide, Article 4 gives the Tribunal jurisdiction to punish conspiracy to commit genocide, direct and public incitement to commit genocide, attempt to commit genocide, and complicity in genocide.[41] Article 4(2) and (3) of the Statute reproduce verbatim Articles II and III of the Convention on the Prevention and Punishment of the Crime of Genocide, adopted on 9 December 1948. The Tribunal found that 'the law set out in the [Genocide] Convention reflect[s] customary international law and that the norm prohibiting genocide constitutes *jus cogens*'.[42]

ICTY case law further defines genocide. The *Krstic* Trial Chamber elaborated on the intent requirement for genocide: 'Genocide refers to any criminal enterprise seeking to destroy, in whole or in part, a particular kind of human group, as such, by certain means. Those are two elements of the special intent requirement of genocide: (1) the act or acts must target a national, ethnical, racial or religious group; (2) the act or acts must seek to destroy all or part of that group'.[43] The *Jelisic* Trial Chamber determined that two legal ingredients are necessary for genocide to exist. They are as follows: '[1] the material element of the offence, constituted by one or several acts enumerated in paragraph 2 of Article 4; [and] [2] the *mens rea* of the offence, consisting of the special intent to destroy, in whole or in part, a national, ethnical, racial or religious group, as such'.[44]

Thus, for genocide to exist, the perpetrators must have targeted a specific group. The Trial Chamber in *Stakic* opined that, '[t]he group must be targeted because of characteristics peculiar to it, and the specific intent must be to destroy the group as a separate and distinct entity. . . . Whereas it is the individuals that constitute the victims of most crimes, the ultimate victim of genocide is the group'.[45] The ICTY determined that the Bosnian Muslim people were a 'specific, distinct national group' covered by Article 4.[46]

Crimes against humanity

The ICTY Statute also gives the Tribunal jurisdiction over crimes against humanity.[47] The Tribunal has jurisdiction to prosecute persons for 'the following crimes when committed in armed conflict, whether international or internal in character, and directed against any civilian population: (a) murder; (b) extermination; (c) enslavement; (d) deportation; (e) imprisonment; (f) torture; (g) rape; (h) persecutions on political, racial and religious grounds; [and] (i) other inhumane acts'[48] The Tribunal determined that an accused could only be responsible for a crime against humanity if the acts of the accused were 'part of a widespread or systematic attack "directed against any civilian population"'.[49] The Trial Chamber went on to enumerate the five requirements for the applicability of Article 5. These are '(i) there must be an attack; (ii) the acts of the perpetrator must be part of the attack; (iii) the attack must be directed against any civilian population; (iv) the attack must be widespread or systematic; and (v) the perpetrator must know that his or her acts constitute part of a pattern of widespread or systematic crimes directed against a civilian population and know that his or her acts fit into such a pattern (i.e. knowledge of the wider context in which his or her acts occur and knowledge that his or her acts are part of the attack)'.[50]

Not only must the acts be committed during an armed conflict for Article 5 to apply[51] but also the acts must be 'linked geographically as well as temporally with the armed conflict'.[52] There must be 'proof that there was an armed conflict at the relevant time and place'.[53] However, this does not require proof of a nexus between the crimes and the armed conflict.[54]

The Tribunal has found that murder committed in the former Yugoslavia amounted to a crime against humanity in various instances. One instance was in the town of Srebrenica. The *Blagojevic and Jokic* Trial Chamber found that 'it has been established beyond reasonable doubt that more than 7,000 Bosnian men any [sic] boys were killed' in Srebrenica. The court went on to find that '[i]t is further proven that the direct perpetrators had the intention to kill or inflict serious injury in the reasonable knowledge that their acts or omissions were likely to cause the death of the victim'.[55] The Tribunal further found that murder as a crime against humanity was committed in Sarajevo.[56] In addition, the Trial Chamber found murder as a crime against humanity to have been committed in Prijedor Municipality.[57]

The Tribunal found destruction of property to amount to a crime against humanity in the Autonomous Region of Krajina, Srebrenica, Bosanski Samac, and Prijedor Municipality. In the Autonomous Region of Krajina, the Tribunal found that 'extensive destruction and appropriation of non-Serb property located in areas predominantly inhabited by Bosnian Muslims and Bosnian Croats' occurred.[58] Unlike non-Serb property, Bosnian Serb property was systematically left intact. The Tribunal found that in Srebrenica, the personal property of the Bosnian Muslim prisoners was confiscated and destroyed.[59] The *Nikolic-Momir* Trial Chamber went on to find that personal property was taken from Bosnian Muslim refugees and from those about to be executed.[60] The ICTY determined that there was looting and property destruction in Prijedor Municipality also, with the victims being predominantly Bosnian Muslims and Bosnian Croats.[61] The Trial Chamber found these acts amounted to crimes against humanity. However, not all property destruction is serious enough to constitute a violation of Article 5. For example, destruction of clothing and wallets was not grave enough.[62]

The ICTY's interpretation of specific international law issues: torture, command responsibility, affirmative defenses, and self-representation

Torture

The ICTY defined torture as 'the intentional infliction, by act or omission, of severe pain or suffering, whether physical or mental, for a prohibited purpose, such as obtaining information or a confession, punishing, intimidating, humiliating, or coercing the victim or a third person, or discriminating, on any ground, against the victim or a third person'.[63] The Appeals Chamber in *Furundzija* defined torture in the same way but also required that the torture 'be linked to an armed conflict'.[64] The *Kvocka* Trial Chamber listed examples of acts that were likely to constitute torture: '[b]eating, sexual violence, prolonged denial of sleep, food, hygiene, and medical assistance, as well as threats to torture, rape, or kill relatives'.[65] The ICTY recognized that the prohibition against torture is a *jus cogens* norm.[66]

Command responsibility

The ICTY has significantly shaped the law of command responsibility. Article 7(3) of the Statute provides '[t]he fact that any of the acts referred to in articles 2 to 5 of the present Statute was committed by a subordinate does not relieve his superior of criminal responsibility if he knew or had reason to know that the subordinate was about to commit such acts or had done so and the superior failed to take the necessary and reasonable measures to prevent such acts or to punish the perpetrators thereof'. The *Delalic* Appeals Chamber found that '[t]he principle that military and other superiors may be held criminally responsible for the acts of their subordinates is well-established in conventional and customary law'.[67] The *Halilovic* Trial Chamber further determined that Article 7(3) of the Statute applies to all acts found in Articles 2, 3, 4, and 5.[68] The Tribunal applied the principle of command responsibility in the context of the duty to punish in *Strugar*, which addressed the shelling of parts of the town of Dubrovnik.[69]

Affirmative defenses

Various affirmative defenses have been tested before the ICTY, some accepted in full, some accepted only partially, and some rejected. The Tribunal accepted the use of an alibi defense, although it clarified that an alibi is technically a denial of committing crime rather than an affirmative defense.[70] The Tribunal accepted duress as a partial defense.[71] Finally, the affirmative defenses the ICTY rejected are the *tu quoque* defense,[72] involvement in a defensive operation,[73] and diminished mental capacity.[74]

Right to self-representation

The ICTY was faced with the difficult issue of defining the parameters of the right to self-representation in the *Milosevic* case. Due to interruptions, outbursts, and delays from Milosevic, the Appeals Chamber relied on 'existing precedent from contemporary war crimes tribunals' to conclude that 'the right to self-representation "is a qualified and not an absolute right" '.[75] The Tribunal addressed the issue of whether or not the right to self-representation could be limited based on the fact that the defendant was 'substantially and persistently obstructing the proper and expeditious conduct of his trial'.[76] The Tribunal ultimately determined that it is able to restrict the right to self-representation based on those reasons. The Tribunal likened the right to self-representation to the right to be tried in one's own presence. Because Rule 80(B) of the Rules of Procedure and Evidence permitted the Trial Chamber to remove an accused due to disruptive conduct, it must follow that an accused may lose his or her right to self-representation if the exercise of this right proves disruptive. When the Appeals Chamber evaluated the Trial Chamber's decision, the Appeals Chamber determined that the Trial Chamber did not abuse its discretion in assigning Milosevic counsel.[77] The Appeals Chamber was persuaded by the fact that permitting Milosevic to continue to represent himself might cause the trial to last for an unreasonable amount of time or never be concluded. However, the Appeals Chamber did limit the Tribunal's ability to encroach on the right to self-representation. Any restrictions on Milosevic's right to self-representation had to 'be limited to the minimum extent necessary to protect the Tribunal's interest in assuring a reasonably expeditious trial'.[78] The Appeals Chamber ordered that the Trial Chamber 'steer a careful course' between safeguarding Milosevic's right to represent himself and the ICTY's interest in expeditiously resolving its cases.[79]

The International Criminal Tribunal for Rwanda

On 8 November 1994, just 18 months after the creation of the Yugoslavia Tribunal, the Security Council established the International Criminal Tribunal for Rwanda (ICTR).[80] This development was in response to systematic killings of Tutsi and moderate Hutu men, women, and children in 1994, amounting to around 800,000 victims.[81] Several thousand people were massacred, mutilated, buried alive, and raped. The Special Rapporteur for Rwanda of the United Nations Commission on Human Rights detailed specific atrocities, such as a street being covered with corpses for an entire kilometer on 10 April; common graves filled with several hundred victims, some still alive; and summary executions.[82]

Only months after the atrocities occurred, the Security Council established the ICTR by Chapter VII Resolution. The Tribunal's Statute is annexed to Security Council Resolution 955. Although the post-conflict government of Rwanda had initially requested the establishment of the Rwanda Tribunal, it ended up voting against the Tribunal as one of the non–Permanent Members of the Council because of the absence of the death penalty in the Tribunal's Statute. Thus, the mode of establishment was important because it obligated neighboring countries to which perpetrators had fled, as well as the Rwandan government itself, to cooperate fully with the Tribunal.

In contrast to the process for establishing the Yugoslavia Tribunal, the Security Council did not request the UN Secretary-General or the Office of Legal Affairs to submit a Statute for the Rwanda Tribunal.[83] Instead, the Council came up with its own draft, closely mirroring the Yugoslavia Tribunal's Statute, with some notable departures. For example, the Rwanda Tribunal's Statute provided for temporal jurisdiction for the period of 1 January 2004 to 31 December 2004, whereas the ICTY's temporal jurisdiction has no end date. In addition, the ICTR Statute stipulated that the Tribunal had jurisdiction over crimes committed in internal armed conflict, while at the same time excluding jurisdiction over crimes committed in an international armed conflict. The Prosecutor of the Yugoslavia Tribunal would serve also as Chief Prosecutor of the Rwanda Tribunal, assisted by a Deputy Prosecutor whose office would be at the Tribunal's headquarters in Africa. The two tribunals would share a single Appeals Chamber in The Hague, while the Trial Chambers of the Rwanda Tribunal would be in Africa.

In making the decision to set up the ICTR's headquarters in Arusha, Tanzania, the Security Council took into consideration the February 2005 report of the Secretary-General, which considered, among other things, administrative efficiency, proximity to witnesses, and economic costs.[84] Therefore, the Tribunal's location is outside of Rwanda because of security concerns.

The Judges adopted the Rules of Procedure and Evidence pursuant to Article 14 of the ICTR Statute. The Tribunal consists of three organs: (1) the Trial and Appeals Chambers, (2) the Office of the Prosecutor, and (3) the Registry.

Current statistics

As of December 2009, no detainees are still awaiting trial or awaiting transfer. The cases of eight accused are pending appeal. Twenty-three accused are currently serving their sentences, 14 in Mali and nine in Benin. Eight individuals have been acquitted. Two cases of two accused have been transferred to the national jurisdiction of France: Munyeshyaka and Bucyibaruta.[85]

Temporal and territorial jurisdiction

The ICTR only prosecutes individuals for crimes committed between 1 January 1994 and 31 December 1994.[86] Jurisdiction *ratione personae* is limited primarily to crimes committed by Rwandans in Rwanda or neighboring states. The Tribunal may also prosecute non-Rwandans if they committed crimes within Rwanda's borders. Jurisdiction *ratione materiae* is limited to genocide, crimes against humanity, and violations of Article 3 common to the Geneva Conventions and of Additional Protocol II.[87]

Crimes covered by the ICTR Statute

The prosecutable crimes are listed in the ICTR Statute. Similar to the ICTY Statute, the ICTR Statute also requires that each accused be individually responsible for a crime before he or she can be convicted for it. The *Kayishema and Ruzindana* Trial Chamber determined that, in order to establish individual criminal responsibility under Article 6(1), there must be a demonstration that (1) the conduct for the accused contributed to the commission of an illegal act, and (2) the accused had awareness of his participation in a crime.[88] Crimes must have been completed before the crime can give rise to criminal responsibility because Article 6(1) does not criminalize inchoate offenses.[89] The exception to this is that there is attempt liability for the crime of genocide.

Genocide

The crime of genocide can be found in Article 2 of the ICTR Statute. The Statute defines genocide as any one of the following acts committed with intent to destroy, in whole or in part, a national, ethnical, racial, or religious group: (1) killing members of the group; (2) causing serious bodily or mental harm to members of the group; (3) deliberately inflicting on the group conditions of life calculated to bring about its physical destruction, in whole or in part; (4) imposing measures intended to prevent births within the group; or (5) forcibly transferring children of the group to another group.[90] Article 2 goes on to make the following acts punishable: (1) genocide; (2) conspiracy to commit genocide; (3) direct and public incitement to commit genocide; (4) attempt to commit genocide; and (5) complicity in genocide.[91]

To prove that an accused committed the crime of genocide, the Prosecution must establish the following elements beyond a reasonable doubt: (1) the accused committed one of the acts listed in Article 2(2) of the Statute and (2) the act 'was committed against a specifically targeted national, ethnical, racial, or religious group, with the specific intent to destroy, in whole or in part, that group'.[92] The Tribunal recognized that the prohibition of genocide is *jus cogens* and found in customary international law.[93]

Crimes against humanity

Article 3 of the Statute gives the ICTR jurisdiction over crimes against humanity. Article 3 states that the Tribunal has 'the power to prosecute persons responsible for the following crimes when committed as part of a widespread or systematic attack against any civilian population on national, political, ethnic, racial or religious grounds: (a) murder; (b) extermination; (c) enslavement; (d) deportation; (e) imprisonment; (f) torture; (g) rape; (h) persecutions on political, racial and religious grounds; and (i) other inhumane acts'.[94] Crimes against humanity have four elements. The enumerated acts must be (1) inhumane in nature and character, causing great suffering, or serious injury to body or to mental or physical health; (2) part of a widespread or systematic attack; (3) committed against civilians; and (4) committed on one or more discriminatory grounds.[95]

In order to be responsible for crimes against humanity, a perpetrator must 'understand the overall context of his act'.[96] In other words, he must have knowledge, actual or constructive, that his act is part of a widespread or systematic attack on a civilian population. Notably, an accused does not need to act with discriminatory intent, except for the crime of persecution, in order to be responsible for a crime against humanity.[97] The Tribunal can hold both state and non-state actors responsible for crimes against humanity.[98]

War crimes

Article 4 of the Statute gives the Tribunal jurisdiction over war crimes. These include, but are not limited to, the following: '(a) violence to life, health and physical or mental well-being of persons, in particular murder as well as cruel treatment such as torture, mutilation or any form of corporal punishment; (b) collective punishments; (c) taking of hostages; (d) acts of terrorism; (e) outrages upon personal dignity, in particular humiliating and degrading treatment, rape, enforced prostitution and any form of indecent assault; (f) pillage; (g) the passing of sentences and the carrying out of executions without previous judgment pronounced by a regularly constituted court, affording all the judicial guarantees which are recognized as indispensable by civilized peoples; (h) threats to commit any of the foregoing acts'.

The Security Council included provisions from international instruments in the ICTR Statute, some of which were not considered customary international law at the time of the drafting of the Statute, which makes the ICTR Statute more expansive than the ICTY Statute.[99] The ICTR concluded that Common Article 3 of the Geneva Conventions was customary international law. However, it determined that only portions of Additional Protocol II constituted customary international law. Further, all of the crimes specifically listed in Article 4 of the Statute were determined to be customary international law.

The *Kayishema and Ruzindana* Trial Chamber took a different approach, noting that Rwanda was a party to the Conventions and that the Conventions were in force prior to the events giving rise to the establishment of the Tribunal.[100] Furthermore, 'all the offences enumerated in Article 4 of the Statute, also constituted crimes under the laws of Rwanda', and the Rwandan Patriotic Front (RPF) even admitted to the International Committee of the Red Cross that it was bound by the rules of International Humanitarian Law.[101]

The elements of a breach of Common Article 3 or Protocol II is (1) a non-international armed conflict must exist; (2) a link must exist between the armed forces and the accused; (3) the crimes must be committed within the *ratione loci* and *ratione personae* of the Tribunal; and (4) a nexus must exist between the crime and the armed conflict.[102] The *Akayesu* Appeals Chamber did not require a showing of the second element.[103]

The ICTR's interpretation of specific international law issues: rape, torture, command responsibility, and equality of arms

Rape

The ICTR was the first international tribunal to find an accused guilty of rape both as a part of genocide and as a crime against humanity. The Tribunal defined rape as a physical invasion of a sexual nature committed on a person under coercive circumstance.[104] The Tribunal found that rape could be an instrument used to commit genocide because 'sexual violence can form an integral part of the process of destruction of a group'.[105] The *Akayesu* Trial Chamber determined that the sexual violence targeted at Tutsi women contributed to the destruction of the Tutsi group as a whole.[106] The *Akayesu* court also found that rape can be punishable as a crime against humanity.

Torture as a crime against humanity

The Tribunal adopted the definition of "torture" found in the United Nations Convention Against Torture and Other Cruel, Inhuman or Degrading Treatment or Punishment.[107] In addition to this definition, torture is a crime against humanity if the torture was a part of a widespread or systematic attack against civilians and launched on discriminatory grounds.[108] When torture is considered a crime against humanity, there is no 'public official' requirement.[109] The *Akayesu* Trial Chamber found that rape can constitute torture 'when inflicted by or at the instigation of or with the consent or acquiescence of a public official or other person acting in an official capacity'.[110]

Command responsibility

The ICTR Statute explains, in Article 6(3) and (4), that a superior can be responsible for the acts of his or her subordinate. Interestingly, the *Kayishema and Ruzindana* Trial Chamber explained that it is possible to find a person individually responsible for a crime and also responsible through command responsibility.[111] The forms of responsibility are not mutually exclusive. The elements of command responsibility include '(i) the existence of a superior-subordinate relationship of effective control between the accused and the perpetrator of the crime; and, (ii) the knowledge, or constructive knowledge, of the accused that the crime was about to be, was being, or had been committed; and, (iii) the failure of the accused to take the necessary and reasonable measures to prevent or stop the crime, or to punish the perpetrator'.[112]

The *Nahimana, Barayagwiza, and Ngeze* Trial Chamber found that Nahimana and Barayagwiza had superior responsibility for particular radio broadcasts. Barayagwiza was consequently found guilty of genocide pursuant to Article 6(3) because of his control over the radio broadcasts.[113] He was additionally found guilty of genocide through command responsibility for his control over a political party, CDR, which promoted extermination of the Tutsi.[114]

Equality of arms

Article 20 of the Tribunal's Statute requires equality of arms between the Prosecution and the Defense. This does not require that each party have the same material resources.[115] Rather, it requires a judicial body to ensure 'that neither party is put at a disadvantage when presenting its case'.[116]

Winding up the ICTR

In May 2005, the Tribunal established Rule 11bis in its Rules of Procedure and Evidence to facilitate the transfer of cases to competent jurisdictions. Rule 11bis provides that the Trial Chamber may refer a case to a competent national jurisdiction at the request of the Prosecutor or *propio motu*.[117] The highest profile cases, however, cannot be transferred. Cases may be transferred to a country where the crime was committed, the country where the accused was arrested, or any other state with jurisdiction that is 'willing and adequately prepared to accept such a case'.[118]

In order to transfer a case, the ICTR must ensure that the accused will receive a fair trial in the receiving state's courts and that the death penalty will not be imposed.[119] The ICTR Prosecutor has the ability to revoke jurisdiction if necessary and can monitor the national court proceedings.[120] The Prosecutor has requested the referral of eight cases to national courts, and only two have been successfully referred.[121]

Conclusion

The establishment of the Yugoslavia Tribunal and the Rwanda Tribunal in the early 1990s initiated a new era of accountability for the international community. As described in other chapters of this book, the successful operation of these first international tribunals since Nuremberg and Tokyo led to the creation of hybrid international tribunals for Sierra Leone, Cambodia, and Lebanon, and ultimately to the establishment of the permanent International Criminal Court. The rules and jurisprudence of the ICTY and ICTR are at the core of an emerging International Criminal Law jurisprudence. Although there are slight deviations in the case law of the different tribunals, each tends to accord substantial weight to the holdings and analysis of its sisters. Together, there has been such a proliferation of judgments and rulings arising from the several tribunals that International Criminal Law is recognized as the fastest developing area in all of international law.

Notes

1 Michael P. Scharf is the John Dever Drinko-Baker & Hostetler Professor of Law and Director of the Frederick K. Cox International Law Center at Case Western Reserve University School of Law.

2 Margaux Day is a federal judicial clerk for Judge Solomon Oliver, Jr, Federal District Court for the Northern District of Ohio, and is an Adjunct Professor at Case Western Reserve University School

of Law. She was an intern for the Office of the Co-Prosecutors of the Extraordinary Chambers in the Courts of Cambodia in 2008 and was a member of the 2008 Philip C. Jessup International Moot Court World Champion Team, winning the award of Best Oralist in the World Championship Final Round.

3 M. Scharf, *Balkan Justice: The Story Behind the First International War Crimes Trial Since Nuremburg*, Durham, NC: Carolina Academic Press, 1997.
4 Ibid., at 37–49.
5 S.C. Res. 808, 22 February 1993.
6 Establishment of the ICTY, http://www.icty.org/sid/319. Visited 7 January 2010.
7 Michael P. Scharf, BALKAN JUSTICE, at 66–9.
8 Ibid., at 75–79.
9 Ibid., at 63–65.
10 P. Williams and M. Scharf, *Peace with Justice? War Crimes and Accountability in the Former Yugoslavia*, London: Roman and Littlefield, 2002, 211–34.
11 Key Figures, http://www.icty.org/sections/TheCases/KeyFigures. Updated: 12 November 2009. Visited 6 December 2009.
12 Statute of the International Criminal Tribunal for the Former Yugoslavia, UN Doc. S/RES/827 (1993) (as amended 7 July 2009 by Resolution 1877), Art. 1.
13 Tadic (IT-94-1-A), Appeals Chamber, Decision on the Defence Motion for Interlocutory Appeal on Jurisdiction, 2 October 1995, para. 2.
14 Ibid., para. 18.
15 Ibid., para. 36.
16 Ibid., para. 47.
17 Nikolic (IT-94-2-PT), Trial Chamber, Decision on Defence Motion Challenging the Exercise of Jurisdiction by the Tribunal, 9 October 2002, para. 70.
18 Blaskic (IT-95-14-A), Appeals Chamber, Judgment, 29 July 2004, para. 78.
19 Ibid., para. 86.
20 Stakic (IT-97-24), Trial Chamber, Judgment, 31 July 2003, para. 414.
21 Ibid.
22 Ibid.
23 Galic (IT-98-29), Trial Chamber, Judgment, 5 December 2003, para. 98.
24 Ibid., para. 91; Stakic (IT-97-24), Trial Chamber, Judgment, 31 July 2003, para. 411.
25 Stakic (IT-97-24), Trial Chamber, Judgment, 31 July 2003, para. 411.
26 Blaskic (IT-95-14), Appeals Chamber, Judgment, 29 July 2004, para. 141.
27 Statute of the International Criminal Tribunal for the Former Yugoslavia, UN Doc. S/RES/827 (1993), Art. 7(1). See also, Jokic (IT-01-42/1), Trial Chamber, Judgment, 18 March 2004, para. 56.
28 Simic, Tadic, and Zaric (IT-95-9), Trial Chamber, Judgment, 17 October 2003, para. 135.
29 Kordic and Cerkez (IT-95-14/2), Trial Chamber, Judgment, 26 February 2001, para. 367.
30 Statute of the International Criminal Tribunal for the Former Yugoslavia, UN Doc. S/RES/827 (1993), Art. 2.
31 Blaskic (IT-95-14-A), Appeals Chamber, Judgment, 29 July 2004, para. 170.
32 Brdanin (IT-99-36-T), Trial Chamber, Judgment, 1 September 2004, para. 121.
33 Blaskic (IT-95-14), Trial Chamber, Judgment, 3 March 2000, para. 152.
34 Statute of the International Criminal Tribunal for the Former Yugoslavia, UN Doc. S/RES/827 (1993), Art. 3.
35 Tadic (IT-94-1-AR72), Appeals Chamber, Decision on the Defence Motion for Interlocutory Appeal on Jurisdiction, October 2, 1995, paras 87, 91; Kunarac, Kovac, and Vokovic (IT-96-23, 23-1), Appeals Chamber, Judgment, 12 June 2002, para. 68; Galic (IT-98-29), Trial Chamber, Judgment, 5 December 2003, para. 10.
36 Furundzija (IT-95-17/1), Trial Chamber, Judgment, 10 December 1998, paras 132–33.
37 Tadic (IT-94-1-AR72), Appeals Chamber, Decision on the Defence Motion for Interlocutory Appeal on Jurisdiction, 2 October 1995, para. 98; Kunarac, Kovac, and Vokovic (IT-96-23, 23–1), Appeals Chamber, Judgment, 12 June 2002, para. 68; Halilovic (IT-01-48), Trial Chamber, Judgment, 16 November 2005, para. 31.
38 Kunarac, Kovac, and Vokovic (IT-96-23, 23-1), Appeals Chamber, Judgment, 12 June 2002, para. 66; Galic (IT-98–29), Trial Chamber, Judgment, 5 December 2003, paras 11, 89; Halilovic (IT-01-48-T), Trial Chamber, Judgment, 16 November 2005, para. 30.

39 Strugar (IT-1-42), Trial Chamber, Judgment, 31 January 2005, para. 218. Compare Kordic and Cerkez (IT-95-14/2-A), Appeals Chamber, Judgment, 17 December 2004, para. 46 (applying treaty law instead of customary international law).
40 Statute of the International Criminal Tribunal for the Former Yugoslavia, UN Doc. S/RES/827 (1993), Art. 4.
41 Ibid., Art. 4(3).
42 Blagojevic and Jokic (IT-02-60), Trial Chamber, Judgment, 17 January 2005, para. 639. See also Brdjanin (IT-99-36), Trial Chamber, Judgment, 1 September 2004, para. 680; Stakic (IT-97-24), Trial Chamber, Judgment, 31 July 2003, para. 500.
43 Krstic (IT-98-33), Trial Chamber, Judgment, 2 August 2001, para. 550.
44 Jelisic (IT-95-10), Trial Chamber, Judgment, 14 December 1999, para. 62.
45 Stakic (IT-97-24), Trial Chamber, Judgment, 31 July 2003, para. 521.
46 Krstic (IT-98-33), Appeals Chamber, Judgment, 19 April 2004, para. 6; Blagojevic and Jokic (IT-02-60), Trial Chamber, Judgment, 17 January 2005, para. 667.
47 Statute of the International Criminal Tribunal for the Former Yugoslavia, UN Doc. S/RES/827 (1993), Art. 5.
48 Ibid.
49 Limaj, *et al.* (IT-03-66), Trial Chamber, Judgment, 30 November 2005, para. 181.
50 Ibid. See also Galic (IT-98-29), Trial Chamber, Judgment, 5 December 2003, para. 140; Simic, Tadic, and Zaric (IT-95-9), Trial Chamber, Judgment, 17 October 2003, para. 37; Stakic (IT-97-24), Trial Chamber, Judgment, 31 July 2003, para. 621.
51 Stakic (IT-97-24), Trial Chamber, Judgment, 31 July 2003, para. 567.
52 Kunarac, Kovac, and Vokovic (IT-96-23, 23-1), Appeals Chamber, Judgment, 12 June 2002, para. 83. See also Simic, Tadic, and Zaric (IT-95-9), Trial Chamber, Judgment, 17 October 2003, para. 38; Stakic (IT-97-24), Trial Chamber, Judgment, 31 July 2003, para. 570.
53 Limaj, *et al.* (IT-03-66), Trial Chamber, Judgment, 30 November 2005, para. 180.
54 Ibid.; Tadic (IT-94-1), Appeals Chamber, Judgment, 15 July 1999, para. 251.
55 Blagojevic and Jokic (IT-02-60), Trial Chamber, Judgment, 17 January 2005, para. 569.
56 Galic (IT-98-29), Trial Chamber, Judgment, 5 December 2009, para. 599.
57 Stakic (IT-27-24), Trial Chamber, Judgment, 31 July 2003, para. 632.
58 Brdanin (IT-99-36), Trial Chamber, Judgment, 1 September 2004, paras 1022, 1024.
59 Obrenovic (IT-02-60/2), Trial Chamber, Sentencing Judgment, 10 December 2003, para. 37.
60 Nikolic, Momir (IT-02-60/1), Trial Chamber, Judgment, 2 December 2003, paras 21, 31, 39.
61 Stakic (IT-27-24), Trial Chamber, Judgment, 31 July 2003, paras 809-10.
62 Blagojevic and Jokic (IT-02-60), Trial Chamber, Judgment, 17 January 2005, paras 615, 620.
63 Kvocka, *et al.* (IT-98-30/1-A), Appeals Chamber, Judgment, 28 February 2005, para. 289. See also Kunarac, Kovac, and Vokovic (IT-96-23, 23-1), Appeals Chamber, Judgment, 12 June 2002, para. 142. See also Limaj, *et al.* (IT-03-66), Trial Chamber, Judgment, 30 November 2005, para. 235.
64 Furundzija (IT-95-17/1), Appeals Chamber, Judgment, 21 July 2000, para. 111.
65 Kvocka, *et al.* (IT-98-30/1), Trial Chamber, Judgment, 2 November 2001, para. 144.
66 Furundzija (IT-95-17/1), Trial Chamber, Judgment, 10 December 1998, paras 139, 153.
67 Delalic, *et al.* (IT-96-21-A), Appeals Chamber, Judgment, 20 February 2001, para. 195. See also; Brdjanin (IT-99-36), Trial Chamber, Judgment, 1 September 2004, para. 275.
68 Halilovic (IT-01-48), Trial Chamber, Judgment, 16 November 2005, para. 55.
69 Strugar (IT-01-42), Trial Chamber, Judgment, 31 January 2005, paras 436, 439, 444.
70 Limaj, *et al.* (IT-03-66), Trial Chamber, Judgment, 30 November 2005, para. 11; Delalic, *et al.* (IT-96-21-A), Appeals Chamber, Judgment, 20 February 2001, para. 581. See also Vaseljevic (IT-98-32), Trial Chamber, Judgment, 29 November 2002, para. 15.
71 Erdemovic (IT-96-22), Appeals Chamber, Judgment, 7 October 1997, para. 19.
72 Kupreskic, *et al.* (IT-95-16) Trial Chamber, Judgment, 14 January 2000, paras 51, 515-20; Limaj, *et al.* (IT-03-66), Trial Chamber, Judgment, 30 November 2005, para. 193.
73 Kordic and Cerkez (IT-95-14/2), Trial Chamber, Judgment, 26 February 2001, paras 448–52.
74 Vasiljevic (IT-98-32), Trial Chamber, Judgment, 29 November 2002, para. 282. See also Delalic, *et al.* (IT-96-21-A), Appeals Chamber, Judgment, 20 February 2001, para. 590.
75 Milosevic (IT-02-54-A), Appeal Chamber, Decision on Interlocutory Appeal of the Trial Chamber's Decision on the Assignment of Defense Counsel, 1 November 2004, para. 12.
76 Ibid., para. 13.

77 Ibid., para. 15.
78 Ibid., paras 16–7.
79 Ibid., para. 19.
80 Statute of the International Criminal Tribunal for Rwanda, UN Doc. S/RES/955 (1994).
81 Alison Des Forges, Human Rights Watch, Leave None to Tell the Story: Genocide in Rwanda 15 (1999).
82 Report by the Special Rapporteur for Rwanda of the United Nations Commission on Human Rights, UN Doc. S/1994/1157 (1994).
83 Virgina Morris and Michael P. Scharf, *The International Criminal Tribunal for Rwanda* 101 (Transnational Publishers, New York, 1998).
84 Report of the Secretary-General Pursuant to Paragraph 5 of Security Council Resolution 955 (1994), UN Doc. S/1995/134 (1995), para. 35.
85 International Criminal Tribunal for Rwanda, http://www.ictr.org/default.htm. Visited 7 January 2010.
86 Statute of the International Criminal Tribunal for Rwanda, UN Doc. S/RES/955 (1994), Art. 1.
87 Ibid., Arts 2, 3, 4; International Criminal Tribunal for Rwanda, http://www.ictr.org/default.htm. Visited 7 January 2010.
88 Kayishema and Ruzindana (ICTR-95-1-T), Trial Chamber, Judgment, 21 May 1999, para. 198.
89 Semanza (ICTR-97-20), Trial Chamber, 15 May 2003, para. 378.
90 Statute of the International Criminal Tribunal for Rwanda, UN Doc. S/RES/955 (1994), Art. 2(2).
91 Ibid.
92 Bagilishema (ICTR-95-1A-T), Trial Chamber, 7 June 2001, para. 55.
93 Kayishema and Ruzindana (ICTR-95-1-T), Trial Chamber, Judgment, 21 May 1999, para. 88; Rutaganda (ICTR-96-3), Trial Chamber, 6 December 1999, para. 46.
94 Statute of the International Criminal Tribunal for Rwanda, UN Doc. S/RES/955 (1994), Art. 3.
95 Akayesu (ICTR-96-4), Trial Chamber, Judgment, 2 September 1998, para. 578. Compare with para. 595, where the Tribunal lists the elements for a crime against humanity in three parts.
96 Kayishema and Ruzindana (ICTR-95-1-T), Trial Chamber, Judgment, 21 May 1999, para. 133. See also Ruggiu, (ICTR-97-32), Trial Chamber, 1 June 2000, paras 19-20; Bagilishema (ICTR-95-1A), Trial Chamber, Judgment, June 7, 2001, para. 94.
97 Niyitegeka (ICTR-96-14), Trial Chamber, 16 May 2003, para. 442; Semanza (ICTR-97-20), Trial Chamber, 15 May 2003, para. 332.
98 Kayishema and Ruzindana (ICTR-95-1-T), Trial Chamber, Judgment, 21 May 1999, paras 125–26.
99 Akayesu (ICTR-96-4), Trial Chamber, Judgment, 2 September 1998, paras 604–7; Statute of the International Criminal Tribunal for the Former Yugoslavia, UN Doc. S/RES/827 (1993).
100 Kayishema and Ruzindana (ICTR-95-1-T), Trial Chamber, Judgment, 21 May 1999, paras 156–58.
101 Ibid. See also Rutaganda (ICTR-96-3), Trial Chamber, Judgment and Sentence, 6 December 1999, paras 86–90.
102 Kayishema and Ruzindana (ICTR-95-1-T), Trial Chamber, Judgment and Sentence, 21 May 1999, para. 169.
103 Akayesu (ICTR-96-4-A), Appeals Chamber, Judgment, 1 June 2001.
104 Akayesu (ICTR-96-4), Trial Chamber, Judgment, 2 September 1998, para. 598; Musema (ICTR-96-13), Trial Chamber, Judgment and Sentence, 27 January 2000, paras 220–1, 226–9. Compare Semanza (ICTR-97-20), Trial Chamber, Judgment and Sentence, 15 May 2003, paras 344–45 (adopting a narrower definition of rape).
105 Akayesu (ICTR-96-4), Trial Chamber, Judgment, 2 September 1998, para. 731.
106 Ibid., para. 731.
107 Ibid., para. 681.
108 Ibid., para. 595.
109 Semanza (ICTR-97-20), Trial Chamber, Judgment and Sentence, 15 May 2003, paras 342–3.
110 Akayesu (ICTR-96-4), Trial Chamber, Judgment, 2 September 1998, paras 597, 687.
111 Kayishema and Ruzindana (ICTR-95-1-T), Trial Chamber, Judgment, 21 May 1999, para. 210.
112 Bagilishema (ICTR-95-1A), Trial Chamber, Judgment, 7 June 2001, para. 38.
113 Nahimana, Barayagwiza, and Ngeze (ICTR-96-11, 97-19, 97-27), Trial Chamber, Judgment and Sentence, 3 December 2003, paras 970–3.
114 Ibid., para. 977.

115 Kayishema and Ruzindana (ICTR-95-1), Appeals Chamber, Judgment (Reasons), 1 June 2001, para. 69.
116 Ibid. [quoting Tadic (IT-94-1), Appeals Chamber, Judgment, 15 July 1999, para. 48].
117 ICTR Rules of Procedures and Evidence, Rule 11bis(B).
118 Ibid., Rule 11bis(A)(iii).
119 Ibid., Rule 11bis(C).
120 Ibid., Rule 11bis(D)(iv), (F).
121 Letter dated 21 November 2008 from the President of the International Criminal Tribunal for Rwanda addressed to the President of the Security Council, S/2008/726, 21 November 2008, para. 50; Letter dated 14 May 2009 from the President of the International Criminal Tribunal for Rwanda addressed to the President of the Security Council, S/2009/247, 14 May 2009, para. 29; G. Norris, 'Closer to Justice: Transferring Cases from the International Criminal Court', *Minnesota Journal of International Law*, 2010, Vol. 19, 210.

5

The International Criminal Court

David Scheffer

The development of international criminal law during the 21st century will arise primarily out of the jurisprudence of the permanent International Criminal Court located in The Hague. The other tribunals covering specific regional situations in the Balkans, Rwanda, Sierra Leone, and Cambodia have established a rich body of procedural and substantive law and will continue to do so for several more years until their mandates and responsibilities expire. But the future lies mostly with the work of the International Criminal Court and, significantly, the deep influence it increasingly will have in generating new national laws and domestic trials for the prosecution of alleged war criminals.

The rationale for negotiating the establishment of the International Criminal Court during the 1990s emerged from several developments that finally enabled the international community to arrive at a level of comfort with the prospect of a permanent tribunal. In previous stages of the 20th century following World Wars I and II, there had been serious proposals for an international criminal court to prosecute the types of leading war criminals who had caused so much death and destruction during those wars. But significant political obstacles prevented the project from proceeding each time it was proposed.[1] The international military tribunals at Nuremberg and Tokyo set examples that many thought could be replicated for a permanent court. The Cold War intervened to put the idea into deep freeze, as did a decades-long project for the International Law Commission to arrive at a definition for the crime of aggression before deciding how to build such a court. The definitional endeavor finally produced a UN General Assembly resolution in 1974 defining an act of aggression between countries (but not the crime of aggression for purposes of individual criminal responsibility).[2]

In 1989, Trinidad and Tobago proposed that the International Law Commission consider creation of an international criminal court to bring drug traffickers to justice. Other governments proposed that such a court's mandate be expanded to include international terrorists. The international drug cartels and terrorist groups had created judicial challenges throughout the 1980s.[3] Then, as the atrocities in the Balkans took their terrible tolls in 1991 and 1992, the original concept of a court to prosecute perpetrators of genocide, crimes against humanity, war crimes, and aggression ('atrocity crimes')[4] came to the fore again in the drafting work of the International Law Commission.

The draft statute approved by the International Law Commission in 1994 covered the four atrocity crimes and added exceptionally serious treaty crimes of international concern, including drug trafficking and international terrorism.[5] Under the Commission's draft, states parties to the statute of the permanent court automatically would be subject to genocide investigations and prosecutions. The preconditions for charges of aggression, war crimes, and crimes against humanity would be the acceptance of the Court's jurisdiction by the state that had custody of the accused and by the state on whose territory the crime was committed. Additionally, the crime of aggression could not be prosecuted without a prior determination by the Security Council that the state of nationality of the accused had committed an act of aggression. Further, no crime that arose from a situation being dealt with by the UN Security Council as a threat to or breach of the peace or an act of aggression as determined by the Council under Chapter VII of the UN Charter could be prosecuted without the express approval of the Council. A state party to the statute could declare its acceptance of specific treaty crimes, like drug trafficking and terrorism, and thus enable the court to prosecute its nationals for such crimes.

The work of the International Law Commission was admirable, but it was not sufficient to convince governments to rush towards adoption of the draft statute. That required intergovernmental negotiations that commenced in early 1995, under the authority of the UN General Assembly, and used the Commission draft as a template.[6] There was momentum behind the venture because many governments, particularly those on the Security Council, began to suffer 'tribunal fatigue' over the financial and political costs of creating *ad hoc* UN criminal tribunals for the atrocities that burdened so many regions of the world. There was considerable logic underpinning a permanent court that would provide greater efficiencies in addressing the investigation and prosecution of atrocity crimes.

For three and one-half years a majority of the world's governments sent legal experts and diplomats to several multi-week sessions annually to negotiate the provisions of the statute for the International Criminal Court. They agreed to go to Rome to finish the statute in the summer of 1998 and, after five intensive weeks of negotiations, a final text emerged on 17 July.[7] The Rome Statute of the International Criminal Court was adopted by an overwhelming majority of votes when 120 governments approved the final text, 21 abstained, and seven voted 'no,' including the United States, the People's Republic of China, and Israel. The United States had long sought the establishment of the International Criminal Court but found certain provisions in the final text, particularly relating to the preconditions for jurisdiction, unacceptable.[8] China objected to the statute's coverage of non-international armed conflicts. Israel rejected the definition of one particular war crime pertaining to the indirect transfer of an occupying power's civilian population into the territory it occupies.

Critical supplemental documents were successfully negotiated at the United Nations for several years after the Rome Conference. They included the Rules of Procedure and Evidence and the Elements of Crimes (both of which were adopted by consensus, including by the United States, China, and Israel),[9] the Negotiated Relationship Agreement between the International Criminal Court and the United Nations,[10] and the Agreement on Privileges and Immunities.[11] By April 2002 more than 60 nations had ratified the Rome Statute and that permitted the Court to become operational on 1 July 2002. By 2010, 113 countries had ratified the Rome Statute. All European and South American countries had joined the Court, while 31 African, 17 Asian and Pacific, and 13 North American and Caribbean nations had become members. Two of the five permanent members of the Security Council—namely, the United Kingdom and France—were states parties. The Court was investigating atrocity crimes and initiating prosecutions of suspects in five situations: Uganda, the Democratic Republic of the Congo, Darfur (Sudan), the Central African Republic, and Kenya. A total of 23 accused had been indicted, with five of them in custody and either in pre-trial or trial proceedings in The Hague. The prosecutor was reviewing other situations in such state parties as Chad, Colombia, Georgia, and Afghanistan, as well as

Palestine for the purpose of possibly seeking authority to investigate one or more of them.

Structure of the Court

The International Criminal Court is a treaty-based tribunal, meaning that its existence derives from an international treaty, the Rome Statute, which governments ratify or accede to and under which they enjoy certain rights and are obligated to perform designated duties. The Court was not established by and is not an organ of the Security Council like the International Criminal Tribunals for the former Yugoslavia and Rwanda. Nor is the International Criminal Court of the hybrid character of either the Special Court for Sierra Leone or the Extraordinary Chambers in the Courts of Cambodia, both of which have treaty relationships with the United Nations.[12] The Negotiated Relationship Agreement between the International Criminal Court and the United Nations establishes means of cooperation between the two institutions and confirms the uniquely crafted role of the Security Council in the Court's operations. But the independence of the Court is a paramount characteristic of its existence.

The Court has four organs: the judicial chambers, the presidency, the prosecutor, and the registry. There are 18 judges elected by majority vote of the Assembly of States Parties for terms of nine years (except for some who had lesser terms in the beginning of the Court). No two judges can share the same nationality, each must be a citizen of a state party, and each judge must have experience either in criminal law or international law.[13] They are divided among the Pre-Trial Chamber, Trial Chamber, and Appeals Chamber. The president of the Court is a judge elected by majority vote among the judges, as are the first and second vice-presidents of the Court.[14] The initial president, serving two consecutive terms of three years each, was Judge Philippe Kirsch of Canada. The first individual elected by the states parties as prosecutor of the Court for a nine-year term was Luis Moreno Ocampo from Argentina. His first deputy prosecutor was Serge Brammertz from Belgium, who was succeeded in 2004 by Fatou Bensouda of the Gambia. The administrative arm of the Court, the registry, was first headed by Bruno Cathala from France and later by Silvana Arbia of Italy. There is a very active defense bar that represents defendants before the Court, and an Office of Public Counsel for the Defence to assist in the early stages of representation and provide support to the defense teams. There is also an Office of Public Victims to provide similar assistance to victims and their legal representatives before the Court.

The Assembly of States Parties of the Court consists of all of the nations that have ratified or acceded to the Rome Statute. They meet periodically to elect Court officials, to approve the budget of the Court, and to undertake other administrative oversight functions.[15] The Assembly has authority to remove Court officials and to vote on amendments to the Rome Statute and to the Rules of Procedure and Evidence and the Elements of Crimes. The Rome Statute mandated the Assembly to hold a review conference on the Rome Statute and to consider amendments to it seven years after the treaty's entry into force. States parties converged on Kampala, Uganda, in mid-2010 for that purpose. Article 112(4) empowers the Assembly to create an independent oversight mechanism for inspection, evaluation, and investigation of the Court. The Assembly was considering such an initiative in 2010.

There are four categories of jurisdiction that frame the work of the International Criminal Court. They cover jurisdictional regimes relating to subject matter (the crimes that can be investigated and prosecuted),[16] personal (individuals who fall under the Court's scrutiny),[17] territorial (where the crimes are committed),[18] and temporal (the time frame during which the Court can consider the commission of crimes in any particular situation).[19] One of the prosecutor's earliest challenges is to construct the matrix of jurisdictional opportunities and obstacles that will determine whether the situation of atrocity crimes and suspected perpetrators of them fall within the Court's overall jurisdiction for purposes of investigation and prosecution.

Subject matter jurisdiction

The subject matter jurisdiction of the Court is set forth in Articles 5 through 8 of the Rome Statute. It consists of the atrocity crimes described earlier: aggression, genocide, crimes against humanity, and war crimes. The crime of aggression, identified in Article 5, was defined and the manner of its referral to the Court was finalized in Kampala in 2010. There were years of negotiation leading to Rome on whether and how to define aggression and determine the procedure by which the Court would be seized with the crime. Despite the heritage of prosecuting crimes against the peace (or aggression) before the Nuremberg and Tokyo International Military Tribunals following World War II, debate ensued in the negotiations for the International Criminal Court over whether the definition for aggression should be wider than simply wars of aggression that result in the occupation of foreign territory. Governments also diverged on whether the Security Council must first determine an act of aggression has occurred between states before the Court can investigate the crime of aggression by particular individuals. Nonetheless, the crime of aggression was included in the Rome Statute with the expectation that in the future both definitional and referral issues could be ironed out to 'activate' the crime with relevant amendments to the Rome Statute.[20]

The crime of genocide in the Rome Statute has its roots in the 1948 Genocide Convention.[21] Negotiators recognized they were on very safe ground in relying upon the Convention's definition of genocide, given the 130 countries that had ratified the treaty by the mid-1990s. The statutes of the International Criminal Tribunals for the former Yugoslavia and Rwanda had recently relied on the Convention definition, and that constituted an important contemporary precedent upon which to build.[22] However, in contrast to the tribunal statutes and the Convention itself, the Rome Statute does not identify the four punishable 'other acts' of genocide: namely, the forms of participation consisting of conspiracy to commit genocide, direct and public incitement to commit genocide, attempt to commit genocide, and complicity in genocide. Negotiators considered that these 'other acts' are better designated within the modes of participation defined for all of the atrocity crimes of the Rome Statute in Article 25 of that document.[23] Indeed, Article 25(e) ensures that direct and public incitement to commit genocide is criminalized, thus reaffirming the Convention's original construct. However in the drafting of the Rome Statute, the inchoate crime of conspiring to commit genocide was eliminated. The prosecutor sought his first genocide charge in the indictment of Sudan President Omar al-Bashir regarding the Darfur situation, but a split Pre-Trial Chamber approved only charges covering war crimes and crimes against humanity.[24] The Appeals Chamber instructed the Pre-Trial Chamber to review the evidence on genocide to determine whether the prosecutor had a "reasonable basis" to believe the crime had been committed.[25]

Article 7 of the Rome Statute provides the most extensive and well-defined listing of crimes against humanity of any of the tribunal statutes of the 1990s. The codification of crimes against humanity was no easy task for the negotiators as there was no international convention to draw upon and there were only the relatively limited precedents of the Nuremberg and Tokyo Tribunal charters and of the statutes of the International Criminal Tribunals for the former Yugoslavia and Rwanda. There had never been a gathering of the international community to determine precisely what acts constituted crimes against humanity and how they should be defined for purposes of individual criminal responsibility. That task was completed in Rome in the summer of 1998.

The first step was to establish a significant threshold of conduct to trigger the Court's jurisdiction over this category of crimes. Negotiators settled on a magnitude and knowledge test of 'widespread or systematic attack directed against any civilian population, with knowledge of the attack ....'[26] That was further defined as 'a course of conduct involving the multiple commission of acts referred to in paragraph 1 [of Article 7] against any civilian population, pursuant to or in furtherance of a State or organizational policy to commit such attack ....'[27] Thus, multiple actions carried out as part of a leadership-driven policy need to be established, alongside the defendant's knowledge about the actual attack on the civilian population, in order to charge crimes against humanity.[28]

The Rome Statute expands the list of crimes against humanity beyond the conventional categories of murder, extermination, enslavement, deportation, imprisonment, torture, rape, persecutions on political, racial, and religious grounds, and other inhumane acts. In addition to those crimes, Article 7 criminalizes forcible transfer of population, severe deprivation of physical liberty in violation of fundamental rules of international law, sexual slavery, enforced prostitution, forced pregnancy, enforced sterilization, or any other form of sexual violence of comparable gravity. It further lists as crimes against humanity persecution on national, ethnic, cultural, gender, or other grounds that are universally recognized as impermissible under international law. But an act of persecution must be connected to any one or more of the other acts designated as crimes against humanity or to the crime of genocide under Article 6 or to war crimes defined in Article 8. With the crime of aggression set to be activated in 2017 under the Rome Statute, it may be possible to link persecution to that atrocity crime as well. Ethnic cleansing, while not a crime *per se* under the Rome Statute, arises from acts of persecution that are conducted with discriminatory intent and involve the commission of any of the other criminal acts under the Statute.[29] The additional crimes against humanity in the Rome Statute include enforced disappearance of persons and the crime of apartheid. 'Other inhumane acts' are codified as being 'of a similar character [to the other crimes against humanity] intentionally causing great suffering, or serious injury to body or to mental or physical health.'[30]

Many of the Rome Statute's crimes against humanity are defined in greater detail in Article 7(2), an exercise intended to fill gaps not otherwise covered by treaty law. For example, arriving at a definition for 'forced pregnancy,' a crime committed during the Balkans conflict of the early 1990s, took considerable time during the negotiations.[31] The influence of religious lobbying was reflected in how negotiators agreed that the definition for 'forced pregnancy' should not be interpreted 'as affecting national laws relating to pregnancy' and how the term 'gender,' which is used as a category of discriminatory conduct for the crime of persecution, can refer only 'to the two sexes, male and female, within the context of society.' Thus, at least in theory, widespread or systematic persecution based on other types of possible gender discrimination (gays, transvestites, bisexuals) might not qualify as a crime against humanity under the Rome Statute. Similarly, 'enforced disappearance of persons' required prolonged discussion to ensure that its definition would provide a comprehensive framework for criminal prosecution.[32]

The subject matter jurisdiction of war crimes covers a wide range of criminal conduct during either international or non-international armed conflicts. Article 8 of the Rome Statute provides a far more extensive listing and definitions of war crimes than found in earlier tribunal charters and statutes.[33] However, the gravity test is uniquely established to point towards the probability, but not the absolute requirement, that the war crime be 'committed as part of a plan or policy or as part of a large-scale commission of such crimes.' This is largely because in the relatively long history of war crimes codification, any violation of, for example, the Geneva Conventions should be well known to soldiers as a war crime. If soldiers were to begin to consider some violations as too insignificant to attract prosecution, then the discipline afforded by the Geneva Conventions might be undermined. Negotiators of the Rome Statute struggled with this dilemma because the International Criminal Court is designed to investigate and prosecute primarily leadership crimes of significant magnitude and not the isolated 'grave breach' (as that violation is defined in the Geneva Conventions) of a foot soldier dealing with civilians or the wounded or guarding prisoners of war. The answer was found in a negotiated formula, by stating in Article 8(1) that the Court shall have jurisdiction over war crimes '*in particular* when committed as part of a plan or policy or as part of a large-scale commission of such crimes' (emphasis added). This particularity requirement, if it might be called that, has become the standard for war crimes prosecutions before the Court.[34]

In addition to the grave breaches and Article 3 common violations of the Geneva Conventions, Article 8 establishes two fairly long lists of 'serious violations of the laws and customs,' one applicable for international armed conflicts and a shorter one for non-international armed conflicts (such as civil wars). These particular war crimes constituted in 1998 what the negotiators viewed as the embodiment of customary international law for which individuals could be prosecuted.[35] They were drawn from The Hague Conventions, Geneva Conventions, Geneva Protocols of 1977, and modern practice that had essentially accelerated recognition of certain conduct as criminal. The latter included attacks on the personnel or assets of humanitarian organizations or UN peacekeepers, enforced prostitution, and forced pregnancy. The fact that serious violations identified for non-international armed conflicts are fewer in number than those for international armed conflicts in the Rome Statute reflected negotiators' conservative approach to the exercise. They wanted to make a persuasive case under customary international law for the listed war crimes rather than follow the logic that there should be no distinction between criminal conduct in one type of armed conflict and the identical conduct in another type of armed conflict.[36] The objective of the Rome Statute was to reflect customary international law with respect to individual criminal responsibility as of the summer of 1998 and not to legislate new law in the process.

Yielding to pressure from such states as China, negotiators carved three caveats into the war crimes provisions: First, regarding non-international armed conflicts, the Court will not investigate and prosecute crimes arising from 'situations of internal disturbances and tensions, such as riots, isolated and sporadic acts of violence or other acts of a similar nature.' Second, the character of the internal armed conflict must be of 'protracted' duration and 'between governmental authorities and organized armed groups or between such groups.'[37] Third, nothing the Court does to investigate violations of the laws and customs applicable in armed conflicts can affect the government's responsibility for law and order or to defend the unity and territorial integrity of the state 'by all legitimate means.'[38] These caveats potentially and purposely create a wide range of situations of armed violence and war crimes within a society that would not fall within the subject matter jurisdiction of the Court.

The Court has approved indictments based in significant part on charges of war crimes. The trial of the Court's first defendant, Thomas Lubanga Dyilo, is centered on the war crime of conscripting or enlisting children under the age of 15 years into armed forces or groups or using them to participate actively in hostilities in the Democratic Republic of the Congo.[39] Other defendants have been charged with the same offense or other war crimes such as rape, pillage, murder of civilians who took no active part in hostilities, destruction of civilian property, direct attacks against a civilian population, cruel treatment of civilians, and intentional direct attacks against a peacekeeping mission.

Personal, territorial, and temporal jurisdiction

The three other types of jurisdiction—personal, territorial, and temporal—are intertwined in the Rome Statute. They should be examined alongside how situations are referred to the Court. In the latter respect, atrocity crime situations (not individual cases) can be referred by the Security Council under a UN Charter Chapter VII resolution, by a state party, or by the prosecutor provided the Pre-Trial Chamber approves.[40] Once a situation has been referred to the Court, the prosecutor has the sole authority to investigate individual suspects and seek indictments against any of them in connection with the referred situation.

Provided that a situation has been referred to the Court, it can exercise its jurisdiction over the citizens of any state party to the Rome Statute who are identified as having committed any of the atrocity crimes in the referred situation. If such crimes were committed on the territory of a state party, then the Court can also exercise jurisdiction over any individual perpetrator of such crimes from a non-party state (unless the temporal jurisdiction argument set forth below prevails).[41] If a non-party state files a declaration with the registrar of the Court consenting to jurisdiction over a particular situation of atrocity crimes, then, provided there is a referral of the situation to the Court, the citizens of that non-party state can be investigated by the Court for commission of such crimes. Nationals of other non-party states who commit atrocity crimes relating to the situation on the declaring non-party's territory can also be investigated.[42] Finally, if the Security Council refers a situation to the Court for investigation and prosecution, then any individual, whether of state party or non-party state nationality, who is linked to the referred situation may fall within the Court's personal jurisdiction, although the Council's decision in the Darfur situation to limit the mandate regarding personal jurisdiction is controversial.[43]

Three of the situations before the Court in 2010—Uganda, Democratic Republic of the Congo, and the Central African Republic—were self-referred by the state party on the territory where the atrocity crimes occurred.[44] A fourth situation, Darfur, concerned atrocity crimes on the territory of a non-party state, Sudan, committed by citizens of that country. The Darfur situation arrived before the Court because the Security Council referred it under Chapter VII authority, as authorized by Article 13(b) of the Rome Statute.[45] A fifth situation, Kenya, was initiated by the prosecutor *proprio motu* and the Pre-Trial Chamber authorized the commencement of an investigation in 2010.[46]

That hard case might arise when temporal jurisdiction is considered. The four self-referred and *proprio motu* situations concerned alleged atrocity crimes committed *after* each of the countries had ratified the Rome Statute. Article 11(1) of the Rome Statute states that the Court exercises jurisdiction only over atrocity crimes committed following the entry into force of the Rome Statute, which was 1 July 2002. However, Article 11(2) addresses temporal jurisdiction for states that ratify the Rome Statute after that date, and permits the Court to 'exercise its jurisdiction only with respect to crimes committed after the entry into force of this Statute for that State, unless that State [as a non-party State] has made a declaration under article 12, paragraph 3.'

One might argue that when read in conjunction with other provisions of the Rome Statute, a non-party national cannot be investigated and prosecuted unless either the suspect's state of nationality accepted the Court's jurisdiction with an Article 12(3) declaration or the Security Council referred the relevant situation to the Court under Chapter VII authority.[47] The possibility could arise, under this theory, where a non-party national commits an atrocity crime on the territory of a state party and cannot be prosecuted by the Court unless the Security Council refers the situation or the suspect's government files an Article 12(3) declaration.

The alternative view would be that Article 12's preconditions to jurisdiction trump other provisions of the Rome Statute so as to neutralize temporal jurisdiction conditionality. After all, there would be little point to the two alternative preconditions, one being commission of the atrocity crime on the territory of a state party, if it were meant to cover only state party nationals involved in the commission of the crime. However, the simple fact that Article 126(1) of the Rome Statute states that it will not enter into force for any nation joining the Court after 1 July 2002, until 60 days after that state's ratification, accession, acceptance, or approval of the treaty only makes common sense if that procedure relates to the liability of the state's nationals.

Otherwise, if every state's nationals (and thus the entire population of the world) are presumed to be potentially covered by the Court's jurisdiction since 1 July 2002 for atrocity crimes committed on the territories of states parties, there would be no incentive for states to join the Court as such an act simply would confirm jurisdiction existing over its nationals since 1 July 2002. What would be the point of becoming a state party if that country's nationals already were subject to the Court's jurisdiction since its opening day? A primary purpose of Article 126(2) is to assure a non-party state that its nationals would *not* be subject to the jurisdiction of the Court prior to such state joining the Court, thus ensuring that the nation's past sins are not fair game for the Court to investigate. The state joins the Court knowing it does so with a clean slate, focusing on the conduct of its nationals in the future (and not the past). No nation that has become a state party to the Court after 1 July 2002 has conceded the liability of its nationals prior to the sixtieth day after that state ratified or acceded to the Rome Statute.[48]

The counter-argument to this reading of the Rome Statute is that every non-party state must accept the reality, whether it wishes to or not, that any of its nationals who commit atrocity crimes on the territory of a state party subject themselves not only to the domestic legal system of that state party but also to the state party's prior decision under the Rome Statute to delegate prosecution of such cases to the jurisdiction of the International Criminal Court. The practical issue remains, of course, regarding custody of such non-party nationals for the purpose of bringing them to The Hague to stand trial. At some point in its practice, the Court will confront the unique dilemma posed by this blending of personal, temporal, and territorial jurisdiction, and when it does the judges will need to determine the parameters of the Court's jurisdiction over a non-party state national.

Applicable law

The Court determines the law of a case in accordance with a cascading priority of sources that provide no surprises but may cause tension in the future when the application of international humanitarian law collides with international human rights law. Priority sources are the Rome Statute itself and its Rules of Procedure and Evidence and the Elements of Crimes. Of second priority are principles of international law and, in particular, the law of armed conflict. The third tier of application pertains to the general principles of law derived from national legal systems.[49] However, the Rome Statute stipulates that '[t]he application and interpretation of law pursuant to this article must be consistent with internationally recognized human rights ….'[50] The growing integration of and conflict between the application of the law of war and of human rights principles originally envisaged for relatively peaceful societies could deeply influence the Court's jurisprudence in years to come.

Complementarity

The International Criminal Court is designed to render international criminal justice in an international courtroom. But it also has a primary duty to afford national court systems the initial opportunity to investigate and prosecute individuals suspected of committing atrocity crimes in the situations referred to the Court. If such national initiatives are faithfully carried out, then the Court must stand down on the particular individuals for whom justice is being or has been rendered at the national level. The importance of this innovative feature of the Rome Statute cannot be understated. In every situation referred to the Court, the prosecutor must look first to the relevant national courts and whether they are bringing the alleged perpetrators to justice before he or she can proceed with confidence to investigate and prosecute such individuals. The negotiators of the Rome Statute labeled the procedure 'complementarity,' although that term appears nowhere in the text of the document. The word is used to describe how the Court complements the judicial efforts of nations. The long-term objective is to strengthen the capabilities of and incentivize national courts to prosecute atrocity crimes and use the Court only for the hopefully declining number of cases over the years that cannot be prosecuted elsewhere.[51]

From a strictly legal perspective, complementarity describes the admissibility of cases before the Court as covered by Articles 17, 18, and 19 of the Rome Statute. When a situation has been referred to the Court by either a state party or by the prosecutor with the approval of the Pre-Trial Chamber, the prosecutor must notify the nations (both states parties and non-party states) that normally would exercise national jurisdiction over the atrocity crimes covered by the referral.[52] The notified states have one month to inform the Court that they are investigating their nationals or others within their jurisdiction with respect to such atrocity crimes.[53] If such notification is made, then the prosecutor must withdraw and permit the state to investigate for at least six months without interference by the Court unless the prosecutor persuades the Pre-Trial Chamber to authorize him or her to investigate because the state proves unwilling or genuinely unable to carry out the investigation nationally.[54] The Rome Statute does not require such notification to states or deferral to national investigations when the Security Council refers a situation to the Court. The Council would be operating under Chapter VII authority in connection with a threat to or breach of international peace and security and thus would be seeking the Court's direct and immediate action to investigate and prosecute the atrocity crimes. The Security Council can frame its resolution so as to encourage a national effort at investigation and prosecution but it also can remain silent on the point or explicitly direct rapid action by the Court, in either case liberating the Court to proceed full steam ahead.

Beyond the initial phase of deferral to national jurisdictions that choose to step forward and commit to authentic investigations, the Rome Statute has a secondary level of complementarity for each case that is prosecuted before the Court.[55] A case is inadmissible before the Court if a state with jurisdiction over the case is investigating or prosecuting it, unless the state 'is unwilling or unable genuinely' to carry out the investigation or prosecution. If, for example, a case has been investigated by a state with jurisdiction over it and there is a decision not to prosecute the suspect, the Court must withdraw unless the state's decision resulted from 'the unwillingness or inability' to genuinely prosecute the individual.[56] The Court must also stand down if the suspect has already been tried for the same conduct, unless the national proceeding sought to shield the individual from criminal responsibility or unless international norms of due process were violated and 'were inconsistent with an intent to bring the person concerned to justice.'[57]

However, a finding of inability in a particular case can arise only when there has been 'a total or substantial collapse or unavailability of [the state's] judicial system.'[58] That may prove to be a very high bar to scale on the issue of a state's inability to investigate or prosecute a case. The possibilities may be limited to failed nations or totally devastated countries in the wake of war or atrocities. Thus, the Court arguably is confined to a finding of inadmissibility only on grounds of unwillingness with respect to highly developed legal systems.

A finding of unwillingness in a particular case can arise under one of three circumstances: a national decision to shield the person from criminal responsibility or, in a manner inconsistent with an intent to bring the person concerned to justice, there is an unjustified delay in the proceedings or there are proceedings that were not or are not being conducted independently or impartially.[59]

There is one additional factor that can terminate the Court's scrutiny: 'The case is not of sufficient gravity to justify further action by the Court.'[60] The gravity test for an individual case is a significant barrier to admissibility. It points to the probability that the Court will focus on leadership crimes where, for example, a political, military, business, or media leader orchestrates widespread or otherwise very significant commission of atrocity crimes by others, some of which may be quite singular and minor in character but when combined, under the leadership of the defendant, constitute an atrocity crime of significant magnitude.[61]

General principles of law

Part 3 of the Rome Statute sets forth 12 general principles of law that guide the Court's administration of justice. These general principles were not all drawn from customary international law in 1998; some were heavily negotiated compromises for the unique requirements of the International Criminal Court. For example, the principle of non-retroactivity *ratione personae*, which does not hold a person criminally responsible for conduct committed prior to entry into force of the Rome Statute and hence the operation of the Court, is one of the pillars of customary international law.[62] In contrast, the defense of superior orders by military or civilian leaders set forth in Article 33 was a negotiated compromise that differs from other statutory and judicial precedents on the subject and thus should not be regarded as customary international law.[63]

The International Criminal Court only investigates and brings to justice individual human beings. It has no criminal jurisdiction over governments and therefore does not seek to establish state responsibility in the same way that the International Court of Justice undertakes that function, including for civil reparations claims. Nor does the International Criminal Court have jurisdiction over organizations or corporations that may be deeply involved in the commission of atrocity crimes, other than through the investigation and prosecution of individual members or officers of those entities. Within the Court's jurisdiction to examine individual criminal responsibility, the Court must choose a mode of liability that describes how the accused participated in the commission of the crime and determine how that mode of liability affects his or her culpability.

The most prominent category of individual criminal responsibility before the Court in Article 25 of the Rome Statute includes the accused as a perpetrator who, in the context of leadership defendants before the International Criminal Court, likely would be a lead planner or organizer of the atrocity crime and act individually or jointly 'with another or through another person.'[64] The second category covers defendants who act with complicity in the commission of the crime. They can act either as someone who 'orders, solicits or induces'[65] the crime or as a person who 'aids, abets or otherwise assists.'[66] This accomplice category can invite considerable complexity in the deliberations of the Court. The Rome Statute does not make it easier by failing to explicitly include some of the guideposts that have arisen in the jurisprudence of the other tribunals. One such requirement, for example, is that the assistance must be 'substantial' in character to attract liability.[67]

An additional and highly significant prong of individual liability—common purpose complicity—described in Article 25(3)(d) of the Rome Statute has helped generate a relatively new doctrine of 'joint criminal enterprise' liability oriented towards leaders of atrocity crimes falling within the jurisdiction of the Court. 'It assigns criminal responsibility to an individual who, sharing in a common criminal purpose with others, contributes to the furtherance of that common criminal purpose with the direct intent to commit at least one crime falling within that purpose.'[68] This type of liability includes circumstances where the accused can be convicted for atrocity crimes committed by others if such crimes were reasonably foreseeable as a consequence of the criminal plan, even though the accused originally had not intended that the particular crime or crimes be part of the plan.

Finally, Article 25(3) of the Rome Statute provides that within several categories of individual criminal responsibility, the mere attempt to commit an atrocity crime can attract liability. Although this serves the deterrence value of the International Criminal Court, acts of such character are unlikely to be prosecuted very often because the prosecutor would have difficulty meeting the gravity test in the case of an attempted commission. But the possibility certainly remains and for good purpose: to stifle atrocity crimes in their infancy.

Perhaps the most profound principle of law in the Rome Statute is stated in Article 27, which denies immunity from prosecution for any government official, civilian or military, and regardless of any individual's official capacity. While this echoes similar provisions in the Nuremberg and Tokyo charters and the tribunal statutes of modern times,[69] and while the most senior officials claiming immunity have been prosecuted before such courts, the Rome Statute represents the first treaty codification among nations of an explicit principle of leadership liability devoid of immunity defenses. Significantly, Article 27 was agreed to as a standing general principle for the unknown events of the future, in contrast to specific conflicts or atrocities that already had occurred or were occurring in connection with all other tribunals. When the Pre-Trial Chamber approved an arrest warrant against Sudan President Omar al-Bashir in March 2009,[70] the Court put Article 27 to the test because, although Sudan is a non-party state, it is the object of a Security Council referral of the Darfur situation to the Court requiring the cooperation of Sudan.

Unique characteristics about how the Court operates

The International Criminal Court conducts its investigations and trials pursuant to a voluminous body of rules set forth in the Rome Statute, the Rules of Procedure and Evidence and the Elements of Crimes. Many of the procedures, rights, and duties found in these constitutional documents reflect and build upon how the other tribunals of the modern era have functioned. However, some characteristics of the Court's operation merit particular emphasis in this chapter.

Security Council deferral of investigation or prosecution

Article 16 of the Rome Statute recognizes the Security Council's power to adopt an enforcement resolution under Chapter VII of the UN Charter that requests that an investigation or prosecution of a case or an overall situation not be commenced or continued for a period of 12 months, a period that can be renewed in the same manner. The origin of this provision arises from the effort by some governments, particularly the United States, to require that all situations be referred to the Court either by the Security Council or by a state party provided the Council approved the referral if the situation pertained to a matter already before the Council. When the Council oversight role was eliminated during the negotiations and the prosecutor gained the power to initiate investigations with Pre-Trial Chamber approval, the Singapore delegation tabled a compromise formula that codified the right of the Security Council to interrupt the Court's work, provided it approved a Chapter VII resolution and avoided the veto of any of its permanent members.[71]

Article 16 was logically intended to be used in connection with referrals by state parties and with respect to investigations launched by the prosecutor, as both held the potential of starting judicial investigations into situations for political or other ill-founded purposes that ran counter to the wishes of the Security Council. Where the Security Council referred a situation to the Court, it was not anticipated that the Council would want to suspend its own requested investigations and prosecutions. The purpose of Article 16 was to assuage the concerns of those delegations deeply concerned about referrals by states parties or the prosecutor. Nonetheless, when the prosecutor initiated his efforts to indict Sudan President Omar al-Bashir in July 2008, Article 16 became the focal point of a campaign to persuade the Security Council to suspend the Court's work on al-Bashir and perhaps others suspected or charged with atrocity crimes in the Darfur situation. This occurred despite the fact that the Council had referred the Darfur situation to the Court in 2005 with full knowledge that it might implicate senior leaders in the government.[72]

Prosecutor's duties

When the prosecutor initiates an investigation, he or she must take into account the gravity of the crime, the interests of the victims, and whether the investigation would serve the interests of justice.[73] These are discretionary powers that the prosecutor can use either widely or narrowly to frame the Court's docket. However, the prosecutor's power to investigate is heavily conditioned by the rights of the person being questioned, including the suspect. In the latter respect, the suspect is entitled to prior notification of the grounds on which he or she is believed to have committed an atrocity crime and is further entitled to legal counsel prior to the initial interview (and long before any indictment of the suspect).[74] The suspect is practically encouraged to remain silent (with no inference of guilt or innocence to be drawn from such silence) despite the fact that no criminal conduct has been charged and the prosecutor may be trying only to collect evidence of what actually happened before determining precisely whom to indict.

The prosecutor has a duty to look for and provide exculpatory, or exonerating, evidence to the defense team of the defendant.[75] This responsibility is taken seriously by the Court. In 2008 the case against Thomas Lubanga Dyilo almost collapsed because of the prosecutor's refusal to provide certain evidence to the defense on the grounds that it had been provided by the UN Peacekeeping Force in the Democratic Republic of the Congo on grounds of strict confidentiality. However, if such information contained exculpatory evidence, the defense would be deprived of potentially vindicating evidence. After months of litigation over this point, with the entire case hanging in the balance, the Court finally resolved the impasse with the disclosure of a sufficient amount of the evidence to enable the trial to commence in 2009.[76]

Summons to appear and national security information

When the Pre-Trial Chamber determines that there are reasonable grounds to believe that a person has committed an atrocity crime, it can approve either an arrest warrant against the individual or a summons to appear.[77] The latter is a tool to encourage cooperation by the indictee with the Court and may result in pre-trial release or mitigation of the sentence. Article 72 of the Rome Statute ensures the protection of national security information from the Court's scrutiny provided a number of steps are undertaken by the state holding the information. This was a hotly contested provision in the negotiations of the Rome Statute and recognizes the reality that governments will not easily hand up very sensitive intelligence derived from sources that cannot be disclosed to an international court.[78] However, if an impasse arises over how to handle particular information, the Court can try to compel production of it from a state party by referring the dispute to the Assembly of States Parties or, if the Security Council referred the situation to the Court, to the Council itself.[79] In neither case is there any guarantee of a response or any enforcement action by the Council. The more critical feature of this provision is the prohibition on the prosecutor or defense counsel from using such information in the courtroom. While this may limit, if not distort, the historical record being generated by the public trial, Article 72 was an essential compromise on the gathering and use of evidence in order for many governments to have greater confidence in the work of the Court.

Role of victims

Victims have a relatively significant role in the proceedings against defendants. They are allowed to be represented by counsel at various stages of a trial for the purpose of obtaining reparations, compensation, and rehabilitation.[80] A special Victims and Witnesses Unit, operated by the registrar of the Court, may advise on protective measures, security arrangements, counseling, and other assistance for these critical players in any trial.[81]

Insulating likely defendants from the Court

There are two means by which likely defendants before the Court can be insulated from appearing in The Hague to stand trial.[82] The first possibility is diplomatic immunity that is binding as a matter of international law for the state in question, thus preventing the surrender of the diplomat-suspect to the Court.[83] At first glance, this may seem inconsistent with Article 27's denial of official capacity as a shield from prosecution. But that provision primarily concerns a state party's obligation to hold its own nationals to account before the Court. It does not address Article 98(1)'s focus, which is what a state party must do with respect to a foreign diplomat in its jurisdiction, even one suspected of committing an atrocity crime. He or she would be entitled to the immunities long provided by international law, including the Vienna Convention on Diplomatic Relations.[84] The Rome Statute does not trump those diplomatic immunities despite the seeming inconsistency that arises between such protection and the treaty's purpose to ensure the investigation and prosecution of atrocity crimes by the nationals of states parties or when committed on the territory of a state party. Even when the Security Council refers a situation to the Court, that referral should not extinguish the defense of diplomatic immunity unless the Council so stipulates in its referral resolution.

The second means of insulating an individual from the jurisdiction of the Rome Statute would avoid the surrender of a person to the Court in the event there is a treaty between two states prohibiting a state from surrendering a person in its custody or jurisdiction to the Court without the consent of the state of nationality of the person's state.[85] The source of this provision is the status of forces agreement that the United States, in particular, negotiates and brings into force with practically every nation where US military forces are deployed. The status of forces agreement establishes how criminal matters for soldiers are managed between the 'sending' state and the 'receiving' state. Again, Article 98(2) may not appear consistent with the rest of the Rome Statute, as it would potentially enable perpetrators of atrocity crimes to avoid prosecution before the Court. But the utility of status of forces agreements and UN status of mission agreements on issues of criminal law for troops stationed in another country was sustained through the years of negotiation of the Rome Statute and survived in this provision.

Unfortunately, the United States diverged from the original purpose behind Article 98(2) when the George W. Bush administration negotiated about 100 special agreements prohibiting surrender not only of official personnel (such as military and diplomatic personnel) to the Court but also of mercenaries, individuals engaged in commerce, journalists, or any private US citizen accused of committing an atrocity crime. Such overreach from the original purpose of Article 98(2) led to significant objections to the American agreements. Many countries feared losing US economic and military assistance if they did not sign the document.[86]

High bar for amendments

Most amendments to the Rome Statute require ratification by seven-eighths of the states parties.[87] That probably means that successful amendment of the treaty will take a number of years to achieve and address issues that can attract near-consensus among the states parties. The Rome Statute prohibits any reservations,[88] so the conventional means to condition an individual state party's obligations under a treaty are absent (although far-reaching declarations and understandings have been attached to some states' ratifications).[89] A government joining the Court must factor in the prospect that any desired modification of the treaty by amendment would be quite problematic and difficult to achieve.

As a permanent judicial body, the International Criminal Court likely will experience periods of heavy caseloads spanning several situations of atrocity crimes and then periods where evil rests and leaders' strategies to ethnically cleanse an entire population, or conduct a war against civilians rather than soldiers, or simply eliminate a racial group, miraculously subside. Through it all, the Court embodies the constitutional framework and an evolving record of investigations and prosecutions to render fair and well-reasoned international justice.

Notes

1 M. Cherif Bassiouni, 'International Criminal Justice in Historical Perspective,' in M. Cherif Bassiouni (ed.), *International Criminal Law*, 2nd edn, Vol. III, Leiden: Koninklijke Brill NV, 2008, pp. 29–65; A. Cassese, 'From Nuremberg to Rome: International Military Tribunals to the International Criminal Court,' in A. Cassese, P. Gaeta, and J. R. W. D. Jones (eds), *The Rome Statute of the International Criminal Court: A Commentary*, Vol. 1, New York: Oxford University Press, 2002, pp. 3–19; B. Ferencz, *An International Criminal Court: A Step Toward World Peace—A Documentary History and Analysis*, 2 vols, New York: Oceana Publications, 1980.

2 G. A. Res. 3314 (1975); Antonio Cassese, *International Criminal Law*, 2nd edn, New York: Oxford University Press, pp. 152–61.

3 G. A. Res. 44/89 (1989); P. Robinson, 'The Missing Crimes,' in *The Rome Statute of the International Criminal Court: A Commentary*, pp. 497–521.

4 An explanation of 'atrocity crimes' can be found in D. Scheffer, 'Genocide and Atrocity Crimes,' *Genocide Studies & Prevention* 1, 2006, 229–50, and in D. Scheffer, 'The Merits of Unifying Terms: "Atrocity Crimes" and "Atrocity Law",' *Genocide Studies & Prevention* 2, 2007, 91–5.

5 *Report of the International Law Commission on the Work of Its Forty-Sixth Session*, UN GAOR, 49th Sess., Supp. No. 10, UN Doc. A/49/10(1994); J. Crawford, 'The Work of the International Law Commission,' in *The Rome Statute of the International Criminal Court: A Commentary*, pp. 23–34.

6 W. A. Schabas, *An Introduction to the International Criminal Court*, 3rd edn, Cambridge: Cambridge University Press, 2007, p. 16, fns. 54, 56.

7 Rome Statute of the International Criminal Court, July 17, 1998, 2187 U.N.T.S. 90 (entered into force on 1 July 2002), available at http://www.icc-cpi.int/library/about/officialjournal/Rome_Statute_English.pdf (access 7 December 2009); A. Bos, 'From the International Law Commission to the Rome Conference (1994–1998),' in *The Rome Statute of the International Criminal Court: A Commentary*, pp. 35–66; P. Kirsch and D. Robinson, 'Reaching Agreement at the Rome Conference,' ibid., pp. 67–92.

8 See D. Scheffer, 'Staying the Course with the International Criminal Court,' 35 *Cornell International Law Journal*, Nov. 2001–Feb. 2002, pp. 47, 69–87; D. Scheffer, 'The United States and the International Criminal Court,' *American Journal of International Law* 93, 1999, 12–22.

9 Rules of Procedure and Evidence, ICC-ASP/1/3 (Part II-A) (9 September 2002), available at http://www.icc-cpi.int/NR/rdonlyres/F1E0AC1C-A3F3-4A3C-B9A7-B3E8B115E886/140164/Rules_of_procedure_and_Evidence_English.pdf; Elements of Crimes, ICC/ASP/1/3 (part II-B) (9 September 2002), available at http://www.icc-cpi.int/NR/rdonlyres/9CAEE830-38CF-41D6-AB0B-68E5F9082543/0/Element_of_Crimes_English.pdf; Fabricio Guariglia, 'The Rules of Procedure and Evidence for the International Criminal Court: A New Development in International Adjudication of Individual Criminal Responsibility,' in *The Rome Statute of the International Criminal Court: A Commentary*, Vol. II, pp. 1111–36; M. Politi, 'Elements of Crimes,' ibid., pp. 443–74.

10 ICC-ASP/3/Res.1 (4 October 2004), available at http://www.icc-cpi.int/NR/rdonlyres/916FC6A2-7846-4177-A5EA-5AA9B6D1E96C/0/ICCASP3Res1_English.pdf; L. Condorelli & S. Villalpando, 'Relationship of the Court with the United Nations,' in *The Rome Statute of the International Criminal Court: A Commentary*, pp 219–34.

11 ICC-ASP/1/3 (Part II-E) (22 July 2004), available at http://www.icc-cpi.int/NR/rdonlyres/23F24FDC-E9C2-4C43-BE19-A19F5DDE8882/140090/Agreement_on_Priv_and_Imm_120704EN.pdf; H. Ascensio, 'Privileges and Immunities,' in *The Rome Statute of the International Criminal Court: A Commentary*, pp. 289–96.

12 See the Agreement between the United Nations and the Government of Sierra Leone on the Establishment of a Special Court for Sierra Leone, Jan. 16, 2002, UN SCOR, 57th Sess., Annex, U.N. Doc. S/2002/246, available at http://www.sc-sl.org/Documents/scsl-agreement.html; Agreement between the UN and the Royal Government of Cambodia Concerning the Prosecution Under Cambodian Law of Crimes Committed During the Period of Democratic Kampuchea, 6 June 3 2003, available at http://www.eccc.gov.kh/english/agreement.list.aspx.

13 Rome Statute, art. 36; J. R. W. D. Jones, 'Composition of the Court,' in *The Rome Statute of the International Criminal Court: A Commentary*, pp. 241–57.

14 Ibid., pp. 257–62.

15 Rome Statute, art. 112.

16 A. Cassese, 'Genocide' and 'Crimes Against Humanity,' in *The Rome Statute of the International Criminal Court: A Commentary*, pp. 335–78; M. Bothe, 'War Crimes,' ibid., pp. 379–426.

17 M. Frulli, 'Jurisdiction *ratione personae,*' ibid., pp. 527–42.

18 S. Bourgon, 'Jurisdiction *ratione loci,*' ibid., pp. 559–70.

19 S. Bourgon, 'Jurisdiction *ratione temporis,*' ibid., pp. 543–58.

20 G. Gaja, 'The Long Journey towards Repressing Aggression,' in *The Rome Statute of the International Criminal Court: A Commentary*, pp. 427–41; ICC Assembly of States Parties Resolution RC/Res. 6, adopted at the 13th plenary meeting on 11 June 2010, by consensus (advance version 28 June 2010); See also David Scheffer, 'Aggression is Now a Crime,' *International Herald Tribune*, 1 July 2010, p. 8; David Scheffer, 'State Parties approve new crimes for International Criminal Court,' *ASIL Insight*, vol. 14, Issue 16, 22 June 2010, at http://www.asil.org/insights100622.cfm.

21 Convention on the Prevention and Punishment of the Crime of Genocide, 1948, 78 UNTS 277.

22 W. A. Schabas, *Genocide in International Law*, 2nd edn, Cambridge: Cambridge University Press, 2009, pp. 454–61; A. Cassese, 'Genocide,' in *The Rome Statute of the International Criminal Court: A Commentary*, pp. 340–7.

23 Ibid., p. 460; Antonio Cassese, *International Criminal Law,* 2nd edn, New York: Oxford University Press, 2008, p. 146.

24 *Warrant of Arrest for Omar Hassan Al Bashir*, in Case of The Prosecutor v. Omar Hassad Ahmad Al Bashir, No. ICC-02/05-01/09, 4 March 2009.

25 *Judgment on the Appeal of the Prosecutor against the 'Decision on the Prosecution's Application for a Warrant of Arrest against Omar Hassan Ahmad Al Bashir,'* in Case of The Prosecutor v. Omar Hassan Ahmad Al Bashir, No. ICC-02/05-01/09-0A, 3 February 2010.

26 Rome Statute, art. 7(1).

27 Ibid., 7(2)(a).

28 W. A. Schabas, *An Introduction to the International Criminal Court*, pp. 101–5.

29 For a discussion of persecution and ethnic cleansing, see A. Zahar & G. Sluiter, *International Criminal Law*, New York: Oxford University Press, 2008, pp. 211–5.

30 Rome Statute, art. 7(1)(k).

31 See *The Oxford Companion to International Criminal Justice*, Antonio Cassese (ed. in chief), New York: Oxford University Press, 2009, pp. 77–8; W. A. Schabas, *An Introduction to the International Criminal Court*, pp. 106–7.

32 A. Cassese, *International Criminal Law*, 2nd edn, New York: Oxford University Press, 2008, p. 113.
33 M. Bothe, 'War Crimes,' in *The Rome Statute of the International Criminal Court: A Commentary*, pp. 379–426.
34 A. Cassese, *International Criminal Law*, p. 113.
35 R.C. Slye and B.V. Schaack, *Essentials International Criminal Law*, New York: Aspen Publishers, 2009, pp. 182–4; A. Cassese, *International Criminal Law*, pp. 94–7.
36 M. Cherif Bassiouni, 'The Normative Framework of International Humanitarian Law: Overlaps, Gaps, and Ambiguities,' in M. Cherif Bassiouni (ed.), *International Criminal Law*, 3rd edn, Vol. III, pp. 505–19; W.A. Schabas, *An Introduction to the International Criminal Court*, pp. 117–18.
37 Rome Statute, art. 8(2)(f).
38 Ibid., 8(3).
39 Ibid., 8(2)(b)(xxvi).
40 Ibid., 13.
41 Ibid.,12(2)(a).
42 Ibid.,12(3); Rules of Procedure and Evidence, rule 44(2).
43 W. A. Schabas, *An Introduction to the International Criminal Court*, pp. 71, 74–5, 155–57.
44 Ibid., pp. 143–51.
45 UN Doc. S/RES/1593 (2005).
46 Rome Statute, art. 15; *Decision Regarding Article 15 of the Rome Statute on the Authorization of an Investigation into the Situation in the Republic of Kenya,* in the Situation in the Republic of Kenya, No. ICC-01/09, 31 March 2010.
47 Rome Statute, arts 11(2), 12(3), 22(1), 24, 121(5), and 126(2); D. Scheffer, 'How to Turn the Tide Using the Rome Statute's Temporal Jurisdiction,' *Journal of International Criminal Justice*, 2004, vol. 2, 26–34.
48 Rome Statute, art. 126(2).
49 A. Pellet, 'Applicable Law,' in *The Rome Statute of the International Criminal Court: A Commentary*, Vol. II, pp. 1051–84.
50 Rome Statute, art. 21(3).
51 W. Schabas, *An Introduction to the International Criminal Court*, pp. 174–86; A. Cassese (ed.), *The Oxford Companion to International Criminal Justice*, pp. 346–8; J.T. Holmes, 'Complementarity: National Courts versus the ICC,' *The Rome Statute of the International Criminal Court: A Commentary*, pp. 667–86.
52 Rome Statute, art. 18(1).
53 Ibid., 18(2).
54 Ibid., 18(2–3).
55 Ibid., 17.
56 Ibid., 17(1)(b).
57 Ibid., 17(1)(c).
58 Ibid., 17(3).
59 Ibid., 17(2).
60 Ibid., 17(1)(d).
61 W. A. Schabas, *An Introduction to the International Criminal Court*, pp. 186–91; B.V. Schaack, 'Atrocity Crimes Litigation: 2008 Year-In-Review,' *Northwestern Journal of International Human Rights*, 2009, Vol. 7, pp. 176–83; R. Rastan, 'Review of ICC Jurisprudence 2008,' *Northwestern Journal of International Human Rights*, 2009, Vol. 7, pp. 276–80.
62 Rome Statute, art. 24; A. Cassese, *International Criminal Law*, pp. 43–7; A. Cassese (ed.), *The Oxford Companion to International Criminal Justice*, pp. 437–8.
63 A. Cassese, *International Criminal Law*, pp. 279–80.
64 Rome Statute, art. 25(3)(a); B.V. Schaack, 'Atrocity Crimes Litigation: 2008 Year-In-Review,' *Northwestern Journal of International Human Rights*, pp. 229–33; R. Rastan, 'Review of ICC Jurisprudence 2008,' *Northwestern Journal of International Human Rights*, pp. 262–9.
65 Rome Statute, art. 25(3)(b).
66 Ibid., 25(3)(c).
67 W.A. Schabas, *An Introduction to the International Criminal Court*, pp. 213–14.
68 A. Cassese (ed.), *The Oxford Companion to International Criminal Justice*, p. 392; Allison Marston Danner, 'Joint Criminal Enterprise,' in M. Cherif Bassiouni (ed.), *International Criminal Law*, 3rd edn, Vol. III, pp. 483–93; B.V. Schaack, 'Atrocity Crimes Litigation 2008 Year-in-Review,' *Northwestern Journal of International Human Rights*, pp. 218–25.

69 Agreement for the Prosecution and Punishment of the Major War Criminals of the European Axis, adopted August 8, 1945, 82 UNTS 279, art. 7; Charter of the International Military Tribunal for the Far East (IMTFE), art. 6; Statute of the International Criminal Tribunal for the former Yugoslavia, art. 7(2); Statute for the International Criminal Tribunal for Rwanda, art. 6(2); Statute for the Special Court for Sierra Leone, art. 6(2); Law on the Establishment of the Extraordinary Chambers in the Courts of Cambodia for the Prosecution of Crimes Committed During the Period of Democratic Kampuchea, art. 29.
70 Warrant of Arrest for Omar Hassan Ahmad Al Bashir, ICC-02/05-01/09-1, 4 March 2009.
71 W. A. Schabas, *An Introduction to the International Criminal Court*, pp. 166–70; L. Condorelli and S. Villalpando, 'Referral and Deferral by the Security Council,' in *The Rome Statute of the International Criminal Court: A Commentary*, pp. 655–64.
72 D. Scheffer, 'The Security Council's Struggle over Darfur and International Justice,' JURIST (20 August 2008), available at http://jurist.law.pitt.edu/forumy/2008/08/security-councils-struggle-darfur.php.
73 Rome Statute, art. 53(1)(c).
74 Ibid., 55(2).
75 Ibid., 51(a).
76 Judgment on the appeal of the Prosecutor against the decision of Trial Chamber I entitled 'Decision on the consequences of non-disclosure of exculpatory materials covered by Article 54(3)(e) agreements and the application to stay the prosecution of the accused, together with certain other issues raised at the Status Conference on 10 June 2008,' ICC-01/04-01/06, Appeals Chamber, The Prosecutor v. Thomas Lubanga Dyilo, 21 October 2008; R. Rastan, 'Review of ICC Jurisprudence 2008,' *Northwestern Journal of International Human Rights*, pp. 270–6.
77 Rome Statute, art. 58; D. Scheffer, 'International Criminal Court: Introductory Note to Decision on the Prosecution Application under Article 58(7) of the Statute In the Case of The Prosecutor v. Ahmad Muhammad Harun ("Ahmad Harun") and Ali Muhammad Al Abd-Al-Rahman ("Ali Kushayb") ICC Pre-Trial Chamber I,' *International Legal Materials*, 2007, Vol. 46, pp. 532–3.
78 W. A. Schabas, *An Introduction to the International Criminal Court*, pp. 299–301; P. Malanczuk, 'Protection of National Security Interests,' in *The Rome Statute of the International Criminal Court: A Commentary*, Vol. II, pp. 1371–86.
79 Rome Statute, arts 72(7)(a)(ii), 87(7).
80 Ibid., 68, 75; T. Markus Funk, *Victims' Rights and Advocacy at the International Criminal Court*, New York: Oxford University Press, 2010; C. Jaorda and J. De Hemptinne, 'The Status and Role of the Victim,' in *The Rome Statute of the International Criminal Court: A Commentary*, Vol. II, pp. 1387–19; C.H. Chung, 'Victims' Participation at the International Criminal Court: Are Concessions of the Court Clouding the Promise?,' *Northwestern Journal of International Human Rights*, 2008, Vol. 6, pp. 459–545.
81 Rome Statute, art. 43(6); W. A. Schabas, *An Introduction to the International Criminal Court*, pp. 323–41.
82 Ibid., pp. 72–5; P. Gaeta, 'Official Capacity and Immunities,' in *The Rome Statute of the International Criminal Court: A Commentary*, pp. 975–1002.
83 Rome Statute, art. 98(1).
84 500 UNTS 95 (1961).
85 Rome Statute, art. 98(2).
86 D. Scheffer, 'Article 98(2) of the Rome Statute: America's Original Intent,' *Journal of International Criminal Justice*, 2005, Vol. 3, pp. 333–53.
87 Rome Statute, arts 121–2.
88 Ibid., 120.
89 W. A. Schabas, *An Introduction to the International Criminal Court*, pp. 372–5, 470–86.

6
Hybrid tribunals

Fidelma Donlon

Introduction

In response to the widespread atrocities committed during the Balkan wars and the Rwandan genocide, in the early 1990s the Security Council established the *ad hoc* international criminal tribunals for the former Yugoslavia and Rwanda under Chapter VII of the Charter of the United Nations.[1] Subsequently, the Security Council was called upon to create other *ad hoc* tribunals to try the massive violations of international law committed in a variety of other conflicts. However, after less than 10 years of operations a number of structural, administrative, and financial problems plagued the international tribunals. This prompted the discussion whether there was a more efficient and cheaper justice model to combat impunity for international crimes.[2]

The Security Council was not willing to create additional international criminal tribunals. Instead the focus shifted to the United Nations Secretariat 'to develop a model similar in form, substance, and international legitimacy to the *ad hoc* tribunals, but one which respects a nation's vision of justice, its choice of means of bringing it about, and its ownership, at least in part, of the judicial process'.[3] Thus a new generation of courts emerged which are commonly referred to as the 'hybrid', 'mixed', or 'internationalized' tribunals. Although each hybrid model is distinctive, in general many of the institutions share a number of common defining features: the hybrid tribunals typically apply a mix of national and international law; they have a mixed staff composition—international judges, prosecutors, and experts work with their national counterparts—and, generally they are located in the country where the atrocities were committed. One commentator has remarked that the existing hybrid models 'are products of judicial accountability-sharing between the states in which they function and international entities, particularly the UN'.[4]

This chapter will examine seven hybrid models of justice created since the late 1990s. The respective models are broadly divided into three categories. First, those created as part of a United Nations territorial administration mandate: the Special Panels for Serious Crimes in East Timor and the so-called Regulation 64 Panels in the courts of Kosovo. Secondly, the models created by mutual agreement between the United Nations and the state concerned: the Extraordinary Chambers in the Courts of Cambodia; the Special Court for Sierra Leone; and the Special Tribunal for Lebanon. The third category incorporates the institutions which were not created by the United Nations: the so-called War Crimes Chamber of Bosnia and Herzegovina and the Supreme Iraqi Criminal Tribunal. To consider the main hybrid characteristics of the various models, their background; founding instruments, applicable law, jurisdiction, and composition will be briefly analyzed.

The special hybrid panels created as part of the United Nations administration of East Timor and Kosovo

The special panels and serious crimes unit in East Timor

In 1999, with the adoption of Resolution 1272, the Security Council established the United Nations Transitional Administration in East Timor (UNTAET). The resolution referred to the systematic and widespread violations of international humanitarian and human rights law committed in East Timor after the 30 August 1999 referendum, and called on all parties to cooperate with investigations. UNTAET had a far-reaching mandate: it was responsible for the administration of East Timor and was 'empowered to exercise all legislative and executive authority, including the administration of justice'.[5] In addition, by promulgating the first UNTAET Regulation No. 1999/1, the Special Representative of the Secretary-General vested all legislative and executive authority including the administration of the judiciary in East Timor in UNTAET. The overall objective of the transitional administration was to build democratic national institutions. Consequently, the internationalized Special Panels and the Serious Crimes Unit were created as an integral part of the East Timor justice sector. They were the first fixed hybrid panels created within national courts to try serious violations of international law.

UNTAET Regulation No. 2000/11 defined the general organization of the courts in the territory and established the District Court of Dili and the Court of Appeal. The District Court was granted exclusive jurisdiction over six categories of crimes, both international and national, committed in East Timor between 1 January 1999 and 25 October 1999. The offences enumerated under Section 14 included genocide; war crimes; crimes against humanity; murder; sexual offences; and torture. The Court of Appeal was conferred with jurisdiction to hear appeals from the District Court. The concept of hybrid panels in the respective courts first appeared in UNTAET Regulation No. 2000/11. Pursuant to Section 10.3 and Section 15.5, the Transitional Administrator, after consultation with the Court Presidency, was authorized to establish panels composed of both East Timorese and international judges.

On 6 June 2000, a specific regulation governing the establishment of panels with exclusive jurisdiction over serious criminal offences was promulgated.[6] Subsequently, the hybrid Special Panels were established in the District Court in Dili and also in the Court of Appeal. International judges were the majority of the bench: each panel consisted of three judges, one East Timorese and two international. In cases of special importance or gravity a panel of five judges—three international and two East Timorese judges—could be established to hear an appeal from the District Court. The Special Panels could exercise jurisdiction irrespective of whether the serious criminal offence was committed within the territory of East Timor; the offence was committed by an East Timorese citizen; or the victim of the offence was an East Timorese citizen. At any stage of the proceedings in relation to serious criminal offences, a Special Panel could have the case deferred to itself from another court in the territory.

The jurisdiction and authority of the East Timorese Public Prosecution Service was defined in accordance with the provisions of UNTAET Regulation No. 2000/16. The hybrid Serious Crimes Unit was created as part of the Office of the General Prosecutor located in Dili.[7]

The Serious Crimes Unit was vested with the exclusive authority to investigate and prosecute persons responsible for the atrocities committed in East Timor in 1999. All cases brought by the Unit were litigated before the Special Panels in the District Court. Following the recommendation of the Transitional Judicial Service Commission, the first international judges and prosecutors were appointed by the Special Representative in 2000.

Pursuant to Regulations No. 1999/1 and No. 2000/11, the law applied in East Timor was a mix of national and international. The Special Panels were required to apply Indonesian law, the law and regulations promulgated by UNTAET, and where appropriate applicable treaties and customary international law.[8] The subject-matter jurisdiction of the Special Panels was defined in Regulations No. 2000/11 and No. 2000/15. Serious criminal offences were defined as genocide; war crimes; crimes against humanity; murder; sexual offences; and torture. In addition, Section 3.1 of Regulation No. 2000/15 provided 'where appropriate, applicable treaties and recognised principles and norms of international law, including the established principles of the international law of armed conflict' were applicable. UNTAET introduced the transitional Criminal Procedure Code to streamline procedures and to ensure that international standards were applied at all stages of criminal proceedings.[9]

East Timor became the independent state of Timor-Leste on 20 May 2002. The transfer of authority of the UNTAET Special Panels and Serious Crimes Unit to the new Timor-Leste institutions was regulated by the Timor-Leste Constitution. Section 163 stated that the Special Panels would continue their work for the time 'deemed strictly necessary' to finish their cases.

Established in May 2002, the United Nations Mission of Support in East Timor (UNMISET) was the follow-on mission from UNTAET.[10] It continued to operate until 2005 and worked with the Government of Timor-Leste to provide assistance to the justice sector in the area of serious crimes. UNMISET provided lawyers to assist the new nation 'cross a critical threshold of self-sufficiency', including advisors in justice-related areas and acting judges and judge mentors to promote the functioning of the court system while training Timorese counterparts.

The Security Council ended its support of UNMISET, the Special Panels and the Serious Crimes Unit operations in 2005. The Serious Crimes Unit filed 95 indictments against 392 persons. The Special Panels completed 55 trials involving 87 defendants. In total, the Special Panels convicted 84 defendants and acquitted three.[11]

The 'Regulation 64 Panels' in the Kosovo courts

In 1999, forces of the Socialist Federal Republic of Yugoslavia and Serbia engaged in a campaign of terror and violence against the Kosovo Albanian population to expel them from the territory.[12] Serb civilians were also the victims of crimes committed by ethnic Albanian paramilitary forces such as the Kosovo Liberation Army. Yugoslav and Serbian forces agreed to withdraw from Kosovo in June 1999 after NATO's bombing campaign. Subsequently, the Security Council adopted Resolution 1244, which established the United Nations Interim Administration Mission in Kosovo (UNMIK). The mission was mandated to administer Kosovo for a transitional period until democratic self-governing institutions were established. Similar to the interim administration mission in East Timor, all executive and legislative authority for Kosovo, including the administration of the judiciary, was vested in UNMIK and performed by the Special Representative of the Secretary-General.[13] Since the International Criminal Tribunal for the former Yugoslavia had concurrent jurisdiction with the Kosovo courts over the crimes committed, in Resolution 1244 the Council demanded the full cooperation by all national and international parties with the tribunal. Around this time the Prosecutor of the Yugoslavia tribunal indicated that her primary focus would be the prosecution of high-level civilian, police and military leaders responsible for the crimes committed during the armed conflict in Kosovo.[14]

In the early stages of its mission UNMIK started to rebuild the Kosovo justice system which was paralyzed by conflict.[15] One commentator has noted that '[i]nstead of operating in a state of lawlessness, the UN took active steps to restore the applicable law and basic judicial functions in the administered territory'.[16] Two special commissions were created to facilitate this process. UNMIK Regulation No. 1999/7 set up the Advisory Judicial Commission to advise the Special Representative on matters related to the appointment of judges and prosecutors.[17] The Technical Advisory Commission on Judiciary and Prosecution Service was authorized to assess the long-term requirements of the Kosovo judicial system.[18] By August 2000, the Special Representative had appointed 662 judges, lay judges, and prosecutors, mainly Kosovo Albanian, to the various institutions.[19] There were concerns that the judiciary did not have the capacity to render impartial judgments in trials of ethnic Albanians charged with war crimes and other violations of international humanitarian law against ethnic Serbs. The fair and effective trial of these cases was further hampered by attacks and threats against the newly appointed judges.[20] To counteract the problems, the Technical Advisory Commission recommended the creation of the hybrid Kosovo War and Ethnic Crimes Court to try war crimes and crimes of interethnic violence.[21] The proposed interim court was to be located in Kosovo and staffed with national and international judges, prosecutors, and experts. It was to have subject matter jurisdiction over genocide, crimes against humanity, war crimes, and serious interethnic offences under domestic law. Ultimately, all plans for the hybrid Court were abandoned due to concerns about the potential cost of the institution and the opposition of the Kosovo Albanian community.

Yet the objective of involving international lawyers in the trial of war crimes cases was achieved in Kosovo. In February 2000, following a rocket attack against a United Nations High Commissioner for Refugees bus carrying Serbs, interethnic attacks escalated in the ethnically divided city of Mitrovica. UNMIK responded by introducing a package of urgent measures to increase security and restore order.[22] Regulation No. 2000/6 empowered the Special Representative to appoint international judges to the District Court of Mitrovica and other courts within its territorial jurisdiction. International prosecutors were also assigned to prosecution offices in the district. The international lawyers were authorized to select new and pending criminal cases to which they would be appointed. In May 2000, Resolution No. 2000/34 extended the authority of the Special Representative to appoint international judges and prosecutors to courts throughout Kosovo, including the Supreme Court. Unlike the East Timor hybrid model, UNTAET did not create fixed hybrid panels in the Kosovo courts. Instead, international judges sat on panels in a variety of courts throughout the territory.

However, the appointment of international lawyers to the Kosovo courts and prosecutors offices did not guarantee that international standards were followed in the investigation and trial of cases. Pursuant to the Criminal Code of the Federal Republic of Yugoslavia and the Kosovo Criminal Code, cases of genocide or war crimes were heard by a panel of five judges: two professional and three lay judges. As a former international prosecutor reported '[t]he international judges were being outvoted by the lay and professional Kosovan judges, resulting in unsubstantiated verdicts of guilt against some Serbian defendants and questionable verdicts of acquittal against some Albanian Kosovan defendants'.[23] In addition, Kosovo prosecutors were initiating investigations and proposing detentions against Serbs based on insufficient evidence while refusing to investigate ethnic Albanians.[24]

Consequently, UNMIK promulgated two key regulations intended to bolster efforts to prosecute crimes which threatened the peace process and the establishment of the rule of law in Kosovo. Regulation No. 2000/64, entitled the 'Assignment of International Judges and Prosecutors and/or Change of Venue', critically ensured an international majority control of voting in the hybrid panels. The regulation authorized the prosecutor, accused, or defense counsel to petition the Department of Judicial Affairs at any stage of the criminal proceedings, except where a trial or appeal had already started, for a change of venue and/or for the assignment of international judges or prosecutors to 'ensure the independence and impartiality of the judiciary or the proper administration of justice'.[25] If a petition was approved, a 'Regulation 64 Panel' composed of three judges, including at least two internationals judges, was designated. Additionally, the Special Representative had the authority to transfer any case to an international prosecutor to be tried by a majority international panel. The second key regulation was Resolution No. 2001/2. It was designed to prevent Kosovar Albanian prosecutors from circumventing the 'Regulation 64 Panels' by rushing cases to trial, abandoning cases, or by failing to notify the international prosecutors of war crimes cases in the first place. The Resolution obligated the prosecutors to inform the international prosecutor in their district within 14 days of abandoning a case and authorized the international lawyers to reopen cases within 30 days of notice.

Unlike the Special Panels in East Timor, the various regulations which created the hybrid system in Kosovo did not limit the subject-matter jurisdiction of the 'Regulation 64 Panels'. Instead, international judges and prosecutors could take part in any criminal proceedings, if their participation would ensure the independence and impartiality of the judiciary. Internationals were actively involved in cases of war crimes; terrorism; murder; organized crime; corruption; and trafficking in persons, drugs, and weapons. In addition, the temporal and personal jurisdiction of the hybrid panels was not limited. Their jurisdiction was the same as other Kosovo courts. UNMIK Regulations No. 1999/24 and No. 1999/25 established that the legal system in the territory would be based on the law in force on 22 March 1989, before Milosevic revoked Kosovo's autonomy.[26] International crimes were included in the Federal Republic of Yugoslavia Criminal Code which was deemed the applicable law. Article 141 of the Criminal Code followed the language of the 1948 Genocide Convention. Interestingly, considering the nature of the conflict in Kosovo, the Criminal Code departed from the Genocide Convention to the extent that it prescribed 'forcible dislocation of the population' as a genocidal act.[27] The Criminal Code also prescribed individual criminal responsibility for a variety of war crimes. Articles 142–153 codified the grave breaches provisions of the first, second, and fourth Geneva Conventions of 1949.[28] However, there was no domestic statutory equivalent for crimes against humanity. The 'Regulation 64 Panels' also adjudicated cases involving crimes enumerated in a variety of UNMIK regulations.[29] The applicable procedural law was prescribed in the Federal Republic of Yugoslavia Code of Criminal Procedure and various UNMIK regulations.[30] In April 2004, the Provisional Criminal Code and Provisional Criminal Procedure Code were introduced as the applicable criminal law in Kosovo.

In 2004, there were 12 international judges and 12 international prosecutors working in the Kosovo justice system.[31]

On 4 February 2008, the European Union established the European Union Rule of Law Mission in Kosovo (EULEX Kosovo).[32] EULEX provides international judges and prosecutors to assist the investigation and trial of war crimes; terrorism; organized crime; corruption; interethnic crimes; financial/economic crimes; and other serious crimes.[33] Kosovo declared its independence from Serbia in February 2008. International supervision and participation in the judiciary will continue until the final implementation of the Comprehensive Proposal for Kosovo Status Settlement.[34]

The tribunals created by agreement between the United Nations and a state

The Extraordinary Chambers in the courts of Cambodia

During the three years and nine month reign of the Khmer Rouge in Cambodia, some of the most flagrant and horrific violations of international law occurred. By January 1979, the regime's activities had resulted in the death of at least three million people. Almost two decades later, in 1997, the co–Prime Ministers of Cambodia requested the assistance of the United Nations to create an international tribunal to try 'persons responsible for the genocide and crimes against humanity [committed] during the rule of the Khmer Rouge from 1975 to 1979'.[35] Subsequently, a group of experts appointed by the Secretary-General recommended that the United Nations establish an *ad hoc* international tribunal under Chapter VII of the UN Charter.[36] The proposal to create a court similar to the tribunals for the former Yugoslavia and Rwanda did not gain traction with the General Assembly or the Security Council. Consequently, the Secretary-General advised that if international standards were to be met in Khmer Rouge trials, any future court would have to be 'international in character' but not 'modelled after either the existing *ad hoc* tribunals or be linked to them institutionally, administratively, or financially'.[37]

The negotiations between the United Nations Secretariat and the Government of Cambodia on the creation of a hybrid tribunal were lengthy and contentious. Key issues for the United Nations included the appointment of independent international prosecutors and a majority of international judges. However, the Government of Cambodia wanted authority to appoint judges; to compose chambers with a majority of Cambodian judges; and to set up the chambers as part of the national legal system.[38] A leading commentator has remarked that the conflict did not relate to the organizational structure of the mixed tribunal; instead, 'it was a conflict of two visions of justice: an independent tribunal meeting international standards of justice, objectivity, fairness, and due process of law, and a politically controlled judicial process'.[39]

The legal basis for the creation of the Extraordinary Chambers was consensual. Its legal status, applicable law, composition, and organizational structure was negotiated and agreed upon by the United Nations and the Government of Cambodia.[40] The draft Agreement creating the Extraordinary Chambers in the Courts of Cambodia was approved by the General Assembly on 17 March 2003 and formally accepted by the Cambodian Government and the United Nations on 6 June 2003. The Agreement was ratified by the Cambodian Parliament on 4 October 2004 as the Law on the Establishment of the Extraordinary Chambers in the Courts of Cambodia for the Prosecution of Crimes Committed during the period of Democratic Kampuchea.[41] In accordance with Article 2, the Extraordinary Chambers are established within Cambodia's existing court structure, in 'the trial court and the supreme court' and are located in Phnom Penh, Cambodia. Upholding the constitutional validity of the Law, the Cambodian Constitutional Council remarked that by using the existing Cambodian court system and selecting Phnom Penh as the location for proceedings the sovereignty of the Kingdom of Cambodia was protected.[42]

Upon the insistence of the Cambodian Government, the Law on the Extraordinary Chambers ensures that the majority of the judges sitting in the respective chambers are Cambodian nationals. In accordance with Article 20, three Cambodian judges and two international judges comprise the hybrid Pre-Trial Chamber. In addition to adjudicating appeals in the pre-trial phase, this Chamber also has jurisdiction, in the event of disagreement between the Co-Investigating Judges and Co-Prosecutors, to make a final determination.[43] The Decisions of this Chamber are not subject to appeal.

The composition of the hybrid Trial Chambers is regulated by Article 9. The Chambers are composed of five judges: three Cambodian and two international judges. The hybrid Appellate Chamber is an integral part of the Supreme Court.[44] It is the final court of appeal. The Chamber is composed of seven judges: four Cambodian and three international judges. The President of each Extraordinary Chamber is a Cambodian judge. As a concession to the United Nations, the decisions of the Extraordinary Chambers are to be reached by super-majority voting. Effectively, this means that at least one international judge presiding in a hybrid chamber must sign onto the opinion of his or her Cambodian colleagues. Both national and international judges are appointed to the Chambers by the Supreme Council of the Magistracy. The international judges are selected from a list of candidates provided by the Secretary-General.

Investigations and prosecutions are the responsibility of the two Co-Investigating Judges and Co-Prosecutors: one Cambodian and one international. They are jointly responsible for execution of their duties. Although the Law on the Extraordinary Chambers only refers to the role of the Co-Prosecutors in preparing indictments, pursuant to the Internal Rules, the Co-Prosecutors can now conduct preliminary investigations. If they suspect a person has committed a crime within the jurisdiction of the Chambers, the case is filed with the Co-Investigating Judges for a judicial investigation. If the accused is indicted, the Co-Prosecutors manage the trial.[45] The Supreme Council of the Magistracy appoints the Co-Prosecutors. Each Co-Proseuctor can choose one or more deputy prosecutors. International Deputy Prosecutors are selected from a list provided by the Secretary-General and appointed by the international Co-Prosecutor.

International *ad hoc* and hybrid tribunals are diverse institutions. They are courts, in the traditional sense, but they also incorporate a number of other offices which in a national context would typically be independent of a court. Thus, the management and administration of the tribunals, trials, detention facilities, external relations, and outreach activities involve a variety of complex tasks and resources. In the International Criminal Court and the *ad hoc* tribunals, the Registry is the key organ responsible for the aforementioned tasks. In the Extraordinary Chambers, the traditional Registry is replaced by the Office of Administration, which is designed to support the hybrid Chambers, the Office of the Co-Prosecutors, the Office of the Co-Investigating Judges, and the Defense Support Section.

In accordance with Rule 11 of the Internal Rules, the Office of Administration established the Defense Support Section to guarantee fair trials through effective representation of the accused. The Section does not provide direct legal defense for accused. Instead, indigent accused are provided with a list of qualified lawyers who can defend them. The Section provides training and legal research to assigned lawyers. Each accused may have two co-lawyers, one Cambodian and one international.

Article 33 of the Law on the Extraordinary Chambers declares that 'the Court shall provide for the protection of victims and witnesses'. Protection measures may include in camera proceedings, protection of the victims' identity by use of a pseudonym or, if appropriate, voice and face distortion. The Victims Unit was established by the Office of Administration in accordance with Rule 12 of the Internal Rules. The Unit assists victims to submit civil party applications and manages lists of lawyers eligible to represent victims or victims associations before the Extraordinary Chambers.

The personal and temporal jurisdiction of the Extraordinary Chambers is clearly defined in the Law. The temporal jurisdiction extends from 17 April 1975 to 6 January 1979, covering the height of the reign of terror of the Khmer Rouge. There is also a statutory limit on the seniority of the accused to be tried before the Chambers. Article 2 dictates that the Chambers have jurisdiction 'to bring to trial senior leaders of Democratic Kampuchea and those who were most responsible' for the crimes committed in Cambodia. The specific limitation of the personal and temporal jurisdiction of the Chambers was, in some part, founded in the desire not to overburden the Chambers and to limit the financial and human resources required.[46] Once created, it was expected that the Chambers would operate for three years and prosecute less than 10 of the most senior Khmer Rouge suspects.

The subject-matter jurisdiction of the Extraordinary Chambers as formulated in the Law is a mix of national and international law. Under Article 2 the Chambers are entitled to prosecute 'serious violations of Cambodian laws . . . international humanitarian law and custom, and international conventions recognized by Cambodia'. Article 3 creates the jurisdiction over the crimes of homicide; torture; and religious persecution as defined in the 1956 Cambodian Penal Code. The statute of limitations set forth in the Penal Code is extended by an additional 30 years for the crimes enumerated in the Law on the Extraordinary Chambers. Cambodia has been a party to the 1948 Genocide Convention since 1951. The definition of Genocide as articulated in Article 4 of the Law mirrors the text of Article 2 and partly Article 3 of the 1948 Genocide convention.[47] The definition of Crimes against Humanity contained in Article 5 is adopted from the Statute of the Rwanda tribunal. Article 6 confers the Chambers with jurisdiction over the grave breaches of the Geneva Conventions of 1949. Article 7 enumerates the crime of the destruction of cultural property during armed conflict, as defined by the 1954 Hague Convention for Protection of Cultural Property in the Event of Armed Conflict. Article 8 states that crimes against internationally protected persons as defined by the Vienna Convention of 1961 on Diplomatic Relations form part of the subject-matter jurisdiction of the Chamber.

Pursuant to Article 40 of the Law on the Extraordinary Chambers, the Cambodian Government is barred from requesting an amnesty or pardon for persons tried before the Extraordinary Chambers. The validity of an amnesty or pardon granted prior to the enactment of the Law, as a bar to prosecution, is a matter to be determined by the Chambers.[48]

Reflecting the hybrid nature of the Extraordinary Chambers, the Law provides for the application of Cambodian procedural law.[49] If a particular matter is not dealt with in existing procedures, 'guidance may be sought in procedural rules established at the international level'. Pursuant to the commitments embodied in the Law, the Extraordinary Chambers judges adopted the Internal Rules and Regulations to consolidate the Cambodian rules of procedure applicable to proceedings in the Chambers and set forth additional rules to address lacunae or instances where existing Cambodian rules were unclear or potentially conflicted with international standards.[50]

The trial of Kaing Guek Eav, alias 'Duch', the former Head of the infamous S-21 detention centre, began on 30 March 2009. The investigation of the case against four other senior politicians from the Democratic Kampuchea regime charged with crimes against humanity is at an advanced stage.

The Special Court for Sierra Leone

The development of the Special Court for Sierra Leone began in earnest in mid-2000. President Kabbah requested the Security Council to establish 'a strong and credible court that will meet the objectives of bringing justice and ensuring lasting peace' in Sierra Leone and the West African subregion.[51] On 14 August 2000 the Council responded to the call from the Government with the adoption of Resolution 1315. The resolution was not intended to be the legal document creating the Court; instead, it directed the Secretary-General to negotiate an agreement with the Government of Sierra Leone with a view to establishing an independent special court.[52] The formal agreement establishing the Special Court was signed in Freetown on 16 January 2002. Implementation of the agreement in the country required its incorporation into national law. Consequently, in March 2002, the Parliament of Sierra Leone enacted the Special Court

Agreement (Ratification) Act. It provides a legal framework for the activities of the Court within the country. Section 11(2) of the Act has been interpreted by the Supreme Court of Sierra Leone as putting beyond all doubt the intention of the Parliament to create the Special Court independent of the national judiciary.[53] The precise institutional character of the Special Court has been the subject of some debate. Reporting to the Security Council on the establishment of the institution, the Secretary-General noted it would be a 'treaty-based *sui generis* court of mixed jurisdiction and composition'.[54] One commentator has remarked that the agreement created a court which 'is not part of the national legal system of Sierra Leone, but constitutes an international judicial institution, although hybrid in character'.[55]

The Special Court is not anchored fully in either the United Nations or the Sierra Leonean constitutional systems. A Management Committee was established that, *inter alia*, considers reports from the Special Court; provides policy advice and policy directions on all the non-judicial aspects of its operations; oversees the Court's annual budget and other financial reports; and advises the Secretary-General on issues related to the operations. The Court is a self-contained entity with its own Registry, Prosecutor's Office, and Trial and Appeals Chambers. The hybrid institutional characteristics of the institution include staffing of all organs of the Court by national and international personnel and the applicability of both international and Sierra Leonean law. Pursuant to Article 12 of the Statute, three judges serve in a Trial Chamber: one appointed by the Government of Sierra Leone and two appointed by the Secretary-General. Five judges serve in the Appeals Chamber: two appointed by Sierra Leone and three by the Secretary-General. Under Article 15, the Prosecutor is appointed by the Secretary-General and the Deputy Prosecutor by the Government of Sierra Leone. Finally, under Article 16, after consultation with the President of the Special Court, the Secretary-General appoints the Registrar.

Unlike the *ad hoc* tribunals, the seniority of the accused to be tried by the Special Court was defined in its Statute. In accordance with Article 1, the Court has jurisdiction to 'prosecute persons who bear the greatest responsibility for serious violations of international humanitarian law and Sierra Leonean law committed in the territory of Sierra Leone since 30 November 1996'. Another hybrid characteristic of the institution is that it derives its subject-matter jurisdiction from both international and national law. Articles 2–4 of the Statute prescribe the subject-matter jurisdiction of the Court for international crimes. Article 2 defines crimes against humanity; Article 3 covers violations of Article 3 common to the Geneva Conventions and of Additional Protocol II. Article 4 of the Statute enumerates other serious violations of international humanitarian law. Article 5 authorizes the Court to prosecute persons under the Sierra Leonean Prevention of Cruelty to Children Act, 1926 and the Malicious Damage Act, 1861. The procedural regime applicable in proceedings before the Court is governed by the Special Courts Rules of Procedure and Evidence. Pursuant to the Statute, the judges can amend and adopt the Rules.

Section IX(2) of the Lomé Peace Agreement declared that '[a]fter the signing of the present Agreement, the Government of Sierra Leone shall also grant absolute and free pardon and reprieve to all combatants and collaborators in respect of anything done by them in pursuit of their objectives, up to the time of the signing of the present Agreement'. Article 10 of the Special Court Statute states, '[a]n amnesty granted to any person falling within the jurisdiction of the Special Court in respect of the crimes referred to in Articles 2–4 of the present Statute shall not be a bar to prosecution'. The offences prescribed in Articles 2–4 are international crimes: namely, crimes against humanity; violations of Article 3 common to the Geneva Conventions and of Additional Protocol II; and other serious violations of international humanitarian law. The Article 10 amnesty exception extends only to the international crimes prescribed in the Statute. The exception does not extend to the Sierra Leonean crimes prescribed in Article 5. Therefore, a suspect who was granted an amnesty under the terms of the Lomé Peace

Agreement could be indicted by the Special Court for the international crimes regulated in Articles 2–4 but not for the national offences outlined in Article 5 of the Statute.

The precise legal nature of the Special Court was a pivotal issue in the case against the former President of Liberia, Charles Taylor. Taylor sought to have his indictment quashed: he argued that as a head of State at the time criminal proceedings were initiated against him, he enjoyed absolute immunity from criminal prosecution.[56] The former Liberian President maintained the Special Court was without jurisdiction: it did not derive its authority under Chapter VII of the UN Charter, and thus could be characterized as a national court. Pointing out that the International Criminal Court, which does not have Chapter VII powers, denies immunity to heads of State for international crimes, the Prosecutor observed that the lack of such powers did not affect the Special Court's jurisdiction. In addition, the Prosecutor noted that customary international law permits international criminal courts to indict acting heads of State in an international court. In its judgment, the Special Court Appeals Chamber definitively characterized the institution as an international criminal court. The Chamber declared:

> We come to the conclusion that the Special Court is an international criminal court. The constitutive instruments of the court contain indicia too numerous to enumerate to justify that conclusion. To enumerate those indicia will involve virtually quoting the entire provisions of those instruments. It suffices that having adverted to those provisions, the conclusion we have arrived at is inescapable.[57]

Consequently, the Chamber held that Taylor's official position as head of State at the time the proceedings were initiated against him was not a bar to his prosecution. As Professor William Schabas has remarked, the Special Court 'is a close relative of the "hybrid tribunals", but is more accurately classified with the *ad hoc* tribunals because it is a creature of international law, not domestic law'.[58]

The Court has completed the Armed Forces Revolutionary Council; the Civil Defence Forces, and the Revolutionary United Front trials. All eight accused were convicted to terms of imprisonment ranging between 15 and 50 years. The trial of Charles Taylor is expected to last until mid-2011; the appeals judgment, if applicable, is expected by the end of 2011. This judgment will bring all current judicial activities of the Special Court to an end.

The Special Tribunal for Lebanon

On 14 February 2005, the former Lebanese Prime Minister Rafiq Hariri and 22 other persons died in a terrorist attack in Beirut. Resolution 1595 established the United Nations International Independent Investigative Commission, the precursor to the Special Tribunal for Lebanon, to support Lebanese investigations in relation to the assassinations. After the joint investigation commenced, the Government of Lebanon requested the assistance of the United Nations to establish a 'tribunal of an international character to try all those who are found responsible for the terrorist crime . . .'.[59]

Resolution 1664 directed the Secretary-General to negotiate an agreement with the Government of Lebanon to create 'a tribunal of an international character based on the highest international standards of criminal justice . . .'.[60] Following the negotiation process, the Agreement between the United Nations and the Lebanese Government on the establishment of the tribunal was signed by the parties in 2007. To this extent, similar to the Cambodian Extraordinary Chambers and the Special Court for Sierra Leone, the legal basis for the creation of the Special Tribunal was consensual. However, the Lebanon Tribunal is distinctive: unlike the other hybrid models, due to a deadlock in the Lebanese ratification process, the Security Council decided to enforce the bilateral treaty creating the court by acting under Chapter VII. Thus, the Agreement on the Special Tribunal for Lebanon and its Statute are annexed to Resolution 1757, which declared that they entered into force on 10 June 2007.[61] The tribunal is located in the Netherlands.

The Statute imposes a limitation on the personal and temporal jurisdiction of the Special Tribunal. In accordance with Article 1, the court is authorized to prosecute persons allegedly responsible for the Beirut terrorist attack. In addition, the tribunal shall have jurisdiction over other attacks between 1 October 2004 and 12 December 2005, or a later date to be decided by the Lebanon with the consent of the Security Council, if the tribunal decides they are connected 'in accordance with the principles of criminal justice' and are of a nature and gravity similar to the attack of 14 February 2005. The elements used to decide a connection with the Hariri assassination are defined under Article 1 as 'criminal intent (motive), the purpose behind the attacks, the nature of the victims targeted, the pattern of the attacks (modus operandi) and the perpetrators'.

A unique feature of the tribunal is its subject-matter jurisdiction. It is distinct from other hybrid courts since it is the first tribunal of an international character to derive its jurisdiction exclusively from national law. The Statute does not incorporate international crimes as part of the subject-matter jurisdiction of the court. Rather, the jurisdiction of the court is defined solely on the basis of the Lebanese Criminal Code. Article 2(a) of the Statute refers to offences in the Code.[62] They include acts of terrorism; crimes and offences against life and personal integrity, including homicide and bodily harm; illicit associations; and failure to report crimes and offences. Although other hybrid tribunals also exercise jurisdiction over national crimes, unlike the Special Tribunal for Lebanon, they also have jurisdiction over crimes defined in international law.

Nevertheless, the influence of international law can be detected in the Statute. Article 3 prescribes the forms of participation in a crime, including committing, instigating, or participating as an accomplice in an offence. Other forms of participation enumerated are adopted from international law: the principle of joint criminal enterprise and command responsibility are contained in the Statute.[63] Unlike other international tribunals, the Statute does not contain provisions which explicitly limit the immunity of heads of State or other senior officials. Heads of State can be tried before the *ad hoc* international criminal tribunals; the International Criminal Court, and the Special Court for Sierra Leone. The applicability of immunities in cases before the Lebanon Tribunal will be a matter for the judges of the tribunal to decide.[64] Article 6 of the Statute provides that an amnesty granted to any person for a crime within the jurisdiction of the tribunal shall not be a bar to prosecution.

Another distinctive feature of the Special Tribunal is that, in accordance with Article 22, if certain conditions are satisfied, the tribunal is empowered to conduct trials *in absentia*.[65] The Lebanese system also allows for trials *in adsentia*; however, other international and hybrid tribunals do not.

In March 2009 the Rules of Procedure and Evidence of the Special Tribunal were adopted. The Rules are influenced by the Lebanese Code of Criminal Procedure; the Rules of Procedure of the International Criminal Court; and the Rules of the tribunals for the former Yugoslavia and Rwanda. The procedure outlined in the Statute, although predominantly based on the adversarial system, also reflects the inquisitorial system embedded in Lebanese law. The rules attempt to blend the two procedural models to set down a procedure which will best fulfill the needs of international proceedings. The Rules of Procedure regulate the conduct of the pre-trial; trial; and appellate proceedings; the admission of evidence; the status and role of victims as participants in proceedings; the role of the Defence Office; and other matters.[66]

Like other hybrid models, the Special Tribunal has a mixed composition of judges, prosecutors, and staff. The tribunal is composed of four organs: the Chambers; the Prosecutor; the Registry; and the Defence Office. Pursuant to Article 8, the Chambers are composed of one international pre-trial judge; up to two Trial Chambers, each consisting of three judges (two international and one Lebanese); and the Appeals Chamber, composed of five judges (three international and two Lebanese). Thus, unlike the Cambodian Extraordinary Chambers, each Chamber has a majority of international judges. The Special Tribunal is the first hybrid institution to include the Defence Office as a fourth organ, which has equal status to the Chambers, Prosecutor, and Registry. Many commentators consider this essential to ensure effective defence for the accused. Under Article 13, the Office will assist assigned lawyers with research, the collection of evidence, and advice, and appear in court as appropriate. The Head of the Defence Office shall be appointed by the Secretary-General.

The international Prosecutor, appointed by the Secretary-General, has a Lebanese Deputy Prosecutor. The Prosecutors are assisted in their work by international and Lebanese staff. Similar to the structure of the International Criminal Court and the *ad hoc* tribunals, the Registry is responsible for the administration and servicing of the Tribunal. The international Registrar is obliged to establish a Victims and Witness Unit 'to protect the safety, physical and psychological well-being, dignity, and privacy' of persons who are at risk on account of testimony before the tribunal.

Similar to the Special Court for Sierra Leone, the Special Tribunal for Lebanon does not have a direct relationship with the Security Council nor is it funded from the United Nations' budget. Instead, the Secretary-General created a Management Committee composed of the tribunal's major donors to give 'policy direction and advice on all non-judicial aspects' of its work.

The non-United Nations tribunals in Bosnia and Iraq

The War Crimes Chamber of Bosnia and Herzegovina[67]

Signed in 1995, the Dayton Peace Agreement was designed to end the protracted conflict in Bosnia and Herzegovina.[68] It successfully did so by dividing Bosnia into a federal system with two sub-entities—the Republika Srpska and the Federation of Bosnia and Herzegovina—and a weak State government.[69] However, Dayton did not create a specific tribunal with the capacity to try the perpetrators of the atrocities committed during the war. Instead, it concentrated efforts for post-war accountability at the international level: Article IX requires the parties to cooperate fully with anyone authorized by the Security Council to investigate or prosecute war crimes and other violations of international humanitarian law. In addition, Article II.8 of the Bosnian Constitution obliges all authorities to comply with orders for cooperation and judicial assistance issued by the tribunal for the former Yugoslavia. Almost seven years after the Dayton summit a culture of impunity had evolved in Bosnia: the majority of war crimes suspects were effectively immune from prosecution.[70]

In May 2002, the Office of the High Representative combined all of the international community's efforts on the rule of law in one comprehensive judicial reform strategy. It was an extremely ambitious strategy which included getting High Judicial and Prosecutorial Councils functioning so that all judges and prosecutors in the country could be reappointed; restructuring all court and prosecutorial systems; reforming substantive and procedural criminal laws; and establishing the Court and Prosecutor's Office as the centerpiece of the new state criminal justice system.[71] In addition, the Office of the High Representative coordinated an expert report which recommended the creation of International Humanitarian Law Divisions in the Court and Prosecutor's Office of Bosnia and Herzegovina to investigate and try cases involving serious violations of international law.[72]

At that time, the international tribunal for the former Yugoslavia was moving towards closure. In June 2002, the tribunal presented its 'completion strategy' to the Security Council containing broad timelines and proposed methods to complete its work.[73] By concentrating on the prosecution and trial of the highest-ranking political and military leaders and referring intermediate-level accused to national courts, it aimed to complete investigations by the end of 2004, all first instance trials by the end of 2008, and all of its work in 2010. Thus, an independent and impartial Bosnian court that respected the principles of the protection of human rights was required. The Security Council endorsed the completion strategy: it advocated the creation of a special Chamber in the State Court of Bosnia and Herzegovina with the jurisdiction to try intermediate and lower-level accused transferred from the tribunal for trial. To facilitate the transfer of cases, the Council also called upon states to assist Bosnia to build its national justice system.[74] The Office of the High Representative established a 'Multi-Agency Implementation Task Force' composed of national and international institutions, including the Court and Prosecutor's Office; the Bosnian Ministry of Justice; and the Yugoslavia tribunal. Various working groups were established which concentrated on a variety of issues, including the legal amendments to the substantive and procedural criminal laws, witness protection mechanisms; the transfer of evidence from the international tribunal, and the renovation of the Court building and the construction of courtrooms and a detention facility.[75] Ultimately, the broader political decision to complete the mandate of the tribunal for the former Yugoslavia provided a catalyst for turning the new commitment to judicial reform in Bosnia into a concrete commitment to build a state justice sector with the ability to try war crimes cases respecting international standards of fair trial and due process of law.[76]

The hybrid War Crimes Sections in the Court and Prosecutor's Office of Bosnia and Herzegovina were officially inaugurated on 9 March 2005. They had jurisdiction to investigate, prosecute and try cases transferred from the tribunal for the former Yugoslavia under Rule 11*bis* of the Rules of Procedure and Evidence; and, highly sensitive national cases. The Court and Prosecutor's Office are independent national legal entities operating under and created by national law. The Court is composed of three divisions: the Criminal Division; the Administrative Division; and the Appellate Division. Within the Criminal and Appellate Divisions, two hybrid sections were created: Section I for War Crimes and Section II for Organized Crime, Economic Crime, and Corruption. During a five-year transitional period 2005–2009, international judges were initially appointed by the High Representative to the hybrid Sections of the Criminal and Appellate Divisions.[77] The authority to appoint international judges to the court subsequently transitioned to the independent national body, the High Judicial and Prosecutorial Council.[78] The War Crimes Section in the Criminal Division was composed of five hybrid trial panels. A panel was composed of three judges: two international and one national. As a rule, the President of a panel was a Bosnian judge.

In the Appellate Division, the War Crimes Section consisted of one second-instance panel. The panel was composed of three judges: two international and one national. Appeals against decisions of the hybrid trial panels were adjudicated by the judges of the Appellate War Crimes Section. The President of the Appellate Panel was Bosnian. The appointment of international judges to the Court was challenged before the Bosnian Constitutional Court in 2007. The appellant, who had been convicted of war crimes, alleged that the participation of international judges appointed by the High Representative violated the independence and impartiality of the court since the judges 'exclusively depend [on] the entity which appointed them'.[79] Examining the jurisprudence of the European Court of Human Rights, the Constitutional Court held that the national laws regulating appointment created the mechanisms required to ensure the independence of judges from interference or influence by the executive or international authorities.

Unlike the Special Court for Sierra Leone or the Cambodian Extraordinary Chambers, the Prosecutor's Office of Bosnia and Herzegovina is not an integral part of the Court. As previously noted, the institution is an autonomous legal entity. There were two hybrid departments in the Proseuctor's Office: the Special Department for War Crimes and the Special Department for Organized Crime, Economic Crime, and Corruption. The office was managed by a Bosnian Chief Prosecutor. Corresponding to the law regulating the hybrid Chambers in the Court, the Law on the Prosecutor's Office declared that during the five-year transitional period international prosecutors could be appointed to the Special Departments.[80] The War Crimes Department had six mixed prosecution teams: five regional teams and a special team dedicated to the Srebrenica massacre.

One commentator has remarked that the role of the Registry in the Bosnian hybrid model should not be underestimated.[81] Established by an international agreement between the High Representative and Bosnia and Herzegovina, the Registry was an independent international institution which provided management and administrative support to the Court and Prosecutor's Office of Bosnia and Herzegovina.[82] The Registry created the Witness and Victims Support Section in the Court. Witnesses were given assistance by psychologists before their appearance in court, during trials, and also after proceedings ended. The Criminal Defense Office was created with responsibility for compiling and maintaining a roster of qualified defense lawyers. The Office organized training in criminal procedure, international criminal law and advocacy. A team of international and national lawyers provided legal advice, research, and support in drafting motions. The Registry also supported and promoted the application of international standards by other actors in the state justice sector. It supported the creation of the State Police Witness Protection Department and provided an international advisor to train and manage the police officers. In addition, the Registry managed the construction of a maximum security detention facility and worked with the Ministry of Justice to guarantee respect for international standards in the detention of accused persons.

A distinctive feature of the Bosnian hybrid model was the pioneering policy developed by the Registry. A five-year transition strategy and implementation timelines were incorporated into the work plan of the institution from its inception.[83] The Registry initially introduced and paid for international staff in management and litigation positions in the Court and Prosecutor's Office. Over the five-year transition period 2005–2009, internationals were gradually phased out by transferring authority to Bosnian staff and financial responsibility to the Bosnian State. Building the long-term sustainable capacity of the national institutions to try cases of genocide, crimes against humanity, and war crimes was a primary objective of the Registry.

The Socialist Federal Republic of Yugoslavia (SFRY) Criminal Code was the effective criminal law in Bosnia during the 1991–1995 war. In 2003, as part of the judicial reform programme in Bosnia, substantive and procedural criminal laws—the Criminal Code and the Criminal Procedure Code of Bosnia and Herzegovina—were introduced at State level.[84] The Law regulating the transfer of cases and the use of evidence collected by the Yugoslavia tribunal was subsequently implemented.[85] The 2003 Criminal Code aimed to clarify the international offences enumerated in the SFRY Code. Effectively, the 2003 law codified international obligations which were applicable in Bosnia at the time of the conflict. Chapter XVII includes detailed provisions on genocide, war crimes, and crimes against humanity.

The death penalty was abolished in Bosnia in 1997. Consequently, under the 2003 Code, the maximum penalty is life imprisonment. Regarding the prohibition on retroactive application of criminal law, Article 4(1) of the Criminal Code provides that the law in effect at the time the offence was perpetrated shall be applied. However, the Code further provides that Article 4(1) 'shall not prejudice the trial and punishment of any person for any act or omission which, at the time when it was committed, was criminal according to the general principles of international law'. In 2007, Abduladhim Maktouf, who had been convicted for war crimes by the Court, challenged his sentence before the Constitutional Court. He argued that the retroactive application of a penalty in the 2003 Criminal Code violated Article 7 of the European Convention on Human Rights, which calls for application of the more lenient law. The Constitutional Court rejected his challenge, noting that the SFRY Code provided for the death penalty, and thus could not be considered more lenient. The Constitutional Court found that the retroactive application of the 2003 Criminal Code in sentencing for war crimes was permissible because such acts, at the time of their commission, were already criminal according to the 'general principles of law recognized by civilized nations'. In addition, Article III(3)(b) of the Constitution established that 'the general principles of international law shall be an integral part' of Bosnian law.[86]

Before the War Crimes Chamber commenced operations it was clear that the use of evidence collected by the Yugoslavia tribunal would be critical for the future trial of national indictments. In addition, the Court had to try cases referred by the tribunal with confirmed indictments. Consequently, a *lex specialis* law was introduced to regulate the admissibility of evidence and the transfer of cases from the tribunal. Under Article 2(1) of the Law on Transfer, the Prosecutor's Office was obliged to adapt the tribunal's indictment to make it compliant with national law. Subsequently, '[t]he Court . . . shall accept the indictment if it is ensured that the ICTY indictment has been adequately adapted and that the adapted indictment fulfils the formal requirements of the [Bosnian] Criminal Procedure Code'. In addition, Article 3(1) of the law prescribes that '[e]vidence collected in accordance with the ICTY Statute and Rules of Procedure and Evidence may be used in proceedings . . .'. before Bosnian Courts.

Since 2005, six cases involving 10 accused have been transferred from the tribunal for the former Yugoslavia to the Court of Bosnia and Herzegovina for trial. By 2008, trial proceedings against an additional 74 accused were ongoing before the hybrid War Crimes Sections of the Court.

The Supreme Iraqi Criminal Tribunal

After the end of major hostilities in Iraq in 2003, the Coalition Provisional Authority was created to exercise the powers of a transitional government. The Provisional Authority was vested with 'all executive, legislative and judicial authority necessary to achieve its objectives'.[87] Recognizing the support of the Security Council for the creation of an Iraqi interim administration run by Iraqis, the Coalition Provisional Authority later recognized the Iraqi Governing Council as the 'principal body of Iraqi interim administration, pending the establishment of an internationally recognized, representative government by the people of Iraq, consistent with Resolution 1483'. In December 2003, the Provisional Authority promulgated Order Number 48 which delegated legislative authority for creating the Iraqi Special Tribunal to the Governing Council. The Council was authorized to establish the tribunal by adopting a national law which would mirror the provisions of the Statute of the Tribunal which was annexed to Order 48.[88]

In accordance with Article 1 of the Statute, the Iraqi Special Tribunal was foreseen as 'an independent entity and not associated with any Iraqi government departments'. The seat of the Iraqi Special Tribunal was Baghdad. Pursuant to Article 3, the Tribunal was composed of Investigative Judges; one or more Trial Chambers; and an Appeals Chamber. Each Trial Chamber consisted of five permanent judges. The Appeals Chamber was composed of nine judges. The Prosecutor of the Iraqi Special Tribunal was Iraqi. In other hybrid models, international judges and prosecutors were appointed to work alongside their national counterparts in the national institutions. Rather than appoint international judges and prosecutors directly to the Special Tribunal, Article 6 prescribed that '[t]he President of the Tribunal shall be required to appoint non-Iraqi nationals to act in advisory capacities or as observers to the Trial Chambers and to the Appeals Chamber. The role of the non-Iraqi nationals shall be to provide assistance to the judges with respect to international law and the experience of similar tribunals (whether international or otherwise), and to monitor the protection by the Tribunal of general due process of law standards'.

Pursuant to Article 7 and Article 8 of the Statute, the Chief Investigative Judge and Chief Proseuctor were also obliged to appoint non-Iraqi nationals, with experience in international war crimes tribunals, to provide the tribunal with assistance with respect to investigations and prosecution of cases. The Coalition Provisional Authority established the Crimes Against Humanity Investigations Unit staffed by American prosecutors and investigators to assist investigations and the tribunal.[89] In May 2004, the Regime Crimes Liaison's Office was established as the lead US Government agency for support to the Iraqi Special Tribunal. International staff provided training to investigators; prosecutors; investigative judges; and they also gathered evidence and provided technical support.[90]

The tribunal was conferred with far-reaching jurisdiction. It had personal jurisdiction over any Iraqi national or resident of Iraq. Its temporal jurisdiction covered crimes committed between 17 July 1968 and 1 May 2003. It had territorial jurisdiction over crimes committed in Iraq 'or elsewhere, including crimes committed in connection with Iraq's wars against the Islamic Republic of Iran and the State of Kuwait'. As one commentator has noted, the expansive jurisdiction underscored the 'expectation that the [tribunal] would review the entire record of the Ba'ath regime, and thus contribute to the de-Ba'athization of Iraq'.[91] Articles 10–14 of the Statute specified that the tribunal had subject-matter jurisdiction for genocide; crimes against humanity; war crimes; and a number of offences prescribed under Iraqi law.

In 2005 the Transitional National Assembly was elected in Iraq and tasked with drafting a permanent constitution. Article 134 of the Iraqi Constitution states that '[t]he Iraqi High Criminal Court shall continue its duties as an independent judicial body, in examining the crimes of the defunct dictatorial regime and its symbols'. The Statute of the Iraqi High Criminal Court was adopted by the Presidency Council on 9 October 2005.[92] It largely mirrors the Special Tribunal Statute and the general nature of the jurisdiction of the new Tribunal remained the same. Article 37 of the High Court Statute revokes the Special Tribunal Statute while Article 38 states '[a]ll decisions and Orders on Procedure issued under the Iraqi Special Tribunal Law No.1 for the year 2003 are correct and conform to the law'.[93]

The Iraqi High Criminal Court is an independent judicial body for the investigation and prosecution of the former Iraqi regime of Saddam Hussein. Its predecessor, the Special Tribunal was required to appoint non-Iraqi nationals to act as advisors. The High Criminal Court is not obliged to appoint internationals. Instead, the Statute permits the discretionary appointment of non-Iraqi judges who have experience conducting trials of international offences.

Unlike international or other hybrid criminal courts established by the United Nations, the Iraqi Criminal Court applies the death penalty. Saddam Hussein and three others were found guilty of crimes against humanity and executed in 2006, after the judgement in the Dujail trial. In 2007, the tribunal found 'Chemical Ali' and four other defendants guilty of genocide, crimes against humanity, and war crimes in the Anfal trial.

Conclusion

Since the late 1990s the international tribunals for the former Yugoslavia and Rwanda and the various hybrid tribunals have played a significant part in the evolution of the international criminal justice system. In spite of their imperfections, there are valuable lessons to be learnt from the various models created. The International Criminal Court increasingly assumes the centre-stage position in the pursuit of accountability for serious violations of international law. There is little support from the international community for the future creation of courts similar to the *ad hoc* tribunals. However, the support for hybrid tribunals remains steady. Many commentators believe that if hybrid courts are implemented properly they can be a powerful mechanism to combat impunity for serious violations of international law.[94] Arguably, together with the International Criminal Court, hybrid tribunals will underpin the future enforcement of international criminal law.

Notes

1 For a discussion on the creation of the tribunals see: William A. Schabas, *The UN International Criminal Tribunals: The former Yugoslavia, Rwanda, and Sierra Leone*, Cambridge: Cambridge University Press, 2006, pp. 3–74.
2 Ralph Zacklin, 'The Failings of Ad Hoc International Tribunals', 2 *Journal of International Criminal Justice,* 2004, pp. 541–5.
3 See generally: Daphna Shraga, 'The Second Generation UN-Based Tribunals: A Diversity of Mixed Jurisdictions in Internationalized Criminal Courts and Tribunals Sierra Leone, East Timor, Kosovo and C. P. R. Romano, A. Nollkaemper and J. K. Kleffner (eds), *Internationalized Criminal Courts*, Oxford: Oxford University Press, 2004, p.15.
4 Etelle R. Higonnet, 'Restructuring Hybrid Courts: Local Empowerment and National Criminal Justice Reform', 23 *Arizona Journal International and Comparative Law*, 2006, p. 347.
5 UN Doc. S/RES/1272 (1999), para.1.
6 UNTAET/REG/No. 2000/15.
7 UNTAET/REG/No.2000/16, Section 14.6 authorized the Deputy General Prosecutor for Serious Crimes to create a Prosecution Support Unit consisting of East Timorese and International Experts.
8 See generally: Håkan Friman, 'Procedural Law of Internationalized Criminal Courts', in C. P. R. Romano, A. Nollkaemper and J. K. Kleffner (eds), *Internationalized Criminal Courts*, Oxford: Oxford University Press, 2004, pp. 317–58.
9 For a discussion in relation to the applicable laws see: Suzannah Linton, 'Rising from the Ashes: The Creation of a Viable Criminal Justice System in East Timor', 25 *Melbourne University Law Review*, pp. 145–75.
10 UN Doc. S/RES/1410 (2002).
11 For statistics see generally: 'Report of the Secretary-General on the United Nations Mission of Support in East Timor', UN Doc. S/2004/333, para. 26.
12 Šainović *et al.* (IT-05-87), Judgment, 26 February 2009.
13 UNMIK/REG/No. 1999/1, para. 1.1.
14 See: ICTY Press Release PR/P.I.S/437-E, 'Statement by Carla Del Ponte Prosecutor of the International Criminal Tribunal for the former Yugoslavia on the Investigation and Prosecution of crimes committed in Kosovo', 29 September 1999, Available at http://www.icty.org/sid/7733 (accessed 29 October 2009).
15 See generally: David Marshall and Shelley Inglis, 'The Disempowerment of Human Rights-Based Justice in the United Nations Mission in Kosovo', 16 *Harvard Human Rights Journal*, 2003, p. 123.
16 Carsten Stahn, *The Law and Practice of International Territorial Administration: Versailles to Iraq and Beyond*, Cambridge: Cambridge University Press, 2008, p. 309.
17 UNMIK REG/No. 1999/7, under Section 2.1 the Commission was composed of eight local and three international experts. The Commission was mandated to advise the SRSG on matters related to complaints against judges and prosecutors.
18 See: Wendy S. Betts, Scott N. Carlson, Gregory Gisvold, 'The Post-Conflict Transitional Administration of Kosovo and the Lessons-Learned in Efforts to Establish a Judiciary and Rule of Law', 22 *Michigan Journal of International Law*, 2001, p. 378.

19 See generally: Jean-Christian Cady and Nicholas Booth, 'Internationalized Courts in Kosovo: An UNMIK Perspective', in C. P. R. Romano, A. Nollkaemper and J. K. Kleffner (eds), *Internationalized Criminal Courts*, Oxford: Oxford University Press, 2004, p. 59.
20 Jean-Christian Cady and Nicholas Booth, 'Internationalized Courts in Kosovo: An UNMIK Perspective', in C. P. R. Romano, A. Nollkaemper and J. K. Kleffner (eds), *Internationalized Criminal Courts*, Oxford: Oxford University Press, 2004.
21 See: International Centre for Transitional Justice Prosecution Case Studies Series: Tom Perriello and Marieke Wierda, 'Lessons from the Deployment of International Judges and Prosecutors in Kosovo', March 2006, Available at http://www.ictj.org/static/Prosecutions/Kosovo.study.pdf (accessed 29 October 2009).
22 See: UNMIK Press Releases PR/150, 'Kouchner describes new measures to restore calm to Mitrovica', 11 February 2000; UNMIK PR/161, 'Measure to Re-establish security and build peaceful co-existence in Mitrovica', 16 February 2000, Available at http://www.unmikonline.org/press/press/pr161.html (accessed 29 October 2009).
23 See: The United States Institute of Peace Special Report No. 112, Michael E. Hartmann, 'International Judges and Prosecutors in Kosovo: A New Model for Post-Conflict Peacekeeping', October 2003, p. 10, Available at http://www.usip.org/resources/international-judges-and-prosecutors-kosovo-new-model-post-conflict-peacekeeping (accessed 29 October 2009).
24 See: The United States Institute of Peace Special Report No. 112, Michael E. Hartmann, 'International Judges and Prosecutors in Kosovo: A New Model for Post-Conflict Peacekeeping', October 2003.
25 UNMIK/REG/2000/64, Section 1.1.
26 UNMIK/REG/1999/24 and UNMIK/REG/1999/25 repealed Section 3 of UNMIK/REG/1999/1 which provided that the laws applicable in the territory of Kosovo prior to March 1999 shall continue to apply.
27 For a discussion in relation to the substantive criminal law see: John Cerone and Clive Baldwin, 'Explaining and Evaluating the UNMIK Court System', in C. P. R. Romano, A. Nollkaemper and J. K. Kleffner (eds), *Internationalized Criminal Courts*, Oxford: Oxford University Press, 2004, p. 44.
28 Organization for Security and Co-operation in Europe, Mission in Kosovo, Department of Human Rights & Rule of Law, Legal Systems Monitoring Section, 'Kosovo's War Crimes Trials: A Review', September 2002, Available at http://www.osce.org/documents/mik/2002/09/857_en.pdf (accessed 29 October 2009).
29 See: UNMIK/REG/2000/4 (On the Prohibition Against Inciting to National, Racial, Religious or Ethnic Hatred, Discord or Intolerance); UNMIK/REG/2001/4 (On the Prohibition of Trafficking in Persons in Kosovo); UNMIK/REG/2001/12 (On Terrorism and Related Offences); UNMIK/REG/2001/22 (On Measures Against Organized Crime).
30 See: UNMIK/REG/2001/1 (On the Prohibition of Trials in absentia for serious violations of international humanitarian law); UNMIK/REG/2001/20 (On the Protection of Victims and Witnesses); UNMIK/REG/1999/26 (On Extension of Periods of Pre-Trial Detention).
31 For statistics see: UNMIK Pillar 1 Police and Justice, Presentation Paper, June 2004, Available at http://www.unmikonline.org/justice/documents/PillarI_Report_June04.pdf (accessed 29 October 2009).
32 See: Council Joint Action 2008/124/CFSP, 'On the European Union Rule of Law Mission in Kosovo, EULEX KOSOVO', art. 1(1), *Official Journal of the European Union* L 42/92.
33 See: Republic of Kosovo Law No. 03/L-052 'On the Special Prosecution Office of the Republic of Kosovo', March 2008; Law No. 03/L-053 'On the Jurisdiction, Case Selection and Case Allocation of EULEX Judges and Prosecutors in Kosovo'.
34 See: Constitution of the Republic of Kosovo, Article 152.
35 UN Doc. A/51/930-S/1997/488.
36 See: 'Report of the Group of Experts for Cambodia established pursuant to the General Assembly resolution 52/135', 1999, A/53/850, Annex.
37 UN Doc A/53/850, 1999, p. 3.
38 See: Suzannah Linton, 'Putting Cambodia's Extraordinary Chambers Into Context', *Singapore Year Book of International Law and Contributors*, 2007, p. 219.
39 See: Daphna Shraga, 'The Second Generation UN-Based Tribunals: A Diversity of Mixed Jurisdictions', in C. P. R. Romano, A. Nollkaemper and J. K. Kleffner (eds), *Internationalized Criminal Courts*, Oxford: Oxford University Press, 2004, p. 18.
40 Daphna Shraga, 'The Second Generation UN-Based Tribunals: A Diversity of Mixed Jurisdictions', in C. P. R. Romano, A. Nollkaemper and J. K. Kleffner (eds), *Internationalized Criminal Courts*, Oxford: Oxford University Press, 2004

41 UN Doc. A/RES/57/228 B, 'Agreement between the United Nations and the Royal Government of Cambodia Concerning the Prosecution under Cambodian Law of Crimes Committed During the Period of Democratic Kampuchea', 2003; Law on the Establishment of the Extraordinary Chambers, with inclusion of amendments as promulgated on 27 October 2004, NS/RKM/1004/006.
42 See: Kingdom of Cambodia Constitutional Council Decision No. 040/002/2001, 12 February 2001, Available at http://www.eccc.gov.kh/english/cabinet/legislation/5/Const_Council_Res_on_KR_Law_12_Feb_2001.pdf (accessed 29 October 2009).
43 Law on the Establishment of the Extraordinary Chambers, 2004, (NS/RKM/1004/006), Article 20; Article 23.
44 Law on the Extraordinary Chambers, Article 9; Article 17; and Article 36.
45 For a detailed discussion in relation to the duties of the Co-Investigating Judges and Co-Prosecutors see: Suzannah Linton, 'Putting Cambodia's Extraordinary Chambers Into Context', *Singapore Year Book of International Law and Contributors*, 2007, pp. 225–59.
46 For a review of the drafting history of the Law see: Ernestine E. Meijer, 'The Extraordinary Chambers in the Courts of Cambodia for Prosecuting Crimes Committed by the Khmer Rouge: Jurisdiction, Organization, and Procedure', in C. P. R. Romano, A. Nollkaemper, and J. K. Kleffner (eds), *Internationalized Criminal Courts*, Oxford: Oxford University Press, 2004, p. 212.
47 As noted by Ernestine E. Meijer, in C. P. R. Romano, Nollkaemper, and Kleffner (eds), *Internationalized Criminal Courts*, Oxford: Oxford University Press, 2004, pp. 212–13, unlike Article 3 of the Genocide Convention , the Law does not prescribe acts of 'direct and public incitement to commit genocide' and 'complicity in genocide' as the subject-matter jurisdiction of the Chambers. Nevertheless, 'participation in acts of genocide', which is not referred to in Article 3 of the Genocide Convention, is referred to in the Law.
48 In 1979 by trial *in absentia* two of the Khmer Rouge leaders Pol Pot and Ieng Sary were convicted of genocide. In 1996 the Cambodian King granted Ieng Sary amnesty. Although the United Nations held that an amnesty could not apply for international crimes the Cambodian Government refused to repeal the Sary amnesty. Article 40 is the compromise with the effect that it is for the Chambers to decide if Sary's amnesty will serve as a bar to prosecution.
49 Law on the Extraordinary Chambers, Articles 20, 23, and 33, regulating the conduct of prosecutions, investigations, and the general conduct of the trials, refer to the application of existing procedures.
50 See: The Extraordinary Chambers in the Courts of Cambodia, Internal Rules and Regulations (Rev. 4), September 2009.
51 Letter from the Permanent Representative of Sierra Leone to the President of the United Nations Security Council, 9 August 2000, UN Doc. S/2000/786.
52 UN Doc.S/RES/1315, (2000), para.1.
53 Sesay, Kondewa & Fofana—v—The President of the SCSL, The Registrar of the SCSL, The Prosecutor of the SCSL and The Attorney General and Minister of Justice, Supreme Court of Sierra Leone SC No. 1/2003.
54 'Report of the Secretary-General on the establishment of a Special Court for Sierra Leone', UN Doc. S/2000/915, 4 October 2000.
55 'Report on the Special Court for Sierra Leone', submitted by the Independent Expert Antonio Cassese, 12 December 2006, Available at http://www.scsl.org/DOCUMENTS/tabid/176/Default.aspx (accessed 29 October 2009).
56 Taylor (SCSL-2003-01-I), Decision on Immunity from Prosecution, 31 May 2004, para. 6.
57 Ibid., para. 42.
58 For the legal nature of the tribunal see: William A. Schabas, *The UN International Criminal Tribunals: The former Yugoslavia, Rwanda, and Sierra Leone*, Cambridge: Cambridge University Press, 2006, p. 6.
59 Letter of the Prime Minister of Lebanon to the Secretary-General, 13 December 2005, S/2005/783; S/RES/1644 (2005).
60 S/RES/1664 2006.
61 UN Doc. S/RES/1757 2007; see also: Nidal Nabil Jurdi, 'The Subject-Matter Jurisdiction of the Special Tribunal for Lebanon', *Journal of International Criminal Justice*, 2007, p. 1125.
62 See: Lebanese Criminal Code, Law No. 340 1943: Articles 314–16, Articles 547–68, Articles 335–39, Article 398–400.
63 See generally: Marko Milanović, 'An Odd Couple: Domestic Crimes and International Responsibility in the Special Tribunal for Lebanon', *Journal of International Criminal Justice*, 2007, pp. 1139–52.
64 See generally: International Centre for Transitional Justice Prosecutions Programme, 'Handbook on The Special Tribunal for Lebanon', 10 April 2008, Available at http://www.ictj.org/images/content/9/1/914.pdf (accessed 29 October 2009).

65 Pursuant to Article 22, *in absentia* trials are permitted under Statute if the accused has waived his right to be present, has fled or cannot be found, or if the State concerned has not handed him over to the Tribunal.

66 See: The Report of the Special Tribunal for Lebanon President. A. Cassese, 'The STL Six Months On: A Bird's Eye View', September 2009.

67 The 'War Crimes Chamber' is the generic phrase used to describe a number of hybrid sections created in a variety of independent State criminal justice institutions in Bosnia.

68 The General Framework Agreement for Peace in Bosnia and Herzegovina and the Annexes initialed in Dayton, Ohio on 21 November 1995 and signed in Paris on 14 December 1995.

69 See generally: Carsten Stahn, *The Law and Practice of International Territorial Administration: Versailles to Iraq and Beyond*, Cambridge: Cambridge University Press, 2008, p. 290.

70 For a discussion in relation to the post-war judiciary and the lack of war crimes trials see: Fidelma Donlon, 'Rule of Law: From the International Criminal Tribunal for the former Yugoslavia to the War Crimes Chamber of Bosnia and Herzegovina', in Dina Francesca Haynes (ed.), *Deconstructing the Reconstruction: Human Rights and Rule of Law in Postwar Bosnia and Herzegovina,* Aldershot, Hampshire: Ashgate Publishers, 2008, pp. 257–84.

71 The Office of the High Representative was created under the Dayton Peace Agreement. It is an international organization responsible for overseeing all civilian aspects of the peace agreement. In August 2002, as part of the judicial reform programme the High Representative appointed international judges and prosecutors to the organized crime sections in the Court and Prosecutors office of Bosnia and Herzegovina.

72 In 2001, the tribunal for the former Yugoslavia asked the High Representative and the Bosnian Presidency to examine the feasibility of setting up a special court or to propose other options within the existing Bosnian judicial system to enable the future referral of cases.

73 UN Doc. S/678 (2002).

74 UN Doc. S/PRST/2002/21 (2002).

75 For details in relation to creation of the Court see: Mechtild Lauth, 'Ten Years after Dayton: War Crimes Prosecutions in Bosnia and Herzegovina', 16 *Helsinki Monitor*, 2005, p. 258.

76 See: Fidelma Donlon, 'Rule of Law: From the International Criminal Tribunal for the former Yugoslavia to the War Crimes Chamber of Bosnia and Herzegovina', in Dina Francesca Haynes (ed.), *Deconstructing the Reconstruction: Human Rights and Rule of Law in Postwar Bosnia and Herzegovina,* Aldershot, Hampshire: Ashgate Publishers, 2008, pp. 257–84.

77 For the structure of the Court, the composition of panels and the appointment of international judges see: Law on Court of Bosnia and Herzegovina—Consolidated Version. *Official Gazette of Bosnia and Herzegovina*, No. 49/09.

78 Article 8 of the amended Agreement between the High Representative and Bosnia and Herzegovina on the establishment of the Registry for the War Crimes and Organized Crime sections of the Court, *Official Gazette of Bosnia and Herzegovina,* No. 93/06.

79 *Abduladhim Maktouf* (AP-1785/06), Decision on Admissibility and Merits, The Constitutional Court of Bosnia and Herzegovina, 30 March 2007.

80 Law on the Amendments to the Law on the Prosecutor's Office of Bosnia and Herzegovina, *Official Gazette of Bosnia and Herzegovina,* No. 61/04.

81 See generally: William W. Burke-White, 'The Domestic Influence of International Criminal Tribunals: The International Criminal Tribunal for the former Yugoslavia and the Creation of the State Court of Bosnia & Herzegovina', *Columbia Journal of Transnational Law*, 2008, pp. 279–350.

82 For the mandate of the Registry see: Agreement between the High Representative and the Bosnian Presidency on the establishment of the Registry, *Official Gazette of Bosnia and Herzegovina*, International Agreements, No. 12/04. Also see: Law on the Amendments to the Law on the Prosecutor's Office of Bosnia and Herzegovina, *Official Gazette of Bosnia and Herzegovina*, No. 61/04; Law on Court of Bosnia and Herzegovina—Consolidated Version, *Official Gazette of Bosnia and Herzegovina*, No. 49/09.

83 In 2006 the Registry Agreement was amended: the international Registrar was replaced by two national Registrars, one for the Court and one for the Prosecutor's Office. A Transition Council with monitoring and advisory role on issues affecting the transition and integration of national staff to the Bosnian institutions and budget was also created.

84 Criminal Code and the Criminal Procedure Code, *Official Gazette of Bosnia and Herzegovina*, No.3/03.

85 Law on the transfer of cases from the International Criminal Tribunal for the former Yugoslavia to the Prosecutor's Offices of Bosnia and the use of evidence collected by the International Criminal Tribunal in proceedings before the Court, *Official Gazette Bosnia and Herzegovina*, No.61/04.

86 *Abduladhim Maktouf* (AP-1785/06), Decision on Admissibility and Merits, The Constitutional Court of Bosnia and Herzegovina, 30 March 2007.
87 CPA/REG/1, May 2003/01, Section 1.2.
88 CPA/Order/48, 'Delegation of Authority Regarding An Iraqi Special Tribunal', December 2003.
89 For the participation of international staff in the work of the tribunal see generally: M. Cherif Bassiouni and Michael Wahid Hanna, 'Ceding the High Ground: The Iraqi High Criminal Court Statute and the Trial of Saddam Hussein', *39 Case Western Reserve Journal of International Law*, 2007, pp. 21–97.
90 For the nature of support provided by international staff see generally: United States Institute of Peace Training Programmes, 'Building the Iraqi Special Tribunal: Lessons from Experiences in International Criminal Justice', 2004, Available at http://www.usip.org/resources/building-iraqi-special-tribunal-lessons-experiences-international-criminal-justice (accessed 29 October 2009).
91 Yuval Shany, 'Does One Size Fit All? Reading the Jurisdictional Provisions of the New Iraqi Special Tribunal Statute in the Light of the Statutes of International Criminal Tribunals', 2 *Journal of International Criminal Justice,* 2004, p. 340.
92 Iraqi High Criminal Court Law, *Official Gazette of the Republic of Iraq* No. 4006, 18 October 2005.
93 For a detailed discussion in relation to the applicable law see: M. Cherif Bassiouni and Michael Wahid Hanna, 'Ceding the High Ground: The Iraqi High Criminal Court Statute and the Trial of Saddam Hussein', *39 Case Western Reserve Journal of International Law*, 2007, p. 54.
94 See: Laura A. Dickinson, 'The Promise of Hybrid Courts', *The American Journal of International Law',* 2003, pp. 295–310; William W. Burke-White, 'A Community of Courts: Toward a System of International Criminal Law Enforcement', 24 *Michigan Journal of International Law,* 2003, pp. 1–101.

Part II
The crimes

7
Genocide

Paola Gaeta

Introduction

The destruction of, or the attempt to destroy entire groups—whether national, racial, religious, cultural, and so on—is by all evidence an ancient phenomenon in the history of mankind. However, the word 'genocide', which etymologically describes it, has only been coined in 1944 by the Polish lawyer R. Lemkin.[1] In just a few short years the term 'genocide' has spread and asserted itself as the authoritative description of an age-old behaviour.[2] The relatively modern construct of the term explains why the word 'genocide' itself, which is now commonly used also to describe the Holocaust of the Jews before and during World War II, cannot be located within the Statute of the International Military Tribunal at Nuremberg (IMT), nor in its final judgment.[3] As a matter of fact, the Holocaust was punished by the IMT under the charges of extermination and persecution, which constituted two of the underlying offences of crimes against humanity.[4]

On 9 December 1948, in the wake of the Nuremberg trial, the UN General Assembly adopted the Convention for the Prevention and Repression of the Crime of Genocide ('the Genocide Convention' or 'the Convention'),[5] the substantive rules of which may largely be considered as declaratory of customary international law.[6] Among those, one can certainly mention Article II, which provides the legal definition for the crime of genocide.[7] In accordance with this definition, genocide consists of five specific enumerated acts, which are listed in the Convention in an exhaustive manner. Secondly, it is requested that the acts in question be carried out with a specific intent: namely, to destroy in whole or in part, 'a national, ethnical, racial or religious group as such'. This is what is normally referred to as *genocidal intent*, characterized by the fact that the perpetrator of one of the prohibited acts does not necessarily need to realize, through their conduct, the destruction of one of the enumerated groups. In fact is it only necessary that the perpetrator, by carrying out that conduct, intends to attain the desired goal.

Article II of the Genocide Convention can certainly be commended for having provided a legal definition to the 'crime without a name'.[8] Nonetheless, the exhaustive enumeration of the protected groups and the prohibited acts has rendered more difficult the evolution of a parallel, and potentially wider, definition of the crime of genocide through customary international law.

Yet it should be recalled that Article II, and the definition of genocide it enshrines, is merely the outcome of a negotiating process that reflects the views on genocide prevailing at the specific time of the adoption of the Genocide Convention. Such a process, involving representatives from a plethora of states, inevitably results in the formation of a text based on compromise. It must be stated that since this time, international law has undergone significant transformation, most noticeably the development of the doctrine of human rights. Therefore it is conceptually more difficult today to understand why attacks against members of groups other then those listed in the Genocide Convention cannot be considered genocide. Furthermore, it is even more difficult to understand why genocide can be carried out only through one of the enumerated acts, since there may be other acts that can be resorted to with a view to destroying one of the protected groups.

The 'rigidity' of the definition of genocide, however, has been softened down by way of judicial interpretation. In particular, the International Criminal Tribunal for Rwanda (ICTR) has adopted specific criteria to widen the categories of groups protected by the definition, and has considered that some acts, such as rape, can fall within the purview of the enumerated genocidal acts.

This chapter discusses the definition of the crime of genocide by taking into account its judicial application, in particular that by international criminal courts and tribunals. It will also focus on two controversial issues that surround that definition: namely: (i) the need for genocide to be committed in the context of a genocidal policy against one of the protected groups and (ii) the applicability of the definition of genocide embodied in the Genocide Convention in the field of state responsibility, as opposed to international criminal liability.

The legal ingredient of the crime of genocide

Every crime consists of a prohibited act (*actus reus*), committed by a person with a culpable mind (*mens rea*). Genocide, as a crime entailing individual liability, is not an exception. Both the *actus reus* and the required *mens rea* are spelt out in the definition of genocide enshrined in Article II of the Genocide Convention.

The actus reus

The acts that may amount to genocide, as pointed out above, are listed exhaustively in Article II of the Convention. They are the following: (a) killing members of the group; (b) causing serious bodily or mental harm to members of the group; (c) deliberately inflicting on the group conditions of life calculated to bring about its physical destruction in whole or in part; (d) imposing measures intended to prevent births within the group; and (e) forcibly transferring children of the group to another group.

It is apparent from this list that although the direct victims of the prohibited acts are usually individuals the ultimate 'victim' is the group itself. It is against the group as such that the perpetrator directs its criminal activity, although to realize the intended objective (to destroy the group in whole or in part), it is necessary to target specific individuals, who are selected by the perpetrator on account of their membership in the group.[9] However, it is not requested that the individual victim actually belongs to the group, for what counts is the perception or belief of the perpetrator that the victim is a member of the targeted group. Therefore, it has been affirmed by a Trial Chamber of the ICTR that 'if a victim was perceived by the perpetrator as belonging to a protected group, the victim could be considered . . . as a member of the protected group, for the purposes of genocide'.[10]

The question may arise of whether the aforementioned acts must be directed against a plurality of individuals, or whether targeting only one member of the group will suffice for a charge of genocide. In *Akayesu*, the Trial Chamber has contended that the plurality of the victims is not requested,[11] although the use of the plural form (members, deaths, children) may induce the opposite conclusion.[12] Nonetheless, with respect to (c), which deals with acts against the group as such, the prohibited conduct by necessity must be carried out against a plurality of members of the group.

As for the enumerated prohibited acts, it must be observed that the (a) has been considered to be equivalent to 'murder', which requires *intentional* killing.[13]Various arguments have been put forward to ground this interpretation, including the fact that the French text refers to *meurtre* and therefore clearly excludes unintentional homicide.

The act of causing harm under (b) does not require that the harm caused be permanent and irremediable,[14] but '[i]t must be harm that results in a grave and long-term disadvantage to a person's ability to lead a normal and constructive life'.[15] The harm caused can be bodily *or* mental, and must be 'serious'. The seriousness of the harm 'must be assessed on a case by case basis and with due regard for the particular circumstances'.[16] In the ICTR case law, serious bodily harm has been interpreted as 'harm that seriously injures the health, causes disfigurement or causes any serious injury to the external, internal organs or senses'.[17] With respect to serious mental harm, it has considered that 'minor or temporary impairment of mental faculties' would not meet the seriousness threshold.[18] Serious bodily or mental hard can also be caused by rape and other acts of sexual violence.[19]

'Deliberately inflicting on the group conditions of life calculated to bring about its physical destruction in whole or in part', provided under (c), includes 'slow death measures', such as 'lack of proper housing, clothing, hygiene and medical care or excessive work or physical exertion'.[20] It is not requested that those conditions of life actually bring to the physical destruction of the group, in whole or in part; it is only requested that they are 'calculated to bring to its destruction': namely, that they intended to achieve this result.[21]

The fourth prohibited act that can amount to genocide, namely 'imposing measures intended to prevent births within the group', intends to cover conduct whose aim is to prevent the biological reproduction of the group. This result can usually be achieved through the sterilization of women (when the transmission of the distinguishing features of the group is matriarchal, as it was the case of the sterilization of Jewish women). It can also be accomplished through the rape of women of the group by members of another group, when rape aims at changing the ethnic composition of the group whose characteristics are transmitted following the patriarchal line. Other measures intended to achieve the same objective can include segregation of sexes, prohibition of marriage, or forced birth control.[22] As in the preceding hypothesis, it is not required that the measures achieve the desired goal, it being only necessary that they are carried out for that particular purpose.

Finally, the last enumerated act skirts along the borderline of 'cultural genocide'.[23] The forcible transfer of the children of the targeted group to another group may not result in the biological or physical destruction, but cause the disappearance of the group through the severance of the links of the youngest generation with the group of origin. In this way, the children will lose their original cultural identity and their original group will be destroyed.

The mens rea

There is a need to distinguish between first, the mental element required for each of the acts that may amount to genocide, and then second, the specific mental element which is necessary to consider those acts as amounting to genocide.

All the prohibited acts must be accomplished *intentionally*, i.e. they require *intent* on the part of the perpetrator. As highlighted above, this is also the case for the killing of members of the group. Premeditation, i.e. the planning and preparation of the prohibited act, is not required, except—in the opinion of a distinguished commentator—in the case of the act listed under (c), because of the use of the word 'deliberately'.[24]

To the general intent of the prohibited act, an additional specific mental element must be added: namely, 'the intent to destroy, in whole or in part' one of the enumerated groups 'as such'. This is the specific intent of genocide, also known as genocidal intent. It is an aggravated form of intent that does not demand realization through the material conduct, but that is nonetheless pursued by the perpetrator. In other words, it is not required that the perpetrator actually manages to destroy a member of a protected group by carrying out one of the five acts prohibited under the Convention. It is only necessary that the perpetrator harbours the specific intent to destroy the group while carrying out one of the prohibited acts, regardless of whether by accomplishing the act the intended ultimate objective is achieved. Therefore, the requirement of the specific intent has a preventative function, since it allows the criminalization of genocide before the perpetrator achieves the actual destruction of the group.

The question arises of whether the specific intent harboured by the perpetrator has to be 'realistic'; must the perpetrator believe that the intended goal can be achieved through the commission of one of the prohibited acts? The case law of the ICTR and the ICTY (International Criminal Tribunal for the former Yugoslavia) has not expressly tackled this issue.[25] In *Mpambara*, however, an ICTR Trial Chamber has stressed that 'even a single instance of one of the prohibited acts' can amount to genocide, 'provided that the accused genuinely intends by that act to destroy at least a substantial part of the group'.[26] The reference to the *genuine* intent to destroy the group is explained by the Trial Chamber in a note to the judgment: 'The perpetrator of a single, isolated act of violence could not possess the requisite intent based on a delusion that, by his action, the destruction of the group, in whole or in part, could be effected'.[27] Therefore, it seems that for the Trial Chamber the genocidal intent can be 'genuine' only to the extent that the perpetrator considers it possible that the destruction of the group can eventually be achieved.

It is worth emphasising that if one contends that the genocidal intent of the perpetrator must be a 'realistic' one, the outcome could be that genocide becomes punishable only when the destruction of a group, at least in part, is already taking place. This could cover situations where there is a genocidal plan or campaign, to which the perpetrator contributes, or even the case of a lone perpetrator who possesses the means for achieving the desired specific intent (an example could be that of a person in possession of a bacteriological weapon, capable of killing many individuals in one attack). To require that the desired specific intent be 'genuine', in the sense of materially possible, will undermine the preventative nature of the prohibition of genocide, and eventually make genocide punishable only when part of the group (even a substantial part) is already being destroyed.

The genocidal intent of the perpetrator must be directed towards one of the enumerated groups. The list of the protected groups, as underlined above, is exhaustive. During the preparatory works of the Genocide Convention, an attempt was made to include in the list cultural and political groups, but to no avail. The exclusion was grounded on the volatile membership of these two categories of groups and the desire to afford protection to groups characterized by a certain degree of stability.[28] The ICTR has tried to identify the distinguishing features of each protected group, and has affirmed that: (i) a national group is a group of people 'who are perceived to share a legal bond based on common citizenship, coupled with reciprocity of rights and duties';[29] (ii) a racial group is made up by members who possess 'hereditary physical traits often identified with a geographical region, irrespective of linguistic, cultural, national or religious factors';[30] (iii) an ethnic group is 'a group whose members share a common language or culture';[31] and (iv) a religious group is made by members who share 'the same religion, denomination or mode of worship'.[32] It is important to stress, however, that the reference to the four enumerated groups is made to the groups as social entities. It would therefore be useless to try to describe the protected groups by applying rigorous scientific or objective notions, also because by so doing one may find that some groups do not scientifically and objectively exist.[33]

It is perhaps because a particular group can be deemed to exist as a national, racial, ethnic or religious group on account of the perception by the community that the question of the identification of a given group as a group protected by the prohibition of genocide has eventually been solved by also applying a subjective test. Thus, in the case of the attacks against the Tutsis in Rwanda, the ICTR has considered they constituted an *ethnic group*, since the official classifications referred to them as an ethnic group and the Rwandans themselves, without hesitation, answered questions regarding their ethnicity.[34] Similarly, the International Commission of Inquiry on Darfur found that the members of the tribes attacked in Darfur constituted an ethnic group distinct from that of the attackers on account of the self-perception of the victims as well as the attackers that they were two different ethnic groups: namely, the 'Africans' as opposed to the 'Arabs'.[35] In addition, as alluded to above, it is not necessary that the specific individual victim of the genocidal conduct belongs to the targeted group. It is sufficient that the perpetrator believes that the victim is a member of the group he or she seeks to destroy.[36]

The genocidal intent must be directed at one of the listed groups 'in whole or in part'. This means that it is not required that the perpetrator seeks to destroy the group in its entirety, since the intent to attain only a 'partial' destruction would suffice. It is, however, not clear what 'in part' exactly means. If one applies a quantitative approach, 'in part' can describe the numeric size of the group with respect to its totality. By contrast, if one uses a qualitative approach, the intrinsic characteristic of the selected part of the group would count, i.e. the leadership of the targeted group. In any case, it has been contended that 'in part' seems to mean 'a substantial part'[37] of the group, and that both a quantitative and a qualitative approach can be used to establish whether or not part of the targeted group constitutes a substantial part.[38]

Finally, the genocidal intent must aim at the destruction of the group 'as such'. This requirement makes it clear that the ultimate intended victim of genocide is the group, whose destruction is sought by the perpetrator through carrying out the prohibited acts against its individual members or the group itself.[39]

Is the existence of a genocidal policy a legal ingredient of the crime of genocide?

The word genocide reminds us of the extermination of thousands, if not millions of people, on account of their membership in a particular group and in the pursuance of a state policy. However, the definition of genocide enshrined in the Genocide Convention does not expressly require the existence of such a policy, and as a matter of fact does not even consider the number of victims of the prohibited acts as relevant. The fact that historically genocide coincides with the actual destruction of a protected group, carried out in furtherance of a genocidal policy, has not been mirrored in the legal definition of genocide, which is aimed at punishing some enumerated acts as genocide on account of the specific intent harboured by the perpetrator. The ICTR and the ICTY have clearly confirmed this view,[40] although they have admitted that the existence of a genocidal plan may be useful to establish whether the perpetrator of one of the prohibited acts of genocide possesses the required genocidal intent.[41]

Some distinguished commentators consider this stand to be incorrect and argue that a contextual element, in the form of genocidal campaign, or at least of a pattern of collective violence against the group, is necessary.[42] To bolster this proposition, it is maintained that it would be unrealistic for a single individual to aim at the destruction of a group; therefore, the genocidal intent must perforce be directed to the result of a collective endeavour to which the single individual contributes.[43] This view has also been echoed in the case law.[44] It also finds some support in the Elements of Crimes of the International Criminal Court (ICC), according to which the conduct must take place 'in the context of a manifest pattern of similar conduct directed against the group or was conduct that could itself effect [the] destruction [of the group]'.

As it is clear, the question of the need for the existence of a genocidal policy is in fact closely intertwined with whether the specific intent to destroy one of the protected groups, in whole or in part, must be 'genuine' (to use the expression of the ICTR Trial Chamber in *Mpambara*).[45] The existence of a genocidal policy or campaign against the targeted group will in fact make it possible for the perpetrator to form a 'realistic' intent to attain the destruction of the group; the conduct of the perpetrator will in fact aim at the same result pursued by others, thus creating a genuine threat to the existence of the group.

Nonetheless, it would be incorrect to conclude that the genocidal policy or campaign is one of the legal ingredients of genocide. Even admitting that historically genocide has been perpetrated within a genocidal context, still it is theoretically possible that a lone perpetrator may realistically aim at the destruction of a targeted group in the absence of such a context. An example is the one already described: namely, that of the individual who possesses a weapon of mass destruction. Another example is the attack, by a single individual, against the leadership of the group, that may realistically endanger its existence at least in part.

It is on account of these considerations that one may perhaps understand why the ICC Elements of Crimes provide, with respect to genocide, that the conduct either must take place in the context of a manifest pattern of similar conduct directed against the group, *or* must be of a kind that *could itself effect* the destruction of the targeted group. If a *single* conduct may pose a threat to the existence of the group, regardless of the existence of a genocidal policy, the act carried out by the perpetrator can amount to genocide. As the Pre-Trial Chamber of the ICC has put it in Al Bashir, the presence of one of these two requirements clarifies that:

> the crime of genocide is only completed when the relevant conduct presents a concrete threat to the existence of the targeted group, or a part thereof. In other words, the protection offered by the penal norm defining the crime of genocide—as an ultima ratio mechanism to preserve the highest values of the international community—is only triggered when the threat against the existence of the targeted group, or part thereof, becomes concrete and real, as opposed to just being latent or hypothetical.[46]

The legal definition of genocide for the purpose of state responsibility

Does the prohibition of genocide, as defined in the Genocide Convention and other subsequent international instruments for the purpose of international criminal liability, also apply to states as such? Or is the definition of genocide different when it comes to issues of international state responsibility?

This question has been tackled for the first time by the International Court of Justice ('the Court') in the so-called *Bosnian Genocide* case (Bosnia Herzegovina v. Serbia). The Court had to establish, *inter alia,* whether Serbia had committed genocide in Bosnia and Herzegovina and had therefore acted in violation of the Genocide Convention. The Court eventually found that it had not, although it found that Serbia had breached its obligation under the Convention to prevent and punish genocide.[47] By so doing, it applied the definition of the crime of genocide enshrined in the Genocide Convention to the field of international state responsibility. In practice, the Court found that a state is responsible for genocide when a person or group whose acts are legally attributable to the state commits genocide. Individual criminal liability for genocide has thus been considered by the Court as a sort of prerequisite for state responsibility to arise, since there arises the need to establish that persons or groups acting on behalf of the state have indeed committed the crime of genocide to make the state internationally responsible for its perpetration.[48]

The approach taken by the Court has the merit of making it clear—although indirectly—that acts constituting international crimes, such as genocide, when perpetrated by state organs in their official capacity, cannot be considered as acts of a private nature.[49] However, this approach is not flawless. The most relevant deficiency concerns the idea that an inter-state tribunal such as the International Court of Justice (ICJ), which clearly is not endowed with criminal jurisdiction, can in fact find that a given individual has committed an act of genocide. In criminal law, it is crystal clear that no one can be considered responsible for having violated a criminal rule until a competent criminal tribunal has so found. This is so because of the basic principle of the presumption of innocence, which mandates that the criminal behaviour of an individual be established at trial, and with all the guarantees and safeguards of a fair trial.[50]

When one deals with acts that can engage the personal responsibility of individuals under international law, one is tempted to believe that the same primary rule—once breached by a state official or person acting on its behalf—can give rise to the state's international responsibility for the corresponding wrongful act. This, however, is an assumption not fully supported by international practice. On the contrary, there are reasons to believe that the two forms of responsibility are fully independent of each other from the start, i.e. because they are triggered by the *violation of non-identical primary rules.*

Consider, for instance, war crimes, and in particular the grave breaches provisions enshrined in the 1949 Geneva Conventions and their relationship with state responsibility. If a soldier kills a prisoner of war, the responsibility of the state for the violation of the rules on the treatment of prisoners of war would automatically follow, unless that state can demonstrate the absence of fault on the part of the soldier. Nobody would contend that for state responsibility to arise it is also necessary to prove that the soldier intended to kill or that he acted out of recklessness. However, to establish the criminal liability of the soldier for the corresponding war crime or grave breach, such proof will be necessary, and the burden of proof will rest upon the prosecution. Moreover, nobody would contend that a state is responsible for war crimes on the basis of a single case or a host of cases of killings of prisoners of war, unless it is established that these crimes are committed on a large scale, i.e. because they constitute what Röling defined as 'system criminality'.[51] When there is evidence of this system criminality, one could argue that to establish the responsibility of the state for war crimes one can avoid inquiring whether, in every single instance, the individual who acted on behalf of the state had a criminal mental attitude (*mens rea*). What suffices here is proof of the existence of a pattern of violence and the possibility of inferring from this pattern the acquiescence in, or even approval of, the criminal behaviour of their subordinates by the state's military and political authorities.[52]

Arguably, *mutatis mutandis* similar reasoning can be applied to genocide. If one contends, contrary to what the Court held, that the Genocide Convention is a treaty that obliges states to prevent and punish genocide as a criminal act committed by individuals, there is no reason to believe that the definition of genocide contained in the Convention also applies to state responsibility. Clearly, the Genocide Convention aims at ensuring the punishment of individuals engaging in genocide regardless of whether or not they acted as state officials. Genocide is defined in the Convention in criminal terms, and this comes as no surprise, since this definition had to be adopted by contracting states within their own criminal legal systems to prevent and punish genocide. Why, then, maintain that the same definition describes the prohibition of genocide incumbent upon states? In fact, arguably the obligation on states not to perpetrate genocide, far from being rooted in the Genocide Convention, originates in customary international law. It evolved from the emergence in contemporary international law of a set of international obligations of fundamental importance for the international community as a whole that constitute the so-called *jus cogens*. This customary rule on the obligation of states not to engage in genocide 'attracted', as it were, many elements of the definition of genocide enshrined in the 1948 Convention, but remained independent of that Convention. It is a fact that, when referred to state responsibility, genocide has generally been considered as a wrongful act requiring a systematic attack on human rights. For instance, back in 1976, the International Law Commission (ILC)—when commenting upon the former Article 19 on the so-called crimes of states—considered that a telling example of international crime was 'a large-scale or systematic practice adopted in contempt of the rights and dignity of the human being', such as 'genocide', thereby recognizing that genocide—as a particularly serious wrongful act of a state—always presupposes systematic practice.[53] The ILC took a similar position in 2001, when it explicitly said that 'the prohibition of . . . genocide, by [its] very nature require[s] an intentional violation on a large scale'.[54]

In addition, there has never been an attempt to maintain that a state was responsible for genocide without an allegation that that state was pursuing a genocidal policy against a particular group. Whenever it has been maintained that a state has engaged in genocide, there has always been a systematic attack on a particular group allegedly in pursuance of a governmental plan or policy. This was the case with the attacks against the Kurds by the Ottoman Empire, or on the Jews by the Nazis, or on the Tutsis in Rwanda. As regards Darfur, the UN Commission of Inquiry found that attacks against the so-called African tribes could not be categorized as acts of genocide committed by Sudan precisely because the Commission was unable to find evidence of the genocidal intent of the supreme political authorities of the state, thereby implying that there was no proof of a plan or policy of genocide.[55] On the contrary, as stated before, genocide as an act of individual criminality does not expressly require the existence of a state plan or policy of genocide.

In sum, it is possible to argue that states are certainly bound not to commit genocide, but in terms not identical to those embodied in the Genocide Convention. As a crime, genocide requires a special intent (*dolus specialis*) of the perpetrator; furthermore, in some instances it can also be committed in the absence of a state genocidal policy or even a collective act of violence. By contrast, as a wrongful act of states of exceptional seriousness, genocide always requires the existence of a genocidal policy and hence a pattern of widespread and systematic violence against a given group. For the international responsibility of the state to arise, however, there would be no need to demonstrate that the state as such—or one or more of its officials—harboured a genocidal intent in the criminal sense. This is a requirement that only pertains to the criminal liability of individuals. Absent direct evidence of the existence of a genocidal policy, it would only be necessary to prove that, because of the overall pattern of violence; the ultimate goal of the state policy cannot but be that of destroying the targeted group as such.

Only by recognizing that criminal responsibility is one thing and state responsibility is quite another is it possible to fully bring to fruition the notion that there is—under international law—a dual regime of responsibility for serious violations of human rights and other norms of concern for the international community as such. These two distinct legal regimes aim to protect the same values, but from different perspectives, and additionally they apply to different subjects. It is only natural that they are triggered by rules that, although pursuing the same objectives, are not identical in content because they operate on different levels. Since states are abstract entities and have a collective dimension, it is not unrealistic or absurd to maintain that they can commit genocide only when there is a policy or plan against a targeted group. This requirement is unnecessary if one wants to ensure that, at the individual level, genocide is not committed. If one shifts from the collective/state dimension to that of individuals, it is only logical to focus upon the frame of mind of those who have a criminal mental attitude towards a particular group, and intend to pursue its destruction—with or without any state support.

Notes

1 R. Lemkin, *Axis Rule in Occupied Europe: Laws of Occupation, Analysis of Governments, Proposals for Redress*, Washington, DC: Carnegie Endowment for International Peace, 1944, p. 79.

2 See in this regard Y. Shany, 'The Road to the Genocide Convention and Beyond', in P. Gaeta (ed.), *The UN Genocide Convention. A Commentary*, Oxford: Oxford University Press, 2009, p. 7.

3 The word genocide was neither used in the Charter establishing the International Military Tribunal for the Far East (the so-called Tokyo Tribunal), nor in the final judgment issued by this Tribunal. It was, however, used in the indictment before the IMT, in some of the speeches of the Prosecutors before such a Tribunal, and in the *Justice* case before a US military court sitting at Nuremberg and operating under Control Council Law No. 10. See, also for the necessary reference, Shany, 'The Road to the Genocide Convention', p. 7.

4 On crimes against humanity, see Chapter 8 in this volume.

5 Convention on the Prevention and Repression of the Crime of Genocide, 9 December 1948, 78 UNTS 277. The process which led to the adoption of the Convention is concisely described by N. Robinson, *The Genocide Convention. A Commentary*, New York: Institute of Jewish Affairs—World Jewish Congress, 1960, pp. 17–28. See also W. A. Schabas, *Genocide in International Law*, Cambridge: Cambridge University Press, 2nd edn, pp. 59–90.

6 Reservation to the Convention on Genocide, 1951 ICJ Rep 23, where the Court stated: 'the principles underlying the Convention are principles that are recognized by civilized nations as binding on states, even without any conventional obligation'. For some remarks on the interplay between customary international law and treaty law with respect to the prohibition of genocide, see Shany, The Road to the Genocide Convention', pp. 15–19.

7 'In the present Convention, genocide means any of the following acts committed with intent to destroy, in whole or in part, a national, ethnical, racial or religious group as such:

(a) killing members of the group;
(b) causing serious bodily or mental harm to members of the group;
(c) deliberately inflicting on the group conditions of life calculated to bring about its physical destruction, in whole or in part;
(d) imposing measures intended to prevent births within the group;
(e) forcibly transferring children of the group to another group'.

This definition has been reproduced *verbatim* in the Statutes of the International Criminal Tribunal for the former Yugoslavia (ICTY) (Article 4), the International Criminal Tribunal for Rwanda (ICTR) (Article 2), and the International Criminal Court (ICC) (Article 6). In addition, it has been adopted, usually unchanged, in most national criminal legislation. See, in the last respect, B. Saul, 'The Implementation of the Genocide Convention at the National Level', in P. Gaeta (ed.), *The UN Genocide Convention*, pp. 62–6.

8 'Prime Minister Winston Churchill's Broadcast To The World About The Meeting With President Roosevelt', 24 August 1941, available at http://www.ibiblio.org/pha/timeline/410824awp.html (accessed 27 April 2010), speaking of the mass killings committed by the Nazis in occupied Russia: 'The aggressor . . . retaliates by the most frightful cruelties. As his Armies advance, whole districts are being exterminated. Scores of thousands—literally scores of thousands - of executions in cold blood are being perpetrated by the German Police-troops upon the Russian patriots who defend their native soil. Since the Mongol invasions of Europe in the Sixteenth Century, there has never been methodical, merciless butchery on such a scale, or approaching such a scale. And this is but the beginning. Famine and pestilence have yet to follow in the bloody ruts of Hitler's tanks. We are in the presence of a crime without a name'.

9 As the Trial Chamber of the ICTR put it in *Akayesu,* 'the victim is chosen not because of his individual identity, but rather on account of his membership of a national, ethnical, racial or religious group'. [Akayesu (ICTR-96-4-T), 2 September 1998, para. 521].

10 Musema (ICTR-96-13-T), 27 January 2000, para. 161. On this issue see Schabas, *Genocide*, pp. 125–6, also for further reference to case law.

11 Akayesu (ICTR-96-4-T), 2 September 1998, para. 521: 'In concrete terms, for any of the acts charged under Article 2(2) of the Statute to be a constitutive element of genocide, the act must have been committed against *one or several individuals*, because *such individual or individuals* were members of a specific group, and specifically because they belonged to this group' (emphasis added). See also Rutaganda (ICTR-96-3-T), 6 December 1999, para. 60; Musema (ICTR-96-13-T), 27 January 2000, para. 165 ('For any of the acts charged to constitute genocide, the said acts must have been committed against one or more persons because such person or persons were members of a specific group, and specifically, because of their membership in this group'); Semanza (ICTR-97-20-T), 15 May 2003, para. 316; Ndindabahizi (ICTR-2001–71-I), 15 July 2004, para. 271. See also the Elements of Crimes of the International Criminal Court (ICC) with respect to genocide, which require, for instance, that the perpetrator killed 'one or more persons'.

12 For instance, a distinguished commentator has argued that 'this broad interpretation is not consistent with the texts of the norms on genocide, which speaks of "members of a group"': A. Cassese, 'Genocide', in A. Cassese (ed.), *The Oxford Companion to International Criminal Justice*, Oxford: Oxford University Press, 2009, p. 333. *Contra* W. Schabas, *Genocide*, p. 179, who argues that 'from a grammatical standpoint, the phrase [killing members of the group] can just as easily apply to a single act of killing'.

13 See, in particular, Akayesu (ICTR-96-4-T), 2 September 1998, paras 500–1; Kayishema and Ruzindana (ICTR-95-1-A), 1 June 2001, para. 151; Semanza (ICTR-97-20-T), 15 May 2003, para. 319.

14 Akayesu (ICTR-96-4-T), 2 September 1998, para. 502.

15 Kristić (IT-98-33-T), 2 August 2001, para. 513.

16 Ibid.

17 Kayishema and Ruzindana (ICTR-95-1-A), 1 June 2001, para. 109.

18 Semanza (ICTR-97-20-T), 15 May 2003, paras 321–2; Ntagerura, Bagambiki and Imanishimwe (ICTR-99-46-T), 25 February 2004, para. 664.

19 Akayesu (ICTR-96-4-T), 2 September 1998 paras 706 and 731.

20 See the Draft of the Convention prepared by the Secretary-General of the UN: Secretariat Draft E/447, reproduced in H. Abtahi and P. Webb, *The Genocide Convention. The Travaux Préparatoires*, Leiden/Boston: Martinus Nijhoff Publisher, 2008, Volume One, p. 233.

21 The relevant comment in the Secretariat Draft explains that '[i]n such cases, the intention of the author of genocide may be less clear. Obviously, if members of a group of human beings are placed in concentration camps where the annual death rate is thirty per cent to forty per cent, the intention to commit genocide is unquestionable. There may be borderline cases where a relatively high death rate might be ascribed to lack of attention, negligence or inhumanity, which, though highly reprehensible, would not constitute evidence of intention to commit genocide. At all events, there are such borderline cases which have to be dealt with on their own merits'. (Ibid.)

22 Akayesu (ICTR-96-4-T), 2 September 1998, para. 507.

23 In this regard, also for additional reference, see F. Jesserberger, 'The Definition and the Elements of the Crime of Genocide', pp. 102–3.

24 Robinson, *The Genocide Convention*, pp. 63–4.

25 The ICC Pre-Trial Chamber, in its decision on Al Bashir, has considered that the case law of the ICTR and ICTY, by excluding that the existence of a genocidal policy constitutes a legal ingredient of genocide (on this issue, see *infra* in the text), entails that 'for the purpose of completing the crime of genocide, it is irrelevant whether the conduct in question is capable of posing any concrete threat to the existence of the targeted group, or a part thereof'. For the ICC Pre-Trial Chamber, this case law implies that 'the protection offered to the targeted groups by the penal norm defining the crime of genocide is dependent on the existence of an intent to destroy, in whole or in part, the targeted group. As soon as such intent exists and materialises in an isolated act of a single individual, the protection is triggered, regardless of whether the latent threat to the existence of the targeted group posed by the said intent has turned into a concrete threat to the existence in whole or in part of that group'. See Al Bashir (ICC-02/05-01/09-3), Decision on the Prosecutor's Application for Warrant of Arrest against Omar Hassan Ahmad Al Bashir, 4 March 2009, paras 119–20.

26 Mpambara (ICTR-01-65-T), 11 September 2006, para. 8.

27 Ibid., note 7.

28 This is the interpretation put forward by the ICTR Trial Chamber in *Akayesu*: Akayesu (ICTR-96-4-T), 2 September 1998, para. 511: 'On reading through the *travaux préparatoires* of the Genocide Convention, it appears that the crime of genocide was allegedly perceived as targeting only "stable" groups, constituted in a permanent fashion and membership of which is determined by birth, with the exclusion of the more "mobile" groups which one joins through individual voluntary commitment, such as political and economic groups. Therefore, a common criterion in the four types of groups protected by the Genocide Convention is that membership in such groups would seem to be normally not challengeable by its members, who belong to it automatically, by birth, in a continuous and often irremediable manner'.

29 Akayesu (ICTR-96-4-T), 2 September 1998, para. 512. This definition of 'national group' has been criticized, among others, by Schabas, who rightly observes that the ICTR Trial Chamber has mixed up the notion of 'nationality' with that of membership in a national group by referring, as it did, to the decision of the International Court of Justice in *Nottembohm* to ground the definition of 'national group'. Schabas correctly underlines that in the *Nottembohm* case the Court focussed on the effectiveness of the nationality, in the sense of citizenship, of an individual, and did not examine at all the question of individuals who, while sharing cultural, linguistic and other bonds of a particular 'nation', have in fact the citizenship of another State or have even stateless: see W. Schabas, *Genocide*, pp. 134–5.

30 Ibid., para. 514.

31 Ibid., para. 513.

32 Ibid., para. 515.

33 The paradigmatic example is that of 'racial group', since the notion of race or racial group does not find room from a scientific point of view.

34 Akayesu (ICTR-96-4-T), 2 September 1998, para. 702.

35 Report of the International Commission of Inquiry on Darfur to the United Nations Secretary General, 25 January 2005 (UN Doc. S/2005/60), paras 509–12.

36 See text *supra* note 10.

37 See the Commentary on Article 17 (on genocide) of the Draft Code of Crimes against the Peace and Security of Mankind, adopted in 1996 by the UN International Law Commission (ILC), p. 45, para. 8., where the ILC observes: 'the intention must be to destroy a group "in whole or in part". It is not necessary to intend to achieve the complete annihilation of a group from every corner of the globe. None the less the crime of genocide by its very nature requires the intention to destroy at least a substantial part of a particular group'.

38 Kayishema and Ruzindana (ICTR-95-1-T), 21 May 1999, paras 96–7. On this issue and for further reference see Jessberger, 'The Definition and the Elements of the Crime of Genocide', pp. 108–9.

39 Akayesu (ICTR-96-4-T), 2 September 1998, para. 521. For further reference in international case, see Jessberger, 'The Definition and the Elements of the Crime of Genocide', p. 109, note 135.

40 Kayishema and Ruzindana, (ICTR-95-1-T), 21 May 1999, para. 94; Jelisić (IT-95-10-A), 5 July 2001, para. 48.

41 Ibid.

42 See, for instance, W. Schabas, *Genocide*, pp. 243–56. See also, among others, A. K. A. Greenawalt, 'Rethinking Genocidal Intent: the Case for a Knowledge-Based Interpretation', *Columbia Law Review*, 1999, vol. 99, p. 2259; C. Kress, 'The Darfur Report and Genocidal Intent', *Journal of International Criminal Justice*, 2005, vol. 3, p. 562. Another distinguished commentator argues instead that three out of the five acts that may amount to genocide 'not only presuppose, but rather take the shape of, some sort of collective or even organized action', namely: (i) deliberately inflicting on a protected group or members thereof conditions of life calculated to bring about its physical destruction, in whole or in part; (ii) imposing measures intended to prevent births within a protected group; (iii) forcibly transferring children of a protected group to another group'. It is maintained that these acts 'are necessarily carried out on a large scale and by a multitude of individuals in pursuance of a common plan, possibly with the support of at least the acquiescence of the authorities'. See A. Cassese, *Genocide*, p. 335. See also A. Cassese, *International Criminal Law*, Oxford: Oxford University Press, 2008, 2nd edn, p. 141; A. Cassese, 'Is Genocidal Policy a Requirement for the Crime of Genocide?', in P. Gaeta (ed.), *The UN Genocide Convention*, pp. 134–6.

43 As Kress put it: 'An individual perpetrator cannot realistically *desire* the destruction of a protected group to occur *as a result* of his or her *individual genocidal conduct*. The perpetrator's desire must rather be related

to the *results* to be brought about by the *collective activity* to which he or she contributes' (C. Kress, 'The Darfur Report', p. 566).

44 In Krstić (IT-98-33-T), 2 August 2001, para. 682, the Trial Chamber has stated that the genocidal acts must be committed 'in the context of a manifest pattern of similar conduct, or themselves [must] constitute a conduct that could in itself effect the destruction of the group, in whole or in part, as such'. What is requested here, as it is clear, is the systematic or widespread attack against a protected group, to use two expressions that describe the contextual element of crimes against humanity.

45 See text *supra* note 26.

46 Al Bashir (ICC-02/05-01/09-3), Decision on the Prosecutor's Application for Warrant of Arrest against Omar Hassan Ahmad Al Bashir, 4 March 2009, para. 124.

47 Case Concerning the Application of the Convention on the Prevention and Punishment of the Crime of Genocide (Bosnia and Herzegovina v. Serbia and Montenegro) ICJ 2007.

48 On this issue, I take the liberty to refer to P. Gaeta, 'On What Conditions Can A State Be Responsible for Genocide?', *European Journal of International Law*, 2007, vol. 18, p. 631. The following part of this contribution is based in part on such writing.

49 The view that international crimes must always be deemed to pertain to the private sphere was propounded in national case law with regard to the question of immunity from foreign criminal jurisdiction of individuals accused of committing an international crime while acting in their official capacity. It served the purpose of denying the applicability of the so-called immunity *ratione materiae*: in sum, national courts and tribunals maintained that a state official cannot enjoy any immunity from foreign criminal jurisdiction by reason of having acted *qua* state official, since international crimes are necessarily committed in a private capacity. This view has been taken, for instance, by some of Their Lordships in Pinochet (*R v. Bartle and the Commissioner of Police for the Metropolis and Others, ex Parte Pinochet, /* House /of /Lords, 24/ March /1999). Available at: www.publications.parliament.uk/pa/ld199899/ldjudgmt/ jd990324/pino1.htm (accessed 27 April 2010), and was even echoed by the Court itself in the *Arrest Warrant* case (Case Concerning the Arrest Warrant of 11 April 2000, ICJ 2002, para. 61). However, as has been aptly noted by a commentator, this legal construct entails that the international crimes perpetrated by state officials, being considered acts of a private nature, cannot be attributed to the state as such and cannot entail its international responsibility (M. Spinedi, 'State Responsibility v. Individual Responsibility for International Crimes: *Tertium Non Datur?*', *European Journal of International* Law, 2002, vol. 13, p. 895). In the present case, the Court, by assuming that persons who committed genocide can entail the state's international responsibility for their conduct if they acted *qua* state officials, implicitly—but indisputably—rejected the notion that the international crimes are, by their very nature, instances of private criminality, and hence can never be attributed to a state.

50 It is perhaps on account of the inevitable practical difficulties it had to face that the Court, in order to adjudicate on the dispute brought before it, relied so heavily upon the case law of the ICTY.

51 B.V. A. Röling, 'The Significance of the Laws of War', in A. Cassese (ed.), *Current Problems of International* Law, Milano: Giuffré, 1975, pp. 137–9.

52 Another example is that of the crime of torture as a discrete crime. If one accepts the view that the crime of torture, as defined in the 1984 UN Convention, is also prohibited in customary international law, it would, however, be at odds with state practice to contend that a state, by virtue of customary law, can be considered responsible for having committed torture by reason of only a single occurrence of the crime. A pattern of state criminality is required to this effect. See, for instance, the *obiter dictum* of the ICTY Trial Chamber II in the judgment delivered on 10 December. 1998 in Furundžija (IT-95-17/1-T), at para. 141, where it held: '[i]f carried out as an extensive practice of State officials, torture amounts to a serious breach on a widespread scale of an international obligation of essential importance for safeguarding the human beings, this constituting a particularly grave wrongful act generating State responsibility'.

53 See *Yearbook of the International Law Commission* at 121, para. 70, Vol. II, Part Two (1976).

54 See the commentary on Art. 40 of the Articles on State Responsibility. Available at http://untreaty.un.org/ilc/texts/instruments/english/commentaries/9_6_2001.pdf (accessed 27 April 2010).

55 Report of the International Commission of Inquiry on Darfur to the Secretary General, Pursuant to SC Res. 1564, 18 September. 2004, Annex to Letter of 31 January 2005 from the Secretary-General to the President of the Security Council, S/2005/60, at para. 518.

8
Crimes against humanity

Margaret M. deGuzman

Crimes against humanity are serious inhumane acts committed in a context that transforms them from crimes of exclusive domestic jurisdiction to crimes under international law. Unlike the other prototypically international crimes—war crimes and genocide—the proscription against crimes against humanity has yet to be enshrined in an international convention. Instead, the law of crimes against humanity has developed piecemeal, primarily through the work of the International Law Commission (ILC), the jurisprudence of various international tribunals interpreting divergent definitions, and most recently the work of the International Criminal Court (ICC). As a result of this disorganized history, important normative and doctrinal questions remain unanswered. In particular, the context required to qualify an inhumane act as a crime against humanity is subject to considerable controversy. After describing the historical origins and evolution of crimes against humanity, this chapter explores the normative debates and doctrinal ambiguities that surround this category of international crimes.

Historical origins

The concept of 'crimes against humanity' emerged in response to the massive government-orchestrated atrocities of the first half of the twentieth century. Until that time, international law, girded by respect for state sovereignty, rarely sought to reach conduct contained within state borders. In the twentieth century, however, the confluence of globalization and massive crimes perpetrated within state borders motivated the rapid development of international laws aimed at protecting people from governments. The emergence of crimes against humanity as a category of international crimes was one manifestation of this phenomenon. Crimes against humanity therefore owe strong allegiance to international human rights law.

At the same time, this category of crimes has deep roots in humanitarian law. The laws of war have long held that certain conduct in war is illegal and even criminal. Moreover, humanitarian law recognized as early as the Hague Conventions, a source of law routed in morality—the 'laws of humanity'. The 1907 Hague Convention's famous 'Martens clause' declares that in cases not otherwise covered in the convention 'the inhabitants and the belligerents remain under the protection and the rule of the principles of the law of nations, as they result from the usages established among civilized peoples, from the laws of humanity, and the dictates of the public conscience'.[1]

The natural law concept of 'laws of humanity' provided a convenient starting point for those seeking to justify punishing the perpetrators of large-scale human rights violations within state borders. It was a short step from 'laws of humanity' to 'crimes against humanity'.

The first official use of the term 'crimes against humanity' came in 1915 when the governments of Great Britain, France, and Russia jointly declared the Turkish atrocities against Turkish Armenians to be 'crimes against humanity and civilization for which all the members of the Turkish Government will be held responsible . . . '.[2] Although this declaration proved merely hortatory, the stage was set for the second attempt to pursue prosecutions outside the strict confines of conventional war crimes. After World War I, there was considerable support among the Allies for trying the losers not only for violations of the laws of war but also for violating the 'laws of humanity'.[3] The American delegation objected, however, that such prosecutions would be based on morality rather than law and the provision was deleted.[4] It took the Nazi massacre of six million Jews to finally catalyze the codification and prosecution of crimes against humanity.

Evolution of the definition

Nuremberg, Tokyo, and Control Council Law No. 10

The Charter of the International Military Tribunal for the Trial of German Major War Criminals ('Nuremberg Charter') represents the first codification of crimes against humanity. The Nuremberg Charter defines crimes against humanity as:

> murder, extermination, enslavement, deportation, and other inhumane acts committed against any civilian population, before or during the war, or persecutions on political, racial or religious grounds in execution of or in connection with any crime within the jurisdiction of the Tribunal, whether or not in violation of the domestic law of the country where perpetrated.[5]

This definition was largely replicated in the Charter of the International Military Tribunal for the Far East ('Tokyo Tribunal').[6] Although rooted in humanitarian law as noted above, the inclusion of crimes against humanity in the Nuremberg and Tokyo Charters was undoubtedly revolutionary: for the first time, international law reached crimes committed within, rather than between, sovereign states. The prosecution of crimes against humanity before these tribunals helped erode the previously sacred precept that 'civilized nations' should not interfere in one another's internal affairs.[7]

The Nuremberg judgment's embrace of the new concept was circumscribed, however, by its requirement that crimes against humanity be committed in connection with the other crimes within the Tribunal's jurisdiction: that is to say, war crimes and crimes against peace. As a result of this 'war nexus', the Tribunal refused to consider crimes that occurred before the outbreak of the war even though the definition explicitly included inhumane acts committed 'before or during the war'.[8] This jurisdictional link to war seems to have been an effort to justify international jurisdiction over these newly minted crimes. Linking crimes against humanity to the ostensibly treaty-based war crimes and crimes against peace provided a shield against charges that prosecutions for these crimes violated the principle of legality or *nullum crimen sine lege*. According to Justice Jackson who negotiated the Charter on behalf of the United States, a 'war connection' was necessary for the Tribunal to adjudicate atrocities, which would otherwise remain internal state affairs.[9] William Schabas has suggested another motivation for the war nexus—the

Allies' unwillingness to open their treatment of minorities to international scrutiny.[10] Whatever its genesis, the war nexus proved a controversial aspect of the law of crimes against humanity for many years to come.

In addition to the Nuremberg and Tokyo Charters, crimes against humanity were enshrined in Control Council Law No. 10 (CCL No. 10), a law enacted to provide a uniform basis for the Allies to prosecute war criminals other than those tried at Nuremberg in their respective zones of occupation.[11] CCL No. 10 eliminated the war nexus, although the judges implementing the law sometimes adhered to the requirement nonetheless.[12] Importantly, CCL No. 10 also added imprisonment, torture and rape to the enumerated inhumane acts and clarified that the list is exemplary rather than exhaustive.[13]

Despite Nuremberg's war nexus, the post-war prosecutions for crimes against humanity have been widely criticized as violations of the principle of legality. After all, before the Nuremberg Charter crimes against humanity existed, if at all, only in the moral realm of the Martens Clause's 'laws of humanity' and 'dictates of the public conscience'. When the defendants raised this defense, however, they received an unsympathetic and generally uncritical response from the judges, with one exception. Justice Pal of the Tokyo Tribunal wrote a now famous dissent rejecting the legality of the trial and describing it as 'a sham employment of legal process for the satisfaction of a thirst for revenge'.[14] Whatever the merits of this view at the time, the law proscribing crimes against humanity soon became firmly entrenched in customary international law.

Genocide Convention

Instead of pursuing an international convention on crimes against humanity in the post-war years, the international community, propelled significantly by the passion of Rafael Lemkin, adopted the Convention on the Prevention and Punishment of the Crime of Genocide ('Genocide Convention').[15] Genocide is a subcategory of crimes against humanity centered on the intent to destroy, in whole or in part, a particular group of people. While Lemkin encountered substantial political resistance as he sought to propel the Genocide Convention forward, there is little doubt that any similar effort at that time to codify the broader concept of crimes against humanity would have been a non-starter. The concept of genocide both captured the essence of the recent Nazi crimes and provided a moral prototype with which it was hard to disagree. Governments were hard pressed to resist international jurisdiction over genocide in the name of state sovereignty. In contrast, crimes against humanity were ill-defined and seemed to present a significantly greater danger of infringing on state sovereignty.

This early international focus on genocide resulted in the fragmentation of the law of atrocity crimes and delayed the process of shaping the norm of crimes against humanity. Genocide acquired a cachet in the popular imagination such that crimes against humanity are often viewed as less serious and therefore less worthy of attention. For example, an international commission of experts provoked an outcry when it declared that crimes against humanity rather than genocide were taking place in Darfur. Although the commission's report stated that the crimes in Darfur were 'no less serious and heinous than genocide',[16] many were outraged and feared that the finding would decrease the world's willingness to take action.

Work of the International Law Commission

Between World War II and the Balkan crisis of the 1990s discussion of crimes against humanity took place primarily at the United Nations International Law Commission (ILC). The ILC undertook several tasks relevant to this category of crimes: it formulated the principles of international law recognized in the Nuremberg Charter and Judgment, drafted a statute for an international criminal court, and prepared a draft code of offences against the peace and security of mankind ('Draft Code'). In discussing the Draft Code, in particular, the ILC debated the appropriate content of the law of crimes against humanity.

The ILC's 1954 Draft Code defined crimes against humanity as inhumane acts or persecutions 'committed against any civilian population on social, political, racial, religious or cultural grounds by the authorities of a State or by private individuals acting at the instigation or with the toleration of such authorities'.[17] This definition omitted the Nuremberg Charter's war nexus but added requirements of state involvement and discrimination. The Commission had decided that what should distinguish crimes against humanity from ordinary crimes was not the wartime context, as Justice Jackson had envisioned, but the involvement of the state and the perpetrator's motives.[18]

When the ILC revisited the definition to produce its 1991 draft, it deleted both of these requirements, however. The commentary to the provision notes that 'private individuals with de facto power or organized in criminal gangs or groups' could also commit these crimes.[19] Instead, what now distinguished crimes against humanity from ordinary crimes was that they were committed 'in a systematic manner or on a mass scale'.[20] In fact, the ILC changed the title of the provision from 'crimes against humanity' to 'systematic or mass violations of human rights'.[21] In addition to highlighting the new defining feature of these crimes, this title change reflected a desire to link this category of crimes more closely to human rights law, which had developed considerably since the post-war period.[22]

The 1996 Draft Code, the ILC's last attempt to define crimes against humanity, significantly influenced the drafters of the Rome Statute of the International Criminal Court ('Rome Statute'). This version returned to the label 'crimes against humanity', retained the requirement of scale or systematicity, and reinstated a modified version of the state action requirement—the crimes now had to be 'instigated or directed by a Government or by any organization or group'.[23] Furthermore, the list of inhumane acts was expanded significantly and was changed from an exhaustive to an exemplary list.

International Criminal Tribunals for former Yugoslavia and Rwanda

In 1993, the International Criminal Tribunal for former Yugoslavia (ICTY) was established to prosecute perpetrators of war crimes, genocide, and crimes against humanity in the Balkan conflict. The ICTY statute defines crimes against humanity as:

> the following crimes when committed in armed conflict, whether international or internal in character, and directed against any civilian population:
> (a) murder;
> (b) extermination;
> (c) enslavement;
> (d) deportation;
> (e) imprisonment;
> (f) torture;
> (g) rape;
> (h) persecutions on political, racial, and religious grounds;
> (i) other inhumane acts.[24]

This definition revived the Nuremberg Charter's war nexus (modified to include internal armed conflict) in an effort to avoid challenges based on the principle of legality. Although the nexus was absent from CCL No. 10, courts operating under that law had left an ambiguous legacy and the work of the ILC did not provide a legal basis for rejecting the nexus. Nonetheless, the ICTY Appellate Chamber recognized as early as 1995 that customary international law did not require a nexus with *international* armed conflict as Nuremberg had, and might not mandate any nexus with armed conflict at all.[25] Additionally, although the ICTY drafters did not follow the ILC's lead in defining crimes against humanity as massive or systematic, the ICTY's judges have read such a requirement into the definition.[26] Finally, the ICTY definition expands the Nuremberg Charter's list of inhumane acts to include imprisonment, torture, and rape.

Although drafted only a year later, the 1994 Statute of the International Criminal Tribunal for Rwanda (ICTR) contains a significantly different definition of crimes against humanity than the ICTY statute. The ICTR statute includes the same non-exhaustive list of inhumane acts but specifies that they must be committed 'as part of a widespread or systematic attack against any civilian population on national, political, ethnic, racial or religious grounds'.[27] The ICTR statute was thus the first binding legal instrument to codify the ILC's notion that what distinguishes crimes against humanity from domestic crimes is their large-scale or systematic nature rather than their connection to armed conflict. In addition, the ICTR statute is the first legal instrument to inject a discrimination requirement into the definition. The inclusion of discriminatory 'grounds' in the ICTR definition is somewhat surprising given that both the drafters of the Nuremberg Charter[28] and later the ILC had rejected this element.

International Criminal Court

In 1998, the international community came together in Rome to draft and adopt the Rome Statute of the International Criminal Court (Rome Statute and ICC). The Rome Statute's provision on crimes against humanity reads as follows:

1. For the purpose of this Statute, 'crime against humanity' means any of the following acts when committed as part of a widespread or systematic attack directed against any civilian population, with knowledge of the attack:
   (a) murder;
   (b) extermination;
   (c) enslavement;
   (d) deportation or forcible transfer of population;
   (e) imprisonment or other severe deprivation of physical liberty in violation of fundamental rules of international law;
   (f) torture;
   (g) rape, sexual slavery, enforced prostitution, forced pregnancy, enforced sterilization, or any other form of sexual violence of comparable gravity;
   (h) persecution against any identifiable group or collectivity on political, racial, national, ethnic, cultural, religious, gender as defined in paragraph 3, or other grounds that are universally recognized as impermissible under international law, in connection with any act referred to in this paragraph or any crime within the jurisdiction of the Court;
   (i) enforced disappearance of persons;
   (j) the crime of apartheid;
   (k) other inhumane acts of a similar character intentionally causing great suffering, or serious injury to body or to mental or physical health.

2. For the purpose of paragraph (1):
   (a) 'Attack directed against any civilian population' means a course of conduct involving the multiple commission of acts referred to in paragraph (1) against any civilian population, pursuant to or in furtherance of a State or organizational policy to commit such attack.[29]

This definition represents some combination of consensus on the appropriate contours of the norm and political compromise. As evidenced above, the precedents that formed the basis for discussions of crimes against humanity in Rome left open important questions about the nature of these crimes. As such, government delegations held divergent views about what the law required as well as what it ought to require. The Rome Statute therefore does not purport to crystallize the international law of crimes against humanity. On the contrary, the Statute itself declares that the definitions of crimes therein should not 'be interpreted as limiting or prejudicing in any way existing or developing rules of international law for purposes other than [the] Statute'.[30] In fact, definitions of crimes against humanity adopted since the Rome Statute have diverged from the latter in important respects, as described below. Nonetheless, the Rome Statute's definition is the only one that has been adopted by a large segment of the world's states[31] and thus carries significant authority. Furthermore, as states enact domestic legislation proscribing crimes against humanity they look to the Rome Statute for guidance. As such, despite the Rome Statute's admonition to the contrary, the ICC definition may well come to embody customary international law over time.

Whatever the relationship between customary law and the Rome Statute, the ICC definition does appear to have laid to rest at least one important and long-standing debate about these crimes: the Nuremberg Charter's nexus with armed conflict has clearly been rejected as an element of crimes against humanity. This was not a foregone conclusion at the Rome Conference. Rather, a number of state delegations argued adamantly in favor of a war nexus. Not surprisingly, however, the vast majority of participants rejected such a limitation as a relic of an age when respect for state sovereignty was significantly stronger than it is today. The timing of the rejection of the nexus under customary law remains important for courts adjudicating pre-1998 crimes but there is no question that by 1998 at the latest the nexus is gone.

Contrary to the vision some held when crimes against humanity were originally conceived then, it is not the context of international conflict that gives rise to international jurisdiction over crimes against humanity. Instead, the Rome Statute reflects the view that the context that transforms an individual inhumane act into a crime against humanity is the connection between the act and a widespread or systematic attack against a civilian population as well as the perpetrator's awareness of that connection. Much of the debate about crimes against humanity at the Rome Conference therefore centered around the appropriate elements of this contextual or 'chapeau' provision. A minority of delegations argued vigorously that the attack should be conducted on discriminatory grounds, as reflected in the ICTR statute. The majority took the view, however, that discrimination was relevant only to the crime of persecution. There was also extensive debate about whether the elements of 'widespread' and 'systematic' should be conjunctive or disjunctive. Although the disjunctive approach prevailed in the first paragraph, the second paragraph undermines or even contradicts the first. The attack is defined to require both multiple acts—which invokes something close to 'widespread'—*and* a policy, which implies a certain level of systematicity. Thus, while the definition was billed as a compromise between those advocating expansive and restrictive norms,[32] in fact it more closely tracks the conservation approach.

The Rome Statute's definition also expands the list of eligible inhumane acts that has been growing since the time of the Nuremberg Charter. The list now includes several forms of sexual violence in addition to rape, as well as enforced disappearance and apartheid. The list of discriminatory grounds for persecution was expanded to include culture and gender as well as other grounds universally recognized as impermissible. At the same time, in a concession to those advocating stricter contours for these crimes, acts of persecution must be committed in connection with other inhumane acts or other crimes within the Court's jurisdiction.

Like its predecessor definitions, the Rome Statute's enumeration of inhumane acts is not exhaustive, although for this Court any 'other inhumane acts' must be 'of a similar character intentionally causing great suffering, or serious injury to body or to mental or physical health'. Finally, the Rome Statute departs from its predecessors in elaborating on the content of a number of the listed inhumane acts. For example, the definition of torture broadens the norm contained in the Convention Against Torture by omitting the requirements that torture be committed for a particular purpose and by someone acting in an official capacity.

Post-Rome conference definitions

A number of courts have been created since the ICC Statute was adopted and, interestingly, none of them has accepted the latter's definition in its entirety. The Special Court for Sierra Leone, established by agreement between the government of that country and the United Nations, defines crimes against humanity simply as any of a non-exhaustive list of inhumane acts committed 'as part of a widespread or systematic attack against any civilian population'.[33] East Timor's Serious Crimes Panel, a creation of the United Nations, adopted the first paragraph of the Rome Statute definition but not the more controversial second paragraph.[34] The Extraordinary Chambers in the Courts of Cambodia (ECCC), established under the laws of Cambodia but with substantial international influence and participation, defines crimes against humanity as inhumane acts 'committed as part of a widespread or systematic attack directed against any civilian population, on national, political, ethnical, racial or religious grounds'.[35] This definition reintroduces the discrimination requirement and does not require multiple acts or a policy, although it remains to be seen whether the judges will interpret 'attack' to include such elements. The drafters of these definitions may have opted not to follow the Rome Statute at least in part because the acts those courts adjudicate largely pre-date the Statute's adoption. Nonetheless, the lack of uniformity in the post-Rome definitions undermines claims that the Rome Statute crystallized customary international law.

In sum, the definition of crimes against humanity has taken numerous turns since first codified in the Nuremberg Charter. In fact, virtually every definition employed by an international or mixed international/domestic institution has differed in significant respects from the others. In some ways the norm has been clarified over time: crimes against humanity are not inhumane acts committed in connection with armed conflict but rather such acts when committed as part of a widespread or systematic attack against a civilian population. The multiplicity of definitions has left many questions unanswered, however. In fact, this legal diversity reveals a lack of consensus on the fundamental normative underpinnings of crimes against humanity.

Competing normative visions

Until the Rome Conference, the international community as a whole had never grappled with foundational normative questions such as: What makes an inhumane act a crime against humanity? What is the purpose of this category of crimes? What differentiates these crimes from war crimes and genocide? Even at the Rome Conference such normative discussions were constrained by various conflicting political goals. Delegations were willing to compromise their vision of crimes against humanity if the alternative was to scuttle entirely the prospect of a permanent international criminal court. As such, the Rome Conference produced a definition of crimes against humanity without an underlying normative consensus. Instead, several normative visions of crimes against humanity continue to compete for recognition in the law, jurisprudence and scholarship related to these crimes.

Threat to international peace and security

First, crimes against humanity can be seen as worthy of international jurisdiction because they threaten the peace and security of the world. This vision was a central justification for the Nuremberg Charter as reflected in the war nexus. It was the context of war—conflict between states—that justified international jurisdiction. Atrocities committed within a state with no connection to a war concerned that state alone. As already noted, some participants in the Rome Conference endorsed this perspective as late as 1998.

A broader view of the peace and security rationale encompasses threats posed by internal armed conflict. This perspective provided the legal basis for the establishment of the *ad hoc* international criminal tribunals for former Yugoslavia and Rwanda under Chapter VII of the United Nations Charter. Ultimately, the elimination of the requirement of any context of armed conflict from the definition undermined the peace and security rationale for these crimes. Of course, crimes committed in peacetime can be so serious as to disrupt fundamentally the peace and security of a state and, in our globalized world, such disruptions inevitably have extraterritorial effects. The horrendous crimes of the Khmer Rouge provide an apt example. In justifying the continued detention of one of the defendants charged with crimes against humanity, the ECCC echoed the peace and security rationale, stating: '[t]hese crimes are of a gravity such that, 30 years after their commission, they still profoundly disrupt public order . . .'.[36] As this quote demonstrates, the peace and security rationale, to the extent it still undergirds crimes against humanity, tends to rest more on the gravity of the crimes than on any concrete threat to international peace and security. Few would argue that thousands of killings on a remote island don't threaten international peace and security, even if the 'threat' evoked is more metaphysical than originally conceived. As such, the 'peace and security' rationale has become almost indistinguishable from a second normative vision that relies on the gravity of the crimes.

Gravity and the conscience of humanity

One of the most frequently invoked justifications for crimes against humanity is that they 'shock the conscience of humanity'.[37] This language evokes the Martens Clause's 'laws of humanity' and 'dictates of the public conscience'. Although the reasons for humanity's 'shock' are rarely given, this emotion seems driven largely by the gravity or seriousness of the atrocities. This view of crimes against humanity can also be conceptualized as the human rights visions—crimes against humanity are simply particularly serious violations of fundamental human rights. According to this perspective, the purpose of the *chapeau* of crimes against humanity is to capture the element of seriousness, particularly through the requirements of a targeted 'population' and a 'widespread or systematic attack'. Proponents of the gravity rationale reject the notion that crimes against humanity should require a government or organizational policy or a discriminatory intent.

The difficulty with this normative vision is that it requires a tricky line-drawing exercise. Doesn't every serious crime against a human being at some level 'shock the conscience of humanity'? And yet quite clearly every such crime is not a legitimate subject of international jurisdiction, much less a crime against humanity. Nevertheless, the gravity of the crimes remains probably the most pervasive normative justification for crimes against humanity and certainly represents the common understanding of these crimes among lay people.

State action

A third normative perspective envisions crimes against humanity as offenses committed exclusively by state actors—the ethos of crimes against humanity is the misuse of state power to attack rather than to protect. Such influential scholars as Cherif Bassiouni and William Schabas believe that the concept of crimes against humanity does not embrace all serious violations of human rights, but only those perpetrated by members of a state, or perhaps, a state-like entity.[38] For them, it is the perversion of state power that makes these crimes particularly evil and the likelihood they will go unpunished mandates the availability of international jurisdiction. Proponents of this view promote the inclusion of a state policy element in the definition of crimes against humanity. Only inhumane acts committed as part of a state policy to commit such acts rise to the level of a crime against humanity.

This vision of crimes against humanity seems accurate from a historically descriptive point of view—most of the crimes society has labeled 'crimes against humanity' have involved state policies. At the same time, this approach to the crimes against humanity norm arguably reflects an overreliance on an outdated understanding of the importance of the state. In our rapidly globalizing society, non-state actors wield ever-increasing power, including the ability to commit atrocious crimes. While it is true that domestic legal systems are generally willing to prosecute non-state actors, they are not always able to do so. Furthermore, it is far from clear that practical considerations, such as the availability of domestic courts, should drive the norm of crimes against humanity. After all, such crimes are intended for prosecution in both international and domestic courts.

Group-based harm

A fourth approach to crimes against humanity considers the particular evil they embody to be the targeting of a group. For David Luban, for example, the rationale for crimes against humanity lies in the interest all humans share 'in ensuring people are not killed by their neighbors solely because of their group affiliation'.[39] In Luban's view, crimes against humanity are 'committed by politically organized groups against other groups in the same civil society'.[40] Another legal philosopher, Larry May, agrees that group-based harm can justify attaching the label crimes against humanity but would make such harm an alternative to state action.[41] One articulation of this approach requires that the targeted group share particular characteristics beyond the geographic proximity of its members, such as nationality, race, religion, or ethnicity. Such an approach brings the norm of crimes against humanity close to the prohibition against genocide, although without the required intent to destroy the group in whole or in part. The focus on group-based harm, like the state actor model, undoubtedly captures a primary feature of past crimes against humanity. It is less clear, however, that this approach fully expresses the appropriate norm. For example, it appears to exclude a large-scale attack on a gathering of international diplomats, surely an appropriate subject of the law of crimes against humanity.

In sum, none of the current normative approaches to crimes against humanity provides a clear and complete rationale for these crimes. For that reason, no single vision of crimes against humanity has predominated in the scholarship, law, and jurisprudence. Instead, the various approaches have competed for attention from Nuremberg to the present day. The Nuremberg Charter reflected a 'peace and security' approach as already noted. Thereafter, the ILC experimented with different rationales: the 1954 Draft Code adopted a combination of state action and discrimination; the 1991 Draft relied on seriousness, introducing the 'systematic' or 'mass scale' formula; and the 1996 Draft combined the seriousness and state action requirements. The post-Nuremberg statutes have been similarly inconsistent in their justifications, with the ICTY resurrecting the nexus with armed conflict, the ICTR requiring both seriousness and discrimination, the ICC injecting a requirement of state—or at least group—action, the Special Court for Sierra Leone (SCSL) relying on seriousness, and the ECCC re-injecting discrimination. This lack of normative uniformity in the law has left a number of important doctrinal questions unresolved.

Open doctrinal questions

What constitutes a 'widespread or systematic attack'?

The requirement that crimes against humanity are part of a widespread or systematic attack is now well established. All definitions since the ICTR statute have included this language. This requirement seems aimed primarily at capturing the seriousness of the crimes. An individual inhumane act is only a crime against humanity if it is part of a more serious attack. The 'widespread' element implies a substantial number of victims and perhaps a geographic spread of victimization. But how many victims are required and how far must they be spread? It is both implausible and morally repulsive to draw a quantitative line. The ICC addresses this issue by requiring 'multiple' inhumane acts, but that clarifies little other than that there must be at least two acts to form an attack. In fact, the ICC provision raises a new question—What is meant by 'act'? If an individual detonates a bomb that kills thousands is that a single 'act' or multiple 'acts' (e.g. acquisition of materials, construction, or detonation)? Or perhaps each of the resulting killings constitutes a separate act for the purposes of the threshold.

The case law of the tribunals has done little to clarify the meaning of 'widespread'. The judges have made some general statements, indicating, for example, that the 'widespread' element 'refers to the scale of the acts perpetrated and to the number of victims' and that a single inhumane act of extraordinary magnitude can fulfill the requirement.[42] They have not, however, identified a minimum number of victims or otherwise indicated what acts fall outside the purview of a 'widespread' attack. The judges of the current international courts probably feel little need to expound on this aspect of the definition because the conflicts at issue involve such notoriously egregious attacks. Some clarification might have been obtained had the Special Tribunal for Lebanon been permitted to try suspects for crimes against humanity. There was discussion of including such crimes in the statute of the Tribunal, which was set up to adjudicate the attack that killed former Lebanese Prime Minister Rafiq Hariri and 22 others, but ultimately the Tribunal was authorized to apply only domestic laws. The meaning of 'widespread' as a delimitation of crimes against humanity therefore remains unclear.

The 'systematic' alternative is designed to capture attacks that may not yet have reached the scale of victimization required for 'widespread' but are nonetheless serious based on their level of planning and organization. The ICC has followed the ICTY and ICTR understandings of systematic to include the following aspects: thorough organization, a regular pattern, a policy, substantial resources, a political objective, large-scale or continuous crimes that are linked, and the implication of high-level political or military authorities.[43] While helpful, this list of considerations leaves open questions regarding the level, quality, and quantity of organization required. It also fails to explain the relationship between the systematicity element and the policy requirement. For example, what sorts of policies, if any, would not qualify as systematic?

Finally, the case law is unclear as to whether the 'attack' must include acts of violence. An ICTY trial chamber has described the required attack as 'a course of conduct involving the commission of acts of violence'.[44] In contrast, an ICTR trial chamber has declared that an attack can be non-violent, including, for example, 'imposing a system of apartheid'.[45] Similarly, the SCSL has interpreted the concept of attack as encompassing 'any mistreatment of the civilian population'.[46] Although the ICC judges have yet to pronounce on the question, the Rome Statute's definition of attack seems to leave open the possibility of an attack comprised entirely of non-violent acts.

The statutes of the ICTR and ECCC require that the attack be committed on discriminatory grounds. This contextual discrimination element and its concomitant normative vision of crimes against humanity were debated and rejected in Rome. Thus, it seems likely this approach to crimes against humanity will eventually fade into history. Nonetheless, the adoption of the discrimination requirement by the post-Rome ECCC leaves open the possibility that the discrimination requirement will survive.

In sum, the outer limits of the requirement of a 'widespread or systematic attack' remain largely uncertain. Clearly, the attack need not rise to the level of armed conflict since the war nexus has been abandoned. At a minimum, the concept of 'attack' excludes individual crimes against isolated victims from the definition of crimes against humanity.[47] In practice, the question has yet to prove particularly important. The contextual element has often been stipulated by the parties or easily established with expert testimony.[48] In fact, the ICTR has been willing simply to take judicial notice of the existence of a widespread or systematic attack against civilians during the Rwandan genocide.[49]

Is a policy required and, if so what kind?

The most important definition of 'widespread or systematic attack' is of course the Rome Statute's, which requires that the attack be 'pursuant to or in furtherance of a State or organizational policy to commit such attack'. This policy requirement is probably the most controversial aspect of the definition of crimes against humanity. Although none of the pre-ICC definitions required a policy, some of the jurisprudence included this requirement. For example, in Kayishema, an ICTR trial chamber stated: 'For an act of mass victimization to be a crime against humanity, it must include a policy element'.[50] In 2002, however, the ICTY Appeals Chamber conducted an extensive review of the law on this question and concluded that proof of a policy is useful but not necessary to establish the existence of an attack against a civilian population.[51] Even after adoption of the Rome Statute, the policy element was excluded from legal instruments such as the statute of the Special Court for Sierra Leone.[52] Thus, it appears that despite the inclusion of the policy element in the Rome Statute, a policy is not a requirement for crimes against humanity under customary international law. Whether this remains true in the future will depend on the relationship between ICC law and customary international law as already discussed.

In any event, the ICC and any state or international courts that adopt the policy element in the future will have to decide the scope and impact of this requirement. In a recent decision, the ICC held that the policy must be that of a group governing a specific territory or an organization capable of committing a widespread or systematic attack against a civilian population.[53] A non-state organization must have 'the capability to perform acts which infringe on basic human values'.[54] The first option raises questions about the degree of governance required: Must the group be in complete control? What level of services and protection must it be providing to the population? The court's elaboration of the 'organization' alternative is even more perplexing. Isn't almost any group, except perhaps a group of children, capable of performing acts that infringe basic human values? Judge Kaul dissented from the decision, arguing that the policy element requires 'policy-making at the high level' and interpreting 'organization' to include only state-like organizations.[55] This debate illustrates the continuing contest between normative visions discussed above. The majority seems to support a broad interpretation of the norm, causing the dissent to worry that it 'may expand the concept of crimes against humanity to any infringement of human rights'.[56] In contrast, Judge Kaul sides with those who believe that the distinctive evil of crimes against humanity is the perversion of state power they reflect.[57]

An additional ambiguity in the policy requirement concerns the extent to which policies of omission can qualify as crimes against humanity. A footnote to the ICC's Elements of Crimes states that the policy 'may, in exceptional circumstances, be implemented by a deliberate failure to take action, which is consciously aimed at encouraging [the] attack'.[58] The question of when policies of omission will meet this 'exceptional circumstances' requirement will have real significance for the law of crimes against humanity. In particular, interpretation of this element will help to determine when state actors who tolerate terrorist attacks are liable for crimes against humanity.

Who is included in the civilian population?

The *ad hoc* tribunals have given a broad interpretation to the requirement of a targeted 'population',[59] reading the term simply to exclude isolated acts unconnected to a broader attack.[60] Furthermore, they have clarified that the attack need not target all members of a population.[61] Nonetheless, it remains unclear what types of connections among the victims will satisfy the requirement of a 'population'. A pre-trial chamber of the ICC has opined that the victims must belong to 'groups distinguished by nationality, ethnicity, or other distinguishing features'.[62] This suggests a requirement of discriminatory group targeting and leaves open which 'distinguishing features' are sufficient. Does a group of peacekeepers qualify, for example?

The requirement that the population be 'civilian' is also problematic. As the ICTY has noted:

> One fails to see why only civilians and not also combatants should be protected by these rules (in particular by the rule prohibiting persecution), given that these rules may be held to possess a broader humanitarian scope and purpose than those prohibiting war crimes.[63]

Nevertheless, the 'civilian' requirement is contained in all definitions of crimes against humanity. Furthermore, during armed conflict at least some of the rules of crimes against humanity would seem inapplicable to combatants. In particular, killing combatants in widespread and systematic attacks is an essential component of armed conflict. Courts interpreting the provision have turned to the definition of civilian in international humanitarian law, broadly including those not actively engaged in hostilities at the time of the crime regardless of their formal status.[64] They have also held that a predominantly civilian population does not lose its protected status simply because some combatants are present.[65]

The 'civilian' requirement is even more problematic when crimes against humanity are committed in peacetime. Judge Cassese, a prominent jurist and scholar of international criminal law, has written that such a limitation in peacetime contravenes international human rights and humanitarian laws.[66] Since most crimes against humanity are committed during armed conflicts, there is little jurisprudence concerning the content of 'civilian population' when such crimes are committed in peacetime. One ICTR decision on this point maintains that in peacetime all persons are civilians 'except those who have the duty to maintain public order and have the legitimate means to exercise force'.[67] No principled basis appears, however, for excluding persons such as police officers from the targeted population during peacetime. It remains to be seen whether future interpretations of crimes against humanity will adhere to this distinction or instead adopt a broader definition of 'civilian'.

What connection is required between the individual inhumane act and the attack?

An inhumane act is only a crime against humanity when it is 'part of' a widespread or systematic attack against a civilian population. This connection to the broader context is the essential element that transforms an individual murder or rape into an international crime with the enhanced moral stigma and broader jurisdiction that such designation entails. Despite the importance of this element, the outer boundaries of the law are rarely tested because most cases involve acts that are obviously linked to a broader attack. Thus, while there is some jurisprudence addressing the nature of the required nexus, further clarification is needed.

The ICTY has enunciated a test for the nexus requirement that includes both objective and subjective components. First, the act must be objectively—'by its nature and consequences'—part of the attack.[68] The judges have not, however, identified any consistent criteria that can be used to determine whether an act is part of an attack. They have stated that the act can be geographically and temporally distant from the attack[69] but have not clarified what kind of connection would satisfy the objective prong under such conditions. Instead, the standard is simply whether, considering the circumstances, the act can 'reasonably be said to have been part of the attack'.[70]

One open question is whether the individual act itself can constitute the attack, making a nexus element superfluous. The tribunals have yet to face this issue and commentators are divided.[71] The ICC's Elements of Crimes, which supplement the Rome Statute, address this question for genocide but not for crimes against humanity.[72] As noted above, the Rome Statute's requirement that the attack be composed of multiple acts may preclude a single act of mass destruction from meeting the definition of crimes against humanity—unless the term 'act' is given a broad construction.

The contextual nexus requirement also has a subjective component or *mens rea*. In addition to the *mens rea* of the inhumane act in question, the perpetrator of a crime against humanity must have some mental state with regard to the connection between that act and the contextual attack. While earlier statutes did not specify a *mens rea* for crimes against humanity, the Rome Statute requires that the perpetrator act with knowledge of the attack. The Elements of Crimes clarify that the *mens rea* is satisfied if the defendant either knew his conduct was part of the attack or intended such a connection. Although other international criminal tribunals have also generally adopted a knowledge standard,[73] some have considered it sufficient that the defendant had reason to know[74] or took the risk[75] that a connection existed between his act and the attack. The *mens rea* under customary international law thus remains unclear.

Moreover, in the case of an 'emerging' attack, the ICC's Elements of Crimes require intent to further the attack rather than mere knowledge of a connection.[76] This detail is absent from earlier law and it remains unclear when an attack should be considered 'emerging'. Finally, the introduction of the policy element in the Rome Statute gives rise to questions about the extent to which perpetrators must understand the policy behind the attack. The Elements of Crimes specify that perpetrators need not have 'knowledge of all characteristics of the attack or the precise details of the plan or policy'.[77] This provision implies that the perpetrator must have some knowledge of the policy, without explaining how much.

What crimes qualify as 'persecution' and 'other inhumane acts'?

The most difficult of the enumerated inhumane acts to define are 'persecution' and 'other inhumane acts'. As a result, the negotiations surrounding these provisions at the Rome Conference were particularly contentious. Persecution is among the most widely charged of the inhumane acts, but courts have struggled to identify the requirements for this crime. International tribunals have found a wide range of acts and omissions can constitute persecution when committed with discriminatory intent, including harassment, humiliation, psychological abuse,[78] destruction of property,[79] and even hate speech.[80] The Rome Statute restricts the contours of persecution in a number of ways. First, the Statute confines persecution to 'the intentional and severe deprivation of fundamental rights contrary to international law by reason of the identity of the group or collectivity'. The Statute also requires that persecution be committed in connection with another inhumane act or crime within the Court's jurisdiction. This is a controversial restriction since it precludes convictions based on persecution alone. Finally, the Statute constrains the judges' ability to elaborate additional grounds of discrimination by mandating that any grounds of persecution other than those listed (political, racial, national, ethnic, cultural, religious, and gender) must be 'universally recognized as impermissible under international law'. It remains unclear whether these restrictions on persecution will become part of customary international law.

The residual category of 'other inhumane acts' is, not surprisingly, another area where the law is continually evolving. In a recent noteworthy ruling, the SCSL Appeals Chamber held that forced marriage falls into this category.[81] The Appeals Chamber followed the Rome Statute and Elements in requiring that other inhumane acts meet the following criteria: (1) inflict great suffering, or serious injury to body or to mental or physical health; (2) be of similar character/gravity[82] to the listed inhumane acts; and (3) the perpetrator must have been aware of the factual circumstances that established the character/gravity of the act.[83] Despite these restrictions, judges have considerable discretion to elaborate the 'other inhumane acts' that constitute crimes against humanity.

Conclusion

Although now more than a half-century old, the law of crimes against humanity remains riddled with doctrinal ambiguities and subject to fundamental normative disagreements. The Rome Statute's consensus definition represents both a major diplomatic accomplishment and a missed opportunity for conceptual clarity. What next? A group of academics, judges, and practitioners, convened by Professor Leila Sadat and including this author, is currently pursuing Professor Bassiouni's 15-year-old call for an international convention on crimes against humanity.[84] Initial discussions of the proposed convention centered on the prospect of drafting a new definition that might clarify the normative basis for these crimes and resolve some of the doctrinal debates. The participants ultimately concluded, however, that a new definition risked undermining the ICC regime and could present a practical challenge for states that have implemented the ICC definition in their domestic-laws. Instead, the current draft convention adopts the ICC definition with only minor technical modifications.[85] If this approach ultimately prevails and the convention is widely ratified, the political compromises of the Rome Conference will be indelibly inscribed on the definition of crimes against humanity. It will be up to courts to interpret the definition in ways that, over time, develop greater conceptual and doctrinal clarity and consistency.

Even if it does not resolve the open definitional questions, a convention on crimes against humanity could make significant contributions to the law governing these crimes. For example, while many believe that universal jurisdiction over such crimes already exists in customary international law, the draft convention would provide such jurisdiction as a matter of treaty law. Moreover, the convention would require states to either prosecute or extradite perpetrators of crimes against humanity found on their territories. Finally, the convention would mandate the prevention and repression of crimes against humanity and establish a cooperative regime for addressing such crimes. If widely ratified, therefore, the convention would play an important role in strengthening the legal regime governing crimes against humanity.

Notes

1 Convention Respecting the Laws and Customs of War on Land (18 October 1907), 36 Stat. 2277, 1 Bevans 631, Preamble.
2 E. Schwelb, 'Crimes Against Humanity', *British Yearbook of International Law* 23, 1946, 181 (quoting Armenian Memorandum Presented by the Greek Delegation to the Commission of Fifteen on 14 March 1919).
3 Commission on the Responsibility of the Authors of the War and on Enforcement of Penalties, Report Presented to the Preliminary Peace Conference, reprinted in *American Journal of International Law* 14, 1920, 95, 117.
4 Memorandum of Reservations Presented by the Representatives of the United States to the Report of the Commission on Responsibilities (4 April 1919), Annex II, reprinted in 'Commission on the Responsibility of the Authors of the War and on Enforcement of Penalties: Report Presented to the Preliminary Peace Conference (29 March 1919)', *American Journal of International Law* 14, 1920, 134.
5 Agreement for the Prosecution and Punishment of the Major War Criminals of the European Axis, Annex, 59 Stat. 1544, 82 UNTS 279 (8 August 1945), Art. 6(c), reprinted in *American Journal of International Law* 39, Supp. 1945, 257 [hereinafter Nuremberg Charter].
6 Charter of the International Military Tribunal for the Far East, 4 Bevans 20 (19 January 1946), Art. 5(c) (Omitting persecutions on religious grounds).
7 *Trial of the Major War Criminals before the International Military Tribunal*, 1948, vol. 19, pp. 471–2 (1948) (remarks by Sir Hartley Shawcross, British Chief Prosecutor).
8 'International Military Tribunal (Nuremberg) Judgment and Sentences', *American Journal of International Law* 41, 1947, 175 (Nuremberg Judgment) (quoting Charter of the International Military Tribunal [Nuremberg), Art. 6(c)].
9 M. Lippman, 'Crimes Against Humanity', *Boston College Third World Law Journal* 17, 1997, 183 (quoting Jackson).
10 W. Schabas, *Genocide in International Law: The Crime of Crimes*, Cambridge: Cambridge University Press, 2000, pp. 10–11.
11 Punishment of Persons Guilty of War Crimes, Crimes Against Peace and Against Humanity, Control Council Law No. 10, 20 December 1945, 3 Official Gazette Control Council for Germany 50 (1946), reprinted in *Trials of War Criminals before the Nuremberg Military Tribunals under Control Council Law No. 10*, 1949, vol. 1, xvi–xix [hereinafter CCL No. 10].
12 M. deGuzman, 'The Road from Rome: The Developing Law of Crimes Against Humanity', *Human Rights Quarterly* 22, 2000, 357.
13 CCL No. 10, Art. 2(1)(c).
14 United States v. Araki *et al.*, Dissenting Opinion of Justice Pal, in 21 The Tokyo Major War Crimes Trial, 1981, pp. 37 (R. John Pritchard and S. Zaide, eds).
15 Convention on the Prevention and Punishment of the Crime of Genocide, 78 UNTS 277 (1951).
16 Report of the International Commission of Inquiry on Darfur to the United Nations Secretary-General, Pursuant to Security Council Resolution 1564 of 18 September 2004 (25 January 2005), 132, para. 522.
17 ILC, 'Draft Code of Offences Against the Peace and Security of Mankind', reprinted in *Yearbook of the International Law Commission*, 1954, vol. 2, 150, Art. 2(11).
18 Ibid.
19 Ibid., 1991, vol. 2, Part 2, 103–04, para. 5 [hereinafter 1991 Draft Code].
20 Ibid., p. 96, Art. 21. Although this requirement did not apply to deportation or forcible population transfer, the commentary notes that 'the crime in itself necessarily entails a mass-scale element'. Ibid. p. 104, para. 11.
21 Ibid., p. 96, Art. 21.
22 Ibid., p. 103, para. 2.

23 Ibid., 1996, vol. 2, p. 47, Art. 18 [hereinafter 1996 Draft Code].
24 Statute of the International Tribunal for the Prosecution of Persons Responsible for Serious Violations of International Humanitarian Law in the Territory of the former Yugoslavia since 1991, Art. 5, UN SCOR, Annex, UN Doc. S/25704 (1993), reprinted in *International Legal Materials* 32, 1994, 1159, 1192 [hereinafter ICTY Statute].
25 Tadic (IT-94-1), Decision on the Defense Motion for Interlocutory Appeal on Jurisdiction, 2 October 1995, para. 141.
26 Blaskic (IT-95-14-T), Judgement, 3 March 2000, para. 202.
27 Statute of the International Criminal Tribunal for the Prosecution of Persons Responsible for Genocide and Other Serious Violations of International Humanitarian Law Committed in the Territory of Rwanda and Rwandan Citizens Responsible for Genocide and Other Such Violations Committed in the Territory of Neighbouring States Between 1 January 1994 and 31 December 1994, UN Doc. S/RES/955 (1994), Art. 3.
28 M. Lippman, 'Crimes Against Humanity', 180–7
29 Rome Statute of the International Criminal Court, 2187 UNTS 90 (1998), Art. 7.
30 Ibid., Art. 10.
31 To date, 113 states are parties to the Rome Statute, although some of the most populous and most powerful states remain outside the regime, including the United States, China, and India.
32 D. Robinson, 'Defining "Crimes Against Humanity" at the Rome Conference', *American Journal of International Law* 93, 1999, 47–51.
33 Statute of the Special Court for Sierra Leone, 2178 UNTS 138 (2002), Art. 2. [hereinafter SCSL Statute].
34 UNTAET Regulation 15/2000. Available at http://www.un.org/peace/etimor/untaetR/r-2000.htm (accessed 1 May 2010); see also K. Ambos and S. Wirth, 'The Current Law of Crimes Against Humanity: An Analysis of UNTAET Regulation 15/2000', *Criminal Law Forum* 13, 2002, 3.
35 Law on the Establishment of the Extraordinary Chambers in the Courts of Cambodia for the Prosecution of Crimes Committed During the Period of Democratic Kampuchea, NS/RKM/1004/006 (2004), Art. 5.
36 Nuon Chea (ECCC-002/14-08-2006), Provisional Detention Order, 19 September 2007, para. 5.
37 Broomhall, 'International Justice and the International Criminal Court', p. 49 (positing 'collective conscience', as the primary normative rationale for crimes against humanity).
38 M. Bassiouni, *The Legislative History of the International Criminal Court*, Ardsley, NY: Transnational Publishers, 2005, pp. 151–2; W. Schabas, 'State Policy as an Element of International Crimes', *Journal of Criminal Law and Criminology* 98, 2008, 959 (Schabas, unlike Bassiouni, would extend the norm to state-like actors). See also, R. Vernon, 'What is a Crime Against Humanity?', *Journal of Political Philosophy* 10, 2002, 242.
39 D. Luban, 'A Theory of Crimes Against Humanity', *Yale Journal of International Law* 29, 2004, pp. 138–9.
40 Ibid., p. 160.
41 L. May, *Crimes Against Humanity*, New York: Cambridge University Press, 2005, 89.
42 Blaskic (IT-95-14-T), Trial Chamber Judgement, 3 March 2000, para. 206. The ICTR and SCSL have followed a similar approach. Akayesu (ICTR-96-4), Judgment, para. 580 (defining 'widespread' as 'massive, frequent, large scale action, carried out collectively with considerable seriousness and directed against a multiplicity of victims'). Fofana & Kondewa (SCSL-04-14-T), Judgment, para. 112 ('the term "widespread" refers to the large-scale nature of the attack and the number of victims').
43 Situation in the Republic of Kenya (ICC-01/09), Decision Pursuant to Article 15 of the Rome Statute on the Authorization of an Investigation Into the Situation in the Republic of Kenya [hereinafter Authorization Decision], 31 March 2010, para. 96.
44 Kunarac (IT-96-23), Judgment, 22 February 2001, para. 415.
45 Akayesu (ICTR-96-4), Judgment, 2 September 1998, para. 581.
46 Fofana (SCSL-04-14-T), Judgment, 2 August 2007, para. 111.
47 Akayesu (ICTR-96-4), Judgment, 2 September 1998, para. 579.
48 P. Wald, 'Genocide and Crimes Against Humanity', *Washington University Global Studies Law Review* 6, 2007, 630.
49 Semanza (ICTR-97-20-A), Judgment, 20 May 2005, para. 192.
50 Kayishema (ICTR-95-1-T), Judgment, 21 May 1999, para. 124.

51 Kunarac (IT-96-23/1-A), Judgment, 12 June 2002, para. 98.
52 The SCSL judges confirmed that a policy is not required in Fofana (SCSL-04-14-T), Judgment, 2 August 2007, para. 113.
53 Situation in the Republic of Kenya (ICC-01/09), Authorization Decision, 31 March 2010, para. 84 (quoting Katanga Decision on Confirmation of Charges para. 396).
54 Ibid., para. 90.
55 Situation in the Republic of Kenya (ICC-01/09), Authorization Decision, Dissenting Opinion of Judge Hans-Peter Kaul, 31 March 2010, paras 43 and 51.
56 Ibid., para. 53.
57 Ibid., para. 60.
58 ICC Elements of Crimes, Art. 7, n. 6.
59 Kupreskic (IT-95-16), Judgment, 14 January 2000, para. 547 ('It would seem that a wide definition of "civilian" and "population" is intended').
60 Kunarac, (IT-96-23/1-A), Judgment, 12 June 2002, para. 90.
61 Kamuhanda, (ICTR-95-54A-T), Judgment, 22 January 2004, para. 669.
62 Situation in the Republic of Kenya (ICC-01/09), Authorization Decision, 31 March 2010, para. 81.
63 Kupreskic (IT-95-16), Judgment, 14 January 2000, para. 547 ('It would seem that a wide definition of "civilian" and "population" is intended').
64 Blaskic (IT-95-14-T), Trial Chamber Judgment, 3 March 2000, para. 214.
65 Ibid.
66 A. Cassese, 'The Multifaceted Criminal Notion of Terrorism in International Law', *Journal of International Criminal Justice* 4, 2006, 949.
67 Kayishema (ICTR-95-1-T), Judgment, 21 May 1999, para. 128 (emphasis omitted).
68 Kunarac (IT-96-23/1-A), Judgment, 12 June 2002, para. 99.
69 Ibid., para. 100.
70 Ibid.
71 *Compare* P. Wald, 'Genocide and Crimes Against Humanity', p. 629 ('Granted, a loner can't commit a crime against humanity all by himself as in genocide, without a wider campaign against civilians in the background') *with* K. Ambos and S. Wirth, 'The Current Law of Crimes Against Humanity', p. 17 (stating that a single perpetrator acting once can commit a crime against humanity by, for example, poisoning the water supply for a large population).
72 Assembly of State Parties to the Rome Statute of the International Criminal Court [ICC-ASP], 'Elements of Crimes', 9 September 2002, Art. 6 and 7.
73 Blaskic (IT-95-14-T), Judgment, 3 March 2000, paras. 251–57; Rome Statute, Art. 7(1). For additional discussion of the mental element see M. deGuzman, 'The Road to Rome', pp. 381–402; K. Ambos and S. Wirth, 'The Current Law of Crimes Against Humanity', pp. 36–42.
74 Fofana (SCSL-04-14-T), Judgment, 2 August 2007, para. 121.
75 Kunarac (IT-96-23), Judgment, 22 February 2001, para. 434; Blaskic (IT-95-14-T), Judgment, 3 March 2000, para. 254.
76 ICC-ASP, 'Elements of Crimes', Art. 7 Intro.
77 Ibid. Note that the Elements' inclusion of 'plan' in addition to 'policy' is overridden by the Statute's exclusion of the plan alternative. Rome Statute, Art. 9(3) (stating that the Elements of Crimes shall be consistent with the Statute).
78 Kvocka (IT-98-30/1-T), Judgement, 2 November 2001, para. 192.
79 Blaskic (IT-95-14-T), Judgment, 3 March 2000, para. 227.
80 Nahimana (ICTR-99-52-T), Judgment, 3 December 2003, para. 1072.
81 Brima (SCSL-2004-16-A), Judgment, 22 February 2008, para. 202.
82 Ibid., para 198, the Rome Statute refers to the 'character' of the act. Rome Statute of the International Criminal Court, 2187 UNTS 90 (1998), Art. 7(1)(k). While the SCSL decision talks about the 'gravity' of the act.
83 Brima (SCSL-2004-16-A), Judgment, 22 February 2008, para. 198.
84 M. Bassiouni, '"Crimes Against Humanity": The Need for a Specialized Convention', *Columbia Journal of Transnational Law* 31, 1994, 457.
85 November Draft Convention 2009, on file with the author.

9
War crimes

Anthony Cullen[1]

Introduction

For the purposes of international criminal law, war crimes constitute violations of international humanitarian law that are criminalized under treaty law or customary international law. International humanitarian law, also referred to as the law of war or the law of armed conflict, may be defined as:

> a set of international rules, established by treaty or custom, which are specifically intended to solve humanitarian problems, directly arising from international or non-international armed conflicts, and which, for humanitarian reasons, limit the right of Parties to a conflict to use the methods and means of warfare of their choice or protect persons and property that are, or may be, affected by conflict.[2]

International humanitarian law concerns the rules that govern relations between parties engaged in armed conflict (*jus in bello*). It is not concerned with the legality of the armed conflict *per se* or the rules governing the resort to the use of force (*jus ad bello*).[3] Often referred to as the law of war, the object and purpose of international humanitarian law concerns the protection of the victims of armed conflict.[4] Guided by principles of military necessity,[5] humanity,[6] distinction[7] and proportionality,[8] it limits the means and methods that may be employed by parties to an armed conflict.

The focus of this chapter is on how war crimes are characterized for the purposes of international criminal law.[9] To provide context for the discussion, I begin by observing the historical development of the concept of war crimes. Next, the significance of the regime introduced by the Geneva Conventions of 1949 and the Additional Protocols of 1977 is examined. The role of the International Criminal Tribunal for the former Yugoslavia in the development of the concept of war crimes is then explored. Finally, the chapter concludes by considering the war crimes included in the Rome Statute of the International Criminal Court.

Historical development of the concept of war crimes

Before the incorporation of war crimes into treaty law, the rules governing the conduct of warfare evolved as part of customary international law. The ancient origins of international humanitarian law are noted by the UK Ministry of Defence in its *Manual on the Law of Armed Conflict*:

> Evidence of practices intended to alleviate the sufferings of war can be found in the writings of the ancient civilizations of India and Egypt. Agreements on the treatment of prisoners of war existed in Egypt around 1400 BC. The edicts of the Indian Emperor Asoka of about 250 BC were based on principles of humanity. In Europe, the idea of imposing rules on the conduct of warfare seems to have emerged in the Middle Ages as a result of the combined influences of Christianity and chivalry. It is said, however, that the first systematic code of war was that of the Saracens, based on the Koran . . .[10]

The conduct of hostilities in medieval Europe was governed by *jus armorum* or the 'Law of Arms'.[11] As noted by Theodor Meron, the medieval ordinances of war that were issued by kings or their commanders '[o]n many questions . . . restated *jus armorum*, as transmitted orally between heralds and other expects'.[12] Until the expansion of treaty law in the nineteenth and twentieth century, customary law constituted the main source of international law regulating the conduct of hostilities in war.

The first introduction of the concept of war crimes into treaty law was in the Peace Treaty of Versailles in 1919. Article 228 of the treaty provided for the punishment of persons for violations of 'the laws and customs of war':

> The German Government recognizes the right of the allied and associated powers to bring before military tribunals persons accused of having committed acts in violation of the laws and customs of war. Such persons shall, if found guilty, be sentenced to punishments laid down by the law. This provision will apply notwithstanding any proceedings or prosecution before a tribunal in Germany or in the territory of her allies.[13]

The next usage of language pertaining to war crimes in treaty law was the Charter of the International Military Tribunal at Nuremberg in 1945. Article 6(b) of the Nuremberg Charter defined war crimes as:

> violations of the laws or customs of war. Such violations shall include, but not be limited to, murder, ill-treatment or deportation to slave labour or for any other purpose of civilian population of or in occupied territory, murder or ill-treatment of prisoners of war or persons on the seas, killing of hostages, plunder of public or private property, wanton destruction of cities, towns or villages, or devastation not justified by military necessity.[14]

The list of war crimes contained in the Nuremberg Charter was not exhaustive but provided examples of the offences that the International Tribunal would have jurisdiction over. The next major development of treaty law with regard to war crimes was the drafting of the four Geneva Conventions of 1949. Three of the four Conventions were revisions of Conventions previously adopted: the Convention (X) for the Adaptation to Maritime Warfare of the Principles of the Geneva Convention (1907); the Convention for the Amelioration of the Condition of the Wounded and Sick in Armies in the Field (1929); and the Convention relative to the Treatment of Prisoners of War (1929). The fourth Geneva Convention established a new regime for the protection of civilian persons in time of war.

Geneva Conventions of 1949 and the Additional Protocols of 1977

The term 'war crimes' is not used in the Geneva Conventions of 1949. Instead, reference is made to 'grave breaches'. Each Convention stipulates 'High Contracting Parties undertake to enact any legislation necessary to provide effective penal sanctions for persons committing, or ordering to be committed, any of the grave breaches of the present Convention'.[15] As noted by the International Committee of the Red Cross (ICRC) Commentary, legislation relating to grave breaches should cover 'any person who has committed a grave breach, whether a national of that State or an enemy'.[16] The obligation to extradite or prosecute persons accused of grave breaches is provided for in each Convention:

> Each High Contracting Party shall be under the obligation to search for persons alleged to have committed, or to have ordered to be committed, such grave breaches, and shall bring such persons, regardless of their nationality, before its own courts. It may also, if it prefers, and in accordance with the provisions of its own legislation, hand such persons over for trial to another High Contracting Party concerned, provided such High Contracting Party has made out a prima facie case.[17]

Under the Geneva Conventions, the following offences constitute grave breaches if committed against protected persons or property:

- Wilful killing;
- Torture or inhuman treatment, including biological experiments;
- Wilfully causing great suffering or serious injury to body or health;
- Extensive destruction and appropriation of property, not justified by military necessity and carried out unlawfully and wantonly;
- Compelling a prisoner of war or other protected person to serve in the forces of a hostile power;
- Wilfully depriving a prisoner of war or other protected person of the rights of fair and regular trial;
- Unlawful deportation or transfer or unlawful confinement;
- Taking hostages.

Additional Protocol I relating to the Protection of Victims of International Armed Conflicts, adopted on 8 June 1977, expands the concept of grave breaches.[18] Article 11 qualifies as grave breaches the following offences committed against protected persons:

> [A]ny medical procedure which is not indicated by the state of health of the person concerned and which is not consistent with generally accepted medical standards which would be applied under similar medical circumstances to persons who are nationals of the Party conducting the procedure and who are in no way deprived of liberty.
>
> . . .
>
> (a) physical mutilations;
> (b) medical or scientific experiments;
> (c) removal of tissue or organs for transplantation, except where these acts are justified in conformity with the conditions provided for in paragraph 1.

Article 85 of Additional Protocol I further states:

> 3. In addition to the grave breaches defined in Article 11, the following acts shall be regarded as grave breaches of this Protocol, when committed wilfully, in violation of the relevant provisions of this Protocol, and causing death or serious injury to body or health:
>   (a) making the civilian population or individual civilians the object of attack;
>   (b) launching an indiscriminate attack affecting the civilian population or civilian objects in the knowledge that such attack will cause excessive loss of life, injury to civilians or damage to civilian objects, as defined in Article 57, paragraph 2 (a)(iii);
>   (c) launching an attack against works or installations containing dangerous forces in the knowledge that such attack will cause excessive loss of life, injury to civilians or damage to civilian objects, as defined in Article 57, paragraph 2 (a)(iii);
>   (d) making non-defended localities and demilitarized zones the object of attack;
>   (e) making a person the object of attack in the knowledge that he is hors de combat;
>   (f) the perfidious use, in violation of Article 37, of the distinctive emblem of the red cross, red crescent or red lion and sun or of other protective signs recognized by the Conventions or this Protocol.
> 4. In addition to the grave breaches defined in the preceding paragraphs and in the Conventions, the following shall be regarded as grave breaches of this Protocol, when committed wilfully and in violation of the Conventions or the Protocol:
>   (a) the transfer by the occupying Power of parts of its own civilian population into the territory it occupies, or the deportation or transfer of all or parts of the population of the occupied territory within or outside this territory, in violation of Article 49 of the Fourth Convention;
>   (b) unjustifiable delay in the repatriation of prisoners of war or civilians;
>   (c) practices of apartheid and other inhuman and degrading practices involving outrages upon personal dignity, based on racial discrimination;
>   (d) making the clearly-recognized historic monuments, works of art or places of worship which constitute the cultural or spiritual heritage of peoples and to which special protection has been given by special arrangement, for example, within the framework of a competent international organization, the object of attack, causing as a result extensive destruction thereof, where there is no evidence of the violation by the adverse Party of Article 53, subparagraph (b), and when such historic monuments, works of art and places of worship are not located in the immediate proximity of military objectives;
>   (e) depriving a person protected by the Conventions or referred to in paragraph 2 of this Article of the rights of fair and regular trial.
> 5. Without prejudice to the application of the Conventions and of this Protocol, grave breaches of these instruments shall be regarded as war crimes.

States are obligated to vest universal jurisdiction in their national courts over the grave breaches referred to above.[19] While many of the offences listed above may be considered war crimes in any situation of armed conflict, the grave breaches regime only applies in situations of international armed conflict as defined by common Article 2 of the Geneva Conventions and Article 1 of Additional Protocol I. As grave breaches may only be committed against protected persons and property, and as these concepts are specific to international armed conflict, a different basis is required for the prosecution of similar offences in situations of internal armed conflict. The section that follows will now examine the significance of jurisprudence of the International

Criminal Tribunal for the former Yugoslavia for the establishment of individual criminal responsibility for war crimes committed in non-international armed conflict.

The International Criminal Tribunal for the former Yugoslavia

The case law of the International Criminal Tribunal for the former Yugoslavia (ICTY) acted as a significant catalyst in the development of the concept of war crimes in the final decade of the twentieth century. This section will focus on the definition of war crimes in the jurisprudence of the ICTY, with particular attention to the requirements established in the *Tadić* case. The tribunal's jurisdiction over violations of the laws or customs of war is set out in Article 3 of its Statute. This provision states:

> The International Tribunal shall have the power to prosecute persons violating the laws or customs of war. Such violations shall include, but not be limited to:
> (a) employment of poisonous weapons or other weapons calculated to cause unnecessary suffering;
> (b) wanton destruction of cities, towns or villages, or devastation not justified by military necessity;
> (c) attack, or bombardment, by whatever means, of undefended towns, villages, dwellings, or buildings;
> (d) seizure of, destruction or wilful damage done to institutions dedicated to religion, charity and education, the arts and sciences, historic monuments and works of art and science;
> (e) plunder of public or private property.[20]

Like the Charter for the Nuremberg Tribunal, the offences listed in Article 3 were intended not to be exhaustive but rather illustrative of the war crimes that the tribunal would have jurisdiction over.[21] With regard to the characterization of war crimes, the ICTY Appeals Chamber in the *Tadić* case stipulated the following four conditions:

> (i) the violation must constitute an infringement of a rule of international humanitarian law;
> (ii) the rule must be customary in nature or, if it belongs to treaty law, the required conditions must be met . . . ;
> (iii) the violation must be 'serious', that is to say, it must constitute a breach of a rule protecting important values, and the breach must involve grave consequences for the victim. Thus, for instance, the fact of a combatant simply appropriating a loaf of bread in an occupied village would not amount to a 'serious violation of international humanitarian law' although it may be regarded as falling foul of the basic principle laid down in Article 46, paragraph 1, of the Hague Regulations (and the corresponding rule of customary international law) whereby 'private property must be respected' by any army occupying an enemy territory;
> (iv) the violation of the rule must entail, under customary or conventional law, the individual criminal responsibility of the person breaching the rule.[22]

These conditions have been followed consistently in the jurisprudence of the Tribunal.[23] Their application to non-international armed conflict was a bold innovation. Historically, the concept of war crimes had developed in relation to international armed conflict and as a consequence it had only been considered applicable in such situations. It was not until the Tribunal's Decision on the Defence Motion for Interlocutory Appeal on Jurisdiction (*Tadić* Jurisdiction Decision) delivered on 2 October 1995, that the existence of war crimes was recognized in non-international armed conflict.[24] As noted by Christopher Greenwood, this was an important development of the law:

> The Tadić decision . . . breaks new ground to the extent that the criminality under international law of violations of the law of internal armed conflict had not previously been asserted by an international tribunal, or, so far as this writer is aware, by an unequivocal decision of a national court in a state other than that in which the conflict has taken place.[25]

The decision of the Appeals Chamber to criminalize violations of international humanitarian law in situations of non-international armed conflict was on the basis of reasoning which cited, *inter alia*, resolutions of the UN Security Council, the content of military manuals and customary international law.[26] While it is questionable whether *opinio juris* existed to support such a finding,[27] the conclusion of the Appeals Chamber on the applicability of individual criminal responsibility in non-international armed conflict has been broadly welcomed. As highlighted by Ilias Bantekas and Susan Nash,

> contrary to the Appeals Chamber conclusion, customary international law had not until 1995 penalised violations of the laws or customs of war occurring in internal conflicts. This notwithstanding, it is undeniable that the pronouncement of such liability is laudable and is in fact now supported by a much larger number of States than prior to the establishment of the ICTY. Whatever the merits of the Appeals Chamber ruling on the criminal nature of common Art 3 in October 1995, that decision has subsequently been relied upon as authoritative by both ICTY and ICTR Chambers; it has influenced the national prosecution of common Art 3 offences committed abroad, and has culminated in the incorporation of an analogous and much more extensive provision in the Statute of the International Criminal Court.[28]

It is difficult to overstate the significance of this decision for the development of international humanitarian law. Besides the assertion of individual criminal responsibility for violations of international humanitarian law in situations of non-international armed conflict, the *Tadić* Jurisdiction Decision also addressed another significant lacuna by providing a definition of armed conflict.[29] The Appeals Chamber stated:

> [A]n armed conflict exists whenever there is a resort to armed force between States or protracted armed violence between governmental authorities and organized armed groups or between such groups within a State. International humanitarian law applies from the initiation of such armed conflicts and extends beyond the cessation of hostilities until a general conclusion of peace is reached; or, in the case of internal conflicts, a peaceful settlement is achieved.[30]

As noted by Professor William Schabas, '[t]hese words have been repeatedly cited in judgements of the international tribunals, and are really beyond any debate'.[31] Commenting on the concept of armed conflict provided by the *Tadić* Jurisdiction Decision, Greenwood emphasized the significance of this development:

> The definitions of international and internal armed conflict are of considerable importance. Neither term is defined in the Geneva Conventions or other applicable agreements.

> Whereas there is an extensive literature on the definition of 'war' in international law, armed conflict has always been considered a purely factual notion and there have been few attempts to define or even describe it.[32]

The existence of armed conflict is the most fundamental requirement for the establishment of subject-matter jurisdiction in the prosecution of war crimes. Another important requirement is that of a nexus between the alleged offence and a situation of armed conflict. Citing the view of the ICTY Appeals Chamber in *Tadić* Jurisdiction Decision, the ICTY Trial Chamber in the *Delalić* case stated:

> It is axiomatic that not every serious crime committed during the armed conflict in Bosnia and Herzegovina can be regarded as a violation of international humanitarian law. There must be an obvious link between the criminal act and the armed conflict. Clearly, if a relevant crime was committed in the course of fighting or the take-over of a town during an armed conflict, for example, this would be sufficient to render the offence a violation of international humanitarian law. Such a direct connection to actual hostilities is not, however, required in every situation. Once again, the Appeals Chamber has stated a view on the nature of this nexus between the acts of the accused and the armed conflict. In its opinion, [i]t is sufficient that the alleged crimes were closely related to the hostilities occurring in other parts of the territories controlled by the parties to the conflict.[33]

The establishment of individual criminal responsibility for war crimes thus requires proof of a link between the alleged offence and a situation of armed conflict. The requirements of this link were elaborated by the Appeals Chamber in the *Kunarac* case. In its judgement in this case, the Appeals Chamber stated:

> 58. What ultimately distinguishes a war crime from a purely domestic offence is that a war crime is shaped by or dependent upon the environment—the armed conflict—in which it is committed. It need not have been planned or supported by some form of policy. The armed conflict need not have been causal to the commission of the crime, but the existence of an armed conflict must, at a minimum, have played a substantial part in the perpetrator's ability to commit it, his decision to commit it, the manner in which it was committed or the purpose for which it was committed. Hence, if it can be established, as in the present case, that the perpetrator acted in furtherance of or under the guise of the armed conflict, it would be sufficient to conclude that his acts were closely related to the armed conflict. The Trial Chamber's finding on that point is unimpeachable.
>
> 59. In determining whether or not the act in question is sufficiently related to the armed conflict, the Trial Chamber may take into account, inter alia, the following factors: the fact that the perpetrator is a combatant; the fact that the victim is a non-combatant; the fact that the victim is a member of the opposing party; the fact that the act may be said to serve the ultimate goal of a military campaign; and the fact that the crime is committed as part of or in the context of the perpetrator's official duties.[34]

In considering the requirement of a nexus between the offence and a situation of armed conflict, it should be noted that knowledge of the classification of the armed conflict as either international or non-international is immaterial with regard to the individual criminal responsibility of the accused.[35] There is also no requirement of discriminatory intent on the part of the accused. According to the ICTY Appeals Chamber in the *Aleksovski* case,

> There is nothing in the undoubtedly grave nature of the crimes falling within Article 3 of the Statute, nor in the Statute generally, which leads to a conclusion that those offences are punishable only if they are committed with discriminatory intent. The general requirements which must be met for prosecution of offences under Article 3 have already been clearly identified by the Appeals Chamber in the Tadić Jurisdiction Decision, and they do not include a requirement of proof of a discriminatory intent or motivation. The Appeals Chamber recognised there that the relevant violation of international humanitarian law must be 'serious' in the sense that it 'must constitute a breach of a rule protecting important values and the breach must involve grave consequences for the victim'. This in no way imports a requirement that the violation must be committed with discriminatory intent.[36]

The jurisprudence of the ICTY has had a tremendous influence on the development of the concept of war crimes. This influence is reflected not only in the writings of experts in the area of international humanitarian law[37] but also in the content of military manuals and case law of national courts.[38] Perhaps the area where the contribution of the tribunal is most widely recognized is in the Rome Statute of the International Criminal Court.[39] The section that follows now examines the Statute with particular attention to Article 8, which grants jurisdiction of the Court over war crimes committed in international and non-international armed conflict.

The Rome Statute of the International Criminal Court

The adoption of the Rome Statute of the International Criminal Court on 17 July 1998 was a significant watershed in the development of treaty law for the prosecution of international crimes.[40] In terms of scope and substance it went much further in the criminalization of violations of the laws and customs of war than any instrument of international humanitarian law that had preceded it. This section examines the content of the Rome Statute relating to war crimes and comments on the strengths and weaknesses of its contribution to the area.

The rules prohibiting war crimes are contained in Article 8 of the Statute.[41] This provision allows for the prosecution of four categories of offences: grave breaches of the Geneva Conventions of 1949;[42] other serious violations of the laws and customs applicable in international armed conflict;[43] violations of Article 3 common to the four Geneva Conventions of 12 August 1949;[44] and other serious violations of the laws and customs applicable in armed conflicts not of an international character.[45] Article 8(1) provides that '[t]he Court shall have jurisdiction in respect of war crimes in particular when committed as part of a plan or policy or as part of a large-scale commission of such crimes'.

With regard to international armed conflict, the war crimes listed in the Rome Statute include intentionally directing attacks against the civilian population; intentionally directing attacks against civilian objects; intentionally directing attacks against personnel, installations, material, units or vehicles involved in a humanitarian assistance or peacekeeping mission in accordance with the Charter of the United Nations; improper use of the flag of truce; killing or wounding treacherously individuals belonging to the hostile nation or army; pillage; use of poison or poisoned weapons; intentionally using starvation of civilians as a method of warfare; and the conscripting or enlisting of children under the age of 15 years.

The crimes applicable in non-international armed conflict in the Rome Statute are fewer in number than those listed for international armed conflict. They include violence to life and person, in particular murder of all kinds, mutilation, cruel treatment and torture; outrages upon personal dignity, in particular humiliating and degrading treatment; the taking of hostages; ordering the displacement of the civilian population for reasons related to the conflict; and the passing of sentences and the carrying out of executions without previous judgement pronounced by a regularly constituted court, affording all judicial guarantees which are generally recognized as indispensable.

The inclusion of war crimes relating to non-international armed conflict was one of the most significant achievements of the Rome Conference. Luigi Condorelli comments:

> There can be no doubt that the Rome Statute represents a major step in the evolution of international humanitarian law, especially with regards to the norms applicable in case of internal armed conflict. The rules it proclaims are fundamentally innovative if compared to those contained in conventional instruments in force (such as the Geneva Conventions of 1949 and the Protocols of 1977). First of all, the Statute articulates in a written form a Hague Law of internal armed conflicts that was almost unknown in previous legal instruments. Secondly, it identifies the cases in which the violation of humanitarian principles applicable in case of internal armed conflicts are to be qualified as war crimes.[46]

However, there are a number of problems with Article 8 of the Rome Statute. One criticism which has been raised by many scholars concerns the reproduction of the distinction between international and non-international armed conflict.[47] In order to determine the applicability of the relevant war crimes provisions, each situation must first be assessed and characterized as either international or non-international. The inclusion of these different categories of armed conflict was viewed by a number of commentators as a regressive development. According to Professor Antonio Cassese,

> one may entertain some misgivings concerning the distinction, upheld in Article 8, between the regulation of *international* armed conflict, on the one side, and *internal* conflicts on the other. In so far as Article 8 separates the law applicable in the former category of armed conflict from that applicable to the latter category, it is somewhat retrograde, as the current trend has been to abolish the distinction and to have simply one corpus of law applicable to all armed conflicts. It can be confusing—and unjust—to have one law for international armed conflict and another for internal armed conflict.[48] [Emphasis in original.]

Another difficulty with Article 8 is its complicated structure.[49] There are two categories of war crimes listed for international armed conflict and two for non-international armed conflict. Each is covered by a clause stating the scope of its applicability. A particular source contention in this regard is the content of 8(2)(f), which stipulates the field of application for the war crimes listed in Article 8(2)(e):

> Paragraph 2(e) applies to armed conflicts not of an international character and thus does not apply to situations of internal disturbances and tensions, such as riots, isolated and sporadic acts of violence or other acts of a similar nature. It applies to armed conflicts that take place in the territory of a State when there is protracted armed conflict between governmental authorities and organized armed groups or between such groups.

This provision has been interpreted by some commentators as introducing a new category of armed conflict, one that had not existed in international humanitarian law prior to the drafting of the Rome Statute.[50] Others have contended that the wording should not be understood as creating a new threshold of application but interpreted as reflecting the existing threshold of non-international armed conflict provided for in common Article 3.[51] Considering the intentions of the drafters, together with a plain reading of the text in light of its object and purpose, the better view is arguably the latter.[52]

A further flaw with the Rome Statute is that, unlike the statute for the Nuremberg Tribunal and the Statutes of the ICTY and ICTR, it only provides the Court with jurisdiction over the war crimes specifically included in Article 8. This is unfortunate as the list of offences, in particular for non-international armed conflict, omits many rules that were recognized at the time as incurring individual criminal responsibility under customary international law. According to Charles Garraway,

> States were not prepared in a treaty of general application to adopt the open-ended approach taken in Nuremberg. It was argued that this went against the principle of legal certainty and so it was decided to adopt a specific list of offences, covering both international and non-international armed conflict. These included both grave breaches and 'other serious violations of the laws and customs applicable in' armed conflict. The list is, however, a compromise, and should not be taken as exhaustive of all serious violations.[53]

As is the case with other multi-lateral treaties, the Rome Statute is the product of a complex process of negotiation between States. While the end achieved is in many respects commendable, the final text of the Statute reflects the compromises inherent in the process which created it. It is unfortunate that the distinctions introduced into the structure of Article 8 create unnecessary complications for the application of its provisions. The achievement of the Rome Statute in relation to war crimes is nevertheless considerable. Prior to the adoption of the Statute, no treaty existed providing individual criminal responsibility for violations of international humanitarian law in situations of non-international armed conflict. Given that such situations make up the majority of contemporary armed conflicts, this innovation is of particular importance. Also, no instrument of international law had hitherto covered violations of international humanitarian law between armed groups without the involvement of government authorities. Following the approach adopted in the *Tadić* Jurisdiction Decision, this expands the scope of application for war crimes provisions consistent with the object and purpose of international humanitarian law, enhancing the protection available to the victims of non-international armed conflict.

Conclusion

The concept of war crimes has evolved very significantly since the drafting of the Geneva Conventions of 1949 and the Additional Protocols of 1977. The jurisprudence of the International Criminal Tribunal for the former Yugoslavia was pivotal in moving it forward, particularly in relation to non-international armed conflicts. With regard to the prospects for future development of war crimes, it is important, as with all areas of international criminal law, that there is clarity concerning the scope and content of the rules. As noted by Michael Bothe,

> Rules concerning the punishment of 'war crimes' are secondary rules in relation to the primary rules concerning behaviour which is prohibited in case of an armed conflict. Thus, the concept of war crimes is a dynamic concept, as it is bound to change with the development of the primary or substantive rules relating to that behaviour. But for that very reason, it is in the interest of the certainty of the law, which in criminal law matters is enshrined in the principle of *nulla poena sine lege*, that the acts which may be punished as war crimes are clearly defined. This is necessary because of the vague and general character of some of the primary rules, but also because not every breach of those rules may necessarily be characterized as a war crime.[54]

As international humanitarian law evolves, so too will the concept of war crimes. As noted by the Nuremberg Tribunal, the laws that govern armed conflict 'are not static, but by continual adaptation follow the needs of a changing world'.[55] In view of this, it is important to recall that the interpretation of international humanitarian law should be guided by its object and purpose, which concerns the protection of the victims of armed conflict.[56] Towards this end, it is essential that the content of this body of law is kept under review to strengthen the protection available to victims and to develop greater accountability for the violations that continue to occur in contemporary situations of armed conflict.

Notes

1 Anthony Cullen is a Researcher on the joint British Red Cross and International Committee of the Red Cross (ICRC) project to update the collection of practice underlying the ICRC's Study on Customary International Humanitarian Law. The opinions expressed herein are those of the author alone and do not necessarily correspond to those of the British Red Cross Society or the International Committee of the Red Cross. The author acknowledges with gratitude the research assistance provided by Robert Miles.

2 ICRC Advisory Service on International Humanitarian law, 'International Humanitarian Law and International Human Rights Law: Similarities and Differences', January 2003, p. 1, available at: http://www.icrc.org/Web/Eng/siteeng0.nsf/htmlall/57JR8L/$FILE/IHL_and_IHRL.pdf (last visited 1 April 2010). The United States Department of Defense defines the laws of war as '[t]hat part of international law that regulates the conduct of armed hostilities. It is often called the "law of armed conflict". The law of war encompasses all international law for the conduct of hostilities binding on the United States or its individual citizens, including treaties and international agreements to which the United States is a party, and applicable customary international law'. Department of Defense (United States), Department of Defense Directive Number 2311.01E, 9 May 2006, para. 3.1. According to Professor Christopher Greenwood, international humanitarian law comprises of 'all those rules of international law which are designed to regulate the treatment of the individual—civilian or military, wounded or active—in armed conflicts'. C. Greenwood, 'Historical Development and Legal Basis' in D. Fleck (ed.), *The Handbook of Humanitarian Law in Armed Conflicts*, Oxford: Oxford University Press, 1995, p. 9. See also: UK Ministry of Defence, *The Manual of the Law of Armed Conflict*, Oxford: Oxford University Press, 2004, p. 3.

3 See: R. Kolb, 'Origin of the twin terms *jus ad bellum/jus in bello*', *International Committee of the Red Cross*, No. 320, 1997, 553–62. See also: C. Greenwood, 'The Relationship between *ius ad bellum* and *ius in bello*', *Review of International Studies*, vol. 20, No. 4, 1983, 221–34.

4 See: Prosecutor v. Akayesu (Case No. ICTR-96-4), Judgement, Appeals Chamber, 1 June 2001, para. 630.

5 See: UK Ministry of Defence, *The Manual of the Law of Armed Conflict*, Oxford: Oxford University Press, 2004, pp. 21–3; International and Operational Law Department (US Department of Defense), *Operational Law Handbook*, Charlottesville, Virginia: The Judge Advocate General's Legal Center and School, 2007, pp. 12–13; Department of National Defence (Canada), *The Law of Armed Conflict at the Operational and Tactical Levels,* Office of the Judge Advocate General, 13 August 2001, p. 2–1.

6 See: UK Ministry of Defence, *The Manual of the Law of Armed Conflict*, Oxford: Oxford University Press, 2004, pp. 23–4; International and Operational Law Department (US Department of Defense), *Operational Law Handbook*, Charlottesville, Virginia: The Judge Advocate General's Legal Center and School, 2007, p. 14; Department of National Defence (Canada), *The Law of Armed Conflict at the Operational and Tactical Levels,* Office of the Judge Advocate General, 13 August 2001, p. 2–1.

7 See: UK Ministry of Defence, *The Manual of the Law of Armed Conflict*, Oxford: Oxford University Press, 2004, p. 24; International and Operational Law Department (US Department of Defense), *Operational Law Handbook*, Charlottesville, Virginia: The Judge Advocate General's Legal Center and School, 2007, pp. 13–14; Department of National Defence (Canada), *The Law of Armed Conflict at the Operational and Tactical Levels,* Office of the Judge Advocate General, 13 August 2001, p. 2–2.

8 See: UK Ministry of Defence, *The Manual of the Law of Armed Conflict*, Oxford: Oxford University Press, 2004, pp. 25–6; International and Operational Law Department (US Department of Defense), *Operational Law Handbook*, Charlottesville, Virginia: The Judge Advocate General's Legal Center and School, 2007, p. 14; Department of National Defence (Canada), *The Law of Armed Conflict at the Operational and Tactical Levels,* Office of the Judge Advocate General, 13 August 2001, p. 2–2.

9 The definition of war crimes under national legal systems is not dealt with in this chapter. For national practice on the definition of war crimes see: J.M. Henckaerts and L. Doswald-Beck, *Customary International Humanitarian Law,* vol. II, Cambridge: Cambridge University Press, 2004, pp. 3857–74.

10 UK Ministry of Defence, *The Manual of the Law of Armed Conflict*, Oxford: Oxford University Press, 2004, pp. 6–7.

11 According to Stephen Neff, this body of law 'was suited to the everyday needs of the practising soldier, dealing with such matters as ransom arrangements for prisoners, the taking and dividing of spoils, truces and safe-conducts and so forth'. S. Neff, *War and the Law of Nations: A General History*, Cambridge: Cambridge University Press, 2005, p. 70.

12 T. Meron, *War Crimes Law Comes of Age*, Oxford: Oxford University Press, 1998, p. 1. Meron states that '[s]everal of the ordinances . . . mentioned customary law as a residuary source to be applied in cases for which explicit provision was not made'. Ibid.

13 The Treaty of Peace between the Allied and Associated Powers and Germany, and other treaty engagements, signed at Versailles, 28 June 1919, Article 228.

14 Agreement by the Government of the United States of America, the Provisional Government of the French Republic, the Government of the United Kingdom of Great Britain and Northern Ireland and the Government of the Union of Soviet Socialist Republics for the Prosecution of the Major War Criminals of the European Axis (1951) 82 UNTS 279 (8 August 1945), Article 6(b).

15 Geneva Convention for the Amelioration of the Condition of the Wounded and Sick in Armed Forces in the Field, 75 U.N.T.S. 31 (1950), Article 49; Geneva Convention for the Amelioration of the Condition of Wounded, Sick and Shipwrecked Members of Armed Forces at Sea, 75 U.N.T.S. 85 (1950), Article 50; Geneva Convention relative to the Treatment of Prisoners of War, 75 U.N.T.S. 135 (1950), Article 129; Geneva Convention relative to the Protection of Civilian Persons in Time of War, 75 U.N.T.S. 287 (1950), Article 146.

16 Jean S. Pictet (ed.), *Commentary IV Convention Relative to the Protection of Civilian Persons in Time of War*, Geneva: ICRC, 1958, p. 592.

17 Geneva Convention for the Amelioration of the Condition of the Wounded and Sick in Armed Forces in the Field, 75 U.N.T.S. 31 (1950), Article 49; Geneva Convention for the Amelioration of the Condition of Wounded, Sick and Shipwrecked Members of Armed Forces at Sea, 75 U.N.T.S. 85 (1950), Article 50; Geneva Convention relative to the Treatment of Prisoners of War, 75 U.N.T.S. 135 (1950), Article 129; Geneva Convention relative to the Protection of Civilian Persons in Time of War, 75 U.N.T.S. 287 (1950), Article 146.

18 Protocol Additional to the Geneva Conventions of 12 August 1949, and Relating to the Protection of Victims of International Armed Conflicts, 1125 U.N.T.S. 3 (1978).

19 J.M. Henckaerts and L. Doswald-Beck, *Customary International Humanitarian Law,* vol. I, Cambridge: Cambridge University Press, 2004, pp. 604–7; C. Garraway, 'War Crimes' in E. Wilmshurst and S. Breau (eds), *Perspectives on the ICRC Study on Customary International Humanitarian Law*, Cambridge: Cambridge University Press, 2007, pp. 377–98, at p. 390. On the concept of universal jurisdiction generally see: R. O'Keefe, 'Universal Jurisdiction: Clarifying the Basic Concept' (2004) *Journal of International Criminal Justice* 735–60.

20 Statute of the International Tribunal for the Former Yugoslavia, SC Res 827, 48 UN SCOR (3217th mtg), UN Doc S/Res/827 (1993), 32 ILM 1203.

21 A similar approach is taken in Article 4 of the Statute of the International Criminal Tribunal for Rwanda in the context of non-international armed conflict:

> The International Tribunal for Rwanda shall have the power to prosecute persons committing or ordering to be committed serious violations of Article 3 common to the Geneva Conventions of 12 August 1949 for the Protection of War Victims, and of Additional Protocol II thereto of 8 June 1977. These violations shall include, but shall not be limited to:
>
> (a) Violence to life, health and physical or mental well-being of persons, in particular murder as well as cruel treatment such as torture, mutilation or any form of corporal punishment;
> (b) Collective punishments;
> (c) Taking of hostages;
> (d) Acts of terrorism;
> (e) Outrages upon personal dignity, in particular humiliating and degrading treatment, rape, enforced prostitution and any form of indecent assault;
> (f) Pillage;

(g) The passing of sentences and the carrying out of executions without previous judgement pronounced by a regularly constituted court, affording all the judicial guarantees which are recognised as indispensable by civilised peoples;
(h) Threats to commit any of the foregoing acts.

22 Tadić (Case No. IT-94-1-AR72), Decision on the Defence Motion for Interlocutory Appeal on Jurisdiction, 2 October 1995, para. 94. See: Jennifer Trahan (ed.), *Genocide, war crimes, and crimes against humanity: a topical digest of the case law of the International Criminal Tribunal for the Former Yugoslavia*, New York: Human Rights Watch, 2006, pp. 55–76.

23 In the *Boškoski and Tarčulovski* case, the ICTY stated:

> The jurisprudence of the Tribunal has consistently held that for an offence to fall under the scope of Article 3 of the Statute, four conditions must be met. Firstly, the violation must constitute an infringement of a rule of international humanitarian law. Secondly, the rule must be customary in nature or, if it belongs to treaty law, the required conditions must be met. Thirdly, the violation must be serious, that is to say that it must constitute a breach of a rule protecting important values and the breach must involve grave consequences for the victim. Finally, the violation of the rule must entail, under customary or conventional law, the individual criminal responsibility of the person breaching the rule.

Boškoski and Tarčulovski (Case No. IT-04-82-T), Judgement, 10 July 2008, para. 296.

24 Tadić (Case No. IT-94-1-AR72), Decision on the Defence Motion for Interlocutory Appeal on Jurisdiction, 2 October 1995, para. 94. See generally: T. Graditzky, 'Individual Criminal Responsibility for Violations of International Humanitarian Law Committed in Non-International Conflicts' (1998) 322 *International Review of the Red Cross* 29.

25 C. Greenwood, 'International Humanitarian Law and the Tadić Case' (1996) *European Journal of International Law* 265–83 at 281.

26 Tadić (Case No. IT-94-1-AR72), Decision on the Defence Motion for Interlocutory Appeal on Jurisdiction, 2 October 1995, paras 128–37.

27 The report issued by the *Ad Hoc* Committee on the Establishment of an International Criminal Court in 1995 indicates the lack of consensus that existed at the time on the question of individual criminal responsibility for violations of international humanitarian law in situations of non-international armed conflict. The position of states engaged in the process is summarized as follows:

> There were different views as to whether the laws and customs applicable in armed conflict, including treaty crimes, should include those governing non-international armed conflicts, notably common Article 3 of the 1949 Geneva Conventions and Additional Protocol II thereto. Those who favoured the inclusion of such provisions drew attention to the current reality of armed conflicts, the statute of the ad hoc Tribunal for Rwanda and the recent decision of the ad hoc Tribunal for the former Yugoslavia recognizing the customary-law status of common Article 3. However other delegations expressed serious reservations concerning the possibility of covering non-international armed conflicts and questioned the consistency of such an approach with the principle of complementarity. As regards Additional Protocol II, the view was expressed that that instrument as a whole had not achieved the status of customary law and therefore was binding only on States party thereto. The view was also expressed that non-international armed conflicts should not fall within the jurisdiction of the Court either with respect to common Article 3 or Additional Protocol II.

Report of the *Ad Hoc* Committee on the Establishment of an International Criminal Court; G.A., 50th Sess., Supp. No. 22, A/50/22, 1995, para. 74.

28 I. Bantekas and S. Nash, *International Criminal Law*, 3rd edn, Abington: Routledge-Cavendish, 2007, pp. 121–2.

29 See generally: A. Cullen, *The Concept of Non-International Armed Conflict in International Humanitarian Law*, Cambridge: Cambridge University Press, 2010, pp. 117–39. See also: A. Cullen and M.D. Öberg, 'Prosecutor v. Ramush Haradinaj et al.: The International Criminal Tribunal for the Former Yugoslavia and the Threshold of Non-International Armed Conflict in International Humanitarian Law' *American Society of International Law: Insight*, 2008, Vol. 12, Issue 7. Available at http://www.asil.org/insights080423.cfm (accessed 24 April 2010).

30 Tadić (IT-94-1-AR72), Decision on the Defence Motion for Interlocutory Appeal on Jurisdiction, 2 October 1995, para. 70.

31 W. A. Schabas, *The UN International Criminal Tribunals: The Former Yugoslavia, Rwanda and Sierra Leone*, Cambridge: Cambridge University Press, 2007, p. 229.

32 C. Greenwood, 'The Development of International Law by the International Criminal Tribunal for the Former Yugoslavia' (1998) 2 *Max Planck Yearbook of United Nations Law* 97 at 114.
33 Delalić (IT-96-21-T), 16 November 1998, para. 193. See also: Aleksovski (IT-95-14/1-T), Judgement, 25 June 1999, para 45.
34 Kunarac (IT-96-23 & IT-96-23/1-A), Judgement, 12 June 2002, paras 58–59. See also: Rutaganda (ICTR-96-3), 6 December 1999, paras 104–5.
35 This is confirmed in the Elements of Crimes of the Rome Statute of the International Criminal Court. With regard to war crimes in the Rome Statute, the Elements of Crimes state:

- There is no requirement for a legal evaluation by the perpetrator as to the existence of an armed conflict of its character as international or non-international;
- In that context there is no requirement for awareness by the perpetrator of the facts that established the character of the conflict as international or non-international;
- There is only a requirement for the awareness of the factual circumstances that established the existence of an armed conflict that is implicit in the terms 'took place in the context of and was associated with'.

ICC, Elements of Crimes, UN Doc. PCNICC/2000/1/Add. 2 (2000), p. 18. See generally: K. Dörmann, L. Doswald-Beck and R. Kolb, *Elements of War Crimes under the Rome Statute of the International Criminal Court: Sources and Commentary*, Cambridge: Cambridge University Press, 2003.
36 Aleksovski (IT-95-14/1-A), Judgement, 24 March 2000, para. 20.
37 See: Ian G. Corey, 'The Fine Line between Policy and Custom: *Prosecutor v. Tadić* and the Customary International Law of Internal Armed Conflict' (2000) 166 *Military Law Review* 145; C. Kress, 'War Crimes Committed in Non-International Armed Conflict and the Emerging System of International Criminal Justice' (2000) 30 *Israel Yearbook on Human Rights* 103; T. Meron, 'International Criminalisation of Internal Atrocities' (1995) 89 *American Journal of International Law* 554; T. Meron, 'The Humanization of Humanitarian Law' (2000) 94 *American Journal of International Law* 239; T. Meron, 'War Crimes in Yugoslavia and the Development of International Law' (1994) 88 *American Journal of International Law* 78; P. Rowe, 'The International Criminal Tribunal for the Former Yugoslavia: The Decision of the Appeals Chamber on the Interlocutory Appeal on Jurisdiction in the Tadić Case' (1996) 45 *International and Comparative Law Quarterly* 691; M. Sassoli and L. Olsen, 'International Decisions: *Prosecutor v. Tadić*' (2000) 94 *American Journal of International Law*, 571; M. P. Scharf, 'Prosecutor v. Tadić' (1997) 91 *American Journal of International Law* 718.
38 For examples see: UK Ministry of Defence, *The Manual of the Law of Armed Conflict*, Oxford: Oxford University Press, 2004, p. 433; and SRYYY v. Minister for Immigration and Multicultural and Indigenous Affairs (2005) FCAFC 42, Federal Court of Australia, Judgement, 17 March 2005, para. 49.
39 See: W. A. Schabas, *An Introduction to the International Criminal Court*, 3rd edn., Cambridge: Cambridge University Press, 2009, p. 13.
40 Rome Statute of the International Criminal Court, UN Doc. A/CONF.183/9 (hereinafter 'Rome Statute').
41 For commentary on the content of Article 8, see: W. A. Schabas, *The International Criminal Court: A Commentary on the Rome Statute*, Oxford Commentaries on International Law, Oxford: Oxford University Press, 2010, pp. 188–257.
42 Article 8(2)(a).
43 Article 8(2)(b).
44 Article 8(2)(c).
45 Article 8(2)(e).
46 L. Condorelli, 'War Crimes and Internal Conflicts in the Statute of the ICC' in M. Politi and G. Nesi (eds), *The Rome Statute of the International Criminal Court: A Challenge to Impunity*, Aldershot: Ashgate, 2001, p. 116.
47 See for example: D. Willmott, 'Removing the Distinction between International and Non-international Armed Conflict in the Rome Statute of the International Criminal Court' (2004) *5 Melbourne Journal of International Law* 196. For arguments against retention of the distinction between international and non-international armed conflict in international humanitarian law see: E. Crawford, 'Unequal before the Law: The Case for the Elimination of the Distinction between International and Non-international Armed Conflicts' (2007) 20 *Leiden Journal of International Law* 441; J. G. Stewart, 'Towards a single definition of armed conflict in international humanitarian law: A critique of internationalised armed conflict' (2003) 85 *International Review of the Red Cross* 313; G. K. McDonald, 'The Eleventh

Annual Waldemar A. Solf Lecture: The Changing Nature of the Laws of War' (1998) 156 *Military Law Review* 30.

48 A. Cassese, *International Criminal Law*, 2nd edn, Oxford: Oxford University Press, 2008, p. 96.

49 See: W. A. Schabas, *An Introduction to the International Criminal Court*, 3rd. edn, Cambridge: Cambridge University Press, 2009, p. 116.

50 Scholars who interpret a new threshold of application include Marco Sassoli and Antoine Bouvier, and Rene Provost; see: M. Sassoli and A. Bouvier (eds), *How Does Law Protect in War* (vol. 1, 2nd edn, 2006) 110; R. Provost, *International Human Rights and International Humanitarian Law* (2002) 268–69.

51 Scholars who support the interpretation of one uniform threshold applicable in non-international armed conflict include Theodor Meron, Michael Bothe and Claus Kress. See: T. Meron, 'The Humanization of Humanitarian Law' (2000) 94 *American Journal of International Law* 239, 260; M. Bothe, 'War Crimes', in A. Cassese, P. Gaeta, J. R.W.D. Jones (eds), *The Rome Statute of the International Criminal Court: A Commentary,* Oxford: Oxford University Press, 2002, 423; and C. Kress, 'War Crimes Committed in Non-International Armed Conflict and the Emerging System of International Criminal Justice', (2001) 30 *Israel Yearbook on Human Rights* 103, 118.

52 A. Cullen, 'The Definition of Non-International Armed Conflict in the Rome Statute of the International Criminal Court: An Analysis of the Threshold of Application Contained in Article 8(2)(f)' *Journal of Conflict and Security Law*, 2007, vol. 12(3), 419–45. See also: Andreas, Zimmermann, 'War Crimes Committed in an Armed Conflict not of an International Character' in O. Triffterer (ed.), *Commentary on Statute of the International Criminal Court: Observers' Notes, Article by Article*, 2nd. rev. edn, Oxford: Hart Publishing, 2008; pp. 500–2.

53 C. Garraway, 'War Crimes' in E. Wilmshurst and S. Breau (eds), *Perspectives on the ICRC Study on Customary International Humanitarian Law*, Cambridge: Cambridge University Press, 2007, pp. 377–98, at pp. 378–9.

54 M. Bothe, 'War Crimes' in A. Cassese, P. Gaeta and J. R. W. D. Jones (eds), *The Rome Statute of the International Criminal Court: A Commentary*, Oxford: Oxford University Press, 2002, pp. 379–426, at p. 381.

55 *Trial of Major War Criminals before the International Military Tribunal*, Nuremberg, 14 November 1945—1 October 1946, vol. I, p. 221.

56 As noted by the ICTR Trial Chamber in the *Akayesu* case, 'the four Geneva Conventions, as well as the two Protocols, were adopted primarily to protect the victims, as well as potential victims, of armed conflicts'. Akayesu (ICTR-96-4), Judgement, 2 September 1998, para. 603.

10
Aggression

Nicolaos Strapatsas

Historical evolution

The League of Nations was established after the First World War, and its Covenant declared any war or threat thereof to be a matter of concern to the whole League.[1] It also required all members to mutually respect and preserve the territorial integrity and political independence of one another against 'external aggression'.[2] Yet the Covenant contained a number of loopholes as well. For instance, states could have recourse to war in order to enforce an arbitral award or a unanimous decision by the League's Council. Moreover, if the Council failed to come to a unanimous decision regarding a dispute submitted to it, member states had the right to take such action as they considered 'necessary for the maintenance of right and justice', including war.[3]

In 1928, the General Treaty for the Renunciation of War as an Instrument of National Policy, commonly referred to as the Kellogg–Briand Pact, was adopted. Under this instrument, states condemned the recourse to war for the solution of international controversies and renounced it as an instrument of national policy in international relations.[4] However, a problem arose based on the sweeping language employed in the Pact, which seemingly outlawed all wars, even those waged in self-defence or in conformity with the Covenant. Consequently, several states issued reservations and declarations safeguarding their rights of self-defence, as well as their rights under the Covenant, and interpreted the outlawry of war as an 'instrument of national policy' as prohibiting aggressive warfare only.[5] In the years following the Pact's adoption, attempts were made at harmonizing it with the Covenant, by closing the latter's loopholes, but these were unsuccessful.[6] Moreover, the League of Nations proved to be impotent in preventing and repelling the acts of aggression by Japan against China in 1931 and by Italy against Abyssinia (Ethiopia) in 1935, not to mention the outbreak of the Second World War in 1939.

The Second World War sparked a fundamental shift in the will of states to outlaw aggressive warfare, which began with a series of declarations by the Allied and associated states[7] and culminated in 1945 with the adoption of the United Nations Charter[8] and the London Charter of the International Military Tribunal at Nuremberg.[9]

The UN Charter

The most notable aspects of the UN Charter were the prohibition of the threat or use of force in international relations,[10] the express recognition of the right of individual and collective self-defence,[11] and the creation of a collective security system under which the Security Council had the power to take coercive measures in the face of threats to and breaches of international peace and security, and acts of aggression.[12]

By prohibiting the 'use of force', as opposed to the narrower notion of 'war' contained in the Covenant and the Pact, the UN Charter excluded the possibility of engaging in armed action, even without the existence of a state of war.[13] Also, by expressly providing for the right of self-defence and limiting its exercise to response to an 'armed attack', the UN Charter excluded the possibility of a state making a far-fetched reservation of this right, as had been the case with Great Britain with regard to the Pact.[14]

The only major drawback of the UN Charter was the lack of a definition of the concept of 'aggression', despite a number of attempts during the drafting process to define this term. At the time, the predominant view was that such a task went beyond the San Francisco Conference's scope, which was the elaboration of a Charter for the United Nations Organization. The first justification given for not defining this concept was that the progress in the methods of modern warfare made it very difficult to properly enumerate all possible 'aggressive acts', which would encourage a would-be aggressor state to exploit the weak points of an incomplete definition. Second, there was the need to avoid any automaticity that could result in the premature application of enforcement measures or sanctions against a presumed aggressor. Thus, in order to ensure that appropriate action would be taken with respect to international peace and security, including in cases of 'aggression', the Security Council's decision-making ability had to remain unfettered.[15]

The London Charter

Even though the London Charter was adopted a few months after the UN Charter, the Allies had agreed in principle as early as 1943 to prosecute the major Nazi war criminals for the atrocities committed during the Second World War in violation of the rules of warfare.[16] In January 1945, the United States pursued the idea of trying the Nazis for waging of an illegal war of aggression in addition to the wartime atrocities committed by German forces.[17] In June 1945, representatives of the United States, the United Kingdom, the Soviet Union and France met in London in order to give effect to these prosecutorial plans.

Despite their somewhat opposing views, the United States and the Soviet Union's positions were consistent throughout the conference. The United States wanted the launching of an 'aggressive war' to be criminalized and argued for defining the notion of 'aggression' either objectively or by reference to existing international instruments, such as the Kellogg–Briand Pact. The Soviet Union wanted the offence of 'aggressive warfare' to be limited specifically to the major Nazi war criminals, but it opposed any definition or reference to international treaties. It argued that the London conference did not have the competence to define the notion of 'aggression' and wished that such a task be left to the future work of the United Nations. It also insisted that the definition of the crime of 'aggressive warfare' be left up to the judges who would try the Nazis.[18]

In contrast, France changed positions a number of times during the London conference. For instance, its representatives initially had misgivings over the criminalization of 'aggressive war' and argued that such an offence would violate the principle of non-retroactivity of criminal law because this offence did not exist under international law. Later on, France accepted the proposal of criminalizing 'aggressive war' and wanted the definition to make reference to the relevant international instruments on the matter. However, by the end of the conference, France was opposed to defining the crime in question, citing, among other things, the need to avoid prejudice to the work of the United Nations. Instead, France wanted the task of defining the crime to be given to more 'impartial' actors—namely, the judges who were to sit at the trial—despite France's previous concerns over retroactive criminality. For its part, the United Kingdom adopted a position essentially along the same lines as the United States, and in its role of conference chair the United Kingdom attempted to find common points between the different positions in order to reach agreement.[19]

The London Charter, which was adopted on 8 August 1945, criminalized 'aggressive warfare' under the heading of 'crimes against peace'. This criminal offence was defined as: 'planning, preparation, initiation or waging of a war of aggression, or a war in violation of international treaties, agreements or assurances, or participation in a common plan or conspiracy for the accomplishment of any of the foregoing'.[20] Firstly, it should be noted that even though the Soviet Union did not succeed in restricting the definition of this offence exclusively to the European Axis, the London conference did agree to limit the International Military Tribunal's jurisdiction to the trial and punishment of individuals who had acted in the interests of the Axis.[21] Secondly, the main element of 'crimes against peace' was not defined. As per the wishes of the Soviet Union and France, the task of determining what constituted a 'war of aggression' or a 'war in violation of international treaties, agreements or assurances' was left to the judges. Thirdly, a separate offence of participating in a 'common plan or conspiracy' was included under the heading of 'crimes against peace' at the behest of the United States, which considered this to be the cornerstone of their prosecutorial strategy against the Nazis.[22]

At Nuremberg in October 1946 the International Military Tribunal rendered its judgment against the major Nazi war criminals and found 12 of the 22 defendants guilty of 'crimes against peace', eight of whom were also guilty of participating in a 'common plan or conspiracy' to commit this crime. The Nuremberg Tribunal found that Nazi Germany had either committed 'acts' of aggression or had waged 'aggressive wars' against 11 European countries; however, it did not go so far as to define these concepts.[23] Despite the fact that Nazi Germany had not attacked the United States, the Tribunal considered the Japanese attack on Pearl Harbour in its discussion of 'aggressive warfare'.[24] Presumably, the Tribunal regarded Germany's encouragement of the attack against the United States as falling under the 'common plan or conspiracy' to wage a 'war of aggression'.

In 1948, the International Military Tribunal for the Far East, sitting in Tokyo, delivered its judgment against the major Japanese war criminals. The Charter of the Tokyo Tribunal had been proclaimed in 1946 by the Supreme Allied Commander in the Far East, General Douglas MacArthur, and was largely based on the London Charter.[25] The Tokyo Tribunal found that Japan had waged 'aggressive warfare' against seven countries, but as had been the case at Nuremberg, the judges did not define this concept. Of the 28 defendants, 26 were found guilty of 'crimes against peace' and of participating in a 'common plan or conspiracy' to commit this crime. One defendant was found guilty only with regard to 'crimes against peace', and the other was acquitted of all charges related to 'aggressive warfare'.[26]

United Nations attempts at defining aggression

In 1946, at the time the Nuremberg judgment was issued, the first session of the United Nations was underway and the General Assembly adopted Resolution 95(I) in which it affirmed the principles of international law contained in both the London Charter and the judgment of the Nuremberg Tribunal. The Assembly also expressed its desire to have these principles spelled out in the context of a general codification of offences against the peace and security of mankind, which would serve as an international criminal code.[27]

In 1950, the International Law Commission adopted the Nuremberg Principles—the principles of international law recognized in the London Charter and the Nuremberg judgment—and submitted them to the General Assembly for consideration. The Principles included the concept of 'crimes against peace', essentially reproducing the terms of the London Charter without specifying what constituted a 'war of aggression'.[28]

The following year, the International Law Commission produced a draft Code of Offences against the Peace and Security of Mankind, which listed the following as an offence under international law: 'Any act of aggression, including the employment by the authorities of a State of armed force against another State for any purpose other than national or collective self-defence or in pursuance of a decision or recommendation of a competent organ of the United Nations'.[29] However, the International Law Commission chose not to define the term 'act of aggression' essentially for two reasons. First, the Commission considered this to be a 'natural' notion that was not susceptible to a 'legal' definition. Second, even if such a definition could be adopted, it would be rendered useless due to the practical difficulties inherent in determining which state was to be labelled an aggressor.[30]

Yet, contrary to the position adopted by the International Law Commission, the General Assembly took the view that it was both possible and desirable to define the 'act of aggression', as this would ensure international peace and security and develop international law.[31] Consequently, it assigned this task to a Special Committee[32] and postponed its consideration of the Draft Code of Offences until such a definition would be adopted.[33] However, this objective was not achieved easily, because it took a total of four Special Committees and 22 years for the United Nations to adopt a definition of 'aggression'.[34]

On 14 December 1974, the General Assembly adopted, by consensus, Resolution 3314 (XXIX), to which was annexed the 'Definition of Aggression'. It defined an 'act of aggression' as: 'the use of armed force by a state against the sovereignty, territorial integrity or political independence of another state, or in any other manner inconsistent with the Charter of the United Nations'.[35] This generic description was supplemented by an open-ended list of seven 'aggressive acts'.[36] The remaining provisions of the 1974 Definition provided a formula for determining the existence of an 'act of aggression' and labelling a state as an aggressor,[37] as well as a number of legal principles that applied to the commission of an 'act of aggression'.[38] Moreover, the Definition specified that it did not affect the uses of force that were lawful under the UN Charter, such as self-defence,[39] or prejudice the right of peoples to self-determination.[40]

With the adoption of the 1974 Definition, the General Assembly instructed the International Law Commission to resume its work on the Draft Code of Offences.[41] After progressively working on the matter throughout the 1980s, the International Law Commission produced a new version of the Draft Code of Offences, which had since been renamed the Draft Code of Crimes against the Peace and Security of Mankind, in 1991, which criminalized aggression in a provision that was an amalgamation of the texts of the London Charter and the 1974 Definition.[42] Thus, for the first time in history, a text had been produced that defined the individual conduct that amounted to the 'crime' of aggression, as well as the crime's main element, i.e. the 'act' of aggression committed by a state. Most of the 25 states that commented on the 1991 Draft Code of Crimes did not indicate any major difficulties with the International Law Commission's reliance on the 1974 Definition as a basis for the provision outlawing aggression.[43] Only the United Kingdom and the United States objected to the use of the 1974 Definition, claiming that this text was not intended for criminal prosecutions and served only as a guide to the Security Council.[44]

Nevertheless, the International Law Commission came back on its position and thereafter did not provide a definition of the 'act' of aggression when dealing with the 'crime' of aggression. Thus, the 1994 Draft Statute for an International Criminal Court included the 'crime' of aggression but specified that a complaint related to an 'act' of aggression could not be brought before the Court unless the Security Council had first determined that a state had committed such an 'act' of aggression.[45] Moreover, the finalized version of the Draft Code of Crimes, adopted in 1996, defined the 'crime' of aggression as follows: 'An individual who, as leader or organizer, actively participates in or orders the planning, preparation, initiation or waging of aggression committed by a state'. Despite acknowledging that individual criminal responsibility for this crime was 'intrinsically and inextricably linked' to the commission of an 'act' of aggression by a state, the commentary to this provision indicated that the definition of such an 'act' was not addressed because it went beyond the scope of the Draft Code of Crimes, which applied to individuals only.[46]

The work of the International Law Commission during the 1990s formed part of a wider post-Cold War phenomenon that sought to put an end to impunity for the commission of serious violations of international law. Another aspect of this phenomenon was the creation by the Security Council of two *ad hoc* International Criminal Tribunals for the former Yugoslavia (1993) and for Rwanda (1994).[47] These developments contributed to the adoption, in 1998, of the Rome Statute of the International Criminal Court, which established a permanent judicial institution with the power to exercise jurisdiction over persons for the most serious crimes of international concern.[48]

Aggression under the Rome Statute

The 'crime' of aggression was included in the Rome Statute but was not defined. The delegations arrived at this compromise toward the end of the Rome diplomatic conference because they could not reach agreement on the definition of the 'crime' of aggression or on the manner in which the International Criminal Court was to adjudicate this crime.[49] Some of the problematic issues during the Rome diplomatic conference included the Security Council's role in determining the existence of an 'act' of aggression, the effect of such a determination on the Court, and the relationship between self-determination and aggression.[50] Consequently, Article 5(2) of the Rome Statute indicates that the Court shall exercise jurisdiction with respect to the 'crime' of aggression under three conditions. First, a provision must be adopted that defines this crime and sets out the conditions under which the Court may exercise its jurisdiction. Second, this provision must be adopted through an amendment to the Statute at the first review conference, which is scheduled to take place in 2010.[51] Third, this provision must be consistent with the relevant provisions of the UN Charter.[52]

After the adoption of the Rome Statute, the Preparatory Commission for the International Criminal Court was given the mandate of preparing certain key documents, such as the rules of procedure and evidence, the elements of crimes, the relationship agreement between the Court and the United Nations, and 'proposals for a provision on aggression' to be submitted to the Assembly of States Parties of the International Criminal Court.[53] By its final session in 2002, the Preparatory Commission had succeeded in adopting most of these documents. Yet, in the case of aggression, it only managed to produce a discussion paper which brought together various proposals on the definition and the Court's exercise of jurisdiction over this crime.[54]

Nevertheless, the work on aggression managed to continue through a Special Working Group, which was created by the Assembly of States Parties in 2002 and was open to all member states of the United Nations.[55] The Special Working Group took as its starting point the Preparatory Commission's discussion paper on aggression. By the end of its work in February 2009, the Special Working Group had managed to produce a series of proposals for a provision on aggression to be inserted into the Rome Statute.[56]

Proposed amendments to the Rome Statute

The definition of the 'crime' of aggression

The proposed amendments to the Rome Statute include the deletion of Article 5(2) and the insertion of a new Article 8*bis* pertaining to the 'crime' of aggression. It is also proposed that Articles 9 and 20(3) of the Statute, which, respectively, relate to the elements of crimes and the *ne bis in idem* principle, be amended in order to include references to Article 8*bis*.[57] Paragraph (1) of draft Article 8*bis* defines the 'crime' of aggression as:

> the planning, preparation, initiation or execution, by a person in a position effectively to exercise control over or to direct the political or military action of a State, of an act of aggression which, by its character, gravity and scale, constitutes a manifest violation of the Charter of the United Nations.[58]

Two of the four components of this definition derive directly from the prosecutions of 'crimes against peace' following the Second World War. First, there is the language used to describe the conduct elements of the 'crime'—namely, the planning, preparation, initiation, or execution—which is inspired by the London Charter. Second, there is the limitation of the 'crime' to the political and military leaders of a state, which is based on the jurisprudence of several allied military tribunals that tried the subordinates of the major Nazi war criminals and concluded that individual criminal responsibility for aggressive warfare had to be limited to the participants who had acted on a 'policy level'.[59] In this respect, a new paragraph (3*bis*) is intended to be added to Article 25(3) of the Rome Statute, in order to restrict the various means of perpetration and participation in the commission of the 'crime' of aggression to those who are in a position effectively to exercise control over or to direct the political or military action of a state.[60]

The third component of the proposed 'crime' of aggression is the 'act' of aggression committed by a state. Paragraph (2) of draft Article 8*bis* offers a generic definition of the 'act' of aggression that is supplemented by an exhaustive list of 'aggressive acts'; both the definition and the list are based on Articles 1 and 3 of the 1974 Definition.[61] The focus on these two Articles of the 1974 Definition is entirely justified when one considers the practice of the organs of the United Nations in determining the existence of an 'act' of aggression. Throughout their history, the Security Council and the General Assembly have made express determinations of 'aggression' in 31 and in 30 resolutions, respectively.[62] Moreover, the acts that the Security Council and the General Assembly have condemned in their resolutions have corresponded to the 'aggressive acts' enumerated in Article 3 of the 1974 Definition. Thus, it has been argued that Articles 1 and 3 of the 1974 Definition can be taken as expressing customary international law,[63] and draft Article 8*bis* merely reflects this fact.

With regard to the fourth component of the definition of the 'crime' of aggression, draft Article 8*bis* stipulates that the use of armed force must, by its character, gravity, and scale, amount to a manifest violation of the UN Charter in order to constitute an 'act' of aggression.

The imposition of such a minimal threshold of violence follows, to some extent, the same logic as the distinction drawn by the International Court of Justice between grave forms of the use of force, which constitute an 'armed attack', and less grave forms, which do not.[64]

The 1974 Definition employed a similar threshold in its Article 2 with regard to the determination of the existence of an 'act' of aggression, which applied in turn to the prohibited acts enumerated in Article 3. Although the remaining provisions of the 1974 Definition are not reproduced in draft Article 8*bis*, these may nevertheless be relied upon by the Court when interpreting what constitutes an 'act' of aggression. In this respect, draft Article 8*bis* specifies that the meaning to be given to this notion shall be in accordance with the 1974 Definition in its entirety.[65]

Thus, under Article 2 of the 1974 Definition, the first use of armed force is considered to be *prima facie* evidence of an 'act' of aggression; however, the Security Council may decide that a determination of aggression would not be justified in light of other relevant circumstances, such as the fact that the acts concerned or their consequences were not of sufficient gravity.[66] Also, the chapeau of Article 3 indicates that the characterization of the enumerated actions as 'aggressive acts' is subject to Article 2. Consequently, the actions listed in Article 3 are only prohibited, and therefore 'aggressive', when they form part of the first use of armed force by a state against another state. In other words, the 1974 Definition prohibits state 'A' from initially invading or attacking state 'B' but would allow state 'B', as a result of its right of self-defence, to attack and perhaps even invade state 'A' as part of a counter-offensive aimed at repelling the aggression.

Moreover, the reference to the gravity of the acts or their consequences in Article 2 of the 1974 Definition serves as a safeguard against a state attempting to mask its aggressive intentions under the guise of self-defence by overreacting to an initial use of armed force which is relatively insignificant. A few stray bullets originating from state 'A' would not be characterized as an 'attack' under Article 3 and therefore would not allow state 'B' to respond by launching a massive armed retaliation. Thus, the acts enumerated in Article 3 must be considered sufficiently grave in nature so as to amount to an 'armed attack' for the purposes of self-defence under Article 51 of the UN Charter.[67]

Exercise of jurisdiction over the crime by the International Criminal Court

Another proposed amendment to the Rome Statute is the inclusion of a new Article 15*bis* which would set out the manner in which the International Criminal Court would exercise its jurisdiction over the 'crime' of aggression. Paragraph (1) of this provision indicates that the three existing trigger mechanisms under Article 13 of the Rome Statute would apply to the 'crime' of aggression—namely, a referral by a state party, a Security Council referral, and a *proprio motu* investigation by the Prosecutor[68]—but would be subject to the rest of the terms of draft Article 15*bis*.[69]

According to paragraph (2) of this provision, in the event that the Prosecutor of the Court has concluded that there is a reasonable basis to proceed with an investigation concerning the 'crime' of aggression, he or she must first ascertain whether the Security Council has determined that the state concerned has committed an 'act' of aggression.[70] If indeed the Security Council has made such a determination, paragraph (3) indicates that the Prosecutor may proceed with an investigation into the 'crime' of aggression.[71]

On the one hand, the deference to the Security Council under paragraphs (2) and (3) of draft Article 15*bis* is premised on a 'best-case scenario', whereby the Council would have successfully made an express determination of an 'act' of aggression and designated a state as an 'aggressor'. This is understandable in light of the Council's primary responsibility for the maintenance of international peace and security,[72] and the obligation under Article 5(2) of the Rome Statute for the proposed provisions on aggression to be consistent with the relevant provisions of the UN Charter.[73]

On the other hand, this scenario does not address a potentially serious problem which is raised by the Security Council making such a determination and subsequently making a referral to the Court. Basically, the Council would be referring the principal element of the 'crime' of aggression to the Court, i.e. the 'act' of aggression, the existence of which it would have determined. This would be contrary to Article 13(b) of the Rome Statute, which only allows the Council to refer a 'situation' to the Prosecutor where one or more crimes appear to have been committed. Consequently, the Court's jurisdiction in such a scenario could be challenged, and the main advantage associated with a Security Council referral—i.e. the ability to subject non-state parties to the Court's jurisdiction—would be lost.[74] Ironically, the Security Council would be a 'victim of its own success' for having actually succeeded in making a rare determination of an 'act' of aggression. In this respect, it would be better for the cause of international criminal justice if the Security Council were to refer a situation to the Court involving the use of armed force between two states, which generally implies that the *jus contra bellum* has been violated, yet without making an express determination of an 'act' of aggression.

In addition to this 'best-case scenario', draft Article 15*bis* contains two alternative versions of paragraph (4), both of which list a number of options pertaining to the procedure to be followed in the event that the Security Council does not make a determination of an 'act' of aggression. The reason these options are proposed in draft Article 15*bis* is that the Special Working Group was not able to resolve the issue of whether the Prosecutor could proceed with an investigation in the absence of a determination by the Council.

The philosophy behind the first alternative version of paragraph (4) is that the Prosecutor should not be allowed to investigate the 'crime' of aggression without either an express determination by the Security Council (Option 1)[75] or, at the very least, a request by the Council to initiate such an investigation (Option 2).[76] In this respect, Option 1 essentially ensures that the Security Council retains complete control over the matter. It would particularly suit the Council's permanent members, who could exercise their veto and prevent any determination of aggression being made against them or their allies. However, this would run squarely against the Court's independence as a judicial institution, as recognized by both the Rome Statute and the Relationship Agreement between the United Nations and the International Criminal Court.[77]

In contrast, Option 2 indicates that the Prosecutor can proceed with an investigation where the Security Council has made a referral to the Court requesting the Prosecutor to proceed with an investigation into the 'crime' of aggression, even though it has not itself made a determination of the existence of an 'act' of aggression.[78] Yet, by subjecting the Court's jurisdiction over the 'crime' of aggression exclusively to a Security Council referral, this option effectively contradicts paragraph (1) of draft Article 15*bis*, which provides for the application of all three trigger mechanisms to this 'crime'. Moreover, Option 2 proposes that the Council refer a 'crime' to the Court, rather than a 'situation', which is contrary to Article 13(b) of the Rome Statute, as mentioned previously. Also, in the event that one or more permanent members of the Security Council were to prevent the adoption of a resolution determining the existence of an 'act' of aggression, it is difficult to see how these same members would allow the matter to be referred to, and potentially decided by, the Court.

The second alternative of paragraph (4) of draft Article 15*bis* is based on an entirely different premise: namely, that the Prosecutor can proceed with an investigation into the 'crime' of aggression despite the absence of a determination by the Security Council. The only question is what modalities, if any, would have to be followed by the Prosecutor in this event. Thus, Option 1 of the second alternative suggests that no additional modalities be made to apply and that the

Prosecutor simply be allowed to proceed with an investigation into the 'crime' of aggression.[79] In contrast, Option 2 proposes that the initiation of such an investigation be expressly subject to the authorization of the Pre-Trial Chamber under Article 15 of the Rome Statute.[80] In fact, there is a large degree of overlap between these two options because Article 15 of the Statute already applies to any *proprio motu* investigation by the Prosecutor, in which case the requirement expressed under Option 2 essentially becomes redundant. However, Option 2 is innovative in relation to an investigation triggered by a state-party referral, because it proposes to extend the Pre-Trial Chamber's role to investigations concerning the 'crime' of aggression, even though Article 14 of the Rome Statute does not specifically require such a procedure with respect to a state-party referral.[81]

Options 3 and 4 attempt to ensure that the determination of an 'act' of aggression be made by an organ of the United Nations other than the Security Council: namely, the General Assembly[82] or the International Court of Justice.[83] These options are based on the reasoning that the Security Council has primary, but not exclusive, competence with regard to international peace and security, a principle that has been confirmed by the International Court of Justice.[84] In this respect, Options 3 and 4 would also meet the requirements of Article 5(2) of the Rome Statute.

In relation to the General Assembly determining that an 'act' of aggression had been committed by a state under Option 3, several precedents exist to this effect, as mentioned previously. However, it should be noted that the adoption of such a resolution would require a two-thirds majority of the General Assembly's members present and voting because it pertains to the maintenance of international peace and security.[85] Thus, it is not definite that such a large number of votes could be obtained in every alleged case of aggression. Furthermore, it is not clear what the effect of such a resolution would be on the International Criminal Court. For instance, could the Prosecutor simply initiate an investigation *proprio motu*, according to Article 15 of the Rome Statute, or would a referral by at least one state party to the Statute have to be made on behalf of the General Assembly, given the fact that the latter cannot itself refer a situation directly to the Court.

With regard to the International Court of Justice, Option 4 allows for a determination of an 'act' of aggression to be made in the context of either an advisory opinion or a contentious case.[86] However, the problem with both of these procedures is the length of time it would take to make a determination, which could span from a few months to several years. Another problem that arises specifically in the case of an advisory opinion is that this is a non-binding procedure in which the International Court of Justice gives advice on a 'legal' question, whereas the determination of an 'act' of aggression is a 'factual' issue. This could perhaps be circumvented by posing a legal question that would require the International Court of Justice to examine the underlying factual issue, such as what are the legal consequences of the use of force by state 'A' against state 'B'? Yet even in such a scenario, the International Court of Justice might choose to exercise its discretion and not to render an advisory opinion. Moreover, the recourse to contentious proceedings is problematic as well because it could be a daunting, if not an impossible, task to secure the consent of the presumed aggressor state(s). Even in the event that the concerned parties consented to such proceedings, history has shown that the International Court of Justice has been reluctant to characterize a particular use of armed force as 'aggression'.[87] Finally, the questions pertaining to the manner in which the jurisdiction of the International Criminal Court would be triggered after a determination by the International Court of Justice remain to be answered and resemble those mentioned above with regard to the General Assembly.

Paragraph (5) of draft Article 15*bis* states that a determination of an 'act' of aggression by an organ outside the International Criminal Court would not prejudice the Court's own findings under the Rome Statute.[88] The purpose of paragraph (5), which in practice would apply only to paragraph (3) and Options 3 and 4 of the second alternative of paragraph (4), is to ensure that a determination by any organ of the United Nations would serve merely as a procedural prerequisite to triggering the Court's jurisdiction and would not affect the substance of the criminal proceedings. It safeguards both the independence and impartiality of the International Criminal Court as a judicial institution, as well as the right to a fair trial of any individual accused of the 'crime' of aggression. Accordingly, the Rome Statute provides that the onus to prove the guilt of an accused is on the Prosecutor[89] and guarantees that no burden of proof or onus of rebuttal be imposed on the accused.[90] Consequently, an accused individual should be allowed to invoke defences and justifications pertaining to the international law on state responsibility, such as self-defence or the 'state of necessity',[91] in order to challenge whether an 'act' of aggression has indeed been committed, irrespective of prior determinations by United Nations organs. Thus, the International Criminal Court might ultimately decide that the determination of the existence of an 'act' of aggression would in fact not be justified based on the evidence or other relevant exonerating circumstances.

Finally, paragraph (6) concludes by stating that draft Article 15*bis* is without prejudice to the provisions regarding the exercise of jurisdiction with respect to other crimes referred to in Article 5 of the Rome Statute.[92] This merely serves as reminder that draft Article 15*bis* creates a *lex specialis* that only applies to the 'crime' of aggression. This is evidenced by Option 2 of the second alternative of paragraph (4), which proposes to modify the state referral system under Article 14 of the Statute only with regard to aggression.

Conclusion

Even though the Special Working Group concluded its work in February 2009, the Assembly of States Parties recommended that the work on the 'crime' of aggression continue. Thus, the Government of Liechtenstein hosted an informal meeting of states in June 2009, producing a draft text on the elements of the 'crime' of aggression.[93] The workings of paragraph (4) of draft Article 15*bis* were also discussed during this meeting and it was stressed that a politically acceptable solution had to be found in relation to the manner in which the International Criminal Court would exercise its jurisdiction over the 'crime' of aggression;[94] however, no consensus was achieved over the various options contained in this provision. In light of the several problems discussed above, it would be useless to reach a political consensus on this provision that would not be legally viable.

The states also discussed whether the formula contained in paragraph (4) of Article 121 of the Rome Statute, or the formula contained in paragraph (5), or both formulas should apply to the proposed provisions relating to aggression. Once again, the delegations reached no consensus and repeatedly expressed the necessity of reaching a politically acceptable solution.[95]

Thus, in relation to the formula under paragraph (4) of Article 121, once seven-eighths of the states parties to the Rome Statute have ratified or accepted a given amendment, it becomes binding on all states parties one year after its entry into force.[96] This could delay the exercise of jurisdiction over the 'crime' of aggression by the International Criminal Court for several years, pending the ratification by seven-eighths of the states parties. Moreover, once this number is reached, certain states parties that would be subjected to the amendment without having expressly accepted it might be driven to withdraw from the Rome Statute entirely, thereby preventing the International Criminal Court from exercising its jurisdiction with respect to genocide, crimes against humanity, and war crimes, in addition to the 'crime' of aggression with regard to these states.[97]

In relation to the formula under paragraph (5) of Article 121, an amendment enters into force only with regard to those states parties that have accepted it, one year after their ratification or acceptance. In this respect, the International Criminal Court could presumably exercise its jurisdiction much earlier than it would if it were to apply paragraph (4) of Article 121. Nevertheless, paragraph (5) is not without problems. For instance, this provision specifically applies to amendments to Articles 5, 6, 7, and 8 of the Rome Statute.[98] Although it can theoretically be argued that Article 5(2) of the Rome Statute will be amended and replaced by draft Article 8*bis,* the latter must in actuality be considered an entirely new provision that is technically not included in the above enumeration, as is the case with draft Article 15*bis*. Moreover, paragraph (5) of Article 121 stipulates that the Court shall not exercise its jurisdiction in relation to a crime covered by a particular amendment when committed by the nationals or on the territory of a state that has not accepted this amendment.[99] This is particularly problematic when one considers that a 'crime' of aggression is typically planned, prepared, and perhaps even initiated by the nationals of the aggressor state acting on the territory of the aggressed state.

No progress was made with regard to these difficult and politically sensitive issues during the first part of the eighth session of the Assembly of States Parties in November 2009. States parties will have another opportunity to find a solution in March 2010, when the eighth session will reconvene.[100] If consensus is not reached, the task will ultimately be left up to the 2010 review conference in Kampala. What is clear, however, is that while the quest to define the 'crime' of aggression and its constituent elements has taken several decades, the most significant progress has been made by the Special Working Group, and it would appear that the likelihood of reaching consensus is greater than ever.

Notes

1 Covenant of the League of Nations, 11 Martens Nouveau Recueil Général de Traités Ser. 3 (1922) 337, Art. 11.
2 Ibid., Art. 10.
3 Ibid., Arts 12, 15.
4 General Treaty for the Renunciation of War as an Instrument of National Policy, 94 LNTS (1929) 59, Art. 1.
5 M. Gonsiorowski, 'The Legal Meaning of the Pact of the Renunciation of War', 30 *American Political Science Review,* 1936, 664–72; G. Wickersham, 'The Pact of Paris: A Gesture or a Pledge?', 7 *Foreign Affairs*, 1929, 357–62.
6 V. H. Rutgers, 'La mise en harmonie du Pacte de la Société des Nations avec le Pacte de Paris', 38 *Recueil de Cours de l'Académie de Droit International*, 1931, 80–118.
7 'Joint Statement by President Roosevelt and Prime Minister Churchill', August 14, 1941 (the 'Atlantic Charter'), in United States Department of State, *Foreign Relations of the United States, Diplomatic Papers*, Washington: Government Printing Office, 1941, vol. 1, pp. 367–8; 'Declaration by United Nations', in Ibid., 1942, vol. 1, pp. 25–6; 'Declaration of Four Nations on General Security', in Ibid., 1943, vol. 1, pp. 755–6.
8 Charter of the United Nations, 59 Stat. 1031, T.S. 993 (1945) [hereinafter UN Charter].
9 'Charter of the International Military Tribunal' annexed to the Agreement for the Prosecution and Punishment of the Major War Criminals of the European Axis, signed at London, on 8 August 1945, 82 UNTS 279 (1951) [hereinafter IMT Charter].
10 UN Charter, Art. 2(4).
11 Ibid., Art. 51.
12 Ibid., Arts 39, 41–2.
13 L. M. Goodrich and E. Hambro, *Charter of the United Nations: Commentary and Documents*, Boston: World Peace Foundation, 1949, p. 104.
14 Great Britain made a reservation according to which it sought to preserve its freedom of action in certain regions of the world in order to safeguard its vital interests. Despite the fact that this reservation was contrary to the Pact's object and purpose (and would most probably have been declared illegal under

modern rules of treaty interpretation), only Persia, the Soviet Union, Egypt, Afghanistan and the Irish Free State objected to it. See A. Mandelstam, 'L'interprétation du Pacte Briand-Kellogg par les gouvernements et les parlements des états signataires', 40 *Revue Générale de Droit International Public*, 1933, 561–3; A. Mandelstam, 'L'interprétation du Pacte Briand-Kellogg par les gouvernements et les parlements des états signataires (Fin)', 41 *Revue Générale de Droit International Public*, 1934, 239–42; Vienna Convention on the Law of Treaties, 1155 UNTS 331 (1980), Art. 19 (c).

15 B. Broms, *The Definition of Aggression in the United Nations*, Turku: Turun Yliopisto, 1968, p. 32; W. Komarnicki, 'La définition de l'agresseur dans le droit international moderne', 75 *Recueil de Cours de l'Académie de Droit International,* 1949, 73–4.

16 'Declaration of German Atrocities', in *Foreign Relations of the United States, Diplomatic Papers,* 1943, vol. 1, pp. 768–9.

17 'Memorandum to President Roosevelt from the Secretaries of State and War and the Attorney General, January 22, 1945', in *Report of Robert H. Jackson: United States Representative to the International Conference on Military Trials, London, 1945*, Washington: Government Printing Office, 1949, p. 6 [hereinafter Report of Robert H. Jackson].

18 See 'Minutes of Conference Session, July 17, 1945'; 'Minutes of Conference Session, July 19, 1945'; 'Minutes of Conference Session, July 20, 1945'; 'Minutes of Conference Session, July 23, 1945'; 'Minutes of Conference Session, July 25, 1945'; 'Minutes of Conference Session, August 2, 1945', in *Report of Robert H. Jackson*, pp. 262–80, 295–310, 315–27, 328–48, 376–90, 399–420.

19 Ibid.

20 IMT Charter, Art. 6(a).

21 'Minutes of Conference Session, July 24, 1945', in *Report of Robert H. Jackson*, pp. 360–73.

22 See 'Minutes of Conference Session, July 2, 1945'; 'Minutes of Conference Session, July 4, 1945'; 'Minutes of Conference Session, July 16, 1945'; 'Minutes of Conference Session, July 19, 1945', in *Report of Robert H. Jackson*, pp. 129–43, 155–65, 246–59, 295–310; B. F. Smith, *The Road to Nuremberg*, New York: Basic Books, 1981, pp. 233–4.

23 'International Military Tribunal (Nuremberg) Judgment and Sentences', 41 *American Journal of International Law*, 1947, 192–213, 333.

24 Ibid., pp. 213–4.

25 Charter of the International Military Tribunal for the Far East, 19 January 1946, TIAS No. 1589, Art. 5(a).

26 R. J. Pritchard and S. M. Zaide (eds), *The Tokyo War Crimes Trial,* New York: Garland Publishing, 1981, vol. 20, pp. 49773–858.

27 'Affirmation of the Principles of International Law recognized by the Charter of the Nürnberg Tribunal', U.N. Doc. A/RES/95 (I) (1946).

28 'Principles of International Law Recognized in the Charter of the Nürnberg Tribunal and in the Judgment of the Tribunal', in *Yearbook of the International Law Commission,* 1950, vol. 2, paras 110–18.

29 'Draft Code of Offences against the Peace and Security of Mankind', in *Yearbook of the International Law Commission*, 1951, vol. 2, p. 135, Art. 2(1).

30 Ibid., p. 131.

31 'Question of Defining Aggression', U.N. Doc. A/RES/599 (VI) (1952), Preamble, para. 4.

32 'Question of Defining Aggression', U.N. Doc. A/RES/688 (VII) (1952), para. 1.

33 'Draft Code of Offences against the Peace and Security of Mankind', U.N. Doc. A/RES/897 (IX) (1954).

34 B. B. Ferencz, *Defining International Aggression,* New York: Oceana Publications, 1975, vol. 2, pp. 4–54.

35 'Definition of Aggression', Art. 1, annexed to U.N. Doc. A/RES/3314 (XXIX) (1974).

36 Ibid., Arts 3–4.

37 Ibid., Art. 2.

38 Ibid., Art. 5.

39 Ibid., Art. 6.

40 Ibid., Art. 7.

41 'Draft Code of Offences against the Peace and Security of Mankind', U.N. Doc. A/RES/33/97 (1978); 'Draft Code of Offences against the Peace and Security of Mankind', U.N. Doc. A/RES/36/106 (1981).

42 'Draft Code of Crimes against the Peace and Security of Mankind', in *Yearbook of the International Law Commission*, 1991, vol. 2, part 2, p. 95, Art. 15.

43 'Draft Code of Crimes against the Peace and Security of Mankind: Comments and Observations Received from Governments', in *Yearbook of the International Law Commission,* 1993, vol. 2, part 1, pp. 59–109.
44 Ibid., pp. 100–3.
45 'Draft Statute for an International Criminal Court', in *Yearbook of the International Law Commission,* 1994, vol. 2, part 2, pp. 43–5, Art. 23(2).
46 'Draft Code of Crimes against the Peace and Security of Mankind', in *Yearbook of the International Law Commission,* 1996, vol. 2, part 2, pp. 42–3, Art. 16.
47 W. A. Schabas, *An Introduction to the International Criminal Court,* 3rd edn, Cambridge: Cambridge University Press, 2007, pp. 8–15.
48 Rome Statute of the International Criminal Court, 2187 UNTS 90 (2002), Art. 1[hereinafter Rome Statute].
49 H. von Hebel and D. Robinson, 'Crimes Within the Jurisdiction of the Court', in R. Lee (ed.), *The International Criminal Court: The Making of the Rome Statute,* The Hague: Kluwer Law International, 1999, p. 85.
50 Ibid., pp. 80–5.
51 'Venue of the Review Conference', in Assembly of States Parties to the International Criminal Court, Seventh Session, ICC-ASP/7/Res.2, The Hague, 14–22 November 2008, Official Records, vol. 1, p. 26.
52 Rome Statute, Art. 5(2).
53 Resolution 'F', in *final Act of the United Nations Diplomatic Conference of Plenipotentiaries on the Establishment of an International Criminal Court,* U.N. Doc. A/CONF.183/10 (1998).
54 'Discussion paper proposed by the Coordinator', U.N. Doc. PCNICC/2002/WGCA/RT.1/Rev.2.
55 'Continuity of work in respect of the crime of aggression', in Assembly of States Parties to the International Criminal Court, First Session, ICC-ASP/1/Res.1, New York, 3–10 September 2002, Official Records, p. 328.
56 'Proposals for a provision on aggression elaborated by the Special Working Group on the Crime of Aggression', in *Assembly of States Parties to the Rome Statute of the International Criminal Court, Seventh Session (first and second resumptions),* ICC-ASP/7/20/Add.1, Appendix I, New York, 19–23 January and 9–13 February 2009, Official Records, pp. 30–2.
57 Ibid.
58 Ibid., Art. 8*bis*, para. 1.
59 See N. Strapatsas, 'Is Article 25(3) of the ICC Statute Compatible with the "Crime of Aggression"?', 19 *Florida Journal of International Law,* 2007, 177–86.
60 ICC-ASP/7/20/Add.1, Appendix I, p. 32.
61 Ibid., Art. 8*bis*, para. 2.
62 For references see N. Strapatsas, 'Rethinking General Assembly Resolution 3314 (1974) as a Basis for the Definition of Aggression under the Rome Statute of the ICC', in Olaoluwa Olusanya (ed.), *Rethinking International Criminal Law: The Substantive Part,* Groningen: Europa Law Publishing, 2007, pp. 177–86. The following seven General Assembly resolutions can be added to those mentioned in the chapter referred to: 'Question of Palestine', U.N. Doc. A/RES/ES-7/5 (1982), Preamble, para. 3; 'Question of Palestine', U.N. Doc. A/RES/ES-7/6 (1982), Preamble, para. 6; 'Question of Namibia', U.N. Doc. A/RES/ES-8/2 (1981), Preamble, para. 2; para. 7; 'The situation in the occupied Arab territories' U.N. Doc. A/RES/ES-9/1 (1982), para. 2; 'The Situation in Bosnia and Herzegovina', U.N. Doc. A/RES/46/242 (1992), Preamble, para. 7; 'The Situation in Bosnia and Herzegovina', U.N. Doc. A/RES/48/88 (1993), Preamble, paras 2, 6, 13; 'The Situation in Bosnia and Herzegovina', U.N. Doc. A/RES/49/10 (1994), Preamble, para. 3.
63 Ibid., p. 190.
64 Case Concerning Military and Paramilitary Activities in and against Nicaragua (Nicaragua v. United States of America), 1986 ICJ Rep 14, para. 191; Case Concerning Oil Platforms (Islamic Republic of Iran v. United States of America), 2003 ICJ Rep 161, para. 51.
65 ICC-ASP/7/20/Add.1, Appendix I, Art. 8*bis*, para. 2.
66 'Definition of Aggression', Art. 2.
67 B. Broms, 'The Definition of Aggression', 154 *Recueil de Cours de l'Académie de Droit International,* 1977, 346.
68 Rome Statute, Art. 13.
69 ICC-ASP/7/20/Add.1, Appendix I, Art. 15*bis*, para. 1.

70 Ibid., Art. 15*bis*, para. 2.
71 Ibid., Art. 15*bis*, para. 3.
72 UN Charter, Art. 24.
73 Rome Statute, Art. 5(2).
74 Ibid., Arts 12, 13(b), 87(5), (7).
75 ICC-ASP/7/20/Add.1, Appendix I, Art. 15*bis*, para. 4 (alternative 1), Option 1.
76 Ibid., Art. 15*bis*, para. 4 (alternative 1), Option 2.
77 Rome Statute, Preamble, para. 9; Relationship Agreement between the United Nations and the International Criminal Court, 2283 UNTS (2006) 196, Art. 2.
78 ICC-ASP/7/20/Add.1, Appendix I, Art. 15*bis*, para. 4 (alternative 1), Option 2.
79 Ibid., Art. 15*bis*, para. 4 (alternative 2), Option 1.
80 Ibid., Art. 15*bis*, para. 4 (alternative 2), Option 2.
81 Antonio Marchesi, 'Article 14: Referral of a Situation by a State Party', in O. Triffterer (ed.), *Commentary on the Rome Statute of the International Criminal Court,* 2nd edn, Munich: C.H. Beck-Hart-Nomos, 2008, pp. 575–9.
82 ICC-ASP/7/20/Add.1, Appendix I, Art. 15*bis*, para. 4 (alternative 2), Option 3.
83 Ibid., Art. 15*bis*, para. 4 (alternative 2), Option 4.
84 Legal Consequences of the Construction of a Wall in the Occupied Palestinian Territory, Advisory Opinion, 2004 ICJ Rep 136, paras 26–7.
85 UN Charter, Art. 18(2).
86 ICC-ASP/7/20/Add.1, Appendix I, Art. 15*bis*, para. 4 (alternative 2), Option 4.
87 Case Concerning Military and Paramilitary Activities in and against Nicaragua, para. 292; Case Concerning Armed Activities on the Territory of the Congo (Democratic Republic of the Congo v. Uganda), 2005 ICJ Rep para. 345.
88 ICC-ASP/7/20/Add.1, Appendix I, Art. 15*bis*, para. 5.
89 Rome Statute, Art. 66(2).
90 Ibid., Art. 67(1)(i).
91 'Draft articles on responsibility of states for internationally wrongful acts', in *Yearbook of the International Law Commission,* 2001, vol. 2, part 2, pp. 27–28, Arts 21, 25.
92 ICC-ASP/7/20/Add.1, Appendix I, Art. 15*bis*, para. 6.
93 'Informal inter-sessional meeting on the Crime of Aggression, hosted by the Liechtenstein Institute on Self-Determination', ICC-ASP/8/INF.2, Annex I, Woodrow Wilson School, at the Princeton Club, New York, from 8 to 10 June 2009.
94 Ibid., paras 42–53.
95 Ibid., paras 32–41.
96 Rome Statute, Art. 121(4).
97 Ibid., Art. 121(6).
98 Ibid., Art. 121(5).
99 Ibid., Art. 121(5).
100 'Assembly of States Parties concludes its eighth session', ICC-ASP-20091126-PR481, Press Release, 27, November 2009.

11

Terrorism as an international crime

Fiona de Londras

Introduction

Although terrorism has become the subject of sustained levels of discussion and scholarship in international law in recent years, these discussions and writings have generally focused on whether acts of terrorism can trigger the right to use force and how counter-terrorist operations and the law of human rights interact with one another in situations of actual or perceived terrorist risk.[1] This chapter, however, is focused more on whether, and if so, how, international criminal law can be employed in the courtroom-level attempts to counter terroristic activity. Following an overview of the long-standing difficulties in international discourses with coming to a general, binding, treaty-based definition of 'terrorism', the chapter proceeds to consider the ways in which existing international criminal law can be said to include within it prohibitions of terrorist activity; whether terrorism *per se* is a crime in international law; and the ways in which international treaty-based prohibitions on certain types of terrorist activity are developing a transnational criminal law relating to terrorism. Finally, the chapter considers the prospects for an international crime of terrorism in the future.

Definitional conundrums

Before considering the extent to which international criminal law encompasses and prohibits what is known or classified as terrorist activity, the definitional difficulties raised by the treatment of terrorism in international law generally must be addressed. It is, by now, almost clichéd to begin considerations of legal treatments of terrorism with an acknowledgement that the international legal system has found itself to be incapable of coming to a binding, general international legal definition of 'terrorism' in treaty law.[2] Clichés notwithstanding, the definitional conundrums posed by terrorism cannot be ignored, particularly in relation to international criminal law in which the principles of certainty and clarity of prohibited activities must be borne in mind just as they must be in domestic law.

The absence of a general definition of terrorism in international law means that attempts to criminalise terrorism *per se* as a crime are prone to run into serious difficulties of clarity and certainty. These same difficulties do not necessarily arise in relation to situations in which terroristic activity is prosecuted within the ambit of recognised international crimes because, in such cases, the activities are being considered as crimes against humanity, genocide, war crimes or grave breaches when the actions grounding the indictments happen to have been terroristic in character. In essence, the fact that these activities might be labelled as 'terrorism' does not necessarily have any impact on the exercise of proving the elements of the crime as defined within international criminal law generally. That said, such labelling may be relevant in the context of sentencing and certainly has a rhetorical impact that ought not to be underestimated.[3]

Tracing the historical difficulties faced by the international community in defining terrorism is beyond the scope of this chapter;[4] however, the process of trying to reach a definition can be characterised by the two primary stumbling blocks that have been encountered: actor and purpose. There has historically been a considerable amount of resistance to the notion that a state could be deemed to engage in terroristic activity. Even where a state acts unlawfully, including by attacking civilians and/or creating and spreading terror among the civilian population, such unlawful acts are generally considered to be breaches of international humanitarian law but *not* acts that ought to attract the label of 'terrorist' within the international legal discourse.

Precisely the same acts carried out by a non-state actor might be deemed terroristic. This suggests that the identity of the actor has a bearing on the legitimacy of the act. Legitimacy here must be understood as something other than lawfulness, for a state can act in an unlawful manner in international law but not, it seems, in a terroristic manner. When a state acts, even if its actions are prohibited by international law, there is some kind of assumed and implicit legitimacy within those acts that flows from the state identity of the actor. Laura Donohue has been particularly effective in arguing against this conflation of legitimacy and statehood and has questioned the assumptive nature of that conflation within international legal discourses around terrorism (and, indeed, the inverse assumption that acts by non-state actors are necessarily *illegitimate*).[5] Notwithstanding those objections, it does not appear to be the case that states and state actors can be said to be terrorists within international legal parlance.

The second point of contestation within the attempts to arrive at a general international legal definition of terrorism centres on the matter of purpose. In general, an act that is unlawful in all circumstances will be terroristic only in circumstances when it is said to have been directed at a particular purpose or, in other words, to have a particular motive. Terrorism is generally conceived of as an activity that is motivated by a desire to spread feelings of terror and lack of security among the civilian population in order to try to influence the actions of a state or an institution. Indeed, it is the targeting of civilians towards a particular purpose or with a particular motivation that is generally said to distinguish terroristic activity from 'simple' criminal activity; it is the distinction between mass murder and a terrorist attack that brings about multiple fatalities. At their core, both of these examples involve the same action and result: causing the death of multiple persons by means of unlawful activity. Rhetorically, politically and legally, however, the latter example is seen as a different and, generally, more challenging and dangerous activity than the former. It is often said that the purpose or motivation of terrorist activity is one of the factors that makes effective counter-terrorism so difficult. If one has a political, ideological or religious motivation, it is thought that the deterrent effect generally associated with the criminal law is less likely to have an impact on prospective offenders. Although political science has developed a body of literature that calls into question whether individual actors within terrorist campaigns can truly be said to have terroristic motivations closely tethered to political, ideological or religious beliefs,[6] the international community has generally approached terrorism in a manner that presupposes the importance of purpose and motive not only as a definitional matter but also as a design matter in counter-terrorism.

Notwithstanding these definitional conundrums, there are numerous international treaties that deal with and prohibit terrorist activities in particular circumstances:

1 UN Convention on Offences and Certain Other Acts Committed on Board Aircraft (1963);
2 UN Convention on the Suppression of Unlawful Seizure of Aircraft (1970);
3 UN Convention for the Suppression of Unlawful Acts against the Safety of Civil Aviations (1971);
4 UN Convention on the Prevention and Punishment of Crimes against Internationally Protected Persons (1973);
5 UN International Convention on the Physical Protection of Nuclear Material (1980);
6 UN Protocol for the Suppression of Unlawful Acts of Violence at Airports Serving International Aviation, Supplementary to the Convention for the Suppression of Unlawful Acts against the Safety of Civil Aviation (1988);
7 UN Convention for the Suppression of Unlawful Acts against the Safety of Maritime Navigation (1988);
8 UN Protocol for the Suppression of Unlawful Acts against the Safety of Fixed Platforms Located on the Continental Shelf (1988);
9 UN Convention on the Marking of Plastic Explosives for the Purpose of Detection (1991);
10 International Convention for the Suppression of Terrorist Bombings (1997);
11 International Convention for the Suppression of the Financing of Terrorism (1999);
12 International Convention for the Suppression of Acts of Nuclear Terrorism (2005).

The conclusion and ratification of these treaties reflect the fact that the difficulty in international law is not with the principle that terrorism ought to be prohibited as a matter of law, but rather with the task of coming to an agreement on what terrorism is as a general matter. Thus, while we have prohibited terrorism in discrete circumstances and of particular types as a matter of positive law, we have not managed to formulate a treaty-based crime of terrorism *per se*.

Elements of terrorism and international crimes

Terrorist activity might well involve the commission of acts that are themselves violations of international criminal law and particularly of the Statute of the International Criminal Court. That Statute provides jurisdiction to the ICC over four types of international crime: crimes against humanity, genocide, war crimes and the crime of aggression. Although a definition of the crime of aggression was agreed upon at the Review Conference of the Rome Statute in the summer of 2010, the crime itself will not operate for some time and can therefore, be left to one side in the current consideration of the Statute's relevance to terrorsim.[7] The capacity of international criminal law to 'capture' terrorist activities within its established international crimes is significant in three ways.

Firstly it recognises that 'new' crimes need not always be created in response to terrorist activity, as such activity is, in almost all cases, constituted of unlawful actions that can be prosecuted under existing legal frameworks. This refutes often-made claims that the international legal system is compelled to amend itself to 'radical' or 'new' challenges posed by terrorism and rather reiterates the fact that international law is sufficiently broad in range to capture the majority of such activities within its pre-existing doctrinal structures.

Secondly, inasmuch as international crimes can be said to be subject to universal jurisdiction, the categorisation of terroristic activity within pre-existing frameworks of international criminal law both enables and compels states to apprehend, prosecute and aid in the apprehension and prosecution of individuals who are indicted in relation to such offences.

Thirdly, and following *a priori* from the second point of significance, as all of these crimes fall within the Rome Statute of the International Criminal Court, it is conceivable that when nation states are unwilling or unable to undergo domestic prosecutions or to facilitate prosecutions elsewhere relating to such activities, the International Criminal Court may be in a position to 'step in' and act in a complementary manner in order to bring such offences within recognised rubrics of criminal justice.

Crimes against humanity

Article 7 of the Rome Statute of the International Criminal Court defines crimes against humanity over which the Court has jurisdiction thus:

> For the purpose of this Statute, 'crime against humanity' means any of the following acts when committed as part of a widespread or systematic attack directed against any civilian population, with knowledge of the attack:
>
> (a) Murder;
> (b) Extermination;
> (c) Enslavement;
> (d) Deportation or forcible transfer of population;
> (e) Imprisonment or other severe deprivation of physical liberty in violation of fundamental rules of international law;
> (f) Torture;
> (g) Rape, sexual slavery, enforced prostitution, forced pregnancy, enforced sterilization, or any other form of sexual violence of comparable gravity;
> (h) Persecution against any identifiable group or collectivity on political, racial, national, ethnic, cultural, religious, gender as defined in paragraph 3, or other grounds that are universally recognized as impermissible under international law, in connection with any act referred to in this paragraph or any crime within the jurisdiction of the Court;
> (i) Enforced disappearance of persons;
> (j) The crime of apartheid;
> (k) Other inhumane acts of a similar character intentionally causing great suffering, or serious injury to body or to mental or physical health.

The crime therefore requires the commission of one or more of the specified acts against a civilian population as part of a widespread or systematic attack of which the perpetrator had knowledge. The difficulty with placing acts of terrorism within this framework is most likely to lie in the requirement of a 'widespread or systematic attack' as, in many cases, terrorist acts are relatively isolated incidents or, when they are part of a wave of incidents (for example, a wave of suicide bombings), it is frequently the case that such acts are not necessarily centrally directed or organised. In addition, even when there is a case of a wave of attacks over a relatively concentrated period of time, for example, there are difficulties with identifying the threshold for a 'widespread or systematic attack' from a definitional perspective—at what point does such a campaign become widespread or systematic? Article 7(2) of the Statute provides that an attack against the civilian population is to be understood as 'a course of conduct involving the multiple commission of acts referred to in [Article 7(1)] against any civilian population, pursuant to or in furtherance of a State or organisational policy to commit such attack'. Regrettably, this does not offer any further clarity in relation to the 'widespread or systematic' requirement. That notwithstanding, it is conceivable that a terrorist attack or series of attacks could constitute crimes against humanity under Article 7.

Although the Statute suggests that what is required is *either* a widespread *or* a systematic attack, the definition of an attack on the civilian population considered earlier suggests that the distinction between these two classifications may be one of degree rather than one of nature, as both will have to have taken place 'pursuant to or in furtherance of a State or organizational policy to commit such attack'.[8] This arguably blurs the distinction between widespread and systematic attacks that had previously been set down by the Trial Chamber of the ICTR in *Prosecutor v Kayishema and Ruzindana*:[9] thus, 'a widespread attack is one that is directed towards a multiplicity of victims. A systematic attack means an attack carried out pursuant to a preconceived policy or plan'.[10]

Although Article 7 causes a question mark to fall over the extent to which the two types of attack are to be doctrinally distinguished, the distinction from *Kayishema and Ruzindana* is still useful in terms of clarifying that it is possible for a single terrorist attack or a wave of attacks to constitute a crime against humanity provided they are reasonably coordinated and involve an element of organisation and orchestration. Thus, one might argue that the attacks of 11 September 2001 involving, as it appears they did, the multiple commission of acts, including murder against a civilian population in a manner that was both widespread and systematic, constituted a crime against humanity. It may, therefore, have been possible to apply the pre-existing international criminal law framework to that attack.

Genocide

The International Criminal Court has jurisdiction over the crime of genocide, which is defined in Article 6 as follows:

> For the purpose of this Statute, 'genocide' means any of the following acts committed with intent to destroy, in whole or in part, a national, ethnical, racial or religious group, as such:
>
> (a) Killing members of the group;
> (b) Causing serious bodily or mental harm to members of the group;
> (c) Deliberately inflicting on the group conditions of life calculated to bring about its physical destruction in whole or in part;
> (d) Imposing measures intended to prevent births within the group;
> (e) Forcibly transferring children of the group to another group.

Whereas acts of terrorism are likely to involve the commission of the *actus reus* of genocide (particularly, perhaps, killing or causing serious harm to individuals), it seems unlikely that many terrorist acts are in fact commissioned with the required *dolus specialis* of genocide, i.e. 'the intent to destroy, in whole or in part, a national, ethnical, racial or religious group'. This does not mean that terrorist acts or campaigns could never fall within the definition of genocide and be prosecuted as such, but rather that it is extremely unlikely that genocidal terrorism would arise or that the offence of genocide would be used in an indictment against individuals suspected of commissioning or carrying out terrorist attacks.

War crimes

War crimes become relevant in international law only when it can be said that there is an armed conflict of either an international or a non-international character. 'Armed conflict' is a deceptively complex concept. It is clear that it is not confined to 'war'—indeed, the inclusion of the term 'armed conflict' rather than 'war' in the Geneva Conventions was intended to ensure that these Conventions' applicability would not be limited to wars in their traditional sense. Rather, it seems that a consensus view exists that an armed conflict has two core characteristics: (1) the existence of organised armed groups and (2) engagement in fighting of some intensity.[11] This corresponds well with the definition of armed conflict used by the International Criminal Tribunal for the former Yugoslavia in *Prosecutor v Tadic*[12]—the first prosecution brought before the Tribunal. In that case, the Appeals Chamber defined armed conflict thus: '[A]n armed conflict exists whenever there is a resort to armed force between States or protracted armed violence between governmental authorities and organised armed groups or between such groups within a State'.[13]

Proceeding on the basis that both identified elements are required in order for an armed conflict to exist, it is clear that terrorist activities might be considered war crimes in some, although not all, contexts. It is true that there have been some scenarios in which terrorist activity was widespread, there were organised armed groups, and there was fighting of some intensity that have *not* been considered to be situations of 'armed conflict'. The Northern Ireland conflict, for example, was never considered to be an armed conflict by the United Kingdom government, which prosecuted individuals within a criminal justice model of counter-terrorism, albeit with some variations on 'normal' criminal procedures, such as the use of non-jury 'Diplock courts'. In contrast, the United States' counter-terrorist operations against Al Qaeda and associated organisations have been undertaken within what was, at least rhetorically, an armed conflict paradigm. While forests have been felled on whether or not the 'war on terrorism' ought properly to be considered an armed conflict, the United States Supreme Court held in *Hamdan v Rumsfeld* that in fact the 'war' against Al Qaeda and associated forces constituted a non-international armed conflict.[14] Where such a classification is undertaken, it is conceivable that terrorist activities falling within that armed conflict might be considered war crimes.

Article 8(2)(b) of the Rome Statute of the International Criminal Court includes the following within its definition of war crimes:

(i) Intentionally directing attacks against the civilian population as such or against individual civilians not taking direct part in hostilities;
(ii) Intentionally directing attacks against civilian objects, that is, objects which are not military objectives;
(iii) Intentionally directing attacks against personnel, installations, material, units or vehicles involved in a humanitarian assistance or peacekeeping mission in accordance with the Charter of the United Nations, as long as they are entitled to the protection given to civilians or civilian objects under the international law of armed conflict;
(iv) Intentionally launching an attack in the knowledge that such attack will cause incidental loss of life or injury to civilians or damage to civilian objects or widespread, long-term and severe damage to the natural environment which would be clearly excessive in relation to the concrete and direct overall military advantage anticipated;

In addition, Article 15 of Additional Protocol One and Article 13 of Additional Protocol Two to the Geneva Conventions provide that:

1 The civilian population and individual civilians shall enjoy general protection against dangers arising from military operations. To give effect to this protection, the following rules, which are additional to other applicable rules of international law, shall be observed in all circumstances.

2 The civilian population as such, as well as individual civilians, shall not be the object of attack. Acts or threats of violence the primary purpose of which is to spread terror among the civilian population are prohibited.

Where the 'armed conflict' requirement is met, it seems clear that terrorist activities could fall within the offence of war crimes. Indeed, war crimes jurisdiction has been used to prosecute and to convict individuals who are accused of having engaged in terroristic activity within the context of an armed conflict. In *Prosecutor v Galic*,[15] for example, General Galic was convicted of Violations of the Laws or Customs of War under Article 3 of the Statute of the International Criminal Tribunal for the former Yugoslavia in respect of the conduct of a campaign of sniping and shelling the civilian population of Sarajevo with the primary purpose of spreading terror among this population. In that case, the Tribunal termed the offence 'the crime of terror against the civilian population' but were explicit in the holding that the consideration of whether the Tribunal had jurisdiction *ratione materiae* was undertaken 'only to the extent relevant to the charge in this case' (i.e. a war crimes charge).[16] In this respect the Tribunal applied the requirements of a crime in international law as laid down in *Tadic* to find that it had jurisdiction. Thus, the Tribunal held that the crime of terror against the civilian population could be rooted in Article 51 of Optional Protocol 1 to the Geneva Conventions;[17] that this is a treaty-based rule (and therefore a consideration of customary international law was not required in this respect);[18] that the alleged violation constituted a serious breach of international humanitarian law;[19] and that an individual could be fixed with criminal liability in international law for such a breach.[20] The offence itself, the Tribunal heard, could be said to occur only where there are acts of violence directed against civilians not taking an active part in hostilities and who suffered death or serious injury as a result thereof, when the accused 'wilfully' made such persons the object of the attack in question; the primary purpose of these acts was to spread terror among the civilian population;[21] and the acts of violence were unlawful attacks on civilians rather than legitimate attacks against combatants.[22] In the view of the Tribunal, all of these elements were proved in relation to Galic, who was convicted of war crimes with respect to the infliction of terror on the civilian population.

Terrorism *per se* as an international crime

The Rome Statute of the International Criminal Court does not include terrorism *per se* as a crime; neither does any other international treaty, although, as considered above, there are numerous treaties that deal with particular types of terroristic crimes, and breach thereof can constitute a treaty crime in itself. The possibility of including a stand-alone offence of terrorism *per se* featured prominently in the negotiation of the Rome Statute; however it was ultimately decided that no crime of terrorism *per se* ought to be included in the Statute, not least because of the difficulties of definition such as those already considered above. This notwithstanding, whether terrorism as a crime ought to be included in the International Criminal Court's jurisdiction was reconsidered at the first review conference of the Rome Statute in the summer of 2010. This is discussed further below.

The absence of a crime of terrorism within the Rome Statute does not mean, however, that no argument can be made that terrorism *per se* is in fact an international crime as a matter of customary international law. Antonio Cassese argues that 'the contention can be made ... that indeed a *customary rule* on the objective and subjective elements of a crime of terrorism in time of peace has evolved'.[23] Cassese argues that parameters of a generally agreed upon definition of terrorism in a time of peace can be extrapolated from the various regional and international treaties that exist dealing with terrorism: namely, (1) conduct that is criminal;[24] (2) conduct that is transnational in nature;[25] (3) conduct that impacts upon both civilian victims and state officials;[26] (4) conduct that is directed towards the purpose of spreading terror among civilian populations or compelling a government or international organisation to behave in a particular way;[27] (5) conduct that spreads fear or anxiety among civilian populations or targets leading buildings or personalities;[28] (6) conduct that has a political, ideological or religious motivation.[29] For Cassese, the recognition of these six general elements of terrorism and the acceptance thereof by the ratification and development of treaties featuring these elements by states and international institutions point towards the recognition of a crime of terrorism *per se* in times of peace.

It might be argued that the *Galic* judgment noted above is, in fact, more properly to be read as a case in which the Tribunal considered a crime of terrorism *per se*. It might also be argued that, although the Tribunal was careful to limit itself to a consideration of the crime of inflicting terror on the civilian population within the framework of war crimes, the elements of the offence identified can be applied in the recognition of a customary international crime of terrorism. Indeed, there is a clear parallel between the elements of the offence identified by the Tribunal and those elements of the definition of terrorism that Cassese alleges point towards the crime of terrorism *per se* as a matter of customary international law. While such an argument can certainly be made, it must be borne in mind in *Galic* the International Criminal Tribunal for the former Yugoslavia did not purport to made any pronouncements whatsoever in relation to customary international law.

'Treaty crimes'

Terrorist activity is prohibited by numerous treaties in the international legal order. There are, as considered above, numerous treaties that prohibit terrorist activity within discrete areas such as financing, hijacking and so on. In the main, these treaties compel states to ensure that the proscribed activities are criminalised within their domestic legal orders. These acts, then, straddle the international and domestic legal areas and are not, strictly speaking, easily definable as 'international crimes'. Rather, these activities are crimes within the domestic legal order, but the contents of those domestic criminal laws are dictated to at least some degree by international instruments. In some cases, as with the extended terrorist asset-freezing regime that has been developed in the light of the attacks of 11 September 2001, those international provisions will be legally entrenched in regional as well as in domestic laws. In such a case, these crimes arguably have more of an 'international' character, although that categorisation is dependent on the nature of the regional organisation that has acted to implement these international obligations within the context of their own regional legal orders. Geographically, for example, the EU's implementation of the terrorist asset-freezing regime[30] designed by the UN Security Council[31] might be said to be international, but in reality the autonomous nature of the European legal order means that these crimes are more supra-national or transnational than they are *inter*national. Indeed, a concerted body of scholarship is evolving that argues that so-called treaty crimes should in fact be considered part of 'transnational criminal law' rather than part of 'international criminal law'.

Transnational law is primarily traced back to Philip Jessup's influential lecture series delivered at the Yale Law School in the 1950s and later developed into *Transnational Law*, published in 1956.[32] For Jessup, transnational law encompasses 'all law which regulates actions or events that transcend national frontiers'.[33] Since then, the idea of transnational law has greatly developed, although whether it constitutes a 'field' or a 'methodology' is increasingly becoming a matter of dispute among transnational scholars themselves. Although transnational law, whether as a field or as a methodology, is now well established, it has only recently (and indeed relatively slowly) begun to be deployed in the area of criminal law and in particular in the international legal developments that have non-international legal and extra-legal effects.[34] Neil Boister, however, has given particular attention to the transnational criminal law character of what he terms 'suppression conventions', i.e. 'crime control treaties concluded with the purpose of suppressing harmful behaviour by non-state actors'.[35] Certainly, numerous international treaties dealing with terrorist activity fall into this category, and, while the offences created thereunder are not *international* in strict terms, they nevertheless reflect at their core the elements of terroristic activity that are to be deemed 'criminal' or deserving of criminal sanctions within the international *milieu* from which they emerged. These crimes are problematic in numerous ways: there can, for example, be inconsistencies in the ways in which these international standards are translated in and between different domestic and regional jurisdictions. Recent litigation concerning the European implementation of asset-freezing measures relating to terrorist activity has also exposed the capacity of transnational criminal law to result in violations of individual rights by the implementing bodies (whether states or regional institutions). In *Kadi and Al Barakaat*[36] the European Court of Justice held that the implementation by the European Union of mechanisms emanating from the UN Security Council for the freezing of the assets of those deemed to be involved or associated in terrorist activity were invalid as they violated the fundamental rights guarantees that lie at the heart of the European Union's autonomous legal system. This recent case illustrates the difficulties that arise for states and organisations in effectively fulfilling all of their international legal obligations in relation to transnational criminal law: the obligation to criminalise certain activity, on the one hand, and the obligation to respect fundamental rights on the other.[37]

Future developments

The first review conference of the Rome Statute of the International Criminal Court took place during the summer of 2010. In advance of that conference, one of the matters that received consideration by participating states was whether or not the omission of a crime of terrorism *per se* within the Statute ought to be rethought. As mentioned above, at the time of the drafting of the Statute it was decided that terrorism itself ought not to be included as a crime within the Statute, not least because of the persistence of the definitional conundrums considered in the first part of this chapter, but also because, at the time, it was not thought that terrorism was one of the most serious crimes of concern to the international community. Developments since that time, however, point towards the fact that, despite these earlier barriers to inclusion of terrorism *per se* as a crime within the jurisdiction of the International Criminal Court, it might now be a more probable prospect than it was in the late 1990s. Not only have the attacks of 11 September 2001 given rise to an internationalised and widespread counter-terrorist movement epitomised by the 'War on Terrorism' led by the United States, but the emergence of organised and widespread piracy on the high seas is also sometimes linked to organised terror organisations and may well motivate some state action.

In advance of the review convention, the Netherlands submitted a proposal for the inclusion of a crime of terrorism *per se* in the Rome Statute of the International Criminal Court, building on Resolution E, adopted at the Rome Conference in 1998. Resolution E provided:

> The United Nations Diplomatic Conference of Plenipotentiaries on the Establishment of an International Criminal Court,
> Having adopted the Statute of the International Criminal Court,

- *Recognizing* that terrorist acts, by whomever and wherever perpetrated and whatever their forms, methods or motives, are serious crimes of concern to the international community,
- *Recognizing* that the international trafficking of illicit drugs is a very serious crime, sometimes destabilizing the political and social and economic order in States,
- *Deeply alarmed* at the persistence of these scourges, which pose serious threats to international peace and security,
- *Regretting* that no generally acceptable definition of the crimes of terrorism and drug crimes could be agreed upon for the inclusion, within the jurisdiction of the Court,
- *Affirming* that the Statute of the International Criminal Court provides for a review mechanism, which allows for an expansion in future of the jurisdiction of the Court,
- *Recommends* that a Review Conference pursuant to article 123 of the Statute of the International Criminal Court consider the crimes of terrorism and drug crimes with a view to arriving at an acceptable definition and their inclusion in the list of crimes within the jurisdiction of the Court.[38]

While the Dutch proposal did not include the elements of a prospective crime of terrorism as it might appear within a revised Rome Statute, it did recommend that the crime of terrorism ought to be included in the Statute in a manner analogous to the original inclusion of the crime of aggression. In other words, the Dutch proposal was that terrorism ought to be listed as a crime under the Statute, but that a working group ought to be established within which the elements and definition of the crime would be worked out in the future. The inclusion of a crime of terrorism *per se* within the Statute on this basis would have sent a clear message of the international criminality of terrorist activity, but would not have enabled prosecutions under the Statute until the Offence is more clearly defined. Given that terrorist activity can already be prosecuted within the established international criminal law offences and that there is at least arguably a customary international crime of terrorism, inclusion of this nature is likely to be primarily symbolic. Resolution E was not discussed in depth at the review conference itself, primarily because of a desire not to overburden the conference and instead to maintain a focus on the crime of aggression but also—as reflected in the preliminary reports—because of concerns around (i) the lack of consensus that remains on a general definition of terrorism and (ii) developing a practice of amending the Statute in this manner (i.e. by general commitments to include an undefined offence for the purpose of future negotiation).[39]

Conclusion

In spite of all of the definitional difficulties that exist in relation to terrorism as a crime within international criminal law, this chapter has outlined the fact that, as it stands, there is a jurisdiction within international law under which terroristic activity could be prosecuted, albeit without the label of 'terrorism' being attached thereto. In addition, there is a raft of international treaties prohibiting terrorism in particular situations as a result of which domestic and regional legal systems have developed criminal prohibitions on terroristic activity. However, until a generally agreed upon the definition of 'terrorism' can be arrived at, it seems unlikely that terrorism as a crime *per se*—either as a matter of customary international law or within a revised Rome Statute of the International Criminal Court—will be recognised with sufficient certainty and clarity within international criminal law for it to be operationalised in discrete cases.

Notes

1 On the legality of the use of force as a counter-terrorist measure see, for example, M. Schmitt, 'Counter-Terrorism and the Use of Force in International Law', *Israeli Yearbook on Human Rights* 32, 2002, 53–116. On the relationship between human rights and counter-terrorism see, for example, R. Wilson (ed.), *Human Rights in the 'War on Terror'*, Cambridge: Cambridge University Press, 2005.

2 As considered later Cassese argues that the basic elements of terrorism are in fact agreed as a matter of states' practice and customary international law notwithstanding the fact that there is no generally agreed, binding, all-encompassing treaty definition of terrorism as a general phenomenon. A. Cassese, 'The Multifaceted Criminal Notion of Terrorism in International Law', *Journal of International Criminal Justice* 4, 2006, 933; A. Cassese, 'Terrorism as an International Crime', in A. Bianchi and Y. Naqvi (eds), *Enforcing International Law Norms against Terrorism*, Oxford and Portland: Hart Publishing, 2004, p. 213.

3 On the rhetorical power of the 'terrorist' label see, for example, J. Friedrichs, 'Defining the International Public Enemy: The Political Struggle behind the Legal Debate on International Terrorism', *Leiden Journal of International Law* 19, 2006, 69 and G. Andréani, 'The "War on Terror": Good Cause, Wrong Concept' *Survival* 46, 2004–05, 31.

4 An excellent survey is provided by B. Saul, *Defining Terrorism in International Law* Oxford; Oxford University Press, 2007 and R. Higgins, 'The General International Law of Terrorism' in R. Higgins & M. Flory (eds), *Terrorism and International Law*, London: Routledge, 1997, 14.

5 L. Donohue, 'Terrorism and the Counter-Terrorist Discourse' in V. Ramraj, M. Hor and K. Roach (eds), *Global Anti-Terrorism Law and Policy*, Cambridge: Cambridge University Press, 2005, p. 13

6 See esp. M. Crenshaw, 'The Causes of Terrorism', *Comparative Politics* 13, 1981, 379.

7 For a thorough consideration of the negotiations and agreements on the crime of aggression at the Review Conference see, e.g. Beth Van Schaack, 'Negotiating at the Interface of Power and Law: The Crime of Aggression' (2010), *Santa Clara University School of Law Legal Studies Research Papers Series No.* 10-09. Available at http://papers.ssrn.com/sol3/papers.cfm?abstract_id=1668661 (last accessed 6 September 2010).

8 See esp. K. Kittichaisaree, *International Criminal Law*, Oxford: Oxford University Press, 2001, pp. 96–7.

9 Prosecutor v Kayishema and Ruzindana (ICTR-95-1-T), Trial Chamber, 21 May 1999.

10 Ibid., para. 123.

11 These are the characteristics as identified by the ILA Use of Force Committee in its 'Initial Report on the Meaning of Armed Conflict in International Law' (2008). Available at: http://www.ila-hq.org/en/committees/index.cfm/cid/1022 (accessed 14 October 2009).

12 (IT-94-1-A), Appeals Chamber, 15 June 1999.

13 Ibid, para. 70.

14 548 U.S. 557, 629–630 (2006).

15 (IT-98-29-T), Trial Chamber, 5 December 2003.

16 Ibid., para. 87.

17 Ibid., para. 96.

18 Ibid., para. 97.

19 Ibid., para. 109.

20 Ibid., paras 127 and 129.

21 Ibid., para. 133.

22 Ibid., para. 135.

23 A. Cassese, 'The Multifaceted Criminal Notion of Terrorism in International Law', *Journal of International Criminal Justice* 4, 2006, 933, 935. Cassese has also argued that terrorist activity can be prosecuted under existing international criminal law when it can be said to have a nexus to an international or internal armed conflict (i.e. as a crime against humanity, a war crime or a grave breach as considered above). See A. Cassese, 'Terrorism as an International Crime' in A. Bianchi and Y. Naqvi (eds), *Enforcing International Law Norms against Terrorism*, Oxford and Portland: Hart Publications, 2006, p. 213.

24 A. Cassese, 'The Multifaceted Criminal Notion of Terrorism in International Law' *Journal of International Criminal Justice* 4, 2006, 933, 938.

25 Ibid.

26 Ibid.

27 Ibid. Cassese also notes that in more limited cases these treaties require conduct that is intended to destabilise a country's structures.
28 Ibid., 939.
29 Ibid.
30 Common Position 2003/140/CFSP OJ 2003 L 53/62; Regulation 561/2003 OJ 2003 L 82/1.
31 SC Resolution 1267 (1999); SC Resolution 1333 (2000); SC Resolution 1390 (2002); SC Resolution 1455 (2003); SC Resolution 1526 (2004); SC Resolution 1617 (2005); SC Resolution 1735 (2006); SC Resolution 1822 (2008).
32 P. Jessup, *Transnational Law*, New Haven: Yale University Press, 1956.
33 Ibid., p. 2
34 See, for example, A. Eser and O. Lagondy (eds), *Principles and Procedures for a New Transnational Criminal Law*, Frieburg: Max Planck Institute, 1992.
35 N. Boister, 'Transnational Criminal Law?', *European Journal of International Law* 14, 2003, 953, 955.
36 Cases C-402/05P and C-415/05P, Kadi and Al Barakaat, Judgment of the Court (Grand Chamber), 3 September 2008.
37 For a more complete commentary on these competing obligations and how they might be resolved see F. de Londras and S. Kingston, 'Rights, Security and Conflicting International Obligations: Exploring Inter-Jurisdictional Judicial Dialogue, in Europe, *American Journal of Comparative Law* 58(2), 2010, pp. 359–413.
38 Netherlands Proposal, Resolution E, http://iccnow.org/?mod=resolutione, Available at: http://www.ila-hq.org/en/committees/index.cfm/cid/1022 (accessed 18 March 2010).
39 For a detailed consideration of whether or not Resolution E ought to be considered in depth see Report of the Working Group on the Review Conference, Annex III: Report of the Working Group on Other Amendments.

12

Drug crimes and money laundering

Robert Cryer

International criminal law means many different things to many different people.[1] For many, and understandably, it is limited to those crimes that are directly criminalized by international law, i.e. those that are covered by the Nuremberg International Military Tribunal's statement that 'crimes against international law are committed by men, not abstract entities, and only by punishing individuals who commit such crimes can the provisions of international law be enforced . . . individuals have international duties which transcend the national obligations of obedience imposed by the individual state'.[2] There are, basically, four of these: aggression, genocide, crimes against humanity, and war crimes. Nonetheless, these 'core' international crimes do not exhaust what can be covered by the term 'international criminal law', which is often taken to also include what Neil Boister calls 'transnational crimes'.[3]

Transnational crimes are those that, while not directly criminalized by international law, are the subject of treaties that require their states parties (and, to the extent to which those treaties reflect custom, all states)[4] to create crimes in their domestic law. As much can be seen from a comparison of Article I of the Genocide Convention[5] and Article 5 of the Nuclear Terrorism Convention (which undoubtedly is, and is seen as, a 'transnational crime' convention).[6] Article I of the Genocide Convention provides that '[t]he Contracting Parties confirm that genocide, whether committed in time of peace or war, is a crime under international law'. Article 5 of the Nuclear Terrorism Convention, on the other hand, merely requires a state 'to establish as criminal offences under its national law the offences set forth . . . [in the convention]'. There is no concomitant in the Nuclear Terrorism Convention to Article I of the Genocide Convention asserting that international law directly creates such an offense.

There are, at least arguably, a number of normative differences that accompany something being considered a direct liability crime and a 'transnational' crime. It may be, for example, the case that there is no material (rather than personal) immunity for direct liability international crimes, on the basis that a state (or a person acting purportedly on behalf of a state) may be able to plead immunity for a normal violation of international law, but not one that international law directly criminalizes.[7] This is not the case for transnational crimes. One relatively uncontroversial outcome of something being directly criminalized by the relevant applicable international law[8] is that it is not a violation of the *nullum crimen sine lege* principle to backdate the jurisdiction of domestic courts over those offenses to the date when they were criminalized in international law.[9]

As much is made clear, for example, in Article 7 of the European Convention on Human Rights, which provides that '[n]o one shall be held guilty of any criminal offence on account of any act or omission which did not constitute an offence under national *or international law* at the time when it was committed [emphasis added]'.[10] The same does not apply to transnational offenses in general, since international law does not directly create the offense, but rather requires states to introduce those offenses in their own domestic law.

Furthermore, although the matter is not beyond dispute, the 'core' international crimes tend to cover cognate conduct, for the most part physical harm committed in a context in which many people are in a position of vulnerability, while transnational crime treaties (and where applicable, their customary equivalents)[11] cover a vast array of conduct, which is not easily reconcilable to any real general principles of criminalization, other than mostly being reactive responses to perceived social harms.[12] For example, transnational offenses include such disparate conduct as the severing of undersea cables,[13] counterfeiting currency,[14] human trafficking,[15] various aspects of terrorism,[16] organized crime,[17] trading in firearms,[18] torture,[19] and disappearances.[20] As the last two examples show, there are overlaps between transnational crimes and international crimes, as torture and disappearances can also be, in the relevant context, war crimes and crimes against humanity.[21] Given that there are, quite literally, hundreds of 'other crimes' than those dealt with in this volume, this chapter will limit itself to explaining two 'pure' transnational offenses: namely, drug trafficking and money laundering.

Drug trafficking

Drugs, both legal and otherwise, have long been a part of human history.[22] In the late nineteenth and early twentieth century, it was decided, in particular given the fact that the drug trade frequently involved the transportation of narcotics over borders, that international cooperation to suppress the trade in such substances was necessary.[23] The impetus of this came from Western states, in particular the USA, although, it ought to be noted, not without a degree of hypocrisy from some Western (and some non-Western) states, who had not been above using narcotics as an element of foreign policy in the past.[24]

There are now a plethora of treaties dealing with drugs, and the vast majority of states are party to at least one major convention relating to drug control.[25] Nonetheless, it has to be borne in mind that the compounds that are often abused can also have legitimate uses. Opiates include heroin, perhaps the stereotypical narcotic, but also morphine, a very widely used medical anaesthetic, and codeine, which, in many countries, is an over-the-counter painkiller. Furthermore, inadequate supply of such drugs is a considerable problem in many countries, as many late-stage cancer patients, who are desperately in need of pain relief, cannot obtain the necessary analgesia.[26]

The 1961 Convention

In spite of the fact that there were other, earlier, treaties on point, the seminal text relating to drug control in international law may be taken to be the 1961 Single Convention on Narcotic Drugs,[27] which codified and streamlined the pre-existing patchwork of treaties, covering opium, coca leaf, and cannabis, and created a supervisory mechanism, the International Narcotics Control Board (INCB).[28] The Convention was amended by the 1972 Protocol to the 1962 Convention to improve its focus on rehabilitation of drug addicts.[29] The previous year (1971), a similar convention was created to cover psychotropic substances.[30] Both conventions, recognising that there may be medicinal or other uses for such substances, take a balanced approach, not prohibiting the creation, cultivation, or transfer of such substances completely *per se*, but rather establishing a Control mechanism. As much can be seen by Article 4 of the 1961 Convention, which provides, in addition, for obligations of states to domestically implement the relevant parts of the Convention and cooperate with respect to suppressing drug trafficking, '[s]ubject to the provisions of this Convention, to limit exclusively to medical and scientific purposes the production, manufacture, export, import, distribution of, trade in, use and possession of drugs'.[31]

The mechanism set up by the 1961 Convention works in a number of ways. The first is by categorizing various drugs, which are subject to different levels of international control. The various drugs subjected to the Convention regime are listed in Schedules to the Convention.[32] Those drugs that are subject to Schedule 1 listing are subject to the most severe controls. Those in Schedules 2 and 3 are subject to control, albeit not to such significant limitations.[33]

One of the main ways in which the 1961 Convention operates at an inter-state level is that states parties to the Conventions are required to submit estimates of their (legitimate) needs for the various compounds to the INCB every year.[34] The Board then monitors the creation, cultivation, and transport of such compounds to each state, checking, in particular if there seems to be some form of inappropriate stockpiling.[35] This is partially enforced by requiring all transfers between states to be authorized by both states.[36] The convention also creates certain supervisory functions for the Commission on Narcotic Drugs of ECOSOC (Economic and Social Council).[37] One of the most important functions delegated to the Commission is to give consideration to amending the Schedules to the Convention, i.e. which drugs are to be subject to which level of control.[38] The Convention also provides various practical limitations on the cultivation, in particular, of opium poppies, the coca bush, and cannabis, including that there are agencies that license cultivation, that the areas in which cultivation may occur are defined, and that all cultivated products are submitted to the agency.[39]

The 1961 Convention, in addition to looking to the prevention of inter-state trafficking, also requires states to domestically criminalize various other activities related to the drug trade. Hence, Article 33 provides that '[t]he Parties shall not permit the possession of drugs except under legal authority', which, in essence, creates a general obligation to criminalize other possession of the relevant substances. Article 36(1)(a) of the 1961 Convention goes further, requiring that

> [s]ubject to its constitutional limitations, each Party shall adopt such measures as will ensure that cultivation, production, manufacture, extraction, preparation, possession, offering, offering for sale, distribution, purchase, sale, delivery on any terms whatsoever, brokerage, dispatch, dispatch in transit, transport, importation and exportation of drugs contrary to the provisions of this Convention, and any other action which in the opinion of such Party may be contrary to the provisions of this Convention, shall be punishable offences when committed intentionally, and that serious offences shall be liable to adequate punishment particularly by imprisonment or other penalties of deprivation of liberty.[40]

Parties are also required to criminalize conspiracies and attempts to commit such offenses, as well as 'financial operations in connexion with' those offenses.[41] The Convention requires states to adopt an *aut dedere aut judicare* approach, mandating prosecution by the territorial state, or the state in which the alleged offender is found, if that state does not extradite that alleged offender.[42] In a slightly odd provision, however, rather than require states to criminalize extraterritorial drug offenses in this circumstance, the Convention provides that Article 36 'shall be subject to the provisions of the criminal law of the party concerned on questions of jurisdiction'. There is thus nothing in the Convention itself that directly requires states to domestically implement jurisdiction over extraterritorial drug offenses, although such an obligation could be inferred from Article 36(2)(a)(iv).

One of the major difficulties associated with the 1961 (and 1971) Conventions is that their enforcement is largely a matter of voluntary compliance.[43] For example Article 14(1) merely provides, even in situations in which 'the Board has objective reasons to believe that the aims of this Convention are being seriously endangered by reason of the failure of any Party, country or territory to carry out the provisions of this Convention, the Board shall have the right to propose to the Government concerned the opening of consultations or to request it to furnish explanations'. Even when a state is at risk, without it being in default of its obligations under the Convention, of becoming a center for drug creation, cultivation trafficking, or consumption, all the Board can do is recommend, in a confidential fashion, that the government open consultations on point.[44] The Board may ask states to study the matter,[45] or to take remedial measures,[46] but these are non-binding. Even in case of governmental failure to explain the situation, initiate studies, or take remedial measures, when 'there is a serious situation that needs co-operative action at the international level with a view to remedying it', all the Board can do is draw 'the attention of the Parties, the Council and the Commission to the matter'. In this regard, the language in the convention is hardly that of strong obligation; indeed, it comes close to soft law levels of suggestion.[47] In the absence of any more sophisticated form of enforcement, the 1961 Convention at least provides for some form of publicity, in that Article 14(3) allows the Board to publish its reports on point, although subject to the caveat that the government has right of reply.

The 1988 UN Convention

Perhaps unsurprisingly, the Conventions, in a word, failed. The drug trade continued to increase at best not unabatedly, at worst exponentially.[48] It is probably the most damning indictment of the 1961 and 1971 Conventions that in 1984, the General Assembly asked for the effectiveness of the drug control treaties to be evaluated.[49] The result of this review was that it was considered necessary to overhaul the system and provide for a further, comprehensive treaty to deal with drug trafficking and taking.

This overhaul led to the most important of the drug control treaties in modern times: the 1988 United Nations Convention against Illicit Traffic in Narcotic Drugs and Psychotropic Substances, which both complements and supplements the 1961 Convention.[50] The 1988 Convention takes a traditional transnational crime approach to the issue. As such, Article 3(1)(a) of the convention requires parties to domestically criminalize certain conduct, namely the following:

(i) The production, manufacture, extraction, preparation, offering, offering for sale, distribution, sale, delivery on any terms whatsoever, brokerage, dispatch, dispatch in transit, transport, importation or exportation of any narcotic drug or any psychotropic substance contrary to the provisions of the 1961 Convention, the 1961 Convention as amended or the 1971 Convention;

(ii) The cultivation of opium poppy, coca bush or cannabis plant for the purpose of the production of narcotic drugs contrary to the provisions of the 1961 Convention and the 1961 Convention as amended;

(iii) The possession or purchase of any narcotic drug or psychotropic substance for the purpose of any of the activities enumerated in (i) above;

(iv) The manufacture, transport or distribution of equipment, materials or of certain substances knowing that they are to be used in or for the illicit cultivation, production or manufacture of narcotic drugs or psychotropic substances;

(v) The organization, management or financing of any of the offences enumerated in (i), (ii), (iii) or (iv) above.

Article 3(1)(c)(iv) also requires parties to criminalize various forms of complicity, namely '[p]articipation in, association or conspiracy to commit, attempts to commit and aiding, abetting, facilitating and counselling the commission of any' of the crimes created pursuant to Article 3.

Furthermore, the 1988 Convention, like the 1961 and 1971 Conventions, requires parties to criminalize the intentional possession, purchase, or cultivation of drugs and psychotropic substances.[51] In relation to these offenses, there are a set of obligations on states to establish jurisdiction over drug offenses in particular circumstances. Parties are obliged to establish jurisdiction over those offenses that are committed in their territories, and when '[t]he offence is committed on board a vessel flying its flag or an aircraft which is registered under its laws at the time the offence is committed' under Article 4(1)(a). Parties are also permitted, by the 1988 treaty,[52] to assert jurisdiction over offenses established under Article 3(1) when the offense is committed by a national or someone who has 'habitual residence' in the relevant state.

Parties to the 1988 Convention are also permitted to establish jurisdiction when the offense has taken place on a ship for which a state has been authorized by the flag state to board and search the vessel to look for drugs pursuant to Article 17 of the Convention, and to prosecute the alleged offenders. In relation to conspiracies of the sort mentioned in Article 3(1)(c)(iv), parties are entitled to assert jurisdiction over extraterritorial conspiracies, the object of which is to commit a crime covered by Article 3(1). None of these provisions provide for any significant extension of what would be permitted under general international law. States are entitled to assert jurisdiction over their nationals under general international law.[53] Similarly, states are entirely entitled to consent to other states 'borrowing' their jurisdiction.[54] Many states, including the UK, have taken the view that the general international law on territorial jurisdiction is sufficiently broad to cover extraterritorial conspiracies to import drugs into their territory.[55] As such, the Convention does not depart in any real way from what states could probably already do under general international law.

Equally, when a state does not extradite a suspect to another state to stand trial for an Article 3(1) crime, it is obliged to establish jurisdiction over that suspect if that person is in the territory of the requested state in certain circumstances. These are that the extradition was rejected on the basis that the relevant offense was committed in its territory (or on a flagged ship or aircraft) or that the alleged offender is a national of the requested state.[56] Parties to the 1988 Convention also agree that other states parties 'may' assert jurisdiction over Article 3(1) offenses 'when the alleged offender is present in its territory and it does not extradite him to another Party'.[57]

Given that drug offenses, in particular trafficking offenses, most usually involve collaboration across state borders, the 1988 Convention, in a significant advance over the rather laconic (although not utterly useless) provisions of the 1961 and 1971 Conventions, provides for a fairly detailed regime for extradition,[58] mutual legal assistance,[59] transfer of proceedings,[60] and, in addition to other forms of assistance, training.[61]

The Convention also, quite rightly, established a regime for the control of what might be termed 'precursor chemicals', i.e. chemicals that are used in the manufacture of prohibited drugs from their base elements and other items that are used in the manufacture or cultivation of drugs. Article 12 of the 1988 Convention thus creates a detailed regime for the monitoring and control of such chemicals, which are included in tables attached to the Convention. Unfortunately, the problem here is similar to the one that arises in relation to chemical weapons, where notionally innocuous chemicals can also have more sinister uses. Nonetheless, Article 3(1)(c)(ii) requires states parties to criminalize the possession of such substances, and tabled equipment, when that possession is accompanied by the knowledge that they are to be used in the cultivation or manufacture of drugs.

In addition, states parties to the Convention are required to criminalize various different concomitants to the drug trade. For example, Article 3(1)(c)(iii) provides for an obligation to criminalize public incitement or inducement of others to commit any Article 3 offense or the illicit use of drugs. This is a matter that has received quite frequent comment from the INCB, who are concerned about popular media, in particular that surrounding pop music, promoting drug use.[62]

With an important understanding of the interrelationship of transnational criminality and the role of the profit motive in the drug trade,[63] Article 3(1)(b) of the 1988 Convention, building upon Article 37 of the 1961 Convention,[64] also requires states to create offenses related to money laundering. These are the following:

(i) The conversion or transfer of property, knowing that such property is derived from any offence or offences established in accordance with subparagraph (*a*) of this paragraph, or from an act of participation in such offence or offences, for the purpose of concealing or disguising the illicit origin of the property or of assisting any person who is involved in the commission of such an offence or offences to evade the legal consequences of his actions;
(ii) The concealment or disguise of the true nature, source, location, disposition, movement, rights with respect to, or ownership of property, knowing that such property is derived from an offence or offences established in accordance with subparagraph (*a*) of this paragraph or from an act of participation in such an offence or offences.[65]

In addition, Article 3(1)(c)(i) provides for the creation of knowing receipt of property, which was derived from an Article 3 offense. On a related issue, the 1988 Convention goes even further, for the first time in a suppression convention providing (in Article 5) for a detailed regime of confiscation of the proceeds of the drug trade and of drugs and related items. In addition to requiring states to take the measures necessary to trace, freeze, and/or seize these things, Article 5 requires states to provide for authorities to require bank records be made available, and that bank secrecy not be a bar to the enforcement of such orders.[66] This is a sensible provision, in that bank secrecy has been a considerable problem in this regard.[67] Similarly useful is the procedure provided for in Article 5(4) for international recognition of confiscation orders. This is particularly necessary given that the proceeds of crime are frequently sent to states with lax financial regulation and/or strict banking secrecy laws.[68]

The 1988 Convention also passes certain powers to the ICND (International Commission on Narcotic Drugs), to supplement those granted to it in the 1961 and 1971 Conventions. The powers in the 1988 Convention are similar to those granted under the earlier Conventions and relate to receiving information from parties and, with respect to matters relating to precursor items, ensuring labelling of exports; if it is not satisfied that a party is living up to its obligations, it may 'call upon' (not demand) that party to take remedial measures.[69] If the party does not take such measures, the enforcement power of the Board is limited to publishing its finding, alongside (should it wish to comment) the views of the party concerned.[70]

The UN Commission on Narcotic Drugs (CND) is also granted additional powers by the 1988 Convention—these are to review the implementation of the Convention, make 'suggestions and general recommendations' about the information received from states parties, and amend the tables on precursor items and compounds.[71] If the CND refers a matter under Article 22(1)(b), the Commission is entitled to take 'such action as it deems appropriate' under Article 21(d), although this does not grant the Commission enforcement powers.

The Commission is not the only body that deals with drugs in the United Nations. Since 2002, the United Nations Office on Drugs and Crime (UNODC), which replaced earlier UN bodies dealing with the matter, has had a broad remit to oversee issues of drug control throughout the world.[72] Its functions are to undertake field work related to technical cooperation, intended to enhance the capacity of states to act against the drug trade, terrorism, and crime in general; engage in research and analysis on drugs and crime, so to inform the policymaking process; and conduct promotional work, such as encouraging ratification of the relevant treaties, preparing model domestic legislation, and assisting the treaty-based bodies such as the Board and other bodies such as the Commission. The UNODC has, for example, given legal assistance to over 140 states on drug-related matters. The UNODC is not limited to drug crime, though—it also deals, *inter alia*, with money laundering, corruption, HIV/AIDS, prison reform, piracy, and organized crime.

As can be seen though, the UNODC has a promotional and advisory role, rather than an enforcement one. Implementation of the Conventions, and the drug control system as a whole, is thus overseen by a series of bodies that do not have any enforcement powers, rather than an international criminal court or compulsory body.[73] There were proposals to include drug trafficking in the jurisdiction of the International Criminal Court (ICC); however, these foundered, and, in spite of Resolution F of the Rome Conference, which suggested the possible inclusion of such crimes at a later date, there was little appetite for such a development when the agenda of first review conference was being set. Nonetheless, the current transnational regime for prosecution of drug offenses favours powerful states (in particular the USA, with its proximity to certain countries in Latin America that are significant sources of cocaine), and as such, they are unlikely to have changed their minds on the advisability of the fundamental change that transforming drug offenses into international crimes subject to an international court would represent.[74]

Money laundering[75]

There is a strong link between drug trafficking and money laundering. For example, General Manuel Noriega, having been convicted of drug trafficking offenses and served 20 years in prison in the USA, was extradited to France in April 2010 to face money-laundering charges. Money laundering is not limited to drug money, though—there are many other organized crime activities that give rise to it. The UNODC estimates that between 2 and 5% of the worlds GDP (roughly $800 million to $2 trillion) is 'laundered'.[76] Money laundering is not a new phenomenon—the term itself originated in the 1920s, owing to organized criminals using launderettes as front operations.[77] However, organized international cooperation relating to it is a relatively modern phenomenon.[78] The first treaty to deal with money laundering was the 1988 Convention, the provisions of which were appraised above. The approach taken in that Convention has proved highly influential. In recent years, the issue has increasingly been rolled up with the issue of terrorist financing.[79] In this latter regard, enforcement bodies, such as the Security Council, have also taken an interest. Given modern technologies, in particular electronic banking, which enables money to be transferred around the world practically instantaneously, international cooperation is vital. It is a notable feature of the anti-money-laundering regime that regional approaches are also flourishing, particularly in Europe.[80] Soft law also has a strong role here.[81] In the past this was due to the fact that some governments were unwilling to see 'hard' law in the area.[82]

The Palermo Convention and other treaties dealing with money laundering

Chronologically, the next global treaty after the 1988 Convention was the 1999 UN Convention on the Suppression of the Financing of Terrorism. This requires states to create crimes in their domestic legal order of 'directly or indirectly, unlawfully and wilfully' providing or collecting 'funds with the intention that they should be used or in the knowledge that they are to be used, in full or in part, in order to carry out' various terrorist activities.[83] Detailed review of the provisions of this Convention lie more within the study of terrorism than money laundering; suffice it to say here that this Convention, like the 1988 Convention, contains a process for identifying, freezing, and seizing assets in this circumstance.[84] This treaty, like the 1988 Convention, though, only applied to specific, defined 'predicate' offenses.[85] The 2000 UN Convention against Transnational Organized Crime (the Palermo Convention) is somewhat broader, as we will see.

Article 6(1) of the Palermo Convention expressly requires states to criminalize money laundering in their domestic legal orders. The offenses states are required to create are defined in Article 6(1)(a) as

> [t]he conversion or transfer of property, knowing that such property is the proceeds of crime, for the purpose of concealing or disguising the illicit origin of the property or of helping any person who is involved in the commission of the predicate offence to evade the legal consequences of his or her action . . . [and] . . . [t]he concealment or disguise of the true nature, source, location, disposition, movement or ownership of or rights with respect to property, knowing that such property is the proceeds of crime.

The influence of the drafting of the 1988 Convention is clear.[86] Like the 1988 Convention, the Palermo Convention also requires states to criminalize knowing receipt of property—in this regard, knowing it is the proceeds of crime—and conspiracy, attempt, and complicity in the above offenses.[87] Article 6(2)(a) provides that parties should apply the offenses in Article 6(1) to 'the widest range of predicate offences'. They are required to include as predicate offenses all serious criminal offenses;[88] being a member of an organized criminal group, as defined in Article 5 of the Convention; corruption, as defined in Article 8; and obstruction of justice, as defined in Article 23.

Again, following the lead of the 1988 Convention, the Palermo Convention requires states to take jurisdiction over all these offenses on the basis of territoriality and flag-state (including airline registration) jurisdiction. The convention also entitles States to assert jurisdiction on the basis of nationality,[89] passive personality,[90] and, for Article 5 and 6 crimes, where the conduct is abroad, but with an intention to commit the relevant offense in the territory of the state.[91] Possibly the only controversial claim here is that passive personal jurisdiction exists here. However, the Palermo Convention can be seen as an agreement between the states parties that, as between themselves, they will consider it so, and therefore cannot oppose its application by another state party.[92] Whether it would be opposable to a non-state party is a different matter. As befits a transnational crime convention, the Palermo Convention opts for an *aut dedere aut judicare* regime, requiring states to establish jurisdiction over offenses committed by its own nationals when it refuses to extradite them for that reason, or when a person is in their territory and the state does not extradite.[93]

Of course, money laundering needs to be combated by more than just the criminalization of the offense—it needs to be detected and prevented.[94] As a result, the Palermo Convention also places obligations on states to initiate domestic banking supervisory and regulatory frameworks for banks, financial institutions, and 'other bodies particularly susceptible to money laundering', which requires customer identification, record-keeping, and that those institutions report suspicious transactions.[95] States are also encouraged to consider measures to monitor the inflow and outflow of money and other financial instruments to and from their territories.[96] Given the importance of international cooperation, states are obliged by the Convention to ensure that their anti-money-laundering authorities are able to cooperate with each other and internationally.[97]

The imprint of the 1988 Convention is also present in the confiscation provisions of the Palermo Convention. Article 12(1) of the latter provides that states shall adopt measures that enable them to confiscate the proceeds of crime that relate to offenses covered in the Convention, or their equivalent value, and 'property, equipment or other instrumentalities used or destined for use' in those offenses. Parties are also required to take action to ensure that they can identify, trace, freeze, and seize those things.[98] Naturally, one of the reasons for money laundering is to obtain 'clean' money that can then be spent. Therefore, it was, sensibly, decided in the Palermo Convention to ensure that anything bought with the proceeds of crime, or income or other benefits from them, was also to be subject to the measures Article 12 provides for, and when these proceeds have been comingled with other, legitimately obtained property, that property is subject to those measures up to the value of the illegitimate money.[99] Yet again along the lines of the 1988 Convention, bank secrecy is not to be a reason for refusal to hand over records.[100] Similarly, Article 13 of the Palermo Convention provides an analogous regime for cooperation in relation to confiscation to that created by the 1988 Convention. Following the same precedent, the Palermo Convention provides for procedures for extradition and adds transfer of prisoners to the assistance states can give one another.[101]

Interestingly, the Palermo Convention allows states to

> consider the possibility of requiring that an offender demonstrate the lawful origin of alleged proceeds of crime or other property liable to confiscation, to the extent that such a requirement is consistent with the principles of their domestic law and with the nature of the judicial and other proceedings.[102]

Care has to be taken here, in that confiscation proceedings can be seen as criminal proceedings, and as such, subject to human rights considerations, and a reversal of the burden of proof here can prove problematic.[103]

There is another side to money laundering—corruption. As Serrano and Kenny have said, the flip side of money laundering is often corruption: 'political laundering produces corrupt presidential campaigns, investment laundering produces absurdly lavish building[s] . . . which betray their illegitimate sources. Far from being a byzantine mystery, criminal laundering is an open secret'.[104] As a result of this realization, the 2003 UN Convention against Corruption[105] provides for a similar regime to the other conventions referred to above.[106]

'Soft law' and money laundering

As mentioned above, in addition to the treaty-based (and Security Council mandated) restrictions on financial activity, soft law remains a very important influence on the international response to money laundering. For example, UNODC has engaged in the development of model laws, both at the generic level, and, specifically, for common law states.[107] In addition, the UN General Assembly has recommended action against money laundering.[108]

Unquestionably, though, the most important of the soft law instruments that relate to money laundering are those that have come from the Financial Action Task Force (FATF). This is a body that initially was created under the auspices of the OECD (Organization for Economic Co-operation and Development), but has achieved a far broader level of influence than simply amongst its membership.[109] In 1990, the FATF adopted 40 recommendations relating to money laundering, which have been updated semi-regularly since.[110] These recommendations are strictly non-binding, but Security Council Resolution 1617 'strongly urges all member states to implement the comprehensive international standards embodied in the Financial Task Force's (FATF) Forty Recommendations and the FATF Nine Special Recommendations on Terrorist Financing'.[111] The General Assembly followed suit a year later, encouraging states to implement the 40 standards (and the nine special recommendations), although in a notable caveat 'recognizing that States may require assistance in implementing them'.[112] As such, the FATF was only slightly overstating the position when it stated that they are 'the international anti-money laundering standard'.[113] The recommendations attempt to track, but provide more detail than, the provisions of the 1988 Convention and the Palermo Convention.[114]

Conclusion

The law relating to drug offenses and money laundering can be criticized, and has been, on the basis that it is technocratic.[115] This criticism is almost certainly true, as is the complaint that it privileges more powerful states, who, in essence, externalize their own criminal law preferences through the various instruments, both in the form of treaties and soft law.[116] That is not to say that the system as it exists is the worst of all possible worlds. Things are probably better than they would be without the drug and money-laundering conventions.

The regime is not optimally effective, though, and there is a disjuncture between the political rhetoric that some states (and the treaties' preambles) engage in and their willingness and/or ability to translate this into practical implementation of the obligations and suggestions into domestic law and policy. The oversight mechanisms (aside from those relating to the Security Council's response to terrorism) are limited, at least in the Austinian sense. In some ways, what can be seen is a disjuncture between what Paul Diehl and Charlotte Ku call the normative and operating systems of international law.[117] The former is highly developed, the latter less so.

Yet this is, to some extent, not simply a failure of law. The extent to which some states are willing to subject their activities, and activities within their territories, to international scrutiny remains in tension with the perceived imperative of suppressing such behavior. It is also true that

> if states are unable or unwilling to conform to the regime's mandate in practice and if deviant or dissident states and groups persistently refuse to conform to the regime's mandate in practice, they can significantly undermine the global prohibition regime . . . but the failure of a global prohibition regime does not necessarily signal its future demise. Regardless of effectiveness, part of the appeal of a global prohibition regime is its symbolic allure and usefulness as a mechanism to express disapproval.[118]

This latter function is one that ought not to be underestimated.

Notes

1 See Robert Cryer, Håkan Friman, Darryl Robinson and Elizabeth Wilmshurst, *An Introduction to International Criminal Law and Procedure*, 2nd edn, Cambridge: Cambridge University Press, 2010, Ch. 1.

2 'Nuremberg IMT: Judgment and Sentences', *American Journal of International Law*, 1947, vol. 21, 172, at 221.

3 Neil Boister, 'Transnational Criminal Law?', *European Journal of International Law*, 2003, vol. 14, 953. See further M. Cherif Bassiouni, 'The Discipline of International Criminal Law', in M. Cherif Bassiouni

(ed.), *International Criminal Law, Volume I: Sources, Subjects and Contents*, 3rd edn, Leiden: Martinus Nijhoff, 2008, p. 3.

4 Which is not frequent. See Case Concerning the Arrest Warrant of 11 April 2000 (DRC v Belgium), 2002 ICJ Rep 3, Separate Opinion of Higgins Kojimans and Buergenthal, paras 41–2.

5 Convention on the Prevention and Punishment of Genocide, 78 UNTS 277 (1948).

6 International Convention for the Suppression of Acts of Nuclear Terrorism, UN Doc. A/RES/59/290 (2005).

7 Nuremberg Judgment, p. 221; Cryer, Friman, Robinson and Wilmshurst, *Introduction*, pp. 542–4.

8 Which can include, when they are applicable, treaties, such as Additional Protocols I and II. For an example see e.g. Statute of the International Criminal Tribunal for Rwanda, UN Doc. S/RES/955 (1994), Art. 4. More generally see Cryer, Friman, Robinson and Wilmshurst, *Introduction*, pp. 9–10.

9 For an example, see the (UK) Coroners and Justice Act 2009, which grants Courts in England, Wales, and Northern Ireland jurisdiction over international crimes back to 1 January 1991. See Robert Cryer and Paul David Mora, 'The Coroners and Justice Act 2009 and International Criminal Law: Back for the Future?', *International and Comparative Law Quarterly*, 2001, vol. 58, 203.

10 See generally, D. J. Harris, M. O'Boyle, E.P. Bates and C.M. Buckley, *Harris, O'Boyle and Warbrick, Law of the European Convention on Human Rights*, 2nd edn, Oxford: Oxford University Press, 2009, Ch. 7.

11 And, in one exceptional situation, Security Council Resolution. See S/RES/1373 (2001), which practically legislates into being the convention on terrorist financing. For critique see Matthew Happold, 'Resolution 1373, UN Doc. S/RES/1373 (2001) and the Constitution of the United Nations', *Leiden Journal of International Law*, 2003, vol. 16, 593. Although see, on the other side, Paul Szasz, 'The Security Council Starts Legislating', *American Journal of International Law*, 2002, vol. 96, 901.

12 Robert Cryer, 'The Doctrinal Foundations of International Criminalization', in Bassiouni (ed.), *International Criminal Law*, p. 107, at 118–20.

13 Convention for the Protection of Submarine Cables, 11 *Martens Nouveau Recueil* (Series 2) 281 1884.

14 International Convention for the Suppression of the Counterfeiting of Currency, 112 LNTS 371 (1929).

15 For example, Convention for the Suppression of the Traffic in Persons and the Exploitation of the Prostitution of Others, 98 UNTS 271 (1950).

16 For example, International Convention for the Suppression of Terrorist Bombings, 2149 UNTS 284 (1997).

17 UN Convention against Transnational Organised Crime (hereinafter the 'Palermo Convention'), UN Doc. A/RES/55/25 (2000).

18 Protocol against the Illicit Manufacturing of and Trafficking in Firearms, UN Doc. A/RES/55/255 (2001).

19 UN Convention against Torture and Other Cruel Inhuman and Degrading Treatment, 1465 UNTS 85 (1984).

20 International Convention for the Protection of all Persons from Enforced Disappearances, UN Doc. A/RES/61/177 (2006).

21 The same may be said for terrorism. See Chapter 11.

22 Although globalization has increased the influences on young people (the demographic most susceptible to drug abuse), see e.g. Hamid Ghodse, 'Introduction', in Hamid Ghodse (ed.), *International Drug Control Into the 21st Century*, Aldershot: Ashgate, 2008, p. 1, at 1. For a brief history of drug use see Ghodse (ed.), *Drug Control*, pp. 89–94. For a history of the development of laws relating to drug use see Peter Andreas and Ethan Nadelmann, *Policing the Globe: Criminalization and Crime Control in International Relations*, Oxford: Oxford University Press, 2006, pp. 37–46.

23 Which is not to say that suppression is necessarily the best, or most liberal, way to deal with drug use. See, for example, Andrew Ashworth, *Principles of Criminal Law*, 6th edn, Oxford: Oxford University Press, 2009, p. 34. For the arguments against legalization see Ghodse (ed.), *Drug Control*, pp. 31–4. For both sides see Bernard Leroy, M. Cherif Bassiouni, and Jean François Thony, 'The International Drug Control System', in Bassiouni (ed.), *International Criminal Law*, p. 855, at 900–4.

24 Leroy *et al.*, 'Drug Control', pp. 865–8. On Japanese policies in China see Judgment of the Tokyo IMT, reprinted in Neil Boister and Robert Cryer (eds), *Documents on the Tokyo International Military Tribunal*, Oxford: Oxford University Press, 2008, pp. 363–5 (transcript, pp. 49, 159–64).

25 Ibid., p. 855.

26 Ghodse (ed.), *Drug Control*, p. 10.
27 18 UST 1407 (1961) (hereinafter '1961 Convention').
28 Leroy *et al.*, 'Drug Control', p. 872. Pursuant to Article 9(1) of the 1961 Convention, '1. The Board shall consist of thirteen members to be elected by the Council . . . [ECOSOC] . . . as follows: a) Three members with medical, pharmacological or pharmaceutical experience from a list of at least five persons nominated by the World Health Organization; and b) Ten members from a list of persons nominated by the Members of the United Nations and by Parties which are not Members of the United Nations'.
29 976 UNTS 13 (1972).
30 1019 UNTS 175 (1971). The most well-known such substances are LSD and amphetamines, including ecstasy (MDMA). For reasons of space, this chapter will focus on the 1961 Convention. The 1971 Convention is similar to the 1961 Convention, although there are differences with respect to estimates and importation. See Leroy *et al.*, 'Drug Control', p. 874.
31 1961 Convention, Art. 4(1)(c).
32 Leroy *et al.*, 'Drug Control', p. 876.
33 Space limitations militate against explaining the relevant levels in detail. For further detail, see Neil Boister, *Penal Aspects of the UN Drug Conventions*, The Hague: Kluwer Law International, 2001.
34 1961 Convention, Art. 19.
35 Leroy *et al.*, 'Drug Control', p. 877.
36 1961 Convention, Art. 17. See Leroy *et al.*, 'Drug Control', p. 878.
37 Ibid., Art. 5.
38 Ibid., Arts 3, 8(a).
39 Ibid., Arts 23, 26, 28.
40 Article 36(b) provides that when such offenses are committed by drug abusers, the parties may provide for treatment rather than punishment.
41 1961 Convention, Art. 26(2)(ii).
42 Ibid., Art. 36(2)(a)(iv). Article 36(b) provides for Parties to consider the relevant drug crimes extraditable between themselves.
43 Leroy *et al.*, 'Drug Control', pp. 864–5.
44 1961 Convention, Art. 14(1)(a).
45 Ibid., Art. 14(1)(b).
46 Ibid., Art. 14(1)(c).
47 On which, see e.g. Dinah Shelton, 'Normative Hierarchy in International Law', *American Journal of International Law*, 2006, vol. 100, 291; Christine M. Chinkin, 'The Challenge of Soft Law: Development and Change in International Law', *International and Comparative Law Quarterly*, 1989, vol. 38, 850.
48 See e.g. William Gilmore, 'International Action against Drug Trafficking: Trends in United Kingdom Law and Practice', *International Lawyer*, 1990, vol. 24, 365, at 365–6.
49 UN Doc. GA/RES/48/12 (1993).
50 1582 UNTS 95 (1998) (hereinafter '1988 Convention').
51 1988 Convention, Art. 3(2).
52 Which does not seek to exclude any other form of jurisdiction that may lawfully be established by national law. 1988 Convention, Art. 4(3).
53 See e.g. Vaughan Lowe, 'Jurisdiction', in Malcolm Evans (ed.), *International Law*, 2nd edn, Oxford: Oxford University Press, 2006, p. 335, at 345–7.
54 Cryer, Friman, Robinson, and Wilmshurst, *Introduction*, p. 46.
55 Criminal Justice Act 1993, ss. 1–2; Liangsiripraesert v Government of the USA, 1 AC 225 (1991).
56 1988 Convention, Art. 4(2)(a). Many states refuse to extradite their own nationals, although the trend is away from such grounds of refusal. See Cryer, Friman, Robinson, and Wilmshurst, *Introduction*, pp. 97–8.
57 1988 Convention, Art. 4(2)(b).
58 Ibid., Art. 6.
59 Ibid., Art. 7. For a treaty of its time, the Convention provides here, as elsewhere, for a remarkably detailed set of procedures.
60 Ibid., Art. 8.
61 Ibid., Art. 9.
62 Ghodse (ed.), *Drug Control*, pp. 80–1.
63 On which see Ghodse (ed.), *Drug Control*, Ch. 6.

64 Which provides that 'drugs, substances, and any equipment used in or intended for the commission of . . . [any of the offenses specified in Article 36 of the 1961 Convention] . . . are subject to seizure and confiscation'.
65 For discussion see Guy Stessens, *Money Laundering: A New International Law Enforcement Model*, Cambridge: Cambridge University Press, 2000, pp. 113–17.
66 1988 Convention, Art. 5(2), (3).
67 Stessens, *Money Laundering*, pp. 92–3.
68 Ibid.
69 1988 Convention, Art. 22(1).
70 Ibid.
71 1988 Convention, Art. 21. Parties are required to supply information to the Commission by Article 20.
72 For an overview, see Leroy *et al.*, 'Drug Control', pp. 889–94.
73 The initial proposals that led to the creation of the ICC, ironically, given its material jurisdiction, came from Trinidad and Tobago, who wanted the court to deal with drug offenses. See e.g. William Schabas, *The International Criminal Court: A Commentary on the Rome Statute*, Oxford: Oxford University Press, 2010, p. 11.
74 See Neil Boister, 'The Exclusion of Treaty Crimes from the Jurisdiction of the Proposed International Criminal Court', *Journal of Armed Conflict Law*, 1998, vol. 2, 27. For some of the domestic reasons for this see Michael P. Scharf, 'Getting Serious About an International Criminal Court', *Pace International Law Review*, 1994, vol. 6, 103, at 171.
75 See generally William Gilmore, *Dirty Money: The Evolution of International Measures to Counter Money Laundering and the Financing of Terrorism*, 3rd edn, Brussels: Council of Europe Publishing, 2004.
76 Estimate available at http://www.unodc.org/unodc/en/money-laundering/globalization.html (accessed 29 April 2010). Equally, Mónica Serrano and Paul Kenny consider such figures to be 'legendary'. Mónica Serrano and Paul Kenny, 'The International Regulation of Money Laundering', *Global Governance*, 2003, vol. 9, 433, at 436.
77 Stessens, *Money Laundering*, pp. 82–3. Although it may be questioned whether this has now become an unhelpful metaphor. See Serrano and Kenny, 'International Regulation', pp. 433–4.
78 For a brief history, see Stessens, *Money Laundering*, pp. 18–28.
79 For example, the FATF 40 recommendations, discussed *infra*, were amended in 2004 to apply to terrorist financing as well as money laundering. For critique of the conflation see Alyssa Philips, 'Terror Financing Laws Won't Wash: It Ain't Money Laundering', *University of Queensland Law Review*, 2004, vol. 23, 81, at 87–8.
80 For example, Convention on Laundering, Search, Seizure, and Confiscation of the Proceeds from Crime, ETS 141 (1990). For a very useful overview of modern developments see Valsamis Mitsilegas and Bill Gilmore, 'The EU Legislative Framework against Money Laundering and Terrorist Financing: A Critical Analysis in the Light of Evolving Global Standards', *International and Comparative Law Quarterly*, 2007, vol. 56, 119. For a general overview see Ilias Bantekas and Susan Nash, *International Criminal Law*, 3rd edn, London: Cavendish, 2007, pp. 247–64.
81 Stessens, *Money Laundering*, pp. 15–18.
82 M. Cherif Bassiouni, *Introduction to International Criminal Law*, Ardsley: Transnational, 2005, p. 360.
83 2178 UNTS 229 (1999), Art. 2. The obligation to criminalize is contained in Article 4.
84 Ibid., Art. 8.
85 Predicate offenses are those offenses that underlie the proceeds that are being laundered.
86 Andreas Schloenhardt, 'Transnational Organized Crime and International Criminal Law', in Bassiouni (ed.), *International Criminal Law*, p. 939, at 955.
87 Palermo Convention, Art. 6(1)(b).
88 Defined in Article 2(b) of the Palermo Convention as being those that can lead to a sentence of four or more years' imprisonment.
89 Which includes jurisdiction over the stateless and habitual residents. Palermo Convention, Art. 15(2)(b).
90 Palermo Convention, Art. 15(2)(a).
91 Palermo Convention, Art. 15(2)(c). Article 15(6) permits states to adopt further jurisdiction that is compatible with international law.
92 For a similar view of the cognate provisions of the anti-terrorism treaties see Louis Henkin, *International Law: Politics and Values*, The Hague, Kluwer, 1995, p. 301: 'At least, they constitute undertakings by the parties to accept such exercises of jurisdiction as permissible *inter se* and to waive any objections they

might otherwise have as territorial States or as States of nationality of the accused .... The anti-terrorist conventions, of course, do not bind States not party to them'.

93 Art.15(3), (4).

94 Stessens, *Money Laundering*, pp. 108–12.

95 Palermo Convention, Art. 7(1)(a).

96 Ibid., Art. 7(2).

97 Ibid., Art. 7(1)(b).

98 Ibid., Art. 12(2).

99 Ibid., Art. 12(3), (4), (5).

100 Ibid., Art. 12(6).

101 Ibid., Art. 17.

102 Ibid., Art. 12(7).

103 Stessens, *Money Laundering*, pp. 60–81.

104 Serrano and Kenny, 'International Regulation', p. 437.

105 UN Doc. A/RES/55/61 (2000), annex.106 Space reasons preclude a detailed review of the provisions of that treaty. Suffice it to say that they are sufficiently similar to those of the 1988 and Palermo Conventions not to require significant separate treatment.

107 Model Legislation on Money Laundering and Financing of Terrorism, 1 December 2005; Model Provisions for Common Law Legal Systems on Money-Laundering, Terrorist Financing, Preventive Measures and the Proceeds of Crime, April 2009.

108 UN Doc. A/RES/49/159; UN Doc. A/S-20/4D (UNGA Special Session on World Drug Problem).

109 They includes the EU. As Mitsilegas and Gilmore note, the FATF and EU measures have tended (unsurprisingly, given the membership of the two bodies) to develop in tandem. Mitsilegas and Gilmore, 'EU', p. 120

110 Which were supplemented by nine specific additional recommendations related to terrorist financing.

111 UN Doc. S/RES/1617 (2005).

112 UN Doc. A/RES/20/288 (2008), annexed plan of action.

113 FATF 40 Recommendations, 20 June 2003 (incorporating the amendments of 22 October 2004) (hereinafter Recommendation), Introduction. To give the FATF its due, 130 states have accepted the standards.

114 In some circumstances, the standards go beyond those required by the relevant treaties. For example, predicate offenses in the Recommendations are those that, depending on the circumstances, are punishable by imprisonment for as low as six months. Recommendation 1.

115 Serrano and Kenny, 'International Regulation'.

116 Andreas and Nadelmann, *Policing*, Ch. 6. This is particularly the case for the FATF, which began as an OECD body and is made up primarily of representatives of more powerful, developed states.

117 Paul Diehl and Charlotte Ku, *The Dynamics of International Law*, Cambridge: Cambridge University Press, 2010, p. 2.

118 Andreas and Nadelmann, *Policing*, pp. 228–9.

Part III

The practice of international tribunals

13

Understanding the complexities of international criminal tribunal jurisdiction

Leila Nadya Sadat

Introduction

The jurisdiction of international criminal courts and tribunals is set forth in their Statutes or Charters, as understood against the backdrop of general international law. It would generally seem preferable to keep these instruments clear and unambiguous to avoid litigation over a given tribunal's jurisdiction from overwhelming it or impairing its ability to decide the cases before it. Unfortunately, however, many international criminal courts and tribunals have had to address complex questions relating to the exercise of their own jurisdiction, arising either from unanticipated factual scenarios, novel interpretations of the law or the insertion of 'constructive ambiguities' in their statutes resulting from compromises agreed during their negotiation. This chapter will briefly survey the basic principles underlying the jurisdiction of international criminal courts and tribunals, as well as some of the complexities applying these jurisdictional principles engenders in practice. I leave to other chapters in this book the question of criminal jurisdiction before national courts and tribunals, including the issue of universal (inter-state) jurisdiction.

The 'Constitutional Basis' for international criminal jurisdiction

International criminal courts and tribunals exercise jurisdiction in cases allocated to them by the international community, under general rules of international law. Their jurisdiction may displace the jurisdiction of national courts that would ordinarily exercise jurisdiction over criminal matters, particularly courts of the State upon the territory of which the crime or crimes were committed (the 'territorial State'), as well as the State of the accused's nationality. Over time, a tentative understanding appears to have developed with respect to which cases properly lie before national courts only, cases involving concurrent jurisdiction between national and international courts and tribunals, and cases most appropriately allocated to international criminal courts or tribunals.[1] However, these jurisdictional boundaries are fluid and, particularly at their interface, controversy remains as to the appropriate allocation of jurisdiction between national and international courts.[2] Nonetheless, several broad principles can be elucidated from a study of international jurisprudence and State practice that suggest which criteria are employed to identify into which of these three groupings a particular situation belongs. These principles have 'constitutional' significance, in the sense that they represent fundamental understandings concerning the proper repartition of authority as between the international legal system and municipal law.[3] All of them, to some extent, reflect the notion articulated by European scholars many years ago that the international community may not exercise jurisdiction unless *l'ordre public international* has been disturbed[4] or some particular interest of the international community has been impinged upon. The factors looked to in identifying which cases are appropriately heard by international courts include (a) the subject-matter jurisdiction of the court or tribunal (i.e. whether crimes under international law have been committed, particularly during wartime); (b) whether the territorial state is unable or unwilling to exercise jurisdiction; (c) whether the United Nations, and particularly, the Security Council, has intervened because the crimes alleged to have been committed pose a threat to international peace and security, and either the Security Council has invoked its Chapter VII powers (possible primacy jurisdiction), or no State is able or willing to exercise its criminal jurisdiction (complementarity); and finally, (d) how grave and/or serious the crimes are and whether the perpetrators are leaders (who may have special responsibilities under international law) or lower-level accused. There are other factors as well, but each one of these will be addressed briefly in turn.

Subject-matter jurisdiction (jurisdiction ratione materiae*)*

The international criminal tribunals and courts established during the twentieth century emerged from the ashes of war, and their jurisdiction was tied to the commission of wartime atrocities. The International Military Tribunal (IMT) at Nuremberg identified three categories of crimes in Article 6 of its Statute: war crimes, crimes against humanity, and crimes against peace (aggressive war).[5] This was also true of the Tokyo Charter for the International Military Tribunal for the Far East (IMFTE),[6] and when the International Criminal Tribunal for the former Yugoslavia (ICTY) was established in 1993, the Secretary-General's report annexed to the ICTY's Statute opined that the Security Council could, through the exercise of its Chapter VII powers, build upon the Nuremberg precedent to establish a tribunal to prosecute persons of 'serious violations of international humanitarian law . . . which are beyond any doubt part of customary law'.[7] The ICTY Statute included grave breaches of the Geneva Conventions and other violations of the laws or customs of war, genocide, and crimes against humanity.[8] Likewise, the Statute for the International Criminal Tribunal for Rwanda (ICTR) included crimes against humanity, genocide, and war crimes—but limited the war crimes provisions (due to the internal nature of the conflict) to violations of Article 3 common to the Geneva Conventions and of Additional Protocol II.[9] By limiting their jurisdiction to international crimes only, indeed, one might argue *jus cogens* offenses, the establishment of these two tribunals followed the Nuremberg precedent directly, asserting jurisdiction over crimes created by international law, taking place within the context of an armed conflict (even if an armed conflict nexus was later found not to be required with respect to crimes against humanity and genocide).[10] The International Criminal Court (ICC) retains this focus on the 'core crimes' but explicitly removes the armed conflict nexus from Article 7 of the Statute, providing that crimes against humanity (and genocide), may be committed in times of peace.[11] On 12 June 2010, the ICC Assembly of States Parties added the crime of aggression to the jurisdiction of the Court, but it will not become operational until 2017, at the soonest.

Other international criminal tribunals of a hybrid variety have been established with subject-matter jurisdiction provisions that deviate from the Nuremberg pattern, due to the specific nature of the situations they address, and their hybrid nature as tribunals that have both an international and domestic character. This is true of the Special Court for Sierra Leone (SCSL), which was given jurisdiction over certain crimes under Sierra Leonean law,[12] in addition to jurisdiction over serious violations of humanitarian law and crimes against humanity. Likewise, the Special Panels with Exclusive Jurisdiction over Serious Criminal Offenses in East Timor include within their ambit, in addition to genocide, war crimes and crimes against humanity, torture (under international law), and murder and sexual offences as defined by the 'provisions of the applicable Penal Code in East Timor'.[13] The Extraordinary Chambers in the Courts of Cambodia (the Khmer Rouge Tribunal or ECCC), established by an Agreement between the United Nations and the Cambodian government to try senior leaders of former Democratic Kampuchea,[14] have jurisdiction over genocide, crimes against humanity, and grave breaches of the 1949 Geneva Conventions as well as 'other crimes defined in Chapter II of the Law on the Establishment of the Extraordinary Chambers',[15] including destruction of cultural property, attacks on internationally protected persons, and murder under Cambodian law.[16] Finally, the Special Tribunal for Lebanon, created essentially to prosecute those individuals who may have been responsible for the assassination of former Lebanese Prime Minister Rafik Hariri, as well as other associated crimes, is perhaps the most unusual hybrid tribunal in that it has a jurisdiction *ratione materiae* that is tied completely to municipal law. Article 2 of the Lebanon Tribunal Statute provides that the applicable criminal laws are the terrorism and related offenses of the Lebanese Criminal Code and certain articles of the Lebanese law of 11 January 1958 on '[i]ncreasing the penalties for sedition, civil war and interfaith struggle'.[17]

Territorial Jurisdiction (jurisdiction ratione loci*)*

The territoriality principle is a cornerstone of criminal law. In general terms, States have the power to punish individuals—whether their own nationals or not—for crimes committed on their territories.[18] Sometimes States may also seek to extend their prescriptive jurisdiction to crimes committed elsewhere that have *effects* upon their territories[19] or, more attenuated yet, affect some important interest they believe entitles them, under international law, to extend their reach beyond their borders, a topic not addressed here. It is generally understood to be preferable for the territorial State to prosecute its own cases, for typically the evidence will be there, its citizens the victims of the offense, and the perpetrators familiar with the procedures of its court system. Yet in cases of international criminality, the principle of territorial jurisdiction may be difficult or problematic in application—the State's legal infrastructure may lie in ruins (Rwanda), a conflict may be ongoing and ethnic groups distrust each other so that using any national/ethnic judicial system would be problematic (the former Yugoslavia), the country may be under administration by the United Nations following conflict and the alleged perpetrators may be foreigners (Timor-Leste), or some other difficulties may arise, such as a perceived or real inability of a national legal system to conduct the investigation and prosecution safely itself (Lebanon). Whatever the rationale, it has been assumed since the Nuremberg judgment that a group of States may do together what any one of them could have done singly (namely, establish an international criminal tribunal)[20] and that one jurisdictional effect attending the establishment of international criminal tribunals is to displace (or replace) ordinary criminal laws of territorial application with a different legal (international) regime. Although this principle, as articulated by the IMT at Nuremberg, was clearly linked by that Tribunal with the fact that Germany had unconditionally surrendered, and was occupied at the time—such that the Allied Powers were in fact sovereign over German territory—many commentators have suggested that the IMT's opinion as a whole stands for a broader proposition that States may together, under certain conditions, establish international criminal tribunals that displace the application of law by the territorial State.[21]

In terms of their territorial jurisdictions, each of the international *ad hoc* tribunals referred to earlier limits its territorial scope to a particular territory: the ICTY to 'the territory of the former Yugoslavia';[22] the ICTR to the 'Territory of Rwanda';[23] and the SCSL to crimes committed 'in the territory of Sierra Leone'.[24] The ECCC Statute is silent as to its scope of territorial application, although it seems obvious from the overall tenor of the Statute that the territorial ambit of the ECCC's jurisdiction is intended to be Cambodia. Curiously, while the Special Panels for Serious Crimes (SPSC) in East Timor are apparently permitted to exercise 'universal jurisdiction' over genocide, crimes against humanity, and war crimes, the SPSC Statute nonetheless provides that the panels have jurisdiction *ratione loci* 'throughout the entire territory of East Timor', suggesting that those courts were territorially based.[25] Finally, the Lebanon Tribunal limits its territorial jurisdiction to the attack on Rafik Hariri, which took place in Lebanon, as well as, potentially, other 'attacks that occurred in Lebanon'.[26]

The International Criminal Court, unlike the *ad hoc* tribunals, is not limited to crimes committed on the territory of a particular State. Nonetheless, territoriality remains a core principle of the ICC Statute, which provides that in cases brought to the Court by a State or by the ICC Prosecutor, the Court's jurisdiction may attach if 'the State on the territory of which the conduct in question occurred' is either a Party to the ICC Statute or accepts the Court's jurisdiction by declaration under Article 12(3) of the Statute.[27] However, territoriality is not the only basis upon which the Court can exercise its jurisdiction; it can also do so if the State of the accused's nationality accepts the Court's jurisdiction (either as a Party or by declaration);[28] and, in cases referred under Article 13(b) to the Court by the Security Council of the United Nations, the geographic scope of the Court's jurisdiction is unbounded. Indeed, its jurisdiction potentially reaches the territory of every State in the world.[29]

Complementarity and primacy

One central feature of the 'Nuremberg Revolution' was Article 6(c)'s proviso that the acts incriminated by the Statute could fall within the jurisdiction of the IMT 'whether or not in violation of the domestic law of the country where perpetrated'.[30] Implicit in the Charter, then, were two ideas: that international law supplanted or took precedence over domestic law, under certain circumstances, and that, concomitantly, the jurisdiction of an international court established to adjudicate cases involving the application of that law also enjoyed 'supremacy' of jurisdiction over national courts. Although the IMT did not directly speak to this, its view could not have been more clearly expressed in the now-celebrated (and canonical) quote from its judgment, that 'the very essence of the Charter is that individuals have international duties which transcend the national obligations of obedience imposed by the individual state'.[31]

This original conception of the relationship between international and national courts and international and national laws as one of vertical hierarchy was simple and clear; but it subsequently proved inadequate once international tribunals and the International Criminal Court itself were finally established in the 1990s, some 50 years after the judgment at Nuremberg.

When the Security Council established the two *ad hoc* tribunals for the former Yugoslavia and Rwanda, it relied upon this notion of vertical hierarchy to endow those institutions with 'primacy' jurisdiction. For example, Article 9(1) of the ICTY Statute states that national courts have 'concurrent' jurisdiction with the ICTY. However, Article 9(2) provides further that the ICTY 'shall have primacy over national courts'. This means, according to the Statute:

> At any stage of the procedure, the International Tribunal may formally request national courts to defer to the competence of the International Tribunal in accordance with the present Statute.[32]

The ICTR Statute has a similar provision (Article 8), and in fact, the first case before the ICTY, *Prosecutor v. Duško Tadić*, involved a situation in which the accused was being pursued by a national jurisdiction (Germany), and the ICTY issued an order to the German government demanding Tadić 's surrender to the tribunal. This kind of 'primacy' jurisdiction could, of course, be attributable to the fact that the ICTY and the ICTR were created by the Security Council pursuant to its Chapter VII authority, endowing these two international tribunals with special powers. The primacy of the ICTY was challenged by the accused in *Tadić* and the ICTY Appeals Chamber responded, holding that 'when an international tribunal such as the present one is created, it *must* be endowed with primacy over national courts. Otherwise, human nature being what it is, there would be a perennial danger of international crimes being characterized as "ordinary crimes" '.[33] The *Tadić* Appeals Chamber opinion is perhaps the strongest statement of verticality posited between national and international criminal tribunals operating upon the same territory to date, and some have questioned whether it was an accurate statement of the law at the time.[34] Nonetheless, the Statutes of other international and hybrid international criminal tribunals follow a similar pattern—vesting exclusive jurisdiction over the offences within their ambit with the hybrid court.[35]

The model chosen for the International Criminal Court could not be more different, eschewing the notion of primacy jurisdiction and replacing it with one of complementarity. Indeed, as I have written elsewhere, it is perhaps the implementation and implications of the jurisdictional theories of the Rome Statute that are its most revolutionary feature, as a matter of substantive international law.[36] The ICC Statute does not articulate a clear legal basis as the source of the Court's jurisdiction, relying, presumably, on the twin precedents evoked above of (a) Nuremberg and (b) the Chapter VII powers of the Security Council set forth in the UN Charter. The Treaty's preamble suggests two additional bases upon which the jurisdictional power of the Court is predicated: our 'common humanity' and the threat that atrocity crimes pose to international peace and security.[37] And indeed, in cases referred to the Court by the Security Council, neither nationality nor territoriality limit the Court's jurisdiction *in loci* or *in personam*; rather, the only remaining limits are jurisdiction *ratione materiae* and, possibly, the doctrine of complementarity whereby the Court is intended as a Court of last, not first, resort.[38]

The notion of complementarity in the ICC Statute is a novelty, and a great deal of literature has been spawned theorizing about its meaning and operation.[39] It was introduced into the Rome Statute by the International Law Commission's 1994 draft, and was the subject of a great deal of criticism at the time. But the idea had a certain appeal to States attempting to sort out which cases 'ought' to be before the Court, and which cases ought not to be, and was ultimately retained as a central feature of the Rome Statute, which provides that the Court's jurisdiction is meant to be 'complementary' to national criminal jurisdictions in the preamble and Article 1 of the Statute. Although the term is not defined in the ICC Statute, procedurally, the notion of complementarity is made operational by the provisions of the Statute on the 'admissibility' of cases before the Court set out in Article 17. Article 17, in turn, provides that the Court may exercise jurisdiction only if (a) national jurisdictions are 'unwilling or unable' to; (b) the crime is of sufficient gravity; and (c) the person has not already been tried for the conduct on which the complaint is based (*ne bis in idem*).[40]

It is still unclear as to what complementarity means precisely in the operation of the Statute of the Court, whether it can be waived by a State,[41] and whether or not it applies in the case of Security Council referrals to the Court. In an informal and important expert paper, the ICC Prosecutor attempted to operationalize the notion of complementarity, focusing on its purpose as ensuring 'respect for the primary jurisdiction of States', as well as 'considerations of efficiency and effectiveness, since States will generally have the best access to evidence and witnesses and the resources to carry out proceedings'.[42] Importantly, the Prosecutor has taken the position, with which the Court has agreed in its early jurisprudence, that if a State is not investigating a specific crime regarding a specific individual, the ICC retains jurisdiction.[43] While some commentators have argued that this represents a departure from the text of Article 17, the better view (consistent with this author's recollection of the Rome Conference negotiations) seems to be that the Statute deprives the Court of jurisdiction only insofar as a case is actually being investigated or prosecuted by national authorities.[44]

Gravity, seriousness of the crimes and high or leadership position of the accused as quasi-jurisdictional requirements

In the Moscow Declaration of 1943, the Allied Powers declared that

> [t]hose German officers . . . who have been responsible for, or have taken a consenting part in . . . atrocities . . . will be sent back to the countries in which their abominable deeds were done in order that they may be judged and punished [there] . . . without prejudice to the case of the major criminals, whose offenses have no particular geographical localization and who will be punished by the joint decision of the Governments of the Allies.[45]

The Moscow Declaration not only addressed the question of jurisdiction *ratione loci,* as discussed above, but also introduced the notion of 'major' criminals, whose positions were presumably of higher rank than those others accused of 'ordinary' crimes, and whose crimes were concomitantly more serious, thereby requiring an international solution. The Nuremberg Charter retained this notion of 'major war criminals',[46] although there was some debate about whether all of those chosen fit properly within that category of offender.

This notion of major offenders is not found directly in the ICTY and the ICTR Statutes, although the notions of 'seriousness' and/or 'gravity' are, with both Statutes limiting their application to 'serious violations of international humanitarian law'. Indeed, the first case brought to trial before the ICTY involved a 'minor' accused, subjecting the Tribunal to criticism from commentators who argued both that this was a waste of resources, and, less clearly, that this was, as a matter of the Tribunal's status as an international criminal tribunal, jurisdictionally inappropriate.[47]

The Special Court for Sierra Leone has a slightly different version of this idea, limiting its jurisdiction to 'persons who bear the greatest responsibility', including 'leaders'. Indeed, although the Secretary-General's Report on the Statute suggested that this was in the nature of 'guidance to the Prosecutor', as opposed to a 'distinct jurisdictional threshold',[48] the Security Council has insisted upon limiting the focus of the SCSL to 'those who played a leadership role',[49] and the Court's Chief Prosecutors have often made clear that they selected which defendants to indict based upon those criteria. As an aside, one wonders whether this jurisdictional limitation had more to do with keeping the cost of the Special Court low than with fidelity to any particular set of legal principles.

Interestingly, the Agreement establishing the ECCC refers to the 'senior leaders of Democratic Kampuchea' *and* those 'most responsible for the crimes *and serious* violations of Cambodian penal law, international humanitarian law and custom, and international conventions'.[50] The ECCC is likely to have even fewer defendants than the Special Court for Sierra Leone, and its jurisdiction is limited in that the accused must either be senior leaders or those 'most responsible' *and* be accused of serious crimes.

Like the Statutes of the ICTY and ICTR, the International Criminal Court's Statute eschews making direct reference to the leadership position (or not) of the accused as a jurisdictional limit on the Court's competence.[51] Instead, the ICC Statute focuses on the seriousness of the crimes committed, and does this in two ways. First, the Court's Statute refers in the Preamble to the 'most serious crimes of concern to the international community as a whole', a provision which is repeated in Article 1, and again in Article 5, setting out the Court's jurisdiction. This jurisdictional component of 'seriousness' is underscored further in the Statute through the notion of 'gravity' in Article 17 of the Statute, on admissibility. Article 17 provides that the Court *shall* determine a case to be inadmissible if it is 'not of sufficient gravity to justify further action by the Court'.[52]

Because gravity, like complementarity, is not a defined term, interpretation of this provision has been left up to the Court and its personnel. There are clues as to its meaning sprinkled within the Statute such as the precatory *chapeau* to Article 8 (War Crimes), which suggests that war crimes are particularly appropriate for the Court's jurisdiction if they are part of a plan or policy or committed on a 'large-scale basis',[53] for example. Combined with the requirement of 'widespread or systematic' crimes (in Article 7 on crimes against humanity), and the intentional destruction of a group (in Article 6 on genocide), it appears that at least one element of 'gravity', therefore, is scale—i.e. the magnitude or widespread nature of the crimes. Another possible interpretation could be how heinous the offenses are, and of course, there is the possibility that the Court could read back in the 'major' war criminals language even though it is not included in the Statute itself.[54]

In 2006 the Office of the Prosecutor issued a set of draft guidelines interpreting the gravity requirement and factors his office would take into consideration in the selection of cases and situations.[55] Although no subsequent guidelines appear to have been published, the Court's Web site lists the criteria upon which gravity is assessed as including: the scale of the crimes; the nature of the crimes; the manner of commission of the crimes; and the impact of the crimes. Interestingly, in the *Ntaganda* case (the first case litigated on these issues), Pre-Trial Chamber I reverted to the Nuremberg 'major leader' idea. It held that the case against Ntaganda was inadmissible as Ntaganda was not a 'central figure' in the decision-making process of the Union of Congolese Patriots, and lacked any authority over policy development or implementation.[56] This holding was reversed by the Appeals Chamber on several grounds. In particular, the Appeals Chamber rejected the idea that only certain categories of perpetrators may be brought before the Court. Instead, it found that 'individuals who are not at the very top of an organization may still carry considerable influence and commit, or generate the widespread commission of, very serious crimes'.[57]

Personal jurisdiction (jurisdiction *ratione personae*)

Natural and juridical persons

Each of the tribunals discussed earlier and the International Criminal Court have jurisdiction over natural persons.[58] The question has arisen upon many occasions whether it would be useful to permit international criminal courts and tribunals to also exercise jurisdiction over States and legal entities such as corporations. Many thoughtful commentators have advocated for an extension of the Nuremberg Tribunal's argument that 'crimes are committed by men, not by abstract entities';[59] however, the general understanding is that any effort to incriminate States would be futile,[60] and corporate liability has been much more successful as a tool in cases involving civil rather than criminal liability.[61]

Nationality of the accused

Article 6 of the Nuremberg Charter (Jurisdiction and General Principles) provided that the Tribunal was established for the 'trial and punishment of the major war criminals of the

European Axis'.[62] This limited the individuals who could be indicted to German defendants only, a fact that subjected the Nuremberg Tribunal to the criticism that it was no more than 'victors' justice'. Although the International Military Tribunal for the Far East had a similar limitation, and was understood to apply only to Japanese accused, in fact the language of Article 1 of the Tokyo Charter provides broadly for the trial of 'the major war criminals in the Far East', not limiting itself to Japanese or even Asian accused.[63]

This is not a purely academic point, for although more recent tribunals and the International Criminal Court use more carefully worded provisions to delineate their jurisdiction, questions have arisen as to the application of these Statutes to particular individuals and/or conflicts. For example, officials from NATO member countries simply assumed that only nationals of the former Yugoslavia could be accused before the ICTY, and were surprised when the Office of the Prosecutor (correctly, in the view of this author), noted that the only jurisdictional limitation in the ICTY's Statute was geographic, extending the Tribunal's jurisdiction to 'the territory of the former Socialist Federal Republic of Yugoslavia'.[64] Indeed, an Expert Commission was convened to examine NATO's 1999 aerial bombardment campaign against Serbia and advise the Office of the Prosecutor whether or not serious violations of international humanitarian law had taken place that warranted opening a criminal investigation into NATO's activities.[65]

In addition to providing jurisdiction over all persons committing serious violations of international humanitarian law in Rwanda, the ICTR Statute contains an express linkage to nationality, providing that it may assert jurisdiction over 'Rwandan citizens responsible for [crimes within the jurisdiction of the Tribunal] committed in the territory of neighbouring States'.[66] There is some evidence that this provision was included to permit the Tribunal to address crimes committed by Hutus in refugee camps in neighbouring States.[67] However, this provision—the only one of its kind in the statute of an *ad hoc* tribunal—has never been used to date.

The SCSL Statute, like the ICTY Statute, while limiting its ambit to 'those who bear the greatest responsibility for serious violations of international humanitarian law and Sierra Leonean law committed in the territory of Sierra Leone'[68] has no nationality limitation. As a matter of fact, the Prosecutor successfully indicted former Liberian President Charles Taylor, who is now on trial in The Hague. Similarly, the Statute of the Lebanon Tribunal does not limit the Tribunal's jurisdiction based on the nationality of the accused.[69] This is also true of the Special Panels created in East Timor with jurisdiction over 'serious criminal offenses' which, by the Regulation establishing the Panels, have 'universal' jurisdiction[70] meaning, *inter alia*, jurisdiction 'irrespective of whether . . . the serious criminal offence was committed by an East Timorese citizen'.[71] However, the jurisdiction of one present-day hybrid international criminal tribunal—the ECCC—reverts to the Nuremberg and Tokyo approach, limiting its application to the 'senior leaders of Democratic Kampuchea and those who were most responsible for [crimes committed] . . . from 17 April 1975 to 6 January 1979'.[72]

Finally, the International Criminal Court, with its theoretically universal application, nonetheless uses nationality of the accused as a limitation on the universality principle. The prescriptive (legislative) and adjudicative jurisdiction of the International Criminal Court is premised on the universality principle, to the extent that the Security Council may refer a case to the Court even as regards the nationals of a State not party to the ICC Statute.[73] However, in cases not referred by the Security Council, either the State of the accused's nationality *or* the territorial State (where the crimes were committed) must be a party to the ICC Statute for the Court's jurisdiction to attach.[74]

Temporal jurisdiction (jurisdiction *ratione temporis*)

'Temporal' jurisdiction refers to the time period to which a Statute creating the international (or mixed) court or tribunal may apply the law. The principal distinction between the eight *ad hoc* tribunals discussed earlier and the permanent International Criminal Court is that the jurisdiction of the *ad hoc* tribunals is invariably retroactive, meaning that the courts in those cases have been established after the crimes they have been created to address have already been committed. Conversely, the ICC was established with prospective jurisdiction only. Under Article 11 of the Statute, the Court's jurisdiction is limited to crimes committed after the Statute entered into force. For States becoming parties after the Statute's entry into force, the Court may exercise jurisdiction only with respect to crimes committed after the entry into force of the Statute with respect to that State, unless the State declares otherwise.[75]

With *ad hoc* tribunals, the situation is quite different. Some *ad hoc* tribunals limit their temporal jurisdiction with a starting date, but no end date, suggesting that they have ongoing jurisdiction over a particular conflict. This is the case with the Yugoslavia Tribunal and the Special Court for Sierra Leone, which have starting dates for their jurisdiction to begin (tied to the conflicts for which they were established), but no end date. However, the more common situation as regards *ad hoc* tribunals is to specify both a start and end date,[76] or even, as in the case of the Lebanon Tribunal, to specify that the jurisdiction of the tribunal relates primarily to the commission of a particular crime on a particular date.[77] The negotiation of these periods opens political questions, because, often, successor governments wish a tribunal's temporal jurisdiction to be tightly constrained to avoid any possibility that its own activities could come under scrutiny. For example, with respect to the temporal jurisdiction of the Rwanda Tribunal, the Kagame government wished the jurisdiction to begin at least some months prior to the commencement of the genocide on 6 April 1994, to include within the Tribunal's ambit the planning of the genocide that later occurred. Conversely, some Security Council members wished to extend the end period of the Tribunal's temporal jurisdiction to permit the Tribunal to exercise jurisdiction over offenses allegedly committed by Kagame's forces against civilians and Hutu forces as the Tutsi-led RPF (Rwandan Patriotic Front) retook the country following the genocide.[78] The resulting compromise was to establish the Tribunal's jurisdiction from 1 January to 31 December 1994. The Rwandan government voted against the establishment of the ICTR, due in part to its frustration with the limited temporal jurisdiction of the Tribunal, which it felt should have included the 'long period of planning' that had begun well prior to the Tribunal's start date of 1 January 1994.[79]

Conversely, the Secretary-General's report on the jurisdiction of the ICTY provides that the jurisdiction of the Tribunal extends to violations committed 'since 1991', understood to mean 'any time on or after 1 January 1991'. This was intended to be a 'neutral date which is not tied to any specific event'.[80] The Statute has no end-point for its jurisdiction, which was supposed to be set out by the Security Council 'upon the restoration of peace', according to Resolution 827 to which the Statute, as adopted, was annexed.[81] The Council has yet to do so, and the Secretary-General has indicated that he is unable to do so.[82] The ICTY has dismissed a challenge arguing that its jurisdiction ended with the 1999 Kosovo ceasefire,[83] and it appears likely that 'the Security Council will close down the ICTY without ever setting the end-date of its temporal jurisdiction'.[84]

Several interesting legal issues are often posited by litigants with respect to the temporal jurisdiction of international criminal courts and tribunals. First, in cases involving *ad hoc* tribunals, it is practically *de rigeur* to challenge the retroactive application of the tribunal's statute to the accused as an *ex post facto* law that violates the legality principle. This was true at Nuremberg, where the defense argued that 'there can be no punishment of crime without a pre-existing law'.[85] However, this contention was rebuffed by the IMT in plain words:

> In the first place, it is to be observed that the maxim *nullum crimen sine lege* is not a limitation of sovereignty, but is in general a principle of justice. To assert that it is unjust to punish those who in defiance of treaties and assurances have attacked neighbouring states without warning is obviously untrue, for in such circumstances the attacker must know that he is doing wrong, and so far from it being unjust to punish him, it would be unjust if his wrong were allowed to go unpunished.[86]

With respect to the International Criminal Court, a key question even as regards the apparently clear non-retroactivity provisions of Article 11 is whether the Court's jurisdiction might apply to so-called continuing crimes, such as disappearances, that occurred prior to the entry into force of the ICC Statute, but continued thereafter. During the negotiations of the Statute, NGOs (non-governmental organizations) lobbied for an understanding that the Court could be seized with cases involving continuing crimes even if the initial acts took place prior to the start date of the ICC's jurisdiction.[87] However, at least as regards enforced disappearances, such an interpretation appears to have been rejected by the States Parties to the Statute, who placed a note into the Elements of Crimes pertaining to this crime that '[it] falls under the jurisdiction of the Court only if the attack . . . occurs *after the entry into force of the Statute*'.[88] Finally, with respect to the temporal jurisdiction of *ad hoc* tribunals, difficult questions can arise as regards crimes completed during the jurisdiction of the court, but begun prior to it (or, presumably, begun during and completed after it). Some of these cases also relate to continuing or inchoate crimes, such as conspiracy to commit genocide and incitement. This has been particularly true in the ICTR, where several cases have addressed this difficulty. Thus, in *Prosecutor v. Nahimana*,[89] the ICTR addressed charges that the accused had conspired to commit genocide and engaged in direct and public incitement to commit genocide. The Trial Chamber found that the crimes of conspiracy and incitement were crimes that 'continued in time "until the completion of the acts contemplated" ' and concluded that since the genocide occurred in 1994, it had jurisdiction to convict for these crimes even if they had begun before that year.[90] The Appeals Chamber, examining the record of the ICTR's establishment, reversed, finding that the 'Trial Chamber was wrong insofar as it convicted [the accused] on the basis of criminal conduct which took place prior to 1994'.[91] Judge Fausto Pocar dissented from this finding, stating '[i]nsofar as offences are repeated over time and are linked by a common intent or purpose, they must be considered as a continuing offence, that is a single crime'.[92] This issue will surely be litigated (and relitigated) at the ICC, given its neutral, but arbitrary, start point for jurisdiction.

Conclusion

The development of international criminal tribunals and the establishment of the International Criminal Court during the past 15 years have led to considerable uncertainty concerning the overlapping jurisdiction of these entities. This chapter attempts to unpack the basic principles underlying their jurisdiction, as well as explain how each of those jurisdictions operates in fact. Even though these tribunals will no longer continue to operate as their mandates end and their work is completed, many of the core jurisdictional principles and jurisprudence developed by them will influence decisions of the International Criminal Court, and remain an important subsidiary source of customary international law.

Acknowledgment

I would like to thank Genevra Alberti for research assistance.

Notes

1 L. Sadat, 'Transjudicial Dialogue and the Rwandan Genocide: Aspects of Antagonism and Complementarity', *Leiden Journal of International Law* 22 (2009), pp. 543–62; see also Y. Shany, *Regulating Jurisdictional Relations between National and International Courts,* New York: Oxford University Press, 2007.

2 The United States, for example, maintained and continues to contend that the International Criminal Court may not lawfully assert criminal jurisdiction over the nationals of ICC non-party States. Statement of David J. Scheffer, Ambassador-at-Large for War Crimes Issues and Head of the US Delegation to UN Diplomatic Conference on the Establishment of a Permanent International Criminal Court, Before the Committee on Foreign Relations of the US Senate, 23 July 1998, reprinted in WL 425945, 21 (F.D.C.H.). Most commentators and other States disagree with the US position. See, e.g. L. Sadat, 'The New International Criminal Court: An Uneasy Revolution', *The Georgetown Law Journal,* 88 (2000), pp. 381–474; P. Kirsch, 'The Rome Conference on the International Criminal Court: A Comment', *ASIL Newsletter* (American Society of International Law, Washington, DC) November–December. 1998, pp. 1, 8.

3 See generally, L. Sadat, 'The International Criminal Court and Universal International Jurisdiction: A return to First Principles', in *International Law and International Relations: Bridging Theory and Practice* (T. Bierseker, *et al.*, eds), London: Routledge, 2007, p. 181.

4 See, e.g. G. Levasseur, 'Les crimes contre l'humanité et le problème de leur prescription', 93 *Journal du Droit International,* pp. 259, 267 (1966) (arguing that international criminal law may apply as a body of law if an individual's behavior has troubled *l'ordre public* of a country other than his own).

5 Charter of the International Military Tribunal at Nuremberg, Annex to the London Agreement, 82 UNTS 279 (1945), Art. 6 [hereinafter Nuremberg Tribunal Charter].

6 Tokyo Charter for the International Military Tribunal for the Far East, *as amended by* General Orders No. 20, TIAS No. 1589 (1946), Art. 5 [hereinafter Tokyo Charter].

7 Report of the Secretary-General Pursuant to Paragraph 2 of Security Council Resolution 808 (1993), UN Doc. S/25704 (May 3, 1993), paras 33 and 34.

8 Statute of the International Criminal Tribunal for the former Yugoslavia, UN Doc. S/RES/827 (1993), Arts 2–5 [hereinafter ICTY Statute].

9 Statute of the International Criminal Tribunal for Rwanda, UN Doc. S/RES/955 (1994), Arts 2–4 [hereinafter ICTR Statute].

10 Prosecutor v. Tadić, Case No. IT-94-1-AR72, Decision on the Defence Motion for Interlocutory Appeal on Jurisdiction, 2 October 1995, paras 140 and 141.

11 Rome Statute for the International Criminal Court, 2187 UNTS 90 (1998), Arts 6–8 [hereinafter Rome Statute].

12 Statute of the Special Court for Sierra Leone, UN Doc. S/RES/1315 (2000), Art. 5 [hereinafter SCSL Statute].

13 Regulation No. 2000/15 On the Establishment of Panels with Exclusive Jurisdiction over Serious Criminal Offences, UN Doc. UNTAET/REG/2000/15 (2000), Sections 8–9 [hereinafter East Timor Agreement].

14 Agreement between the United Nations and the Royal Government of Cambodia Concerning the Prosecution under Cambodian Law of Crimes Committed during the Period of Democratic Kampuchea, 2329 UNTS 117 (2003), Art. 9 [hereinafter ECCC Statute].

15 Ibid.

16 Law on the Establishment of the Extraordinary Chambers in the Courts of Cambodia for the Prosecution of Crimes Committed during the Period of Democratic Kamppuchea, as amended 27 October 2004 (NS/RKM/1004/006), Arts. 3 (new), 7, 8. So far, at least one defendant at the ECCC has been charged, *inter alia,* with crimes under the Cambodian Penal Code. See Kaing Guek Eay (001/18-07-2007-ECCC-TC), Trial Day 1 Transcript, 30 March 2009, p. 1 (murder and torture).

17 Statute of the Special Tribunal for Lebanon, UN Doc. S/RES/1757 (2007), Art. 2 [hereinafter Lebanon Tribunal Statute].

18 A. Cassese, *International Criminal Law,* Oxford, 2003, p. 277.

19 Ibid., p. 278.
20 International Military Tribunal (Nuremberg), Judgment and Sentences, October 1, 1946, *American Journal of International Law* 41, 1947, p. 216 [hereinafter Nuremberg Judgment].
21 See, e.g. E. Schwelb, 'Crimes against Humanity', 23 *British Yearbook of International Law*, pp. 210–1.
22 ICTY Statute, Art. 1.
23 Ibid. The ICTR also has a competence premised upon the Rwandan nationality of the accused, *see infra* note 65, but this jurisdiction has never been used by the Tribunal.
24 SCSL Statute, Art. 1.
25 East Timor Agreement, Section 2.5. For a general discussion of the establishment of the Special Panels in East Timor, see W. Burke-White, 'A Community of Courts: Toward a System of International Criminal Law Enforcement', *Michigan Journal of International Law* 24, 2002, p. 46.
26 Lebanon Tribunal Statute, Art. 1(1).
27 ICC Statute, Art. 12(2).
28 Ibid.
29 Ibid. See also L. Sadat, *The New International Criminal Court and the Transformation of International Law: Justice for the New Millenium,* Ardsley: Transnational, 2002, p. 105.
30 Nuremberg Tribunal Charter, Art. 6(c).
31 Nuremberg Judgment, p. 221.
32 ICTY Statute, Art. 9(2).
33 Prosecutor v. Duško Tadić, Case No. IT-94-1-AR72, Decision on the Defence Motion for Interlocutory Appeal on Jurisdiction, 20 Oct. 1995, para. 58.
34 For a discussion of the issues with such assertions of primacy, and of statements made by members of the UN Security Council purporting to limit the ICTY's jurisdiction, see B. Brown, 'Primacy or Complementarity: Reconciling the Jurisdiction of National Courts and International Criminal Tribunals', 23 *Yale Journal of International Law*, 1998, pp. 403–6.
35 East Timor Agreement, Section 1.1; See also Lebanon Tribunal Statute, Art. 4(1) ('The Tribunal shall have primacy over the national courts of Lebanon.'); accord SCSL Statute, Art. 8(2) ('The Special Court shall have primacy over the national courts of Sierra Leone.') The ECCC Statute is silent on this issue.
36 L. Sadat, *The International Criminal Court and the Transformation of International Law*, p. 107.
37 Rome Statute, Preamble, Cls 1 and 3.
38 The Statute itself does not contain this language, but is the inference that most authors, including this one, have drawn from the text. See L. Sadat, *The International Criminal Court and the Transformation of International Law*; J. Kleffner, *Complementarity in the Rome Statute and National Criminal Jurisdictions*, Oxford: Oxford University Press, 2008, p. 101.
39 See, e.g. M. El Zeidy, 'Some Remarks on the Question of the Admissibility of a Case during Arrest Warrant Proceedings before the International Criminal Court', 19 *Leiden Journal of International Law*, 2006, pp. 741–51; D. Robinson, 'The Mysterious Mysteriousness of Complementarity', *Criminal Law Forum* (forthcoming 2010); C. Stahn, 'Complementarity: A Tale of Two Notions', 19 *Criminal Law Forum*, (2008), pp. 87–113.
40 Rome Statute, Art. 17(1); L. Sadat, *The International Criminal Court and the Transformation of International Law*, p. 119.
41 One of the earlier incarnations of the Rome Statute, the *Zutphen Intersessional Draft*, contained a footnote querying whether a State could waive complementarity-related admissibility requirements. See Preparatory Committee on the Establishment of an International Criminal Court, Report of the Inter-Sessional Meeting from 19 to 30 January 1998 in Zutphen, The Netherlands, UN Doc A/AC.249/1998/L.13 (1998), Art. 11, 140 n. 53.
42 ICC Office of the Prosecutor, 'Informal Expert Paper: The Principle of Complementarity in Practice', 2003, available at http://www.icc-cpi.int/iccdocs/doc/doc654724.pdf (accessed 21 February 2010).
43 See, e.g. Prosecutor v. Katanga and Ngudjolo Chui, Case No. ICC-01/04-01/07 OA8, Judgment on the Appeal of Mr. Germain Katanga against the Oral Decision of Trial Chamber II of 12 June 2009 on the Admissibility of the Case, at para. 75–8; Prosecutor v. Omar Al Bashir, Decision on the Prosecution's Application for a Warrant of Arrest, Case No. PTC-I, ICC02/05-0, 4 March 2009, at paras 48–9.
44 Robinson, 'The Mysterious Mysteriousness of Complementarity'.
45 Declaration of German Atrocities, November 1, 1943, 3 Bevans 816, 834, *Department of State Bulletin,* 6 November 1943, pp. 310–1.
46 Nuremberg Tribunal Charter, Art. 1.

47 M. Scharf, *Balkan Justice: The Story Behind the First International War Crimes Trial since Nuremberg*, Durham: Carolina Academic Press, 1997, pp. 222–3; M. Zaid, 'Trial of the Century? Assessing the Case of Dusko Tadić Before the International Criminal Tribunal for the Former Yugoslavia', *International Law Students Association Journal of International and Comparative Law* 3, 1997, 593–4.

48 Report of the Secretary-General on the Establishment of a Special Court for Sierra Leone, UN Doc. S/2000/915 (2000), paras 29–30.

49 Letter dated 22 December 2000 from the President of the Security Council Addressed to the Secretary-General, UN Doc. S/2000/1234 (2000), p. 1.

50 ECCC Agreement, Art. 1.

51 This is also true of the Special Panels in East Timor.

52 Rome Statute, Art. 17(1)(d).

53 Ibid. Art. 8(1).

54 L. Sadat, *The International Criminal Court and the Transformation of International Law*, pp. 124–5.

55 ICC Office of the Prosecutor, *Draft for Discussion: Criteria for Selection of Situations and Cases* (June 4–5, 2006).

56 Prosecutor v. Ntaganda, Case No. ICC-01/04-02/06, Decision on the Prosecutor's Application for Warrants of Arrest, Article 58, 10 February 2006, para. 87.

57 Prosecutor v. Ntaganda, Case No. ICC-01/04-02/06, Judgement on the Prosecutor's Appeal against the Decision of Pre-Trial Chamber I Entitled 'Decision on the Prosecutor's Application for a Warrant of Arrest, Article 58' 13 July 2006, para. 77. For an interesting analysis see M. de Guzman, 'Gravity and the Legitimacy of the International Criminal Court', 32 *Fordham International Law Journal*, pp. 1424–9 (2009).

58 Nuremberg Tribunal Charter, Art. 6; Tokyo Charter Art. 5; ICTY Statute, Art. 6; ICTR Statute, Art. 5; SCSL Statute, Art. 1(1), 6; Lebanon Tribunal Statute, Art. 1; ECCC Statute, Art. 2(1); East Timor Agreement, Section 14; Rome Statute, Art. 25. The ICC's jurisdiction is limited to persons 18 years or older. Rome Statute, Art. 26. The other Tribunals are silent on the issue of minimum age, presumably because it was not thought to be an issue that would arise in practice. The Special Court of Sierra Leone does provide that it shall not have jurisdiction over any person who was under 15 at the time of the offense. SCSL Statute, Art. 7.

59 Nuremberg Judgment, p. 221.

60 The International Law Commission, in early discussions on the question of an international criminal court, discussed the idea of State culpability, which was rejected as 'science fiction'. L. Sadat Wexler, 'The Proposed Permanent International Criminal Court: An Appraisal', 29 *Cornell International Law Journal* , at pp. 665, 678 n. 75 (1996).

61 For a discussion of the theoretical possibility that the SCSL could have exercised jurisdiction over juridical persons such as corporations, see W. Schabas, *The UN International Criminal Tribunals: The Former Yugoslavia, Rwanda and Sierra Leone*, Cambridge: Cambridge University Press, 2006, p. 139.

62 Nuremberg Charter, Art. 6.

63 Tokyo Charter, Art. 1; See also J. Gordon, 'The Concept of Human Rights: The History and Meaning of its Politicization', *Brooklyn Journal of International Law* 23, 1998, note 260 ('[A]lthough the tribunal in principle could have exercised jurisdiction over American war crimes, it obviously did not choose to do so.').

64 ICTY Statute, Art. 8.

65 See ICTY Office of the Prosecutor (2000), 'Prosecutor's Report on the NATO Bombing Campaign', ICTY Online, available at http://www.icty.org./sid/7846 (accessed 19 January 2010); P. Benvenuti, 'The ICTY Prosecutor and the Review of the NATO Bombing Campaign against the Federal Republic of Yugoslavia', *European Journal of International Law* 12, 2001, pp. 503–5; 'Final Report to the Prosecutor by the Committee Established to Review the NATO Bombing Campaign against the Federal Republic of Yugoslavia', 2000, ICTY Online, available at http://www.icty.org/x/file/Press/nato061300.pdf.

66 ICTR Statute, Art. 7.

67 V. Morris and M. Scharf, I *The International Tribunal for Rwanda,* Ardsley: Transnational, 1998, p. 71

68 SCSL Statute, Arts 1(1), 1(2).

69 Lebanon Tribunal Statute, Art. 1.

70 East Timor Agreement, Section 2.1.

71 Ibid., Section 2.2(b).

72 ECCC Statute, Art. 1.

73 Rome Statute, Art. 13(b); see also L. Sadat, *The International Criminal Court and the Transformation of International Law,* pp. 116–17.
74 Ibid., Art. 12(2); ibid., p. 117.
75 Rome Statute, Art. 11.
76 The Nuremberg and Tokyo Charters were silent on this issue, but it was understood that they applied to the war. The Nuremberg Tribunal determined the beginning of the war to be 1 September 1939, the date upon which Germany invaded Poland. See B.V. A Röling and C. F. Rüter, 1 *The Tokyo Judgment: The International Military Tribunal for the Far East (I.M.T.F.E)* 29 April 1946–12 November 1948, Amsterdam: APA University Press Amsterdam, 1977, pp. 20, 22, 27–8. The Rwanda, Khmer Rouge, and Lebanon Tribunals and the East Timor Special Panels all have both start and end dates specifying their temporal jurisdiction.
77 Lebanon Tribunal Statute, Art. 1(1) (the Tribunal is established 'to prosecute persons responsible for the attack of 14 February 2005 resulting in the death of former Lebanese Prime Minister Rafiq Hariri and in the death or injury of other persons. If the tribunal finds that other attacks that occurred in Lebanon between 1 October 2004 and 12 December 2005, *or any later date decided by the Parties and with the consent of the Security Council are connected* . . . to the attack of 14 February 2005, it shall also have jurisdiction over persons responsible for such attack.').
78 Morris and Scharf, I *The International Tribunal for Rwanda*, p. 71.
79 Address of Mr. Bakuramutsa to UN Security Council, UN Doc. S/PV.3453 (1994), p. 14.
80 Report of the Secretary-General Pursuant to Paragraph 2 of Security Council Resolution 808 (1993), UN Doc. S/25704 (1993), para. 62; ICTY Statute, Arts 1 and 8.
81 Security Council Resolution 827, UN Doc. S/RES/827 (1993).
82 Report of the Secretary-General Pursuant to Paragraph 6 of Security Council Resolution 1329 (2000), UN Doc S/2001/154 (2001), para. 16.
83 Boskovski & Tarculovski (IT-04-82-PT), Decision on Johan Tarculovski's Motion Challenging Jurisdiction, 1 June 2005, para. 10.
84 W. Schabas, *The UN International Criminal Tribunals*, p. 133. The date for closing down the ICTY was recently extended; first in July 2009, and again in December 2009, the Security Council passed resolutions extending the ICTY judges, terms of office because the ICTY announced it would be unable to complete its cases by 2010 as previously requested by the Security Council. See Security Council Resolution 1877, UN Doc. S/RES/1877 (2009); Security Council Resolution 1900, UN Doc. S/RES/1900 (2009).
85 Nuremberg Judgment, p. 217.
86 Ibid.
87 L. Sadat, *The International Criminal Court and the Transformation of International Law*, p. 158.
88 Elements of Crimes, Article 7(1)(I), Crime against humanity of enforced disappearance of persons, n. 23 (emphasis added).
89 Nahimana, Barayagwiza & Ngeze, Case No. ICTR-99-52-A, Judgment, Appeals Chamber, 28 November 2007.
90 Ibid., para. 308 (quoting para. 1017 of the Trial Chamber Judgment).
91 Ibid., para. 314.
92 Ibid., para. 2 (partly dissenting opinion of Judge Fausto Pocar).

14

Admissibility in international criminal law

*Mohamed M. El Zeidy**

Introduction

The concept of 'admissibility', whether in the context of domestic criminal law or international criminal law, has different connotations and may vary depending on the circumstance of its application. The notion is commonly related or attached to evidentiary rules: i.e. the admissibility of evidence.[1] The purpose of this chapter is to discuss the concept of admissibility from a different perspective; namely, the admissibility of cases before international criminal institutions.

The theory of admissibility in international criminal law generally concerns the allocation of a case between national and international criminal jurisdictions. Thus, the concept tends to solve the possible conflict of jurisdiction that might arise between the two tiers of legal fora. In the sphere of international criminal law, when two judicial systems coexist, whether in a horizontal or vertical relationship,[2] each capable of exercising competence over the same matter(s) or case(s), it became quite common to establish some mechanism to regulate which system proceeds and under what conditions.[3]

When we speak about the admissibility of a case within the context of international criminal law, one would unswervingly think of the classical regime reflected in the Rome Statute establishing the International Criminal Court (Rome Statute).[4] Although the admissibility regime enshrined in the Rome Statute deserves special attention, as it is the prevailing framework for current and future application of the concept of admissibility in international criminal law, for the sake of properly understanding the broader framework in which the concept applies, a review that goes beyond the scope of the Rome Statute and the International Criminal Court (ICC) is warranted.

Admissibility was not an issue before the Nuremberg International Military Tribunal (IMT), the first international criminal forum to try core crimes in modern history. However, with the establishment of the *ad hoc* tribunals in the early 1990s, the international community rejected the idea that these judicial bodies would exercise exclusive jurisdiction over the core crimes referred to in their statutes, and instead retained the competence of national courts. It was thus to be expected that the statutory provisions governing these institutions would set up a procedure to resolve any conflict of jurisdiction between the domestic and international legal orders. The Statutes of the International Criminal Tribunal for the former Yugoslavia (ICTY)[5] and the

International Criminal Tribunal for Rwanda (ICTR),[6] as well as their respective Rules of Procedure and Evidence (ICTY/ICTR RPE),[7] embody identical provisions that tackle this matter. Later, the Statute of the Special Court for Sierra Leone (SCSL) followed the same approach.[8] The respective statutes of these tribunals do not address the question of conflict of jurisdiction by using the term 'admissibility', as is the case with the Rome Statute. Rather, they serve this goal without explicitly referring to the term.

With the advent of a plan for the completion strategy of the ICTY and ICTR, most recently pursuant to Security Council Resolutions 1503 and 1534, the Tribunals and in particular the ICTY, started to develop new methods to reallocate cases by amending the RPE. The revisions actually created a filtering system more akin to an admissibility mechanism, which ensures that not every case that comes before, or is already before, each tribunal should be dealt with. This idea might have been inspired by the existing system of admissibility embodied in the Rome Statute.

This chapter will highlight the different forms of admissibility in international criminal law. It will address the subject matter by way of reviewing the statutory provisions and the practice of international criminal bodies such as (1) the IMT; (2) the ICTY, ICTR and SCSL; and finally, (3) the ICC.

The Nuremberg International Military Tribunal

Before the Allies reached an agreement to establish the IMT to judge Nazi leaders for the crimes committed during the course of the Second World War, there were several attempts undertaken throughout the period of 1941–43 by official, unofficial and even semi-official bodies to create an international judicial forum or an inter-Allied court to serve this purpose. One of the compelling questions discussed at the time of the establishment of an international criminal court or an inter-Allied court was the relationship such a court would have with domestic courts and the role which each judicial organ should play. Different proposals regarding regulation of the proposed court's jurisdiction in relation to national courts were tabled during discussions before a number of bodies, including the London International Assembly,[9] the International Commission for Penal Reconstruction and Development[10] and the United Nations War Crimes Commission.[11] There was a growing tendency to organize the relationship between the proposed court and domestic jurisdictions by creating a procedure that allowed the proposed international machinery to exercise its competence only under exceptional circumstances. Thus, the idea was to give preference to the role of domestic courts and solve any possible conflict of jurisdiction at both levels through a sort of admissibility procedure aimed at filtering the cases to be dealt with before the international forum.

The situation in relation to the IMT was quite different. The legal instruments creating and organizing the functioning of the IMT envisaged a different regime for the allocation of cases between domestic courts, including military courts, and the Tribunal. There was no need to set out conditions or criteria to regulate which forum was to proceed with the case under consideration, given that the issue was initially resolved by the Allies' statement in the Moscow Declaration of 30 October 1943,[12] later referred to in the London Agreement of 8 August 1945 establishing the IMT.[13] In the declaration concerning atrocities made at the Moscow Conference, known as the Moscow Declaration, the three main Allied powers (Britain, the United States and the Soviet Union) declared that German war criminals should be judged and punished in the countries in which their crimes were committed:

> At the time of granting of any armistice to any government which may be set up in Germany, those German officers and men and members of the Nazi party who have been

> responsible for or have taken a consenting part in the (...) atrocities, massacres and executions will be sent back to the countries in which their abominable deeds were done in order that they may be judged and punished according to the laws of these liberated countries and of free governments which will be erected therein. Lists will be compiled in all possible detail from all these countries having regard especially to invaded parts of the Soviet Union, to Poland and Czechoslovakia, to Yugoslavia and Greece including Crete and other islands, to Norway, Denmark, Netherlands, Belgium, Luxembourg, France and Italy. Thus, Germans who take part in wholesale shooting of Polish officers or in the execution of French, Dutch, Belgian or Norwegian hostages of Cretan peasants, or who have shared in slaughters inflicted on the people of Poland or in territories of the Soviet Union which are now being swept clear of the enemy, will know they will be brought back to the scene of their crimes and judged on the spot by the peoples whom they have outraged.[14]

However, this statement was rather categorically limited to the case of relatively minor offenders, since 'German criminals whose offenses have no particular geographical localization [and who were labelled as major war criminals] would be punished by joint decision of the government of the Allies'.[15] This joint decision resulted in the creation of the IMT, which judged 22 Nazis, of whom 19 were found guilty and three were acquitted.[16] Thus, the IMT was established to judge only the 'major war criminals', while the remaining offenders referred to in the Moscow Declaration and the London Agreement were to be dealt with before national criminal jurisdictions. The governments of the occupying powers themselves established national courts with competence to adjudicate war crimes at the places where they were committed, each within its own zone, with its own set of courts, and applying its own scheme of law.[17] To establish a minimum common basis for the trials to be conducted in the four zones of occupation, the Allied Control Council, acting as a legislative body for all of Germany, enacted Law No. 10 entitled 'Punishment of Persons Guilty of War Crimes, Crimes against Peace and Crimes against Humanity' on 20 December 1945. It was the responsibility of each zone commander to implement Law No. 10 in his zone.[18] However, the execution of Law No. 10 was ignored by the British and the Soviet Union, who followed a different path with respect to the trials of war criminals not dealt with before the IMT.[19]

Accordingly, the Allies' decision to divide responsibilities between the two tiers of jurisdiction in this categorical manner, based on the accused's level of responsibility solved from the outset any possible conflict of jurisdiction that might have arisen and thus actually served as an admissibility procedure. This filtering process was carried out in accordance with Article 14 of the IMT Charter, which provided that the Committee of Chief Prosecutors of the signatory Powers was mandated to, *inter alia*, 'settle the final designation of major war criminals' to be judged before the IMT.[20] Indeed, in Berlin, on 18 October 1945, the said Committee, acting pursuant to this provision, lodged its indictment against those who were deemed the major war criminals.[21]

The *ad hoc* tribunals (ICTY, ICTR and SCSL)

The ICTY and ICTR were established *ad hoc* by decisions of the United Nations Security Council to contribute to the restoration and maintenance of peace in the former Yugoslavia and Rwanda, respectively.[22] A third *ad hoc* tribunal, the SCSL, is an internationalized tribunal which was created in response to a call by Sierra Leone's President Kabbah[23] to address the 'very serious crimes' committed in Sierra Leone and also to contribute 'to the restoration of and maintenance of peace in that country'.[24] However, unlike the ICTY and ICTR, the SCSL was not directly set up by virtue of a Security Council resolution, but rather by way of an agreement between the

United Nations and the Government of Sierra Leone. It is therefore considered 'a treaty-based sui generis court of mixed jurisdiction and composition'.[25]

Article 9 of the ICTY Statute[26] and Article 8 of the ICTR[27] and SCSL Statutes[28] define the relationship between these Tribunals and national courts. The three Tribunals function on the basis of concurrent jurisdiction with national courts. However, such concurrence between the Tribunals and national courts is coupled with the principle of primacy, which provides the tribunals with priority over national courts in exercising jurisdiction.[29] Unlike the ICTY and ICTR, which enjoy primacy over national courts even in third states, the primacy granted to the SCSL is confined to Sierra Leonean courts.[30] Practically speaking, primacy means that, at any stage of the procedure, the international tribunals may formally request national courts to defer to their competence pursuant to the terms of their statutory provisions. Nonetheless, invoking the principle of primacy is subject to the fulfilment of one or more of the requirements defined under Rules 8 and 9 of the ICTY, ICTR and SCSL RPE.

According to Rule 9 of the ICTY RPE, the Tribunal may request deferment of a case to its jurisdiction on the basis of the principle of primacy in circumstances where (1) the act subject to domestic proceedings 'is characterized as an ordinary crime'; (2) it was detected that the domestic proceedings lacked 'impartiality or independence' or were 'designed to shield the accused from international criminal responsibility' or the case was not diligently prosecuted; or (3) the investigations or criminal proceedings undertaken by the national authorities of the state are 'closely related and otherwise involve factual or legal questions which may have implications for the Prosecutor's investigations or prosecutions'. This is not exactly the case with respect to the conditions outlined in Rule 9 of the ICTR and SCSL RPE, which lack any direct reference to sham proceedings and instead make these Tribunals' intervention subject to, *inter alia*, an assessment of the gravity of the case in terms of the seriousness of the crime or the status of the accused when the crime was committed.[31] However, despite such divergence, Rule 9 as formulated in the three Tribunals' RPE actually operates as an admissibility provision, although the drafters have not placed it in the RPE under such a heading. The rule settles possible positive conflicts of jurisdiction between the two tiers of jurisdiction and sets out the conditions under which the Tribunals could intervene and exercise primary jurisdiction over certain cases. This ensures that a certain category of cases is litigated or tried before the tribunals, while those of relatively less significance are left to domestic jurisdictions.

The experience of the ICTY and ICTR shows that Rule 9 of the Tribunals' RPE might have functioned as an admissibility provision to relocate cases that were already before national jurisdictions after the Prosecutor was satisfied that at least one of the conditions set out in that rule was met. In *Tadić*,[32] *Mrkšić*[33] and *Re: Republic of Macedonia*[34] before the ICTY and in *Musema*,[35] *Bagosora*[36] and *Radio Television Libre des Mille Collines SARL*[37] before the ICTR, the respective Prosecutors stepped in and requested deferral on the basis of Rule 9(iii) of the ICTY and ICTR RPE, as they believed, as did the judges, that these cases were better tried before the international tribunals. On other occasions, save for policy considerations, the Prosecutor of the ICTY arguably, after considering the requirements of Rule 9, decided to defer to the jurisdiction of national courts, as none of the conditions under this rule was fulfilled to justify the Tribunal's intervention. This seemed to be the situation with respect to the *Djajić* and *Jorgić* cases investigated by the German authorities.[38] Explaining the reasons to arrive at this decision, the Prosecutor said

> The Djajic and Jorgic cases were initiated and investigated by the German authorities, who consulted with the Office of the Prosecutor of the International Tribunal. The Prosecutor assessed that it was not appropriate to seek a deferral of these cases, and the decision was made that they continue to be prosecuted by the German authorities. There is on-going

co-operation between the Prosecutor and the German authorities on these and other cases.[39]

With the introduction of a plan for completing the mandates of the *ad hoc* tribunals, the judges of the three Tribunals amended their respective RPE in order to ensure compliance with the deadlines for the Tribunals' closure. Due to some of these changes, other forms of admissibility mechanisms were introduced as an integral part of the amended rules. According to the former President Claude Jorda of the ICTY, the completion strategy embodied two main components: namely, to prosecute before the Tribunal 'those presumed responsible for crimes which most seriously violate international public order and to give cases of lesser significance to the national courts'.[40] A year later, the Security Council stressed this goal in similar words when it adopted Resolution 1503 (2003).[41] Paragraph 7 of the Resolution's preamble called on the ICTY to concentrate 'on the prosecution and trial of the most senior leaders suspected of being most responsible for crimes within the ICTY's jurisdiction and transferring cases involving those who may not bear this level of responsibility to competent national jurisdictions'.[42] The Security Council also urged the ICTR to follow the same path by 'formaliz[ing] a detailed strategy, modelled on the ICTY Completion Strategy'.[43] A few months later, the Security Council adopted Resolution 1534 (2004),[44] which in more concrete language directed both Tribunals to the method perceived as appropriate for limiting the number of cases to be tried before the two bodies. Paragraph 5 of the Resolution called upon the two Tribunals, in 'reviewing and confirming any new indictments, to ensure that any such indictments concentrate on the most senior leaders suspected of being most responsible for crimes within the jurisdiction of the relevant Tribunal'.[45]

The ICTY plenary of judges responded to the Security Council's call by amending, *inter alia*, Rule 28 of the RPE.[46] According to the new amendment, the Bureau, which consisted of the ICTY's President, Vice-President and the Presiding Judges of the Trial Chambers, shall review any indictments presented by the Office of the Prosecutor in order to ensure they focus on those high-ranking suspects who had allegedly committed crimes within the jurisdiction of the tribunal.[47] If the Bureau finds that the seniority test is satisfied, the indictment moves to the next step, which is the regular review process referred to in Rule 47 of the RPE. However, if it finds that the seniority requirement is not met, the Bureau will block the indictment from reaching the normal review process, and accordingly, the case under consideration cannot proceed before the Tribunal unless the Prosecutor succeeds in a subsequent attempt to show the judges that this condition has been fulfilled.

Introducing a judicial role to assess an element of gravity of the case at the confirmation of indictment stage resembles an admissibility procedure, which aims at filtering the type of cases that do not warrant the Tribunal's intervention. The completion strategy, which also resulted in the amendment of Rule 28 of the ICTY RPE, led to a change in the prosecutorial policy, which has not 'historically limited itself to trials of senior leaders'.[48]

Neither the ICTR nor the SCSL followed the ICTY's route. As for the ICTR, the judges considered that the amendment of Rule 28 'limit[ed] the independence of the prosecutor' and thus was in violation of the Tribunal's Statute.[49] Meanwhile, the SCSL did not need to follow the ICTY example.[50] Security Council Resolution 1315 (2000) initially 'indicated' that the Court should only 'prosecute persons who bear the greatest responsibility'.[51] This requirement also appeared in the text of the agreement between the United Nations and the government of Sierra Leone, as well as in the Court's Statute.[52] As one commentator stated

> [A]lthough the Secretary-General's report did not refer to the experience of the [... ICTY and ICTR] as a justification for some of its proposals, the configuration of the [... SCSL] was

> clearly influenced by lessons the United Nations had learned from its experience with international justice in the former Yugoslavia and Rwanda. From the earliest days of the ICTY, an area of great controversy had been whether prosecution should be directed towards certain categories of offenders. Especially in its early years, the ICTY had proceeded against a number of very minor and insignificant participants in the conflict, and even the ICTR had pursued some relatively low-level culprits.[53]

Actually, the requirement of 'persons who bear the greatest responsibility' as reflected in Article 1 of the Statute of the SCSL suggests that this is more akin to a jurisdictional threshold, rather than an admissibility test. This conclusion holds notwithstanding the Secretary-General's observation that this must be seen not as 'a test criterion or a distinct jurisdictional requirement, but as a guidance to the Prosecutor in the adoption of a prosecution strategy and in making decisions to prosecute in individual cases'.[54]

The completion strategy has also led to further amendments of the Tribunals' RPE, which arguably created additional tiers of admissibility at a later stage of the proceedings: namely, after an indictment has been confirmed. Rule 11 *bis* as amended in the Tribunals' RPE permits the relocation or referral of a case that was already being heard before any of the three Tribunals to the national authorities of a state 'having jurisdiction and being willing and adequately prepared to accept such a case'.[55] The requirements of 'willingness' and 'adequate preparation' are common conditions that must be satisfied before a positive decision on referral is taken by any of the three Tribunals. Also, as is ensuring that the accused will receive a fair trial at the domestic level, is another common prerequisite.[56] The provision as drafted under the ICTY RPE imposes an additional element—namely, that the Tribunal 'consider the gravity of the crimes charged' as well as the 'level of responsibility of the accused'[57]—thus ensuring compliance with paragraphs 4 and 5 of Security Council Resolution 1534 (2004).[58] These elements collectively shape another tier of admissibility that comes into play after the confirmation of an indictment. This process serves as an additional filter to the sort of cases that should not continue to be heard before the Tribunals.

An order from the Referral Bench to refer a case to a designated state does not end the process. The Prosecutor is empowered to send observers to follow the proceedings before the respective state's courts in order to ensure that they are properly conducted. This task is mainly carried out by the Organization for Security and Cooperation in Europe (OSCE).[59] If, after having heard the state concerned, the Tribunal determines failure on the part of the state to properly proceed with the transferred case, it may step in to 'revoke' the referral order in accordance with Rule 11 *bis* (F) of the ICTY and ICTR RPE.[60] Although the latter provision does not mention the phrase 'failure to proceed', it is implicit from reading sub-rules 11 *bis* (A) (iii) and 11 *bis* (F) together that the Referral Bench would not step in pursuant to sub-rule (F) unless there is a clear deficiency in the proceedings conducted before domestic courts.

In *Stankovic* the ICTY Referral Bench said that 'Rules 11 *bis* (D) (iv) and 11 *bis* (F) serve as remedies against a failure of the relevant State to diligently prosecute a referred case or conduct a fair trial of the accused in a referred case'. The ICTY Referral Bench followed the same approach in *Trbić*,[61] *Kovačević*,[62] *Mejakic et al.*,[63] *Jankovic*[64] and *Norac et al.*[65] On appeal of the *Jankovic* decision, the Appeals Chamber stated, 'the Referral Bench did not err in its finding that "Rules *11bis* (D) (iv) and *11bis* (F) serve as precautions against a failure to diligently prosecute a referred case or conduct a fair trial"'. This arguably reveals that a lack of 'diligent prosecution'[66] and 'a fair trial' are the main conditions that trigger the Tribunal's powers to 'revoke the order and make a formal request of deferral'.[67] This process also reflects an additional mechanism of admissibility, which sets out the conditions on the basis of which the Tribunal may re-exercise its jurisdiction over a transferred case, thus reducing a potential impunity gap.

Unlike the ICTY and ICTR, Rule 11 *bis* of the SCSL RPE does not provide the Referral Bench with the power to revoke an order concerning a referred case. This is not surprising, because the amendment to Rule 11 *bis* in May 2008 seemed to have been introduced to overcome a specific situation facing the Tribunal. The provision was amended in anticipation of the end of the Special Court's activities by early 2011[68] and to facilitate the process of referring the case of Johnny Paul Koroma, the only indicted person[69] who remains at large,[70] to a 'competent' domestic jurisdiction 'if he is not confirmed deceased by the end of the duration of the Court'.[71] Accordingly, including a provision to revoke the referral order is certainly unnecessary in this context.

The practice of the International Criminal Court

Among the different forms of admissibility, including those presented earlier, the Rome Statute embodies the most complex and elaborate system of admissibility in international criminal law. This is quite understandable since the ICC, as a permanent international institution, was envisaged by its drafters to be a mere residual jurisdiction that functions only in very limited circumstances: namely, when there is no prospect of relying on domestic efforts. Thus, the drafters created a sophisticated admissibility regime that balances the supranational power entrusted in the Court with that of national jurisdictions, thereby ensuring states that 'they would remain master over their own judicial proceedings' as long as they do not allow perpetrators of serious crimes to go unpunished.[72]

As is the situation with the *ad hoc* Tribunals, the ICC regime is based on the idea of concurrent jurisdiction with national courts, and thus any potential conflict of jurisdiction is resolved by the Court declaring a case 'inadmissible' when certain conditions are met. The conditions or criteria on the basis of which a 'case' is declared 'inadmissible' are elaborated in Article 17 of the Rome Statute.[73] The interpretation of the different paragraphs under Article 17 and of the related provisions governing admissibility has been addressed in detail in many academic writings,[74] and thus it is not to be reiterated in this chapter, except to the extent necessary to disclose the present stage in the Court's case law. However, to date, the Court's practice concerning admissibility reveals a number of significant observations that warrant attention.

Stages of admissibility determinations

At the outset, it is significant to shed light on the main stages in which the admissibility assessment takes place, before delving into the current practice of the ICC. Admissibility determinations may arise throughout one or more of the three main stages enunciated in the following articles: (1) Article 53; (2) Article 18; and (3) Article 19 of the Statute.

With respect to the Article 53 stage, the determination of admissibility is confined to the Prosecutor. This stage encompasses two phases: the first, before the initiation of an investigation under Article 53(1)(b); and the second, after investigations are concluded under Article 53(2)(b). In the context of Article 53(1), the examination of admissibility is mandatory and must be fulfilled before the Prosecutor can 'initiate' an investigation into a situation. The test at this stage focuses on whether one or more potential cases within the context of a given situation 'would be admissible' before the Court.[75] During the Article 53(2) phase, the assessment of admissibility is essential in determining whether there is a sufficient basis for prosecution.

The situation is quite different during the Articles 18 and 19 stages where admissibility determinations lie mainly within the competence of the Chambers, save for Article 18(3) and (5) which provides for a review by the Prosecutor. Once the Prosecutor has made a determination under Article 53(1) to initiate an investigation into a situation, he must 'notify all States Parties', as well as those states that 'would normally exercise jurisdiction over the crimes concerned', of his conclusion. An interested state is given one month from the date of the Prosecutor's notification to request ICC deferment to its domestic investigations. If a state so requests, the Prosecutor should defer unless the Pre-Trial Chamber, upon application of the Prosecutor, decides to authorize an ICC investigation. In reaching a decision on whether to authorize the investigation, the Pre-Trial Chamber shall consider, *inter alia*, the conditions prescribed by Article 17.[76]

An admissibility determination could also arise during the Article 19 stage, which is only reached when there is a 'concrete case' against an identified suspect.[77] This may result from a challenge lodged by either a state referred to in Article 19(2)(b) or (c) or by an 'accused or a person for whom a warrant of arrest or a summons to appear has been issued' pursuant to Article 19(2)(a).[78] Further, Chambers may decide to make a *proprio motu* determination on the admissibility of a given case,[79] or the Prosecutor may request the relevant Chamber to provide him with a ruling concerning any question on the issue.[80]

State of practice before the court

Certainly, in each of the five situations which are currently before the Court—Uganda, Democratic Republic of the Congo (DRC), Central African Republic (CAR), Darfur and Kenya—the Prosecutor has made an initial admissibility determination pursuant to Article 53(1)(b). This is clear because, as mentioned above, the admissibility determination on the part of the Prosecutor at this stage is not a choice.[81] The admissibility test was rather facilitated with respect to the first three situations because they were received by way of 'self-referrals' from states which, despite having direct territorial links to the crimes,[82] nevertheless decided to refrain from conducting domestic proceedings and instead rely on the ICC. This evidently led to a simple, affirmative finding of admissibility due to each state's inactivity in conducting the relevant domestic proceedings.

So far, ICC case law lacks any reference to an admissibility assessment during the Article 18 proceedings. In particular, Rule 55(2), which mandates a Pre-Trial Chamber to consider the requirements of Article 17, remains a dead letter. The reason also relates in part to the so-called self-referrals, which guaranteed, at least in theory, that no self-referring state would request the Prosecutor to defer his investigations. Insofar as the Darfur situation is concerned, Article 18 is, in any event, not applicable, given that the referral was received from the Security Council.[83] The Prosecutor's approach pointed towards a different direction in the Kenya situation. He invoked his *proprio motu* powers under Article 15 and requested Pre-Trial Chamber II to authorize the commencement of an investigation in this situation.[84] By so doing, the Prosecutor opened the door for potential admissibility litigation under Article 18, which comes into play right after the authorization request is granted. In its decision granting the Prosecutor's request, Pre-Trial Chamber II revealed that there is interplay between Articles 15 and 18 to the effect that the scope of admissibility examination under the former 'may well serve an effective application' of the latter.[85] Thus, the Chamber foresaw the possibility of ruling on issues of admissibility at the Article 18 stage.

As far as Article 19 is concerned, the admissibility examination by the Chambers to date has been rather limited and perhaps marginal, save for a handful of rulings, including those issued by the Appeals Chamber, which designed some parameters for this process and the interpretation of Article 17, as discussed below. The bulk of the existing admissibility rulings were carried out by the Pre-Trial Chambers during the issuance of warrants of arrest under Article 58 of the Statute,[86] except for two decisions that briefly touched on the issue in decisions on confirmation of charges.[87] The Chambers acted within the framework of Article 19(1) of the Statute, which provided them with the discretion to examine, *proprio motu*, the admissibility of the cases under consideration in accordance with Article 17.

The first ruling on admissibility emerged in the context of issuing warrants of arrest in the cases against five suspects from the Lord Resistance Army, a rebel group fighting the Ugandan government. In a passing reference, Pre-Trial Chamber II stated that the cases against the suspects 'appear[ed] to be admissible'.[88] This was without prejudice to subsequent determinations on admissibility.[89] Indeed, the same Chamber, albeit with a different composition, revisited its determination on the admissibility of this case four years later in a more elaborate ruling on the subject. However, this time the ruling was not for the sole purpose of reiterating that the case was admissible, but rather was intended to send a clear message to states, including Uganda, that it is the Court that has the upper hand in making such a determination once its jurisdiction has been triggered. The decision came in response to contradictory statements made by the government of Uganda, to the effect that, if any of the suspects were to be arrested, it would be for the state to decide to try any of them before a special division of the High Court of Uganda,[90] which appeared to disregard the Rome Statute's admissibility procedure regulating the allocation of cases. In this context, the Chamber said that the statements made by the government 'seem[ed]' to ignore the reality of the situation: namely, that 'once the jurisdiction of the Court is triggered, it is for the latter and not for any national judicial authorities to interpret and apply the provisions governing the complementarity regime and to make a binding determination on the admissibility of a given case'.[91]

Apart from the foregoing, the most developed decision on admissibility under Article 19(1) issued by a Pre-Trial Chamber to date was prepared in the context of the issuing of warrants of arrest for Thomas Lubanga Dyilo and Bosco Ntaganda in the situation of the DRC. This decision contains the only detailed treatment of the criterion of gravity yet to be issued by the Court. Save for certain portions that warrant criticism,[92] the decision established the parameters on the basis of which the gravity assessment could be undertaken. The Pre-Trial Chamber referred to elements such as the

> position of the persons (most senior leaders), the roles such persons play[ed], when the State entities, organisations or armed groups to which they belong commit systematic or large-scale crimes within the jurisdiction of the Court, and the role played by such State entities, armed groups or organisations in the overall commission of crimes within the jurisdiction of the Court in the relevant situation (those suspected of being most responsible).[93]

The decision was reversed by the Appeals Chamber in its 13 July 2006 judgment based on its finding that the case against Bosco Ntaganda was inadmissible due to insufficient gravity under Article 17(1)(d).[94] The crux of the problem identified by the Appeals Chamber was, *inter alia*, that the Pre-Trial Chamber considered that the Court could not but focus on the most senior leaders, and thus refused to issue a warrant of arrest against Bosco Ntaganda, who was only third in the chain of command of the military wing of the broader *Union des Patriotes Congolais/Forces Patriotiques pour la Libération du Congo* movement (UPC/FPLC).[95] Although the Appeals Chamber rejected, *inter alia*, the Pre-Trial Chamber's finding on this point, its judgment lacked clear guidance on how to assess gravity,[96] leaving the elaboration of a definition open for another Chamber, or perhaps the Prosecutor, as the situation currently stands.[97] However, the decision of Pre-Trial Chamber I was the first to lay down some rules concerning the interpretation of Article 17 and continues to be followed by other Chambers. It was most recently even upheld by the Appeals Chamber in its judgment issued on 25 September 2009, addressing an admissibility challenge lodged by Germain Katanga before Trial Chamber II pursuant to Article 19(2)(a) (25 September 2009 Judgment).

Until the Appeals Chamber rendered its 25 September 2009 Judgment, the interpretation of Article 17 remained controversial, although the decision of Pre-Trial Chamber I in Lubanga and Ntaganda had gone to a certain extent,[98] in the correct direction. There was a clear misconception about how Article 17 was intended to operate. Some scholars expressed the view that the ICC must not exercise its jurisdiction unless it is first proven that the relevant state is 'unwilling' or 'unable' genuinely to conduct national proceedings.[99] This construction, had it prevailed, would have created a lacuna in the text of Article 17. The Appeals Chamber expressed concerns about this interpretation in the 25 September 2009 Judgment when it stated

> Such an interpretation is not only irreconcilable with the wording of the provision, but is also in conflict with a purposive interpretation of the Statute. The aim of the Rome Statute is 'to put an end to impunity' and to ensure that 'the most serious crimes of concern to the international community as a whole must not go unpunished'. This object and purpose of the Statute would come to naught were the said interpretation of article 17 (1) of the Statute as proposed by the Appellant to prevail. It would result in a situation where, despite the inaction of a State, a case would be inadmissible before the Court, unless that State is unwilling or unable to open investigations. The Court would be unable to exercise its jurisdiction over a case as long as the State is theoretically willing and able to investigate and to prosecute the case, even though that State has no intention of doing so. Thus, a potentially large number of cases would not be prosecuted by domestic jurisdictions or by the International Criminal Court.[100]

Actually, a proper interpretation of Article 17 calls for a close look at its first paragraph, which is also central to the application of the remaining parts of the provision. Article 17(1) requires the Court to initially check one or more of four scenarios before making its determination on the admissibility of a given case:

- whether the case is being investigated or prosecuted by a state having jurisdiction [Article 17(1)(a)]
- whether a state has investigated and concluded that there is no basis on which to prosecute [Article 17(1)(b)]
- whether the person has already been tried for this conduct [Article 17(1)(c)]
- whether the case is of insufficient gravity to proceed before the Court [Article 17(1)(d)].

The first three scenarios mainly organize the relationship between national jurisdictions and the ICC by way of testing the domestic efforts with respect to a given case. Thus, they are commonly represented by the term 'complementarity', and they are also treated as the first limb of the admissibility provision. The fourth scenario, which is gravity, represents the second limb of the admissibility provision. The ICC has endorsed this distinction in its case law.[101]

If, for instance, under the first scenario the case is not being investigated or prosecuted by a state having jurisdiction, the plain language of Article 17(1) will render the case admissible, and, accordingly, there is no need to examine a state's 'unwillingness' or 'inability' under Article 17(2) and (3), as has been mistakenly suggested by some and rejected by the Appeals Chamber in the 25 September 2009 Judgment. The 'unwillingness' or 'inability' tests will only come into play if there is an affirmative finding on the part of the Court that national proceedings are underway (i.e. in a scenario of action as opposed to inaction on the part of the state), such that the Court should test their quality.

A finding by the Court that a state is pursuing a given matter will render a case inadmissible only if the investigation, prosecution or trial are genuine and target the same case that is the subject of the Court's consideration. It follows that not every investigation, prosecution or trial conducted at the national level will satisfy the first three scenarios under Article 17 for the purpose of securing a decision of inadmissibility in favour of the state concerned. As Pre-Trial Chamber I stated in the *Lubanga, Harun and Kushayb* and *Katanga* cases, 'it is *a conditio sine qua non* for a case arising from the investigation of a situation to be inadmissible that national proceedings encompass both the person and the conduct which is the subject of the case before the Court'.[102]

Also, a state may have investigated, prosecuted or tried the case involving the person as well as the conduct, but the ICC may still determine that the case is admissible, if it has been demonstrated that the state is 'unwilling' or 'unable' to conduct 'genuine' national proceedings. In *Lubanga*, Pre-Trial Chamber I noted that

> [W]hen a State with jurisdiction over a case is investigating, prosecuting or trying it, or has done so, it is not sufficient to declare such a case inadmissible. The Chamber observes on the contrary that a declaration of inadmissibility is subject to a finding that the relevant State is not unwilling or unable to genuinely conduct its national proceedings in relation to that case within the meaning of article 17(1)(a) to (c), (2) and (3) of the Statute.[103]

The Chamber refrained from elaborating on the notions of 'unwillingness' and 'inability' in this decision, nor has it developed the underlying meaning of the term 'genuinely'. This is justified, given that the Court was mainly acting within the framework of the first part of Article 17(1): namely, to determine whether there were ongoing proceedings with respect to the same case under consideration. Since then, these concepts have not been the subject of judicial interpretation, save for a decision issued recently by Trial Chamber II in the Katanga case, arising out of the DRC situation. In this decision, the Trial Chamber attempted to link the DRC's national inactivity with the criterion of unwillingness.[104] However, the interpretation provided by the Trial Chamber failed to stand on appeal. Instead, the Appeals Chamber considered that the question remains one of inactivity on the part of the state, rather than unwillingness. In this respect, the Appeals Chamber stated:

> [A]t the time of the proceedings before the Trial Chamber, there were [not] in the DRC any investigations or prosecutions of any crime allegedly committed by the Appellant, at Bogora or anywhere else in the DRC [...] the DRC confirmed that there were no investigations to establish the alleged criminal responsibility of the Appellant. For that reason alone, and irrespective of the willingness of the DRC to investigate or to prosecute the Appellant, the Appeals Chamber considers that article 17(1)(a) does not present a bar to his prosecution before the International Criminal Court.[105]

Although the judgment of the Appeals Chamber solved one of the controversial questions on the interpretation of Article 17, it failed to address another question of no lesser significance concerning the timing of a challenge to the admissibility of a case. According to Article 19(4), a challenge to the admissibility of a case 'shall take place prior to or at the commencement of the trial', and in exceptional circumstances it may be brought with leave of the Court 'at a time later than the commencement of the trial'. The issue of the proper timing to lodge a challenge was first discussed before the Trial Chamber. The Chamber was to determine the underlying meaning of 'commencement of the trial' in order to determine whether the accused filed his motion in time. The Chamber gave two interpretations on the basis of different provisions of the Statute. The first interpretation considers that the trial commences 'as soon as the Trial Chamber is constituted pursuant to article 61(11) of the Statute', while the second holds that a trial begins 'when the participants make their opening statements before the Chamber prior to the first witnesses testifying' as per Article 64.[106] The Trial Chamber opted for the former interpretation for practical considerations: namely, to solve the issue of admissibility at the earliest opportunity.[107] The Chamber found that the defence filed the motion out of time, and only challenges based on *ne bis in idem* under Article 17(1)(c) were permitted at this stage. However, the Chamber considered it 'appropriate' for several reasons outlined in the decision to 'rule on the merits of the Motion'.[108] The issue came before the Appeals Chamber, which refused to pronounce on the matter by stating,

> In the present case, the alleged error in relation to the time limit for an admissibility challenge cannot be said to have materially affected the decision on admissibility, because the Trial Chamber did not dismiss the admissibility challenge on the basis that it had not been made in time. Instead, the Trial Chamber considered the merits of the challenge and found the case to be admissible. Thus, even if the Appeals Chamber were to conclude that the Trial Chamber made an error in respect of its interpretation of the term 'commencement of the trial' in article 19(4) of the Statute, this error would not, in itself, be a reason to reverse the Trial Chamber's decision on the admissibility of the case. It is for these reasons that the Prosecutor correctly states that the findings of the Trial Chamber were mere *obiter dicta*. The Appeals Chamber considers it inappropriate to pronounce itself on *obiter dicta*. To do so should be tantamount to rendering advisory opinions on issues that are not properly before it. [...]. The Appeals Chamber nevertheless wishes to stress that the fact that the Appeals Chamber is refraining from pronouncing itself on the merits of the issue raised under the first ground of appeal does not necessarily mean that it agrees with the Trial Chamber's interpretation of the term 'commencement of the trial' in article 19(4) of the Statute.[109]

By so doing, the Appeals Chamber left unresolved one of the most pertinent issues related to admissibility, which has a direct impact on the work of the other Chambers. Until there is another opportunity for the Appeals Chamber to rule on this question, there is a possibility of producing conflicting jurisprudence, which might create double standards for suspects who wish to challenge the admissibility of their cases.

Conclusion

The existence of an idea to solve potential vertical conflict of jurisdictions through a system of admissibility is not a novelty *per se*. What turned out to be new and significant is the development of the mechanisms implementing such an idea. The statutory provisions of the *ad hoc* Tribunals were initially designed with built-in admissibility provisions, which aimed at resolving the problems of concurrent jurisdiction and the distribution of cases between the international Tribunals and domestic courts. The compelling need to meet their respective completion strategies led these Tribunals to think of different methods to achieve this goal. These methods included developing other forms of admissibility that operate at different stages of the proceedings. This is mostly the case with the ICTY, where it is evident that the amended RPE created multiple admissibility tiers—for example, Rule 28(A)—which exceeded those found in the ICTR and the SCSL. The methods that were developed are very useful to meet the specific purpose they are designed to serve. However, as the mandates of these Tribunals are coming to an end, these methods will be of lesser significance, save for historical purposes. This is not the case with the ICC, where the admissibility regime embodied in the Rome Statute is designed to serve current and future application.

Hitherto, the bulk of the ICC's admissibility rulings have been carried out on the initiative of the Court, save for the case of Germain Katanga, which led to issuing the 25 September 2009 Judgment referred to above.[110] Moreover, as for the situation concerning Article 18 proceedings, neither a state party nor a third state has challenged the admissibility of any of the cases before the Court in accordance with Article 19(2)(b) or (c). This is understandable with respect to the first three situations before the Court (Uganda, DRC and CAR), as mentioned earlier, but it remains quite surprising. It was a common understanding when the complementarity or admissibility-related provisions were drafted that states would insist on retaining their sovereign rights and investigating their own nationals, thus marginalizing the Court, or at least reducing the instances in which it should intervene. This turned out not to be the case. The situation of Darfur is easier to justify, given its political sensitivity and the persistent refusal of the Sudanese government and its allied countries to interact with the Court. Thus, the limited context in which admissibility has been addressed led to a lack of sufficient interpretations of the relevant provisions governing its application, with the exception of a few rulings on the interpretation of the first part of Article 17. This lacuna in the current jurisprudence cannot be solely attributed to the Court, but also results from the unexpected attitude of states.

Notes

* The views expressed in this article are those of the author and do not necessarily reflect those of the International Criminal Court.

1 See, for example, *Black's Law Dictionary*, 7th edn, B. A. Garner (ed.), St Paul, Minn.: West Group, 1999, p. 48.

2 In this context, horizontal refers to the conflict of jurisdiction between national judicial systems and vertical means conflict of jurisdiction between one or more domestic judicial systems and an international judicial body.

3 See also, W. A. Schabas, *An Introduction to the International Criminal Court*, 3rd edn, Cambridge: Cambridge University Press, 2007, p. 171. For instance, at the horizontal level, there is a growing tendency to solve possible conflicts of jurisdiction in the context of crimes against international law through the principle of 'subsidiarity'. According to this principle, the territorial state or the state of nationality enjoy 'jurisdictional priority' as far as they prove ability and willingness to prosecute. In other words, any other state that demands to prosecute international crimes on the basis of, for example, universal jurisdiction, can do so only as far as the state directly affected fails to do so. Thus, there is a type of admissibility test, which helps resolve issues of competing jurisdictional claims. See C. Ryngaert, *Jurisdiction in International Law*, Oxford: Oxford University Press, pp. 211–18.

4 Rome Statute of the International Criminal Court, Adopted by the United Nations Diplomatic Conference of Plenipotentiaries on the Establishment of an International Criminal Court, 17 July 1998, UN Doc. A/CONF.183/9, Art. 17 [hereinafter Rome Statute].

5 Statute of the International Criminal Tribunal for the former Yugoslavia, UN Doc. S/RES/827 (1993), Art. 9.

6 Statute of the International Criminal Tribunal for Rwanda, UN Doc. S/RES/955 (1994), Art. 8.

7 See ICTY, Rules of Procedure and Evidence, UN Doc. IT/32/Rev.7 (1996), Rule 9; ICTR, Rules of Procedure and Evidence, UN Doc. ITR/3/REV.1 (1995), Rule 9.

8 See Agreement between the United Nations and the Government of Sierra Leone on the Establishment of a Special Court for Sierra Leone, signed at Freetown on 16 January 2002, annex: Statute of the Special Court for Sierra Leone, UN Doc. S/2002/246, Art. 8; Rules of Procedure and Evidence, Rule 9 [hereinafter SCSL RPE].

9 The London International Assembly was established in 1941 under the auspices of the League of Nations Union, although it was not an official body. Its mandate was mainly to make recommendations in relation to the question of war crimes committed during the course of World War II and to find

solutions to ensure effective punishment for those who bore responsibility for these crimes. See, on the London International Assembly, Historical Survey of the Question of International Criminal Jurisdiction, UN Doc. A/CN.4/7/Rev.1, p. 18 [hereinafter Historical Survey].

10 International Commission for Penal Reconstruction and Development: Proceedings of the Conference held in Cambridge on 14 November 1941, Between Representatives of Nine Allied Countries and of the Department of Criminal Science in the University of Cambridge, p. 11.

11 United Nations War Crimes Commission Progress Report, C.48 (1944).

12 The Tripartite Conference at Moscow, 19–30 October 1943, reprinted in International Conciliation, No. 395, pp. 599–605 (1943) [hereinafter Moscow Declaration].

13 London Agreement of 8 August 1945, reprinted in 1 Trial of Major War Criminals Before the International Military Tribunal 8, pp. 8–9 (1947) [hereinafter London Agreement].

14 Moscow Declaration, Statement on Atrocities.

15 Ibid.

16 International Military Tribunal (Nuremberg), Judgment and Sentences, 1 October 1946, reprinted in *American Journal of International Law*, 1947, vol. 41, 333 [hereinafter The Nuremberg Judgment].

17 A. Cassese, 'From Nuremberg to Rome: International Military Tribunals to the International Criminal Court', in A. Cassese *et al.* (eds) *The Rome Statute of the International Criminal Court*, vol. I, Oxford: Oxford University Press, 2002, p. 7.

18 Allied Control Council Law No. 10, Punishment of Persons Guilty of War Crimes, Crimes against Peace and Crimes against Humanity, 20 December 1945, Official Gazette of the Control Council for Germany, no. 3 (1946).

19 D.A. Mundis, 'Completing the Mandates of the *Ad hoc* International Criminal Tribunals: Lessons from the Nuremberg Process?', *Fordham International Law Journal*, 2005, vol. 28, 598–600.

20 Charter of the International Military Tribunal, 8 August 1945, 82 UNTS 279, Art. 14(b). Available at http://avalon.law.yale.edu/imt/imtconst.asp.

21 The Nuremberg Judgment, p. 172.

22 ICTY Statute, ICTR Statute.

23 'Letter dated 9 August 2000 from the Permanent Representative of Sierra Leone to the United Nations addressed to the President of the Security Council', UN Doc. S/2000/786, annex.

24 SC Res 1315(2000), UN Doc. S/RES/1315 (2000), preamble, para. 1; 'Report of the Secretary-General on the establishment of a Special Court for Sierra Leone', para. 74 [hereinafter SCSL Secretary-General Report].

25 Ibid., para. 9.

26 Art. 9 of the ICTY Statute reads as follows:

   1 The International Tribunal and national courts shall have concurrent jurisdiction to prosecute persons for serious violations of international humanitarian law committed in the territory of the former Yugoslavia since 1 January 1991.
   2 The International Tribunal shall have primacy over national courts. At any stage of the procedure, the International Tribunal may formally request national courts to defer to the competence of the International Tribunal in accordance with the present Statute and the Rules of Procedure and Evidence of the International Tribunals.

27 Art. 8 of the ICTR Statute reads as follows:

   1 The International Tribunal for Rwanda and national courts shall have concurrent jurisdiction to prosecute persons for serious violations of international humanitarian law committed in the territory of Rwanda and Rwandan citizens for such violations committed in the territory of neighbouring States, between 1 January 1994 and 31 December 1994.
   2 The International Tribunal for Rwanda shall have primacy over the national courts of all States. At any stage of the procedure, the International Tribunal for Rwanda may formally request national courts to defer to its competence in accordance with the present Statute and the Rules of Procedure and Evidence of the International Tribunal for Rwanda.

28 Art. 8 of the SCSL Statute reads as follows:

   1 The Special Court and the national courts of Sierra Leone shall have concurrent jurisdiction.
   2 The Special Court shall have primacy over the national courts of Sierra Leone. At any stage of the procedure, the Special Court may formally request a national court to defer to its competence in accordance with the present Statute and the Rules of Procedure and Evidence.

29 See, for example, Tadić (IT-94-1-AR72), Decision on the Defence Motion for Interlocutory Appeal on Jurisdiction, 2 October 1995; Kanyabashi (ICTR-96-15-T), Decision on the Defence Motion on Jurisdiction, 18 June 1997; Kallon *et al.* (Case Nos SCSL-2004-15-AR72(E), SCSL-2004-14-AR72(E), SCSL-2004-16-AR72(E)), Decision on Constitutionality and Lack of Jurisdiction, Appeals Chamber, 13 March 2004.

30 Kallon *et al.* [Case Nos SCSL-2004-15-AR72(E), SCSL-2004-14-AR72(E), SCSL-2004-16-AR72(E)], Appeals Chamber, Decision on Constitutionality and Lack of Jurisdiction, 13 March 2004, para. 69.

31 Nevertheless, Rule 9 as drafted under the ICTR and SCSL RPE could arguably accommodate a scenario of sham proceedings, since the list of conditions outlined under the provision is illustrative.

32 Tadić (IT-94-1-AR72), Decision on the Defence Motion for Interlocutory Appeal on Jurisdiction, 2 October 1995, para. 52.

33 Mrkšić, Šlijvančanin and Radić (IT-95-13-R61), Decision on the Proposal of the Prosecutor for a Request to the Federal Republic of Yugoslavia (Serbia and Montenegro) to Defer the Pending Investigations and Criminal Proceedings to the Tribunal, 10 December 1998.

34 Re: Republic of Macedonia (IT-02-55-MISC.6), Decision on the Prosecutor's Request for Deferral and Motion for Order to the former Yugoslav Republic of Macedonia, 4 October 2002.

35 Musema (ICTR-96-5-D), Decision on the Formal Request for Deferral Presented by the Prosecutor, 12 March 1996.

36 Bagosora (ICTR-96-7-D), Decision on the Application by the Prosecutor for a Formal Request for Deferral, 17 May 1996.

37 Radio Television Libre des Mille Collines SARL (ICTR-96-6-D), Decision on the Formal Request for Deferral Presented by the Prosecutor, 12 March 1996.

38 This author previously argued elsewhere that the allocation of cases under the practice of the *ad hoc* tribunals with respect to the Prosecutor's decisions to defer to national authorities in the two German cases was merely part of the prosecutorial discretionary power. I am still of the same view insofar as one considers the Prosecutor's decision *purely* from the policy perspective without being driven by the requirements of Rule 9. However, if one considers that, in exercising his discretion, he could have been guided by Rule 9 which actually served as a sort of admissibility provision, then it could be argued that the practice of the Prosecutor of the *ad hoc* tribunals also relied on a system of admissibility in the selection of cases. Therefore, I admit that I have developed my thoughts on this issue. Cf. my view in, M. M. El Zeidy, 'From Primacy to Complementarity and Backwards: (Re)Visiting Rule 11 *bis* of the Ad hoc Tribunals', *International & Comparative Law Quarterly*, 2008, vol. 57, 408.

39 S. D. Murphy, 'Progress and Jurisprudence of the International Criminal Tribunal for the former Yugoslavia', *American Journal of International Law*, 1999, vol. 93, 65 (citing Justice Arbour's Statement Regarding War Crimes Related Trials Currently Underway in Germany, ICTY Doc. CC/PIO/171-E, 19 March 1997).

40 'Address by His Excellency, Judge Claude Jorda, President of the International Criminal Tribunal for the former Yugoslavia, to the United Nations Security Council on 23 July 2002', Press Release The Hague, 26 July 2002 (JDH/P.I.S./690-e). Available at: http://www.un.org/icty/pressreal/p690-e.htm.

41 SC Res 1503 (2003), UN Doc. S/RES/1503.

42 Ibid., preamble, para. 7.

43 Ibid., preamble, para. 8.

44 SC Res 1534 (2004), UN Doc. S/RES/1534.

45 Ibid., para. 5.

46 'Judges Amend Rule 28 at Extraordinary Plenary', The Hague, 8 April 2004. Available at: http://www.icty.org/sid/8438. Rule 28(A) reads 'On receipt of an indictment for review from the Prosecutor, the Registrar shall consult with the President. The President shall refer the matter to the Bureau which shall determine whether the indictment, prima facie, concentrates on one or more of the most senior leaders suspected of being most responsible for crimes within the jurisdiction of the Tribunal. If the Bureau determines that the indictment meets this standard, the President shall designate one of the permanent Trial Chamber Judges for the review under Rule 47. If the Bureau determines that the indictment does not meet this standard, the President shall return the indictment to the Registrar to communicate this finding to the Prosecutor'.

47 See generally, S. Williams, 'The Completion Strategy of the ICTY and the ICTR', in M. Bohlander (ed.), *International Criminal Justice: A Critical Analysis of Institutions and Procedures*, London: Cameron May, 2007, pp. 153ff; Mundis, 'Completing the Mandates of the *Ad hoc* International Criminal Tribunals: Lessons from the Nuremberg Process?', pp. 612.

48 Actually the amendment to Rule 28(a) was a way to reduce the ICTY's caseload in order to implement the completion strategy. See for instance, D. Raab, 'Evaluating the ICTY and its Completion Strategy: Efforts to Achieve Accountability for War Crimes and their Tribunals', *Journal of International Criminal Justice*, 2005, vol. 3, 89–90.

49 D.A. Mundis, 'The Judicial Effects of the "Completion Strategies" on the *Ad hoc* International Criminal Tribunals', *American Journal of International Law*, 2005, vol. 99, 148.

50 It is notable that Security Council Resolutions 1503 (2003) and 1534 (2004) only addressed the ICTY and ICTR. See UN Doc. S/RES/1503 and UN Doc. S/RES/1534.

51 SC Res 1315 (2000), UN Doc. S/RES/1315 (2000), para. 3.

52 The phrase 'persons who bear the greatest responsibility' was used despite the fact that in his report on the establishment of the tribunal, the Secretary-General proposed that the 'more general term "persons most responsible" should be used'. See, SCSL Secretary-General Report, paras 29–30.

53 W. A. Schabas, *The UN International Criminal Tribunals: The former Yugoslavia, Rwanda and Sierra Leone*, Cambridge: Cambridge University Press, 2006, pp. 37–8.

54 SCSL Secretary-General Report, para. 30.

55 ICTY, Rule 11 *bis* (A); ICTR, Rule 11 *bis* (A); SCSL, Rule 11 *bis* (A).

56 ICTY, Rule 11 *bis* (B); ICTR, Rule 11 *bis* (C); SCSL, Rule 11 *bis* (B).

57 ICTY, Rule 11 *bis* (C).

58 This last requirement concerning the 'level of responsibility of the accused', which also appears under Rule 28(a) of the ICTY RPE, forms part of a further admissibility tier, as discussed later. Thus, it is as if the ICTY has established a double layer of admissibility on the basis of the same gravity criterion, which serves different purposes at different stages of the proceedings.

59 See most recently, 'Assessment and Report of Judge Patrick Robinson, President of the International Criminal Tribunal for the Former Yugoslavia, provided to the Security Council pursuant to paragraph 6 of Council Resolution 1534 (2004), covering the period from 15 May to 15 November 2009', UN Doc. S/2009/589, Annex I, p. 5.

60 The decision to revoke an order pursuant to Rule 11 *bis* must be done before the accused is convicted or acquitted by a court of the relevant State. See, ICTY, Rule 11 *bis* (F); ICTR, Rule 11 *bis* (F). The plain reading of sub-rule (F) suggests that even if the person was acquitted after sham proceedings, the Tribunal could not revoke the order unless it learned about this failure before the domestic court had rendered its verdict.

61 Trbić (IT-05-88/1-PT), Decision on Referral of Case under Rule 11 *bis* with Confidential Annex, 27 April 2007, para 44.

62 Kovačević (IT-01-42/2-I), Decision on Referral of Case pursuant to Rule 11 *bis* with Confidential and Partly Ex Parte Annexes, 17 November 2006, paras 80–1 (noting that the non-compliance with the requirements of a fair trial would also trigger the power of the Tribunal to revoke an order of referral).

63 Mejakic *et al.* (IT-02-65-PT), Decision on Prosecutor's Motion for Referral of a Case pursuant to Rule 11 *bis*, 20 July 2005, para 134.

64 Jankovic (IT-96-23/2-PT), Decision on Referral of Case under Rule 11 *bis*, 22 July 2005, paras 102–3.

65 Ademi and Norac (IT-04-78-PT), Decision for Referral to the Authorities of the Republic of Croatia Pursuant to Rule 11 *bis*, 14 September 2005, para. 57.

66 The term 'diligent prosecution' was proposed during the 1996 Preparatory Committee negotiations concerning the establishment of an International Criminal Court, to be inserted in the provision on admissibility, but the proposal was finally rejected as too subjective. See, Report of the Preparatory Committee on the Establishment of an International Criminal Court, UN GAOR, 51st Sess., Vol. 1, Supp. No. 22, UN Doc. A/51/22 (1996), para. 164.

67 Nonetheless, neither the RPE nor the jurisprudence of the *ad hoc* tribunals clearly define 'diligent prosecution' or explain the criteria for its satisfaction. Although the jurisprudence of the ICTY, for example, has restricted revocation of an order of referral due to a failure of the state to conduct 'diligent prosecution' or a 'fair trial', by reading the conditions set out in Rule 9, one could argue that the conditions could be reconciled within the entire system in question. In determining whether a referred case has been 'diligently prosecuted', the Prosecutor may therefore take these conditions listed under Rule 9 into assessment as being part of the mechanism established.

68 Sixth Annual Report of the President of the Special Court for Sierra Leone, June 2008 to May 2009, p. 6 [hereinafter SCSL Sixth Annual Report].

69 See Koroma also known as JPK (Case No. SCSL-2003-03-I), Indictment, 7 March 2003.

70 SCSL Sixth Annual Report, p. 6.

71 Ibid., p. 51.

72 A. Bos, 'Foreword', in C. Stahn and G. Sluiter (eds), *The Emerging Practice of the International Criminal Court*, Leiden, Boston: Martinus Nijhoff, 2009, p. xvii.

73 Rome Statute, Art. 17.

74 See, *inter alia*, J. T. Holmes, 'Jurisdiction and Admissibility', in R. S. Lee *et al.* (eds), *The International Criminal Court, Elements of Crimes and Rules of Procedure and Evidence*, Ardsley, NY: Transnational, 2001, p. 321; J. T. Holmes, 'Complementarity: National Courts *Versus* the ICC', in A. Cassese *et al.* (eds), *The Rome Statute of the International Criminal Court: A Commentary*, vol. II, Oxford: Oxford University Press, 2002, p. 667; S. A. Williams and W. A. Schabas, 'Article 17: Issues of Admissibility', in O. Triffterer (ed.), *Commentary on the Rome Statute: Observers' Notes, Article by Article*, Germany, Oxford: C.H. Beck/Hart/Nomos, 2008, p. 605; D. D. Ntanda Nsereko, 'Article 18: Preliminary Rulings Regarding Admissibility', in O. Triffterer (ed.), *Commentary on the Rome Statute: Observers' Notes, Article by Article*, Germany, Oxford: C. H. Beck/Hart/Nomos, 2008, p. 627; C. K. Hall, 'Challenges to the Jurisdiction of the Court or the Admissibility of a Case', in O. Triffterer (ed.), *Commentary on the Rome Statute: Observers' Notes, Article by Article*, Germany, Oxford: C.H. Beck/Hart/Nomos, 2008, p. 637; I. Tallgren and A. Reisinger Coracini, 'Article 20: *Ne Bis In Idem*', in O. Triffterer (ed.), *Commentary on the Rome Statute: Observers' Notes, Article by Article*, Germany, Oxford: C. H. Beck/Hart/Nomos, 2008, p. 669; J. K. Kleffner, *Complementarity in the Rome Statute and National Criminal Jurisdictions*, Oxford: Oxford University Press, 2008; M. M. El Zeidy, *The Principle of Complementarity in International Criminal Law: Origin, Development and Practice*, Leiden, Boston: Martinus Nijhoff, 2008 [hereinafter *Complementarity*].

75 Kenya (ICC-01/09-19-Corr), Decision Pursuant to Article 15 of the Rome Statute on the Authorization of an Investigation into the Situation in the Republic of Kenya, 31 March 2010, para. 48.

76 Rome Statute, Art. 17; Report of the Preparatory Commission for the International Criminal Court, UN Doc. PCNICC/2000/1/Add. 1 (2000), Rule 55(2) [hereinafter ICC Rule].

77 See, Kenya (ICC-01/09-19-Corr), Decision Pursuant to Article 15 of the Rome Statute on the Authorization of an Investigation into the Situation in the Republic of Kenya, 31 March 2010, para. 48; Situation in the DRC (ICC-01/04-101-etEN-Corr), Decision on the Applications for Participation in the Proceedings of VPRS1, VPRS2,VPRS3, VPRS4, VPRS5 and VPRS6 (public redacted), 17 February 2007, para. 65.

78 See also, ICC Rule 58.

79 Rome Statute, Art. 19(1).

80 Ibid., Art. 19(3); ICC Rule 59.

81 In the Kenya situation, Pre-Trial Chamber II confirmed this view when it reviewed for the first time the Prosecutor's assessment of admissibility under Articles 53(1)(b) in the course of its decision authorizing the Prosecutor's request to investigate the situation in accordance with Article 15. Kenya (ICC-01/09-19-Corr), Decision Pursuant to Article 15 of the Rome Statute on the Authorization of an Investigation into the Situation in the Republic of Kenya, 31 March 2010, para. 40.

82 On self-referrals and their implications, see, A. Cassese, 'Is the ICC Still Having Teething Problems?', *Journal of International Criminal Justice*, 2006, vol. 4, 434; C. Kress, '"Self-Referrals" and "Waivers of Complementarity": Some Considerations in Law and Policy', *Journal of International Criminal Justice*, 2004, vol. 2, 944; P. Gaeta, 'Is the Practice of "Self-Referrals" a Sound Start for the ICC?', *Journal of International Criminal Justice*, vol. 2, 949 (2004); M. M. El Zeidy, 'The Ugandan Government Triggers the First Test of the Complementarity Principle: An Assessment of the First State's Party Referral to the ICC', *International Criminal Law Review*, 2005, vol. 5, 83.

83 Rome Statute, Art. 18(1); see, for example, L. N. Sadat and S. R. Carden, 'The New International Criminal Court: An Uneasy Revolution', *Georgetown Law Journal*, 2000, vol. 88, 420; El Zeidy, *Complementarity*, pp. 247–8.

84 Kenya (ICC-01/09-3), Request for authorisation of an investigation pursuant to Article 15, 26 November 2009.

85 Kenya (ICC-01/09-19-Corr), Decision Pursuant to Article 15 of the Rome Statute on the Authorization of an Investigation into the Situation in the Republic of Kenya, 31 March 2010, para. 51.

86 Lubanga (ICC-01/04-01/06-8-US-Corr), Decision on the Prosecutor's Application for a Warrant of Arrest, Article 58, 10 February 2006, para. 18, unsealed pursuant to Decision (ICC-01/04-01/06-37) dated 17 March 2006; Harun and Kushayb (ICC-02/05-01/07-1-Corr), Decision on the Prosecution Application under Article 58(7) of the Statute, 27 April 2007, para. 18; Ngudjolo Chui (ICC-01/04-02/07-1-tENG), Warrant of Arrest for Mathieu Ngudjolo Chui, unsealed pursuant to Decision

ICC-01/04-02/07-10 dated 7 February 2008; Ngudjolo Chui (ICC-01/04-02/07-3), Decision on the Evidence and Information provided by the Prosecution for the Issuance of a Warrant of Arrest for Mathieu Ngudjolo Chui, para. 17, reclassified as public pursuant to Oral Decision dated 12 February 2008; Al Bashir (ICC-02/05-01/09-3), Decision on the Prosecution's Application for a Warrant of Arrest against Omar Hassan Ahmad Al Bashir, 4 March 2009; Abu Garda (ICC-02/05-02/09-1), Decision on the Prosecutor's Application under Article 58, 7 May 2009 (in which the Chamber expressly stated that it declined to examine the admissibility of the case).

87 Bemba (ICC-01/05-01/08-424), Decision Pursuant to Article 61(7)(a) and (b) of the Rome Statute on the Charges of the Prosecutor against Jean-Pierre Bemba Gombo, 15 June 2009, paras 25–26; Abu Garda, (ICC-05-02/09-243-Red), Decision on the Confirmation of Charges, 8 February 2010, paras 28–30.

88 See warrants of arrest for: Joseph Kony (ICC-02/04-01/05-53), 13 October 2005, para. 38; Vincent Otti (ICC-02/04-01/05-54), 13 October 2005, para. 38; Okot Odhiambo (ICC-02/04-01/05-56), 13 October 2005, para. 28; Dominic Ongwen (ICC-02/04-01/05-57), 13 October 2005, para. 26, and Raska Lukwiya (ICC-02/04-01/05-55),13 October 2005, para. 26. Pre-Trial Chamber II terminated proceedings against Raska Lukwiya as he was killed. Kony *et al.* (ICC-02/04-01/05-248), Decision to Terminate the Proceedings against Raska Lukwiya, 11 July 2007.

89 Ibid.

90 Kony *et al.* (ICC-02/04-01/05-320), Decision initiating proceedings under Article 19, requesting observations and appointing counsel for the Defence, 21 October 2008, p. 6.

91 Kony *et al.* (ICC-02/04-01/05-377), Decision on the admissibility of the case under Article 19(1) of the Statute, 10 March 2009, para. 45.

92 See, M. M. El Zeidy, 'The Gravity Threshold under the Statute of the International Criminal Court', *Criminal Law Forum*, 2008, vol. 19, 49–50; R. Murphy, 'Gravity Issues and the International Criminal Court', *Criminal Law Forum*, 2006, vol. 17, 291.

93 Situation in the DRC (ICC-01/04-02/06-20-Anx2), Decision on the Prosecutor's Application for Warrants of Arrest, Article 58, 10 February 2006, paras 51–3, 64.

94 Situation in the DRC (ICC-01/04-169), Appeals Chamber, Judgment on the Prosecutor's appeal against the decision of Pre-Trial Chamber I entitled 'Decision on the Prosecutor's Application for Warrants of Arrest, Article 58', unsealed pursuant to Decision (ICC-01/04-538-PUB-Exp), p. 2 [hereinafter 13 July 2006 Judgment].

95 Situation in the DRC (ICC-01/04-02/06-20-Anx2), Decision on the Prosecutor's Application for Warrants of Arrest, Article 58, 10 February 2006, paras 86–9; 13 July 2006 Judgment, paras 73–9; see also, for the remaining problems identified by the Appeals Chamber, ibid., paras 69–72, 80–2.

96 See also, R. Rastan, 'Complementarity—Contest or Collaboration?', *FICHL Publication Series No. 7,* forthcoming 2010, noting that the Appeals Chamber's reluctance to define gravity 'is perhaps understandable in the light of the role of the appellate chamber to provide sufficient flexibility for future jurisprudence to develop on the basis of case by case assessment'.

97 With regard to the relevant factors applied by the Prosecutor in assessing gravity, see *Report on the Activities Performed during the First Three Years* (June 2003–June 2006), p. 6; *Report on Prosecutorial Strategy*, 14 September 2006, and the most recent *Prosecutorial Strategy* (2009–2012), 1 February 2010, p. 6. More recently, the same Chamber, although differently composed, issued its decision in the case against Abu Garda arising from the Darfur situation. In this decision, the Chamber, in three paragraphs, reintroduced its understanding of gravity by deviating to some extent from its 2006 decision and referring to ICC Rule 145(1)(c) concerning sentencing, as well as to the criteria identified by the Prosecutor for his assessment of this criterion as being applicable. The Chamber also for the first time endorsed the idea that gravity may be assessed quantitatively as well as qualitatively. See, Abu Garda (ICC-02/05-02/09-243-Red), Decision on the Confirmation of Charges, 8 February 2010, paras 30–2; see also, Kenya (ICC-01/09-19-Corr), Decision Pursuant to Article 15 of the Rome Statute on the Authorization of an Investigation into the Situation in the Republic of Kenya, 31 March 2010, para. 62.

98 El Zeidy, *Complementarity*, pp. 228–32; see also, M. M. El Zeidy, 'Some Remarks on the Question of the Admissibility of a Case during Arrest Warrant Proceedings before the International Criminal Court', *Leiden Journal of International Law*, 2006, vol. 19, 741.

99 See the useful review of the literature in D. Robinson, 'The Inaction Controversy: Neglected Words and New Opportunities', in C. Stahn and M. M. El Zeidy (eds), *The International Criminal Court*

and Complementarity: From Theory to Practice, Cambridge: Cambridge University Press, forthcoming 2010.

100 Katanga (ICC-01/04-01/07-1497), Appeals Chamber, Judgment on the Appeal of Mr Germain Katanga against the Oral Decision of Trial Chamber II of 12 June 2009 on the Admissibility of the Case, 25 September 2009, para. 79 [hereinafter 25 September 2009 Judgment].

101 Lubanga (ICC-01/04-01/06-8-US-Corr), Decision on the Prosecutor's Application for a Warrant of Arrest, Article 58, 10 February 2006, para. 29, unsealed pursuant to Decision (ICC-01/04-01/06-37) dated 17 March 2006. However, the Appeals Chamber in one of its early decisions divided the admissibility provision into three prongs. The Appeals Chamber stated that admissibility refers 'in the first place to complementarity (article 17(1)(a) to (b), in the second place to *ne bis in idem* (articles 17(1)(c), 20) and thirdly to the gravity of the offence (article 17(1)(d))'. Lubanga (ICC-01/04-01/06-772), Appeals Chamber, Judgment on the Appeal of Mr Thomas Lubanga Dyilo against the Decision on the Defence Challenge to the Jurisdiction of the Court pursuant to article 19(2)(a) of the Statute of 3 October 2006, 14 December 2006, para. 23.

102 Lubanga (ICC-01/04-01/06-8-US-Corr), Decision on the Prosecutor's Application for a Warrant of Arrest, Article 58, 10 February 2006, paras 31, 37, unsealed pursuant to Decision (ICC-01/04-01/06-37) dated 17 March 2006; Harun and Kushayb (ICC-02/05-01/07-1-Corr), Decision on the Prosecution Application under Article 58(7) of the Statute, 27 April 2007, paras 24–5; Katanga (ICC-01/04-01/07-4), Decision on the Evidence and Information provided by the Prosecution for the Issuance of a Warrant of Arrest for Germain Katanga, 6 July 2007, para. 20.

103 Lubanga (ICC-01/04-01-06-8-US-Corr), Decision on the Prosecutor's Application for a Warrant of Arrest, Article 58, 10 February 2006, para. 32, unsealed pursuant to Decision (ICC-01/04-01/06-37) dated 17 March 2006.

104 Katanga and Ngudjolo Chui (ICC-01/04-01/07-1213-tENG), Reasons for the Oral Decision on the Motion Challenging the Admissibility of the Case (Article 19 of the Statute), 16 June 2009, paras 76–81 [hereinafter Katanga Trial Decision].

105 25 September 2009 Judgment, para. 80.

106 Katanga Trial Decision, para. 30.

107 Ibid., para. 44; see also, G. Bitti and M. M. El Zeidy, 'The Katanga Trial Chamber Decision in Perspective: Some Selected Issues', *Leiden Journal of International Law* 2010, vol. 23, 322–6.

108 Katanga Trial Decision, paras 56, 58.

109 25 September 2009 Judgment, para. 38.

110 However, there is a more recent admissibility challenge lodged by Jean-Pierre Bemba, which is still pending before Trial Chamber III. See Bemba (ICC-01/05-01/08-704-Red3), Requête en vue de contester la recevabilité de l'Affaire conformément aux articles 17 et 19 (2) (a) du Statut de Rome, 25 February 2010.

15
Defences to international crimes

Shane Darcy

Introduction

The label 'defences' can be used to describe a range of excusing or justificatory answers to a criminal charge, or as 'grounds for excluding criminal responsibility', according to Article 31 of the Rome Statute of the International Criminal Court.[1] Defences are often categorized as excuses or justifications, with a justification being a challenge as to whether the act was wrongful and an excuse involving acceptance that the act was wrongful but seeking to avoid attribution of criminal responsibility.[2] This chapter addresses defences to international crimes and is structured in two parts: the first considers those defences which have a counterpart in domestic criminal laws, such as duress, self-defence, mistake, or mental incapacity; and the second those defences which can be considered in some ways unique to international criminal law, such as superior orders and reprisal.

Defences to international crimes are discussed within the framework provided by the Rome Statute in Articles 31–33, as this can be considered an authoritative statement of those defences which are presently accepted in international criminal law. Recourse will be made to the jurisprudence of other relevant international criminal courts, such as the International Military Tribunal at Nuremberg, the *ad hoc* criminal tribunals for Rwanda and the Former Yugoslavia and the Special Court for Sierra Leone. It is worth noting that, at times, such jurisprudence has been at odds with the provisions of the Rome Statute.[3] The Rome Statute allows the judges of the International Criminal Court (ICC) to consider defences not enumerated in the Statute, such as those that may be drawn from the international law of armed conflict or general principles of law derived from national systems.[4] This approach is in keeping with the ICTY (International Criminal Tribunal for the former Yugoslavia) precedent whereby the United Nations Secretary-General had advocated that silence in the instrument did not mean that other defences could not be considered, 'drawing upon general principles of law recognised by all nations'.[5] The approach to defences in the Rome Statute is seen as being 'broad enough to accommodate the different legal traditions' of civil and common law countries.[6] In raising defences, including those not explicitly enumerated, Defence counsel are required to notify the Prosecutor in advance, specifying 'the names of witnesses and any other evidence upon which the accused intends to rely to establish the ground'.[7] The practice before the *ad hoc* international criminal tribunals reveals that defences, as strictly understood, have tended to play a more marginal role for an accused seeking exoneration, than challenges on jurisdictional grounds or to the proof of the legal elements of offences.[8]

Standard criminal law defences

Mental incapacity, disease or defect

The list of defences set out in Article 31 of the Rome Statute begins by stating that a person shall not be criminally responsible for their actions if at the time of their conduct: '[t]he person suffers from a mental disease or defect that destroys that person's capacity to appreciate the unlawfulness or nature of his or her conduct, or capacity to control his or her conduct to conform to the requirements of law'. The issue of mental incapacity is often addressed prior to the commencement of trial, rather than as a defence during the proceedings, although fitness to stand trial does not automatically exclude a defence of mental incapacity. In April 2006, an ICTY Trial Chamber found that Vladmi Kovačević did not 'have the capacity to enter a plea and to stand trial, without prejudice to any future criminal proceedings against him should his mental condition change'.[9] Prior to his being transferred to The Hague, the accused had been confined to a psychiatric institution in Serbia.[10] An accused capable of standing trial and who seeks to raise a defence of mental incapacity would need to contend with the presumption of sanity. As the ICTY Appeals Chamber observed regarding this ground for excluding criminal responsibility:

> This is a defence in the true sense, in that the defendant bears the onus of establishing it—that, more probably than not, at the time of the offence he was labouring under such a defect of reason, from disease of the mind, as not to know the nature and quality of his act or, if he did know it, that he did not know that what he was doing was wrong.[11]

The Chamber noted that a successful plea is a complete defence leading to an acquittal.[12] At the *ad hoc* tribunals, the burden of proving this defence lies with the accused, with the standard of proof required being 'on the balance of probabilities', while at the ICC, it is unclear as yet where the burden of such proof will lie.

In comparison with mental incapacity, an individual who argues they were of diminished mental capacity at the time of the offences might not evade conviction, but could receive a mitigated sentence.[13] While mental incapacity will *destroy* an accused's ability to appreciate the unlawfulness of their conduct or to control it so as to conform with the law, a diminished mental capacity is seen to *impair* that ability.[14] Before the International Criminal Court, a 'substantially diminished mental capacity' is considered to fall short of being a ground for excluding criminal responsibility, but should be taken into account as a mitigating factor in sentencing.[15] The ICTY Rules of Procedure and Evidence, on the other hand, classify diminished mental responsibility as a 'special defence',[16] although as practitioners have noted this defence has suffered from definitional difficulties and 'has enjoyed little or no traction at the tribunals despite repeated defence efforts'.[17]

Intoxication

In contemporary wars and conflicts, alcohol and drugs have often played a significant role in the commission of the physical acts amounting to genocide, crimes against humanity and war crimes. The Truth and Reconciliation Commission of Liberia reported that '[t]housands of children and youth were forced to take drugs as a means to control and teach them to kill, maim and rape'.[18]

A state of intoxication clearly raises the issue as to whether an accused who may have carried out the *actus reus* of a particular international crime, also possessed the necessary *mens rea*. As a general rule, criminal liability under the Rome Statute only arises if the material elements of a crime are committed 'with intent and knowledge', and accordingly, involuntary intoxication is included as a ground for excluding criminal responsibility:

> a state of intoxication that destroys that person's capacity to appreciate the unlawfulness or nature of his or her conduct, or capacity to control his or her conduct to conform to the requirements of law, unless the person has become voluntarily intoxicated under such circumstances that the person knew, or disregarded the risk, that, as a result of the intoxication, he or she was likely to engage in conduct constituting a crime within the jurisdiction of the Court.[19]

The limited relevant jurisprudence of the ICTY treated involuntary intoxication, where it was forced or coerced, as a possible mitigating circumstance, but in a situation where an accused had an 'intentionally procured diminished mental state', the Trial Chamber held that 'in contexts where violence is the norm and weapons are carried, intentionally consuming drugs or alcohol constitutes an aggravating rather than a mitigating factor'.[20] This assertion was considered to be overly severe and inconsistent with the Rome Statute, in that the state of intoxication was a factor to be considered in assessing the extent of an accused's knowledge and intent.[21] In *Vasiljević*, the ICTY rejected the defence claim that the accused's mental responsibility was diminished as a result of chronic alcoholism.[22]

Self-defence, defence of others or defence of property

That a person acted to defend themselves, their property or other persons is a defence frequently invoked in domestic criminal proceedings.[23] One is not expected to stand idly by while a crime is committed upon their person or property, although there are obvious limits to the extent to which a victim may use force to end or prevent the commission of a crime. Any use of force in self-defence is subject to the objective requirements of necessity, reasonableness and proportionality.[24] These criteria are incorporated in Article 31(1)(c) of the Rome Statute, which includes self-defence as a ground for excluding criminal responsibility where:

> The person acts reasonably to defend himself or herself or another person or, in the case of war crimes, property which is essential for the survival of the person or another person or property which is essential for accomplishing a military mission, against an imminent and unlawful use of force in a manner proportionate to the degree of danger to the person or the other person or property protected. The fact that the person was involved in a defensive operation conducted by forces shall not in itself constitute a ground for excluding criminal responsibility under this subparagraph.

The Statute adopts the standard requirements of reasonableness and proportionality for the defence of oneself or others against an 'imminent and unlawful use of force', although it introduces something of a novel concept with regard to the defence of property in the context of war crimes.

Self-defence as a ground for excluding criminal responsibility in international criminal law needs be distinguished from self-defence in public international law, which is an exception to the prohibition on the use of force by States triggered in the event of an 'armed attack' against a State.[25] The latter concept would likely feature in the determination of whether a use of armed force by a State amounts to an act of aggression under the *jus ad bellum*, but that is a separate issue as to whether an individual accused can raise an argument that their actions were in self-defence. To assert that a particular use of armed force is defensive and not contrary to the *jus ad bellum*, and that therefore any measures taken pursuant to such a use of force are not unlawful is not permitted according to the last sentence of Article 31(1)(c) of the Rome Statute. The ICTY noted correctly in *Kordic* that 'military operations in self-defence do not provide a justification for serious violations of international humanitarian law'.[26] A Trial Chamber of the Special Court for Sierra Leone alluded to the notion of a 'just war' in the sentencing stage of the *Civil Defences Force* case:

> although the commission of these crimes transcends acceptable limits, albeit in defending a cause that is palpably just and defendable, such as acting in defence of constitutionality by engaging in a struggle or a fight that was geared towards the restoration of the ousted democratically elected Government of President Kabbah, it certainly, in such circumstances, constitutes a mitigating circumstance in favour of the two Accused Persons.[27]

However, the Appeals Chamber ruled that '"just cause" as a motive for the purposes of sentencing should not be considered as a defence against criminal liability' or as a mitigating factor.[28]

The extent to which force can be used to defend property has proved a controversial issue in domestic jurisdictions,[29] and the inclusion in Article 31 of the defence of using force to protect 'property which is essential for the survival of the person or another person or property which is essential for accomplishing a military mission' has also been criticized. It has been described as 'a disturbing compromise'.[30] According to the ICTY, this aspect of self-defence 'takes into account the principle of military necessity',[31] although this may not be in line with the meaning of military necessity, as described next. Self-defence may not arise as an issue before the International Criminal Court if practice to date is considered; this ground for excluding criminal responsibility has not featured prominently in international proceedings,[32] perhaps owing to the nature of the crimes and the seniority of the accused with whom international criminal tribunals are concerned.

Duress and necessity

International criminal law, like its domestic counterparts, pays heed to the fact that individuals may be forced against their will to commit crimes and, accordingly, allows for a defence of either duress or necessity in such circumstances. Where a threat of harm is made against an individual by other persons, then resort may be made to a defence of duress, and where the harm arises from natural occurrences beyond an individual's control, then a defence of necessity might arise.[33] Duress has generated much scholarship and little in the way of practice at the international criminal tribunals, with the interest perhaps attributable to the moral quandary which it can give rise to.[34] This dilemma is apparent when one considers the ingredients of the defence:

> (a) the act charged was done to avoid an immediate danger both serious and irreparable;
> (b) there was no other adequate means of escape;
> (c) the remedy was not disproportionate to the evil.[35]

A person claiming the defence of duress will have been forced to choose between committing crimes or allowing for either themselves or other persons to be harmed. Although duress and necessity are absent from the statutes of the *ad hoc* international criminal tribunals, Article 31(d) of the Rome Statute considers that criminal responsibility will not arise if:

> The conduct which is alleged to constitute a crime within the jurisdiction of the Court has been caused by duress resulting from a threat of imminent death or of continuing or imminent serious bodily harm against that person or another person, and the person acts necessarily and reasonably to avoid this threat, provided that the person does not intend to cause a greater harm than the one sought to be avoided. Such a threat may either be:
>
> (i) Made by other persons; or
> (ii) Constituted by other circumstances beyond that person's control.

The adoption of the Rome Statute put paid to some of the uncertainty that had existed following the ICTY Appeals Chamber judgment in *Erdemović*, in which a majority had ruled that 'duress does not afford a complete defence to a soldier charged with a crime against humanity and/or a war crime involving the killing of innocent human beings'.[36] Nevertheless, judges at the ICC confronted with a defence of duress will be required to consider the defence's somewhat taxing requirements of necessity, reasonableness and 'lesser evil'. In their separate opinion in *Erdemović*, Judges McDonald and Vohrah considered that no 'remedy' taken by an accused could be deemed proportionate 'to a crime directed at the whole of humanity'.[37] Although the majority did accept that duress could be a mitigating factor in sentencing,[38] it is the minority opinion in *Erdemović* that will likely provide guidance for any future considerations of the defence. Judge Cassese set out the following conditions:

> i the act charged was done under an immediate threat of severe and irreparable harm to life or limb;
> ii there was no adequate means of averting such evil;
> iii the crime committed was not disproportionate to the evil threatened (this would, for example, occur in case of killing in order to avert an assault). In other words, in order not to be disproportionate, the crime committed under duress must be, on balance, the lesser of two evils;
> iv. the situation leading to duress must not have been voluntarily brought about by the person coerced.[39]

The *Erdemović* case also demonstrates that in the context of international crimes, a defence of duress will often arise in connection with superior orders, where an individual soldier, for example, was ordered to commit offences under a threat to their life. Superior orders is a distinct defence and is discussed later in the chapter.

Mistake of fact and mistake of law

The Rome Statute allows mistakes of fact or law as defences where the mistakes are such as to prevent the accused from having formulated the necessary *mens rea* for the offence. Article 32 of the instrument specifies that

> 1 A mistake of fact shall be a ground for excluding criminal responsibility only if it negates the mental element required by the crime.
> 2 A mistake of law as to whether a particular type of conduct is a crime within the jurisdiction of the Court shall not be a ground for excluding criminal responsibility. A mistake

> of law may, however, be a ground for excluding criminal responsibility if it negates the mental element required by such a crime, or as provided for in article 33.

The second paragraph gives expression to the general position that 'ignorance of the law is no excuse', with the exceptions being where the mistake negates the crime's mental element, or with regard to the defence of 'superior orders', discussed further below. It has been noted that Article 30 of the Rome Stature requires that offences be committed with intent and knowledge, while crimes such as genocide and the crime of humanity of persecution require additional special intent. The ICC has asserted that 'the defence of mistake of law can succeed under Article 32 of the Statute only if [an accused] was unaware of a normative objective element of the crime as a result of not realising is social significance (its everyday meaning)'.[40] The specialized and, at times, technical nature of international humanitarian law, as evidenced by the concept of reprisals, for example, should see a more flexible approach to this defence.[41]

The Hartmann contempt trial before the ICTY was one of the rare occasions when mistake was raised as a defence before international criminal tribunals, although of course the accused in that instance was not charged with an international crime. Defence argued that the accused was not aware of the illegality of her conduct and that she acted under a reasonable belief that the information she disclosed was public.[42] The Chamber did not accept that the accused was reasonably mistaken in fact regarding the confidential material and as regards the mistake of law defence, it noted 'that a person's misunderstanding of the law does not, in itself, excuse a violation of it'.[43] In dismissing the claim, the Chamber found that the accused had demonstrated knowledge, rather than ignorance of the law.[44]

Alibi

Although not considered as a defence 'in its true sense',[45] hence its omission from the defences listed in Article 31 of the Rome Statute, alibi is a defensive argument that is nonetheless relied upon by defence lawyers where it is claimed that an accused was not present when the offence in question was committed. The argument of alibi is envisaged in proceedings before the International Criminal Court, as Rule 79 of the Rules of Procedure and Evidence requires the Defence to disclose to the Prosecutor if they intend to:

> Raise the existence of an alibi, in which case the notification shall specify the place or places at which the accused claims to have been present at the time of the alleged crime and the names of witnesses and any other evidence upon which the accused intends to rely to establish the alibi.[46]

The possible existence of an alibi is an issue of fact that will need to be disproved by the Prosecution in order to establish the presence of an accused at the location of the offence's commission. Alibi is more relevant for those persons accused of directly participating in the commission of crimes, as military or civilian superiors or those who may have ordered, induced or aided and abetted in the carrying out of an offence need not be present at the scene for criminal liability to arise. That being said, alibi may be raised with regard to presence at particular meeting where an agreement was made to pursue a course of action involving aggression, genocide, crimes against humanity or war crimes.

Commentators have observed that alibi may be 'the wrong *kind* of defence for most cases before the tribunals', and it has succeeded in only one case to date.[47] In *Rwamakuba*, the Prosecution failed to rebut the significant alibi evidence presented, and an ICTR (International

Criminal Tribunal for Rwanda) Trial Chamber found that this was 'sufficient to cast reasonable doubt upon the allegations regarding the Accused's participation in public meetings and gatherings'.[48] On the other hand, the ICTY rejected the defence of alibi in *Tadić*, 'in view of the overwhelming credible testimony to the contrary'.[49] Therefore, in raising an alibi for an accused, there is an evidentiary burden for the Defence to the extent that they must 'indicate proof to raise a reasonable doubt', although the burden of proof overall clearly remains with the Prosecution.[50] As the ICTR observed, 'the Prosecution's burden is to prove the accused's guilt as to the alleged crimes beyond reasonable doubt in spite of the proffered alibi'.[51]

Provocation

Provocation has not been explicitly included as a defence in the Rome Statute and although it may be difficult to envisage the so-called heat of the moment defence being relevant for high-ranking accused charged with international crimes, such as war crimes 'committed as part of a plan or policy', or crimes against humanity involving a 'widespread or systematic attack against any population', it cannot with certainty be fully excluded from international criminal law.[52] Carla Del Ponte, in the Prosecution's opening statement in the *Bagosora* trial before the ICTR, contended that '[t]he abhorrent nature of the crime of genocide necessarily negates the idea of provocation as an acceptable defence to that crime'.[53] Nonetheless, the possibility of provocation as a defence is alluded to by the *ad hoc* international criminal tribunals, and an ICTY Trial Chamber in *Milutinović* referred to numerous killings as being 'unprovoked and without legal justification'.[54]

In national jurisdictions, a successful plea that a killing was provoked by the words or deeds of the victim would usually see a charge of murder reduced to manslaughter.[55] International criminal law does not allow for such gradations in offences, and Defence counsel before the ICTY sought to use such an argument to have a killing that was allegedly provoked considered as manslaughter and thus outside the Tribunal's jurisdiction.[56] The judgment reads

> The Trial Chamber does not accept that Gojko Vujičić's curses constituted provocation such as to exclude the required *mens rea* for murder on the part of the Mujahedin who killed him. Apart from the fact that Gojko Vujičić's curses seem to have been themselves a reaction to the conditions of his detention and his injury, firing a shot into Vujičić's temple would be completely out of proportion to the alleged provocation.[57]

In the trial of Dragomir Milošević, the Trial Chamber took the view that the Defence argument of provocation was a challenge to the intent element of the crime of unlawful attacks against civilians:

> In this respect, the Trial Chamber recalls that in prohibiting attacks against civilians and civilian objects, Article 49 of Additional Protocol I defines 'attacks' as meaning 'acts of violence against the adversary, whether in offence or defence'. There is an unconditional and absolute prohibition on the targeting of civilians in customary international law: Any attack directed at the civilian population is prohibited, regardless of the military motive.[58]

Consent

The absence of consent by a victim is generally considered as an element of certain crimes, although the claimed presence of consent might sometimes be raised as a defence. Lack of consent is a specific element for the war crimes of pillage, enforced sterilization, rape, sexual violence and enforced prostitution in the Rome Statute.[59] Particular attention is paid to the issue of consent with regard to crimes of sexual violence in the jurisprudence and Rules of Procedure and Evidence of the various contemporary international tribunals.[60] Rule 96 of the ICTY and ICTR Rules of Procedure and Evidence sets out that 'consent shall not be allowed as a defence' in cases where the victim:

(a) has been subjected to or threatened with or has had reason to fear violence, duress, detention or psychological oppression, or
(b) reasonably believed that if the victim did not submit, another might be so subjected, threatened or put in fear.[61]

This approach to the issue of consent is seen as 'just the mirror image of the definition of rape'.[62] Moreover, it has been contended that 'sexual violence that qualifies as genocide, a crime against humanity, or a war crime, occurs under circumstances that are inherently coercive and negate any possibility of genuine consent'.[63] Consent, of course, can never be a defence to murder and would not be relevant for many international crimes, although where it might arise, its classification as either a defence or an element of the crime would impact on the burden of proof.[64]

International criminal law defences

Superior orders

The highly regimented structure of military forces, where lawful orders should be met with 'prompt, immediate, and unhesitating obedience',[65] has given rise to a defence of superior orders, whereby an accused claims that they acted on the basis of orders from a superior which as a subordinate they were bound to follow. International criminal law has evolved in its treatment of the defence, from its rejection as an absolute defence at Nuremberg, to a more nuanced approach under the Rome Statute of the International Criminal Court.[66] Article 8 of Nuremberg Charter established the standard approach:

> The fact that the Defendant acted pursuant to order of his Government or of a superior shall not free him from responsibility, but may be considered in mitigation of punishment if the Tribunal determines that justice so requires.

This approach ruled out superior orders as a defence, and rendered it relevant only at the sentencing stage, although in finding Keitel guilty on all four counts, the Nuremberg Tribunal concluded that the defence of superior orders 'cannot be considered in mitigation where crimes as shocking and extensive have been committed consciously, ruthlessly and without military excuse or justification'.[67] Other tribunals operating in the post–Second World War period considered the defence of superior orders beyond the context of mitigation.[68] The statutes of the contemporary *ad hoc* international criminal tribunals have included a provision on superior orders largely replicating the approach taken at Nuremberg.[69] However, according to Zahar and Sluiter, the practice is that despite the considerable academic commentary on superior orders, it is 'almost by definition not a live defence at the tribunals' given the seriousness of crimes charged and the seniority of the accused.[70] The limited consideration of the defence of superior orders at the *ad hoc* tribunals has taken place at the sentencing stage, and has usually been unsuccessful, as was the case in *Erdemović*.[71]

The Rome Statute dedicates a separate article to the defence of 'superior orders and prescription of law'. Article 33 reads

> 1 The fact that a crime within the jurisdiction of the Court has been committed by a person pursuant to an order of a Government or of a superior, whether military or civilian, shall not relieve that person of criminal responsibility unless:
> (a) The person was under a legal obligation to obey orders of the Government or the superior in question;
> (b) The person did not know that the order was unlawful; and
> (c) The order was not manifestly unlawful.
>
> 2 For the purposes of this article, orders to commit genocide or crimes against humanity are manifestly unlawful.

This is a departure from the approach taken at Nuremberg and by the *ad hoc* tribunals, in that the defence is allowed in limited circumstances: only those under a duty to obey orders can raise the defence, it is limited to war crimes charges, and will succeed where it is proved that the individual did not know that the order was unlawful and the order itself was not manifestly unlawful. Antonio Cassese has contended that the provision is out of step with customary international law by treating war crimes differently from genocide and crimes against humanity in terms of manifest unlawfulness.[72]

Reprisals

The concept of reciprocity often cast a dark shadow over observance of the laws of armed conflict,[73] although according to the ICTY, '[t]he defining characteristic of modern international humanitarian law is . . . the obligation to uphold key tenets of this body of law regardless of the conduct of enemy combatants'.[74] Persons accused of international crimes have occasionally sought to raise a defence of *tu quoque*, claiming that similar acts were also carried out by their opponents, although such an argument has invariably been rejected and often serves more as a political denunciation of the relevant tribunal, rather than a genuine defence to criminal charges.[75] Until such a time as international criminal justice is applied evenly to all international crimes, then such claims of justification will continue to be made.[76] Defence arguments seeking to rely on reciprocity may gain some traction by resort to the doctrine of reprisals.

Reprisals are a somewhat anachronistic international law enforcement mechanism, and although largely of academic interest in the present day, with little actual reliance on the doctrine, reprisals have been invoked as a defence before the international tribunals recently[77] and cannot with certainty be ruled out as a defence to war crimes or even perhaps to the crime of aggression. The defence of reprisals was used frequently in the trials conducted after the Second World War as an attempt to justify conduct which would otherwise be viewed as being contrary to the laws of war.[78] The appeal of the defence is obvious, when one considers that belligerent reprisals are deliberate violations of the laws of war by a party to an armed conflict in response to the prior violation of those same laws by the opposing party, and for the purpose of forcing a return to observance of the law.[79] The concept of reprisal also exists outside the context of armed conflict, in the form of so-called peacetime reprisals. Such countermeasures involve a use of force falling short of war, by one State in response to a prior violation of the *jus ad bellum* by another State – a forcible means of self-help.[80]

Belligerent reprisals have historically served as a blunt instrument of law enforcement during times of war, although not without limitation, as customary international law prescribed certain rules governing their use. Reprisals could only be in response to a breach of the laws of war, any resort to the doctrine required observance of the principle of proportionality and reprisals could only be used in an attempt to force compliance with the law, if other means would not prove effective.[81] Positive international humanitarian law began progressively protecting certain categories of persons from reprisals when such a rule was introduced for prisoners of war in 1929,[82] and this was followed by similar protections for various categories of persons and property protected by the Geneva Conventions of 1949, such as the wounded, sick and shipwrecked members of armed forces and civilians in occupied territory.[83] Additional Protocol I added to this growing list by including, for example, the civilian population, objects indispensable to the survival of the civilian population and the natural environment,[84] although the attempt to include reprisal prohibitions applicable to non-international armed conflicts in Additional Protocol II proved unsuccessful.[85] A complete ban of belligerent reprisals has not yet been brought about, and while no State disputes the reprisal prohibitions in the Geneva Conventions, the rules in Additional Protocol I have not been agreed to by all States and doubts exist over the customary international law status of some of those provisions.[86] The laws applicable to internal armed conflicts are silent on the question of belligerent reprisals, although it is arguable that this concept does not apply outside of the context of inter-State conflict.[87]

The defence of belligerent reprisal in the Allied trials after the Second World War yielded little if any success for those accused who sought to raise it, often because of the excessively disproportionate nature of the reprisals taken; in the notorious 'Ardeatine Cave' incident, 10 prisoners were killed for each German policeman who had been killed in a partisan bomb attack.[88] The ICTY has discussed belligerent reprisals as a possible defence in its jurisprudence, holding somewhat controversially that the rule that protects civilians from being the target of reprisal action applies in all armed conflicts and that the rule in Additional Protocol I prohibiting reprisals against the civilian population is a rule of customary international law.[89]

Where the law relating to belligerent reprisals is either contested or permissive, as is the case with reprisals against active combatants and military objects, recourse to the reprisal argument may act as a possible legitimate defence to a charge of war crimes.[90] The issue of reprisals as a defence had been addressed with some concern in the preparatory work leading to the adoption of the Rome Statute,[91] and the instrument itself does not include reprisals in Article 31. It is likely that some reprisals, particularly those against military forces or objects or involving the use of prohibited weapons, could be in accordance with 'the established principles of the international law of armed conflict',[92] and depending on the circumstance, admissible as a defence to war crimes contained in the Rome Statute.

The question of reprisals as a defence to a charge of aggression may also be an unresolved one, although interestingly the answer was perhaps clearer when international criminal law was in its infancy. Peacetime reprisals consist of 'modes of putting stress upon an offending state which are of a violent nature, although they fall short of actual war',[93] and in 1946, the Nuremberg Charter defined a crime against peace as a 'war of aggression, or a war in violation of international treaties, agreements or assurances'.[94] The United Nations Declaration of Aggression distinguished between acts of aggression, which give rise to international responsibility, and wars of aggression, which amount to crimes against international peace.[95] Reprisals would constitute *prima facie* aggressive acts, and the International Law Commission, in its 1996 Draft Code of Crimes Against the Peace and Security of Mankind, omitted the reference to 'wars' and referred only to 'aggression'.[96] The ICC Special Working Group on the Crime of Aggression recently proposed the following definition of the offence:

> the planning, preparation, initiation or execution, by a person in a position effectively to exercise control over or to direct the political or military action of a State, of an act of

> aggression which, by its character, gravity and scale, constitutes a manifest violation of the Charter of the United Nations.[97]

Yoram Dinstein contends that it is an open question as to whether 'the practice of States, and the future definition to be incorporated in the revised Statute of the ICC, will confirm the broadening of criminal liability in this sphere'.[98] This more expansive approach to aggression would seem to encompass unlawful reprisals, and it may be the case that under contemporary international law all armed reprisals are now unlawful following the adoption of the rules limiting resort to the use of force in the Charter of the United Nations and as interpreted in the 1970 General Assembly 'Declaration on Principles of International Law Concerning Friendly Relations'.[99]

Military necessity

The concept of military necessity plays an important role in the assessment of the legality of wartime conduct under the laws of armed conflict. In planning military actions, forces 'are permitted to take into account the practical requirements of a military situation at any given moment and the imperatives of winning'.[100] Certain rules of international humanitarian law are subject to an exception of military necessity, such as Article 53 of the Fourth Geneva Convention, which states that:

> Any destruction by the Occupying Power of real or personal property belonging individually or collectively to private persons, or to the State, or to other public authorities, or to social or cooperative organizations, is prohibited, except where such destruction is rendered absolutely necessary by military operations.

The concept of military necessity appears in various war crimes under international criminal law, including the list in Article 6 of the Nuremberg Charter, which considered criminal 'wanton destruction of cities, towns or villages, or devastation not justified by military necessity'. In the Rome Statute, a similar war crime appears, defined as '[e]xtensive destruction and appropriation of property, not justified by military necessity and carried out unlawfully and wantonly'.[101] The Statute also includes a war crime of '[o]rdering the displacement of the civilian population for reasons related to the conflict, unless the security of the civilians involved or imperative military reasons so demand'.[102] Military necessity, or more accurately, the lack of a justification of military necessity, is an inherent element of the crime, rather than a defence *per se* to criminal conduct. That being said, it is worth considering it in this context of defences, as the concept invariably gives rise to subjective assessments as to whether a particular course of action was justified by military necessity and, accordingly, there is some room for debate regarding the concept amongst the parties in criminal proceedings.

The application of the concept of military necessity is not without limitations. It can only be raised in the context of attacks aimed at the military defeat of the enemy and, moreover, such attacks must respect the principle of proportionality: i.e. they 'must not cause harm to civilians or civilian objects that is excessive in relation to the concrete and direct military advantage anticipated'.[103] As the concept of military necessity is an explicit aspect of several humanitarian law rules, it cannot be relied upon to breach other rules where no such reference exists. A US Military Tribunal sitting after the Second World War correctly noted that '[m]ilitary necessity or expediency do not justify a violation of positive rules'.[104] An ICTY Trial Chamber interpreted the concept incorrectly in the *Blaškić* case, when it asserted that 'targeting civilians is an offence when not justified by military necessity'.[105] The Appeals Chamber made a correction and reiterated that there is an absolute prohibition of the targeting of civilians in customary international law.[106] Military necessity may be raised to an accused's defence with regard to charges of property destruction, displacement and detention of civilians, for example, and in the context of either war crimes or crimes against humanity,[107] although such arguments are viewed as 'controversial because of their potential to subvert the legal regulation of armed conflict'.[108] Such an argument was rejected by the *Krstić* Trial Chamber in relation to the transfer of civilians at Srebrenica, as the evacuation of civilians 'was itself the goal and neither the protection of the civilians nor imperative military necessity justified the action'.[109]

Notes

1 Rome Statute of the International Criminal Court, UN Doc. A/CONF.183/9, 2187 UNTS 90 (1998).
2 A. Cassese (ed.), *The Oxford Companion to International Criminal Justice*, Oxford: Oxford University Press, 2009, pp. 318–19. Zahar and Sluiter question the need for such a theoretical distinction in light of practice, contending that '[a]ny submission seeking acquittal may be regarded as a kind of defence', A . Zahar and G. Sluiter, *International Criminal Law*, Oxford: Oxford University Press, 2008, p. 396.
3 See generally A. Cassese, 'Justifications and Excuses in International Criminal Law', in A. Cassese, P. Gaeta and J. R. W. D. Jones (eds), *The Rome Statute of the International Criminal Court: A Commentary*, Vol. I, Oxford: Oxford University Press, 2002, p. 951.
4 Rome Statute, Art. 31(3), referring to Art. 21.
5 *Report of the Secretary-General Pursuant to Para. 2 of Security Council Resolution 808 (1993)*, UN Doc. S/25704, 3 May 1993, para. 58.
6 J. Gilbert, 'Justice not Revenge: The International Criminal Court and the "Grounds to Exclude Criminal Responsibility": Defences or Negation of Criminality?', *Journal of Human Rights* 10:2, 2006, 143, 144.
7 International Criminal Court Rules of Procedure and Evidence, adopted by the Assembly of States Parties, 2002, ICC-ASP/1/3, Rules 79 and 80.
8 Zahar and Sluiter, *International Criminal Law*, p. 443.
9 ICTY Chambers, Press Release, 'Vladmir Kovačević declared unfit to stand trial', The Hague, 12 April 2006, OK/MOW/1069e
10 Zahar and Sluiter, *International Criminal Law*, p. 441.
11 Delalić *et al.* (Case No. IT-96-21-A), Appeals Chamber, 20 February 2001, para. 582.
12 Ibid.
13 W. A. Schabas, *The UN International Criminal Tribunals*, Cambridge: Cambridge University Press, 2006, p. 333.
14 Vasiljević (IT-98-32-T), 29 November 2002, para. 283.
15 ICC Rules of Procedure and Evidence, Rule 145(2)(a)(i).
16 International Criminal Tribunal for the former Yugoslavia, Rules of Procedure and Evidence, IT/32/Rev.43, 24 July 2009, Rule 67(B)(i)(b).
17 Zahar and Sluiter, *International Criminal Law*, pp. 437, 440.
18 *Final Report of the Truth and Reconciliation Commission of Liberia*, Volume I: Findings and Recommendations, 2009 p. 51.
19 Rome Statute, Art. 31(1)(b).
20 Kvočka *et al.* (IT-98-30/1/T), 2 November 2001, para. 706.
21 Schabas, *The UN International Criminal Tribunals*, p. 335.
22 Vasiljević (IT-98-32-T), 29 November 2002, para. 284.
23 See F. Leverick, *Killing in Self-Defence*, Oxford: Oxford University Press, 2007; C. Hanly, *An Introduction to Irish Criminal Law*, Dublin: Gill & Macmillan, 1999, pp. 99–109.
24 See generally A. Ashworth, *Principles of Criminal Law*, 4th edn., Oxford: Oxford University Press, 2003, pp. 135–49.
25 See Charter of the United Nations, T.S. 993 (1945), Art. 51.
26 Kordić and Čerkez (IT-95-14/2-T), 26 February 2001, para. 452.
27 Fofana and Kondewa (SCSL-04-14-T), Sentencing Judgment, 9 October 2007, para. 86.

28 Fofana and Kondewa (SCSL-04-14-A), 28 May 2008, paras 523, 534.
29 Ashworth, *Principles of Criminal Law*, p. 144.
30 W. A. Schabas, *An Introduction to the International Criminal Court*, Cambridge: Cambridge University Press, 2007, pp. 228–9.
31 Kordić and Čerkez (IT-95-14/2-T), 26 February 2001, para. 451.
32 A. Cassese, *International Criminal Law*, Oxford: Oxford University Press, 2003, pp. 223–4.
33 Ashworth, *Principles of Criminal Law*, pp. 221–31.
34 See, for example, L. E. Chiesa, 'Duress, Demanding Heroism, and Proportionality', *Vanderbilt Journal of Transnational Law*, 41, 2008, 741; V. Epps, 'The Soldier's Obligation to Die when Ordered to Shoot Civilians or Face Death Himself', *New England Law Review*, 37, 2003, 987; R. Ehrenreich Brooks, 'Law in the Heart of Darkness: Atrocity and Duress', *Virginia Journal of International Law*, 43, 2003, 861.
35 Erdemović (IT-96-22-A), Appeals Chamber, 7 October 1997, Separate and Dissenting Opinion of Judge Li, para. 5.
36 Erdemović (IT-96-22-A), Appeals Chamber, 7 October 1997, para. 19.
37 Ibid., Joint Separate Opinion of Judge McDonald and Judge Vohrah, para. 37.
38 Ibid., Joint Separate Opinion of Judge McDonald and Judge Vohrah, para. 66; Separate and Dissenting Opinion of Judge Li, para. 5.
39 Ibid., Separate and Dissenting Opinion of Judge Cassese, para. 16.
40 Lubanga (ICC-01/04-01/06), Decision on the Confirmation of Charges, 29 January 2007, para. 316. See T. Weigend, 'Intent, Mistake of Law and Co-perpetration in the Lubanga Decision on Confirmation of Charges', *Journal of International Criminal Justice* 6, 2008, 471, p. 476.
41 Schabas, *An Introduction to the International Criminal Court*, p. 230.
42 Hartmann (IT-02-54-R77.5), Special Appointed Chamber, Judgment, 14 September 2009, paras 63–4.
43 Ibid., paras 64–5.
44 Ibid., para. 66.
45 Delalić *et al.* (IT-96-21-A), Appeals Chamber, 20 February 2001, para. 581.
46 ICC Rules of Procedure and Evidence, Rule 79(1)(a). See also ICTY Rules of Procedure and Evidence, Rule 67.
47 Zahar and Sluiter, *International Criminal Law*, pp. 423–4.
48 Rwamakuba (ICTR-98-44C-T), 20 September 2006, paras. 82–3.
49 Tadić (IT-94-1-T), 7 May 1997, para. 434.
50 Schabas, *The UN International Criminal Tribunals*, p. 340.
51 Kajelijeli (ICTR-98-44A-A), Appeals Chamber, 23 May 2005, para. 43.
52 Rome Statute, Arts 7 and 8.
53 Bagosora *et al.* (ICTR-98-41), Prosecution Opening Statement, 2 April 2002, available at: http://www.ictr.org/ENGLISH/PRESSREL/2002/312chile&delponte.htm
54 Milutinović (IT-05-87-T), 26 February 2009, paras 538–40, 543.
55 See K. J. Heller, 'Beyond the Reasonable Man? A Sympathetic but Critical Assessment of the Use of Subjective Standards of Reasonableness in Self-Defense and Provocation Cases', *American Journal of Criminal Law* 26, 1998, 1.
56 Delić (IT-04-83-T), 15 September 2008, para. 262.
57 Ibid., para. 263. See also Orić (IT-03-68-T), 30 June 2006, para. 384.
58 Milošević (IT-98-29/1-T), 12 December 2007, para. 906. See also ibid., paras 775–80.
59 International Criminal Court Elements of Crimes, ICC-ASP/1/3(part II-B) (2002), Art. 8(2)(b)(xvi); Art. 8(2)(b)(xxii)-5; Art. 8(2)(b)(xxii)-6; Art. 8(2)(e)(vi)-3.
60 See generally W. Schomburg and I. Peterson, 'Genuine Consent to Sexual Violence under International Criminal Law', *American Journal of International Law* 101: 1, 2007, 121.
61 ICTY Rules of Procedure and Evidence, Rule 96(ii). See also ICC Rules of Procedure and Evidence, Rule 70.
62 Schabas, *The UN International Criminal Tribunals*, p. 341.
63 Schomburg and Peterson, 'Genuine Consent to Sexual Violence', p. 124.
64 Schabas, *The UN International Criminal Tribunals*, pp. 342–3.
65 United Kingdom War Office, *Manual of Military Law*, London: HMSO, 1907, p. 18.
66 See J. N. Maogoto, 'The Defence of Superior Orders', in Olaoluwa Olusanya, *Rethinking International Criminal Law: The Substantive Part*, Groningen: Europe Law Publishing, 2007, 89.

67 International Military Tribunal (Nuremberg), *Judgment and Sentences*, 1 October 1946, reprinted in *American Journal of International Law* 41: 1, 1947, 172, 283.
68 C. Garraway, 'Superior Orders and the International Criminal Court: Justice Delivered, or Justice Denied', *International Review of the Red Cross*, No. 836, 1999, 785.
69 Statute of the International Tribunal for the Prosecution of Persons Responsible for Serious Violations of International Humanitarian Law Committed in the Territory of the former Yugoslavia since 1991, UN Doc S/25704 at 36, Annex (1993) and S/25704/Add.1, (1993) UN Doc S/RES/827, Art. 7, para. 4, Statute of the International Criminal Tribunal for the Prosecution of Persons Responsible for Genocide and Other Serious Violations of International Humanitarian Law Committed in the Territory of Rwanda, UN Doc. S/Res/955 (1994), Art. 6, para. 4; Statute of the Special Court for Sierra Leone, having been established by an Agreement between the United Nations and the Government of Sierra Leone pursuant to Security Council Resolution 1315 (2000) of 14 August 2000, Art. 6, para. 4.
70 Zahar and Sluiter, *International Criminal Law*, p. 425.
71 Erdemović (IT-96-22-T), Sentencing Judgment, 29 November 1996, paras 13–20.
72 Cassese, *International Criminal Law*, p. 241.
73 F. Kalshoven and L. Zegveld, *Constraints on the Waging of War*, 3rd edn, Geneva: International Committee of the Red Cross, 2001, pp. 75–6.
74 Kupreškić *et al.* (IT-95-16-T), 14 January 2000, para. 511.
75 Ibid., paras 511, 515. See also Kunarac *et al.* (IT-96-23 and IT-96-23/1-A), Appeals Chamber, 12 June 2002, para. 87; S. Yee, 'The Tu Quoque Argument as a Defence to International Crimes, Prosecution or Punishment', *Chinese Journal of International Law*, 3, 2004, 87.
76 See generally R. Cryer, *Prosecuting International Crimes: Selectivity and the International Criminal Law Regime*, Cambridge: Cambridge University Press, 2005.
77 See Martić (IT-95-11-T), 12 June 2007, paras 464–8; Martić (IT-95-11-A), Appeals Chamber, 8 October 2008, paras 263–7.
78 See, for example, *United States of America* v. *Wilhelm List et al.*, Judgment, 19 February 1948, Case No. 7, XI *Trials of War Criminals before the Nuernberg Military Tribunals under Control Council Law No. 10* 757, pp. 1252–3; *United States of America* v. *Wilhelm von Leeb et al.*, Judgment, 27 October 1948, Case No. 12, XI *Trials of War Criminals before the Nuernberg Military Tribunals under Control Council Law No. 10* 462, p. 528; *United States of America* v. *Otto Ohlendorf et al.*, Judgment, 8–9 April 1948, Case No. 9, IV *Trials of War Criminals before the Nuernberg Military Tribunals under Control Council Law No. 10* 1, pp. 493–4; *In re Rauter,* Holland, Special Criminal Court, 4 May 1948, Special Court of Cassation, 12 January 1949, Case No. 193, 16 *Annual Digest and Reports of Public International Law Cases* (1949) 526, p. 539; *Trial of General von Mackensen and General Maelzer*, British Military Court, Rome, 18–30 November 1945, Case No. 43, VIII *Law Reports of Trials of War Criminals* 1, pp. 3–7.
79 See generally F. Kalshoven, *Belligerent Reprisals,* Leyden: A.W. Sijthoff, 1971.
80 See generally Y. Dinstein, *War, Aggression and Self-Defence*, 2nd edn., Cambridge: Cambridge University Press, 1994, pp. 215–26; Derek Bowett, 'Reprisals Involving Recourse to Armed Force', 66 *American Journal of International Law* 1 (1972); Jason S. Wrachford, 'The 2006 Israeli Invasion of Lebanon: Aggression, Self-Defence of Reprisal Gone Bad?', *Air Force Law Review*, 60, 2007, 29.
81 S. Darcy, 'The Evolution of the Law of Belligerent Reprisals', *Military Law Review*, 175, 2003, 184, pp. 189–96.
82 Convention Relative to the Treatment of Prisoners of War (1929), Art. 2, para. 3.
83 See, for example, Geneva Convention I for the Amelioration of the Condition of Wounded and Sick in Armed Forces in the Field, 75 UNTS 31 (1949), Art. 46; Geneva Convention II for the Amelioration of the Condition of Wounded, Sick and Shipwrecked Members of Armed Forces at Sea, 75 UNTS 85 (1949), Art. 47; Geneva Convention III Relative to the Treatment of Prisoners of War, 75 UNTS 135 (1949), Art. 13, para. 3; Geneva Convention IV Relative to the Protection of Civilian Persons in Time of War, 75 UNTS 287 (1949), Art. 33, para. 3. See also Convention for the Protectionof Cultural Property in the Event of Armed Conflict, 249 UNTS 240 (1954), Art. 4, para. 4.
84 Protocol Additional to the Geneva Conventions of 12 August 1949, and Relating to the Protection of Victims of International Armed Conflicts (Protocol I), 1125 UNTS 3 (1977), Art. 20, Art. 51, para. 6, Art. 52, para. 1, Art. 53, para. c, Art. 54, para. 4, Art. 55, para. 2, Art. 56, paras 1 and 4.
85 See S. Darcy, *Collective Responsibility and Accountability under International Law*, Ardsley, New York: Transnational Publishers, 2006, pp. 152–4.

86 J. M. Henckaerts and L. Doswald-Beck, *Customary International Humanitarian Law, Volume I – Rules*, Cambridge: Cambridge University Press, 2007, pp. 519–26; Darcy, *Collective Responsibility and Accountability*, pp. 154–6.
87 See Darcy, *Collective Responsibility and Accountability*, pp. 166–75.
88 *In re Kappler*, Italy, Military Tribunal of Rome, 20 July 1948, Case No. 151, 15 *Annual Digest and Reports of Public International Law Cases* (1948) 471, pp. 472–6.
89 See, respectively, Martić (IT-95-11-R61), Decision, 8 March 1996, 39, p. 47; Kupreškić *et al.* (IT-95-16-T), 14 January 2000, paras 527–35. The Martić Trial Chamber seems to have softened its approach in its final judgment, see Martić (IT-95-11-T), 12 June 2007, paras 464–8.
90 M. Bothe, 'War Crimes' in Cassese, Gaeta and Jones (eds), *The Rome Statute of the International Criminal Court*, 379, p. 387; Cassese, 'Justifications and Excuses in International Criminal Law', pp. 951–2; E. van Sliedregt, *The Criminal Responsibility of Individuals for Violations of International Humanitarian Law*, The Hague: T. M. C. Asser Press, 2003, pp. 291–4.
91 *Report of the Preparatory Committee on the Establishment of an International Criminal Court*, G.A. O.R. 51st session, Supp. no. 22, UN Doc. A/51/22, Vol. I, (1996), para. 209; *Report of the Preparatory Committee on the Establishment of an International Criminal Court*, UN Doc. A/51/22, Vol. II, (1996), p. 103.
92 Rome Statute, Art. 21, para. (b).
93 T. J. Lawrence, *The Principles of International Law*, 6th edn, Boston/New York/Chicago: D.C Heath & Co., 1917, p. 334.
94 Charter of the International Military Tribunal at Nuremberg (1945), Art. 6.
95 United Nations General Assembly Resolution 3314 (XXIX), 14 December 1974, Art. 5(2).
96 Draft Code of Crimes against the Peace and Security of Mankind, *Report of the Commission on the work of its forty-eighth session* (1996), Volume II, Part 2, *Yearbook of the International Law Commission*, UN Doc. A/CN.4/SER.A/1996/Add.1 (Part 2), Art. 16.
97 *Report of the Special Working Group on the Crime of Aggression*, ICC-ASP-6/20/Add.1/Annex 2, 6 June 2008, p. 12.
98 Dinstein, *War, Aggression and Self-Defence*, p. 126.
99 'Declaration on Principles of International Law Concerning Friendly Relations and Co-operation Among States in Accordance with the Charter of the United Nations', UNGA Res. 2625 (1970). See, however, Dinstein, *War, Aggression and Self-Defence*, pp. 221–31; M. Shaw, *International Law*, 6th edn, Cambridge: Cambridge University Press, 2008, pp. 1129–30.
100 F. Hampson, 'Military Necessity', in R. Gutman and D. Rieff (eds), *Crimes of War: What the Public Should Know*, New York/London: W.W. Norton & Company, 1999, p. 251.
101 Rome Statute, Art. 8(2)(a)(iv). See Kordić and Čerkez (IT-95-14/2-T), 26 February 2001, paras 329–347.
102 Rome Statute, Art. 8(2)(e)(xiii).
103 Hampson, 'Military Necessity', p. 251.
104 *United States of America* v. *Wilhelm List et al.*, p. 1256.
105 Blaškić (IT-95-14-T), 3 March 2000, para. 180.
106 Blaškić (IT-95-14-A), Appeals Chamber, 29 July 2004, para. 109. See also Galic (IT-98-29-T), 5 December 2003, para. 44.
107 Schabas, *The UN International Criminal Tribunals*, p. 347.
108 Zahar and Sluiter, *International Criminal Law*, p. 430.
109 Krstić (IT-98-33-T), 2 August 2001, para. 527.

16

Participation in crimes in the jurisprudence of the ICTY and ICTR

Mohamed Elewa Badar

Introduction

The Statutes of the International Criminal Tribunal for the former Yugoslavia[1] (ICTY) and the International Criminal Tribunal for Rwanda[2] (ICTR) explicitly provide that these Tribunals are concerned with natural persons only.[3] Legal entities such as associations or organizations cannot be declared criminal as such, thereby excluding membership in such entities as a legal basis for criminal responsibility.[4] Articles 7(1)(3) and 6(1)(3) of the ICTY and ICTR Statutes, respectively, are the general provisions governing whether and through what mode of liability an accused may be held responsible for a crime within the jurisdiction of these Tribunals. The full text of these provisions reads as follows:

> Individual Criminal Responsibility
>
> 1 A person who planned, instigated, ordered, committed or otherwise aided and abetted in the planning, preparation or execution of a crime referred to in Articles 2 to 5 of the present [ICTY] Statute [and Articles 2 to 4 of the ICTR Statute] shall be individually responsible for the crime . . . .
>
> 2 The fact that any of the acts referred to in Articles 2 to 5 of the present Statute [and Articles 2 to 4 of the ICTR Statute] was committed by a subordinate does not relieve his or her superior of criminal responsibility if he or she knew or had reason to know that the subordinate was about to commit such acts or had done so and the superior failed to take the necessary and reasonable measures to prevent such acts or to punish the perpetrator thereof. [5]

The principle underlying the aforementioned provisions is that an individual is responsible for his or her acts and omissions.[6] That is to say, an individual may be held criminally responsible for the direct commission of a crime, whether as an individual or jointly,[7] or through his or her omissions with regard to the crimes of subordinates when under obligation to act.[8] This chapter uses a systematic analysis of the Tribunals' case law to examine the subjective and objective elements of different modes of perpetration and participation in criminal conduct.

Responsibility under Articles 7(1) and 6(1) of the ICTY and ICTR Statutes

Planning

Actus reus

The notion of planning implies that one or several persons plan or design the commission of a crime within the jurisdiction of the Tribunals at both the preparatory and the execution phases.[9] The crime planned must be completed in order to trigger the criminal responsibility of the planner.[10] The level of participation in planning to commit a crime must be substantial, such as actually formulating a plan or endorsing a plan proposed by another individual.[11] It is sufficient to demonstrate that the planning substantially contributed to the criminal conduct.[12] The crime, however, need not be executed by the planners, nor is their intervention in the commission of the offence required in any other way. However, in situations which the planner is found to have committed the crime, he or she will not be found responsible for planning the same crime.[13] In other words, responsibility as the planner of a crime is subsumed within responsibility for the same crime as a perpetrator.[14] As noted by William Schabas, '[t]here have been no convictions for the stand-alone crime of planning a crime within the jurisdiction of the [Yugoslavia and Rwanda] tribunals'.[15]

Mens rea

Criminal responsibility for planning requires that the accused directly or indirectly intended that the crime in question be committed.[16] Thus, if D planned the ethnic cleansing of a village by force, D could incur criminal responsibility for planning the wilful killings of any of the civilians who are killed during the execution of the plan. In *Limaj*, the ICTY ruled that '[a] person who plans an act or omission with an intent that a crime will be committed in the execution of that plan, has the requisite *mens rea* for establishing responsibility under Article 7(1) of the Statute for planning'.[17] The Trial Chamber gave no further clarification with regard to the degree of intent required in order to trigger the criminal responsibility of planning under Article 7(1) of the ICTY Statute. In *Nahimana et al.* and *Dragomir Milošević*, the Appeals Chambers of the ICTR and ICTY, respectively, extended the *mens rea* requisite for this mode of liability to reach the one of *dolus eventualis*: 'the intent to plan the commission of a crime or, at a minimum, the awareness of the substantial likelihood that a crime will be committed in the execution of the acts or omissions planned'.[18]

For an individual to be criminally liable for planning a crime, it is not necessary to prove that any of the persons executing the plan had the requisite *mens rea* for the offence committed. Suppose high-level political and military leaders, from a distant location, plan the widespread destruction of civilian hospitals and schools in a particular area in order to demoralize the enemy, without the soldiers responsible for carrying out the attacks sharing the objective in question, or even knowing the nature of the relevant targets. In this hypothetical example, the high-level political and military leaders should bear the criminal responsibility for planning, even though none of their troops are criminally liable with respect of execution of the plan.

Instigating

Actus reus

According to the Yugoslavia and Rwanda Tribunals, instigating entails prompting another to commit an offence.[19] Instigation encompasses incitement, but it is much broader than incitement.

In particular, there is no requirement that instigation be direct and public.[20] In contrast to ordering as a form of participation under Articles 7(1) and 6(1) of the ICTY and ICTR Statutes, instigation does not necessarily presuppose a hierarchical relationship.[21] Instigation can be expressed or implied and can also occur by omission rather than by a positive act.[22] It is not necessary that the original idea or plan to commit the crime be created by the instigator. The *Orić* Trial Chamber stated,

> [e]ven if the principal perpetrator was already pondering on committing a crime, the final determination to do so can still be brought about by persuasion or strong encouragement of the instigator. However, if the principal perpetrator is an '*omnimodo facturus*' meaning that he has definitely decided to commit the crime, further encouragement or moral support may merely, though still, qualify as aiding and abetting.[23]

Instigation influence can be generated both face to face and by intermediaries. It can also be excreted over either a small or a large audience provided that the instigator has the corresponding *mens rea*.[24] The '*actus reus* is satisfied if it is shown that the conduct of the accused [instigator] was a factor substantially contributing to the perpetrator's conduct.'[25] The *Gacumbitsi* Trial Chamber found that the accused incited the killing of Tutsi in Rusumo commune based on the following evidence: the accused, at various locations, publicly instigated the population to kill the Tutsi; and the accused made speeches at the Rwanteru commercial centre, where shortly after his instigation, those who listened to his speeches participated in looting property belonging to the Tutsi and killing the Tutsi.[26]

One issue is left unresolved under the jurisprudence of the Yugoslavia and Rwanda Tribunals. For situations in which the *actus reus* of an offence was carried out by several perpetrators, it is questionable whether it must be demonstrated that the instigator have provoked the conduct of all the perpetrators. One might suggest that it is sufficient that the accused instigated the conduct of any one of the perpetrators. A chain of instigation would then be punishable under Articles 7(1) and 6(1) of the ICTY and ICTR Statutes.

Mens rea

With regard to the *mens rea* of instigating, the ICTY has consistently held that it is necessary to prove that the instigator either '(a) intended to provoke or induce the commission of the crime [direct intent], or (b) was aware of the substantial likelihood that the commission of a crime would be a *probable* consequence of his acts'.[27] This runs contrary to the Trial Chamber's ruling in the *Kordić* case. In this case, the Trial Chamber required proof of the accused's direct intent 'to provoke the commission of the crime'.[28]

Ordering

Actus reus

The *actus reus* of ordering 'requires that a person in a position of authority instructs another person to commit an offence'.[29] There is no requirement that a person giving orders be a sole decision-maker or be the highest or only person in a chain of command. It is possible that a commander who is himself acting on the orders of a hierarchical superior, or who is acting in concert with, or at the command of, other political or military leaders, may nevertheless be criminally responsible for ordering crimes.[30] With regard to the existence of a formal superior–subordinate relationship between the person giving the order and the one executing it, the two *ad hoc* Tribunals have ruled differently.[31]

It is sufficient that the orderer possesses the authority, either *de jure* or *de facto*, to order the commission of an offence or that his authority can be reasonably implied.[32] However, in the absence of such a relationship, the prosecution has to demonstrate that the accused's words of incitement were perceived as orders within the meaning of Articles 7(1) and 6(1) of the ICTY and ICTR Statutes.[33]

There is no requirement regarding the form in which the order must be given;[34] its existence 'may be proven through direct or circumstantial evidence'.[35] A causal link between the act of ordering and the physical perpetration of the crime at issue is an ingredient of the *actus reus* of ordering.[36] This causal link, however, 'need not be such as to show that the offence would not have been perpetrated in the absence of the order'.[37]

Mens rea

The authoritative judgment concerning the *mens rea* of ordering was delivered by the ICTY Appeals Chamber in the *Blaškić* case.[38] In examining the issue of whether a standard of *mens rea* lower than direct intent may apply in relation to ordering under Article 7(1) of the Statute, the Appeals Chamber reversed the Trial Chamber's articulations of the *mens rea* required for ordering:

> The knowledge of any kind of risk, however low, does not suffice for the imposition of criminal responsibility for serious violations of international humanitarian law. The Trial Chamber does not specify what degree of risk must be proven. Indeed, it appears that under the Trial Chamber's standard, any military commander who issues an order would be criminally responsible, because there is always a possibility that violations could occur. The Appeals Chamber considers that an awareness of a higher likelihood of risk and a *volitional* element must be incorporated in the legal standard.[39]

The Appeals Chamber concluded as follows:

> A person who orders an act or omission with the awareness of the substantial likelihood that a crime will be committed in the execution of that order, has the requisite *men rea* for establishing liability under Article 7(1) pursuant to ordering. Ordering with such awareness has to be regarded as accepting that crime.[40]

Giving orders to a particular unit with the awareness of the existence of criminals in its rank amounts to accepting the risk that violent crime may result from their participation in the offensives.[41] It is unnecessary to establish that those who execute the order possess the same mental state as the one who has issued it. If a commander gives an order to attack a specific position that he knows with certainty is not a military target and civilians are taking refuge there, he could be held criminally liable pursuant to Articles 7(1) and 6(1) of the ICTY and ICTR Statutes for having ordered the wilful killing of civilians, even if those who executed the order lacked the knowledge that they were shelling civilians. In a situation in which none of the subordinates had the relevant *mens rea* and were merely executing apparently legitimate orders, it may be that the commander could be regarded as having committed wilful killing as an indirect perpetrator (*mittelbarer Täter*), using his subordinates as instruments. Addressing this point, the Blaškić Trial Judgment ruled that 'what is important is the commander's *mens rea*, not that of the subordinate executing the order'.[42] Evidence that a crime has been committed by members of a unit and that its commander was present at the scene 'may be perceived as a significant *indicium* of his or her encouragement or support', but it does not constitute *prima facie* evidence of the responsibility of the commander.[43]

Aiding and abetting

Actus reus

Aiding and abetting is a form of accessorial liability or secondary participation in the commission of a crime.[44] It applies to situations in which the *actus reus* of the crime is carried out by a person or persons other than the principal perpetrator. If the offender performes the *actus reus* of the offence, then the offender is no longer liable as an aider or abettor, but rather as a perpetrator or co-perpetrator of the crime at issue. One might discern that when the accused is responsible for aiding or abetting, and for other forms of liability under Articles 7(1) and 6(1) of the ICTY and ICTR Statutes, the *lex specialis* principle may lead to the conclusion that ordering or instigating the commission of a crime prevails over responsibility for aiding and abetting.

Although the case law of the ICTY conflates aiding and abetting into a broad, singular legal concept,[45] ICTR case law views the two terms as distinct legal concepts.[46] Aiding is the provision of assistance to another in the commission of a crime, whereas abetting is the facilitation of, or the provision of advice in relation to, the commission of an act.[47] The *actus reus* for aiding and abetting is that the accused carried out an act that consisted of practical assistance, encouragement, or moral support to the principal offender of the crime.[48] The crime that the accused is said to have aided or abetted must actually have been committed.[49] Mere presence at the scene of the crime without taking action to prevent the occurrence of a crime does not *per se* constitute aiding and abetting.[50] However, in cases of an 'approving spectator', or if the presence of a superior can be a significant *indicium* of encouragement or moral support, mere presence at the scene of a crime that is about to be committed can trigger criminal responsibility for aiding and abetting.[51]

A causal link between the act of assistance and the conduct of the principal offender need not be such as to show that the offence would not have been committed in the absence of such assistance, 'but it must have had a substantial effect on the commission of the crime by the principal offender'.[52] The assistance may consist of an act or an omission, and it may occur before, during, or after the act of the actual perpetrator.[53] No prior agreement is required except in *ex post facto* aiding and abetting.[54] *Ex post facto* aiding and abetting requires 'that at the time of the planning, preparation or execution of the crime, a prior agreement exists between the principal and the person who subsequently aids and abets in the commission of the crime'.[55]

Mens rea

The *Orić* Trial Chamber noted that while it is undisputed that aiding and abetting requires a subjective element to be proved on the part of the accused, the structure and contents of this mental element are described by the two *ad hoc* Tribunals in different ways.[56] Several judgments of the Yugoslavia and Rwanda Tribunals identify intent from the knowledge or awareness of the aider and abettor that his conduct assisted or facilitated the commission of a crime by the principal offender,[57] whereas other judgments require that the aider or abettor be aware of the essential elements of the crime committed by the principal offender, including the principal offender's state of mind.[58] Recent judgments demand some sort of volitional element—acceptance of the final result—in addition to the knowledge requirement.[59] Bearing in mind the evolving law of *mens rea* in the jurisprudence of the *ad hoc* Tribunals, the *Orić* Trial Chamber ruled as follows:

> (i) aiding and abetting must be intentional; (ii) the aider and abettor must have 'double intent', namely both with regard to the furthering effect of his own contribution and the intentional completion of the crime by the principal perpetrator; (iii) the intention must

> contain a cognitive element of knowledge and volitional element of acceptance, whereby the aider and abettor may be considered as accepting the criminal result of his conduct if he is aware that in consequence of his contribution, the commission of the crime is more likely than not; and (iv) with regard to the contents of his knowledge, the aider and abettor must at the least be aware of the type and the essential elements of the crime(s) to be committed.[60]

The above Orić test indicates that the mental state of the aider and abettor has to encompass the two components of intent, namely the cognitive and the volitional components. However, the aider and abettor need not share the intent of the principal offender, nor is it necessary that he or she be aware of the specific crime that will be committed by the perpetrator.[61] If the aider and abettor is aware that one of a number of crimes will probably be committed by the perpetrator, and one of those crimes is in fact committed, then he or she has intended to assist or facilitate the commission of that crime and is guilty as an aider and abettor.[62]

It has been said that the nature of *mens rea* required for this mode of secondary participation may differ somewhat depending upon whether the participation involves aiding or whether it involves abetting. As stated by William Schabas,

> [i]n the case of aiding, the accomplice will often be responsible for a neutral or ambiguous act – for example, procuring insecticide, which might be used to exterminate pests in a labour camp, but which might also be used for gas chambers in an extermination camp [as in *Zyklon B* case]. In such cases the Prosecutor will have difficulty convincing judges that the accomplice intended the consequences of his or her acts, because two or more hypotheses may exist.[63]

Committing – direct perpetration

The jurisprudence of the two *ad hoc* Tribunals is consistent in holding that committing 'covers physically perpetrating a crime or engendering a culpable omission in violation of criminal law'.[64] In this sense, there can be several principal offenders in relation to the same offense when the conduct of each offender satisfies the requisite elements of the substantive offence.[65] This is the most straightforward form of perpetrating an offence within the subject-matter jurisdiction of the two *ad hoc* Tribunals, and the plain meaning of the word 'committed' under Articles 7(1) and 6(1), respectively, of the Statutes of these Tribunals.

As will be discussed below, the word 'committed' was defined by the Appeals Chamber of both *ad hoc* Tribunals to encompass not only those perpetrators who physically perform the criminal conduct but also, in certain circumstances, those who contribute to the crime's commission in execution of a common criminal purpose or joint criminal enterprise.[66]

Actus reus

With regard to the *actus reus* required for committing, it must be established that 'the accused participated, physically or otherwise directly, in the material elements of a crime provided for in the Statute[s], through positive acts or omissions'.[67]

Mens rea

The *mens rea* for committing under Articles 7(1) and 6(1) of the ICTY and ICTR Statutes differs from the one required for other modes of participation (for example, instigating and aiding and abetting) in that the accused who physically performs the material elements of the offence must possess the full *mens rea* required for the crime, including any specific intent or grounds required by its definition. Thus, to incur criminal responsibility for committing a specific intent crime (for example, terror against the civilian population), 'the Prosecution is required to prove not only that the Accused accepted the likelihood that terror would result from the illegal acts – or, in other words, that he was aware of the possibility that terror would result – but that that was the result which he specifically intended'.[68] Thus, knowledge, *dolus eventualis* or advertent recklessness are not sufficient mental states to hold an accused criminally liable for committing specific intent crimes, although these mental states may be sufficient to trigger criminal responsibility for the same type of offences with respect to other modes of participation under Articles 7(1) and 6(1) of the ICTY and ICTR Statutes.

Committing through participation in a joint criminal enterprise

Although the Statutes of the two *ad hoc* Tribunals do not make explicit reference to the notion of joint criminal enterprise (JCE), the Appeals Chambers of these Tribunals have held that participating in a JCE is a form of liability that exists in customary international law and is a form of commission under Articles 7(1) and 6(1) of the Statutes.[69] Discussing the concept of joint criminal enterprise, the Tadić Appeals Chamber stressed the importance of expanding the concept of primary participation, as opposed to secondary participation, beyond those who physically carry out the criminal conduct:

> Although only some members of the group may physically perpetrate the criminal act … the participation and contribution of the other members of the group is often vital in facilitating the commission of the offence in question. It follows that the moral gravity of such participation is often no less – or indeed different – from that of those who actually carry out the acts in question.[70]

Evidentially, JCE as a mode of criminal liability has become the prosecution's 'darling notion',[71] though legal commentators doubt its validity.[72]

General requirements for joint criminal enterprise liability

It is settled in the jurisprudence of the two *ad hoc* Tribunals that the word 'committed', as provided for in Articles 7(1) and 6(1) of the ICTY and ICTR Statutes, includes three forms of joint criminal enterprise: namely, the basic, the systemic, and the extended forms.[73] The required *actus reus* for each of these forms comprises three elements: (1) a plurality of persons; (2) the existence of a common purpose that amounts to or involves the commission of a crime provided for in the Statutes;[74] and (3) the participation of the accused in the common purpose.

This mode of liability need not involve the physical commission of a specific crime by all the members of JCE but may take the form of assistance in, or contribution to, the execution of the common purpose.[75] Thus, 'once a participant in a joint criminal enterprise shares the intent of that enterprise, his participation may take the form of assistance or contribution with a view to carry out the common plan or purpose'.[76] While a Trial Chamber must identify the plurality of persons belonging to the JCE, it is not necessary to identify each of the persons involved by name. Rather, it is sufficient to refer to categories or groups of persons.[77] The 'common objective need not have been previously arranged or formulated, and . . . . it may materialise extemporaneously and be inferred from the fact that a plurality of persons acts in unison to put into effect a joint criminal enterprise'.[78] The same applies to the expansions of criminal means.[79] A Trial Chamber need not to decide whether there was 'a consensus or shared understanding amounting to a psychological causal nexus' between the accused and other members of the JCE.[80]

The basic form of JCE (JCE I)

The first form of JCE arises when all co-perpetrators, acting pursuant to a common purpose, possess the same criminal intent.[81] An example is a plan formulated by the co-defendants in the JCE to commit the act of murder; although each of the co-defendants may carry out a different role, they all have the intent to murder.[82] This basic form of JCE encompasses two different types of participation in a crime within the *ratione materiae* jurisdiction of the two *ad hoc* Tribunals. The first scenario, direct perpetration, appears when the conduct of each of the co-defendants satisfies the *actus reus* of the crime at issue. The second scenario appears when a participant in a JCE does not carry out, or cannot be proven to have carried out, the *actus reus* at issue. In this situation, the following objective and subjective prerequisites have to be established in order to hold the accused criminally responsible as a co-perpetrator in the JCE:

> (i) the accused must voluntarily participate in one aspect of the common design (for instance, by inflicting non-fatal violence upon the victim, or by providing material assistance to or facilitating the activities of his co-perpetrators; (ii) the accused, even if not personally effecting the killing, must nevertheless intend this result.[83]

It has been argued whether a member of the JCE can incur criminal responsibility for the acts of persons who were not members of the JCE and who potentially did not even know of the existence or purpose of the JCE.[84] Recent case law of the ICTY has answered this in the affirmative, provided that 'it has been established that the crimes can be imputed to at least one member of the JCE and that this member—when using the principal perpetrators—acted in accordance with the common objective'.[85]

The argument that a co-perpetrator in a JCE must physically commit part of the *actus reus* of a crime in order to be criminally liable was rejected by the *Kvočka* Appeals Chamber, which stated that, on the grounds that 'a participant in a joint criminal enterprise need not physically participate in any element of any crime, so long as the requirements of joint criminal enterprise responsibility are met'.[86]

Mens rea

The *mens rea* required for the basic form of JCE is the intent to take part in a criminal enterprise and to further—individually and jointly—the criminal purpose of that enterprise. It must be established that the accused voluntarily participated in one aspect of the common design while being aware of the criminal character of the enterprise. The accused need not have knowledge of every criminal incident committed in furtherance of the enterprise. In the words of *Tadić* Appeals Chamber, 'what is required is the intent to perpetrate a certain crime (this being the shared intent on the part of all co-perpetrators).'[87]

In this category of JCE, all co-perpetrators must possess the *mens rea* required for the crime at issue. For instance, when the crime committed is extermination, it must be established that all the co-perpetrators, even those not physically perpetrating the killing, had the conscious objective of killing persons on a massive scale, inflicting serious bodily injury or creating conditions of life that lead to the death of a large number of persons. In the alternative, it must be shown that the co-perpetrators proceeded in the knowledge that mass extermination would be the probable outcome and reconciled themselves to this and made peace with this fact.

The systemic form of JCE (JCE II)

The systemic form of JCE is based on the post–World War II concentration camp cases, in which the notion of common purpose was applied to situations in which the offences charged were alleged to have been committed by members of military or administrative units, such as those running concentration camps—groups acting pursuant to a concerted plan.[88] This mode of liability can be attached to those responsible for carrying out a task within a criminal design that is implemented in an institutional framework, such as an internment or concentration camp.[89]

Actus reus

The *actus reus* of the systemic form of JCE entails the same objective elements as the first category. The participation in this form of JCE need not involve the commission of a particular crime within the subject-matter jurisdiction of the Tribunals but may take the form of assistance in, or contribution to, the execution of the common purpose.[90]

Given the fact that the general rule governing JCE liability does not require proof of substantial contribution to the enterprise,[91] it was argued that 'opportunistic visitors' who enter a camp occasionally and mistreat its detainees could be held responsible as participants in the enterprise.[92] Addressing this point, the *Kvočka* Appeals Chamber asserted that in the case of 'opportunistic visitors', a substantial contribution to the overall effect of the Omarska detention camp would be necessary to establish responsibility under the JCE doctrine.[93]

Mens rea

There is consensus within the jurisprudence of the ICTY that the mental state required for the systemic form of JCE is the participant's personal knowledge of the nature of the system in question and the intent to further the concerted system of ill treatment.[94] Similar to the basic form, the participants in the systemic form of JCE must be shown to share the required intent of the principal perpetrators.[95] The *Krnojelac* Appeals Chamber distinguished between three different scenarios with respect to crimes committed in the 'KP Dom': (1) crimes within the system's common purpose, (2) crimes beyond the system's common purpose, and (3) crimes that implicated several co-perpetrators but could not be recognized as constituting a purpose common to all the participants in the system.[96]

As for the *mens rea* required by a participant in a system in which a 'common denominator' exists among all the participants in that system, it is sufficient to prove that the accused participating in the system was aware that particular crimes were being committed by another participant and that the accused intended to further the system in place.[97] The *Krnojelac* Appeals Chamber held that in such scenarios, all the participants in the system should be considered as coming under a first-category JCE without reference to the concept of system.[98]

The extended form of JCE (JCE III)

The third form of joint criminal enterprise concerns those participants who share a common purpose – for instance, to forcibly transfer civilians from an occupied territory – but do not share the intent to commit a criminal act that falls beyond the common purpose—for instance, murdering one or more members of the transferred group. Under this category of JCE, participants who did not intend to commit murder would still be held criminally responsible upon proof that they were nevertheless in a position to foresee the commission of murder and willingly took the risk. According to the *Stakić* Appeals Judgment, for the application of third-category JCE liability, the following elements must be satisfied:

> (a) crimes outside the Common Purpose have occurred; (b) these crimes were a natural and foreseeable consequence of effecting the Common Purpose; and (c) the participant in the joint criminal enterprise was aware that the crimes were a possible consequence of the execution of the Common Purpose, and in that awareness, he nevertheless acted in furtherance of the Common Purpose.[99]

The distinctive feature of the extended form of JCE is the 'fault element', which, subject to certain conditions, permits criminal liability to be extended to crimes other than those initially agreed upon in the plan or design. This third category of JCE requires not only that an individual, by his or her controlled acts, has taken unlawful risks in violation of international humanitarian law but also that he or she has assumed the risk of criminal results arising from the common criminal design, regardless of who commits those crimes.

One serious problem that confronted the two *ad hoc* Tribunals is the applicability of the extended form of JCE to specific intent crimes: notably, genocide. It is questionable whether individuals should be convicted of such high-profile and morally culpable crimes on the basis of mere foresight. Addressing this point, the *Stakić* Trial Chamber spelled out its concerns in the following words:

> [T]he application of a mode of liability can not replace a core element of a crime. The Prosecution confuses modes of liability and the crimes themselves. Conflating the third variant of joint criminal enterprise and the crime of genocide would result in the *dolus specialis* being so watered down that it is extinguished.[100]

In addition, those crimes that require specific intent are generally regarded as the most serious, and an attempt to undermine the mental element—charging individuals for specific intent crimes under the extended form of JCE—devalues the seriousness of these crimes. These concerns were spelled out by the *Brđanin* Trial Chamber. It held that the specific intent required for a conviction of genocide cannot be reconciled with the *mens rea* standard for an extended form of joint criminal enterprise.[101] The Trial Chamber concluded that the accused's awareness of the risk that genocide would be committed by other members of the joint criminal enterprise was incompatible with and fell short of the threshold needed to satisfy the specific intent required for a genocide conviction.[102] Notably, the *Brđanin* Trial Chamber's finding was reversed by the Appeals Chamber Decision on Interlocutory Appeal.[103]

A major source of concern with regard to the applicability of the extended form of JCE in the sphere of international criminal law is that under both the objective and subjective standards, the participant is unfairly held liable for criminal conduct that they did not intend and in which they did not participate. It is also unjust that the liability of the actual perpetrator, who carried out the crime outside the common plan, is tested subjectively, whereas the liability of the participant is tested objectively. Moreover, if the accused had actually participated in crimes outside the initial 'common purpose' as an aider or abettor, he or she would arguably have an increased chance of acquittal, as the Prosecution would be confronted with having to prove a higher level of mental awareness: namely, that the accused knew that the principal perpetrator had the state of mind required for the crime at issue.[104] This author is of the opinion that if, one day, the

Prosecution succeeds in securing a conviction for one of the 'specific purpose crimes' under the third category of joint criminal enterprise, this will alter the JCE doctrine to become a device used to 'just convict everyone'.[105]

Co-perpetration as a form of 'committing'

In examining the criminal responsibility of Dr Milomir Stakić for the crimes alleged, a Trial Chamber of the ICTY applied a mode of liability that it termed 'co-perpetratorship', committing 'jointly with another person, in lieu of JCE'.[106] In the words of the *Stakić* Trial Chamber, the main features of co-perpetration are that the 'co-perpetrators must pursue a common goal, either through an explicit agreement or silent consent, which they can only achieve by coordinated action and joint control over the criminal conduct. Each co-perpetrator must make a contribution essential to the commission of the crime'.[107] In order to meet the requirements of co-perpetratorship as a mode of liability, the Prosecution must prove beyond reasonable doubt that there was an explicit agreement or silent consent between two or more individuals to reach a common goal by coordinated cooperation with joint control over the criminal conduct.[108] Under the *Stakić* Judgment, this form of liability will occur when co-perpetrators can only realize their plan insofar as they act jointly, but each individual can ruin the whole plan if he does not carry out his part. To this extent, each of the co-perpetrators is considered to be in control of the criminal act.[109]

In addition to the *mens rea* required for the particular crime, this mode of liability, co-perpetratorship, requires proof of (1) mutual awareness of substantial likelihood that crimes would occur and (2) the defendant's awareness of the importance of his or her own role.[110]

Despite the fact that the *Stakić* Trial Judgment limited itself to the clear wording of the Statute when interpreting 'committing' in the form of 'co-perpetration' in lieu of JCE, the *Stakić* Appeals Chamber's recent judgment marked the death of this mode of liability in the jurisprudence of the ICTY.[111]

Responsibility under Articles 7(3) and 6(3) of the ICTY and ICTR Statutes

The principle of individual criminal responsibility of commanders for failure to prevent or punish crimes committed by their subordinates is not alien to international criminal law. It is a well-established rule of customary international law applicable to both international and internal armed conflicts.[112] Articles 7(3) and 6(3) of the ICTY and ICTR Statutes, in contrast to Articles 7(1) and 6(1), create a form of indirect liability 'predicated upon the power of the superior to control the acts of his subordinates'.[113] A recent judgment expressly stated that command responsibility as provided for in Article 7(3) of the ICTY Statute is responsibility for an omission.[114]

General requirements under Articles 7(3) and 6(3) of the ICTY and ICTR Statutes

For a superior, military or civilian,[115] to be found criminally responsible under Articles 7(3) and 6(3) of the Statutes, the following elements have to be established beyond reasonable doubt:

> (i) an act or omission incurring criminal responsibility within the subject matter jurisdiction of the Tribunals has been committed by other(s) than the accused ('principal crime'); (ii) there existed a superior-subordinate-relationship between the accused and the principal perpetrator(s) ('superior-subordinate-relationship'); (iii) the accused as a superior knew or had reason to know that the subordinate was about to commit such crimes or had done so

('knew or had reason to know'); and (iv) the accused as a superior failed to take the necessary and reasonable measures to prevent such crimes or punish the perpetrator(s) thereof ('failure to prevent or punish').[116]

A crime was committed

The first element requires that a perpetrator or group of perpetrators other than the accused has committed a crime within the subject-matter jurisdiction of the two *ad hoc* Tribunals. It has been argued that because Article 7(3) of the ICTY Statute merely refers to committing and does not expressly mention the other modes of liability set out in Article 7(1) of the Statute, a superior can incur criminal responsibility only if his subordinates committed the crimes themselves and not if they merely aided and abetted the crimes of others.[117] Addressing this point, the *Orić* Judgment, as well as the *Boškoski* Decision, ruled that superior responsibility is not limited to crimes committed physically by the subordinates as principal perpetrators, as this form of liability also encompasses situations in which the subordinates merely aided and abetted the crimes of others as accessories or secondary participants.[118]

A superior's criminal responsibility is not limited to situations of a subordinate's active perpetration or participation, but also comprises the commission of crime by omission.[119] The following hypothetical example given by the *Orić* Trial Chamber is illustrative:

> if for instance the maltreatment of prisoners by guards, and/or by outsiders not prevented from entering the location, is made possible because subordinates in charge of the prison fail to ensure the security of the detainees by adequate measures, it does not matter any further by whom else, due to the subordinates' neglect of protection, the protected persons are being injured, nor would it be necessary to establish the identity of the direct perpetrators.[120]

The ICTY emphasized that in any mode of criminal participation, 'omission can incur responsibility only if there was a duty to act in terms of preventing the prohibited result from occurring.'[121]

Superior authority over the subordinates

The requirement of a superior–subordinate relationship, which 'lies in the very heart of a commander's liability for crimes committed by his subordinates',[122] is best encapsulated by the *Ntagerura* Trial Chamber:

> (i) a superior–subordinate relationship is established by showing a formal or informal hierarchical relationship; (ii) the superior must have possessed the power or the authority, *de jure* or *de facto*, to prevent or punish an offence committed by his subordinates; (iii) the superior must have had effective control over the subordinates at the time the offence was committed.[123]

Effective control—material ability

The concept of effective control, which is the decisive criterion for establishing the superior–subordinate link, is defined by the *Čelebići* Appeals Chamber as connoting the commander's material ability to prevent and punish criminal conduct.[124] Effective control is more a matter of evidence than of law, and 'those indicators [of effective control] are limited to showing that the accused had the power to prevent, punish or initiate measures leading to proceedings against the alleged perpetrators where appropriate.'[125] Thus, the effective control requirement is not satisfied by a showing of mere general influence on the part of the accused.[126]

De jure and/or de facto

The jurisprudence of the ICTY and the ICTR confirms that formal designation as a commander or a superior is not a prerequisite for superior responsibility and that such responsibility may be imposed by virtue of a person's *de facto*, as well as *de jure*, position of authority or powers of control.[127] In the words of the *Orić* Trial Chamber, 'regardless of which chain of command or position of authority the superior-subordinate relationship may be based on it is immaterial whether the subordination of the perpetrator to the accused as superior is direct or indirect, and formal or factual'.[128]

Mens rea—*'knew or had reason to know'*

It has been repeatedly cautioned, at least as it is understood and applied within the framework of the Yugoslavia and the Rwanda Tribunals, that command responsibility is not a mode of strict liability.[129] A commander, whether military or civilian, will be found to possess the requisite *mens rea* sufficient to hold him responsible under Articles 7(3) and 6(3) of the ICTY and ICTR Statutes when the commander knew (actual knowledge) or had reason to know (imputed or constructive knowledge) that the subordinate was about to commit or had committed a crime.[130] It must be established either that the commander had actual knowledge that his or her subordinates were committing or about to commit crimes within the subject-matter jurisdictions of the Tribunals or that the commander had in his or her possession information that would at least put him or her on notice of the risk of such offences.[131] With regard to the latter form (imputed knowledge), one Trial Chamber of the Yugoslavia Tribunal noted that

> by permitting the attribution of criminal responsibility to a superior for what is in actual fact a lack of due diligence in supervising the conduct of his subordinates, Article 7(3) in this respect sets itself apart being satisfied with a *mens rea* falling short of the threshold requirement of intent under Article 7(1) of the Statute.[132]

Mens rea—actual knowledge

As a mode of liability, command responsibility requires the Prosecution to establish that a commander, whether military or civilian, 'knew' of the criminality of subordinates. Thus, this mode of liability does not require proof of intent in its strict sense on the part of the superior before criminal liability can attach.[133] The term 'knew', as provided for in Articles 7(3) and 6(3) of the Statutes, implies actual knowledge—the superior's awareness that the relevant crimes were committed or were about to be committed.[134] This is the highest standard of knowledge and the hardest to prove, as it requires evidence establishing beyond reasonable doubt that the commander actually knew of the crimes committed or about to be committed by his subordinates.[135] It is not required, on the one hand, to prove that the commander possesses any volitional element with regard to the crimes committed by his subordinates. On the other hand, under this formulation of 'actual knowledge', recklessness or negligence is not a sufficient fault element to trigger the criminal responsibility of a commander for the proscribed acts committed by his or her subordinates.[136]

It is worth stressing that in situations in which there is sufficient evidence to establish that superiors, in addition to possessing knowledge that crimes were committed or were about to be committed by their subordinates, have substantially contributed to the commission of these crimes, this may transform their responsibility to 'complicity' under Articles 7(1) and 6(1) of the ICTY and ICTR Statutes. As one Trial Chamber of the Yugoslavia Tribunal noted,

> [i]n cases where the evidence presented demonstrates that a superior would not only have been informed of subordinates' crimes committed under his authority, but also exercised his powers to plan, instigate or otherwise aid and abet in the planning, preparation or execution of these crimes, the type of criminal responsibility incurred may be better characterised by Article 7(1). Where the omissions of an accused in a position of superior authority contribute (for instance by encouraging the perpetrator) to the commission of a crime by a subordinate, the conduct of the superior may constitute a basis for liability under Article 7(1).[137]

The *Čelebići* Trial Chamber rightly emphasised that 'in the absence of direct evidence of the superior's knowledge of the offences committed by his subordinates, such knowledge cannot be presumed, but must be established by way of circumstantial evidence'.[138] Types of circumstantial evidence include

> the number, type and scope of illegal acts, time during which illegal acts occurred, number and types of troops and logistics involved, geographical location, whether the occurrence of the acts is widespread, tactical tempo of operations, *modus operandi* of similar illegal acts, officers and staff involved, and location of the commander at the time.[139]

Imputed knowledge – had reason to know

The standard of 'had reason to know', which constitutes the alternative type of knowledge as set out in Articles 7(3) and 6(3) of the ICTY and ICTR Statutes, is based on Articles 86 and 87 of Additional Protocol I to the 1949 Geneva Conventions. The 'had reason know' standard does not require proof of 'actual knowledge' on the part of the superior.[140] Thus, if the superior is in possession of sufficient information to put him or her on notice of the likelihood of illegal acts by his or her subordinates—if the information available is sufficient to justify further inquiry—he or she may be regarded as 'having reason to know'.[141]

Mere expectation that offences were about to be committed is not sufficient to imply that the superior 'had reason to know'.[142] According to the *Blaskić* Appeals Chamber, a superior can incur responsibility 'for *deliberately* refraining from finding out but not for negligently failing to find out.'[143]

Superiors' knowledge of the criminal reputation of their subordinates may be sufficient to meet the 'had reason to know' standard if it amounts to information that would put them on notice of the present and real risk of offences within the jurisdiction of the Tribunals.[144] The findings of the Israeli Commission of Inquiry responsible for investigating the massacre perpetrated in the Sabra and Shatilla refugee camps in Beirut in 1982 is illustrative.[145] In examining the responsibility of the Chief of Staff of the Israel Defence Forces, the Commission held that 'his knowledge of the feelings of hatred of the particular forces involved towards the Palestinians did not justify the conclusion that the entry of those forces into the camps posed no danger.'[146] The Commission went on to hold as follows:

> [t]he absence of a warning from experts cannot serve as an explanation for ignoring the danger of a massacre. The Chief of Staff *should have known and foreseen*—by virtue of *common knowledge*, as well as the special information at his disposal—that there was a possibility of harm to the population in the camps at the hands of the Phalangists. Even if the experts did not fulfil their obligation, this does not absolve the Chief of Staff of Responsibility.[147]

It should be noted that a superior cannot be found responsible for failing to acquire information in the first place.[148] In the words of the *Čelebići* Appeals Chamber

> [n]eglect of a duty to acquire such knowledge, however, does not feature in the provision [Article 7(3)] as a separate offence, and a superior is not therefore liable under the provision for such failures but only for failing to take necessary and reasonable measures to prevent or to punish.[149]

However, in situations in which the superior had the means to obtain the relevant information of a crime and deliberately refrained from doing so, he or she may be held responsible under the doctrine of command responsibility.[150]

Some Trial Chambers of the Yugoslavia and Rwanda Tribunals considered criminal negligence to be a sufficient fault element to hold a superior criminally responsible for crimes committed by his or her subordinates.[151] The Appeals Chamber, however, overturned these findings, assuring that 'criminal negligence' is not a basis of liability in the context of command responsibility[152] and that such references to negligence are 'likely to lead to confusion of thought'.[153] The Appeals Chamber, while rejecting criminal negligence as a sufficient fault element for superior responsibility, failed to identify which degree of knowledge is sufficient in cases in which the superior 'had reason to know'. Recent judgments rendered by the ICTY provide further clarification as to the nature of the definition of 'had reason to know':

> By contenting itself with having had 'reason to know' instead of requiring actual knowledge, superior criminal responsibility under Article 7(3) of the Statute obviously does not presuppose intent of the superior with regard to crimes of his subordinates, let alone a malicious one. What is required though, beyond solely negligent ignorance, is the superior's factual awareness of information which, due to his position, should have provided a reason to avail himself or herself of further knowledge. Without any such subjective requirement, the alternative basis of superior criminal responsibility by having had 'reason to know' would be diminished into a purely objective one and, thus, run the risk of transgressing the borderline to 'strict liability'. This is not the case, however, as soon as he or she has been put on notice by available information as described above.[154]

Failure to prevent or punish

To establish criminal responsibility under Articles 7(3) and 6(3) of the ICTY and ICTR Statutes, the Prosecution must demonstrate, in addition to the superior's actual or imputed knowledge of crimes that are about to be committed or have been committed by his or her subordinates, that he or she failed to take necessary and reasonable measures to prevent such acts or to punish the perpetrator thereof. Thus, as already stated by the ICTY Appeals Chamber, the neglect of a duty to acquire such knowledge does not feature within Article 7(3) of the Statute as a separate offence. Rather, it is merely an element within the superior criminal responsibility for failure to prevent or punish.

The superior's obligations to prevent and punish are consecutive and do not provide the accused with two alternative and equally satisfactory options.[155] Thus, 'where the accused knew or had reason to know that subordinates were about to commit crimes and failed to prevent them, he cannot make up for the failure to act by punishing the subordinates afterwards'.[156] Professor William Schabas once noted that 'the superior is being punished for failure to supervise rather than for the offence itself'.[157] He continued, 'to the extent that the superior can demonstrate that he or she actually fulfilled the duty to prevent such crimes, we are indeed in the presence of a strict liability offence, as this concept is generally understood in criminal law'.[158]

General remarks and observations

The systematic analysis of the jurisprudence of the Yugoslavia and Rwanda Tribunals reveals that the case law of these Tribunals does not state a consistent *mens rea* for accomplice liability. Sometimes the Tribunals require a *dolus directus* of the first degree on the part of the accomplice to bring about the crime; sometimes *dolus directus* of the second degree; sometimes knowledge; and sometimes they use a language that embraces recklessness.[159]

Recent judgments delivered by the Appeals and Trial Chambers have required proof of some sort of volitional element on the part of the accused in addition to the cognitive element of knowledge.[160] They also ruled out recklessness and gross negligence from being sufficient fault elements for accessorial liability. On this particular point, one might recall the Commentaries of the Model Penal Code:

> The culpability required to be shown of the principal actor, is normally higher than negligence .... To say that the accomplice is liable if the offence committed is 'reasonably foreseeable' or the 'probable consequence' of another crime is to make him liable for negligence, even though more is required in order to convict the principal actor. This is both incongruous and unjust; if anything, the culpability level for the accomplice should be higher than that of the principal actor, because there is generally more ambiguity in the overt conduct engaged in by the accomplice, and thus a higher risk of convicting the innocent.[161]

In light of these developments it is submitted that accomplice liability requires the existence of a mental element on the part of the accused. That is to say both a cognitive element of knowledge (awareness or contemplation) and a volitional element (acceptance of the result) must be incorporated into the legal standards.[162]

As for the third category of JCE, it is submitted that the 'reasonable foreseeable' test applied by the two *ad hoc* Tribunals is unfair. On that particular point, one might recall the strong dissenting judgment delivered by Justice Michael Kirby in the High Court of Australia in a murder case:

> To hold an accused liable for murder merely on the foresight of a possibility is fundamentally unjust. It may not be truly a fictitious or 'constructive liability'. But it countenances what is 'undoubtedly a lesser form of mens rea'. It is a form that is an exception to the normal requirements of criminal liability. And it introduces a serious disharmony in the law, particularly as that law affects the liability of secondary offenders to conviction for murder upon this basis.[163]

Thus, this author recommends the reform of the 'reasonably foreseeable' standard of the extended form of joint criminal enterprise through the adoption of a *dolus eventualis* standard, requiring that the accused have foreseen the commission of the crime that went beyond the common plan as not merely a possibility, but rather as a high probability, and that he or she accepted its occurrence and made peace with it.

Notes

1 Statute of the International Criminal Tribunal for the former Yugoslavia, UN Doc. S/RES/827 (1993).
2 Statute of the International Criminal Tribunal for Rwanda, UN Doc. S/RES/955 (1994).
3 See ICTY Statute, Art. 6; ICTR Statute Art. 5.
4 Report of the Secretary-General pursuant to para. 2 of the Security Council Resolution 808 (1993), S/25704, 3 May 1993, paras 50–51. Some legal scholars hold the opinion that corporate entities should be held criminally liable for violations of international criminal law. See, for instance, R. C. Slye, 'Corporations, Veils, and International Criminal Liability', *Brookline Journal of International Law* 33, 2008, 955–73; K. Magraw, 'Universally Liable? Corporate-Complicity Liability under the Principle of Universal Jurisdiction', *Minnesota Journal of International Law* 18, 2009, 458–97; J. Kyriakakis, 'Corporations and the International Criminal Court: The Complementarity Objection Stripped Bare', *Criminal Law Forum* 19, 2008 115–151; W. Schabas, 'Enforcing International Humanitarian Law: Catching the Accomplices', *International Review of the Red Cross* 83, 2001, 439–58; A. Clapham, 'The Question of Jurisdiction under International Criminal Law over Legal Persons: Lessons from the Rome Conference on an International Criminal Court', in M. T. Kamminga and S. Zia-Zarifi (eds), *Liability of Multinational Corporations under International Law*, Hague, Kluwer, 2000, pp. 139–95; A. Clapham, 'Extending International Criminal Law beyond the Individual to Corporations and Armed Opposition Groups', *Journal of International Criminal Justice* 6, 2008, 899–926.
5 See ICTY Statute Art. 7(1)(3); ICTR Statute Art. 6(1)(3).
6 Tadić (IT-94-1-A), Appeals Chamber, 15 July 1999, para. 186; Kordić & Čerkez (IT-95-14/2-T), 26 February 2001, para. 364.
7 Tadić (IT-94-1-A) Appeals Chamber, 15 July 1999, paras 220, 227–8; Furundžija (IT-95-17/1-T), 10 December 1998, para. 216; Kordić & Čerkez (IT-95-14/2-T), 26 February 2001, para. 364.
8 Tadić (IT-94-1-A), Appeals Chamber, 15 July 1999, para. 188; Delalić *et al.* (Čelebići Case) (IT-96-21-A), Appeals Chamber, 20 February 2001, paras 215-268; Kordić & Čerkez (IT-95-14/2-T), 26 February 2001, para. 364; Aleksovski (IT-95-14/1-T), 25 June 1999, paras. 69–81. See also Report of the Secretary-General pursuant to para. 2 of the Security Council Resolution 808 (1993), S/25704, 3 May 1993 (Secretary-General Report) paras 53–8.
9 Gacumbitsi (ICTR-2001-64-T), 17 June 2004, para. 271, citing Blaškić (IT-95-14-T), 3 March 2000, para. 386; Musema (ICTR-96-13-T), 27 January 2000, para. 119; Akayesu (ICTR-96-4-T), 2 September 1998, para. 480; Kajelijeli (ICTR-98-44A-T), 1 December 2003, para. 761; Kamuhanda (ICTR-95-54A-T), 22 January 2004, para. 592. For the ICTY, see Limaj (IT-03-66), 30 November 2005, para. 513; Brđanin (IT-99-36-T), 1 September 2004, para. 268; Krstić (IT-98-33-T), 2 August 2001, para. 601; Stakić (IT-97-24-T), 31 July 2003, para. 443; Milošević (IT-98-29/1-A), Appeals Chamber, 12 November 2009, para. 268; Kordić and Čerkez (IT-95-14/2-A), Appeals Chamber, 17 December 2004, para. 26.
10 Akayesu (ICTR-96-4), 2 September 1998, para. 473; Limaj (IT-03-66), 30 November 2005, para. 513; Kordić and Čerkez (IT-95-14/2-A), Appeals Chamber, 17 December 2004, para. 26. But see G. Mettraux, *International Crimes and the Ad hoc Tribunals*, Oxford: Oxford University Press, 2005, 279–80. For different opinion see W. Schabas, *The UN International Criminal Tribunals: The former Yugoslavia, Rwanda and Sierra Leone*, Cambridge: Cambridge University Press, 2006, p. 299.
11 Bagilishema (ICTR-95-1A-T), 7 June 2001, para. 30.
12 Milošević (IT-98-29/1-A), Appeals Chamber, 12 November 2009, para. 268.
13 Galić (IT-98-29-S), 30 March 2004, fn. 280.
14 Ibid.
15 Schabas, *The UN International Criminal Tribunals*, p. 299.
16 Blaškić (IT-95-14-T), 3 March 2000, para. 278; Kordić & Čerkez (IT-95-14/2-T), 26 February 2001, para. 386.
17 Limaj (IT-03-66), 30 November 2005, para. 513, citing with approval Kordić and Čerkez (IT-95-14/2-A), Appeals Chamber, 17 December 2004, para. 31.

18 Dragomir Milošević (IT-98-29/1-A), Appeals Judgment, 12 November 2009, para. 268.
19 Limaj (IT-03-66), 30 November 2005, para. 514; Brđanin (IT-99-36-T), 1 September 2004, para. 269; Kamuhanda (ICTR-95-54A-T), 22 January 2004, para. 593; Akayesu (ICTR-96-4), 2 September 1998, para. 482; Blaškić (IT-95-14-T), 3 March 2000, para. 280; Krstić (IT-98-33-T), 2 August 2001, para. 601; Kordić (IT-95-14/2-T), 26 February 2001, para. 387; Gacumbitsi (ICTR-2001-64-T), 17 June 2004, para. 279; Kajelijeli (ICTR-98-44A-T), 1 December 2003, para. 762; Bagilishema (ICTR-95-1A-T), 7 June 2001, para. 30.
20 Gacumbitsi (ICTR-2001-64-T), 17 June 2004, para. 279, citing Semanza (ICTR-97-20-T), 15 May 2003, para. 381; Bagilishema (ICTR-95-1A-T), 7 June 2001, para. 30; Akayesu (ICTR-96-4), Appeals Chamber, 1 June 2001, paras 478–82; Kajelijeli (ICTR-98-44A-T), 1 December 2003, para. 762.
21 A. Cassese, *International Criminal Law*, Oxford: Oxford University Press, 2003, p. 189.
22 Limaj (IT-03-66), 30 November 2005, para. 514; Brđanin (IT-99-36-T), 1 September 2004, para. 269, citing Blaškić (IT-95-14-T), 3 March 2000, para. 280; Kajelijeli (ICTR-98-44A-T), 1 December 2003, para. 762; Kamuhanda (ICTR-95-54A-T), 22 January 2004, para. 593.
23 Orić (IT-03-68-T), 30 June 2006, para. 271 (footnotes omitted).
24 Ibid., para. 273 (emphasis added, footnotes omitted).
25 Kordić and Čerkez (IT-95-14/2-A), Appeals Chamber, 17 December 2004, para. 27. See also Brđanin (IT-99-36-T), 1 September 2004, para. 269.
26 Gacumbitsi (ICTR-2001-64-T), 17 June 2004, para. 279.
27 Kordić and Čerkez (IT-95-14/2-A), Appeals Chamber, 17 December 2004, para. 32; Limaj (IT-03-66), 30 November 2005, para. 514; Brđanin (IT-99-36-T), 1 September 2004, para. 269 (emphasis added).
28 Kordić and Čerkez (IT-95-14/2-T), 26 February 2001, para. 387.
29 Limaj (IT-03-66), 30 November 2005, para. 515, citing Kordić and Čerkez (IT-95-14/2-A), Appeals Chamber, 17 December 2004, para. 28; Strugar (IT-01-42-T), 31 January 2005, para. 331. Krstić (IT-98-33-T), 2 August 2001, para. 601.
30 Partial Dissenting Opinion of Judge Weinberg De Roca, para. 41, Blaškić (IT-95-14-A), Appeals Chamber, 29 July 2004.
31 Some judgments take the position that ordering implies the existence of a superior–subordinate relationship between the individual who gives the order and the one who executes it, Akayesu (ICTR-96-4-T), 2 September 1998, para. 483; Semanza (ICTR-97-20-T), 15 May 2003, para. 382, citing with approval Bagilishema (ICTR-95-1A-T), 7 June 2001, para. 30. Other Chambers hold the opinion that a formal superior–subordinate is not a requirement for a finding of 'ordering' as a form of criminal participation , see Kajelijeli (ICTR-98-44A-T), 1 December 2003, para. 763; Kordić & Čerkez (IT-95-14/2-T), 26 February 2001, para. 388; Strugar (IT-01-42-T), 31 January 2005, para. 331.
32 Limaj (IT-03-66), 30 November 2005, para. 515, citing Brđanin (IT-99-36-T), 1 September 2004, para. 270; Gacumbitsi (ICTR-2001-64-T), 17 June 2004, para. 282.
33 Gacumbitsi (ICTR-2001-64-T), 17 June 2004, para. 283.
34 Galić (IT-98-29-S), 30 March 2004, para. 168, citing Krstić (IT-98-33-T), 2 August 2001, para. 601; Akayesu (ICTR-96-4), 2 September 1998, para. 483; Blaškić (IT-95-14-T), 3 March 2000, para. 281; Kordić and Čerkez (IT-95-14/2-T), 26 February 2001, para. 388.
35 Strugar (IT-01-42-T), 31 January 2005, para. 331, citing Blaškić (IT-95-14-T), 3 March 2000, para. 281; Kordić and Čerkez (IT-95-14/2-T), 26 February 2001, para. 388. Galić (IT-98-29-S), 30 March 2004, para. 171. See also the Final Report of the Commission of Experts established pursuant to Security Council Resolution 780 (1992), 27 May 1994 (S/1994/674) at 17.
36 Strugar (IT-01-42-T), 31 January 2005, para. 332. In Gacumbtsi, the ICTR found that the accused incurred liability for having ordered the policemen to kill the Tutsi, since the participation of those policemen was a direct consequence of the orders given by the accused, Gacumbitsi (ICTR-2001-64-T), 17 June 2004, para. 284.
37 Strugar (IT-01-42-T), 31 January 2005, para. 332.
38 Blaškić (IT-95-14-A), Appeals Chamber, 29 July 2004.
39 Ibid., para. 41 (emphasis added).
40 Ibid., para. 42. Limaj (IT-03-66), 30 November 2005, para. 515; Kordić and Čerkez (IT-95-14/2-A), Appeals Chamber, 17 December 2004, para. 30; Brđanin (IT-99-36-T), 1 September 2004, para. 270.
41 Blaškić (IT-95-14-T), 3 March 2000, para. 592.
42 Ibid., para. 282.
43 Kajelijeli (ICTR-98-44A-T), 1 December 2003, para. 769.

44 Kunarac (IT-96-23/1-T), 22 February 2001, para. 391.
45 On this point see Orić (IT-03-68-T), 30 June 2006, para. 280.
46 Several judgments rendered by the Rwanda Tribunal defined aiding to mean 'giving assistance to someone' and abetting to involve 'facilitating the commission of an act by being sympathetic thereto'; see Akayesu (ICTR-96-4), 2 September 1998, para. 484; Kayishema (ICTR-95-1-T), 21 May 2001, para. 196; Ntakirutimana [(ICTR-96-10-T) and (ICTR-96-17-T)], 21 February 2003, para. 787. Concerning abetting in particular, the Semanza Trial Chamber refers to it as 'encouraging, advising or instigating the commission of a crime': Semanza (ICTR-97-20-T), 15 May 2003, para. 384. Other cases further include 'facilitating' as well; see Kajelijeli (ICTR-98-44A-T), 1 December 2003, para. 765; Kamuhanda (ICTR-95-54A-T), 22 January 2004, para. 596. See also Limaj (IT-03-66), 30 November 2005, para. 516.
47 Muhimana (ICTR-95-1B-T), 28 April 2005, para. 507; Gacumbitsi (ICTR-2001-64-T), 17 June 2004, para. 286; Ntakirutimana [(ICTR-96-10-T) and (ICTR-96-17-T)], 21 February 2003, para. 787; Semanza (ICTR-97-20-T), 15 May 2003, para. 384; Kajelijeli (ICTR-98-44A-T), 1 December 2003, para. 763; Kvočka (IT-98-30/1-T), 2 November 2001, para. 254.
48 Blagojević (IT-02-06-T), 17 January 2005, para. 726; Brđanin (IT-99-36-T), 1 September 2004, para. 271; Tadić (IT-94-1-A), Appeals Chamber, 15 July 1999, para. 229; Aleksovski (IT-95-14/1-A), Appeals Chamber, 24 March 2000, paras 163–4; Čelebići (IT-96-21-A), Appeals Chamber, 20 February 2001, para. 352; Furundžija (IT-95-17/1-T), 10 December 1998, paras 235, 249; Vasiljević (IT-98-32-A), Appeals Chamber, 25 February 2004, para. 102; Naletilić (IT-98-34-T), 31 March 2003, para. 63; Simić (IT-95-9-T), 17 October 2003, para. 161. In Tadić, the Appeals Chamber held that the principal offender may not even be aware of the accomplice's contribution: Tadić (IT-94-1-A), Appeals Chamber, 15 July 1999, para. 229.
49 Akayesu (ICTR-96-4-T), 2 September 1998, paras 473-5; Aleksovski (IT-95-14/1-A), Appeals Chamber, 24 March 2000, para. 165; Blagojević (IT-02-06-T), 17 January 2005, para. 726; Brđanin (IT-99-36-T), 1 September 2004, para. 271.
50 Orić (IT-03-68-T), 30 June 2006, para. 283; Kvočka (IT-98-30/1-T), 2 November 2001, para. 257; Krnojelac (IT-97-25-T), 15 March 2002, para. 89; Vasiljević (IT-98-32-T), 29 November 2002, para. 70; Limaj (IT-03-66), 30 November 2005, para. 517.
51 Orić (IT-03-68-T), 30 June 2006, para. 283.
52 Ibid., para. 284; Vasiljević (IT-98-32-A), Appeals Chamber, 25 February 2004, para. 102; Blagojević (IT-02-06-T), 17 January 2005, para. 726; Furundžija (IT-95-17/1-T), 10 December 1998, paras 223–4, 249; Aleksovski (IT-95-14/1-T), 25 June 1999, para. 61; Kunarac (IT-96-23/1-T), 22 February 2001, para. 391; Kordić and Čerkez (IT-95-14/2-T), 26 February 2001, para. 399; Vasiljević (IT-98-32-T), 29 November 2002, para. 70. The Kajelijeli Trial Chamber stated as follows: 'Such act of assistance before or during the fact need not have actually caused the consummation of the crime by the actual perpetrator, but it must have had a substantial effect on the commission of the crime by the actual perpetrator', Kajelijeli (ICTR-98-44A-T), 1 December 2003, para. 766.
53 Kamuhanda (ICTR-95-54A-T), 22 January 2004, para. 597; Blagojević (IT-02-06-T), 17 January 2005, para. 726; Blaškić (IT-95-14-A), Appeals Chamber, 29 July 2004, para. 165; Čelebići (IT-96-21-A), Appeals Chamber, 20 February 2001, para. 352; Blagojević (IT-02-60-A), Appeals Chamber, 9 May 2007, para. 127.
54 Blagojević (IT-02-06-T), 17 January 2005, para. 731.
55 Ibid.; Blagojević (IT-02-60-A), Appeals Chamber, 9 May 2007, paras 177–181.
56 Orić (IT-03-68-T), 30 June 2006, para. 286.
57 Vasiljević (IT-98-32-A), Appeals Chamber, 25 February 2004, para. 102; Blaškić (IT-95-14-A), Appeals Chamber, 29 July 2004 paras 46, 49–50; Aleksovski (IT-95-14/1-A), Appeals Chamber, 24 March 2000, para. 162; Tadić (IT-94-1-A), Appeals Chamber, 15 July 1999, para. 229; Brđanin (IT-99-36-T), 1 September 2004, para. 272; Kajelijeli (ICTR-98-44A-T), 1 December 2003, para. 768; Kayishema (ICTR-95-1-A), Appeals Chamber, 1 June 2001, paras 186–7; Semanza (ICTR-97-20-T), 15 May 2003, para. 387; Bagilishema (ICTR-95-1A-T), 7 June 2001, para. 32. This awareness need not have been explicitly expressed, it may be inferred from all relevant circumstances, see Limaj (IT-03-66), 30 November 2005, para. 518.
58 Aleksovski (IT-95-14/1-A), Appeals Chamber, 24 March 2000, para. 162; Blagojević (IT-02-06-T), 17 January 2005, para. 727; Krnojelac (IT-97-25-T), 15 March 2002, para. 90.
59 Orić (IT-03-68-T), 30 June 2006, para. 288; In *Blaskic*, as in *Begilishema*, the Trial Chamber required that the aider and abettor 'intended to provide the assistance, or as a minimum, accepted that such assistance would be a possible and foreseeable consequence of his conduct', in addition to requiring knowledge

that the conduct of the accused assisted and facilitated the commission of the crime.: see Blaškić (IT-95-14-T), 3 March 2000, para. 286; Bagilishema (ICTR-95-1A-T), 7 June 2001, para. 32.

60 Orić (IT-03-68-T), 30 June 2006, para. 288 (emphasis added, footnotes omitted).

61 Limaj (IT-03-66), 30 November 2005, para. 518; Aleksovski (IT-95-14/1-A), Appeals Chamber, 24 March 2000, para. 162; Krnojelac (IT-97-25-T), 15 March 2002, para. 90.

62 Limaj (IT-03-66), 30 November 2005, para. 518, citing Blaskić (IT-95-14-A), Appeals Chamber, 29 July 2004, para. 50.

63 Schabas, *The UN International Criminal Tribunals*, pp. 306–37.

64 Limaj (IT-03-66), 30 November 2005, para. 509; Krstić (IT-98-33-A), Appeals Chamber, 19 April 2004, para. 188; Kunarac (IT-96-23/1-T), 22 February 2001, para. 390; Gacumbitsi (ICTR-2001-64-T), 17 June 2004, para. 285.

65 Kajelijeli (ICTR-98-44A-T), 1 December 2003, para. 764.

66 It is to be noted that unlike the ICC Statute, the Statutes of the ICTY and the ICTR lack a provision concerning 'intermediary perpetration', in which the accused, as an indirect perpetrator, uses another innocent person as his or her instrument to perform the relevant conduct.

67 Limaj (IT-03-66), 30 November 2005, para. 509, citing Kordić and Čerkez (IT-95-14/2-T), 26 February 2001, para. 376.

68 Galić (IT-98-29-S), 30 March 2004, para. 136.

69 See Kvočka (IT-98-30/1-A), Appeals Chamber, 28 February 2005, paras 79–80, 99; Tadić (IT-94-1-A), Appeals Chamber, 15 July 1999, paras 188, 195–226; Milutinović *et al.* (IT-99-37-AR72), Decision in Dragoljub Ojdanić's Motion Challenging Jurisdiction – Joint Criminal Enterprise, 21 May 2003, para. 20; Vasiljević, (IT-98-32-A) Appeals Chamber, 25 February 2004, para. 111; Ntakirutimana (ICTR-96-17-A), Appeals Chamber, 13 December 2004, para. 462; Karemera *et al.* (ICTR-98-44-T), Decision on Jurisdictional Appeals: Joint Criminal Enterprise, Appeals Chamber, 12 April 2006, para. 16.

70 Tadić (IT-94-1-A), Appeals Chamber, 15 July 1999, para. 191; Furundžija (IT-95-17/1-T), 10 December 1998, para. 256.

71 A. Cassese, 'The Proper Limits of Individual Responsibility under the Doctrine of Joint Criminal Enterprise', *Journal of International Criminal Justice* 5, 2007, 109–133, 110.

72 JCE has been a source of endless fascination for commentators, generating an enormous amount of literature. A. O'Rourke, 'Joint Criminal Enterprise and Brđanin: Misguided Over-Correction', *Harvard International Law Journal* 47, 2006, 307; A. Danner and J. Martinez, 'Guilty Associations: Joint Criminal Enterprise, Command Responsibility, and the Development of International Law', *California Law Review* 93, 2005, 75; K. Ambos, 'Joint Criminal Enterprise and Command Responsibility', *Journal of International Criminal Justice* 5, 2007, 159; M. Elewa Badar, '"Just Convict Everyone!" 'Joint Perpetration: From Tadić to Stakić and Back Again', *International Criminal Law Review* 6, 2006, 293; J. Ohlin, 'Three Conceptual Problems with the Doctrine of Joint Criminal Enterprise', *Journal of International Criminal Justice* 5, 2007, 69; K. Gustafson, 'The Requirement of an "Express Agreement" for Joint Criminal Enterprise Liability: A Critique of Brđanin', *Journal of International Criminal Justice* 5, 2007, 134; H. van der Wilt, 'Joint Criminal Enterprise, Possibilities and Limitations', *Journal of International Criminal Justice* 5, 2007, 91; E. van Sliedregt, 'Pathway to Convicting Individuals for Genocide', *Journal of International Criminal Justice* 5, 2007, 184.

73 Stakić (IT-97-24-A), Appeals Chamber, 22 March 2006, para. 64; Kvočka (IT-98-30/1-A), Appeals Chamber, 28 February 2005, paras 82–3; Vasiljević (IT-98-32-A), Appeals Chamber, 25 February 2004, paras 96–9; Krnojelac (IT-97-25-A), Appeals Chamber, 17 September 2003, para. 30; Simba (ICTR-01-76-T), 13 December 2005, para. 386. It is worth pointing out that while joint criminal enterprise liability has been firmly established in the jurisprudence of the ICTY since the *Tadić* Appeal Judgment in 1999, the ICTR was first called upon to address the issue in two cases in 2004. See André Rwamakuba (ICTR-98-44-AR72.4), Decision on Interlocutory Appeal Regarding Application of Joint Criminal Enterprise to the Crime of Genocide, 22 October 2004, and Ntakirutimana (ICTR-96-17-A), Appeals Chamber, 13 December 2004.

74 The Krnojelac Appeals Chamber held that 'using the concept of joint criminal enterprise to define an individual's responsibility for crimes physically committed by others requires a strict definition of common purpose', Krnojelac (IT-97-25-A), Appeals Chamber, 17 September 2003, para. 116

75 Stakić (IT-97-24-A), Appeals Chamber, 22 March 2006, para. 64; Kvočka (IT-98-30/1-A), Appeals Chamber, 28 February 2005, para. 96; Ntakirutimana (ICTR-96-17-A), Appeals Chamber, 13 December 2004, para. 466; Vasiljević (IT-98-32-A), Appeals Chamber, 25 February 2004, para. 100; Krnojelac (IT-97-25-A), Appeals Chamber, 17 September 2003, para. 31; Simba (ICTR-01-76-T),

13 December 2005, para. 386; Brdjanin (IT-99-36-T), Decision on Motion for Acquittal Pursuant to Rule 98 *bis*, 28 November 2003, para. 26.
76 Krnojelac (IT-97-25-A), Appeals Chamber, 17 September 2003, para. 81.
77 Krajišnik (IT-00-39-A), Appeals Chamber, 17 March 2009, para. 156; Limaj *et al.* (IT-03-66-A), Appeal Judgment, 27 September 2007, para. 99.
78 Brđanin (IT-99-36-A), Appeals Chamber, 3 April 2007, para. 418; Krajišnik (IT-00-39-A), Appeals Chamber, 17 March 2009, para. 163.
79 Krajišnik (IT-00-39-A), Appeals Chamber, 17 March 2009, para. 163.
80 Ibid.; para. 185.
81 Tadić (IT-94-1-A), Appeals Chamber, 15 July 1999, para. 196; Krnojelac (IT-97-25-A), Appeals Chamber, 17 September 2003, para. 84; Ntakirutimana (ICTR-96-17-A), Appeals Chamber, 13 December 2004, para. 467.
82 Tadić (IT-94-1-A), Appeals Chamber, 15 July 1999, para. 196; Vasiljević (IT-98-32-A), Appeals Chamber, 25 February 2004, para. 97; Ntakirutimana (ICTR-96-17-A), Appeals Chamber, 13 December 2004, 463.
83 Tadić (IT-94-1-A), Appeals Chamber, 15 July 1999, para. 196.
84 This argument was raised by the *Amicus Curiae* in their Notice of Appeal in the Krajišnik case. See Krajišnik (IT-00-39-A), Appeals Chamber, 17 March 2009, para. 220, quoting the *Amicus Curiae*'s Notice of Appeal, para. 50
85 Krajišnik (IT-00-39-A), Appeals Chamber, 17 March 2009, para. 225, quoting Brđanin (IT-99-36-A), Appeals Chamber, 3 April 2007, para 413.
86 Kvočka (IT-98-30/1-A), Appeals Chamber, 28 February 2005, paras 99, 112; Tadić (IT-94-1-A), Appeals Chamber, 15 July 1999, para. 192.
87 Tadić (IT-94-1-A), Appeals Chamber, 15 July 1999, para. 228.
88 Kvočka (IT-98-30/1-A), Appeals Chamber, 28 February 2005, para. 82; Tadić (IT-94-1-A), Appeals Chamber, 15 July 1999, paras 202–3; Krnojelac (IT-97-25-A), Appeals Chamber, 17 September 2003, para. 89: ('The Appeals Chamber holds that, although the second category of cases defined by the *Tadić* Appeals Judgment "systemic" clearly draws on the Second World War extermination and concentration camp cases, it may be applied to other cases and specially to the serious violations of international humanitarian law committed in the territory of the former Yugoslavia since 1991'); Kvočka (IT-98-30/1-T), 2 November 2001, para. 202.
89 Cassese, 'The Proper Limits', p. 112.
90 Kvočka (IT-98-30/1-A), Appeals Chamber, 28 February 2005, para. 96.
91 Krajišnik (IT-00-39-A), Appeals Chamber, 17 March 2009, para. 675; Brđanin (IT-99-36-A), Appeals Chamber, 3 April 2007, para. 430; Kvočka (IT-98-30/1-A), Appeals Chamber, 28 February 2005, para. 97.
92 Kvočka (IT-98-30/1-A), Appeals Chamber, 28 February 2005, para. 599.
93 Ibid.
94 Krnojelac (IT-97-25-A), Appeals Chamber, 17 September 2003, paras 89, 96.
95 Kvočka (IT-98-30/1-A), Appeals Chamber, 28 February 2005, para. 110.
96 Krnojelac (IT-97-25-A), Appeals Chamber, 17 September 2003, paras 118–4.
97 Ibid., para. 122.
98 Ibid.
99 Stakić (IT-97-24-A), Appeals Chamber, 22 March 2006, para. 87.
100 Stakić (IT-97-24-T), 31 July 2003, para. 530
101 Barđanin (IT-99-36-T), Decision on Motion for Acquittal Pursuant to Rule 98 *bis*, 28 November 2003, para. 57.
102 Ibid.
103 Barđanin (IT-99-36-A), Decision on Interlocutory Appeal, 19 March 2004, paras 5–10.
104 Tadić (IT-94-1-A) Appeals Chamber, 15 July 1999, para. 229.
105 The term 'just convict everyone' was used by Professor William Schabas as an alternative to the third category of JCE during a lecture at the fifth annual International Criminal Court Summer Course in Galway in 2005 hosted by the Irish Centre for Human Rights, National University of Galway, Ireland. See Badar, "Just Convict Everyone".
106 Stakić (IT-97-24-T), 31 July 2003, paras 438–41. The Stakić Trial Chamber applied a combination of two forms of commission, known in German criminal law as *Mittäterschaft* (co-perpetration) and *mittelbare Täterschaft* (indirect perpetratorship); for more information on joint principles in

German Criminal Law see M. Bohlander, *General Principles of German Criminal Law*, Oxford: Hart Publishing, 2009, pp. 161–66.

107 Stakić (IT-97-24-T), 31 July 2003, para. 440.

108 Ibid.

109 Ibid., quoting Claus Roxin, *Täterschaft und Tatherrschaft*, Berlin, New York, 1994, 278.

110 Ibid., paras 495–7.

111 See Badar, '"Just Convict Everyone!"'.

112 Halilović (IT-01-48-T), 16 November 2005, para. 55, citing Čelebići (IT-96-21-A), Appeals Chamber, 20 February 2001, para. 195; Čelebići (IT-96-21-T), 16 November 1998, para. 343; Strugar (IT-01-42-T), 31 January 2005, para. 357.

113 Čelebići (IT-96-21-A), Appeals Chamber, 20 February 2001, para. 197; Kordić and Čerkez (IT-95-14/2-T), 26 February 2001, para. 369; Kayishema (ICTR-95-1-T), 21 May 1999, para. 217; Musema (ICTR-96-13-T), 27 January 2000, para. 148.

114 Halilović (IT-01-48-T), 16 November 2005, para. 54. For more details on omission as a culpable conduct, see M. Duttwiller, 'Liability for Omission in International Criminal Law', *International Criminal Law Review* 6, 2006, 1–61.

115 There is a consensus in the jurisprudence of the ICTY and ICTR that the doctrine of command responsibility extends beyond the responsibility of military commanders to encompass civilian superiors in positions of authority; see Bagilishema (ICTR-95-1A-T), 7 June 2001, paras 41–3;

116 Orić (IT-03-68-T), 30 June 2006, para. 294. See also Ntagerura (ICTR-99-46-T), 25 February 2004, para. 627; Semanza (ICTR-97-20-T), 15 May 2003, para. 400; Blaškić (IT-95-14-A), Appeals Chamber, 29 July 2004, para. 484; Aleksovski (IT-95-14/1-A), Appeals Chamber, 24 March 2000, para. 72.

117 Ibid., para. 297, referring to the Defence Final Brief, paras 507ff. and the Defence Closing Argument, T. 16438.

118 Boškoski and Tarčulovski (IT-04-82-PT), Decision on Prosecution's Motion to Amend the Indictment, 26 May 2006, paras 18–48.

119 Orić (IT-03-68-T), 30 June 2006, para. 302.

120 Ibid., para. 305.

121 Ibid., para. 304.

122 Limaj (IT-03-66), 30 November 2005, para. 521; Strugar (IT-01-42-T), 31 January 2005, para. 359.

123 Ntagerura (ICTR-99-46-T), 25 February 2004, para. 628; Halilović (IT-01-48-T), 16 November 2005, para. 58; Galić (IT-98-29-S), 30 March 2004, para. 173.

124 Čelebići (IT-96-21-A), Appeals Chamber, 20 February 2001, para. 256. See also Blaškić (IT-95-14-A), Appeals Chamber, 29 July 2004, para. 69.

125 Blaškić (IT-95-14-A), Appeals Chamber, 29 July 2004, para. 69.

126 Orić (IT-03-68-T), 30 June 2006, para. 311; Ntagerura (ICTR-99-46-T), 25 February 2004, para. 628; Semanza (ICTR-97-20-T), 15 May 2003, para. 402.

127 Čelebići (IT-96-21-T), 16 November 1998, paras 353–354, 370, 736, confirmed by Čelebići (IT-96-21-A), Appeals Chamber, 20 February 2001, paras 195ff. Aleksovski (IT-95-14/1-T), 25 June 1999, para. 76; Blaškić (IT-95-14-T), 3 March 2000, para. 301; Kunarac (IT-96-23/1-T), 22 February 2001, para. 396; Kordić and Čerkez (IT-95-14/2-T), 26 February 2001, para. 416; Naletilić (IT-98-34-T), 31 March 2003, para. 67; Stakić (IT-97-24-T), 31 July 2003, para. 459; Halilović (IT-01-48-T), 16 November 2005, paras 58, 60; Musema (ICTR-96-13-T), 27 January 2000, para. 148; Kayishema (ICTR-95-1-T), 21 May 1999, paras 218, 222.

128 Orić (IT-03-68-T), 30 June 2006, para. 310.

129 Ibid., para. 318; Čelebići (IT-96-21-A), Appeals Chamber, 20 February 2001, para. 239; Čelebići (IT-96-21-T), 16 November 1998, para. 383; Halilović (IT-01-48-T), 16 November 2005, para. 65; Brđanin (IT-99-36-T), 1 September 2004, para. 278; Blagojević (IT-02-06-T), 17 January 2005, para. 792; Kajelijeli (ICTR-98-44A-T), 1 December 2003, para. 776.

130 Limaj (IT-03-66), 30 November 2005, para. 523; Halilović (IT-01-48-T), 16 November 2005, para. 64; Ntagerura (ICTR-99-46-T), 25 February 2004, para. 629.

131 Ntagerura (ICTR-99-46-T), 25 February 2004, para. 629; Semanza (ICTR-97-20-T), 15 May 2003, para. 405; Halilović (IT-01-48-T), 16 November 2005, para. 65.

132 Orić (IT-03-68-T), 30 June 2006, para. 317.

133 Barđanin (IT-99-36-A), Decision on Interlocutory Appeal, 19 March 2004, para. 7.

134 Kordić and Čerkez (IT-95-14/2-T), 26 February 2001, para. 427.

135 K. Keith, 'The *Mens Rea* of Superior Responsibility as Developed by ICTY Jurisprudence', *Leiden Journal of International Law* 14, 2001, 617–34, 619.
136 Bagilishema (ICTR-95-1A-A), Appeals Chamber, 3 July 2002, paras 34–5; Blaškić (IT-95-14-A), Appeals Chamber, 29 July 2004, para. 63; Halilović (IT-01-48-T), 16 November 2005, para. 71.
137 Kordić and Čerkez (IT-95-14/2-T), 26 February 2001, para. 371.
138 Čelebići (IT-96-21-T), 16 November 1998, para. 386; Trial Judgment, para. 524; Halilović (IT-01-48-T), 16 November 2005, para. 66; Aleksovski (IT-95-14/1-T), 25 June 1999, para. 80; Blaškić (IT-95-14-T), 3 March 2000, para. 308. The Aleksovski and Blaškić Judgments indicated that the position of authority of the superior over the subordinate may in some circumstances of itself be an indicator that the superior must have known of the subordinate's conduct. Kayishema (ICTR-95-1-T), 21 May 1999, para. 225.
139 Limaj (IT-03-66), 30 November 2005, para. 524; Kordić and Čerkez (IT-95-14/2-T), 26 February 2001, para. 427; Blaškić (IT-95-14-T), 3 March 2000, para. 307; Strugar (IT-01-42-T), 31 January 2005, para. 368.
140 Bagilishema (ICTR-95-1A-A), Appeals Chamber, 3 July 2002, para. 28.
141 Halilović (IT-01-48-T), 16 November 2005, para. 68.
142 Strugar (IT-01-42-T), 31 January 2005, para. 416.
143 Blaškić (IT-95-14-A), Appeals Chamber, 29 July 2004, para. 406 (emphasis in original).
144 Čelebići (IT-96-21-A), Appeals Chamber, 20 February 2001, paras 223 and 241; Brđanin (IT-99-36-T), 1 September 2004, para. 278; Halilović (IT-01-48-T), 16 November 2005, para. 68; Galić (IT-98-29-S), 30 March 2004, para. 175.
145 Final Report of the Commission of Inquiry into the Events at the Refugee camps in Beirut, 7 February 1983 (Kahan Report), reproduced in 22 *International Legal Materials* (1983) 473–520, cited by Halilović (IT-01-48-T), 16 November 2005, fn. 164 and Blaškić (IT-95-14-T), 3 March 2000, paras 330–1.
146 Blaškić (IT-95-14-T), 3 March 2000, para. 331, citing the Kahan Report.
147 Ibid., (emphasis added). See also Halilović (IT-01-48-T), 16 November 2005, fn. 164. See also L. Malone, 'Kahan Report, Ariel Sharon and the Sabra-Shatila Massacres in Lebanon; Responsibility under International Law for Massacres of Civilian Populations, 1985 *Utah Law Review*, 373.
148 Čelebići (IT-96-21-A), Appeals Chamber, 20 February 2001, para. 226; Blaškić (IT-95-14-A), Appeals Chamber, 29 July 2004, para. 62; Halilović (IT-01-48-T), 16 November 2005, para. 69.
149 Čelebići (IT-96-21-A), Appeals Chamber, 20 February 2001, para. 226, endorsed by Blaškić (IT-95-14-A), Appeals Chamber, 29 July 2004, para. 62.
150 Halilović (IT-01-48-T), 16 November 2005, para. 69.
151 Bagilishema (ICTR-95-1A-T), 7 June 2001, para. 897.
152 Blaškić (IT-95-14-A), Appeals Chamber, 29 July 2004, para. 63, citing Bagilishema (ICTR-95-1A-A), Appeals Chamber, 3 July 2002, paras 34–5.
153 Bagilishema (ICTR-95-1A-A), Appeals Chamber, 3 July 2002, para. 35; Blaškić (IT-95-14-A), Appeals Chamber, 29 July 2004, para. 63; Orić (IT-03-68-T), 30 June 2006, para. 324; Halilović (IT-01-48-T), 16 November 2005, para. 71.
154 Orić (IT-03-68-T), 30 June 2006, para. 324.
155 Ibid., para. 326.
156 Blaškić (IT-95-14-T), 3 March 2000, para. 336.
157 Schabas, *The UN International Criminal Tribunals*, p. 320.
158 Ibid.
159 Orić (IT-03-68-T), 30 June 2006, para. 277.
160 See Blaškić (IT-95-14-A), Appeals Chamber, 29 July 2004, para. 41; Orić (IT-03-68-T), 30 June 2006, para. 279.
161 *Model Penal Code and Commentaries: Official Draft and Revised Comments*, Philadelphia: The American Law Institute, 1980 § 2.06 Comment at 312, fn. 42.
162 See Blaškić (IT-95-14-A), Appeals Chamber, 29 July 2004, para. 41.
163 *Clayton v. The Queen*, [2006] High Court of Australia 58, para. 108.

17

International criminal procedures

Trial and appeal procedures

Håkan Friman

International criminal jurisdictions require their own criminal procedures and procedural systems have been created for each international court from the Nuremberg trials and onwards. Each system is *sui generis* in the sense that it departs from any one domestic system or tradition, but they are still inspired by and have elements from the major domestic legal systems. This is important for the perceived legitimacy of the court and its procedures, but the *sui generis* nature of the procedures and mix of elements from different domestic systems also give rise to uncertainty and sometimes to unfortunate combinations.[1] Those who practice in these jurisdictions will have to become specialists with respect to the criminal procedures in question.

The criminal procedures of the International Criminal Court (ICC), International Criminal Tribunal for the former Yugoslavia (ICTY) and International Criminal Tribunal for Rwanda (ICTR) are laid down in their respective Statute and Rules of Procedure and Evidence (hereinafter 'Rules'). The Statutes of the ICTY and ICTR contain only a few basic procedural provisions and most of the procedures are regulated in the Rules which are adopted by the judges and have been amended on numerous occasions over the years. On the other hand, the ICC Statute, sets forth a much more comprehensive procedural scheme and additional directions are provided in the Rules which are also developed and adopted by States. In addition, practice directives and other regulatory instruments exist at the Tribunals and the ICC has got Regulations of the Court, adopted by the judges, and special regulations for the Office of the Prosecutor and for the Registry. Hence, the procedures of each institution are voluminous, multi-layered and rather complex.

Criminal investigation and prosecution

The jurisdictional parameters of the ICTY and ICTR are clear and within these the prosecutor is authorized to initiate investigations on his own initiative whenever there is 'sufficient basis to proceed'.[2] Hence, it is a discretionary power, not subject to any judicial supervision,[3] and no obligation to investigate (or prosecute) applies. At the ICC the requirements for the commencement of an investigation are more complex. Firstly, the jurisdiction of the Court must be 'triggered' by a State or Security Council referral of 'the situation' or by the prosecutor *proprio motu* with the authorization of the Pre-Trial Chamber. Secondly, the prosecutor shall, regardless of the 'trigger mechanism', determine whether an investigation may be initiated in accordance with set criteria: a reasonable suspicion of a crime within the Court's jurisdiction, the admissibility of the case in accordance with the 'complementarity principle' and the requirement of 'sufficient gravity', and a determination of 'the interests of justice'.[4] The ICC prosecutor's discretion is a little more circumvented and a decision not to initiate an investigation may be reviewed by the Pre-Trial Chamber.[5]

All three institutions have adopted an explicit strategy to target those most responsible for the most serious violations of international humanitarian law. At the ICC, the Prosecutor has so far opted for opening the investigations concerning entire 'situations' and not with respect to more defined 'cases' or incidents.[6]

The investigation is normally conducted by investigators and experts within the Tribunal's or Court's Office of the Prosecutor and led by a prosecutor. No international police forces are available and in practice most investigative measures depend upon the cooperation of States, international organisations and other entities. Cooperation by States and others are also required for the crucial issue of arrest and surrender of the suspects, and generally for other coercive measures that are required for the investigation.[7] However, there is a preference for conducting most of the activities with as little involvement of other authorities as possible. Internal directives and regulations are issued for the conduct of the investigation.[8]

Prosecution is also a matter for the prosecutor to decide, although a decision in the ICC not to prosecute may be subject to review by the Pre-Trial Chamber.[9]

Preparations for trial

The trials of the international criminal jurisdictions have often been long, partly due to the fact that each party, in an adversarial fashion, has presented a distinct 'case' to the court; the prosecution case first and the defence case thereafter. The parties have had much room for strategic considerations and adjustment of the evidence depending on how the trial has developed and without the Chambers taking control over the proceedings. However, this has changed over time into more structured and regulated preparations for trial and stricter court control. The judges now have better tools and are more prone to intervene.

Confirmation of the charges

The charges must stand a test of judicial scrutiny before going to trial. At the ICTY and ICTR, a single judge examines each charge of the indictment in order to determine if a *prima facie* case exists against the suspect.[10] This is an *ex parte* process in which the suspect is not allowed to make representations.[11] The ICC Statute provides instead for an adversarial process with the prosecution and defence present.[12] The test is whether there are 'substantial grounds to believe' that the accused has committed the crimes charged. In all instances the Prosecutor must support the charges with sufficient evidence, at this stage normally documentary and summary evidence. However, the defendant at the ICC is entitled to challenge the prosecutor's evidence and to present evidence. Hence, the ICC confirmation hearings have run over a number of days, including the examination of some witnesses, and resulted in very long and detailed decisions.[13] The Tribunals and the ICC also provide for special confirmation proceedings in the absence of the accused, proceedings that have proven to be controversial.[14]

Disclosure and admissibility of evidence

Disclosure of evidence is a fundamental element in the preparation of any criminal trial, in particular the prosecutor's disclosure to the defendant. In procedural terms, domestic systems deal with this matter very differently and the regimes adopted for the international criminal jurisdictions are based on an adversarial trial model. They are presented in Chapter 20. It is important to note that a very large part of the work of the Chambers before trial, and many decisions, relate to disclosure matters. A particular issue is whether the evidence should also be disclosed in advance to the Chamber, something that, according to the ICTY Appeals Chamber, the Trial Chamber has a discretionary power to order.[15] This measure assists the judges to plan and direct the trial, but raises concerns regarding them being unduly influenced by the information. Moreover, the Chambers determine questions of admissibility of evidence.

Protective measures, provisional release and other preliminary matters

The procedures being unique, it is not surprising that the Chambers have had to address numerous motions on pre-trial matters. Sometimes the determination has been very important for the development of the law: for example, the ICTY's decision in *Tadić* on jurisdiction.[16] The Tribunals make a distinction between 'preliminary matters' (for example, jurisdiction, form of the indictment, severance of cases, denial of defence counsel) and other matters (for example, the issuance of warrants and orders).[17] Numerous motions and decisions have also occurred at the ICC, where special provisions apply for challenges to jurisdiction or the admissibility of the case and for the issuance of orders.[18]

The protection of victims and witnesses is a demanding task for the international criminal jurisdictions. Great reliance upon live evidence, the nature of the crimes and the widely publicized nature of the proceedings necessitate thorough protection regimes and this need is further exacerbated for the ICC which operates in ongoing violent conflicts. However, the lack of enforcement organs and the dependence upon cooperation by States and others reduce the tools available. In practice, protective measures in order to prevent disclosure to the public (screening, voice or image distortion, pseudonyms, photo prohibition etc.) are regularly applied. This complicates the proceedings and infringes the principle of public trial, which means that a careful balancing of interests is required and routine application must be avoided.[19]

An important pre-trial matter is pre-trial detention of the accused (or suspect) and interim release. ICTY and ICTR arrest warrants are based upon a confirmed indictment, while the ICC warrants are issued in a separate process and independently of the formal charges against the accused.[20] At the Tribunals, the accused are automatically detained upon their surrender.[21] Interim release may be ordered by a Trial Chamber and the prerequisites have changed over time in a pro-release direction;[22] while many accused at the ICTY have been released awaiting trial, no one has yet secured this at the ICTR. The ICC process is substantially different and apart from adjudicating requests for interim release the Pre-Trial Chamber is tasked with regular reviews, each time having to assess whether the conditions for the warrant of arrest are met.[23] The Tribunals and the ICC may also entertain challenges to the lawfulness of the detention and review violations of procedural rights.[24]

Joinder or severance of crimes and cases

Another important pre-trial matter is decisions on joinder or severance of cases against multiple accused[25] and joinder of crimes against a single accused. At the ICTY and ICTR, persons accused of the same or different crimes committed in the course of 'the same transaction' may be jointly charged and tried. Consideration will also be given to whether joinder would be in the interests of justice, and a similar test is applied by the ICC.[26] As to joinder of crimes in the same indictment, both legal and efficiency reasons may be held in support, but there are also instances where it has led to unmanageably large trials.[27]

Place of the trial

The trial shall normally be conducted at 'the seat' of the Tribunal or Court, that is in The Hague or Arusha. However, the ICC may sit elsewhere 'whenever it considers it desirable'.[28] Similarly, the Chambers of the ICTY and ICTR may exercise their functions away from the seat of the Tribunal.[29] While the ICC provisions aim at conducting court proceedings elsewhere, the Tribunals are more focused on site visits. A site visit, and even more to move a trial, involves considerable logistical challenges and costs, which means that the reasons for the measure must be very strong[30] and the conditions favourable, including securing the consent of the State in question.

Trial management

Much time and effort has been devoted at the ICTY and ICTR to increase the efficiency and decrease the length of the trials. Different procedural tools have been developed by the Tribunals and for the ICC, such as pre-trial (or pre-appeal) judges,[31] status conferences[32] and pre-trial and pre-defence conferences.[33] A common feature is that the judges have assumed an increasingly active and controlling role, which requires information in advance concerning the respective 'cases' and the intention to call evidence. Most controversially, this includes powers to restrict, *inter alia*, the scope of the charges, the number of witnesses at trial and the time available to the respective party for presenting evidence at trial; discretionary powers that must of course be exercised with utmost diligence.[34]

Witness preparations

The trial can be a cumbersome and even frightening experience for witnesses, not the least in international criminal proceedings. Like in many domestic systems, efforts to familiarize the witnesses with the process are considered very useful. This is accepted practice in the international criminal jurisdictions as well. More controversial are the parties' preparation in substance of witnesses that they intend to call at trial, so-called witness proofing. Whereas this is allowed in the ICTY and ICTR, the ICC Prosecutor has been prohibited from doing so.[35]

Participation of victims

At the ICTY and ICTR, victims participate in the proceedings as witnesses. At the ICC, however, the victims have been afforded an independent additional role as participants in the proceedings.[36] Furthermore, the ICC may award reparations, including restitution, compensation and rehabilitation to, and in respect of, victims.[37] The right to participation relates to the personal interests of the victims and shall include the presentation and consideration of their views and concerns. However, the exercise of this right is to be firmly controlled by the relevant Chamber and done in a manner that is not prejudicial to or inconsistent with the rights of the accused and a fair and impartial trial. In practice, the ICC Chambers, and thus also the parties and victims, have invested much time and effort in these issues and the emerging case law is, in part, rather far-reaching and controversial.[38]

Trial

The ICTY, ICTR and ICC all have Trial Chambers with three judges, but the quorum rules differ. While only a judge who has been present throughout the trial may take part in the judgment at the ICC, a judge may under certain conditions be substituted during the trial at the ICTY and ICTR.[39] For example, this has occurred when a judge has died or failed re-election, sometimes a long way into the trial.[40] The ICTR Appeals Chamber has concluded that this mechanism does not prejudice the rights of the accused since there are certain safeguards,[41] but serious concerns may still be raised.[42] This problem, and the impractical alternative of restarting the trial, is nowadays avoided at the ICTY by the possibility to appoint a fourth member to the bench, a 'reserve judge', which is regularly applied for longer trials.[43]

As the main rule, the trial shall be public, but exceptions may be made for reasons of public order and morality, protection of victims and witnesses and if required in 'the interests of justice'.[44] Extensive use of protective measures for victims and witnesses has in practice limited the publicity principle in many cases. The presence of the accused is a necessary prerequisite for trial and so-called trials *in absentia* are not allowed.[45] The prohibition is one of principle and reflects the adversarial trial model.[46] However, others have argued that absence should not frustrate the efforts of bringing the perpetrators to justice and, thus, that trials *in absentia* should be possible under certain conditions.[47] Disruptive persons may be excluded and removed from the courtroom, which may also include the accused.[48]

The trial follows an adversarial, common law-inspired model whereby the parties each present their own 'case' to the court: the prosecution case and the defence case. As has already been explained, this informs the entire criminal process, including the preparations for trial. However, there are deviations from the common law adversarial trial model and some of the main features will be indicated in the following. The rather informal law of evidence that applies also contributes to less formalistic and regulated trial procedures.[49]

The trial proper, the trial hearing, commences at the ICTY and ICTR with the opening statement of the prosecution. The defence may also make its opening statement at this time or wait until after the conclusion of the prosecution case.[50] In the ICTY, the defendant is explicitly entitled to make a statement without being sworn (make a 'solemn declaration') or be examined concerning the content of the statement;[51] a feature with roots in the civil law tradition.

The ICC trial hearing is characterized by a degree of discretion for the trial judges, particularly the presiding judge, to set the procedures by providing directions.[52] Nevertheless, certain procedural elements are set forth in the statutory law of the Court. The hearing begins with the charges being read out followed by the Chamber satisfying itself that the accused understands the nature of the charges and allowing him or her to plead to the charges. While the Statute leaves room for a two-case trial as well as a more unified trial, the experience so far has been trials quite similar to those of the Tribunals with distinct prosecution and defence cases. Opening statements may be made not only by the parties but also by participating victims.[53]

Presentation and examination of evidence constitute the major part of the hearing and the primary responsibility for these tasks rests with the parties.[54] However, the judges may also order evidence to be presented, for example, by summoning a witness,[55] which has also occurred in practice.[56] At the ICC, a Trial Chamber has emphasized that witnesses are 'witnesses of the Court' and not 'owned' by either of the parties.[57] Witnesses may be heard by means of video and audio technology:[58] for example, when they are unable to appear in person or due to security concerns. As already mentioned, the Chambers have extensive powers to reduce the length of the trials, *inter alia*, by limiting the number of witnesses and the time available for presenting evidence.

Unless otherwise directed, the presentation of evidence in the ICTY and ICTR follows the order customary for adversarial trials: prosecution evidence, defence evidence, prosecution rebuttal evidence and defence rejoinder evidence.[59] This is followed by evidence ordered by the Trial Chamber and evidence relevant for sentencing. Examination-in-chief, cross-examinations, and re-examinations shall be allowed in each case and a judge may at any stage put questions to the witness. The cross-examination is surrounded by certain limitations.[60] This common law-inspired model proved controversial when the ICC Statute and Rules were negotiated. Instead, the organization rests upon an agreement between the parties and, as a fallback, the judges' power to issue directions.[61] The directions are sometimes rather extensive and comprehensive.[62] However, certain principles must always be adhered to, such as the right of a party to question a witness that he or she has called and the right of the defence to be the last to examine a witness. The parties have the right to question witnesses about 'relevant matters related to the witness's testimony and its reliability, the credibility of the witness and other relevant matters'.[63] The Trial Chamber may put questions to the witness before or after the parties. In the ICC, legal representatives of victims participating in the process may also be permitted to put questions to witnesses.[64]

The accused may give testimony in his or her defence, which will take place after the closing of the prosecution case and the defendant is entitled to choose the timing of the testimony.[65]

The prosecution and the defence make closing statements, which in the ICC may also be extended to participating victims.[66] The Trial Chamber thereafter deliberates in private and the deliberations shall remain confidential.[67] Each count of the indictment shall be considered separately. Majority decisions are allowed, but the ICC Statute underlines that the judges shall attempt to achieve unanimity.[68] Joint trials against multiple accused will result in a single judgment. In practice, deliberations and drafting of judgments last for a long time. Judgments shall be in writing and contain a reasoned opinion, including any separate or dissenting opinions, and be delivered in open court.[69]

Admission of guilt and 'guilty pleas'

In common law jurisdictions a guilty plea leads to abbreviated trial proceedings whereby the trial court restricts itself to assessing whether the plea is voluntary and informed; the formal plea constitutes a waiver of the right to trial by the accused.[70] If the plea is accepted, the court will move to deciding the penalty. No equivalent process exists in civil law jurisdictions where a confession or admission of the facts is considered to form part of the evidence that the court shall assess in the case.[71]

The Statutes of the ICTY and ICTR do not provide for abbreviated proceedings in case of a guilty plea, but appear instead to presuppose that a trial shall be held in each case.[72] Nonetheless, such a procedure was applied in some cases. In *Erdemović*, the majority of the ICTY Appeals Chamber found that the guilty plea was uninformed, and hence involuntary, which led to the judgment being quashed and the case being remitted to a new Trial Chamber.[73] In *Kambanda*, the accused unsuccessfully sought to withdraw his guilty plea after having received a life sentence for the admitted crimes.[74] Subsequently, the Rules were amended to include such proceedings.[75] If the accused pleads guilty, the Trial Chamber shall assess whether the plea has been made voluntarily, is informed and is unequivocal. More recently, and most likely inspired by the ICC provisions, the Chamber must also assess whether there is a sufficient factual basis for the crime and the accused's participation in it. When these conditions are met, the Chamber may enter a finding of guilt and order a sentencing hearing. The procedure has been applied in a number of cases, usually in combination with a plea agreement between the accused and the prosecutor.

The ICTY and ICTR regime is drafted on the assumption that the plea is entered at the initial appearance by the accused before the Tribunal. However, nothing hinders a change of plea at any time and there are examples of guilty pleas being made late into the trial.[76]

For a long time the ICTY and ICTR have also accepted plea-bargaining, which is now regulated in the Rules.[77] This practice exists in many common law jurisdictions and is generally associated with a formal guilty plea regime. This is a controversial practice and its acceptance by the ICTY and ICTR has generated considerable debate.[78] If the proceedings are essentially a contest between the parties, they may also conclude the matter by settlement. If, on the other hand, the procedural model is based upon an official determination of the facts of the case, as in civil law jurisdictions, formal pleadings and agreements are objectionable.

Proponents of plea-bargaining stress judicial economy, sparing victims the stress of giving evidence, and the possibility to catch other, higher-ranked perpetrators by insider evidence given by the first accused. The special difficulties of the international criminal jurisdictions with respect to, *inter alia*, the conduct of the criminal investigation, securing evidence, including witness testimony, and witness protection, make this alternative particularly attractive. However, the drawbacks are also obvious. The fact-finding mission of the criminal procedure is affected and the practice may lead to judgments that are factually incorrect. Generally, a full trial produces a more reliable and complete historical record, although some argue that plea-bargaining contributes more effectively to a general acceptance of the historical record and to a greater number of completed cases and thus to a broader factual base.[79] Moreover, plea-bargaining concerning international crimes may be considered inappropriate due to the vagueness with respect to their legal elements for criminal responsibility.[80]

Nonetheless, in many cases the ICTY, and to a lesser extent the ICTR, have accepted plea agreements as the basis for convictions, although it has been underlined that the practice should be used with caution and only when it satisfies the interests of justice.[81] The judges are not bound by the agreement, but in the majority of cases the sentence falls within the range agreed by the parties and includes a substantive sentencing rebate.[82]

The ICC regime, which, as already stated, has influenced the current ICTY and ICTR Rules, refers to an 'admission of guilt' and represents a middle way between the traditional common law and civil law approaches.[83] The procedure allows for abbreviated trial proceedings while providing the judges with a high level of control and a responsibility to be satisfied that the admission is supported by the facts of the case. All the essential facts that are required to prove the crime to which the admission relates must be established and the Chamber may request the prosecutor to present additional evidence if 'required by the interests of justice, in particular the interests of victims'.[84] In case the admission of guilt is not accepted as the basis for a conviction, the trial will be continued under the ordinary trial procedures, possibly by another Chamber. Unlike the Tribunals, the ICC scheme is primarily designed for the admission of guilt to take place at the very beginning of the trial; if it is made earlier, the pre-trial procedures must still be followed.[85] The provisions have not yet been applied in practice.

Plea-bargaining was a hotly contested issue in the ICC negotiations and many were advocating strongly against allowing this practice, and thus were initially reluctant to accept the admission of guilt proceedings. On the insistence of the opponents, the ICC Statute explicitly sets forth that discussions between the prosecution and the defence concerning 'modification of the charges, the admission of guilt or the penalty' shall not be binding on the Court.[86]

However, this provision supports rather than prevents plea agreements, in particular when read together with the provision that the prosecutor may '[e]nter into such arrangements or agreements, not consistent with this Statute, as may be necessary to facilitate the cooperation of [...] a person'.[87] It remains to be seen if any plea-bargaining, however controversial, will take place at the ICC.

Sentencing

Domestic practice differs with respect to bifurcated trial proceedings, where issues of guilt and of sentencing are dealt with separately, or a unified trial. In the first cases to be adjudicated, the ICTY took the former approach and sentencing issues were addressed in a separate process once the criminal responsibility of the accused had been established.[88] Thereafter, rules were adopted prescribing that 'any relevant information that may assist the Trial Chamber in determining an appropriate sentence' should normally be presented already at the trial, and allowing the Chamber to address guilt and penalty issues at the same time.[89] Since then, unified trial proceedings have been applied by both Tribunals. Also at the ICC the main rule is a unified trial unless the Trial Chamber decides otherwise.[90] However, here the parties play a decisive role and the prosecutor or the accused may request bifurcated trial proceedings. Simplified trial proceedings due to the admission of guilt shall always be unified. In case of a bifurcated trial, issues concerning reparations to victims shall be addressed in the sentencing hearing and, if necessary, during additional hearings.

Mid-trial acquittal

The ICTY and ICTR procedures provide for a judgment of acquittal at the close of the prosecution case on any count 'if there is no evidence capable of supporting a conviction'.[91] The test is whether the evidence, if believed, is sufficient for a reasonable trier of fact to find that guilt has been proved beyond reasonable doubt, i.e. whether the accused has a case to answer.[92] It is not meant to be a full evaluation of the prosecution evidence at this point in time, but instead an assessment of whether the evidence could sustain a conviction.[93] The reliability and credibility of the evidence will be regarded only if 'the Prosecution's case has completely broken down'.[94] No equivalent procedure is provided for the ICC, but, as in the early practice of the ICTY,[95] the Court could consider that such an assessment may be made based upon an inherent power of the Trial Chamber to dismiss counts of the indictment. The procedure promotes judicial economy but the impartiality of the judges may be questioned in case the motion for acquittal is rejected.

Appeal

Appeal against convictions, acquittals and sentences

Today the right of appeal is generally recognized as a fundamental human right in criminal proceedings.[96] The ICTR, ICTR and ICC all allow appeals and, like in many civil law jurisdictions, appeals are not only allowed with respect to convictions and sentences but also to acquittals.[97] In practice, acquittals have been replaced by convictions on appeal concerning specific counts in the indictment.[98] Hence, the interest of achieving materially correct verdicts, and thus not considering a verdict of acquittal as final until the time for appeal has run out, takes precedence over the interest of protecting the individual against repeated charges by public authorities. In the

ICC, the prosecutor is also entitled to appeal a conviction, which underscores the prosecutor's role as an organ of justice and not merely a party to the proceedings.[99]

On appeal, the Appeals Chamber may affirm, reverse or revise the appealed decision.[100] Alternatively, it may set aside the judgment and order a new trial before a different trial chamber.[101] At the ICTY, cases have been remitted to the Trial Chamber when a guilty plea was invalid[102] or for resentencing subsequent to the reversal of acquittals.[103] The ICTR Appeals Chamber ordered a retrial because of insufficient reasoning in the trial judgment.[104] However, there are examples where the Appeals Chamber has reversed the trial judgment in part and reduced the sentence, based on extensive additional material in the appeals proceedings, as will be seen further in this chapter.[105] Moreover, the ICTY Appeals Chamber has established that it may choose the remedy when overturning an acquittal and decline to remit the case back to the Trial Chamber for trial.[106]

The Appeals Chambers consist of a panel of five judges. Detailed procedures are set forth for each jurisdiction.[107] Naturally, the standard of review has a decisive influence on the procedures, a point which is addressed further in this chapter. It is primarily a written process in which additional evidence may be admitted.[108] However, the ICC Statute leaves room for a greater degree of oral proceedings.

A safeguard in domestic jurisdictions where acquittals are subject to appeals is a prohibition against *reformatio in peius* (worsening of an earlier verdict). Hence, a verdict or sentence may not be changed to the detriment of the accused if only he or she appeals. The principle is set forth in the ICC Statute and is also applied by the Tribunals.[109] In practice, the principle is easy to apply to penalties but more difficult concerning convictions, since no formal hierarchal order has been established between the different crimes and thus there is no clear indication concerning which crime shall be considered more or less serious than another crime.

Grounds of appeal and standard of review

Appeals against trial judgments at the ICTY and ICTR—verdicts and sentences—are appeals *strictu sensu* in the meaning that they are of a corrective nature and do not constitute new trials (trials *de novo*), a fact that is repeatedly stated by the Appeals Chambers.[110] Hence, the process is limited to correcting errors of law invalidating the decision and errors of fact resulting in a 'miscarriage of justice'. The parties must limit their arguments within the confines of the applied standard, but it is not sufficient to merely repeat unsuccessful arguments at the trial; the party must also demonstrate that rejecting them was an error that warrants the intervention of the Appeals Chamber.[111]

With respect to errors of law, the Appeals Chamber will not only correct the legal error but also apply the correct legal standard to the evidence in the trial record and determine whether it is itself convinced that the evidentiary standard for a conviction is met.[112] However, by also applying the correct legal standard to the case at hand, instead of ordering a retrial before a Trial Chamber, the Appeals Chamber will turn into a trier of fact to an extent that it was unwilling to assume in earlier cases. The reason for the shift was the Appeals Chambers increasingly being faced with additional evidence on appeal and mindful of the long trials and limited resources.

The threshold for intervention in factual determinations is high and requires that the conclusion of the Trial Chamber is one 'which no reasonable trier of fact could have reached',[113] leading to a 'grossly unfair outcome in judicial proceedings, as when the defendant is convicted despite a lack of evidence on an essential element of the crime'.[114] When applying this principle of 'reasonableness', the ICTY and ICTR Appeals Chambers have stressed that it 'will not lightly disturb findings of fact by a Trial Chamber',[115] i.e. hearing, assessing and weighing the evidence presented at trial is primarily the task for the Trial Chamber. However, this practice could be criticized for doing away with the possibility to appeal the findings.

In addition to this, the ICTY and ICTR Appeals Chambers have established an inherent power, deriving from their judicial function, to ensure that justice is done by assuming a discretionary power to correct an error of law on their own motion if the interests of justice so require;[116] the Appeals Chamber applies the principle of *jura novit curia*. Hence, the burden of proof is not absolute regarding points of law, but the party is required to identify the alleged error and present arguments explaining how the error invalidates the Trial Chamber's determination.[117] Being a precedence-setting body in a new and unique procedural system, the Appeals Chambers has also assumed the power to 'determine issues which, though they have no bearing on the verdict reached by a Trial Chamber, are of general significance to the Tribunal's jurisprudence'.[118]

With respect to penalties, the ICTY and ICTR Appeals Chambers have taken the view that the sentence should not be revised unless the Trial Chamber has committed a 'discernible error' in exercising its discretion or has failed to follow applicable law.[119] At the ICC, a verdict or sentence may be appealed on the ground of a procedural error, an error of fact or an error of law, but also against a conviction on 'any other ground that affects the fairness or reliability of the proceedings or decision'.[120] The main ground for appeal against a sentence is disproportion between the crime and the sentence.[121] In addition, however, it is clarified that a reversal, amendment or remittal to a new trial before a Trial Chamber requires that the 'proceedings were unfair in a way that affected the reliability of the decision or sentence' or that 'the decision or sentence ... was materially affected by error of fact or law or procedural error'.[122] Concerning errors of law, 'materially affected' means that 'the Pre-Trial or Trial Chamber would have rendered a decision that is substantially different from the decision that was affected by the error, if it had not made the error'.[123] Moreover, the Appeals Chamber may also on its own motion raise the question to set aside a conviction or reduce a sentence, i.e. a power that is only applicable to the benefit of the defendant.[124]

The nature of the appeals review at the ICC is less clear and no appeal against a verdict or sentence has yet been heard. The Statute leaves the Appeals Chamber with broad discretion; it has all the powers of the Trial Chamber and evidence may be presented in the appeals proceedings, including evidence called by the Chamber itself.[125] It is possible to interpret the provisions to leave room for a trial *de novo*, but a better reading is that the enumerated grounds for an appeal point towards a corrective procedure with a possibility of admitting additional evidence.[126]

Interlocutory appeals

The ICTY and ICTR Statutes do not provide for interlocutory appeals, but such appeals were nevertheless soon accepted in practice and have now statutory support.[127] The ICC Statute also allows interlocutory appeals.[128] This applies to decisions on jurisdiction and in the ICC also to decisions regarding admissibility of a case. Moreover, the ICC Statute allows interlocutory appeals against decisions concerning provisional release and certain Pre-Trial Chamber–ordered measures during the investigation. For all other decisions leave to appeal (or certification) by the Chamber issuing the decision is required, which in turn requires that the decision 'involves an issue that would significantly affect the fair and expeditious conduct of the proceedings or the outcome of the trial' and for which 'an immediate resolution by the Appeals Chamber may materially advance the proceedings'.[129] At the ICC, leave to appeal may also be granted by the Pre-Trial or Trial Chamber on its own accord.[130] Since interlocutory appeals are time and resource consuming, the Tribunals and the ICC all apply restrictions.[131] Apart from the limited scope of the right to interlocutory appeals, the ICTY and ICTR have adopted a restrictive approach to reviews of the Trial Chamber's exercise of discretionary powers, confining it to whether the discretion was correctly exercised, but not to whether the Appeals Chamber agrees in substance.[132] A matter determined in an interlocutory decision is not open for reconsideration unless 'a clear error of reasoning has been demonstrated or if it is necessary to do so to prevent an injustice'. At the ICTR, frivolous motions may cause refusal of payment to counsel under the legal aid scheme.[133]

Early practice of the ICC has also been restrictive and most applications for leave to appeal have been denied, although inconsistent approaches to different procedural issues have prompted a more generous practice.[134] By addressing the 'admissibility of an appeal', the Appeals Chamber has explained the requirements for such an appeal, both concerning the matters specifically mentioned in Article 82(1) of the ICC Statute and the 'issues' that may be appealed if leave for appeal is granted.[135] The Appeals Chamber has stated that the lack of specified grounds for appeal means that the parties are at liberty to raise any grounds, including those that apply to appeals against a verdict or sentence.[136] However, with respect to interlocutory appeals that require leave to appeal, the Chamber has concluded that only procedural errors or errors of law or of fact may be relied upon as grounds.[137]

Review or revision

Extraordinary challenges – review or revision – after the time for appeal has lapsed, are possible at the ICTY, ICTR and ICC.[138] It is a remedy against miscarriage of justice, which goes beyond errors of fact or law. While revision at the ICC may only be directed against a conviction or sentence, the remedy is also available against acquittals at the ICTY and ICTR. The prosecutor of the ICTY or ICTR must seek review within one year after the final judgment, but the convicted person is not restricted by any time limit.[139] At the ICC, no time constraints apply to any of the parties, or certain relatives, if the accused is deceased. Through their case law, the Tribunals have extended the scope of the review proceedings to final decisions other than those which contain a verdict or sentence: for example, to final decisions resulting in the dismissal of the case with prejudice to the prosecutor.[140] This issue is not regulated for the ICC.

The exceptional nature of the remedy is underlined by strict requirements. The ICTY and ICTR demand a new fact that was not known to the applicant at the time of the original proceedings and, thus, could not be considered when the verdict was reached.[141] In addition, it is required that the failure to discover the new fact was not due to the applicant's lack of due diligence,[142] and that the new fact could have been a decisive factor in reaching the original decision. In extraordinary circumstances, however, the Tribunal may grant review although the fact was known to or discoverable by the applicant; this is in order to prevent a miscarriage of justice.[143]

Also, at the ICC, revision requires that 'new evidence', which was not available at the time of the trial by reasons not wholly or partially attributable to the moving party, be sufficiently important so that the verdict is likely to have turned out differently. Arguably, the notion of 'new evidence' should be understood as a broader concept than 'new facts'.[144] Additional grounds for revision are the new discovery that decisive evidence at trial turns out to be false, forged or falsified, or the occurrence of serious misconduct or breach of duty by a participating judge. The provisions have not yet been applied in practice and different views have been advanced as to how the additional grounds relate to the 'new evidence' criterion.[145]

The procedures of the ICTY and ICTR, on the one hand, and the ICC, on the other hand, differ.[146] At the Tribunals, the admissibility of the application for revision and, if successful, the review as such are normally dealt with at the same time and by the Chamber that handed down the decision under review. The ICC instead applies a two-step process where the Appeals Chamber first determines the admissibility of the application and the revision is to be conducted thereafter by itself or another Chamber.

Notes

1 See V. Tochilovsky, 'International Criminal Justice: "Strangers in the Foreign System"', *Criminal Law Forum*, vol. 15, 2004, 319–44.
2 Article 18(1) of the ICTY Statute and Article 17(1) of the ICTR Statute.
3 However, as part of the ICTY's completion strategy, new indictments were made subject to a pre-screening process, Rule 28(A) of the ICTY Rules. No equivalent rule was adopted by the ICTR.
4 Article 53(1) of the ICC Statute and Rule 48 of the ICC Rules.
5 Ibid. Article 53(3).
6 An attempt to clarify the difference between a 'situation' and a 'case' is made in *Lubanga* (ICC-01/04-01/06), Decision on the Applications for Participation in the Proceedings of VPRS1, VPRS2, VPRS3, VPRS4, VPRS5 and VPRS6, Pre-Trial Chamber 17 January 2006, para. 65; see also R. Rastan, 'What Is a "Case" for the Purpose of the Rome Statute?', *Criminal Law Forum*, vol. 19, 2008, 435–48.
7 See further Chapter 19.
8 For the ICC, e.g. the *Regulation of the Office of the Prosecutor* (ICC-BD/05-01-09), adopted on 23 April 2009.
9 Article 53(2)–(3) of the ICC Statute.
10 Rule 47(E) of the ICTY and ICTR Rules.
11 For example, *Kordić et al.* (IT-95-14/2), Order concerning documents to be transmitted by the defence to the judge reviewing the proposed amended indictment, Trial Chamber 26 August 1998.
12 Article 61 of the ICC Statute and Rule 121 of the ICC Rules.
13 See, e.g. M. Miraglia, 'Admissibility of Evidence, Standard of Proof, and Nature of the Decision in the ICC Confirmation of Charges in Lubanga', *Journal of International Criminal Justice*, vol. 6, 2008, 489–503.
14 Rule 61 of the ICTY and ICTR Rules, Article 61(2) of the ICC Statute, and Rules 123–6 of the ICC Rules. On the debate, see, e.g. M. Thieroff and E. Amley, 'Proceeding Justice and Accountability in the Balkans: The International Criminal Tribunal for the former Yugoslavia and Rule 61', *Yale Journal of International Law*, vol. 23, 1998, 231–74.
15 *Blagojević & Jokić* (IT-02-60), Decision, Appeals Chamber 8 April 2003, para. 18. See also Rule 73*bis*(B) of the ICTR Rules.
16 *Tadić* (IT-94-1), Decision on the defence motion for interlocutory appeal on jurisdiction, Appeals Chamber 2 October 1995.
17 Rules 54, 72 and 73 of the ICTY and ICTR Rules.
18 Articles 19, 57 and 64 of the ICC Statute and Rules 58–62 of the ICC Rules.
19 For a critical view, see G. Sluiter, 'The ICTR and the Protection of Witnesses', *Journal of International Criminal Justice*, vol. 3, 2005, 962–76.
20 Rules 47(H)(i) and 54 of the ICTY and ICTR Rules, and Article 58 of the ICC Statute.
21 For example, *Brđanin & Talić* (IT-99-36), Decision on motions by Momir Talić (1) to dismiss the indictment, (2) for release, and (3) for leave to reply to response of prosecution to motion for release, Trial Chamber 1 February 2000, paras 20–3.
22 Rule 65 of the ICTY and ICTR Rules.
23 Article 60 of the ICC Statute and Rules 118–19 of the ICC Rules.
24 For example, *Barayagwiza* (ICTR-97-19), Decision, Appeals Chamber 3 November 1999, and *Lubanga Dyilo* (ICC-01/04-01/06), Judgment of the appeal of Mr Thomas Lubanga Dyilo against the decision on the defence challenge to the jurisdiction of the Court pursuant to Article 19(2)(a) of the Statute of 3 October 2006, Appeals Chamber 14 December 2006.
25 Rules 48, 49 and 82 of the ICTY Rules, Rules 48, 48*bis*, 49 and 82 of the ICTR Rules, Article 64(5) of the ICC Statute, and Rule 136 of the ICC Rules.
26 For example, *Bagosora et al.* (ICTR-96-7), Decision on the Prosecutor's motion for joinder, Trial Chamber 29 June 2000, paras 145–56, and *Katanga & Ngudjolo Chui* (ICC-01/04-01/07), Decision on

the joinder of the cases against Germanin Katanga and Mathieu Ngudjolo Chui, Pre-Trial Chamber 10 March 2008.

27 For example, *Milošević* (IT-99-37 a.o.), Decision on the Prosecutor's motion for joinder, Trial Chamber 13 December 2001, and Reasons for decision on prosecution interlocutory appeal from refusal to order joinder, Appeals Chamber 18 April 2002. See also G. Boas, *The Milošević Trial*, Cambridge: Cambridge University Press, 2007, pp. 115–21.

28 Articles 3(3) and 62 of the ICC Statute and Rule 100 of the ICC Rules.

29 Rule 4 of the ICTY and ICTR Rules.

30 For example, *Bagosora et al.* (ICTR-98-41), Decision on Prosecution's motion for site visits in the Republic of Rwanda, Trial Chamber 29 September 2004.

31 Rules 65*ter* and 108*bis* of the ICTY Rules, Articles 39(2)(b)(iii) and 57(2)(b) of the ICC Statute, Rule 7 of the ICC Rules, and Regulation 47 of the ICC Regulations of the Court.

32 Rule 65*bis* of the ICTY and ICTR Rules, Rule 132 of the ICC Rules and Regulation 54 of the ICC Regulations of the Court.

33 Rules 73*bis* and 73*ter* of the ICTY and ICTR Rules, Regulation 54 of the ICC Regulations of the Court.

34 See, e.g. *Orić* (IT-03-68), Interlocutory Decision on Length of Defence Case, Appeals Chamber 20 July 2005.

35 *Lubanga Dyilo* (ICC-01/04-01/06), Decision on the practice of witness familiarization and witness proofing, Pre-Trial Chamber 8 November 2006; cf. *Limaj et al.* (IT-03-66), Decision on defence motion on prosecution practice of 'proofing' witnesses, Trial Chamber 10 December 2004, *Milutinović et al.* (IT-05-87), Decision on Ojdanić motion to prohibit witness proofing, Trial Chamber 12 December 2006, and *Karemera et al.* (ICTR-98-44), Decision on interlocutory appeal regarding witness proofing, Appeals Chamber 11 May 2007. See also S. Vasiliev, 'Proofing the Ban on "Witness Proofing": Did the ICC Get it Right?', *Criminal Law Forum*, vol. 20, 2009, 193–261, and K. Ambos, 'Witness Proofing before the ICC: Neither Legally Admissible nor Necessary' in C. Stahn and G. Sluiter (eds), *The Emerging Practice of the International Criminal Court,* Leiden/Boston: Martinus Nijhoff Publishers, 2009, pp. 599–614.

36 Articles 15(3), 19(3) and 68(3) of the ICC Statute, and Rules 89–93 of the ICC Rules.

37 Article 75 of the ICC Statute and Rules 94–9 of the ICC Rules.

38 See, e.g. H. Friman, 'Participation of Victims before the ICC: A Critical Assessment of the Early Developments' in G. Sluiter and S. Vasiliev (eds), *International Criminal Procedure: Towards a Coherent Body of Law,* London: CMP Publishing, 2009, pp. 205–36, and 'The International Criminal Court and Participation of Victims: A Third Party to the Proceedings?', *Leiden Journal of International Law*, vol. 22, 2009, 485–500.

39 Article 74(1) of the ICC Statute; cf. Rule 15*bis* in the ICTY and ICTR Rules.

40 For example, *Nyiramasuhuko et al.* (ICTR-98-42), Decision in the matter of proceedings under Rule 15*bis*(D), Trial Chamber 15 July 2003, and *Krajišnik* (IT-00-39&40), Decision pursuant to Rule 15*bis*(D), Trial Chamber 16 December 2004.

41 *Nyiramasuhuko et al.* (ICTR-98-42), Decision in the matter of proceedings under Rule 15*bis*(D), Appeals Chamber 24 September 2003, paras 17–18.

42 For example, M. Fairlie, 'Adding Fuel to Milosevic's Fire: How the Use of Substitute Judges Discredits the UN War Crimes Tribunals', *Criminal Law Forum*, vol. 16, 2005, 107–57.

43 Rule 15*ter* of the ICTY Rules.

44 Rules 79–80 of the ICTY and ICTR Rules, and Articles 63 and 64(7) of the ICC Statute. See further, J. D'Aoust, 'The Conduct of Trials' in J. Doria *et al.* (eds), *The Legal Regime of the ICC: Essays in Honour of Prof. I Blishchenko*, Antwerp: Intersentia, 2009, pp. 868–9.

45 Article 21(4)(d) of the ICTY Statute, Article 20(4)(d) of the ICTR Statute, and Article 63 of the ICC Statute.

46 For example, H. Friman, 'Rights of Persons Suspected or Accused of a Crime' in R. S. Lee (ed.), *The International Criminal Court: The Making of the Rome Statute*, The Hague: Kluwer Law International, 1999, pp. 247–61, and W. Schabas, 'In Absentia Proceedings before the International Criminal, Courts', in G. Sluiter and S. Vasiliev (eds), *International Criminal Procedure: Towards a Coherent Body of Law*, 335–80.

47 For example, R. Wedgwood, 'War Crimes: Bosnia and Beyond – War Crimes in the former Yugoslavia: Comments on the International War Crimes Tribunal', *Virginia Journal of International Law*, vol. 34, 1994, 267–75; A. Pellet, 'Le Tribunal criminel pour l'ex-Yougoslavie. Poudre aux yeux ou avancée

décisive?', *Revue générale de droit international public*, vol. 98, 1994, 7, 48; H. Schwartz 'Trials in Absentia', *Human Rights Brief*, vol. 4, 1996, 18.

48 Rule 80 of the ICTY and ICTR and Article 71 of the ICC Statute.

49 See further Chapter 20.

50 Rule 84 of the ICTY and ICTR Rules.

51 Rule 84*bis* of the ICTY Rules.

52 Article 64(8) of the ICC Statute.

53 For example, *Lubanga Dyilo* (ICC-01/04-01/06), Decision on opening and closing statements, 22 May 2008.

54 Rule 85(A) of the ICTY and ICTR Rules, and Article 69(3) of the ICC Statute. See also J. D'Aoust, 'The Conduct of Trials', in J. Doria *et al.* (eds), *The Legal Regime of the ICC*, pp. 874–89.

55 Rule 98 of the ICTY and ICTR Rules, and Articles 64(6)(d) and 69(3) of the ICC Statute.

56 See, e.g. a series of decisions in *Blaškić* (IT-95-14) on 25 March, 13 May and 21 May 1999, and *Lubanga Dyilo* (ICC-01/04-01/06), Instructions to the Court's expert on child soldiers and trauma, 6 February 2009.

57 *Lubanga Dyilo* (ICC-01/04-01/06), Second Decision on disclosure by the defence and Decision on whether the prosecution may contact defence witnesses, 19 November 2009, para. 49.

58 Rules 71 and 81*bis* of the ICTY Rules, Rule 71 of the ICTR Rules, and Article 69(2) of the ICC Statute.

59 Rule 85 of the ICTY and ICTR Rules.

60 Rule 90(H) of the ICTY Rules and Rule 90(G) of the ICTR Rules.

61 Rule 140 of the ICC Rules. See also P. Lewis, 'Trial Procedure' in R. S. Lee *et al.* (eds), *The International Criminal Court: Elements of Crimes and Rules of Procedure and Evidence*, Ardsley, NY: Transnational Publishers, 2001, pp. 547–50.

62 For example, *Katanga & Ngudjolo Chui* (ICC-01/04-01/07), Directions for the conduct of the proceedings and testimony in accordance with rule 140, 20 November 2009.

63 Rule 140 of the ICC Rules. Compared with different practices within the common law-tradition, the scope of cross-examination in the ICC is more similar to English law than to American practice in that it allows the examination to go beyond the subject matters of direct examination. In the ICTY and ICTR the 'American rule' applies; see J. R. W. D. Jones and S. Powles, *International Criminal Practice*, Oxford: Oxford University Press, 3rd edn, 2003, pp. 718–19.

64 Rule 91(3) of the ICC Rules.

65 For example, *Bagosora et al.* (ICTR-98-41), Decision on motion to compel accused to testify prior to other defence witnesses, Trial Chamber 11 January 2005, and *Kordić & Čerkez* (IT-95-14/2), Decision on Prosecutor's motion on trial procedure, Trial Chamber 19 March 1999.

66 Rule 86 of the ICTY and ICTR Rules, and Rules 89(1) and 141 of the ICC Rules.

67 Rules 29 and 87 of the ICTY and ICTR Rules, Article 74(5) of the ICC Statute, and Rule 142 of the ICC Rules.

68 Article 74(3) of the ICC Statute.

69 Rule 98*ter* of the ICTY Rules, Rule 88 of the ICTR Rules, Article 74(5) of the ICC Statute, and Rule 142 of the ICC Rules.

70 The guilty plea also constitutes the waiver of other rights, such as the right to remain silent, to conduct his or her own defence, to raise defences, and to cross-examine witnesses; see also F. Guariglia and G. Hochmayr, 'Article 65' in O. Triffterer (ed.), *Commentary on the Rome Statute of the International Criminal Court: Observers' Notes, Article by Article*, Munich/Oxford/Baden-Baden: C.H. Beck, Hart, Nomos, 2nd edn, 2008, p. 1227.

71 See Y. Ma, 'Prosecutorial Discretion and Plea Bargaining in the United States, France, Germany, and Italy: A Comparative Perspective', *International Criminal Justice Review*, vol. 12, 2002, 22–52.

72 Article 20(3) of the ICTY Statute and Article 19(3) of the ICTR Statute.

73 *Erdemović* (IT-96-22), Appeals Chamber Judgement, 7 October 1997 (a minority also found the guilty plea to be equivocal).

74 *Kambanda* (ICTR-97-23), Appeals Chamber Judgement, 19 October 2000.

75 Rule 62*bis* of the ICTY Rules and Rule 62 of the ICTR Rules. For a critical view, see Jones and Powles, *International Criminal Practice,* p. 641.

76 Examples at the ICTY are Sikirica and Došen who pleaded guilty first when genocide charges were dismissed by the Trial Chamber by way of a (partial) so-called mid-trial acquittal, and M. Simić who changed his plea to guilty on day 83 of the prosecution presenting its evidence at trial.

77 Rule 62*ter* of the ICTY Rules and Rule 62*bis* of the ICTR Rules.
78 For example, M. Bohlander, 'Plea-Bargaining before the ICTY' in R. May *et al.* (eds), *Essays on ICTY Procedure and Evidence – In Honour of Gabrielle Kirk McDonald,* The Hague: Brill, 2001, pp. 151–63; N. Combs, 'Copping a Plea to Genocide: The Plea Bargaining of International Crimes', *University of Pennsylvania Law Review*, vol. 151, 2002, 1–57; M. Damaška, 'Negotiated Justice in International Criminal Courts', *Journal of International Criminal Justice*, vol. 2, 2004, 1018–39; J. Cook, 'Plea Bargaining at the Hague', *Yale Journal of International Law*, vol. 30, 2005, 473–506; R. Henham and M. Drumbl, 'Plea Bargaining at the International Criminal Tribunal for the former Yugoslavia', *Criminal Law Forum*, vol. 16, 2005, 49–87; M. Harmon, 'Plea Bargaining: The Uninvited Guest at the International Criminal Tribunal for the former Yugoslavia' in J. Doria *et al.* (eds), *The Legal Regime of the ICC,* pp. 163–82.
79 See Damaška, 'Negotiated Justice', pp. 1031–3. Cf. M. Scharf, 'Trading Justice for Efficiency: Plea-Bargaining and International Tribunals', *Journal of International Criminal Justice*, vol. 2, 2004, 1070–81, and A. Tieger and M. Shin, 'Plea Agreements in the ICTY: Purpose, Effects and Propriety', *Journal of International Criminal Justice*, vol. 3, 2005, 666–79, 671.
80 See Damaška, 'Negotiated Justice', p. 1033.
81 *Momir Nikolić* (IT-02-60/1), Sentencing Judgement, Trial Chamber 2 December 2003, para. 73.
82 For example, *Todorović* (IT-95-9/2), Sentencing Judgement, Trial Chamber 31 July 2001, paras 80–2. See also R. Dixon and A. Demirdjian, 'Advising Defendants about Guilty Pleas before International Courts', *Journal of International Criminal Justice*, vol. 3, 2005, 680–94, 681.
83 Article 65 of the ICC Statute. See Guariglia and Hochmayr, 'Article 65', in Triffterer (ed.), *Commentary on the Rome Statute of the International Criminal Court*, p. 1223, and H. D. Bosly, 'Admission of Guilt before the ICC and in Continental Systems', *Journal of International Criminal Justice*, vol. 2, 2004, 1040–9.
84 Article 65(4) of the ICC Statute.
85 See also Guariglia and Hochmayr, 'Article 65', in Triffterer (ed.), *Commentary on the Rome Statute of the International Criminal Court*, pp. 1225–6.
86 Article 65(5) of the ICC Statute.
87 Article 54(3)(d) of the ICC Statute. See also Bohlander, 'Plea-Bargaining', in May *et al.* (eds), *Essays on ICTY Procedure and Evidence*, p. 157, and H. Friman, 'Inspiration from the International Criminal Tribunals when developing Law on Evidence for the International Criminal Court', *The Law and Practice of International Courts and Tribunals*, vol. 3, 2003, 373, 393.
88 See the *Erdemović* (IT-96-22) and *Tadić* (IT-94-1) cases.
89 Rules 85 and 87 of the ICTY and ICTR Rules.
90 Article 76 of the ICC Statute and Rule 143 of the ICC Rules.
91 Rule 98*bis* of the ICTY and ICTR Rules.
92 For example, *Delalić et al.* (IT-96-21), Appeals Chamber Judgement, 20 February 2001, para. 434.
93 See *Jelisić* (IT-95-10), Judgement, Appeals Chamber 5 July 2001, paras 34–7 (also warning against the term 'no case to answer' since it could lead to incorrect domestic analogies).
94 *Kordić & Čerkez* (IT-95-14/2-T), Decision on defence motions for judgement of acquittal, Trial Chamber 6 April 2000, para. 28.
95 For example, *Delalić et al.* (IT-96-21), Order on motion to dismiss the indictment at the close of the Prosecutor's case, Trial Chamber 18 March 1998.
96 For example, Article 14(5) of the International Covenant on Civil and Political Rights. Cf. the Nuremberg and Tokyo Tribunals where appeals were not provided for.
97 Article 25 of the ICTY Statute, Article 24 of the ICTR Statute, and Article 81 of the ICC Statute.
98 For example, *Tadić* (IT-94-1), Judgement, Appeals Chamber 15 July 1997, and *Rutaganda* (ICTR-96-3), Judgement, Appeals Chamber 26 May 2003.
99 Article 81(1)(b) of the ICC Statute. See also R. Roth and M. Henzlin, 'The Appeal Procedure of the ICC', in A. Cassese *et al.* (eds), *The Rome Statute of the International Criminal Court: A Commentary*, Oxford: Oxford University Press, 2002, p. 1543.
100 Article 25(2) of the ICTY Statute, Article 24(2) of the ICTR Statute, and Article 81(2) of the ICC Statute.
101 Article 81(2) of the ICC Statute. See also Rule 117(C) of the ICTY Rules and Rule 118(C) of the ICTR Rules.
102 *Erdemović* (IT-96-22), Judgement, Appeals Chamber 7 October 1997.
103 *Tadić* (IT-94-1), Order remitting sentencing to a Trial Chamber, Appeals Chamber 10 September 1999.

104 *Muvunyi* (ICTR-2000-55A), Judgement, Appeals Chamber 29 August 2008.
105 See *Blaškić* (IT-95-14), Judgement, Appeals Chamber 29 July 2004.
106 *Jelisić* (IT-95-10), Judgement, Appeals Chamber 5 July 2001, paras 72–7; cf. the dissenting opinion of Judge Wald to the ruling.
107 Rules 107–18 of the ICTY Rules, Rules 107-19 of the ICTR Rules, Rules 149–58 of the ICC Rules and Regulations 57–65 of the ICC Regulations of the Court.
108 Rule 115 of the ICTY and ICTR Rules. See U. Lundqvist, 'Admitting and Evaluating Evidence in the International Criminal Tribunal for the former Yugoslavia Appeals Chamber Proceedings. A Few Remarks', *Leiden Journal of International Law*, vol. 15, 2002, 641–65.
109 Article 83(2) of the ICC Statute. See also *Bralo* (IT-95-17), Judgement on sentencing appeals, Appeals Chamber 2 April 2007, para. 85, and *Muvunyi* (ICTR-2000-55A), Judgement, Appeals Chamber 29 August 2008, para. 170.
110 Article 25 of the ICTY Statute and Article 24 of the ICTR Statute; see also, e.g. *Kupreškić et al.* (IT-95-16), Judgement, Appeals Chamber 23 October 2001, para. 408. For an analysis of the grounds and standards, see, e.g. J. Doria, 'Standards of Appeals and Standards of Revision' in J. Doria *et al.* (eds), *The Legal Regime of the ICC*, pp. 945-72.
111 For example, *Blaškić* (IT-95-14), Judgement, Appeals Chamber 29 July 2004, para. 13.
112 Ibid., para. 15.
113 For example, *Tadić* (IT-94-1), Judgement, Appeals Chamber 15 July 1999, para. 64, and *Akayesu* (ICTR-95-4), Judgement, Appeals Chamber 1 June 2001, para. 178.
114 For example, *Furundžija* (IT-95-17/1), Judgement, Appeals Chamber 21 July 2000, para. 37.
115 For example, *Tadić* (IT-94-1), Judgement, Appeals Chamber 15 July 1999, para. 35, and *Musema* (ICTR-96-13), Judgement, Appeals Chamber 16 November 2001, para. 18.
116 For example, *Delalić et al.* (IT-96-21), Judgement on sentence appeal, Appeals Chamber 8 April 2003, para. 16, and *Kambanda* (ICTR-97-23), Judgement, Appeals Chamber 19 October 2000, para. 98.
117 For example, *Krnojelac* (IT-97-25), Judgement, Appeals Chamber 17 September 2003, para. 10.
118 For example, *Akayesu* (ICTR-95-4), Judgement, Appeals Chamber 1 June 2001, para. 21, and *Furundžija* (IT-95-17/1), Judgement, Appeals Chamber 21 July 2000, para. 35.
119 For example, *Tadić* (IT-94-1), Judgement in sentencing appeals, Appeals Chamber 26 January 2000, para. 22, and *Musema* (ICTR-96-13), Judgement, Appeals Chamber 16 November 2001, para. 395.
120 Article 81(1) of the ICC Statute.
121 Article 81(2)(a) of the ICC Statute.
122 Article 83(2) of the ICC Statute.
123 See *Situation in the Democratic Republic of the Congo* (ICC-01/04), Judgment on the Prosecutor's appeal against the decision of Pre-Trial Chamber I entitled 'Decision on the Prosecutor's Application for Warrants of Arrest, Article 58', Appeals Chamber 13 July 2006, para. 84; cf. Lubanga Dyilo (ICC-01/04-10/06), Judgement on the Prosecutor's appeal against the decision of Pre-Trial Chamber I entitled 'Decision Establishing General Principles Governing Applications to Restrict Disclosure pursuant to Rule 81 (2) and (4) of the Rules of Procedure and Evidence', Appeals Chamber 13 October 2006, para. 19, where the grounds were limited to those enumerated in Article 81(1)(a) of the ICC Statute (Judge Pikis dissenting, para. 14).
124 Article 81(2) of the ICC Statute; similarly, see *Erdemović* (IT-96-22), Judgement, Appeals Chamber 7 October 1997, para. 39 (exercising an 'inherent power').
125 Article 83(1)–(2) of the ICC Statute; see also Rule 149 of the ICC Rules and Regulation 62 of the Regulations of the Court.
126 See H. Brady, 'Appeal and Revision' in R. S. Lee (ed.), *The International Criminal Court: The Making of the Rome Statute*, pp. 585–6, and A. Orie, 'Accusatorial v. Inquisitorial Approaches in International Criminal Proceedings Prior to the Establishment of the ICC and in the Proceedings before the ICC' in A. Cassese *et al.* (eds), *The Rome Statute of the International Criminal Court* pp. 1490–1.
127 Rules 72 and 73 of the ICTY and ICTR Rules. For earlier practice, see, e.g. *Tadić* (IT-94-1), Decision on the defence motion for interlocutory appeal on jurisdiction, Appeals Chamber 2 October 1995 paras 4–6.
128 Article 82 of the ICC Statute and Rules 154–8 of the ICC Rules.
129 Rules 72(B)(ii) and 73(B) of the ICTY and ICTR Rules, and Article 82(1)(d) of the ICC Statute. On what constitutes an appealable 'issue', see *Situation in the Democratic Republic of the Congo* (ICC-01/04), Judgment on the Prosecutor's application for extraordinary review of Pre-Trial Chamber I's 31 March 2006 decision denying leave to appeal, Appeals Chamber 13 July 2006, paras 9–10.

130 *Situation in the Democratic Republic of the Congo,* ibid., para. 20.
131 On concerns regarding too many interlocutory appeals, see D. Mundis, 'Improving the Operation and Functioning of International Criminal Tribunals', *American Journal of International Law*, vol. 94, 2000, 759, 763.
132 For example, *Milošević* (IT-02-54), Decision on interlocutory appeal of the Trial Chamber's decision on the assignment of defence counsel, Appeals Chamber 1 November 2004, paras 9–10.
133 Rule 73(D) of the ICTR Rules.
134 For a critical view, see H. Friman, 'Interlocutory Appeals in the Early Practice of the International Criminal Court' in C. Stahn and G. Sluiter (eds), *The Emerging Practice of the International Criminal Court*, pp. 445–61; cf. W. Schabas, *An Introduction to the International Criminal Court*, Cambridge: Cambridge University Press, 3rd edn, 2007, pp. 308–9.
135 For example, *Situation in the Democratic Republic of the Congo* (ICC-01/04), Judgment on the Prosecutor's appeal against the decision of Pre-Trial Chamber I entitled 'Decision on the Prosecutor's Application for Warrants of Arrest, Article 58,' Appeals Chamber 13 July 2006, and Judgment on the Prosecutor's appeal against the decision of Pre-Trial Chamber I entitled 'Decision on the Prosecutor's application for warrants of arrest, Article 58', Appeals Chamber 13 July 2006. See also Franziska Eckelmans, 'The First Jurisprudence of the Appeals Chamber of the ICC', in C. Stahn and G. Sluiter (eds), *The Emerging Practice of the International Criminal Court*, pp. 527–52.
136 *Situation in the Democratic Republic of the Congo* (ICC-01/04), Judgment on the Prosecutor's appeal against the decision of Pre-Trial Chamber I entitled 'Decision on the Prosecutor's Application for Warrants of Arrest, Article 58,' Appeals Chamber 13 July 2006, para. 34.
137 *Lubanga Dyilo* (ICC-01/04-01/06), Judgment on the Prosecutor's appeal against the decision of Pre-Trial Chamber I entitled 'Decision establishing general principles governing application to restrict disclosure pursuant to rule 81(2) and (4) of the Rules of Procedure and Evidence', Appeals Chamber 13 October 2006, para. 19; cf. the dissenting opinion of Judge Pikis, para. 14.
138 Article 26 of the ICTY Statute, Article 25 of the ICTR Statute, and Article 84 of the ICC Statute.
139 Rule 119 of the ICTY Rules and Rule 120 of the ICTR Rules.
140 For example, *Barayagwiza* (ICTR-97-19), Decision (Prosecutor's request for review of reconsideration), Appeals Chamber 31 March 2000, paras 45–50, and *Delalić et al.* (IT-96-21), Decision on motion for review (Delić), Appeals Chamber 25 April 2002, para. 5.
141 For example, *Barayagwiza,* ibid., para. 41, *Delalić et al.*, ibid., para. 8, and *Tadić* (IT-94-1), Decision on motion for review, Appeals Chamber 30 July 2002, para. 25. See also Jean Galbraith, 'New Facts in the ICTY and ICTR Review Proceedings', *Leiden Journal of International Law*, vol. 21, 2008, 131–50.
142 Rule 119 of the ICTY Rules and Rule 120 of the ICTR Rules.
143 For example, *Baryagwiza* (ICTR-97-19), Decision (Prosecutor's request for review of reconsideration), Appeals Chamber 31 March 2000, para. 65, and *Tadić* (IT-94-1), Decision on motion for review, Appeals Chamber 30 July 2002, para. 27.
144 See Doria, 'Standards of Appeals', pp. 968–72.
145 Compare Doria, ibid., 968–9, and A. M. La Rosa, 'Revision Procedure under the ICC Statute', in A. Cassese *et al.* (eds), *The Rome Statute of the International Criminal Court,* p. 1569.
146 Rules 119–22 of the ICTY Rules; Rules 120–3 of the ICTR Rules; Article 84(2) of the ICC Statute, Rules 159–61 of the ICC Rules, and Regulation 66 of the ICC Regulations.

18

Sentencing and penalties

Nadia Bernaz

Introduction

The fact that numerous individuals are currently serving prison sentences following their conviction by international criminal tribunals for international crimes of genocide, crimes against humanity and war crimes constitutes one of the most visible signs of the extraordinary evolution of international criminal law over the past 20 years. Persons who might previously have evaded prosecution are now incarcerated. While the implementation of international law is often seen as lacking, it is somewhat satisfying to be able to point to imprisoned individuals who are 'paying for their crimes'. The imprisonment of these criminals seems to be an almost natural way of addressing the public's indignation towards their crimes and, arguably, it provides the surviving victims with some form of closure and a sense of justice.

International criminal law does not thoroughly address the practicalities of sentencing. The provisions on penalties in existing statutes are brief and sketchy and the written law as it stands provides no proper sentencing scale to be used by international tribunals. States, who remain the primary authorities responsible for the implementation of international criminal law, are free to apply their own sentencing guidelines domestically, which can include the death penalty and any other sentence they deem appropriate, provided that such are not contrary to the State's human rights obligations. They are unlikely to be influenced by the unsettled practice that has developed at the international level. International criminal law generally does not influence which penalties states ultimately choose in their domestic criminal justice systems, although this is perhaps not one of its purposes. This is made clear by Article 80 of the Statute of the International Criminal Court (ICC): 'Nothing in this Part [Part 7—Penalties] affects the application by states of penalties prescribed by their national law'. This provision was introduced in the Statute as a consolation for the states that had unsuccessfully pushed for the Court to be able to sentence persons to death, and who wanted to make sure they could freely continue with domestic executions in the future.[1] In effect, it means that the discussion of the issue of penalties in international criminal law is necessarily limited to *international* criminal tribunals' law and practice regarding sentencing and does not extend to the domestic sphere. One exception concerns the enforcement of penalties since sentences of international tribunals are served domestically, which will be addressed in the final section of this chapter.

A recurrent discussion regarding penalties in international criminal law concerns the principle of legality. This two-fold principle encompasses the principle of legality of crimes and the principle of legality of penalties and is of particular relevance in civil law countries.[2] It means that persons can only be charged if the acts they committed were criminal—i.e. criminalised, preferably in a statute—at the time they were committed. Also, they can only be sentenced if the statute provided for a specific penalty for the commission of the crime. In its purest form, the principle of legality of penalties implies that a set of sentences should be determined prior to the commission of the crime. The tribunal then mathematically applies the law to come up with the appropriate penalty for each crime. The principle of individual sentencing, according to which individual mitigating and aggravating circumstances should be taken into account, tempers such rigidity. In a number of domestic systems, the two principles are balanced against each other.[3] By contrast, in international criminal law, the principle of individual sentencing plays a more decisive role since the different tribunals' statutes do not provide any precise list of penalties. The question of whether they should include such a codification 'has been debated for decades'.[4] Some even argue that the absence of a sentencing scale is not problematic since the principle of legality of penalties 'is not applicable at the international level'.[5]

The statutes of international tribunals contain no sentencing scale but they do contain specific provisions on penalties, which will be presented in the first section of this chapter. The second section will focus on the practice of sentencing by international tribunals and the discretion judges enjoy in this respect, while the third section will briefly address the issue of enforcement of sentences.

The provisions on penalties

Considering that the punishment of criminals is one of the primary functions of international criminal law, the contemporary tribunals' provisions on penalties are strikingly short and lacking in detail. Yet, they are much more developed than the single article on penalties contained in the Charter of the International Military Tribunal (IMT),[6] on the basis of which 12 individuals were sentenced to death by hanging following the Nuremberg trial.[7]

Nuremberg and Tokyo: minimal provisions on penalties

As early as 1941, Winston Churchill, referring to the atrocities committed by the Nazis, stated that 'the punishment of these crimes should now be counted among the major goals of the war'.[8] For the United Kingdom, there was no doubt that the Nazi leaders should be promptly executed and they suggested to impose summary executions:

> H.M.G. [Her Majesty's Government] thoroughly appreciate the arguments which have been advanced in favour of some form of preliminary trial. But H.M.G. are also deeply impressed with the dangers and difficulties of this course, and they wish to put before their principal Allies (...) the arguments which have led them to think that execution without trial is the preferable course.[9]

The United States strongly opposed such a proposal[10] and the four Allied Powers eventually agreed on the creation of a tribunal to try the leaders of the Nazi regime. While the Allies were in agreement regarding the principle of prosecution and punishment during the negotiations for the adoption of the Statute of the IMT, the practicalities of the sentencing process led to ardent discussions between, on the one hand, the United Kingdom, the United States and France, and on the other hand, the Soviet Union, about the role of the Allied Control Council, the military occupation governing body, in the administration of sentences. Paragraphs 20 and 21 of the initial draft of the proposed Tribunal's Charter presented by the United States in San Francisco in April 1945 stated:

> 20. Defendants brought to trial before an International Military Tribunal as provided in this Agreement shall, upon conviction, suffer death or such other punishment as shall be determined by the Tribunal before which they are tried and approved by the Control Council acting by majority vote. The Control Council, by such vote, may approve, reduce, or otherwise alter the sentences determined by the Tribunal, but may not increase the severity thereof.
>
> 21. The sentences, when and as approved by the Control Council, shall be carried into execution in accordance with the written orders of the Control Council.[11]

On 29 June 1945, the British delegate proposed that the Control Council retain the powers referred to in paragraph 21, but without any role in relation to the judgements as such. Conversely, the Soviet delegate wanted the Council to retain the competence to intervene in order to alter the sentences.[12] In the end, the United Kingdom proposed that the Control Council be allowed to pass on to the Tribunal possible new evidence having emerged after the judgement.[13] This way the Council would retain the ability to intervene in the procedure but without keeping the fate of the judgements completely in their hands. All parties eventually agreed upon this arrangement.

The Americans presented their initial draft of April 1945, together with a memorandum in which they stated that

> The defendant in each case should, upon conviction, suffer death or such other punishment as the tribunal may direct, depending upon the gravity of the offense and the degree of culpability of the defendant. In general, except upon proof of very substantial individual participation in specific atrocities, the less prominent defendants might well be sentenced to perform useful reparational labor, etc., rather than to capital punishment.[14]

The study of the drafts and minutes of the different meetings reveals that the Allies never actually discussed the suggested penalties themselves. Also, it seems as though it went without saying that the death penalty, then used by most countries including the Allied Powers, was to be included in the set of penalties. Article 27 of the Charter reads as follows: 'The Tribunal shall have the right to impose upon a Defendant, on conviction, death or such other punishment as shall be determined by it to be just'. There is nothing else in the Statute concerning penalties, which means that the task of choosing the appropriate penalty for the crimes committed was left entirely to the judges' discretion.

Article 16 of the Statute of the International Military Tribunal for the Far East is virtually identical and was most probably simply copied from Article 27. This Statute granted the judges an almost unlimited power regarding sentencing and granted a high degree of political control over sentences to the Supreme Commander for the Allied Powers.[15]

The provisions on penalties of the ad hoc *Tribunals*

In the report in which the UN Secretary-General suggested the creation of an international criminal tribunal to address the atrocities that were being committed on the territory of the former Yugoslavia, he insisted on the necessity of respecting the principle of legality of crimes.[16] He rejected the idea of giving the future tribunal the competence to apply domestic law, arguing that international humanitarian law provided 'a sufficient basis for subject-matter jurisdiction' but pointed out that there was 'one related issue which would require reference to domestic practice, namely, penalties'.[17] In his report, the Secretary-General also declared that 'the International Tribunal should not be empowered to impose the death penalty'[18] but provided no explanation for adopting this position.

Article 24 is the only article on penalties in the Statute. It reads as follows:

1 The penalty imposed by the Trial Chamber shall be limited to imprisonment. In determining the terms of imprisonment, the Trial Chambers shall have recourse to the general practice regarding prison sentences in the courts of the former Yugoslavia.

2 In imposing the sentences, the Trial Chambers should take into account such factors as the gravity of the offence and the individual circumstances of the convicted person.

3 In addition to imprisonment, the Trial Chambers may order the return of any property and proceeds acquired by criminal conduct, including by means of duress, to their rightful owners.

The official UN records do not mention any discussion within the Security Council on this article.

Article 23 of the Statute of the International Criminal Tribunal for Rwanda (ICTR) is identical to the International Criminal Tribunal for the former Yugoslavia's (ICTY) except that it refers to 'the general practice regarding prison sentences in the courts of Rwanda'. Clearly, this article was drafted on the basis on Article 24 of the ICTY Statute. Interestingly, the members of the Security Council did enter into discussions on the issue of penalties, and Rwanda itself voted against the adoption of the Statute, partly because of the absence of the death penalty in the Statute. At the time, Rwanda had not abolished the death penalty and argued that the Statute:

> establishes a disparity in sentences since it rules out capital punishment, which is nevertheless provided for in the Rwandese penal code. Since it is foreseeable that the Tribunal will be dealing with suspects who devised, planned and organized the genocide, these may escape capital punishment whereas those who simply carried out their plans would be subjected to the harshness of this sentence. That situation is not conducive to national reconciliation in Rwanda.[19]

The United States indicated that they understood some of Rwanda's concerns about the Statute, in particular with regard to the death penalty, but added that securing the adoption of the Statute was their priority and that meeting such concerns would have jeopardised the consensus.[20] Conversely, New Zealand made clear that they would not have supported the creation of the Tribunal had the death penalty been included in the Statute.[21]

The Rules of Procedure and Evidence of both Tribunals cover the sentencing procedure in areas ranging from guilty pleas[22] to the place of imprisonment,[23] the key rule being Rule 101, which provides short guidelines about determining sentences. Rule 101 falls short of a proper list of penalties matching the list of offenses and, in truth, it does not add much to the Statutes, except on one point: it indicates that the prison sentences can go up to life imprisonment, which is not explicitly mentioned in the Statutes. The Rule also indicates that aggravating and mitigating circumstances, as well as 'the general practice regarding prison sentences in the courts' of the former Yugoslavia and Rwanda should be taken into account in the sentencing process.

Negotiating the International Criminal Court's Statute: the difficult exclusion of capital punishment

During the negotiations that led to the establishment of the International Criminal Court, there were limited discussions regarding penalties generally. However, the question of whether or not capital punishment would be included in the Statute was a contentious issue and one which was vigorously debated. In the Draft Statute for an International Criminal Court presented in 1994, the International Law Commission proposed two types of penalties: imprisonment, either for life or for a given period of time, and a fine.[24] Draft Article 47 provided that

> in determining the length of a term of imprisonment or the amount of a fine to be imposed, the Court may have regard to the penalties provided for by the law of: (a) The State of which the convicted person is a national; (b) The State where the crime was committed; (c) The State which had custody of and jurisdiction over the accused.[25]

The International Criminal Court Preparatory Commission discussed the issue of penalties during the session of August 1996. In order to secure a fair representation of all the legal systems of the world, several states such as Egypt and Malaysia wanted the death penalty to be included in the Statute. By contrast, Denmark, Italy, Mexico, New Zealand and Portugal supported the exclusion of the death penalty from the Statute.[26] Hence, 'debates revealed deep divisions of opinion on this issue, and it became clear that it would not be possible to work out a consensual approach, let alone solve the issue, before the Diplomatic Conference'.[27] As far as establishing a set of penalties was concerned, the consensus among states was precisely that no set be established.[28] Within the Sixth Committee of the UN General Assembly, the death penalty was discussed again. Ecuador, the Russian Federation, Haiti, Nicaragua, Paraguay, Poland, Slovakia and the Ukraine did not want it in the statute, while Kuwait did.[29] In December 1997, a working group on penalties was established, chaired by Rolf Einar Fife, the Head of the Norwegian delegation. He deliberately avoided entering into discussions about capital punishment.[30] Hence, the final version of Draft Article 75(e) read as follows:

> Option 1
> [death penalty, as an option, in case of aggravating circumstances and when the Trial Chamber finds it necessary in the light of the gravity of the crime, the number of victims and the severity of the damage.]
>
> Option 2
> No provision on death penalty.[31]

The issue of whether or not the death penalty was going to be included in the Statute was therefore to be settled during the Rome Conference.

Rolf Einar Fife also chaired the working group on penalties during the Conference itself. The issue of the death penalty continued to give rise to tensions and was much discussed until the very last days of the Conference.[32] Two separate groups of states made proposals for an article on penalties that would include, directly or indirectly, the death penalty. On the one hand, a group of Islamic states proposed that the Court be empowered to sentence the accused to penalties existing in the domestic law of the state on the territory of which the crime was committed,[33] which amounted to implicitly allow the Court to sentence people to death. This proposal was much criticised because it created a discriminatory system by which not all defendants would be treated equally.[34] On the other hand, Singapore and a group of Caribbean states made a proposal which directly included the death penalty.[35] On 3 July 1998, the United States representative indicated that he was against the inclusion of the death penalty in the Statute, while defending the use of capital punishment in his own country and pointing out that the death penalty would be used against people accused of international crimes and judged at the domestic level.[36]

On 6 July 1998, the Chairperson noted that there were 'no grounds for establishing a consensus'[37] on the issue of the death penalty between the delegations who 'strongly favour an inclusion of the death penalty as one of the penalties to be applied by the Court'[38] and other ones who were 'strongly opposed to such an inclusion'.[39] At this point, he highlighted the fact that by virtue of the principle of complementarity, excluding the death penalty from the Statute would not constitute an obstacle for states who wished to continue using it.[40] On 16 July, just one day before the signature of the Statute, the question of whether or not the death penalty would be included in its final version had still not been decided.[41]

Moreover, as it is often the case, the debates on the death penalty went hand in hand with discussions about life imprisonment. The inclusion of the latter in paragraph 1(b) of the final version of the Article, albeit under strict conditions, is the result of a compromise and stands as a consolation prize for states who favoured the death penalty and who eventually relinquished in the very last days of the Conference.

Article 77 ('Applicable penalties') now reads as follows:

> 1 Subject to article 110, the Court may impose one of the following penalties on a person convicted of a crime referred to in article 5 of this Statute:
> (a) Imprisonment for a specified number of years, which may not exceed a maximum of 30 years; or
> (b) A term of life imprisonment when justified by the extreme gravity of the crime and the individual circumstances of the convicted person.
> 2 In addition to imprisonment, the Court may order:
> (a) A fine under the criteria provided for in the Rules of Procedure and Evidence;
> (b) A forfeiture of proceeds, property and assets derived directly or indirectly from that crime, without prejudice to the rights of bona fide third parties'.

Moreover, Article 78 ('Determination of the sentence') states that

> 1 In determining the sentence, the Court shall, in accordance with the Rules of Procedure and Evidence, take into account such factors as the gravity of the crime and the individual circumstances of the convicted person.
> 2 In imposing a sentence of imprisonment, the Court shall deduct the time, if any, previously spent in detention in accordance with an order of the Court. The Court may deduct any time otherwise spent in detention in connection with conduct underlying the crime.
> 3 When a person has been convicted of more than one crime, the Court shall pronounce a sentence for each crime and a joint sentence specifying the total period of imprisonment. This period shall be no less than the highest individual sentence pronounced and shall not exceed 30 years imprisonment or a sentence of life imprisonment in conformity with article 77, paragraph 1 (b).

The sentencing process: a wide degree of discretion

On the basis of the provisions presented in the previous section, the international tribunals, with the exception of the International Criminal Court which has yet to complete a trial, have imposed sentences on a considerable number of defendants. This section will explain the way the sentencing decisions are made at the international level and will point out the wide degree of discretion enjoyed by the judges.

Nuremberg and Tokyo

Before the International Military Tribunal of Nuremberg, the defendants raised the defence of *nullum crimen sine lege* (there is no crime without law), arguing that the acts they were being charged with had been criminalised after their commission (*ex post facto*) in violation of the principle of legality of crimes but they did not raise the parallel defence of *nulla poena sine lege* (there is no penalty without law, an alleged violation of the principle of legality of penalties). Hence, while the Tribunal addresses and dismisses the defence based on the principle of legality of crimes,[42] there is no mention of the fact that the appropriate penalties had not been established prior to the commission of the crimes.[43] Yet, as far as punishment was concerned, the principle of legality in its purest form was clearly violated. No precise set of penalties had been established prior to the trial. The judgement makes no mention of the penalties pronounced in previous trials. As seen in the previous section, the Statute itself granted the judges a virtually limitless power regarding the determination of penalties. The only guidance the Statute gave them was that they were allowed to sentence the defendants to death if they thought it was appropriate.

The International Military Tribunal sentenced to death 12 defendants out of 22. The others received penalties ranging from 10 years in jail to life imprisonment.[44] While in Nuremberg the judges agreed on the appropriate penalties for most defendants, in Tokyo the sentencing process was somewhat chaotic, as will be seen further.

The judgement of the IMT does not mention anything in relation to the notion of 'just' punishment as referred to in the Charter and the judges do not seem to have discussed it as such. The Soviet Judge Nikitchenko is responsible for the only crack in the apparent unanimity of the judges with regards to penalties. In his separate opinion he criticised the acquittals of Hjalmar Schacht, Franz Von Papen and Hans Fritzsche as being ill-founded. He also disagreed with Rudolf Hess's life imprisonment. He argued that Rudolf Hess was 'Hitler's closest personal confident', that he 'played a decisive role in the crimes of the Nazi regime' and that, therefore, 'the only justified sentence in his case can be death'.[45]

In Tokyo, the issue of sentencing was treated in a significantly different manner. The 11 judges were far from unanimous regarding the degree of guilt and the appropriate sentence of a good number of the 25 defendants who were actually tried. Judge Bernard (France), Judge Pal (India) and Judge Röling (the Netherlands) wrote dissenting opinions, while Judge Webb (Australia) and Judge Jaranilla (the Philippines) wrote separate opinions.[46] In the subsequent series of interviews he gave to Professor Cassese, Judge Röling provided some insider comments regarding those opinions. He confirmed that which Judge Pal had made clear in his dissenting opinion, that the Indian Judge was opposed to the Tribunal as a matter of principle because he believed that only Asian people should be judging other Asian people.[47] Judge Bernard refused to vote with the other judges, neither regarding guilt, nor regarding penalties, since he considered the accused had not received a fair trial.[48] Judge Jaranilla thought the penalties pronounced against certain defendants were 'too lenient, not exemplary and deterrent, and not commensurate with the gravity of the offense or the offenses committed'.[49] While the Filipino judge voted with the majority, he would have preferred more defendants to be sentenced to death. Conversely, Judge Webb was in favour of milder penalties. He pointed out that the International Military Tribunal at Nuremberg had not sentenced anyone to death on the count of initiating an aggressive war only, probably to take into account the fact that 'aggressive war was not universally regarded as a justiciable crime when they made war'.[50] According to the Australian judge, it was inappropriate to sentence to death solely on this count. Moreover, he stated that

> It is universally acknowledged that the main purpose of punishment for an offence is that it should act as a deterrent to others. It may well be that the punishment of imprisonment for life under sustained conditions of hardship in an isolated place or places outside Japan—the usual conditions in such cases—would be a greater deterrent to men like the accused than the speedy termination of existence on the scaffold or before a firing squad. Another consideration is the very advanced age of some of the accused. It may prove revolting to hang or shoot such old men.[51]

Despite his strong reservations, he concluded that he was 'unable to say that any sentence is manifestly excessive or manifestly inadequate'[52] and that, as a result, he was going to vote with the majority.

Judge Röling indicated in his dissenting opinion his view that Takasumi Oka, Kenryo Sato and Shigaterō Shimada, three military officers, should have been sentenced to death as opposed to life imprisonment, because of their high degree of responsibility in the commission of war crimes.[53] Shunroku Hata, Kōichi Kido, Mamoru Shigemitsu and Shigenori Tōgō should have been acquitted instead of being sentenced to imprisonment.[54] Finally, Judge Röling argued that Kōki Hirota was in fact not guilty and should have been acquitted whereas he was sentenced to death and hanged with the others on 23 December 1948.[55]

Regarding sentencing as such, Judge Röling, while presenting himself as a 'strong believer in the secrecy of chambers' attempted to guess what each judge had voted. According to him, Pal did not vote in favour of the death sentences because he was convinced that all the accused should be acquitted. Judge Bernard did not even vote. The Soviet Judge Zaryanow had received instructions from his government, who had just officially abolished the death penalty, and who did not want it to be used against the accused before the International Tribunal in Tokyo.[56] These three judges being excluded, eight judges remain who could have voted in favour of the death sentences.[57] It seems as though Judge Webb, the President of the Tribunal, was opposed to the use of the death penalty as a matter of principle because the Emperor himself had managed to escape justice.[58] Finally, Judge Röling pointed out that, at most, seven judges out of 11 voted in favour of the death sentences and only six in the case of Kōki Hirota, since he himself voted against it. Regarding Kōki Hirota, he wrote that it was 'a scandalous way of arriving at the penalty of hanging'.[59]

In the end, the Tribunal sentenced seven defendants out of 25 to death. The others received penalties ranging from seven years to life imprisonment.

At both International Military Tribunals, the statement of each defendant's sentence was included in the judgement and no separate sentencing hearings were held. Today, the International Criminal Tribunals for the former Yugoslavia and Rwanda do not hold separate sentencing hearings or issue separate sentencing decisions either, although they initially did. By contrast, sentencing will be a distinct phase before the International Criminal Court.[60]

The ad hoc *Tribunals*

Working around the reference to domestic law

Relying on domestic law is not uncommon in international criminal law since, historically, international criminal law has been primarily implemented by states applying their own domestic set of penalties.[61] However, the Statutes of the *ad hoc* Tribunals have created a system of implementation of international criminal law at the international level. Therefore, there could be 'no assumption that national legislation will fill *lacunae*'[62] in relation to penalties and an alternative way needed to be set up. This is the reason why Articles 24 ICTY and 23 ICTR state that 'in determining the terms of imprisonment, the Trial Chambers shall have recourse to the general practice regarding prison sentences in the courts' of, respectively the former Yugoslavia and Rwanda, a recommendation reiterated in Rule 101 ICTY and ICTR.

This reference gives rise to a number of issues. First, by simply reading the wording 'the general practice regarding prison sentences in the courts' of the former Yugoslavia or Rwanda, it is not clear whether the Trial Chamber should refer to the applicable statutory law or to the practice strictly speaking.[63] In the former Yugoslavia, the existing penalty for persons guilty of genocide and crimes against humanity (the law stipulated that the two crimes had to be prosecuted together) was a minimum of five years imprisonment, up to capital punishment. Crimes against humanity did not exist as a separate category of crimes; therefore, the law did not mention any penalty for these crimes specifically and, in any event, almost no prosecutions had occurred.[64]

In Rwanda, before the genocide occurred there was no law regarding international crimes; therefore, no case law either. While the penal code mentioned the death penalty, as well as life imprisonment for murder and rape, the defendants were sentenced to much less stringent penalties and, in practice, there were no executions.[65]

In this context, it is hard to see how having 'recourse to the general practice regarding prison sentences in the courts of' the former Yugoslavia and Rwanda can be of any help for the Trial Chamber to determine sentences. Indeed the gap is wide between the crimes the *ad hoc* Tribunals are dealing with and the contents of domestic law prior to their commission. This is probably the reason why the ICTR has already referred to the Rwandan statute adopted after the genocide since it was tailored precisely to address these types of crimes.[66] It should be noted, however, that such a reference contradicts one of the purposes of the provision, which was to cover the Tribunals against allegations of violation of the principle of legality. A reference to a piece of legislation adopted after the Statute entered into force does not make much sense in this respect.

Early on in their practice, both Tribunals made clear that they were not bound to have recourse to domestic practice but that the Statutes had opened a possibility they were free to use or not.[67] And it is fair to say they have not really taken such practice into consideration. To take one example, the maximum imprisonment penalty in the former Yugoslavia was 20 years, even when such a penalty was used as an alternative to capital punishment. Yet, the ICTY has condemned defendants to much longer penalties.[68] The Appeals Chamber even stated that 'a Trial Chamber's discretion in imposing sentence is not bound by a maximum term of imprisonment applied in a national system' and that

> accordingly, the reliance by the Appellant on the law of the former Yugoslavia which prescribed a maximum sentence of 20 years as an alternative to the death penalty is misplaced, and more especially having regard to the fact that, at the time when the offences were committed, a death penalty could have been imposed under that law for similar offences.[69]

It is as though the Appeals Chamber used the exclusion of the death penalty from the list of penalties that the ICTY can impose as a justification for lengthy prison sentences, with the implication being that the defendants should not complain about such terms of imprisonment, since, had they been judged in their own country according to the law then in force, they could have faced a death sentence!

A few states, including the United States, argued that since the defendants were to escape death they should at least face life imprisonment. This reasoning explains why life imprisonment is mentioned as a possibility in the Rules of Procedure and Evidence.[70] This is questionable because excluding the death penalty does not necessarily go hand in hand with establishing life imprisonment. Additionally, life imprisonment is simply contrary to the law of the former Yugoslavia which was supposed to be used as a reference in the sentencing process.[71]

Leaving judges with the possibility to impose life imprisonment when they are addressing such horrendous crimes has naturally resulted in severe sentences. The ICTR has already imposed 10 life sentences out of the 30 cases it has now completed. Out of its 60 completed cases, the ICTY has only imposed one life sentence,[72] but it has also sentenced eight persons to penalties exceeding the maximum prison term of 20 years, which was in force in the former Yugoslavia.

Finding the just penalty: an impossible quest?

The determination of just penalties is a thorny exercise at the domestic level, one which gives rise to extra-legal considerations and is deeply impacted by cultural values. Unsurprisingly, figuring out the appropriate penalties at the international level, where judges from different backgrounds have to work together to address crimes committed in contexts of large-scale violence, turns out to be even more difficult.

First, it must be noted that international human rights law generally has no impact on the determination of sentences at the domestic level, which remains a symbolic attribute of state sovereignty. International human rights treaties[73] prohibit inhuman or degrading treatments or punishments but the international case law based on these treaties actually focuses on treatments.[74] The notion of unjust criminal punishment as inhuman or degrading is not addressed and states are left free to choose the appropriate sentences themselves.[75] In the context of international criminal law, the judges' discretion in the sentencing process is not regulated by international human rights law either. In other words, human rights law is of no help when it comes to the determination of penalties. Human rights–related *considerations*, for instance age and health, can be used as mitigating circumstances but human rights *law* cannot be used as such.

Second, international judges cannot rely on the otherwise key notion of proportionality in the same way as their domestic counterparts can. As pointed out by Judge Harhoff, of the ICTY:

> In every national jurisdiction, the crime of murder is considered a serious crime with sentences ranging from 12 years to life imprisonment. If this sentencing range was designed to cover a single or perhaps a few murders in peacetime, then how do we administer a meaningful sentence to the perpetrator of mass scale killings of hundreds of even thousands of innocent victims committed in armed conflict? I can find no reasonable answer to this question, except to say that for the purpose of punishing mass atrocities committed in wartime, it is probably impossible to make the punishment—indeed any punishment—fit that sort of crime.[76]

The ratio between the time spent in prison and the number of victims in the various contexts in which international criminal law applies tends to remain unsatisfying, at least from the victims' point of view. This is not to say that proportionality plays no role at the international level. Different categories of criminal conducts can be identified that attract different penalties and aggravating as well as mitigating circumstances are also taken into consideration to modulate the penalties.[77] This results in penalties ranging from a couple of years to life imprisonment. While acknowledging the reassuring logic of all this, it is hard to see the practical, rather than symbolic, purpose of sentencing someone to life imprisonment, or for that matter to 30 or 40 years in prison. Does it achieve more than sentencing him or her to 20 years? This leads us to our third point: the purpose of sentencing by the *ad hoc* Tribunals.

Uncertainties about the purpose of sentencing

The Tribunals have made some conflicting pronouncements regarding the purpose of sentencing. In 1997, the ICTY declared that the purpose of sentencing should 'include such aims as just punishment, deterrence, incapacitation of the dangerous and rehabilitation'[78] after having said one year earlier that 'the particularities of crimes falling within the jurisdiction of the International Tribunal rule out consideration of the rehabilitative function of punishment'.[79] The Tribunal also stated that both retribution and deterrence served as 'the primary purposes of sentence',[80] which was also highlighted by the ICTR:

> it is clear that the penalties imposed on accused persons found guilty by the Tribunal must be directed, on the one hand, at retribution of the said accused, who must see their crimes punished, and over and above that, on the other hand, at deterrence, namely dissuading for good those who will attempt in future to perpetrate such atrocities by showing them that the international community was not ready to tolerate the serious violations of international humanitarian law and human rights'.[81]

A Trial Chamber of the ICTY criticised retribution, pointing out that 'a consideration of retribution as the only factor in sentencing is likely to be counter-productive and disruptive of the entire purpose of the Security Council, which is the restoration and maintenance of peace in the territory of the former Yugoslavia. Retributive punishment by itself does not bring justice'.[82] By contrast, the Appeals Chamber chose to highlight the importance of retribution, which 'is not to be understood as fulfilling a desire for revenge but as duly expressing the outrage of the international community at these crimes'.[83] Hence, the difference between a sentence of 35 years in prison and life imprisonment may be that they represent different degrees of outrage. For the accused, who are often middle-aged or older, the practical difference between the two is tenuous.

On the whole, no consensus has emerged on the purpose of sentencing within the different institutions of international criminal justice, and even from one trial Chamber to another. As noted by Judge Harhoff: 'on the international level (...) the sentencing practice has not yet reached a dependable stage of predictability and proportionality; this practice and the theory behind it are still in their making'.[84]

Enforcement of sentences

The *ad hoc* Tribunals and the International Criminal Court possess detention facilities to detain the accused before and during their trials but there is no international prison for the convicted, who must serve their sentence in states who have volunteered to accept them.

As provided by Regulation 113 of the International Criminal Court, an Enforcement Unit under the responsibility of the Presidency is specifically in charge of these questions. Once the sentence is decided, the Court will officially choose a state within a list of volunteers where the convicted prisoner will be sent. Once it has committed itself to become the state of detention, that state will not be able to modify the penalty, hence creating an inequality between a person convicted by the International Criminal Court and an ordinary local detainee. Sentences will only be reviewed by the Court itself after two-thirds of the penalty have elapsed or after 25 years in case of people sentenced to life imprisonment.

Before the *ad hoc* Tribunals, the rules are different since the tribunals are temporary bodies and are expected not to remain in existence in their present form beyond the foreseeable future. Articles 27(2) ICTY and 26(2) ICTR provide that 'imprisonment shall be in accordance with the applicable law of the State concerned'. For instance, in accordance with Norwegian law, Drazen Erdemović was released after having served two-thirds of his sentence.[85] In practice, this creates a discrepancy between people sentenced by the same institution but who serve their prison sentence in different places.

So far, 16 countries have signed agreements with the ICTY for the enforcement of sentences[86] and seven countries are linked to the ICTR by similar agreements.[87]

Notes

1 As suggested by the Chairman of the Working Group on penalties during the Rome Conference: Chairman's Working Paper on Article 75, Paragraph 1, A/CONF.183/C.1/WGP/L.3/Rev.1, 6 July 1998, 3.
2 For a useful discussion on this principle in the context of international criminal law, see A. Cassese, *International Criminal Law*, Oxford: Oxford University Press, 2008, p. 36.
3 For a discussion on the tensions between 'legality' and 'fine-grainedness' (i.e. the taking into account of moral considerations in sentencing) see K. Huigens, 'Solving the *Williams* Puzzle', *Columbia Law Review*, 2005, 1063–5.
4 W. Schabas, *An Introduction to the International Criminal Court*, Cambridge: Cambridge University Press, 2007, p. 312.
5 Cassese, *International Criminal Law*, p. 51.
6 Article 27, Charter of the International Military Tribunal, annex to the Agreement for the Prosecution and Punishment of the Major War Criminals of the European Axis, 8 August 1945, 82 UNTS 279.
7 France *et al. v.* Goering *et al., American Journal of International Law* 41, 1947, 331.
8 Nuremberg Trial Proceedings, Vol. 5, Thirty-Sixth Day, Thursday, 17 January 1946, p. 411, Avalon Project Web site, Yale Law School, http://avalon.law.yale.edu/imt/01-17-46.asp (accessed 15 September 2009).
9 Aide Mémoire from the United Kingdom, 23 April 1945, Avalon Project Web site, Yale Law School, http://avalon.law.yale.edu/imt/jack02.asp (accessed 24 July 2009).
10 American Memorandum presented at San Francisco, 30 April 1945, Part IV, Avalon Project Web site, Yale Law School, http://avalon.law.yale.edu/imt/jack05.asp (accessed 24 July 2009).
11 American Draft of Definitive Proposal presented to Foreign Ministers at San Francisco, April 1945, Avalon Project Web site, Yale Law School, http://avalon.law.yale.edu/imt/jack04.asp (accessed 24 July 2009).
12 Minutes of Conference, 29 June 1945, and Draft Showing Soviet and American Proposals in Parallel Columns, 1945, Avalon Project Web site, Yale Law School, http://avalon.law.yale.edu/imt/jack17.asp and http://avalon.law.yale.edu/imt/jack23.asp (accessed 24 July 2009).
13 Draft Agreement and Charter, Proposed by British Delegation, 11 July 1945, Avalon Project Web site, Yale Law School, http://avalon.law.yale.edu/imt/jack26.asp (accessed 24 July 2009).
14 See note 10.
15 Statute of the International Military Tribunal for the Far East, Article 17(2).
16 Report of the Secretary-General pursuant to the Paragraph 2 of Security Council Resolution 808 (1993), S/25704, 3 May 1993, para. 34.

17 Ibid., para. 36.
18 Ibid., para. 112.
19 UN Security Council, S/PV.3453, 16.
20 Ibid., 17.
21 Ibid., 5.
22 Rules of Procedure and Evidence, International Criminal Tribunal for the former Yugoslavia and International Criminal Tribunal for Rwanda, Rule 100.
23 Ibid., Rule 103.
24 Report of the International Law Commission on the Work of his Forty-Sixth Session, Draft Statute for an International Criminal Court, A/49/355, Draft Article 47.
25 Ibid.
26 UN Press release, L/2805, *Discussion turns to range and definition of penalties in draft statute in preparatory committee on international criminal court*, 22 August 1996; UN Press release, L/2806, *Preparatory committee for international criminal court discusses definition of crimes; potential use of capital punishment*, 23 August 1996.
27 R. Fife, 'Penalties', in R.S. Lee (ed.) *The International Criminal Court, Issues, Negotiations, Results*, The Hague: Kluwer Law International, 1999, p. 326.
28 Ibid., p. 327.
29 UN General Assembly, Sixth Committee, Press Releases GA/L/3044, 21 October 1997; GA/L/3046, 23 October 1997; GA/L/3047, 23 October 1997.
30 W. Schabas, 'Life, Death and the Crime of Crimes, Supreme Penalties and the ICC Statute', *Punishment and Society*, 2000, 271.
31 Report of the Preparatory Committee on the Establishment of an International Criminal Court, A/CONF.183/2/Add.1, 14 April 1998, 121.
32 W. Schabas, 'The Penalty Provisions of the ICC Statute', in D. Shelton (ed.), *International Crimes, Peace and Human Rights, The Role of the International Criminal Court*, Ardsley: Transnational Publishers, 2000, pp. 109–110.
33 Algeria, Bahrain, Djibouti, Egypt, Iran, Iraq, Kuwait, Nigeria, Oman, Qatar, Saudi Arabia, Sudan, Syria, United Arab Emirates and Yemen, A/CONF.183/C.1/WPG/L.11, 3 July 1998.
34 Fife, 'Penalties', p. 334.
35 Barbados, Dominica, Jamaica, Singapore and Trinidad and Tobago, A/CONF.183/C.1/WGE/L.13, 4 July 1998.
36 Schabas, 'The Penalty Provisions of the ICC Statute', p. 120.
37 Chairman's Working Paper on Article 75, Paragraph 1, A/CONF.183/C.1/WGP/L.3/Rev.1, 6 July 1998, 2.
38 Ibid.
39 Ibid.
40 Ibid., p 3.
41 Report of the Working Group on Penalties, A/CONF.183/C.1/WGP/L.14/Add.3/Rev.1, 17 July 1998, 1.
42 France *et al. v.* Goering *et al.*, 39.
43 The only time the issue of the legality of penalties was raised in relation to international crimes was during the Eichmann trial in Israel. In 1950, the Knesset adopted the law on the punishment of Nazis. The death penalty was in the list of possible penalties. In 1954, Israel abolished the death penalty for ordinary crimes and, also, deleted the paragraph of the Criminal Code which mentioned hanging as the method of execution. This paragraph was later reintroduced and Eichmann's defence lawyers argued that this was a violation of the principle of non retroactivity of penalties. The tribunal dismissed the argument (L. Green, 'Aspects juridiques du procès Eichmann', *Annuaire français de droit international*, 1963, 172–3).
44 France *et al. v.* Goering *et al.*, 333.
45 Judgement: Dissenting Opinion of Judge Nikitchenko, Avalon Project Web site, Yale Law School, http://avalon.law.yale.edu/imt/juddiss.asp (accessed 23 July 2009).
46 Judge Röling's opinion is labelled as a separate opinion in the official documents but it is in fact a dissenting opinion. See J. R. Pritchard, S. Magbuna Zaide (eds), *The Tokyo War Crimes Trial, the Complete Transcripts of the Proceedings of the International Military Tribunal for the Far East in Twenty-Two Volumes*, New York, London: Garland Publishing Inc., 1981, vol. 21, Separate opinions.
47 B. V. A. Röling, A. Cassese, *The Tokyo Trial and Beyond*, Cambridge: Polity Press, 1993, p. 29. See also Pritchard and Magbuna Zaide, *The Tokyo War Crimes Trial*, vol. 21, Dissenting Opinion of the Member for India (Rabhabinod B. Pal) pp. 42–62.

48 Röling, Cassese, *The Tokyo Trial and Beyond*, p. 4. See also Pritchard and Magbuna Zaide, *The Tokyo War Crimes Trial*, vol. 21, Dissenting Opinion of the Member from France (Henri Bernard), pp. 20–23.
49 See also Pritchard and Magbuna Zaide, *The Tokyo War Crimes Trial*, vol. 21, Concurring Opinion of the Member for the Philippines (Delfin Jaranilla), p. 34.
50 Ibid., Separate Opinion of the President of the Tribunal, Sir William Flood Webb (the Member for Australia), p. 14.
51 Ibid., p. 17.
52 Ibid., p. 19.
53 Pritchard and Magbuna Zaide, *The Tokyo War Crimes Trial*, vol. 21, The Separate Opinion of the Member for the Netherlands (Bernard Victor Röling), p. 178.
54 Ibid. For detailed explanations: 179–90 (Hata), pp. 211–27 (Kido), pp. 228–42 (Shigemitsu) and pp. 243–9 (Togo).
55 Ibid., p. 191–210.
56 Röling, Cassese, *The Tokyo Trial and Beyond*, p. 30.
57 Ibid., p. 64.
58 Ibid., p. 42.
59 See note 57.
60 Schabas, *An Introduction to the International Court*, p. 305.
61 C. Bassiouni, P. Manikas, *The Law of the International Criminal Tribunal for the Former Yougoslavia*, Irvington-on-Hudson, New York: Transnational Publishers, 1996, p. 269.
62 Ibid.
63 W. Schabas, 'Perverse Effects of the *nulla poena* Principle: National Practice and the *Ad hoc* Tribunals', *European Journal of International Law* 11, 2000, 526.
64 Ibid.
65 Ibid., 527.
66 Kambanda (ICTR-97-23-S), Sentencing Judgement, 4 September 1998, paras 18–25.
67 Ibid., para. 23 and Erdemović (IT-96-22), Sentencing Judgement, 29 November 1996, para 39.
68 For instance: Stakić (IT-97-24) was sentenced to 40 years, Martić (IT-95-11) and Krstić (IT-98-33) to 35 years.
69 Tadić (IT-94-I-A), Appeals Chamber, 26 January 2000, para. 21.
70 The Statute of the International Criminal Court allows for a maximum sentence of life imprisonment but it is strictly limited since it must be 'justified by the extreme gravity of the crime and the individual circumstances of the convicted person'. Hence, the *ad hoc* Tribunals' Rules of Procedure and Evidence leave the judges freer to impose life imprisonment.
71 Schabas, 'Perverse Effects of the *nulla poena* Principle : National Practice and the *Ad hoc* Tribunals', 528.
72 Galić (IT-98-29).
73 European Convention on Human Rights, International Covenant on Civil and Political Rights, American Convention on Human Rights.
74 Treatments include interrogation techniques (ECtHR, Ireland *v.* UK, 18 January 1978, paras 165–8; Human Rights Committee, Safarmo Kurbanova *v.* Tajikistan, No. 1096/2002, 12 November 2003, para. 7.4), conditions of detention (ECtHR, Iovchev *v.* Bulgaria, 2 February 2006, para. 129–38 ; Human Rights Committee, Mukong *v.* Cameroun, No. 458/1991, 10 August 1994, paras 9.3–9.4.) and punishment in school (ECtHR, Costello-Roberts *v.* UK, 25 March 1993, paras 29–32).
75 The exception is ECtHR, Tyrer *v.* UK, 25 April 1978, paras 28–35). Interestingly, Article 5(6) of the IACHR states that 'punishments consisting of deprivation of liberty shall have as an essential aim the reform and social readaptation of the prisoners'. This is a unique provision in international human rights law. It expressly links the prohibition of inhuman treatments with imprisonment, which becomes contrary to the Convention if the social readaptation of the prisoners is not taken into account.
76 F. Harhoff, 'Sense and Sensibility in Sentencing—Taking Stock of International Criminal Punishment', in C. Greenwood and L. H. McCormack (eds), *Law at War: The Law as It Was and the Law as It Should Be: Liber Amicorum Ove Bring*, Leiden, Boston: Martinus Nijhoff Publishers, 2008, p. 125.
77 Ibid., pp. 134–5.
78 Tadić (IT-94-I-A), Sentencing judgment, 14 July 1997, para. 61.
79 Erdemović (IT-96-22), Sentencing judgment, 29 November 1996, para. 66.
80 Tadić (IT-94-I-A), Sentencing judgment, 11 November 1999, para. 9.

81 Kambanda (ICTR-97-23-S), Sentencing Judgement, 4 September 1998, para. 28.
82 Delalić et al. (IT-96-21), 16 November 1998, para. 1231.
83 Aleksovski (IT-95-14/1-A), Appeals Chamber, 24 March 2000, para. 185.
84 Harhoff, 'Sense and Sensibility in Sentencing—Taking Stock of International Criminal Punishment', p. 122.
85 Case information sheet, Web site of the ICTY.
86 Albania, 19 Sep. 2008; United Kingdom, 11 March 2004; Finland, 7 May 1997; Poland, 18 Sep. 2008; Denmark, 4 June 2002; Italy, 6 Feb. 1997; Slovakia, 7 April 2008; Spain, 28 March 2000; Estonia, 11 Feb. 2008; France, 25 Feb. 2000; Portugal, 19 Dec. 2007; Sweden, 23 Feb. 1999; Ukraine, 7 Aug. 2007; Austria, 23 July 1999; Belgium, 2 May 2007; Norway, 24 April 1998. Moreover, Germany signed *ad hoc* agreements for three detainees (Galić, 16 Dec 2008; Kunarac, 14 Nov. 2002; Tadić, 17 Oct. 2000).
87 Rwanda, 4 March 2008; Sweden, 27 April 2004; Italy, 17 March 2004; France, 14 March 2003; Swaziland, 30 August 2000; Benin, 26 August 1999; Mali, 12 February 1999.

19

State cooperation and transfers

Kimberly Prost

Introduction

The unique nature of international criminal tribunals and courts is perhaps no better illustrated than in the context of state cooperation and transfer. Whether the adjudicative body is established by the Security Council, created by resolution or agreement or constituted through a negotiated instrument, all face the same distinct reality. To gather evidence, obtain witnesses, arrest suspects and bring those suspects before them, these bodies depend on the cooperation of states. This reality has important consequences for the legal systems adopted by the various tribunals and courts and perhaps even more significantly, the effectiveness or lack thereof of the cooperation regimes, is pivotal to their success or failure on a practical level.

This chapter examines regimes for cooperation in terms of evidence gathering and the arrest and transfer of suspects. The analysis is confined to the International Criminal Tribunal for the former Yugoslavia (ICTY), the International Criminal Tribunal for Rwanda (ICTR) and the International Criminal Court (ICC) which provide a comprehensive exemplification of the relevant principles and issues in the area of cooperation and transfer.

The *ad hoc* Tribunals

The cooperation and transfer regime for the two *ad hoc* Tribunals established by the Security Council has developed through a combination of statutory provisions, judicial law making and interpretation and general practice. Albeit there are some distinctions, generally the principles and approach are similar for both Tribunals and thus will be considered together.

The Statutes

The obligations regarding state cooperation are identical in both the Statute of the ICTY (ICTY Statute) and the Statute of the ICTR (ICTR Statute). Articles 29 and 28, respectively, provide:

1 States shall co-operate with the International Tribunal in the investigation and prosecution of persons accused of committing serious violations of international humanitarian law.

2 States shall comply without undue delay with any request for assistance or an order issued by a Trial Chamber, including, but not limited to

(a) the identification and location of persons;
(b) the taking of testimony and the production of evidence;
(c) the service of documents;
(d) the arrest or detention of persons;
(e) the surrender or the transfer of the accused to the International Tribunal.[1]

Surprisingly, this is the sole statutory provision governing state cooperation with, and the transfer of persons to, the two *ad hoc* Tribunals.

While not specified, the inference from the cooperation obligations imposed is that a failure to cooperate in accordance with the article can be reported to and sanctioned by the Security Council.

The Rules

The Rules of Procedure and Evidence of the ICTY (ICTY Rules) and The Rules of Procedure and Evidence of the ICTR (ICTR Rules) have expanded considerably on this obligation, even though state cooperation is not a subject matter specifically mentioned in the rule-making power.[2] While Article 15 of the ICTY Rules does not purport to contain an exhaustive list of subjects for rules, the unique external reach of rules relating to state cooperation makes them quite distinct from the subject areas specified in Article 15. Though it was clearly contemplated that the judges would adopt rules to better define and expand on internal procedure and powers, it is not evident that rules to extend the obligations on states beyond that specified by the Statute were envisaged. In essence, it is one thing for the Security Council acting under Chapter VII to impose decisions on states and another for the elected judges of the court to do so.

In terms of content, the relevant rules on cooperation and transfer can be summarized as falling into the following categories:

(a) Orders and related compulsory measures for arrest, transfer and evidence gathering;[3]
(b) General cooperation obligations; and[4]
(c) Procedures for non compliance.[5]

The ICTR Rules on state cooperation and transfer are almost identical to those of the ICTY. The only substantive exception is Rule 55 on the execution of arrest warrants, where the procedure is somewhat different as between the two Tribunals, albeit the fundamental obligations on States remain the same.

Cooperation in evidence gathering

States are required to cooperate with the Tribunals with respect to the listed assistance prescribed in Article 29. In addition, as foreshadowed, both Tribunals have extended the statutory cooperation obligations through the rules. While the Statute provision is short and vague, the practice with reference to the general types of assistance outlined therein is similar to that found in state-to-state cooperation, at least in terms of the measures of assistance sought. Thus, the Tribunals seek assistance in various forms such as interviewing witnesses and suspects, obtaining testimony, compelling the production of documents, search and seizure and the transfer of persons in custody to give evidence.

The subpoena power

The Tribunals' practice departs sharply from state-to-state regimes with respect to compelling witness testimony and the production of documents. Rule 54 of both Statutes empowers the Judges to issue 'such orders, summonses, *subpoenas*, warrants and transfer orders as may be necessary for the purposes of an investigation or for the preparation or conduct of trial' [emphasis added].

While upon first glance this rule might not appear extraordinary, it is, in so far as Article 29 obligates states to comply with any such orders. By including 'subpoena' amongst the possible orders, the rule vested power in the Tribunal to issue an 'international subpoena' to compel the attendance of a witness 'cross border'. Such an instrument had not existed prior to the enactment of Rule 54, as state-to-state cooperation never involved cross-border compulsion of witnesses. What makes the rule even more radical is that there is no reference to such a power in the Tribunal Statute. In contrast, Article 29 reflects a scheme for evidence gathering premised on state responsibility and cooperation. Notably, the only mention of assistance with witness evidence in Article 29 is the obligation on states to comply with a request or order for 'the taking of testimony'. This is in stark contrast to the specific reference to compliance with any request or order for arrest or detention and surrender of an accused. As a result of Rule 54, and the judicial interpretation of it, the system for cooperation in securing the attendance of witnesses before the ICTY and ICTR is unique in international cooperation.

Compelled transfer of detained persons as witnesses

Another addition to the types of assistance mandated under Article 29 is found in Rule 90*bis*, which provides for the transfer of detained persons as witnesses. The rule provides for the issuance of a transfer order provided two conditions are met—the transfer will neither interfere with pending proceedings in the state nor extend the period of detention for the person. The rule further elaborates the applicable procedures for the physical transfer of the detainee. Once again, however, the rule is unique in international cooperation in that the consent of the person to be transferred is not required. This approach of 'compulsion across borders' is of course consistent with the incorporation of an international subpoena power as discussed above.

Production of documents by states

Finally, uniquely to the ICTY,[6] the rules were amended in November of 1999 to expand on the compulsory powers relating to evidence gathering with the addition of Rule 54*bis*, which sets out a detailed procedure for the production of documents by States. This rule was adopted in light of the *Blaskić* decision,[7] which considered the powers of the Tribunal in that respect.

In brief, the rule provides that a party seeking an order for the production of documents by a state must, as far as possible, identify the documents or information sought and establish their relevance. In addition, the applicant must explain the steps that have been taken to secure the state's voluntary assistance.

Notice of an application will be served on the interested state, unless the application is rejected *in limine* or exceptionally if the judge or trial chamber decides to issue the order without notification to the state. In the latter circumstance, the state is given a limited ability to challenge the order subsequently on the basis of national security only. In cases where prior notice is given, a state will have the opportunity to make submissions, not limited to any particular issue, before the order is issued. Provision is made for any decision on production to be both appealed and reviewed at the request of the state involved.

Paragraph (F) of this Article addresses in some detail the issue of national security objections to the production of documents. Procedurally, the State must notify its objection and the grounds for it to the Chamber not less than five days before the hearing. The State can request and the Chamber can order protective measures for the hearing, including *in camera* and *ex parte* proceedings, redaction of documents, no transcripts, return of unnecessary material and methods to ensure restricted access to the material.[8] Any ultimate order of production issued can also provide for protective arrangements to protect the state's interests, including the measures previously outlined with respect to the hearing.

Rule 70—confidential material

Interestingly, a Rule which has played an important role in facilitating the production of evidence to the Tribunals is Rule 70, ironically entitled 'Matters not subject to disclosure'. In addition to restrictions on prosecutorial disclosure obligations related to work product, the rule carves out a protection for material disclosed to the prosecutor in confidence. Specifically, where the Prosecutor has received documents and information on a confidential basis and has used the same only for the purpose of generating new evidence, he or she is prohibited from disclosing that original information without the consent of provider. At the same time, that initial information may also not be used in evidence unless it is disclosed to the accused.

The rule not only shields the material from disclosure but also it authorizes the Prosecutor to accept information under the condition of confidentiality. As a further safety measure, if permission is ultimately received from the provider to use the evidence in court, the Trial Chamber, despite its general powers, is precluded from ordering further evidence from the provider either directly or through the parties.

The effect of these protections has been to generate a 'comfort zone' for states such that material which might not have been disclosed otherwise has been made available to the Prosecutor and subsequently has been used in trial proceedings. While it is open to providers to impose conditions on evidence, the Trial Chambers remain competent to determine whether the 'conditioned evidence' can be admitted in those circumstances. Should the Chamber consider the conditions unacceptable, the evidence may be excluded in accordance with the general provisions of Rule 89, especially paragraph (D) relating to the balance between probative value and fair trial rights.[9] While Rule 70 is included in the rules of the ICTY and the ICTR, in the case of the former only, it has been amended to make the Rule applicable *mutatis mutandis* to material in the possession of the accused.

Arrest and transfer

The Statutes provide only for the general obligation on states to cooperate with the arrest, detention, transfer or surrender of persons to the Tribunal, while the Rules set forth in a fair amount of detail the procedures to be followed in such cases.

Importantly in this regard, the Statutes provide no direction as to the manner in which surrender or transfer are to be carried out. Specifically, there is nothing to preclude resort to extradition as a procedure by which the obligations under Article 29 can be met. In this context, Rule 58 is an interesting example of use of the rules to 'amend' the statutory obligation on states. Rule 58, entitled 'National Extradition Provisions' can be found in both Statutes. While not going so far as to prohibit the use of extradition as a means for transfer or surrender, the rule does provide that Article 29 prevails over any legal impediment to surrender arising from national extradition law or extradition treaties. Though arguably more consistent with Article 29 than the subpoena power created under Rule 54, it is still striking that the rule-making power is used to override national law and international treaties. As to the practical effect of the rule, it is limited in so far as there is no evidence that the Tribunals' rules have been 'internalized' such that they provide a legal basis for a state to override either its' laws or treaties.

Urgent provisional measures

Rule 40 allows for urgent provisional measures including provisional arrest and measures to prevent escape or the intimidation of witnesses. It also contemplates the urgent seizure of physical evidence. Provisional arrest requests would be made where immediate action is required but the formal request for arrest and surrender is not ready for transmission to the State. This is analogous to state practice in extradition.

Notably, Rule 40 of the ICTR Statute replicates the ICTY Rule but adds provisions which allow for the transfer to the Tribunal of a person provisionally arrested in cases where the state is unable to keep the person in custody or to prevent escape. Such provisional detention is limited to 20 days and certain prescribed rights are accorded.[10] This provision gives the ICTR the capacity to take over custody of a suspect provisionally arrested where continued detention might otherwise be jeopardized.

Rule 40*bis*, found in both Rules, is a curious provision adopted in 1996 which is analogous, in part, to the additional paragraphs of the ICTR Rule 40. The rule allows for the transfer of a suspect to The Hague at the request of the Prosecution when the suspect has been provisionally arrested or otherwise detained in a state. Before issuing the 'transfer' order, the judge must be satisfied that the person is detained, there is material to show the suspect may have committed a crime within the jurisdiction of the Tribunal and the transfer is necessary. The period for detention post transfer is 30 days, though it can be renewed. Protections are afforded to the detainee. Thus both Tribunals are empowered to safeguard the custody of a suspect when he or she is arrested before the Prosecutor is in a position to transmit the full request for arrest and surrender or even a provisional request. In essence it was aimed at unique arrest opportunities that might otherwise be unavailable.

Procedure for transmission of arrest warrants/requests for transfer

Generally, however, requests for arrest and transfer will be transmitted once the internal Tribunal procedures have resulted in the issuance of the indictment and an arrest warrant and the relevant documentation is compiled for transmission. In those circumstances, the Registrar will retain the original signed warrant and make certified copies of the same for distribution to states. The Registrar is empowered to transmit the warrant to relevant authorities in states where the accused resides, where he or she was last known to be or where the Registrar believes he or she may be found. Though not explicitly provided, this latter requirement would appear to import some requirements for a basis for the Registrar's belief. In addition, a Judge or Chamber could authorize transmission to a specific addressee.

The Rules reiterate the statutory obligation on states to cooperate in the arrest and further seek to ensure that upon arrest the accused will be informed of the indictment and his or her rights, in a language understood by the person. While it is recognized that the arrest and detention will be carried out by state authorities, the Office of the Prosecutor may be represented. States are obligated to inform the Registrar when an accused has been arrested and, subsequently, arrangements will be made between the relevant authorities for the transfer of the accused to The Hague.

There are also procedures in place for the special transmission of the arrest warrant to an authority or international body or the Prosecutor on order of a judge in circumstances where an accused has been taken into custody by that authority, body or the Prosecutor. This Rule is aimed at situations where authorities other than states have taken custody of the accused such as the international forces engaged in the region. Presumably the Prosecutor was included in this Rule by amendment in 1996 to address situations where he or she might find herself in custody of an individual turned over through a process other than a state transfer.

The Rules further authorize a form of 'wanted poster' in allowing for the transmission to states of an advertisement for publication through various media. The advertisement would have the goal of publicizing indictments and seeking information regarding the whereabouts of suspects.

Failure to execute

Not surprisingly, the Rules address in considerable detail the ramifications of a failure to execute an arrest warrant or transfer order. States to which a warrant of arrest or transfer order has been transmitted are mandated to report back in circumstances where they have been unable to execute the warrant and to provide reasons for the failure to do so. A presumption of failure to execute will arise when a reasonable time has passed since the transmission of the warrant and no report has been provided. In the latter circumstances, the possibility of a report by the President to the Security Council is explicitly mentioned. Presumably, a report which fails to provide adequate reasons for the failure to execute may result in a similar action by the President.

In the circumstances where, after a reasonable period of time, the warrant has not been executed through the normal request channels, an international arrest warrant may be issued. There are internal procedural steps that must be taken before a Trial Chamber can issue such a warrant but, once issued, the warrant will be transmitted to all states. Notably the provisions of Rule 61 are also unique in that there is no precedent in state-to-state cooperation for an international arrest warrant *per se*.

It is an understatement to note that both *ad hoc* Tribunals have a troubled history with the arrest and surrender of accused persons. In early days both bodies were plagued by an inability to locate, capture and obtain the surrender of suspects. While there have been some improvements, even as the Tribunals work towards completion, state cooperation with arrest and surrender remains a major concern for the Tribunals and for states. However, the problems have rarely related to legal impediments and almost exclusively arise from political or practical realities such as lack of will to cooperate or inability to locate persons subject to arrest warrants.

Judicial interpretation

There have been a few key decisions of the ICTY Appeals Chamber which have considered and further defined or expanded upon the cooperation practice before the Tribunals.

Orders for production

In the *Blaskić* decision,[11] which predated the adoption of the ICTY Rule 54*bis*, the Appeals Chamber confirmed wide sweeping powers on the part of the Tribunal to compel witnesses and documents. In summary, the decision recognized a power to:

(a) subpoena individuals;
(b) issue binding orders to states and state officials to compel testimony and to produce documents; and
(c) contact witnesses directly.

The decision also confirmed that where national security issues were implicated in such orders, the ultimate power to decide rested with the Tribunal.

Subsequent Tribunal decisions have extended the power of the Tribunal to issue binding orders to international organizations. Although the decisions have employed the broad terminology of 'international organizations', the orders to date have been issued only to intergovernmental organizations[12] on the basis that such organizations involve states operating cooperatively and are thus encompassed by the Article 29 obligations on states.

Rule 70

There have been some decisions relating to the application of Rule 70. Of note is the Appeals Chamber ruling in *Milutinović et al.*[13] that an accused seeking information from a state must first accept documentation pursuant to Rule 70, if offered by the state, before seeking an order for the production of the material under Rule 54*bis*.

Arrest and transfer

Two significant issues have been addressed in the jurisprudence related to surrender—allegations of misconduct and illegal acts during the course of bringing the accused before the Tribunal and the interrelationship of the surrender obligations of States in terms of the newly adopted 'referral' process.

The seminal case on the issue of illegal arrest and mistreatment is the decision of the Appeals Chamber in the *Nikolić* case.[14] Factually, it was alleged that Dragan Nikolić had been illegally arrested, abducted from the territory of the former Yugoslavia by unknown individuals and transferred to the territory of Bosnia and Herzegovina, where he was taken into custody by the Stabilization Forces for Bosnia and Herzegovina (SFOR) and eventually handed over to the Office of the Prosecutor (OTP). The issue considered was whether the ICTY could exercise jurisdiction over the accused, notwithstanding the allegation of a violation of Serbia and Montenegro's sovereignty and of the rights of the accused by SFOR and, by extension, the OTP.

The Appeals Chamber concluded that in the case of universally condemned crimes, a violation of state sovereignty, brought about by the apprehension of fugitives from international justice, would not be sufficient to justify setting aside jurisdiction. As to alleged human rights violations during an arrest, the Appeals Chamber recognized that some violations may be of such a serious nature as to warrant declining jurisdiction. But, aside from those exceptional circumstances of very grave abuse, the remedy of setting aside jurisdiction in these types of cases would be disproportionate. In the *Nikolić* case, the Appeals Chamber found that the circumstances were not egregious as to fall into the category of cases where jurisdiction should be declined. Similarly, none of the subsequent cases where there has been alleged misconduct during arrest has led the Tribunal to decline jurisdiction.

The second issue on arrest and surrender arose in the consideration of a request for referral of the case of Milan Lukić to Bosnia and Herzegovina.[15] While the initial decision was ultimately overturned by the Appeals Chamber, it was for reasons unrelated to the relevant question as to state cooperation. Factually, Milan Lukić was arrested in Argentina in August of 2005 on the strength of an ICTY indictment and warrant of arrest. In January 2006, a judge in Argentina ordered him to be surrendered to the ICTY stating:

> I hereby decide to grant the request for the transfer of and surrender of Milan Lukić *for him to be tried at the seat of the Tribunal* prohibiting that he be sent without the prior

> authorization of the State of Argentina to another hereby unauthorized place in order to be charged, prosecuted or harassed for previous acts that are different from those constituting the crimes for which his surrender has been requested.[16] [emphasis added]

Pursuant to this decision, in February 2006 Milan Lukić was transferred into the custody of the ICTY. In April of 2007, the Referral Bench of the ICTY considered a request by the Prosecutor, dating from February of 2005, for referral of the case of Milan Lukić and Sredoje Lukić under Rule 11*bis* to Bosnia and Herzegovina for trial. Amongst the issues considered by the Bench were the objections raised by Argentina to the transfer, in light of the conditions of the original surrender to the ICTY.

The Referral Bench considered whether the conditions applied by the extradition judge in Argentina were binding on the Tribunal such that they should affect the determination on transfer. In summary, the Referral Bench found that the ICTY has primacy over national courts, the cooperation obligation to surrender prevails over any impediment in national law or treaties and determinations of national courts are not binding on the Tribunal. The effect of the decision is that a state surrendering a person to the Tribunal in accordance with its Article 29 obligations retains no control over the subsequent determinations regarding that person, even in so far as transfer to another state for trial may be concerned. Further more, the normal protections of 'specialty' applicable in extradition do not apply in the case of transfer to the Tribunal.

Practice before the Tribunals

As described previously, neither the Statute nor Rules provide much by way of procedural detail as to the practical aspects of cooperation between the Tribunal and States. That gap in procedure has been filled by practices implemented by the OTP and the Registrar to facilitate the transmission of cooperation requests to States. Both have established contact networks identifying the relevant authorities for the transmission of requests along with computerized and hard copy databases for the collection of information on state practices. There is also a dedicated tracking system for the requests transmitted and guidance by way of sample requests and format documents have been developed to assist with the drafting of requests.

Requests to the Tribunals for assistance

The Statute and Rules of the Tribunals are silent as to requests to the Tribunal for cooperation and assistance with respect to national cases. The only arguable exception is the ICTY Rule 75H – recently adopted – which allows for a variation of protective measures to be granted upon the request of a court in another jurisdiction. This provision facilitates the transmission of confidential material to a state which may be prosecuting related cases or using witnesses who have testified before the Tribunal with protective measures. The provision is of particular importance given the adoption of the 11*bis* referral procedure in the latter days of the life of the Tribunal.

Despite the absence of statutory or rule-based powers to provide assistance, the Tribunals have acceded to requests from States for the taking of statements and evidence from persons detained under its auspices and other requests for assistance. The obvious limitation is that types of assistance requiring judicial orders would not be available given the absence of powers for that in the Statute and Rules.

The International Criminal Court

In stark contrast to the Statutes of the *ad hoc* Tribunals, the Rome Statute of the International Criminal Court sets out in Part IX a detailed scheme of the cooperation obligations of states parties. In some instances, it also provides guidance as to the applicable procedures. As a result, the main principles on cooperation are found in the Statute, with the Rules providing supplementary information and detailed procedural guidance. The analysis below focuses on the Statute, with reference to the Rules as may be necessary.

Overview of cooperation regime

The cooperation scheme of the Rome Statute is generally framed in terms analogous to state-to-state cooperation, providing for the Court to make requests and placing a corresponding obligation on states parties to comply with those requests. The scheme operates in the context of a general obligation on states parties to fully cooperate with the Court's investigations and prosecutions.

The Articles of Part IX can be divided into three subject areas broadly speaking:

1 General/miscellaneous provisions
2 Arrest and surrender
3 Other forms of cooperation (evidence gathering).

General or miscellaneous provisions

While the Rome Statute addresses the two main forms of 'cooperation' separately—arrest/surrender and evidentiary/related assistance—some issues were best addressed globally because of their applicability to all forms of assistance.

The communication of requests

Requests are to be transmitted through diplomatic or other designated channels and they must be in or accompanied by a translation into an official language of the state or a working language of the Court, depending on the State's election.[17] The related Rules of Procedure and Evidence (Rules) provide guidance to states as to the timing and content of relevant notifications and the channels and languages of communication.[18] Similar to the *ad hoc* Tribunals' practice, the Court has a cooperation unit in place with an extensive database, along with a request tracking system and various tools for the preparation of the requests.

Requests to other than states parties

Part IX specifically authorizes the Court to 'invite' non-states parties to provide assistance pursuant to an *ad hoc* agreement or otherwise.[19] The Court is further empowered to 'ask' intergovernmental organizations to provide documents and information or other forms of assistance.[20] It is interesting that while arguably the Court is free to ask any organization or person for information and assistance, the Statute specifically restricts the remit of Article 89(6) to intergovernmental organizations in contrast to the broader 'international organizations' term coined by the ICTY.

Confidentiality and protective measures

Article 87 obligates states to keep requests confidential except as may be necessary for execution and provides specifically for the application of protective measures to both the request and the responses as may be necessary to protect victims and witnesses.[21]

Non-compliance

Part IX includes a 'sanction' provision for instances where a state party fails to comply with a request of the Court. In such circumstances the matter is to be referred to the Assembly of States Parties or, where the case was referred by the Security Council, to that body. A similar sanction process is applicable where there has been non-compliance by a non-state party when an arrangement or agreement was entered into by that state. However, the Statute is silent as to the general obligations of cooperation of non-states parties in circumstances where the case under investigation has been referred by the Security Council.

Costs

Ordinary execution costs are to be borne by the state, with the Court covering matters such as costs for the travel and security of witnesses/experts, as well as those associated to transporting an accused, translation, interpretation/transcription, court travel, expert opinions/reports and, after consultation, any extraordinary expenses.

Article 98—conflicting obligations

It is ironic that one of the most controversial articles of the Rome Statute is best classified as a miscellaneous provision—Article 98. Obviously the scope of this chapter does not permit a detailed consideration of the controversies surrounding the operation of this single provision. What is provided therefore is a descriptive analysis of Article 98 in terms of its intent and language.

Article 98 was introduced as a procedural provision designed to address the practical situations of conflicting international obligations which might arise in the operation of the Rome Statute. Thus, if a state party were to receive a request seeking the arrest and surrender of a diplomat accredited to it or the search of diplomatic premises, that state would be placed in a situation of conflict in terms of its international law obligations. Similarly, there was recognition that pursuant to Status of Forces agreements, a request for surrender or another form of cooperation could place a receiving state under such an agreement in a conflict position. Thus Article 98 was incorporated to provide a procedural redress in such situations. It was framed so as to accord the ICC with the responsibility not to transmit requests where it would place a state in conflict with its international obligations. Instead, the Court should seek consent from the other state involved with regard to the cooperation sought.

Neither the placement nor content of Article 98 suggests that it was intended as a substantive article or that it was designed to conflict with, amend or countermand the clear obligations on states parties flowing from the adoption of Article 27 on official capacity. Importantly, there are two key characteristics to Article 98. First, the article envisages pre-existing obligations under international law which would conflict with the obligations undertaken by the state party in respect of the Rome Statute. It was never contemplated nor does the language suggest that a state could create an international obligation of such a nature in contradiction to its obligations under the Rome Statute once those are undertaken. Second, as the mandate is for the Court not to proceed with the request when there is an international obligation or agreement which places the state in conflict, it naturally falls to the Court to make that essential determination as to the existence of that obligation or agreement.

Arrest and surrender

The obligation with respect to arrest and surrender of persons was a highly contentious issue in the negotiation of the Rome Statute. Central to the debate was whether states could follow extradition law and practice in effecting surrender or a different form of process should be employed. There was also considerable debate as to whether the Statute should reflect any grounds of refusal for such requests.

In the end, the position adopted was analogous to the practice before the Tribunals in that the obligation of states parties is to comply with the Court's request but the way in which that compliance is achieved under national law is a matter left to states to determine. The only limitation is that if extradition laws are employed, the requirements as to the material which must be submitted in support of the request cannot be more burdensome than that applicable in state-to-state practice and it should be less onerous.

The compromise resolution of the issue as to 'extradition' or 'surrender' also necessitated the inclusion of Article 102, where these terms are defined as 'delivery of a person to the Court' and 'delivery of a person by one state to another state', respectively.

Situations affecting compliance

Ultimately, no grounds of refusal were incorporated such that the arrest and surrender obligations are also analogous to those applicable to the Tribunal. However, there are a few situations where practical circumstances may impede or prevent execution of requests for arrest and surrender.

Competing requests

Article 90 seeks to resolve the myriad of circumstances that may arise where a state receives a request from the ICC and a competing request from a state for the same person. Two features of the Rome Statute made the analysis of the various scenarios particularly complex – the principle of complementarity and the different obligations depending on whether the request emanates from a state party or a non-state party. The scheme adopted is divided into cases where the competing requests relate to the same or different conduct. For the former, where the request emanates from a state party, if the case has been or is ruled admissible, priority should be accorded to the ICC. In the case of a non-state party request, if there is no international obligation to extradite to that state, the ICC request has priority. Where such an obligation does exist, the requested state party should make a decision between the two requests weighing relevant factors.

Where the requests relate to different conduct, the ICC request will have priority in the absence of an international obligation to the other state. If such an obligation exists, again the decision will involve a weighing of the factors relative to both requests, but with special focus on the gravity of the offence.

Conflicting proceedings in the requested state

The Statute also addresses the situation where the person sought for surrender is being proceeded against or is serving a sentence in the requested state for a different crime. Despite tortured and lengthy discussion, no resolution could be agreed, so the decidedly vague Article 89(4) requires that such a request be granted with 'consultations' to ensue. One of the solutions to this problem – temporary surrender – could not be agreed for inclusion in the Statute but an optional provision in this regard can be found in Rule 183.

Documents/information in support

The second caveat relates to procedural requirements for such requests. Article 91 sets out the content of a request for arrest and surrender and recognizes that a state may request documents, statements or information in support, to meet the requirements of national law for the arrest and surrender of the person. This additional component was included in recognition of the common law extradition practice which can require the submission of 'evidence' in support of a request. Ironically, the provision was of particular concern to the United States because of its constitutional requirements for surrender of a person. While the Statute does not contemplate a 'refusal' of surrender based on the absence of information in the request, obviously there could be situations where compliance would be impeded or, in the worst scenario, precluded on such a basis. This would be a particular danger where the national law of the requested state places the determination on sufficiency of material in the hands of the judiciary. It is notable that most of the implementing laws in common law jurisdictions have avoided this potential problem by adopting streamlined procedures for surrender which avoid traditional extradition requirements.

Ne bis in idem

Because of complementarity, it was necessary to address the question of *ne bis in idem* challenges brought before national courts by an accused. If the case has been ruled admissible by the Court, the request should be executed despite such objections. Otherwise, execution may be postponed pending a decision on admissibility.[22] Under the Rules, in these latter circumstances, the Chamber hearing the admissibility challenge should seek all the relevant[23] information regarding the *ne bis in idem* challenge.[24]

Provisional arrest

The Rome Statute specifically recognizes requests for 'provisional arrest' of a suspect pending the presentation of a full request for arrest and surrender. It is aimed at instances where an arrest may be required on a very urgent basis. If a person is arrested on the basis of such a request, a 'full' request for arrest and surrender must follow within 60 days.[25] The Statute also provides for the transit of a person in custody through other states for the purpose of surrender to the Court. Proper documentation needs to be submitted in advance of such transit or in the case of unscheduled landings, the person can be held for up to 96 hours pending receipt of the relevant information.[26]

Speciality, state prosecution and re-extradition

Apposite to the views expressed by the Referral Bench of the ICTY, the Rome Statute accepts the application of the rule of specialty to cases before the ICC. Article 101 precludes proceedings by the ICC against a person for conduct which preceded that person's surrender and for which he or she was not surrendered. The restriction may be waived by the surrendering state upon a request from the ICC. The person surrendered is granted the opportunity to make submissions regarding the decision on speciality.[27] The same principle was recognized in Article 108, which precludes an enforcement state from proceeding against a person or extraditing him or her to another state, unless after 30 days from release the person remains in the territory of that state. In addition, the Court has the capacity to waive the requirement at the request of the enforcement state.

While the situation of release after service of a sentence was addressed in the Statute, other circumstances where the person may be released were not. Rule 185 was adopted in an attempt to remedy this lacuna by providing transfer options in such a case. Significantly, the rule provides that where the person is released because of a successful challenge to admissibility, the Court shall arrange for the transfer of the person to the State whose investigation or prosecution formed the basis for that successful challenge. However, recognizing that this could result in 're-extradition', such a transfer will not take place if the state which originally surrendered the person requests his or her return.

In the case of a state of enforcement seeking to prosecute or extradite, no opportunity or rights are accorded to the original surrendering state. If the person in question is a national of the surrendering state, the effect of surrender to the ICC could be prosecution or extradition of a national by another state without any input from the original surrendering state. Attempts to remedy this 'gap' in the Statute can be found in Rule 214 where the Presidency is mandated to consult with the original surrendering state in the case of a request for prosecution or extradition, unless that state is the state seeking to prosecute or extradite.

Other forms of cooperation

The nature of the states parties' obligation to cooperate in evidence gathering was the subject of much debate during the negotiation of the Rome Statute. There was a division of views between those seeking a scheme where national law would apply and those advocating for a purely 'vertical' relationship in favour of the ICC. In the end, a compromise was adopted between the two positions. Compliance with the Court's requests will be carried out in accordance with Part IX and 'under the procedures of national law'.[28] However, to avoid the use of national law as an impediment to execution, states parties must have procedures available under national law for all the forms of cooperation specified.[29] By this approach, there is a clear obligation on states parties to cooperate in evidence gathering.

At the same time, unlike under the regime applicable to the Tribunals, the obligatory types of assistance are those specified in the Statute. While Article 93(l) provides a 'catch all' for other types of measures, a state could not be in breach of its obligations with respect to such a request in the absence of a specification of the type of assistance in the Statute. However, there is a strong encouragement on states to provide such additional assistance in so far as it is not 'prohibited' by the law of that State. To further that obligation, the Statute provides for consultations in such circumstances to determine if assistance can still be provided perhaps on a conditioned basis or at a later time or in an alternative manner.[30]

Types of assistance

The other forms of cooperation identified in the Rome Statute are primarily related to assistance with gathering evidence and procuring testimony.[31] There is also specific reference to requests related to protection for witnesses and victims and the preservation of evidence. Given the Statute regime for forfeiture of assets, there is further provision for assistance in gathering information with that aim. The major types of assistance are all reflected in the list, including identifying and locating persons, provision of records and documents, search and seizure and the temporary transfer of persons to provide evidence or assist the investigation.

In light of the subpoena approach of the ICTY/ICTR, it is interesting to note that Part IX of the Statute makes no reference to such a power. The system adopted in the ICC Statute places the responsibility for securing the evidence of witnesses on the state. With regard to witnesses, the states are obliged to provide the following types of assistance:

> The taking of evidence, including testimony under oath, and the production of evidence, including expert opinions and reports necessary to the Courts; ...
> Facilitating the voluntary appearance of persons as witnesses or experts before the Court'[32]

As the obligation to assist is framed, it is for the state to determine how its obligation to arrange for the 'the taking of evidence' will be fulfilled, which could include arranging for the attendance of the witness before the Court in The Hague on a voluntary basis, adducing evidence via technology or having the court take the evidence of the witness in the state.

The ICC scheme also differs from the Tribunal in that while temporary transfer of detained persons as witnesses is specifically provided for, consent of the person to be transferred is mandatory.[33]

Article 93(1)(c) also foresees state cooperation in 'the questioning of any person being investigated or prosecuted'. This would suggest an obligation on states parties to compel a person to appear for such an examination, albeit other statutory provisions and rules would apply in terms of the obligation of the person to answer any questions posed in such a context.

Content of requests

In contrast to the ICTY/ICTR Statutes, detail is provided in the Rome Statute both as to the measures and the applicable process and procedures. There is detail provided as to the content of the requests for assistance, as an aid to both court officials and states. No ground of refusal is premised upon insufficiency in the content of the request. Instead, Article 97 on consultations specifically envisages that a lack of information for execution would be one of the problems that should trigger consultations with the Court.

Grounds of refusal

Unlike the surrender of persons, there are two grounds for a request for other cooperation to be refused by a state. The first concerns circumstances where cooperation would require the state to breach a fundamental principle of its constitution or law. Examples often cited in the discussion were cases where compelling the testimony of the witness would breach a privilege or where the measure sought, e.g. freezing of an asset which was a marital home, was fundamentally impermissible in the state. Whereas those situations would be rare and they were made even more so by the extensive privileges ultimately recognized in the Rules, given the absolute cooperation obligation it was considered necessary to include such protection. However, the ground of refusal is limited to where the particular measure of assistance is prohibited by an already existing fundamental legal principle of general application. In those circumstances, consultations and consideration of conditioned assistance should result and only if no solution can be found would the Court then be obliged to 'modify the request' as necessary.[34]

The second circumstance for 'refusal' is in relation to national security information. Objections to the production of documents or evidence on the basis of national security are the subject of a very detailed regime in Part VI of the Statute.[35] Part IX simply recognizes that, at the end of the process, production of material may be denied or restrictions may be applied to witness testimony,[36] in which case it constitutes an exception to the general cooperation obligation. In any circumstances of refusal, it is incumbent on the state to provide reasons.

Procedure for execution

The intersection of national procedural law with the procedural regime of the ICC, in the context of execution of requests, was a very vexing matter which ultimately required specific statutory treatment.

Article 99(1) recognizes that states will use relevant national procedures in the execution of requests. However, so that the material will be admissible before the ICC, the manner of execution should conform to what the Court specifies in the request unless execution in that way is prohibited by national law. The Statute also recognized the obvious—that in urgent cases documents and evidence should be provided urgently.

Direct execution of requests

One further challenge was the issue of 'direct' execution of requests by ICC officials. Motivated by the wide sweeping comments of the ICTY Appeals Chamber in *Blaskić*, the original proposal sought to accord to the ICC the right to directly carry out various measures in the territory of states. The proposal was considered an important one in so far as the ICC might well encounter situations of hostility and resistance from a state during the course of an investigation. However, there were political and practical concerns about any such provision and state sovereignty. The compromise achieved was premised on two underlying principles. A distinction should be drawn between requests to the territorial state and requests to other states. Furthermore, any 'right' of direct contact and execution should be restricted to forms of cooperation which did not require compulsory measures. Thus, the Statute provides for direct execution of a request not involving compulsory measures (such as an interview or taking of evidence from a witness on a voluntary basis or examining a site) where it is necessary for the successful execution of the request. In such cases, where it is the territorial state, execution may proceed 'following all possible consultations with the requested state party'. For all other states, it can proceed 'following consultations and subject to reasonable conditions or concerns raised by the Requested state'.[37]

Competing requests

The issue of competing requests was considered less significant in the context of other forms of cooperation, since in many instances the evidence can be provided to both parties. Article 93(9) recognizes that principle and only if it is not possible to meet both requests will the regime in Article 90 for competing surrender requests be applied to other forms of cooperation.

Timing of assistance/postponement

The Statute recognizes that in the case of requests for other forms of cooperation, the timing of the assistance may be an issue and thus there is provision for the postponement of assistance. Basically, two scenarios were contemplated—where immediate execution of the request would interfere with an investigation or proceeding in a different matter or where there is an admissibility challenge pending and the Court has not ordered the collection of evidence in any event. In the former case, the state is mandated to keep the delay as short as possible and to consider conditioned assistance as a solution. It is further recognized that in those circumstances the Prosecutor may seek measures to preserve evidence.[38] In the latter case, assistance may be postponed pending a determination of the admissibility question.

Judicial interpretation

The ICC case law is of course still evolving and thus there is little jurisprudence relating to the cooperation regime.[39] However, one issue has arisen surprisingly in the context of provisional release. In the case of Jean-Pierre Bemba Gomba, a single judge granted a request for interim release but deferred implementation of the decision pending a decision as to which state he would be released to and the conditions to be imposed.[40] Furthermore, the decision invited the states identified as possible receiving states to participate in public hearings which would be held to make those determinations. While the decision to grant release and the 'two-step' approach employed were ultimately overturned by the Appeals Chamber, there is a lingering question as to the view regarding state obligations to cooperate with provisional release. At least the single judge appears to have interpreted Part IX to mandate state cooperation in this respect.

There are two significant problems with the analysis. Whereas the list of types of assistance incorporated in Article 93 is indicative and not exclusive, the 'catch all' provision encompasses other types of assistance 'with a view to facilitating the investigation and prosecution of crimes'. Provisional release does not constitute such a measure. Support for this position comes from an examination of the listed types of assistance, all of which relate to evidence gathering or the protection of evidence or asset confiscation. Provisional release is not analogous to any of those types of assistance.

In addition, what was being sought is more properly categorized as assistance with the enforcement of orders and thus falls more properly to be considered under Part X of the Statute. Unlike the regime of the ICTY and ICTR, Part IX is premised on cooperation obligations related to requests and Part X deals with the obligation to comply with courts orders. However, Part X identifies only an obligation with respect to the enforcement of fines and forfeiture measures. States parties have no obligation to cooperate with the enforcement of ICC sentences in terms of providing for the service of the sentence on their territory. Only states indicating a willingness to do so are subject to the provisions of Part X in this regard. In light of that limitation and the fact that the Statute and Rules are silent as to state obligations regarding provisional release, it cannot be assumed that a state, other than one to which the accused has an existing right of entry, has any obligation to accept the person during provisional release.

Requests to the ICC for cooperation

In contrast to the Tribunals, the Rome Statute provides for cooperation by the Court with states on a discretionary basis.[41] Two broad types of assistance are referenced—production of documents and questioning of persons detained by the Court. Protections are afforded with respect to statements or documents obtained with the assistance of a state or a person by requiring consent for disclosure. On a discretionary basis such cooperation may be extended to non-states parties.

Notes

1 Statute of the International Criminal Tribunal for the former Yugoslavia, UN Doc. S/RES/827 (1993), Art. 29; Statute of the International Criminal Tribunal for Rwanda, UN Doc. S/RES/955 (1994), Art. 28.

2 Article 15 of the ICTY Statute accords to the (permanent) judges a power to adopt rules of procedure and evidence for 'the conduct of the pre-trial phase trials and appeals, the admission of evidence, the protection of victims and witnesses and other appropriate matters'. Under Article 14 of the ICTR Statute the (permanent) judges are to adopt the rules of procedure and evidence of the ICTY in relation to the same listed matters with 'such changes as they deem necessary'.
3 Rule 54 general power to issue orders, summonses, subpoenas, etc.; Rule 54*bis* orders to states for the production of documents; Rule 55 issuance/transmission of arrest warrants or transfer orders; Rule 59*bis* on transmission of arrest warrants when accused in custody; Rule 61(D) creating an international arrest warrant; Rule 98 additional power to order evidence.
4 Rule 56 obligation to cooperate in arrest and transfer; Rule 57 procedure post arrest; Rule 58 overriding national extradition provisions; Rule 70 on exceptions to disclosure.
5 Rule 7*bis* providing for referral to the Security Council based on the finding of a chamber or judge or information from the Prosecutor which satisfies the President; Rule 11 non compliance with a request for deferral; Rule 59 on failure to execute arrest warrant or transfer order; Rule 61(E) on failure to effect service.
6 No such rule has been incorporated into the ICTR Rules of Procedure and Evidence.
7 *Blaskić* (IT-95-14-AR108*bis*), Judgement on the Request of the Republic of Croatia for Review of the Decision of Trial Chamber II of 18 July 1997, 29 October 1997.
8 Methods would include assigning a single judge to examine the material or allowing for the State to use its own translators and interpreters.
9 See, for example, *Milutinović et al.* (IT-O5-87-T), Second Decision on Prosecution Motion to Amend its *65ter* list to add Wesley Clark, 16 February 2007 where the Prosecution request to add General Clark to the 65ter list was denied on the basis of the restrictive nature of the Rule 70 conditions imposed. The decision was upheld by the Appeals Chamber.
10 The accused shall enjoy the rights accorded suspects in an investigation (Rule 42) and have the right of review.
11 See note 7.
12 See, for example, *Simić et al.*(IT-95-9-PT), Decision on Motion for Judicial Assistance to be Provided by SFOR and others, 18 October 2000; *Milutinović et al.*(IT-05-87-AR108*bis*), Decision on Request of the North Atlantic Treaty Organization for Review, 15 May 2006.
13 (IT-5-87-AR108*bis*.2), Decision on Request of the United States of America for Review, 12 May 2006.
14 *Nikolić* (IT-94-2-AR73), Decision on Interlocutory Appeal Concerning Legality of Arrest, 5 June 2003.
15 *Milan Lukić* (IT-98-32/1-PT), Decision on Referral of Case Pursuant to Rule 11*bis*, *Prosecutor v. Lukic,* 5 April 2007 (*Lukić decision*).
16 Ibid., para. 38.
17 Rome Statute of the International Criminal Court, Art. 87.
18 Rules of Procedure and Evidence, Rules 176–180.
19 ICC Statute, Art. 87(5).
20 Ibid., Art. 87(6).
21 Paragraphs 3 and 4.
22 ICC Statute, Art. 89(2).
23 See, for example, Australia, *International Criminal Court Act,* 2002; New Zealand, *International Crimes and ICC Act*, 2000; United Kingdom, *International Criminal Court Act, 2001* (Chapter 17).
24 ICC RPE, Rule 181.
25 ICC Statute, Art. 92; ICC RPE, Rule 198.
26 ICC Statute, Art. 89(3).
27 ICC RPE 196 and 197.
28 ICC Statute, Art. 93.
29 Ibid., Art. 88.
30 ICC Statute, Art. 97.
31 See note 28.
32 Ibid., Art. 93 (1)(b) and (e).
33 Ibid., Art. 93(7).
34 Ibid., Art. 93(3).
35 Ibid., Art. 72.
36 Ibid., Art. 99(5).

37 Ibid., Art. 99(4).
38 Ibid., Art. 93(1)(j).
39 While the decisions relating to the consequences of non-disclosure in the case of *Prosecutor v. Thomas Lubanga Dyilo* also touch on cooperation issues with respect to the United Nations, as the core of the cases relate to Article 54(3)(e) and disclosure obligations they will not be analyzed here.
40 *Bemba* (ICC 01/05-01/08), Decision on Interim Release of Jean-Pierre Bemba Gomba, 14 August 2009.
41 ICC Statute, Art. 93(10).

20
Evidence

Nancy Amoury Combs

Prosecuting perpetrators of mass atrocities in international tribunals gives rise to unique evidentiary challenges. The crimes prosecuted in these tribunals feature large-scale violence that frequently takes place over protracted periods of time in locations far from the courtrooms in which the crimes are ultimately prosecuted. Credible evidence can be hard to come by because recalcitrant states erect obstacles that impede prosecutors or defense counsel seeking to investigate the crimes, because witnesses fear retaliation for their testimony, and because considerable time typically elapses between the crimes and the trials. Given the unique nature of international criminal trials and the unique challenges they pose, it should come as no surprise that a unique system has developed to govern the treatment of evidence at the international tribunals. Although many discussions of international criminal evidence focus primarily on admissibility and consequently observe that the evidentiary schemes of international criminal tribunals follow the civil law model, evidentiary issues at the international tribunals cover far broader ground and include both civil law and common law features. Space constraints prevent me from presenting a thorough discussion of international criminal evidence as a whole, but I will endeavor here to touch upon the most prominent evidentiary issues that arise during the pre-trial, trial and post-trial phases of international criminal proceedings.

Pre-trial evidentiary issues

The primary evidentiary issues that arise during a case's pre-trial phase concern the collection of evidence and the disclosure of evidence. As for the former, international criminal tribunals—like common law domestic courts—bestow on each party the obligation to identify witnesses and collect the evidence that the parties will later present at trial. Some commentators have noted the structural advantages that the prosecution enjoy over the defense in the collection of evidence. These advantages stem primarily from the fact that the prosecution is one of the main organs of each of the international criminal tribunals; consequently, the Tribunals' statutes bestow on the prosecution distinct powers to collect evidence, and members of the office of the prosecutor enjoy privileges and immunities that facilitate their on-site investigations.[1] In certain tribunals, defense counsel are also at a comparative disadvantage when it comes to their ability to gain access to crime sites and locate witnesses. The International Criminal Tribunal for

Rwanda (ICTR) defense counsel, for instance, have at various times accused the government of Rwanda of impeding investigations by harassing and intimidating defense witnesses to prevent them from testifying.[2] In other cases, defense counsel have lacked sufficient funds to carry out adequate investigations.[3] Although the Trial Chambers cannot remedy insufficient funding, they have acknowledged the difficulties that have sometimes confronted parties seeking access to evidence and they have committed themselves to providing 'every practicable facility' that they can provide 'when faced with a request by a party for assistance in presenting its case.'[4]

International criminal tribunals require the disclosure of much of the evidence that will eventually be presented at trial. As a comparative matter, the International Criminal Tribunal for the former Yugoslavaia (ICTY) and ICTR rules on pre-trial disclosure steer a middle course between the broad and narrow disclosure frameworks prevailing in civil law and common law jurisdictions, respectively. In the United States, for instance, the parties are required to disclose little or no information to the judge or jury prior to trial[5] because the judge or jury has little or no reason to possess that information prior to trial. The same is not true in civil law jurisdictions, where judges take primary control over the questioning. For such judicial questioning to be effective, judges must have substantial knowledge about the case. To that end, investigating authorities in civil law countries record all the documents pertaining to the pre-trial investigation in a *dossier*[6] and make that *dossier* available to the presiding judge,[7] among others.[8]

Although ICTY and ICTR prosecutors are not obliged to create a *dossier* containing all of the documents relevant to the case, they are obliged to disclose a substantial quantity of supporting information. For instance, the ICTY, ICTR and Special Court for Sierra Leone (SCSL) prosecutors must disclose, among other things, a witness list which summarizes each witness's testimony; an exhibits list;[9] all material which accompanied the indictment when confirmation was sought; and copies of all statements of witnesses that the prosecution intends to call at trial.[10] The defense has similar disclosure obligations and consequently must provide the prosecution with a witness list, a summary of witness testimony, and an exhibits list.[11] Additionally, the defense must notify the prosecution if it intends to raise certain defenses, such as alibi or lack of mental responsibility, and it must provide certain information regarding the defenses.[12] International Criminal Court (ICC) parties have similar, though slightly more complex, disclosure requirements because some disclosure obligations come into play before the confirmation hearing, while others arise later, before trial.[13] Although the disclosure of the above information is typically expected to take place prior to trial, concerns about witness safety have recently led the ICTR, SCSL and the ICC to permit 'rolling disclosure,' in which witnesses' identities are disclosed after the trial has commenced but well before the witnesses' actual testimony.[14]

Tribunal prosecutors are also obliged to disclose exculpatory material, typically defined as 'material which in the actual knowledge of the Prosecutor may suggest the innocence or mitigate the guilt of the accused or affect the credibility of Prosecution evidence.'[15] Moreover, ICC prosecutors are obligated not only to disclose exculpatory evidence but also to search for it.[16] The defense may also request exculpatory materials from prosecutors, but before such a request will be granted, the defense must make a *prima facie* showing that the materials are apt to be relevant and exculpatory and that they are in the custody of the Prosecution.[17] The responsibility of determining whether material is exculpatory rests in the first instance with the prosecution,[18] and the prosecution must exercise this responsibility in good faith.[19] It is this good-faith obligation that is so frequently in question at the Tribunals because, although the legal standards governing the disclosure of exculpatory evidence are relatively clear-cut, defense counsel frequently claim prosecutorial violations of the standard.[20] As a consequence, commentators have suggested that Tribunal judges take a more active role in monitoring disclosure and that they apply heavy penalties when disclosure obligations are violated.[21]

Evidentiary issues arising during trial

Most evidentiary issues occur during trial. This section will consequently discuss (1) the way in which evidence is presented to the Tribunals; (2) the admissibility standards governing evidence in international criminal trials; and (3) the exclusionary rules that prevent evidence from being considered.

How is evidence presented in international criminal proceedings?

The presentation of evidence at the ICTY, ICTR and SCSL follows an adversarial model. That is, international criminal trials in those bodies feature two cases—a prosecution case and a defense case—and each party presents its own evidence at trial. Rule 85 of both the ICTY and ICTR Rules of Procedure and Evidence (RPE) reflects this model and provides that evidence will be presented in the following sequence: evidence for the prosecution, evidence for the defense, prosecution evidence in rebuttal, defense evidence in rejoinder, evidence ordered by the Trial Chamber and finally any relevant information to assist the Trial Chambers in sentencing.[22] Furthermore, each party must be permitted to examine and re-examine the witnesses they call and to cross-examine the opposing party's witnesses. Judges, however, are permitted to ask questions of witnesses at any time,[23] and the Chambers also have the discretion to vary the order of the presentation of evidence if it is in the interests of justice to do so. In *Rukundo*, for instance, an ICTR Trial Chamber called as its own witness a witness who had originally testified for the Prosecution but who had subsequently recanted his testimony. Rule 85 typically requires Trial Chambers that wish to call witnesses to do so after the close of both the prosecution and defense cases. However, in light of its interest in determining the validity of these accusations as well as the seriousness of retracting sworn testimony, the Trial Chamber decided to depart from the normal sequence of evidence presentation in order to recall the witness during the Prosecution's case.[24]

Sequencing issues also arise when Trial Chambers receive motions to present rebuttal evidence or to reopen a case. As a general rule, the prosecution must present evidence pertaining to the defendant's guilt as part of its case in chief.[25] Rule 85 does anticipate that the prosecution may seek to present evidence in rebuttal, as just noted, but such evidence must be 'limited to matters that arise directly and specifically out of defense evidence.'[26] Consequently, Trial Chambers have proven reluctant to permit evidence in rebuttal where that evidence is probative of the accused's guilt or is designed to fill some gap that was reasonably foreseeable to the prosecution.[27] If the evidence sought to be presented does not meet the standards for rebuttal evidence, then a party may seek to reopen its case,[28] but such a request is not apt to be granted unless the evidence sought to be presented is 'fresh evidence.' Fresh evidence has been defined not merely as 'evidence that was not in fact in the possession of the prosecution at the time of the conclusion of its case, but as evidence by which the exercise of all reasonable diligence could not have been obtained by the prosecution at that time.'[29] If a Trial Chamber does conclude that the evidence sought to be presented is 'fresh,' it must consider a number of additional factors in determining whether to exercise its discretion to reopen the case. These include the stage of the trial at which the evidence is sought to be adduced, the delay likely to be caused by reopening the case,[30] and the effect of presenting new evidence against one accused in a multi-accused case.[31]

The ICC employs a more flexible approach than the *ad hoc* Tribunals when it comes to the sequencing of evidence presentation at trial. In particular, Article 64(8)(b) of the Rome Statute gives the Presiding Judge of the Trial Chamber complete discretion over the procedural model to be followed at trial.[32] That is, the judge may follow the ICTY and ICTR and adopt an adversarial model of evidence presentation, as just described, but the judge also has the discretion to adopt a civil law mode of evidence presentation in which the judge takes the primary role in questioning witnesses.[33] Thus far, the emerging practice of the ICC is veering toward an adversarial evidence presentation at trial. In the ICC's first trial, for instance, the Trial Chamber issued instructions that permitted the party calling the witness to ask the first questions of the witness, with this questioning followed by questioning from the party not calling the witness.[34]

What evidence is admissible?

General admissibility rules

The international tribunals have adopted lenient and flexible admissibility rules. Pursuant to Rule 89(C), an ICTY Trial Chamber 'may admit any relevant evidence which it deems to have probative value.' The other *ad hoc* Tribunals and the ICC follow a similarly flexible approach.[35] The Rome Statute authorizes ICC Trial Chambers to 'rule on the relevance or admissibility of any evidence, taking into account, *inter alia*, the probative value of the evidence and any prejudice that such evidence may cause to a fair trial or to a fair evaluation of the testimony of a witness.'[36] The ICC's Rules of Evidence and Procedure maintain this flexibility by authorizing the Trial Chambers to 'assess freely all evidence submitted in order to determine its relevance or admissibility.'[37]

Although the admissibility standard in use at the international tribunals requires that evidence be both relevant and probative, the threshold for relevance and probity is rather low. As the Musema Trial Chamber put it, the standard of admissibility embodied in Rule 89(C) requires the evidence merely to have 'some relevance and some probative value.'[38] As I will discuss below, hearsay evidence is admissible at the international tribunals, and, as a general matter, the Trial Chambers have exhibited 'a fairly uniform tendency . . . towards admitting evidence in the first place leaving its weight to be assessed when all the evidence is being considered by the Trial Chamber in reaching its judgement.'[39] However, one controversial question has pertained to the role of reliability in the admissibility decision. For instance, some Trial and Appeals Chambers have concluded that the reliability of a piece of evidence is relevant to its admissibility. Under this approach, then, evidence that is lacking in reliability should be excluded as without probative value under Rule 89(C).[40] The alternative approach is to admit the evidence but to consider its reliability when determining its weight.[41] This approach has been endorsed by several commentators, who point out that it is 'consistent with the free system of evidence that the Tribunal has adopted.'[42] As for the ICC, a proposal was introduced during one of the Preparatory Commissions to include reliability as a factor to be freely assessed by a Chamber in determining relevance or admissibility. However, because no consensus was reached on this question, the ICC evidentiary rules do not address it.[43]

The admissibility of specific categories of evidence

Because an international criminal defendant has the right to 'examine, or have examined, the witnesses against him and to obtain the attendance and examination of witnesses on his behalf,'[44] the international tribunals generally favor oral testimony. Rule 90(A) of the ICTY's and the ICTR's initial Rules of Procedure provided that 'witnesses shall, in principle, be heard directly by the Chambers.' The Rome Statute also expresses a preference for live evidence through Article 69(2), which states that 'the testimony of a witness at trial shall be given in person.' Oral presentation of evidence has been seen as providing the best opportunity for a party to challenge the evidence of an opposing party and for the Trial Chambers to evaluate the credibility of the presented evidence.[45] These benefits notwithstanding, exceptions to the principle of orality have always existed, and in recent years some tribunals have chosen to temper their preference for orality as a means of expediting trials.

The Tribunals' above-mentioned willingness to admit hearsay evidence constitutes one long-standing exception to the principle of orality. A hearsay statement is defined as a 'statement, other than one made by the declarant while testifying at the trial or hearing, offered in evidence to prove the truth of the matter asserted.'[46] Although the admission of hearsay statements contravenes both the principle of orality and the right to confront witnesses upon which that principle is based, international tribunals have refused to exclude hearsay statements categorically. Early ICTY decisions held that there existed 'no blanket prohibition on the admission of hearsay evidence,' but that its admission depended on its relevance, probative value, and reliability.[47] Trial Chambers thus have considerable discretion in determining the admissibility of specific hearsay statements; as mentioned above, some Trial Chambers consider the reliability of the hearsay statement in determining its admissibility while other Trial Chambers are inclined to admit all hearsay statements but to consider their reliability when determining the weight to afford them.[48]

Other exceptions to the principle of orality are of more recent vintage and stem from the Tribunals' understandable desire to expedite trial proceedings. As noted above, the original version of the ICTY's Rule 90(A) expressed the Tribunal's preference for oral testimony. However, later amendments to the ICTY rules eliminated that preference[49] and created mechanisms to introduce written evidence in lieu of oral witness testimony. For instance, although all of the Tribunals provide for the admission of depositions, the ICTY amended its rule to lower the burden on those seeking to introduce deposition testimony.[50] The admission of deposition testimony does not compromise the confrontation rights of the accused in the same way that the admission of witness statements does because, during a deposition, the defense has the opportunity to cross-examine the witness. No such cross-examination is envisaged for written statements that are tendered in lieu of oral testimony, but Rule 92*bis* nonetheless permits ICTY, ICTR and SCSL Trial Chambers to admit such statements so long as they go to proof of a matter other than the acts and conduct of the accused as charged in the indictment. The version of Rule 92*bis* in effect at the ICTY and ICTR delineates a series of factors that Trial Chambers should consider in determining whether to admit the statements,[51] and it requires that certain formalities be observed in order to enhance the reliability of the statements.[52] Because Rule 92*bis* does not permit the introduction of written statements to prove the acts and conduct of the accused, the rule has been useful primarily for expediting the presentation of 'crime-base' evidence.[53] Moreover, some commentators have noted that because rule 92*bis* does not permit the introduction of written statements to prove the acts and conduct of the accused, the rule is a 'mandatory exclusionary rule' that constitutes 'a significant departure from the initial flexible nature of the ICTY's law of evidence.'[54]

The ICC takes a more restrictive approach to the admission of documentary evidence. Pursuant to Rule 68 of the ICC's RPE, documentary evidence of a witness may be admitted only when both parties have had the opportunity to question the witness during the taking of testimony or the witness is available to be cross-examined at trial.

What evidence is excluded?

Although the international tribunals do utilize liberal admissibility standards, they are nonetheless permitted, and in some cases required, to exclude certain evidence. ICTY Trial Chambers, for instance, are authorized under Rule 89(D) to exclude evidence if its probative value is substantially outweighed by the need to ensure a fair trial. The Rome Statute instructs ICC Trial Chambers similarly, not with a specific exclusionary rule, but by inserting fair trial considerations into the Trial Chamber's decision on admissibility. Thus, Article 69(4) of the Rome Statute requires Trial Chambers that are considering the admissibility of a piece of evidence to take account of 'the probative value of the evidence and any prejudice that such evidence may cause to a fair trial or to a fair evaluation of the testimony of a witness.' The ICTR does not have a similar rule, and this omission arguably has affected the Trial Chambers' recourse to the most prominent mandatory exclusion that is included in the rules of all of the Tribunals.

That mandatory exclusion, included at Rule 95 of the ICTY's and ICTR's RPE, requires Trial Chambers to exclude evidence if 'its admission is antithetical to, and would seriously damage, the integrity of the proceedings' or if it has been 'obtained by methods which cast substantial doubt' on the reliability of the evidence.[55] ICTY Trial Chambers have made little use of this provision, preferring instead to exclude evidence pursuant to Rule 89(D), discussed above.[56] By contrast, ICTR Trial Chambers, having no Rule 89(D) at their disposal, have made greater use of the mandatory exclusion appearing in Rule 95. Of course, even at the ICTR, 'Rule 95 does not require automatic exclusion of all unlawfully obtained evidence.'[57] As a consequence, ICTR Trial Chambers have refused to exclude witness testimony when the contemporaneous notes of the witness's interview were not preserved;[58] they have refused to exclude a statement taken one week after the accused's arrest, when he had not yet been taken before a judge,[59] and they have refused to exclude a document seized during an illegal arrest, unless there is a specific showing that the document was not reliable or that the admission of the document would seriously damage the integrity of the proceedings.[60] By contrast, evidence will be excluded if the integrity of the proceedings would otherwise be seriously damaged.[61] Consequently, ICTR Trial Chambers will exclude statements taken in violation of the defendant's right to the assistance of counsel,[62] statements taken without informing the accused of the charges against him,[63] and statements taken in violation of a witness protection order.[64]

The analogous ICC rule appears to require that a higher standard be met before evidence will be excluded. In particular, to exclude evidence under Rome Statute Article 69(7), the Trial Chamber must find that the evidence was both 'obtained by means of a violation of this Statute or internationally recognized human rights' *and* that 'the violation casts substantial doubt on the reliability of the evidence' or that the 'admission of the evidence would be antithetical to and would seriously damage the integrity of the proceedings.' Zahar and Sluiter find fault with this formulation, asking rhetorically: 'Does admission of evidence obtained in violation of human rights not by definition damage the integrity of the proceedings?'[65] These commentators go on to opine that an 'interpretation of Article 69(7), according to which not every human rights violation damages the integrity of the proceedings, amounts to a departure from the original purpose of Rule 95 of the ICTY and ICTR RPE, and also makes a mockery of human rights law as an indivisible set of minimum legal standards.'[66]

Post-trial evidentiary issues – weighing evidence

As noted, international tribunals boast liberal admissibility rules that result in the admission of a great deal of evidence, much of which would be excluded in common law criminal trials. However, the fact that Trial Chambers admit a great deal of evidence does not tell us anything about how they weigh the evidence that they admit. The ICTR Appeals Chamber warned that it is 'neither possible nor proper to draw up an exhaustive list of criteria for the assessment of evidence, given the specific circumstances of each case and the duty of the judge to rule on each case in an impartial and independent manner,'[67] but general principles regarding the weight accorded to certain classes of evidence can be discerned.[68] It goes almost without saying that hearsay evidence is afforded less weight than the testimony of a witness who has given that testimony under oath and has been cross-examined.[69] Moreover, in keeping with their adherence to the principle of orality, Trial Chambers have also held live testimony to be weightier than video link testimony.[70] Live testimony not only better respects the accused's right to confrontation but also it affords the Trial Chamber the best opportunity to evaluate the demeanor and credibility of the witness. Video link testimony, however, has been held to be weightier than testimony given by deposition.[71] In determining what weight is appropriate for documentary evidence, Trial Chambers consider its authenticity as well as its source or authorship. In particular, in determining the authenticity of a document, a Trial Chamber will consider its form, contents and the purported use of the document, among other factors.[72]

Conclusion

International criminal evidence rules constitute a unique amalgam. The Tribunals' basic approach to evidence derives from civil law systems, but that civil law approach must be utilized in trial proceedings that are primarily common law in character. Not surprisingly, this blending creates certain tensions, as do recent efforts to speed up trial proceedings, which can be seen as compromising certain fair trial rights. Indeed, safeguarding the accused's right to an expeditious trial while simultaneously protecting his or her other fair trial rights stands as one of international criminal law's most pressing challenges.

Notes

1 A. Zahar and G. Sluiter, *International Criminal Law*, Oxford: Oxford University Press, 2008, pp. 364–5.

2 See, e.g. Simba (ICTR-01-76-T), Judgement and Sentence, 13 December 2005, paras 41–3; Bagosora *et al.* (ICTR-98-41-T), Defense Motion Concerning Alleged Witness Intimidation, 28 December 2004, para. 1; see also K. Ambos, 'International Criminal Procedure: "Adversarial," "Inquisitorial" or Mixed,' 3 *International Criminal Law Review* 1, 2003, 36; F. Harhoff, 'The Role of the Parties Before International Criminal Courts', in Fischer *et al.* (eds), *International and National Prosecution of Crimes under International Law*, Berlin: Berlin Verlag Arno Spitz, 2001, pp. 655–6; S. Kay and B. Swart, 'The Role of the Defense', in A. Cassese *et al.* (eds), *II The Rome Statute of the International Criminal Court*, Oxford: Oxford University Press, 2002, p. 1424.

3 See S. Kendall and M. Staggs, U.C. Berkeley War Crimes Studies Center, *From Mandate to Legacy: The Special Court for Sierra Leone as a Model for 'Hybrid Justice:' Interim Report on the Special Court for Sierra Leone* 14–15 (April 2005) (arguing that SCSL defense counsel lack sufficient funding to conduct thorough investigations). Moreover, the woefully insufficient funds provided to early defense counsel at the Special Panels in East Timor substantially impeded the ability of counsel to investigate. Defense counsel called not a single defense witness to testify in the first 14 Special Panels trials, not even in the massive *Los Palos* case, in which 10 defendants were prosecuted for crimes against humanity. D. Cohen, 'Seeking Justice on the Cheap: Is the East Timor Tribunal Really a Model for the Future?' *in Asia Pacific Issues* No. 61, at 5 (East-West Center 2002). Special Panels defense counsel complained that they lacked both cars and the time to travel to the districts to interview potential witnesses. In addition, they lacked resources to provide witnesses with transportation to the court in Dili and to pay for their food and lodging while there. Judicial System Monitoring Programme, *The General Prosecutor v. Joni Marques and 9 Others (The Los Palos Case): A JSMP Trial Report*, §3.2.2.1 (March 2002).

4 Tadić (IT-94-1-A), Judgement, 15 July 1999, para. 52.

5 In some states, prosecutors are required only to disclose exculpatory evidence and statements of the defendant in their possession. See C. Bradley, 'United States', in C. M. Bradley (ed.), *Criminal Procedure: A Worldwide Study*, Durham, NC: Carolina Academic Press, 1999, pp. 416–17. In recent years, American jurisdictions have begun granting criminal defendants greater discovery rights, see W. R. LaFave *et al.*, *Criminal Procedure*, St. Paul, MN: West, 4th edn, 2004, pp. 924–5, but those rights are

still comparatively limited. Only slightly more than one-third of American jurisdictions require prosecutors to disclose the statements of co-defendants and witnesses, but a majority of American jurisdictions now require the disclosure of scientific reports relating to the case, the defendant's criminal record, and documents and tangible items which will be used at trial. Ibid., at 933–6. For a discussion of the disclosure obligations placed on British and Irish prosecutors, see D. J. Feldman, 'England and Wales', in C. M. Bradley (ed.), *Criminal Procedure: A Worldwide Study*, pp. 119–21; F. McAuley and J. O'Dowd, 'Ireland', in C. Van den Wyngaert *et al.* (eds), *Criminal Procedure Systems in the European Community*, London: Butterworths, 1993, p. 195.

6 M. Daly, 'Some Thoughts on the Differences in Criminal Trials in the Civil and Common Law Legal Systems', *Journal of the Institute for the Study of Legal Ethics* 2, 1999, 67–8; C. Van den Wyngaert, 'Belgium', in C. Van den Wyngaert *et al.* (eds), *Criminal Procedure Systems in the European Community*, p. 30; N. Jörg *et al.*, 'Are Inquisitorial and Adversarial Systems Converging?', in P. Fennell *et al.* (eds), *Criminal Justice in Europe: A Comparative Study*, Oxford: Clarendon Press, 1995, p. 47 (discussing the nature of the *dossier* in The Netherlands).

7 G. van Kessel, 'Adversary Excesses in the American Criminal Trial', *Notre Dame Law Review* 67, 1992, 423; C. Van den Wyngaert, 'Belgium', in C. Van den Wyngaert *et al.* (eds), *Criminal Procedure Systems in the European* Community, p. 35.

8 Typically, the *dossier* is also made available in its entirety to the defendant or his counsel and is supposed to contain all the evidence relevant to the case, exculpatory as well as inculpatory. See, e.g. M. Damaška, 'Evidentiary Barriers to Conviction and Two Models of Criminal Procedure: A Comparative Study', *University of Pennsylvania Law Review* 121, 1973, 533–4; R. Frase, 'Comparative Criminal Justice as a Guide to American Law Reform: How Do the French Do It, How Can We Find Out, and Why Should We Care?', *California Law Review* 78, 1990, 672.

9 ICTY Rules of Procedure and Evidence, Rule 65*ter*(E) (2009) [hereinafter ICTY RPE]; ICTR Rules of Procedure and Evidence, Rule 73*bis*(B) (2008) [hereinafter ICTR RPE]; SCSL Rules of Procedure and Evidence, Rule 73*bis*(B) (2008) [hereinafter SCSL RPE].

10 ICTY RPE, Rule 66(A)(i)–(ii); ICTR RPE, Rule 66(A)(i)–(ii); SCSL RPE, Rule 66(A)(i)–(ii).

11 ICTY RPE, Rule 65*ter*(G); ICTR RPE, Rule 74*ter*(B); SCSL RPE, Rule 73*ter*(B).

12 ICTY RPE, Rule 67(B)(i)(a)–(b); ICTR RPE, Rule 67(A)(ii)(a)–(b); SCSL RPE, Rule 67(A)(ii)(a)–(b). With respect to an alibi defense, the defendant must inform the prosecution of the places where he claims to have been, and with respect both to alibis and special defenses, the defendant must disclose the names and addresses of the witnesses and any other evidence on which he or she intends to rely. See note 12.

13 For instance, Article 61(3) of the Rome Statute requires prosecutors to disclose – within a reasonable amount of time before the confirmation hearing – the charge document and the evidence upon which the prosecutor intends to rely at the confirmation hearing. Rome Statute of the International Criminal Court, United Nations Diplomatic Conference of Plenipotentiaries on the Establishment of an International Criminal Court, UN Doc. A/CONF.183/9 (1998), Article 61(3) [hereinafter Rome Statute]. Rule 121 of the ICC's Rules of Procedure and Evidence implements Article 61(3) and provides a detailed regime governing the disclosure of evidence prior to the confirmation hearing. Articles 64(3)(c) and 64(6)(d), by contrast, govern the disclosure that must take place prior to trial. Those articles are implemented by Rules 76 and 84, which require prosecutors to disclose, among other things, witness lists, witness statements, and the statements of accused. Similarly, pursuant to Rule 79, the defense must disclose its intent to raise an alibi or a ground for excluding criminal responsibility and the identity of the witnesses that it will call to prove those defenses.

14 See ICTR RPE, Rule 69(C); SCSL RPE, Rule 69(C); ICC Rules of Procedure and Evidence, Rule 140(2) (2002) [hereinafter ICC RPE]. See also G. Sluiter, 'The ICTR and the Protection of Witnesses', *Journal of International Criminal Justice* 3, 2005, 972–3. The ICTY continues to require that witness identities be disclosed before trial. See ICTY RPE, Rule 69(C) ('Subject to Rule 75, the identity of the victim or witness shall be disclosed in sufficient time prior to the trial to allow adequate time for preparation of the defence.')

15 ICTY RPE, Rule 68(i); ICTR RPE, Rule 68(A); SCSL RPE, Rule 68(B); Rome Statute, Article 67(2). Although the text of the ICTY, ICTR and SCSL rules suggests that the prosecutor must disclose any exculpatory evidence about which he has 'actual knowledge,' those tribunals have sensibly limited the disclosure obligation to material that is also in the possession of the prosecution. Karemera *et al.* (ICTR-98-44-T), Decision on Joseph Nzirorera's Notices of Rule 68 Violations and Motions for Remedial and Punitive Measures, 13 November 2007, para. 5; Kajelijeli (ICTR-98-44A-A), Judgement, 23 May 2005, para. 262.

16 Rome Statute, Article 54(1).

17 Blaškić (IT-95-14-PT), Decision on the Defence Motion for 'Sanctions for Prosecutor's Repeated Violations of Rule 68 of the Rules of Procedures and Evidence', 29 April 1998; Blaškić (IT-95-14-PT), Decision on the Defence Motion for Sanctions for the Prosecutor's Continuing Violation of Rule 68, 28 September 1998.

18 Nahimana *et al.* (ICTR-99-52-A), Decision on Appellant Jean-Bosco Barayagwiza's Motion Requesting that the Prosecution Disclosure of the Interview of Michel Bagaragaza be Expunged from the Record, 30 October. 2006, para. 6; Karemera *et al.* (ICTR-98-44-AR73.7), Decision on Interlocutory Appeal Regarding the Role of the Prosecutor's Electronic Disclosure Suite in Discharging Disclosure Obligations, 30 June 2006, para. 9; Karemera *et al.* (ICTR-98-44-AR73.6), Decision on Joseph Nzirorera's Interlocutory Appeal, 28 April 2006, para. 16; Kordić and Čerkez (IT-95-14/2-A), Judgement, 17 December 2004, para. 183; Brđanin (IT-99-36-A), Decision on Appellant's Motion for Disclosure Pursuant to Rule 68 and Motion for an Order to the Registrar to Disclose Certain Materials, 7 December 2004; Blaškić (IT-95-14-A), Judgement, 29 July 2004, para. 264.

19 Blaškić (IT-95-14), Decision on the Appellant's Motions for the Production of Materials, Suspension or Extension of the Briefing Schedule, and Additional Filings, 26 September 2000, para. 45.

20 S. Zappalà, 'The Prosecutor's Duty to Disclose Exculpatory Materials and the Recent Amendment to Rule 68 ICTY RPE', *Journal of International Criminal Justice* 2, 2004, 623; A. Zahar and G. Sluiter, *International Criminal Law*, p. 375 and note 132 (citing cases).

21 S. Zappalà, *Human Rights in International Criminal Proceedings*, Oxford: Oxford University Press, 2003, p. 145; A. Zahar and G. Sluiter, *International Criminal Law*, p. 375.

22 Rule 85 of the SCSL RPE is very similar, but it does not authorize defense evidence in rebuttal.

23 ICTY RPE, Rule 85(B); ICTR RPE, Rule 85(B); SCSL RPE, Rule 85(B).

24 Rukundo (ICTR-2001-70-T), Decision on Defence Motion to Recall Prosecution Witness BLP, 30 April 2007, para. 7.

25 Blagojević & Jokić (IT-02-60-T), Decision on Prosecution's Case on Rebuttal and Incorporated Motion to Admit Evidence under Rule 92*bis* in its Case on Rebuttal and to Re-open its Case for a Limited Purpose, 13 September 2004, paras 5–6; Delalić *et al.* (IT-96-21-T), Decision on the Prosecution's Alternative Request to Reopen the Prosecution's Case, 19 August 1998, para. 18 [hereinafter Delalić Decision on Request to Reopen]; Halilović (IT-01-48-T), Decision on Prosecution Motion to Call Rebuttal Evidence, 21 July 2005 [hereinafter Halilović Decision on Rebuttal Evidence]; Orić (IT-03-68-T), Decision on the Prosecution Motion With Addendum and Urgent Addendum to Present Rebuttal Evidence Pursuant to Rule 85(A)(iii), 9 February 2006 [hereinafter Orić Decision on Motion to Request Rebuttal Evidence].

26 Delalić Decision on Request to Reopen, para. 23; see also Orić Decision on Motion to Request Rebuttal Evidence; Ntagerura *et al.* (ICTR-99-46-T), Decision on the Prosecutor's Motion for Leave to Call Evidence in Rebuttal Pursuant to Rules 54, 73, and 85(A)(iii) of the Rules of Procedure and Evidence, 21 May 2003, para. 34 (holding that the Prosecutor has failed to show that the subject of the proposed rebuttal evidence arose for the first time in the Defence's case).

27 Delalić Decision on Request to Reopen, paras 22–3; see also Orić Decision on Motion to Request Rebuttal Evidence (finding that 'admission of the rebuttal evidence proposed by the Prosecution, even if permissible under a more flexible application of the high or strict standard of admissibility, would be outweighed by the need to ensure a fair and expeditious trial.'); Halilović Decision on Rebuttal Evidence.

28 Karemera *et al.* (ICTR-98-44-T), Decision on the Prosecution Motion to Reopen its Case and on the Defence Motion to File Another Rule 98*bis* Motion, 19 April 2008, para. 11 [hereinafter Karemera Decision on Motion to Reopen].

29 Delalić Decision on Request to Reopen, para. 26. For instance, in *Karemera,* prosecution witness BTH recanted his testimony after the Prosecution case had closed, so the Prosecution sought to call three additional witnesses in an effort to bolster its case. Karemera Decision on Motion to Reopen, paras 1–3, 8. In denying the motion, the Trial Chamber noted that the three additional witnesses initially had been on the Prosecution's witness list, but the Prosecution had chosen not to call them and had instead relied on the testimony of BTH. In addition, the Prosecution itself had described the testimony of the three proposed witnesses 'as corroborating evidence that was already on the record.' Id. at para. 12. Under these circumstances, the Trial Chamber could not consider the evidence 'new,' and it additionally considered that the interests of justice would not be served by permitting a party to call additional witnesses 'every time they consider a witness may have been discredited.' Id. at paras 12–3; see also

Bagosora *et al.* (ICTR-98-41-T), Decision on Bagosora Motion to Present Additional Witnesses and Vary its Witness List, 17 November 2006, para. 13 (rejecting the Prosecution's motion with regards to specific witnesses because 'the interests of justice do not favor altering the trial schedule to accommodate a witness whose appearance is both unnecessary and unlikely').

30 Delalić Decision on Request to Reopen, para. 27.

31 Zigiranyirazo (ICTR-01-73-T), Decision on the Prosecution Joint Motion for Reopening its Case and for Reconsideration of the 31 January 2006 Decision on the Hearing of Witness Michel Bagaragaza by Video-Link, 16 November 2006, para. 16.

32 Rome Statute, Article 64(8)(b) provides: 'At the trial, the presiding judge may give directions for the conduct of proceedings, including to ensure that they are conducted in a fair and impartial manner. Subject to any directions of the presiding judge, the parties may submit evidence in accordance with the provisions of this Statute.'

33 Should the judge decline to set out the order of evidence presentation, Rule 140(1) of the ICC's Rules of Procedure and Evidence authorizes the parties to reach their own agreement on the question. However, since it may prove difficult for the parties to agree on such an important issue, Rule 140(1) provides a back-up plan by requiring the judge to issue directions. However, Rule 140(2) limits the judge's discretion by establishing certain rules concerning witness questioning that apply 'in all cases.' In particular, no matter what procedural model the judge chooses, in each case each party maintains the essential right to question the witnesses they call, and to question the witnesses their opponent calls.

34 Lubanga (ICC-01/04-01/06-T-104-ENG), Transcript, 16 January 2009, at 37–8.

35 The ICTR's Rule 89(C) is identical to that of the ICTY, but the ICTR has not adopted Rule 89(D) which permits a Trial Chamber to 'exclude evidence if its probative value is substantially outweighed by the need to ensure a fair trial.' The pertinent SCSL Rule seems to contemplate an even more lenient standard, for it provides simply that a 'Chamber may admit relevant evidence.' SCSL RPE Rule 89(C).

36 Rome Statute, Article 69(4).

37 ICC RPE, Rule 63(2).

38 Musema (ICTR-96-13), Judgement and Sentence, 27 January 2000, para. 56 (emphasis in original) [hereinafter Musema Judgement].

39 Brđanin and Talić (IT-99-36-T), Order on the Standards Governing the Admission of Evidence, 15 February 2002, para. 13.

40 See, e.g. Kordić & Čerkez (IT-95-14/2), Decision on Appeal Regarding Statement of a Deceased Witness, 21 July 2000, para. 28; Musema Judgement, paras 35–8.

41 See, e.g. Blaškić (IT-95-14-T), Decision on Standing Objection of the Defence to the Admission of Hearsay with no Inquiry as to its Reliability, 21 January 1998, paras 11–13 [hereinafter Blaškić Decision on Admission of Hearsay]; Aleksovski (IT-95-14/1-T), Decision Granting Leave for the Admission of Evidence, 22 October 1998.

42 A. Rodrigues and C. Tournaye, 'Hearsay Evidence', in R. May *et al.* (eds), *Essays on ICTY Procedure and Evidence in Honour of Gabrielle Kirk McDonald*, The Hague: Kluwer Law International, 2001, p. 303; R. May and M. Wierda, *International Criminal Evidence*, Ardsley, NY: Transnational, 2002, pp. 109–10; see also Stakić (IT-97-24-PT), Provisional Order on the Standards Governing the Admission of Evidence and Identification, 25 February 2002, p. 6.

43 D. Piragoff, 'Article 69 – Evidence', in O. Triffterer (ed.), *II Commentary on the Rome Statute of the International Criminal Court – Observers' Notes, Article by Article*, Munich/Oxford/Baden-Baden: C.H. Beck, Hart, Nomos, 2nd edn, 2008, p. 1306.

44 ICTY Statute, SC Res. 827, UN SCOR, 48th Sess., 3217th mtg., UN Doc. S/RES/827, Article 21(4)(e) (1993); ICTR Statute, SC Res. 955, UN SCOR, 49th Sess., 3453d mtg., UN Doc. S/RES/955 & Annex, Article 20(4)(e) (1994); Statute of the Special Court for Sierra Leone, Article 17(4)(e) (2002).

45 See Tadić (IT-94-1-T), Decision on the Defence Motions to Summon and Protect Witnesses and on the Giving of Evidence by Video Link, 25 June 1996, para. 11; Kupreškić (IT-95-16-AR73.3), Decision on Appeal by Dragan Papić against Ruling to Proceed by Deposition, 15 July 1999, para. 18; Aleksovski, (IT-95-14/1-A), Judgement, 24 March 2000, paras 62–64.

46 *Black's Law Dictionary*, St. Paul, Minn: West Publishing Co. 6th ed., 2009, p.790.

47 Tadić, (IT-94-1-T), Decision on Defence Motion on Hearsay, 5 August 1996, para. 7; see also Aleksovski (IT-95-14/1-AR73), Decision on Prosecutor's Appeal on Admissibility of Evidence, 16 February 1999, para. 15 [hereinafter Aleksovski Decision on Admissibility of Evidence]; Blaškić Decision on Admission of Hearsay, para. 9.

48 See A. Rodrigues and C. Tournaye, 'Hearsay Evidence', in R. May *et al.* (eds), *Essays on ICTY Procedure and Evidence in Honour of Gabrielle Kirk McDonald*, pp. 300–01.

49 The current SCSL's rules also express no preference for oral testimony. SCSL Rule 90 provides that '[w]itnesses may give evidence directly or as described in Rules 71 [governing depositions] and 85(D) [governing testimony given through video media].'

50 The original text of Rule 71(A) at the ICTY, ICTR and SCSL provided that, 'at the request of either party, a Trial Chamber may, in exceptional circumstances and in the interests of justice, order that a deposition be taken for use at trial.' Subsequent case law established that the temporary unavailability of a judge did not satisfy the 'exceptional circumstance' requirement under Rule 71(A). Rather, the Appeals Chamber strictly construed the rule to permit depositions only in instances in which witnesses were unavailable or possibly where the accused agreed to the admission. Kupreškić (IT-95-16-A), Decision on Appeal by Dragan Papić against Ruling to Proceed by Deposition, 15 July 1999, paras 19–22. The ICTY then amended Rule 71 to eliminate the 'exceptional circumstances' requirement. Consequently, the rule now permits a Trial Chamber to order a deposition so long as doing so is 'in the interests of justice', and regardless of 'whether or not the person whose deposition is sought is able physically to appear before the Tribunal to give evidence.'

51 Factors arguing in favor of the admission of written evidence include instances in which the relevant evidence: (a) is cumulative to other evidence given orally; '(b) relates to relevant historical, political or military background; (c) consists of a general or statistical analysis of the ethnic composition of the population in the places to which the indictment relates; (d) concerns the impact of crimes upon victims; (e) relates to issues of the character of the accused; or (f) relates to factors to be taken into account in determining sentence.' ICTR RPE, Rule 92*bis* (A)(i)(a)–(f); ICTY RPE, Rule 92*bis* (A)(i)(a)–(f). Factors arguing against the admission of written evidence include instances in which '(a) there is an overriding public interest in the evidence in question being presented orally; (b) a party objecting can demonstrate that its nature and source renders it unreliable, or that its prejudicial effect outweighs its probative value; or (c) there are any other factors which make it appropriate for the witness to attend for cross-examination.' ICTY RPE, Rule 92*bis* (A)(ii)(a)–(c); ICTR RPE, Rule 92*bis* (A)(ii)(a)–(c).

52 ICTY RPE, Rule 92*bis* (B); ICTR RPE, Rule 92*bis* (B).

53 R. May and M. Wierda, *International Criminal Evidence*, p. 222.

54 A. Zahar and G. Sluiter, *International Criminal Law*, pp. 388–9.

55 ICTY RPE, Rule 95; ICTR RPE, Rule 95. The SCSL's rule on the subject provides that '[n]o evidence shall be admitted if its admission would bring the administration of justice into serious disrepute.' SCSL RPE, Rule 95.

56 A. Zahar and G. Sluiter, *International Criminal Law*, pp. 381–2.

57 Karemera *et al.* (ICTR-98-44-T), Decision on the Prosecutor's Motion for Admission of Certain Exhibits into Evidence, 25 January 2008, para. 11 [hereinafter Karemera Decision on Motion for Admission of Exhibits].

58 Niyitegeka (ICTR-96-14-A), Judgement, 9 July 2004, para. 39.

59 Karemera *et al.* (ICTR-98-44-T), Decision on the Prosecution Motion for Admission into Evidence of Post-Arrest Interviews with Joseph Nzirorera and Mathieu Ngirumpatse, 2 November 2007, para. 17 [hereinafter Karemera Decision on Motion for Admission of Post-Arrest Interviews].

60 Karemera Decision on Motion for Admission of Exhibits, para. 16.

61 Id. at para. 11.

62 Bagosora *et al.* (ICTR-98-41-T), Decision on the Prosecutor's Motion for the Admission of Certain Materials Under Rule 89(C), 14 October 2004, para. 21; Zigiranyirazo (ICTR-2001-73-T), Decision on the Voir Dire Hearing of the Accused's Curriculum Vitae, 29 November 2006, para. 13; Karemera Decision on Motion for Admission of Post-Arrest Interviews, para. 25.

63 Karemera Decision on Motion for Admission of Post-Arrest Interviews, paras. 9, 11–3, 30, 32.

64 Kajelijeli (ICTR-98-44A-T), Decision on Kajelijeli's Motion to Hold Members of the Office of the Prosecutor in Contempt of the Tribunal [Rule 77(C)], 15 November 2002, para. 14.

65 A. Zahar and G. Sluiter, *International Criminal Law*, p. 382.

66 Id.

67 Kayishema and Ruzindana (IT-95-1-A), Judgement, 1 June 2001, para. 319.

68 See G. Sluiter, *International Criminal Adjudication and the Collection of Evidence: Obligations of States*, Antwerp: Intersentia, 2002, p. 237.

69 See, e.g. Aleksovski Decision on Admissibility of Evidence, para. 15; Tadić (IT-94-1-A-R77), Judgment on Allegations of Contempt against Prior Counsel, Milan Vujin, 31 January 2000, para. 93.

70 As the Tadić Trial Chamber put it, 'It is preferable for the Trial Chamber to have the benefit of the physical presence of the witnesses at trial.' Tadić (IT-94-1-T), Decision on the Defence Motions to Summon and Protect Defense Witnesses and on the Giving of Evidence by Video Link, 25 June 1996, para. 21.

71 Id.

72 Musema Judgement, at para. 67.

Part IV
Key issues in international criminal law

21

The rise and fall of universal jurisdiction

Luc Reydams

Introduction

For the last two decades most of the international human rights movement has advocated the exercise of universal jurisdiction—civil and criminal—by individual states over 'gross human rights violations' wherever committed and regardless of the nationality of the victim or perpetrator. The most spectacular criminal case was the arrest and detention in 1998 of former Chilean President (and dictator) Augusto Pinochet by British authorities at the request of Spain. His arrest and the adoption in the same year of the Rome Statute of the International Criminal Court (ICC) were hailed as global civil society achievements.

But that was then. Pinochet was never extradited and by late 2009—the time of writing of this chapter—Spain had *de facto* repealed its controversial universal jurisdiction law and the first trial before the ICC, of a minor actor by all standards in Africa's Great War, continued its slow but rocky course. International criminal justice *anno* 2009 is probably not what proponents anticipated a decade ago.

This chapter considers the rise and fall of universal jurisdiction. It begins by revisiting the unique trend of the 1990s and by broaching the actors behind the campaign for universal jurisdiction. Then it discusses how these actors, mainly non-governmental organizations (NGOs), framed the issue and how policy-oriented international lawyers constructed the legal argument. Thereafter, it reviews the (alleged) historical sources of universal jurisdiction and their contemporary (distorted) interpretation. The subsequent examination of post–World War II multilateral treaty practice finds little enthusiasm among *states* for universal jurisdiction. After that, cases of the last 15 or so years are assessed, distinguishing between 'hard' cases (in courts) and 'virtual' cases (in the media). Next, it is shown in a brief *post mortem* how a backlash in Africa, the United States, Israel, and China against virtual trials in Europe caused the premature end of universal jurisdiction. The final section draws some lessons and ponders universal jurisdiction's future.

It may be useful for the reader to know what prompted me to write this chapter. In July 1997, I participated in a residential seminar 'National Adjudication of International Crimes' organized by the Dutch section of Amnesty International (AI). I was invited as an 'expert' because I was preparing a doctoral dissertation on the subject. At the seminar, which brought together experts, activists, and government officials, we brainstormed and strategized on how individuals like

Pinochet could be held accountable outside Chile. The following year Pinochet *was* under arrest. Reflecting back on this memorable event, I realize how for a while, through publications and participation in events like the AI seminar, I unwittingly—but not unwillingly—was part of a so-called *transnational advocacy network*.[1] My being part of the network ended with my book on universal jurisdiction[2] in which I doubted that *Pinochet* would ever be repeated and concluded that '[i]n the end it may well be that [it was] an aberrant intermezzo between Nuremberg and the ICC'. A decade later I revisit my conclusion and take stock.[3]

Trend and actors

The end of the Cold War and its coincidence with the countdown towards a new century triggered a flurry of writing about a New World Order. The main ingredients thereof would be great power cooperation, nuclear disarmament, multilateralism, and 'preventive diplomacy, peace-making and peace-keeping'.[4] In this climate the doctrines of just war and humanitarian intervention re-emerged, as did the concomitant idea of international criminal justice. After all, if military intervention is acceptable to protect human rights then judicial intervention[5] surely is too.

Both ideas, of universal jurisdiction and of an international criminal court, cannot be dissociated from the 'endism' and 'sans-frontièrism'[6] that pervaded 1990s discourses—end of history, end of politics, and end of the Westphalian State.[7] In a post-ideological and increasingly borderless world, deterritorialization of criminal justice became conceivable for 'gross human rights violations' (and 'terrorism').[8] A globalized world called for global jurisdiction over universal wrongs.

But this trend alone does not explain the spectacular advances of the international criminal justice project in the 1990s. Actors to push it forward were needed too. During the 1990s the number of international human rights NGOs grew exponentially[9] and both states and inter-governmental organizations opened up to them 'on a scale qualitatively different from what went before'.[10] At the Rome Diplomatic Conference for an International Criminal Court, officially accredited NGOs nearly equaled the number of states.[11] In this ever denser and competitive field, AI and Human Rights Watch (HRW) achieved superpower status with global reach.[12] Like Greenpeace and *Médecins Sans Frontières* they grew into professional, media savvy organizations capable of waging strategic campaigns. One such campaign launched in the 1990s was 'ending impunity for gross human rights violations'.[13] And so it happened that in the quasi-criminal extradition proceedings against Pinochet before the venerable House of Lords, AI, and three other NGOs were granted leave to intervene as third parties, which symbolizes the human rights movement's ascendency.

Issue framing and legal argument

In the long history of transnational activism, the international criminal justice campaign stands out for its extraordinary successful issue framing.[14] There are countless victims of gross human rights violations and impunity has been the norm. The juxtaposition of these facts suggests a causal relation; hence, fighting impunity through universal jurisdiction or an international criminal court becomes a moral imperative. While creating a legitimate international criminal court requires a substantial number of states, universal jurisdiction can be exercised by *any state* with the necessary courage and will, *right now*. The idea was so obvious, so simple, and so readily accessible that it appeared brilliant. What was demanded was a leap of faith, and if things did not work out as hoped, the flaws would be in the world (self-interest, indifference, parochialism) and not in the doctrine.

Once framed in such simple moral and practical terms it became politically difficult to question universal jurisdiction or, for that matter, the idea of an international criminal court. The latter in particular was presented as historically inevitable and in line with the progress of history. The history of international criminal justice—according to the conventional account—begins in 1474 with the trial of Peter von Hagenbach. As a long-time advocate put it in 1991: 'The time has come for an International Criminal Court'.[15]

But a moral argument, however powerful, is not a legal argument, nor is something legal because it sounds legal (universal *jurisdiction*). The legal argument went as follows: universal jurisdiction was legal lore, it had always existed 'out there', scattered in the writings of publicists or legal-philosophers and in criminal codes, judicial dicta, and treaties here and there. The task at hand was to piece together from this amalgam of sources an international legal 'principle' and then put it into practice. This task was to be undertaken by adepts of policy-oriented schools of international law, such as the New Haven School, for whom international law is not a fixed set of rules that regulate state behavior but an ongoing process of decision making through which 'the international community' identifies, clarifies, and secures common interests. Scholars and lawyers must advocate and develop law to address issues of concern to that community. An example thereof is the Princeton Project on Universal Jurisdiction created 'to contribute to the ongoing development of universal jurisdiction'.[16] The Project's *Principles on Universal Jurisdiction* (2001)

> are intended to be useful to legislators seeking to ensure that national laws conform to international law, to judges called upon to interpret and apply international law and to consider whether national law conforms to their state's international legal obligations, to government officials of all kinds exercising their powers under both national and international law, to nongovernmental organizations and members of civil society active in the promotion of international criminal justice and human rights, and to citizens who wish to better understand what international law is and what the international legal order might become.

Despite the acknowledgement that the *Principles* are a mixture of *lex lata* and *lex desiderata*, the text itself reads like a confident statement of the law:

> Principle 1—Fundamentals of Universal Jurisdiction
>
> 1 For purposes of these Principles, universal jurisdiction is criminal jurisdiction based solely on the nature of the crime, without regard to where the crime was committed, the nationality of the alleged or convicted perpetrator, the nationality of the victim, or any other connection to the state exercising such jurisdiction.
>
> 2 Universal jurisdiction may be exercised by a competent and ordinary judicial body of any state in order to try a person duly accused of committing serious crimes under international law as specified in Principle 2(1), provided the person is present before such judicial body.
>
> 3 A state may rely on universal jurisdiction as a basis for seeking the extradition of a person accused or convicted of committing a serious crime under international law as specified in Principle 2(1) provided that it has established a prima facie case of the person's guilt and that the person sought to be extradited will be tried or the punishment carried out in accordance with international norms and standards on the protection of human rights in the context of criminal proceedings.
>
> 4 In exercising universal jurisdiction or in relying upon universal jurisdiction as a basis for seeking extradition, a state and its judicial organs shall observe international due

process norms including but not limited to those involving the rights of the accused and victims, the fairness of the proceedings, and the independence and impartiality of the judiciary (hereinafter referred to as international due process norms).

5 A state shall exercise universal jurisdiction in good faith and in accordance with its rights and obligations under international law.

Principle 2—Serious Crimes Under International Law

1 For purposes of these Principles, serious crimes under international law include: (1) piracy; (2) slavery; (3) war crimes; (4) crimes against peace; (5) crimes against humanity; (6) genocide; and (7) torture.

2 The application of universal jurisdiction to the crimes listed in paragraph 1 is without prejudice to the application of universal jurisdiction to other crimes under international law.

Another example is *Hard Cases: Bringing Human Rights Violators to Justice Abroad—A Guide to Universal Jurisdiction* (1999) by the Swiss-based International Council on Human Rights Policy.[17] The 72-page report asserts with similar certainty that

> universal jurisdiction is a system of international justice that gives the courts of any country jurisdiction over crimes against humanity, genocide and war crimes, regardless of where or when the crime was committed, and the nationality of the victims or perpetrators. It allows the prosecution of certain crimes before the courts of any country even if the accused, the victim, or the crime, has no link to that country.[18]

Through endless recycling of reports like these, universal jurisdiction—however radical and counter-intuitive – became dogma in no time.

The above statements are presented by their authors as definitions but, in truth, they are *petitii principii*.[19] Proclaiming that any state has broader jurisdiction—subject matter, temporal, territorial—than the ICC is all the more extraordinary because universal jurisdiction originally was explained by the absence of an international criminal court.[20] The possibilities for abuse and conflict in such a free-for-all system seem obvious, which brings to mind what social writer and philosopher Eric Hoffer wrote in *The True Believer*: '[i]t is the certitude of his infallible doctrine that renders the true believer impervious to uncertainty, surprises and the unpleasant realities of the world around him'.[21] To be sure, there has been no shortage of surprises and unpleasant realities since *Pinochet* and some are discussed in this contribution. First, universal jurisdiction's historical sources and their contemporary interpretation are succinctly considered.

Historical roots and contemporary interpretation

The claim that universal jurisdiction is time-honored, and therefore not in need of further proof, is based on an appeal to authority and on state practice regarding piracy on the high seas. Let us begin with the argument from authority. Universal jurisdiction has been traced to the first general treatises on modern international law and international relations. Covarruvias in the sixteenth century, Grotius in the seventeenth century, and de Vattel in the eighteenth century, these so-called founding fathers, all elaborated on the question of crime and punishment in the emerging Westphalian order.

However, it should be noted that they wrote from a pragmatic sovereign perspective. They wanted to make sovereignty a workable organizing principle and their primary concern was good neighbourship among the new sovereign entities in Western Europe. Grotius (Holland) and de Vattel (Switzerland) were particularly concerned about the interests of small countries like their own; hence, the emphasis on reasonableness and reciprocity. To stay with Grotius, the title of his classic *De Jure Belli ac Pacis* (*On the Law of War and Peace*)[22] reflects the author's pragmatism and realism. (Compare with Kant's *Zum ewigen Frieden* or *Toward Eternal Peace.*) The sections on crime and punishment carefully balance the requirements of justice, *ordre public*, and sovereignty:

> The matter that necessarily comes next under consideration is the case of those, who screen delinquents from punishment. It was before observed that, according to the law of nature, no one could inflict punishment, but a person entirely free from the guilt of the crime which he was going to punish. But since established governments were formed, it has been a settled rule, to leave the offences of individuals, which affect their own community, to those states themselves, or to their rulers, to punish or pardon them at their discretion. But they have not the same plenary authority, or discretion, respecting offences, which affect society at large, and which other independent states or their rulers have a right to punish, in the same manner, as in every country popular actions are allowed for certain misdemeanors. Much less is any state at liberty to pass over in any of its subjects crimes affecting other independent states or sovereigns, On which account any sovereign state or prince has a right to require another power to punish any of its subjects offending in the above named respect: a right essential to the dignity and security of all governments.
>
> [...]
>
> But as it is not usual for one state to allow the armed force of another to enter her territories under the pretext of inflicting punishment upon an offender, it is necessary that the power, in whose kingdom an offender resides, should—*upon the complaint of the aggrieved party*—either punish him itself, or deliver him up to the discretion of that party. Innumerable instances of such demands to deliver up offenders occur both in sacred and profane history. [...] Yet all these instances are to be understood not as strictly binding a people or Sovereign Prince to the actual surrender of offenders, but allowing them the alternative of *either punishing or delivering* them up. [emphasis added]
>
> [...]
>
> What has been said of punishing or giving up aggressors, applies not only to those, who always have been subjects of the sovereign, in whose dominions they are now found, but to those also, who, after the commission of a crime, have fled to some place for refuge.[23]

Thus, all Grotius said was that a sovereign cannot shield from punishment somebody who has aggrieved another sovereign. Upon complaint of the latter, the former should either punish or extradite the offender. The underlying idea is that there should be no safe havens for *fugitives*. Saying that any state to which an offender flees must either try or extradite him evidently is not the same as saying that any state can request extradition; much less does it follow that any state can seek arrest and extradition of somebody who, like Pinochet, is no fugitive at all.

Why, then, mention Grotius (or Covarruvias or de Vattel) in a discussion on universal jurisdiction? Some extrapolate from these paragraphs a right for any state to exercise jurisdiction over human rights offences.[24] This is textually and contextually indefensible: textually because punishment (or the alternative, extradition) is something between 'the power, in whose kingdom an offender resides' and 'the *aggrieved* party'; contextually because at odds with the pragmatism of *De Jure Belli ac Pacis* and with Grotius' other magnum opus *Mare Liberum* (*The Free Sea*).[25] In the latter, Grotius distinguished 'between that jurisdiction which is competent to each in common and that which is competent to each one properly speaking' and went on to say that 'all peoples or their princes in common can punish pirates and others, who commit delicts on the sea against the law of nations'.[26] Had Grotius, in the above-quoted paragraphs from *De Jure Belli ac Pacis*, meant a 'jurisdiction which is competent to each in common' he would probably have said so. The statesman-diplomat who Grotius was, would probably cringe at the contemporary interpretation of his words.

The second argument is based on state practice regarding the repression of piracy on the high seas and by analogy vests any state with universal jurisdiction ('jurisdiction which is competent to each in common') over modern crimes under international law. However, piracy was a *delictum iuris gentium* (and the pirate a *hostis humanis generum*) because, as argued in *Mare Liberum*, the high seas were outside the jurisdiction of any state and belonged to all humanity. The analogy with modern crimes under international law is fallacious and results in putting piracy in the category of 'serious crimes under international law', as in the *Princeton Principles*, together with war crimes, crimes against peace, crimes against humanity, genocide, and torture, which is rather a stretch. This was illustrated recently when no country was willing to try a dozen Somali pirates captured by the Dutch navy. Accordingly, they 'were put back on their own speedboat with some food and fuel'.[27]

Even though universal jurisdiction over piracy is uncontroversial today[28] it was not when *Mare Liberum* was published in 1609. Until the late Middle Ages, European governments officially or unofficially sponsored piracy, but with the broad expansion of European maritime commerce in the sixteenth and seventeenth century[29] the advantages to be derived from stealing from one another was giving way to the greater advantage of stable commercial relations. Early in the seventeenth century, Turkish corsairs began expanding their piratical activities from the Mediterranean to the Atlantic.[30] To the seventeenth-century European mind, '[...] the prospect of infidels carrying Christians into bestial captivity in North Africa gave efforts to eradicate piracy an urgency and crusading zeal which they had previously lacked. In a Europe strongly divided by political and religious differences, the one objective on which all Christian nations were agreed (sic) was the desirability of crushing the Turkish pirates'.[31] 'At the same time, non-European states and even some colonies regarded European efforts against piracy and privateering as unwarranted and unwelcome infringements into local struggles over power and wealth'.[32] As will be seen later, similar complaints could be heard four centuries later.

It seems clear that the claim that universal jurisdiction has deep historical roots is unconvincing. In this context, how should the Nuremberg trial, *the* milestone in international criminal law, be viewed? Proponents of universal jurisdiction draw support from a passage in the Nuremberg judgment that '[t]he Signatory Powers created this Tribunal, defined the law it was to administer, and made regulations for the proper conduct of the Trial. In doing so, *they have done together what any of them might have done singly*' [emphasis added]. However, the edge of this argument can be taken off by a passage from the Tokyo judgment:

> This is a special tribunal set up by the Supreme Commander under the authority conferred on him by the Allied Powers. It derives its jurisdiction from the Charter. […] In the result, *the members of the Tribunal, being otherwise wholly without power in respect to the trial of the Accused*, have been empowered by the documents, which constituted the Tribunal and appointed them as members, to try the Accused but subject always to the duty and responsibility of applying to the trial the law set forth in the Charter. [emphasis added]

The Allied Powers' rationale for establishing *international* tribunals after World War II can be found in a paragraph in the 1943 Moscow Declaration:

> Those German officers and men and members of the Nazi party who have been responsible for or have taken a consenting part in the above atrocities, massacres and executions will be sent back to the countries in which their abominable deeds were done in order that they may be judged and punished according to the laws of these liberated countries and of free governments which will be erected therein. [...] The above declaration is without prejudice to the case of German criminals whose offenses have no particular geographical localization and who will be punished by joint decision of the government of the Allies.

One could argue that the Allies deliberately avoided any reference to universal jurisdiction and instead pointed to the absence of a 'particular geographical localization' of certain crimes as justification for not following the territoriality principle.

In summary, advocates of universal jurisdiction have gone out of their way to invoke historical authority. The founding fathers and defining events like Nuremberg were used to demonstrate that the doctrine was not invented overnight, but the wisdom of ages. However, a closer look at these sources and events showed that the claim of historical authority does not stand scrutiny.

Multilateral treaty practice

Having found little historical evidence (yet much contemporary distortion), this section will now consider whether universal jurisdiction over the 'most serious crimes under international law' has any basis in treaty law because, as Grotius said, 'jurisdiction over a person results either from the institution of the state itself, as that of the supreme power over subjects, or from agreement over allies'.

In the course of the twentieth century, states have entered into a considerable number of agreements with penal characteristics. Most are 'law and order' instruments, aimed at repressing offences typically committed by non-state actors and in an international context: e.g. piracy, terrorism, drug trafficking, and mercenary activities. The suppression of these types of crimes presumably serves parallel state interests; sovereignty and reason of state hardly seem an issue. However, gross violations of human rights (and humanitarian law) typically are *crimes of state*: by its agents, in its name, and often against its own citizens. Alleged offenders may range from a mere bureaucrat or foot soldier to the commander-in-chief. Therefore, an interesting question is whether states have consented to universal jurisdiction in human rights or humanitarian law treaties. Put differently, have they accepted that crimes of state can be prosecuted by any other (contracting) state?

The first human rights treaty adopted by the United Nations—and the first convention to use the term 'crime under international law'—was the Convention for the Prevention and Punishment of the Crime of Genocide of 1948 ('Genocide Convention'). As previously pointed out, the Allies, when establishing the Nuremberg and Tokyo Tribunals, conspicuously avoided any reference to universal jurisdiction. After Nuremberg, however, legal scholars like the drafters of the *Princeton Principles*, almost unanimously took the position that the emerging new category of 'international crimes' was subject to universal jurisdiction.

The first draft of the Genocide Convention, prepared by the UN Secretariat with the assistance of international criminal law scholars, reflected their view. Article VII stated: 'The High Contracting Parties pledge themselves to punish any offender under this Convention within any territory under their jurisdiction, irrespective of the nationality of the offender or the place where the offence has been committed'. However, the then great powers strongly opposed draft Article VII. The delegate of the United States called the principle of universal punishment 'one of the most dangerous and unacceptable of principles'; the representative of the Soviet Union, Platon Morozov, stated that it was to be expected that the state where the offence was committed 'jealous of its sovereignty, would not consent to surrender its penal jurisdiction to another state since the principal of universal punishment was even more incompatible with the sovereignty of states than [punishment by an international court]'. The proposal was decisively rejected by vote.

The final clause on jurisdiction and punishment (Article VI) reads as follows:

> Persons charged with genocide or any of the other acts enumerated in article III shall be tried by a competent tribunal of the State in the territory of which the act was committed, or by such international penal tribunal as may have jurisdiction with respect to those Contracting Parties which shall have accepted its jurisdiction.

To give effect to the second option the UN General Assembly, immediately after the adoption of the Convention, invited the International Law Commission to study the desirability of establishing an international judicial organ for the trial of persons charged with genocide. The court envisaged was established on 1 July 2002 when the ICC Statute entered into force.

Despite the unambiguous phrasing of the Genocide Convention, some argue that the Convention, much like the ICC Statute, does not exclude universal jurisdiction. States parties to these treaties somehow reserved themselves the right to act unilaterally. This brings to mind the implausible interpretation of a bilateral extradition treaty by the United States Supreme Court. In United States *v.* Alvarez-Machain[33] the court contemptuously held that forcible abduction (by US agents) of a criminal suspect (from Mexico) does not constitute a violation of the US–Mexico extradition treaty—because the treaty does not prohibit it.

Less than a year after the Genocide Convention, states adopted the Geneva Conventions Relating to the Protection of Victims of Armed Conflicts ('Geneva Conventions'). The Conventions were supplemented in 1977 by two Additional Protocols. A jurisdiction/extradition clause common to the Conventions and Additional Protocol I provides as follows:

> The High Contracting Parties undertake to enact any legislation necessary to provide effective penal sanctions for persons committing, or ordering to be committed, any of the grave breaches of the present Convention defined in the following Article. Each High Contracting Party shall be under the obligation to search for persons alleged to have committed, or to have ordered to be committed, such grave breaches, and shall bring such persons, regardless of their nationality, before its own courts. It may also, if it prefers, and in accordance with the provisions of its own legislation, hand such persons over for trial to another High Contracting Party *concerned* [emphasis added], provided such High Contracting Party has made out a *prima facie* case.

The clause resembles Grotius' formulation that 'it is necessary that the power, in whose kingdom an offender resides, should—upon the complaint of the *aggrieved* party—either punish him itself, or deliver him up to the discretion of that party' [emphasis added]. Therefore, the clause provides an example of a 'try or extradite' regime which conforms to the teachings of the classics.

However, as with Grotius' work, some read universal jurisdiction into the Geneva Conventions by pointing to the expression 'regardless of their nationality'.[34] To accept this interpretation is to believe that the drafters of the Genocide Convention had a complete change of mind on the jurisdiction issue when negotiating the Geneva Conventions less than a year later.[35] This is unlikely. The jurisdiction clause of the Geneva Conventions should be read in light of the recommendations of the United Nations War Crimes Commission (UNWCC) during World War II.[36] The Commission acknowledged that there were no fixed rules regarding the surrender of war criminals and that the ordinary rules of extradition were 'defective'.[37] Besides this general problem, it feared that Axis war criminals might thwart attempts to hold them accountable by fleeing to a neutral country. To avoid a repeat of history—after World War I the German Kaiser found safe haven in the neutral Netherlands which had no obligation to extradite or try him—the Commission prepared a draft convention for the extradition of Axis war criminals from neutral countries.[38]

Though never adopted, the draft convention and states' official reactions formed the basis for the jurisdiction clause in the Geneva Conventions.[39] The obligation for all countries, including neutral ones, to search for persons suspected of grave breaches of the Conventions 'regardless of their nationality' is a reference to displacement and migration of millions and the redrawing of national borders at the end of World War II. An alternative to the obligation to prosecute a suspect found within one's territory is handing over to another High Contracting Party *concerned* which has made out a *prima facie* case. This corollary refers to the involvement of dozens of countries in a war that spanned the entire globe. It is a *non sequitur* to read in this secondary sentence an unqualified right for neutral countries to prosecute grave breaches; one simply cannot seriously believe that the drafters ever contemplated universal jurisdiction.[40] The authoritative article-by-article commentary on the Geneva Conventions[41]—by staff of the International Committee of the Red Cross 'who [....] were closely associated with the discussions of the Diplomatic Conference of 1949 and the meetings of experts which preceded it'—surely would have mentioned it.[42]

The above review of two important post-Nuremberg instruments shows that states were far less enthusiastic than scholars about universal jurisdiction over 'human rights offences'.[43] Yet there seems to be one exception. In 1971, the Soviet Union and Guinea together submitted early drafts of a convention to deal with the suppression and punishment of apartheid.[44] Two years later a divided UN General Assembly adopted the International Convention on the Suppression and Punishment of the Crime of Apartheid ('Apartheid Convention'). The Convention is modeled after the Genocide Convention, except for its jurisdiction clause, which reads

> Persons charged with the acts enumerated in Article II of the present Convention may be tried by a competent tribunal of any State Party to the Convention which may acquire jurisdiction over the person of the accused or by an international penal tribunal having jurisdiction with respect to those States Parties which shall have accepted its jurisdiction (Article 5).

Why had universal jurisdiction become acceptable for a majority when it had failed to gain support in the drafting process of the Genocide Convention? The prospect of establishing an international criminal court, which both conventions envisage was much bleaker in 1973 than in 1948, and the prospect of the countries who were being targeted adhering to the Convention was zero. More importantly, the Apartheid Convention was clearly drafted with three regimes in mind: namely, the white minority regimes in the former Rhodesia, Namibia, and the Republic of South Africa. The Convention is in fact tailored to the officials of regimes that were the last vestiges of colonialism in Africa. Therefore, states parties have little reason to fear reciprocity. No former apartheid official has ever been prosecuted in a third state. Interestingly, and tellingly, none of the countries that are now in the forefront of universal jurisdiction has signed the convention, let alone ratified it. During the drafting, Western countries considered the initiative redundant[45] and took issue with the definition of the crime of apartheid (overly broad), its qualification as a crime against humanity—and the jurisdiction clause.[46]

Let us now consider the treaty at issue in *Pinochet*, the United Nations Convention against Torture and other Cruel, Inhuman, or Degrading Treatment or Punishment (UN Torture Convention). Adopted in 1984 in response to the brutal political repression in Chile and other Latin American countries in the 1970s, the Convention outlaws the intentional infliction of severe pain and suffering 'by or at the instigation of or with the consent or acquiescence of a public official or other person acting in an official capacity'. Because no international element is required, the Convention basically protects the right of citizens to be free from torture by their own officials—like the Genocide Convention protects citizens from genocide by their rulers. Nonetheless, the UN Torture Convention provides that a state on whose territory an alleged torturer 'is found' or 'is present' must submit the case to its competent authorities for the purpose of prosecution if it does not extradite him. It is an extreme historical twist of fate that Pinochet was the first to step in this legal trap. Opposition against a try or extradite regime during the drafting came from a number of Latin American countries—as one could expect—but not from the great powers. The United States, in a complete change from its opposition during the drafting of the Genocide Convention, even advocated the inclusion of a try or extradite clause.

In light of allegations of torture against the United States in the prosecution of its war on terror after 11 September 2001 it is worth quoting the US delegate's reply to Argentine objections:

> Such jurisdiction was intended primarily to deal with situations where torture is a state policy and, therefore, the state in question does not, by definition, prosecute its officials who conduct torture. For the international community to leave enforcement of the convention to such a state would be essentially a formula for doing nothing. Therefore in such cases universal jurisdiction would be the most effective weapon against torture which could be brought to bear.[47]

The delegate presciently added that 'it could be utilized against official torturers who travel to other states, a situation which was not at all hypothetical'.[48] Given the US opposition to the ICC and its pressure on the British not to allow the Law Lord's judgment on Pinochet's extradition to stand, its embrace of 'universal jurisdiction' in the UN Torture Convention appears in hindsight almost an accident. One explanation for this apparent lapse may be that the United States was not yet the pre-eminent power which it is today.

What the US delegate referred to as 'universal jurisdiction' is in fact a typical try or extradite clause. Article 7.1 provides that

> [t]he State Party in the territory under whose jurisdiction a person alleged to have committed any offence referred to in Article 4 is found shall *in the cases contemplated in Article 5*, if it does not extradite him, submit the case to its competent authorities for the purpose of prosecution [emphasis added]

Which are the cases contemplated in Article 5?

> Article 5
>
> 1 Each State Party shall take such measures as may be necessary to establish its jurisdiction over the offences referred to in article 4 in the following cases:
>
> 1 When the offences are committed in any territory under its jurisdiction or on board a ship or aircraft registered in that State;

2 When the alleged offender is a national of that State;
3 When the victim was a national of that State if that State considers it appropriate.

2 Each State Party shall likewise take such measures as may be necessary to establish its jurisdiction over such offences in cases where the alleged offender is present in any territory under its jurisdiction and *it does not extradite him* pursuant to article 8 *to any of the States mentioned in Paragraph 1 of this article.* [emphasis added]

Accordingly, *not contemplated* by Articles 5 and 7—or by any state delegate during the drafting[49]—is the scenario of a state exercising jurisdiction *without its having a link with the offense.* An arrest warrant or extradition request from such a state has no basis in the Convention.

In summary, the Grotian try or extradite formula has been incorporated into the Geneva Conventions and the UN Torture Convention. The more radical (Princeton) view, according to which any state may request arrest and extradition in cases involving 'serious crimes under international law', has not been codified in a multilateral treaty. Human rights and 'law and order' treaties alike require a meaningful link for the exercise of jurisdiction. Admittedly, the Apartheid Convention is an exception, but also a revealing one.

Perhaps some consistent practice has developed meanwhile that makes the original intent irrelevant and the genuine link requirement superfluous, which is why the next section briefly discusses state practice.

State practice

'State practice' is used here to refer to actual 'deeds', not the obligatory lofty declarations in multilateral forums.[50] NGOs have reported plenty of deeds but the problem is that they tend to cherry-pick evidence and leave out critical context. A good example of cherry-picking and also of leaving out context, is the argument that *Eichmann*[51] and *Demjanjuk*[52] are precedents for universal jurisdiction. This ignores Israel's thinly veiled threats against the recent use of universal jurisdiction against Israeli officials. In the United States, a federal court, in *Demjanjuk*, once held that

> Israel's assertion of jurisdiction over the respondent based on the Nazi statute conforms with the international law principle of 'universal jurisdiction'. [...] The power to try and punish an offense against the common law of nations, such as the law and customs of war, stems from the sovereign character of each independent State, not from the State's relationship with the perpetrator, victim, or act.[53]

Yet, after 9/11, the US government has made clear that other countries should not even think about prosecuting US officials.[54] The point is that for any claim of state practice in support of universal jurisdiction, evidence can be adduced that undercuts the original claim.

The second problem with NGO reports is that they leave out the critical context. Upon closer examination, in nearly all 'hard' cases (actual trials) there appear to be significant links between offender and forum. Let us briefly review these links and other relevant contextual elements.

'Hard' cases

All in all, some two dozen individuals have been tried by courts in Austria, Canada, Germany, Denmark, Belgium, the United Kingdom, the Netherlands, Finland, France, Spain, and

Switzerland for 'war crimes' committed abroad. Without exception the defendants had taken up permanent residence in the forum state—as refugee, exile, fugitive, or immigrant—and resisted being 'sent back to the countries in which their abominable deeds were done'.[55] In most cases the other states concerned acquiesced in or even supported prosecution. The majority of these cases concerned atrocities committed in the former Yugoslavia and in Rwanda. The Prosecutor of the *ad hoc* international criminal tribunals for these countries and the UN Security Council had encouraged all states to search for and try suspects on their territory, as prescribed by the Geneva Conventions. Finally, extradition was often impossible, if not legally then practically.

A good example is the *Butare Four* case in Belgium.[56] The defendants had fled Rwanda in the aftermath of the armed conflict and genocide in 1994. They applied for political asylum in Belgium (where three of them had lived before) but were arrested after being denounced by other Rwandan refugees. Extradition to Rwanda was legally impossible under Belgian law and under the European Convention for the Protection of Human Rights and Fundamental Freedoms. The International Criminal Tribunal for Rwanda (ICTR) declined to take over the proceedings. Belgium was thus faced with a dilemma of whether to grant asylum to so-called *génocidaires*,[57] or to prosecute them.

This, of course, is the kind of impasse Grotius had in mind and for which he proposed an obligation for the asylum state to either punish or deliver the suspect. It is also the scenario covered by the jurisdiction/extradition clauses of the Geneva Conventions and the UN Torture Convention which merely codify Grotius' proposal. Not so long ago, such individuals would have been left in peace by the authorities of the asylum state for lack of interest, lack of capacity, lack of expertise, lack of a constituency, lack of political will, or a lack of legal basis in domestic law – or expelled.[58] This has changed after nearly two decades of campaigning against impunity for gross human rights violations. The application of the try or extradite principle in the various cases proved Grotius right: justice was done *and* relations between the states concerned were furthered.

Another example, but less typical, is the case of Ephrem Nkezabera, a Rwandan banker, who was prosecuted in Belgium in 2009 at the specific request of the ICTR Prosecutor as part of a strategy to transfer cases involving intermediate and lower-rank accused to national courts, as demanded by UN Security Council Resolution 1503.[59] Belgium was chosen because it already had conducted three Rwanda genocide trials and Nkezabera was in Belgium at the time of the ICTR request. There was thus an objective link *and* a mandate from a legitimate international authority.

In the above cases prosecution (in the forum state) was just and reasonable both from the defendants' perspective and from the perspective of the states concerned. The proceedings unfolded in a sphere of mutual assistance in criminal matters[60] and international law was used to *solve* problems, as it should. This form of jurisdiction is universal *ratione loci* but not *ratione personae* because of the objective pre-existing link between forum and suspect. Yet media[61] and NGO[62] reports lump together these uncontroversial cases of judicial *cooperation* and highly contentious cases of judicial *intervention* under the single rubric of 'universal jurisdiction'. This is unhelpful and distortive; the former, it is submitted, have no precedential value for the latter.

'Virtual' cases

This category refers to the headline-making NGO-driven[63] cases against a host of (former) senior officials, from Pinochet in 1998 to Tzipi Livni in 2009 – and, in between, Fidel Castro, Yerodia Ndombasi, George H. Bush, Ariel Sharon, Amos Yaron, Hissène Habré, Donald Rumsfeld, Paul Kagame, and many others. They are called 'virtual' cases because, with the exception of *Pinochet*, they produced little more than headlines and diplomatic headaches as well as fame for a Spanish Judge. Apart from immunity questions, these cases raised the issue of the meaning or definition of universal jurisdiction.

Many activists—but also the drafters of the *Princeton Principles*—interpret 'universal' in universal jurisdiction *literally* and do not seem to accept anything less. Their goal appears to be to enshrine in law a right for any state—or for any judge for that matter because in their worldview the territorial state is obsolete—to exercise criminal jurisdiction over *anybody, anywhere in the world* suspected of 'gross human rights violations'. It is rather remarkable that professed multilateralists are willing to advocate a free for all.

Two Belgian cases will prove this point. The first concerned an international arrest warrant against the minister of foreign affairs of the Democratic Republic of the Congo, Yerodia Ndombasi. Tired of catching only small fry, the judge responsible for the above-mentioned Rwanda dossiers went after an alleged big fish in Africa's Great War. Alas, the prospect of a Congo genocide trial in the colossal palace of justice in Brussels—commissioned by Congo's erstwhile sovereign King Leopold II—ended when the International Court of Justice ruled that a foreign minister enjoys absolute immunity abroad, while sidestepping the universal jurisdiction question.[64]

The second case targeted Chad's former president Hissène Habré, or 'Africa's Pinochet' according to Human Rights Watch, which has spared no means in its pursuit of the deposed ruler.[65] In fact, HRW has taken *Pinochet* (which involved rival Amnesty International) a step further.[66] After failed attempts to bring charges in Senegal where Habré has been living since 1990, HRW showed three Chadians the way to the palace of justice in Brussels.[67] Acting upon their complaint, a Belgian rogatory mission visited Chad in 2002. The following year, however, the Belgian Parliament, under US and Israeli pressure, repealed the famous universal jurisdiction statute, thereby effectively scuttling all cases—except one. A mysterious transition clause sneaked into the new law appeared to be tailored to *Habré*, thus saving the investigation. In 2005 then, the Belgian government officially requested Habré's extradition on charges of genocide, crimes against humanity, war crimes, and torture. However, for unknown reasons, by 2009 Habré was still in Senegal. What followed then is a real *coup* for an NGO because it involved the highest Belgian echelons: Belgium instituted proceedings against Senegal before the International Court of Justice (ICJ) on the grounds that Senegal was in non-compliance with its try or extradite obligation under the UN Torture Convention.[68] After Amnesty International had its day in the House of Lords, Human Rights Watch will have its day in the International Court of Justice – albeit through a proxy.

Post mortem

Habré showed how, after *Pinochet*, all kinds of actors—sometimes from opposing sides—found their way to courts in Europe where things quickly escalated. African countries countered by petitioning the International Court of Justice to rein in European judges[69] and by putting the issue on the agenda[70] of the UN General Assembly[71] and the African Union–European Union (AU–EU) Ministerial Troika.[72] Powerful countries like Israel, the United States, and China used other means to stop the 'lawfare'[73] against them. The Belgian[74] and Spanish[75] governments obliged and repealed their controversial universal jurisdiction statutes. At the time of writing, the British government was reconsidering its law after a UK court issued an arrest warrant for former Israeli foreign minister Tzipi Livni who was believed to be on a visit.[76] So far, Germany has maintained the universal jurisdiction provision in its much heralded Code of Crimes against International Law, but it has not really used it yet.[77]

The cases mentioned above showed that universal jurisdiction was anything but universal in practice. As an almost exclusively European affair, they represented a curious mixture of *mission civilisatrice* and resistance against US hegemony and Israeli exceptionalism. This dual undercurrent, it is submitted, ultimately provoked a fatal backlash.

The cases also showed an interesting 'small fry—big fish' dimension. The hard cases concerned mostly small fry swept ashore in Europe, whereas the virtual cases targeted the big fish. While understandable—which NGO, judge, or country is willing to spend time, resources, and political capital on a virtual case against a minor player?—it would seem that, by going after big fish, judges in Spain, Belgium, and the United Kingdom entered the territory of international tribunals. Also worthy of note is that none of the countries jostling for indicting inaccessible foreign 'war criminals' was willing to try a dozen ragtag Somali pirates captured by the Dutch navy. No one seemed to be outraged by the release of these *hostis humanis generum*.

Lessons and prospects

With the benefit of hindsight, it is now submitted that universal jurisdiction was essentially a post–Cold War discourse and self-feeding hype generated by NGOs, activist lawyers and judges, academic conferences and papers, and mass media. The degree of consensus and self-imposed political blindness within the 'invisible college of international (criminal) lawyers' was truly amazing.[78] Universal jurisdiction was legal lore but few noticed—or wanted to notice—that the debate was fraught with circular arguments and flawed analogies, and self-serving.[79]

Perhaps it is time to admit that 'universal jurisdiction' is an unhelpful misnomer. Just like 'free market' does not refer to an absolute freedom of markets, 'universal jurisdiction' does not refer to an absolute right for individual states to prosecute gross human rights violations committed abroad. It simply cannot, because limitations on states' jurisdiction are the logical precondition for the existence of a multi-state system. Universal jurisdiction, as advocated by true believers, belongs to the realm of cosmopolitanism. Trying to reconcile a Kantian idea with the Grotian international legal order is like trying to square the circle.

It is noteworthy that *laissez faire* capitalism and *laissez faire* jurisdiction crashed into reality around the same time and that regulation is the order of the day again. Rather than strengthening international (criminal) law, the virtual proceedings in some West European countries against officials from non-European countries made a mockery of it. There is only so much room for symbolic actions and stunts in a legal system worthy of its name. The thinking probably was that enough 'precedents'—no matter how frivolous or controversial—would help 'crystallize' a legal norm before the gains could be reversed. Unsurprisingly, that point already has been reached: universal jurisdiction—according to a recent NGO position paper—is now 'firmly enshrined in international treaty and customary law'.[80]

The question of the scope and application of the principle of universal jurisdiction is now on the international judicial and diplomatic agenda. The parties in the ICJ litigation[81] are taking their time to plead their case. In the UN General Assembly Sixth Committee and in the AU–EU Troika legal experts and state representatives continue their semantic disputes about the 'universal' in universal jurisdiction, while NGOs prepare a counter-offensive.[82] For the UN Sixth Committee it is *déjà vu* all over again 60 years after the negotiation of the Genocide Convention. Bad ideas never die and universal jurisdiction is probably one.

Notes

1 See the by now classic work by M. Keck and K. Sikkink, *Activists beyond Borders: Advocacy Networks in International Politics*, Ithaca: Cornell University Press, 1998. The story of the actors behind the Pinochet cases is masterfully told by N. Roht-Arriaza, *The Pinochet Effect: Transnational Justice in the Age of Human Rights*, Philadelphia: University of Pennsylvania Press, 2004.

2 L. Reydams, *Universal Jurisdiction: International and Municipal Legal Perspectives*, Oxford: Oxford University Press, 2003. Other books on the subject include S. Macedo (ed.), *Universal Jurisdiction: National Courts and the Prosecuting of Serious Crimes under International Law*, Philadelphia: University of Pennsylvania Press, 2004; M. Inazumi, *Universal Jurisdiction in Modern International Law: Expansion of National Jurisdiction for Prosecuting Serious Crimes under International Law*, Antwerp & Oxford: Intersentia, 2005; W. Kaleck, M. Ratner, T. Singelnstein, and P. Weiss (eds), *International Prosecution of Human Rights Crimes*, Berlin: Springer Verlag, 2006; W. N. Ferdinandusse, *Direct Application of International Criminal Law in National Courts*, The Hague: TMC Asser Instituut, 2006.

3 Rather than subdivide and limit my examination of the problem, I look at the larger picture this time. I reject the tendency of legal scholars to reduce universal jurisdiction to an abstract legal question. On the contrary, it is hard to think of a more *political* question. I consider the issue therefore *non-justiciable* and resist determining whether universal jurisdiction is 'legal/permissible' or 'illegal/impermissible' under international law, and if none of these, whether it is an 'emerging norm'. This being said, I do engage in the legal debate and answer the legal arguments but without claim to comprehensiveness. Cases, statutes, and reports cited are cited as mere illustrations.

4 As outlined in the *Agenda for Peace* of the then UN Secretary-General Boutros Boutros-Ghali.

5 The term, I believe, was coined by then US Ambassador-at-Large for War Crimes *David Scheffer* in the context of the *ad hoc* international criminal tribunals: D. Scheffer, 'International Judicial Intervention', *Foreign Policy*, 102, 1996.

6 It is no coincidence that *Médecins sans Frontières*, the forerunner of all sorts of NGOs 'without borders', was awarded the Nobel Peace Prize in 1998.

7 See most famously F. Fukuyama, *The End of History and the Last Man*, New York: Free Press, 1992.

8 I use quotation marks because both are pliable, ill-defined concepts.

9 J. Smith, 'Exploring Connections between Global Integration and Political Mobilization', *Journal of World-Systems Research*, vol. X, 1, 2004, 255–85, 266.

10 M. Kaldor, *Global Civil Society: An Answer to War*, Cambridge: Polity Press, 2003, p. 115.

11 A/CONF.183/INF/3 contains the complete list of the 134 accredited NGOs. Available at http://daccess-dds-ny.un.org/doc/UNDOC/GEN/N98/158/99/PDF/N9815899.pdf?OpenElement. On the role of NGOs at the Rome Conference, see J. Van der Vyver, 'Civil Society and the International Criminal Court', *Journal of Human Rights*, vol. 2, 2003, 425–39; M. Glasius, *The International Criminal Court: A Global Civil Society Achievement*, London and New York: Routledge, 2005.

12 Human Rights Watch (HRW) in particular grew dramatically in the 1990s. As a centralized, non-membership NGO with headquarters in New York and offices in a dozen other world cities, HRW organizationally resembles a multinational corporation. Its budget ($42 million in 2008) brings HRW nearly on par with Greenpeace International (€48 million in 2008).

13 Many NGOs would join the campaign and new ones would be created around 'international criminal justice' specifically. The result is an international criminal justice 'cottage industry'.

14 On successful issue framing by transnational advocacy networks, see Keck and Sikkink, *Activists beyond Borders*, Chapter 1.

15 M. C. Bassiouni, 'The Time Has Come for an International Criminal Court', *Indiana International and Comparative Law Review*, 1, 1991, 1–43.

16 Available at http://www.derechos.org/nizkor/icc/princeton.html and reprinted in Macedo, *Universal Jurisdiction*, pp. 18–25. Another example is the International Law Association's Committee on International Human Rights Law and Practice, 'Final Report on the Exercise of Universal Jurisdiction in Respect of Gross Human Rights Offences', *Report of the 69th Conference of the International Law Association*, 2000, 403–31.

17 Available at http://www.ichrp.org/files/reports/5/201_report_en.pdf.

18 International Council on Human Rights Policy, *Hard Cases*, 4.

19 An extreme example of begging the question can be found in International Federation of Human Rights, *Position Paper to the United Nations General Assembly at Its 64th Session, October 2009*: 'Universal jurisdiction gives a State the competence to prosecute an alleged perpetrator of serious human rights violations or international crimes, regardless of the location of the crime and the nationality of the victim or the perpetrator'. Available at http://www.fidh.org/IMG/pdf/FIDH_Position_Paper_to_the_GA_-_64.pdf.

20 'The inability of the world community to reach political consensus on the creation of an international criminal court [...] has lead to the furthering of the indirect enforcement system', M. C. Bassiouni 'Penal Characteristics of Conventional International Criminal Law', *Case Western Reserve Journal of International Law*, vol. 15, 1983, 27, 34.

21 E. Hoffer, *The True Believer: Thoughts on the Nature of Mass Movements*, New York: Harper and Row, 1951, p. 76.
22 H. Grotius, *The Rights of War and Peace, Including the Law of Nature and of Nations,* translated from the original Latin by A. C. Campbell, with an Introduction by D. J. Hill, New York: M. Walter Dunne, 1901. Available at http://oll.libertyfund.org/index.php?option=com_staticxt&staticfile=show.php%3Ftitle=553&Itemid=28.
23 Grotius, *Law and Peace*, Chapter XXI, 'On the Communication of Punishment'.
24 For example, D. Hawkins, 'Universal Jurisdiction for Human Rights: From Legal Principle to Limited Reality', *Global Governance*, vol. 9, 2003, 347–65.
25 H. Grotius, *The Freedom of the Seas, or the Right Which Belongs to the Dutch to Take Part in the East Indian Trade*, translated by R. Van Deman Magoffin, New York: Oxford University Press, 1916. Available at http://oll.libertyfund.org/index.php?option=com_staticxt&staticfile=show.php%3Ftitle=552&Itemid=28.
26 Ibid.: Hugo Grotius's Reply: Defense of Chapter V of the *Mare Liberum* Which had been attacked by William Welwod, Professor of Civil Law, in Chapter XXVII of that book written in English to which he gave the title 'An Abridgement of All Sea-Lawes'.
27 'Suspected Somalia pirates freed by Dutch navy', BBC News, 18 December 2009, available at http://news.bbc.co.uk/2/hi/8420207.stm.
28 Universal jurisdiction over piracy is codified in the 1958 (Geneva) Convention on the High Seas (article 19) and in the 1982 (United Nations) Convention on the Law of Sea (article 105).
29 Demonstrated, for example, by the founding in 1602 of the Dutch East India Company. The latter actually commissioned *Mare Liberum*, which explains its full title: *Mare Liberum: The Freedom of the Seas, or the Right Which Belongs to the Dutch to Take Part in the East Indian Trade.*
30 See R. Davis, *Christian Slaves, Muslim Masters: White Slavery in the Mediterranean, the Barbary Coast, and Italy, 1500–1800,* New York: Palgrave Macmillan, 2003.
31 E. A. Nadelmann, 'Global Prohibition Regimes: The Evolution of Norms in International Society', *International Organization*, vol. 44, 1990, 479–562, 487, quoting C.M. Senior.
32 Ibid., p. 489.
33 United States *v.* Alvarez-Machain, 504 U.S. 655 (1992)
34 I earlier shared that opinion, but after studying the work of the United Nations War Crimes Commission (see note 36) I reverse myself.
35 The Geneva Conference (1946–1949) and the drafting of the Genocide Convention (1946–1948) involved some of the same state representatives. Platon Morozov, for example, simultaneously served as deputy head of the Soviet delegation in Geneva and Soviet representative in the Sixth Committee. The biography of Morozov, later a judge at the ICJ, is available at http://www.icj-cij.org/presscom/files/7/9947.pdf.
36 *History of the United Nations War Crimes Commission and the Development of the Laws of War*, London: HMSO, 1948. Available at http://www.heinonline.org (subscription required for access).
37 Ibid. Chapter XIII: 'Arrangements for the Surrender of War Criminals', pp. 392–434.
38 The text of the draft convention unfortunately is not included in the *History* but a reconstruction is possible on the basis of the commentary.
39 I cannot prove that the drafters of Geneva Conventions were familiar with the work and recommendations of the UNWCC. The *Pictet* commentary on the Geneva Conventions (see note 41) mentions a number of sources but not the UNWCC. That being said, it is hard to image that they were not.
40 The members of the UN General Assembly certainly did not at the time of the Geneva Conference. See Resolution 3 (I) of 13 February 1946 'Extradition and Punishment of War Criminals', in which the General Assembly '*recommends* that Members of the United Nations forthwith take all the necessary measures to cause the arrest of [...] war criminals [...], and to cause them to be sent back to the countries in which their abominable deeds were done, in order that they may be judged and punished according to the laws of those countries; *and calls upon* the governments of States which are not Members of the United Nations also to take all the necessary measures for the apprehension of such criminal in their respective territories with a view to their immediate removal to the countries where the crimes were committed for the purpose of trial and punishment according to the laws of those countries'.
41 J. S. Pictet (ed.), *Commentary on the Geneva Conventions of 12 August 1949 for the Amelioration of the Condition of the Wounded and Sick in Armed Forces in the Field*, Geneva: International Committee of the Red Cross, 1952.

42 The commentary on jurisdiction/extradition clause (Article 49 of Geneva Convention I) runs nine pages, pp. 362–70.

43 M. C. Bassiouni deplores states' lack of deference to 'the specialists in international criminal law' in 'Penal Characteristics of Conventional International Criminal Law', *Case Western Reserve Journal of International Law*, vol. 15, 1983, 27, 31.

44 For the convention's procedural history see http://untreaty.un.org/cod/avl/ha/cspca/cspca.html.

45 After the Genocide Convention (1948) and the Convention for the Elimination of All Racial Discrimination (1965).

46 See audio files of discussions in Third Committee of General Assembly, 2006th meeting, 25 October 1973, available at http://untreaty.un.org/cod/avl/ha/cspca/cspca_audio.html.

47 Quoted in J. H. Burgers and H. Danelius, *The United Nations Convention Against Torture: A Handbook on the Convention against Torture and other Cruel, Inhuman or Degrading Treatment or Punishment*, Dordrecht: Martinus Nijhoff, 1988, pp. 78–9.

48 Ibid.

49 See exhaustively, M. Nowak and E. McArthur, *The United Nations Convention against Torture: A Commentary*, Oxford: Oxford University Press, 2008.

50 For example, UN General Assembly, Sixth Committee, 21 October 2009, available at http://www.un.org/News/Press/docs/2009/gal3372.doc.htm. Even if one considers these statements as practice, they are non-committal and inconsistent.

51 Attorney General of Israel *v.* Eichmann, Jerusalem District Court (1961) and Attorney General of Israel *v.* Eichmann, Supreme Court of Israel (1962).

52 Matter of Extradition of John Demjanjuk, United States District Court, N. D. Ohio, Eastern Division, 15 April 1985, 612 F. Supp. 544.

53 District Court judgment under section 'Israeli Jurisdiction'.

54 One can also cite the US pressure on the British government not to allow the Law Lords' judgment on Pinochet's extradition to stand. See G. Hawthorn, 'Pinochet: The Politics', *International Affairs*, vol. 75, 1999, 253–8, 253.

55 Cf. the 1943 Moscow Declaration quoted above in the section 'Historical Roots and Contemporary Interpretation'.

56 I discuss this case at length in *Journal of International Criminal Justice*, vol. 1, 2003, 428–36. A similar case in the Netherlands against a Rwandan is discussed by L. van den Herik, 'A Quest for Jurisdiction and an Appropriate Definition of Crime: Mpambara before the Dutch Courts', *Journal of International Criminal Justice*, vol. 7, 2009, 1117–31.

57 *Génocidaires* is a term used in Rwanda for all people 'with blood on their hands'. The *Butare Four,* it should be noted, were convicted of war crimes, not genocide.

58 Canada, for example, before the enactment in 2000 of the Crimes against Humanity and War Crimes Act, would deport foreigners suspected of war crimes. See Reydams, *Universal Jurisdiction*, p. 122. Now it prosecutes them. See R v. Munyaneza (2009 QCCS 2201), available at http://www.haguejusticeportal.net/Docs/NLP/Canada/Munyaneza_Judgement_22-5-2009_EN.pdf.

59 Completion strategy of the International Criminal Tribunal for Rwanda, S/2007/323, paras 7 and 35. Available at http://www.ictr.org/ENGLISH/completionstrat/s-2007-323e.pdf.

60 A Finnish court in Bazaramba and a Swiss court in Nyonteze went to Rwanda to hear evidence. See 'Finnish genocide trial in Rwanda', BBC News, 16 September 2009, available at http://news.bbc.co.uk/2/hi/8258113.stm and '*Nyonteze* v. Public Prosecutor', American Journal of International Law, vol. 96, 2002, 231.

61 'The long arm of Universal Jurisdiction', Radio Nederland Wereldomroep, 11 November 2009, available at http://www.rnw.nl/int-justice/article/long-arm-universal-jurisdiction.

62 FIDH and Redress, *Universal Jurisdiction Developments: January 2006–May 2009*. Available at http://www.fidh.org/IMG/pdf/UJ_Informal_Update_Draft020609.pdf.

63 For an example of NGO strategizing, see Lawyers Committee for Human Rights, 'Universal Jurisdiction: Meeting the Challenge through NGO Cooperation: Report of a Conference Organized by the Lawyers Committee for Human Rights'. Available at http://www.humanrightsfirst.org/international_justice/w_context/meeting_challenge310502.pdf.

64 Arrest Warrant of 11 April 2000 (Democratic Republic of the Congo *v.* Belgium), Judgment of 14 February 2002.

65 One might therefore also refer to the case as 'Human Rights Watch's Pinochet'.

66 Perhaps it is more appropriate to say that Reed Brody has taken *Pinochet* a step further. Brody is Counsel and Spokesperson for Human Rights Watch in Brussels and the main character in the movie

The Dictator Hunter. 'He hunts dictators for a living as a lawyer for Human Rights Watch. For seven years, Brody has been chasing one former dictator in particular: Hissène Habré, the former leader of Chad, who is charged with killing thousands of his own countrymen in the 1980s. Now Habré lives in Senegal where Brody is attempting to have him brought to trial or extradited' (http://www.thedictatorhunter.com/reedbrody.php). The HRW web site features a detailed chronology of *Habré*: http://www.hrw.org/en/news/2009/02/12/chronology-habr-case.

67 'But by then, Brody, Guengueng, and their colleagues had already filed charges against Habré in Belgium, whose anti-atrocity law allowed its courts to hear cases from all over the world' (http://www.thedictatorhunter.com/hissenehabre_about.php).

68 Questions relating to the Obligation to Prosecute or Extradite (Belgium *v.* Senegal). Earlier in this Chapter I have argued that an extradition request from a state without any link to the offense has no basis in the Convention.

69 Arrest Warrant of 11 April 2000 (Democratic Republic of the Congo *v.* Belgium) and Certain Criminal Proceedings in France (Republic of the Congo *v.* France).

70 African Union Assembly Decision on the *Report of the Commission on the Abuse* of the Principle of *Universal Jurisdiction*. Doc. Assembly/AU/14 (XI). Available at http://www.minec.gov.mz/index2.php?option=com_docman&task=doc_view&gid=12&Itemid=48.

71 'The scope and application of the principle of universal jurisdiction', Report of the Sixth Committee, A/64/452. Available at http://www.un.org/ga/sixth/64/ActionbyGA.shtml.

72 The AU-EU Expert Report on the Principle of Universal Jurisdiction, 8672/1/09 REV1. Available at http://www.africa-eu-partnership.org/pdf/rapport_expert_ua_ue_competence_universelle_en.pdf.

73 'Lawfare' is a term used by Israel supporters to denounce the legal 'harassment' of Israel in national and international forums. See, for example, 'Lawfare against Israel', *Wall Street Journal*, 5 November 2008, opinion page. Available at http://online.wsj.com/article/SB122583394143998285.html

74 See L. Reydams, '*Belgium Reneges* on Universality: The 5 August 2003 Act on Grave Breaches of International Humanitarian Law', *Journal of International Criminal Justice*, 2003, 679–89.

75 Ley Orgánica 1/2009, de 3 de noviembre, complementaria de la Ley de reforma de la legislación procesal para la implantación de la nueva Oficina judicial, por la que se modifica la Ley Orgánica 6/1985, de 1 de julio, del Poder Judicial. Available at http://noticias.juridicas.com/base_datos/Admin/lo1-2009.html

76 'UK ponders law change after Tzipi Livni arrest warrant', BBC News, 15 December 2009, available at http://news.bbc.co.uk/2/hi/8415161.stm

77 So far all complaints against foreign officials have dismissed. See Amnesty International, 'Germany: End Impunity through Universal Jurisdiction', *No Safe Haven Series No. 3*, EUR23/003/2008, 102-105. Recently two long-time residents of Rwandan origin were arrested and charged under the Code of Crimes against International Law. Ignace Murwanashyaka and Straton Musoni are accused of leading *from Germany* one of the rebel armies in the Easter Congo. See statement of the German federal prosecutor, available at http://www.generalbundesanwalt.de/de/showpress.php?themenid=11&newsid=347 and 'Germany Arrests Rwandan War Crimes Suspects', *Spiegel Online*, 18 November 2009, available at http://www.spiegel.de/international/world/0,1518,661965,00.html.

78 I am paraphrasing the late Oscar Schachter, '*The Invisible College of International Lawyers*', *Northwestern University Law Review*, vol. 72, 1977, 217–26.

79 Activists and scholars often dismiss a priori criticism of self-servingness by saying that they defend 'values' – universal values – not 'interests'.

80 International Federation of Human Rights, *Position Paper to the United Nations General Assembly at its 64th Session, October 2009*. Available at http://www.fidh.org/IMG/pdf/FIDH_Position_Paper_to_the_GA_-_64.pdf.

81 Certain Criminal Proceedings in France (Republic of the Congo *v.* France); Questions relating to the Obligation to Prosecute or Extradite (Belgium *v.* Senegal).

82 For example, International Federation of Human Rights, Position Paper and Amnesty International, 'International Law Commission: The obligation to extradite or prosecute (*aut dedere aut judicare*)', IOR 40/001/200. Available at http://www.amnesty.org/en/library/info/IOR40/001/2009/en.

22

Immunities

Rémy Prouvèze

Immunities, or immunity in a broad sense, has become a very important issue with the development of international criminal law. Immunity evolved over the course of history[1] in response to the needs of international relations.[2] It is a deeply rooted institution of the international legal order, but it is also a complex issue.

Immunity exempts certain entities or property from proceedings or legal obligations. Immunity encompasses several meanings and appears, in fact, as a vast category of rules covering various situations.[3] Among the immunities covering individuals in international criminal law,[4] immunity from criminal jurisdiction, which exempts the beneficiaries from the jurisdiction of foreign criminal courts, is the main obstacle to the prosecution of international crimes. Thus, this type of immunity is often seen as the first step in the struggle against impunity and in the establishment of a truly efficient system of international criminal law.

Despite the extensive history and significance of immunity for positive inter-state relations, it remains an uncertain and contested topic. These debates have been renewed by the recent developments in international criminal law. The number of proceedings against state officials for international crimes has increased, and some of these prosecutions have been successful, calling the contents, and perhaps even the existence, of the rule of immunity into question.

Immunity may be seen as a principle or as an exception. According to one view, due to its importance and its recognition in international law, immunity is the rule rather than the exception, and thus a wide circle of persons, perhaps even all state agents, can benefit from it. While this thesis has many supporters,[5] the theory that immunity is the exception rather than the rule is also valid, perhaps even more so. Considering the many different immunity regimes which benefit as many different actors, immunity should be seen as an exception to state jurisdictional freedom or competence,[6] what is in accordance with a more realistic view of international law and society.[7] Immunity must be strictly defined in consequence, directly benefitting only a limited number of people.

Thus, the size of the circle of people who benefit from immunity before foreign courts depends on the choice made between these two alternatives. The issue is still controversial and both points of view have their supporters. Whatever the adopted postulate, immunity remains a complex institution.

One reason for this complexity is that immunity is twofold. On the one hand, immunity *ratione materiae*, or functional immunity, protects official acts. As regards state agents, this immunity seems linked to State immunity[8] and the Act of State doctrine.[9] As state agents act on behalf of the state, meaning the state itself acts through its agents, their acts are attributed to the state. Thus, as states cannot be held liable before foreign tribunals due to immunity, agents of the state cannot be held liable for acts performed in their official capacity.

On the other hand, a few high-ranking agents may also be protected by a *ratione personae* immunity.[10] This personal immunity is of a different kind: attached to a particular office with representative functions, it aims at avoiding any interference with the conduct of the official duties of a few state agents by protecting their persons and not only their acts. Consequently, it covers official and private acts performed before or while in office.

This distinction is important because these two faces of immunity do not apply in the same way to all beneficiaries or to every situation in which immunity could be invoked.

The determination of a legal basis for immunity represents another illustration of the complexity of this issue because of the number of theories that attempt to explain and to justify immunity. Far from being based on a single explanation, immunity in international law is founded on a series of principles, among which the theory of functional necessity has become dominant. Many legal grounds have been invoked in the discussion of international immunity, as shown by the debate on heads of state immunity, which has included the concepts of the Latin maxim *par in parem non habet imperium*, meaning no peer has jurisdiction or can exercise authority over another peer;[11] the independence and sovereignty of the state;[12] the dignity of the sovereign;[13] the theory of extraterritoriality;[14] and the theory of comity or international courtesy, among others.[15] Nevertheless, while sovereignty remains an important basis for the immunity of state officials,[16] as well as, for example, the representative character of diplomatic agents, the current trend is to consider that immunities exist mainly to allow representatives or agents of state and international organizations to act freely and independently in the framework of their official missions.[17]

As previously described, immunity covers a large number of different situations. The main categories of individuals who enjoy immunity are state officials, such as heads of state, heads of government, and ministers; diplomatic and consular agents; members states' representatives; agents of international organizations; and members of the armed forces. Some of these individuals benefit from an immunity regime governed by conventional law, while others are ruled by the more uncertain regime of customary international law. A comparable uncertainty surrounds the phenomenon of the recognition of exceptions to immunity, which is a more recent development in criminal proceedings, though not in civil proceedings, and has surely been one of the most problematic issues in international criminal law in recent years.

Conventional immunities

Many immunities are codified by treaties or are the object of international agreements or texts. Customary international law only applies when there are no applicable conventional provisions.

Diplomatic and consular agents

Diplomatic agents

Immunity of diplomatic agents is one of the oldest rules of international relations. Its origins date back to antiquity and the creation of a protection for envoys sent abroad by their sovereigns. This specific category of agents benefited from special treatment because such agents were considered to be sacred and to be the representation of the person of their sovereign.[18] Prosecuting these persons would have been like prosecuting the sovereign.

Primarily, these diplomatic agents' missions were limited in time and they benefited from the protection of immunity from the jurisdiction of the receiving state only for such time as they were on a given mission. With the establishment of permanent missions, diplomatic immunity developed and was finally codified in the Convention on Diplomatic Relations, signed in Vienna on 18 April 1961.

Diplomatic agents are granted extensive immunity. While diplomatic agents must comply with the law of the receiving states, under the 1961 Vienna Convention, diplomats are entitled to a personal immunity, considered as absolute, on the territory of their receiving state for the duration of their mission. Diplomats cannot be prosecuted before the domestic tribunals of the receiving state and they cannot be required to give evidence as witnesses.[19] Actually, diplomatic immunity is twofold, encompassing immunity *ratione personae* and *ratione materiae*. As a result, unless the sending state waives immunity, diplomatic envoys are fully exempt from the criminal jurisdiction of the receiving state with regard to official and private acts for as long as they are in office. Immunity for acts performed in relation to official functions continues even after diplomats leave their duties.

Consular agents

The Convention on Consular Relations was adopted in 1963. As a multilateral treaty, it codifies consular practices that developed through customary international law and numerous bilateral or regional treaties.[20] According to this instrument, consular agents are afforded a less extensive immunity than diplomatic agents. Consular agents' immunity is limited to 'acts performed in the exercise of consular functions'.[21] This *ratione materiae* immunity prevents these agents from being prosecuted or called to testify as witnesses.[22] However, consular agents may be prosecuted or required to give evidence before local tribunals with respect to private acts.[23]

International organizations

State representatives to and agents of international organizations enjoy immunity derived from the organization's own immunity. This immunity may be provided for by the founding document of the organization, the agreement between the host state and the organization, a general convention on privileges and immunities, or, in some cases, the national legislation of the host state.[24] Consequently, immunities in this area vary according to the text that provides for them.[25]

With respect to the United Nations (UN), while the UN Charter contains a general provision on immunities in Article 105, the Convention on the Privileges and Immunities of the United Nations, adopted on 13 February 1946,[26] is the primary instrument in a large collection of treaties concerning immunity.[27] According to this text, state envoys and the agents of UN institutions are entitled to special treatment.

Representatives of states

Article IV(11) of the Convention on the Privileges and Immunities of the United Nations provides jurisdictional immunity for 'Representatives of Members to the principal and subsidiary organs of the United Nations and to conferences convened by the United Nations', but only 'while exercising their functions and during the journey to and from the place of meeting'. This immunity remains after representatives have left office for 'words spoken or written and all acts done by them in discharging their duties'.[28]

Nevertheless, the status of the representatives of non-member states or other entities who are accredited as observers is not specified in the UN Convention on Privileges and Immunities. While the UN Secretary-General considered that these representatives should be granted immunity for acts performed in their official capacity,[29] the actual status of these envoys is far from clear due to a lack of conventional regulation and practice.[30]

UN agents

As regards UN agents, their situations vary. Despite this diversity, officials and experts who belong to the organization enjoy an immunity principally limited to acts related to their official functions.[31] However, the UN Secretary-General and all Assistant Secretaries General are afforded the same status as diplomatic agents, enjoying *ratione personae* immunity for as long as they are in office.[32] These immunities are said to be *erga omnes*, unlike those of state representatives.[33]

Another category of individuals whose status may be problematic is UN peacekeepers. These individuals are considered neither officials nor experts, and their status depends on agreements concluded by the United Nations with receiving states. In this context, these armed forces enjoy a general immunity before the host state's tribunals, servicemen coming under the exclusive jurisdiction of their respective sending states.[34] However, some questions remain about the status of UN peacekeepers with regard to third-party states, though in practice, peacekeepers seem to be considered experts in mission.[35]

Members of state armed forces

The situation of state armed forces is less clear than the categories described above and depends mainly on bilateral and multilateral agreements.[36]

During wartime the detaining power can exercise its criminal jurisdiction over members of the armed forces of a party to the conflict who have fallen into its power.[37] However, during peacetime, members of foreign armed forces are, more often than not, entitled to a special treatment and may be exempt from the receiving state's jurisdiction. While the principle of immunity from criminal jurisdiction developed early on in the history of international law,[38] applying, for example, to UN peacekeepers and North Atlantic Treaty Organization (NATO) forces,[39] this principle did not receive universal application. As a result, the status of foreign armed forces depends on complicated and varied regimes of shared jurisdiction as provided for by agreements between the sending state or international organization and the receiving state. This system does not preclude problems of interpretation and application.[40]

It is also significant to note that, following the US campaign against the International Criminal Court (ICC), which led US authorities to call for the support of the Security Council in protecting members of the US armed forces participating in UN peacekeeping or peace enforcement operations abroad,[41] UN Security Council resolutions dealt with the issue of the immunity of a contributing state's armed forces in a multinational force when the contributing state is not a party to the Rome Statute by recognizing the exclusive jurisdiction of the contributing state.[42]

These conventions, international agreements and resolutions concerning immunities do not solve all the problems that may arise from the immunities. Questions remain regarding, for example, the extent *ratione temporis* and *ratione loci* of immunity and the issue of acts of function and officials acts,[43] just to mention a few common issues concerning all types of immunities and not only conventional ones. However, these instruments related to immunity provide a written basis to the special status recognized for certain individuals by international law. The situation is somewhat different with regard to state officials.

Immunity of state officials

The immunity of state officials is perhaps the most complicated and contested issue in this field due to the lack of international general instruments on the subject.[44] Because of the absence of conventional law in this area, the immunity of high-ranking state officials is governed by customary international law.[45]

Heads of state

Heads of state are the state officials dealt with most often in doctrine and case law.[46] Traditionally, heads of state are not subject to criminal responsibility for their acts because they are considered to be exempted from foreign jurisdiction,[47] meaning that tribunals of a foreign state cannot prosecute this type of state representative. More precisely, '[i]ncumbent Heads of State enjoy a twofold immunity from criminal process before foreign domestic courts on the one hand an absolute immunity *ratione personae*, and on the other hand, a limited immunity *ratione materiae*'.[48]

Few senior state officials are afforded the 'twofold immunity' of the diplomats' regime. Heads of state enjoy both types of immunity as long as they are serving. Consequently, they cannot be prosecuted or forced to testify before a foreign tribunal.[49] *Ratione personae* immunity covers official and private acts performed before or during the period the officials are in office. However, personal immunity ceases when heads of state leave their functions, while functional immunity remains for official acts. Thus, former heads of state do not benefit from the same immunity as their counterparts who are still in charge: they only enjoy a *ratione materiae* immunity with respect to public or official acts they performed as heads of state.

Heads of government

By analogy, heads of government seem to be entitled to the same immunity conferred on heads of state.[50] International law is unclear on this point, and because this type of state representative is not a head of state, and thus does not personify or symbolize the state,[51] there remains much debate.[52] Nevertheless, heads of government exercise functions that can become similar to those of heads of state, particularly when the latter exercise no real powers within the state.[53] For this reason, heads of government are usually assimilated to heads of state and thus are accorded head of state immunity[54] or, at least, should be granted this immunity due to the functions they exercise.

Foreign ministers and other members of a government

Whereas there are relatively few doubts regarding the type of immunity granted to heads of government, the question remains controversial with respect to other ministers. However, the trend is to consider these state officials to be immune from the domestic jurisdiction of foreign states, even if this immunity is more limited compared to the immunity regime international law recognizes for heads of state and heads of government.[55]

The International Court of Justice (ICJ) tried to brush aside hesitations concerning foreign ministers' immunity in the *Congo v. Belgium* case. The ICJ judgement claimed that under customary international law, foreign ministers are entitled to full immunity (*ratione personae*) as long as they are in office, and after the end of their mandate, they remain protected from the criminal jurisdiction of foreign states for acts connected with their function (immunity *ratione materiae*).[56] With this decision, the ICJ recognized that due to their functions and position in international law, foreign ministers enjoy the same special treatment as heads of state and heads of government despite a small body of case law,[57] which could be (and was) criticized.[58]

Though heads of state, heads of government, and foreign ministers benefit from full (personal and functional) immunity, the immunity of other members of government remains debated. However, this immunity appears to be limited to *ratione materiae* immunity, and members of the government enjoy personal immunity only in the event of official visits to foreign states. Immunity in this situation is due to the development of the international functions of these state representatives.[59]

Thus, each state representative is not entitled to the same proportion of both types of immunity, which contributes to the complexity of immunity as an institution.

Another important issue regarding state officials concerns how the theory of recognition influences the application of the inter-state rule of immunity. This issue arises when an illegitimate change in government brings a new head of state, or even a new state, onto the international scene. Recognition allows the new government, or the new state, to enjoy all the rights international law grants to such an entity, including immunity. According to practice, it appears that if a government or a head of state is recognized by a foreign state, the head of state, or the members of the government are considered to be immune from domestic prosecutions before the foreign state's tribunals. This is not the case if the government or the head of state is not recognized.[60] This point shows that the question of immunity is at the intersection of law and politics[61] and in fact is not as absolute as it seems. Another illustration of the complexity of immunity can be found in the development of international crimes.

Immunity and international crimes

The question of immunity in case of international crimes is a very important aspect of the international law on immunities. This question allows the determination of the content of the rule, which can often only be expressed when immunity is contested before a judge, and plays an important role in the movement to restrict immunity.[62] Attempts to contest the notion of immunity itself, and not only its limits, before the European Court of Human Rights (ECHR) have not been successful,[63] but there has been a trend toward general restriction of immunities in international criminal law. The immunity of state officials is the focus of several cases dealing with immunity and its limits, particularly the existence of exceptions to immunity with regard to international crimes. Because international crimes can be prosecuted by two types of tribunals, it is important to distinguish between prosecutions before international criminal tribunals and prosecutions before foreign courts.

Irrelevance of immunity before international tribunals

The indictment and arrest warrant against the Sudanese President Omar Al-Bashir issued by the Pre-Trial Chamber I of the ICC[64] shed light on an often-mentioned problem with international criminal tribunals.[65] The statutes of these specific jurisdictions, as well as others international instruments, are commonly said to deal with the question of immunity from criminal jurisdiction. The most commonly referenced provisions regarding immunity are the following: Article 7 of the Charter of the Nuremberg tribunal; Article 6 of the Charter of the International Military

Tribunal for the Far East; Article IV of the Convention on the Prevention and Punishment of the Crime of Genocide; Principle III of the Nuremberg Principles; Article 7(2) of the Statute of the International Criminal Tribunal for the former Yugoslavia; Article 6(2) of the Statute of the International Criminal Tribunal for Rwanda; Article 7 of the Draft Code of Crimes against the Peace and Security of Mankind; Article 6(2) of the Statute of the Special Court for Sierra Leone; and Article 27 of the Rome Statute of the International Criminal Court.[66]

In fact, except for Article 27(2) of the Rome Statute of the International Criminal Court, these provisions address questions of responsibility rather than immunity. Immunity from criminal jurisdiction is a procedural question,[67] and this is an issue most of the statutes do not mention explicitly. However, according to some authorities, international tribunals have taken this aspect into account in their judgements by interpreting their statutes in light of the nature of the tribunals themselves.[68] It is this last point that is perhaps the most important. A better explanation and justification for the non-applicability of immunity before international criminal tribunals could lie not in the above-mentioned provisions, but rather in the particular nature and position of these tribunals, which stand outside strict inter-state relations,[69] while immunity appears as a classical institution of relations between states. Moreover, these international courts were created to prosecute international crimes and persons who bear the greatest responsibility for the commission of these crimes when justice is not possible before national tribunals, especially when high-ranking state officials are involved. International tribunals appear as a special resort in situations in which national courts cannot discharge their functions correctly and when serious violations of international humanitarian law or a few other international crimes are at stake.

Be that as it may, immunity is not generally considered as a valid claim before international tribunals. This was confirmed by the ICJ judgement in the Congo *v.* Belgium case.[70] Practice also confirms this assertion. Prosecutions before international criminal tribunals have been mainly focused on senior state officials[71] and immunity has not prevented the tribunals from exercising jurisdiction.[72]

Exceptions to immunity before national tribunals

The practice of foreign criminal tribunals in relation to immunities of individuals is quite scarce. Long considered to be absolute, immunity, particularly heads of state immunity, was a bar to the admissibility of cases before foreign tribunals and appeared to be impossible to overcome in criminal proceedings. Nevertheless, several recent decisions help define the limits of immunity from criminal jurisdiction.

While there have been other significant cases,[73] the British Lords' decisions in the *Pinochet* case opened the door to exceptions to immunity before national courts.[74] The House of Lords recognized the *ratione materiae* immunity of the former head of state[75] but took the nature of crimes committed by Augusto Pinochet into account in excluding acts of torture from the benefit of immunity, even when perpetrated in an official capacity.[76] The prohibition of such crimes by the UN Convention against Torture and Other Cruel, Inhuman or Degrading Treatment or Punishment of 10 December 1984 provided a conventional basis for the recognition of this exception. The numerous separate opinions issued by the Lords made it difficult to identify the *ratio decidendi* of the British decision, allowing various interpretations. It explains that other cases followed and challenged the immunity of state agents.[77]

The *Ghaddafi* case provided another significant element of the answer to the issue of possible exceptions to immunity. The French *Cour de cassation* held that customary international law prohibits criminal proceedings against sitting heads of state before foreign tribunals in the absence of a contrary international provision binding on states parties.[78] While this decision confirmed the *ratione personae* immunity of incumbent heads of state, it implicitly admits that conventional exceptions are possible for certain crimes,[79] even if terrorism is not one of them.

However, this interpretation is partially contradicted by the ICJ decision in the Congo *v.* Belgium case, which confirms the absolute *ratione personae* immunity of high-ranking officials and refuses to recognize customary exceptions while beneficiaries remain in office.[80] Moreover, the ICJ stated that former foreign ministers enjoy immunity before national courts, except for private acts.[81] This conclusion suggests that a serious international crime must be considered as a private act in order for a prosecution to proceed, which is hardly consistent with modern practice and case law.[82] Rather, there is a large trend to consider core international crimes—war crimes, crimes against humanity and genocide[83]—and maybe other internationally prohibited crimes—such as torture[84]—exceptions to the *ratione materiae* immunity of state officials.[85] The *jus cogens* nature of the rules prohibiting such crimes is often mentioned to explain and justify this conclusion.[86]

In summary, it appears that individuals who enjoy *ratione personae* immunity cannot be prosecuted, even for international crimes, until the beneficiaries are no longer in mission or in charge and personal immunity ceases, but there may be exceptions to *ratione materiae* immunity for international crimes.

Although immunity is very well established in international law, the development of international criminal law indicates a shift in the approach to the notion of immunity and allows, in spite of persistent hesitations, the acknowledgment of certain exceptions to immunity for international crimes. Eventually, considering the increasing demands for international criminal justice and the possible application to *ratione personae* immunity of the argument justifying exceptions to *ratione materiae* immunity based on the nature of international crimes, the movement for the restriction of immunities will continue to develop. Thus, immunity from criminal jurisdiction in international law may become still more questioned or even disappear completely.

Notes

1 According to several authors, immunity is a classical notion that goes back to the beginning of International Law. See L. S. Frey and M. L. Frey, *The History of Diplomatic Immunity*, Columbus: Ohio State University Press, 1999, pp. 3, 5.

2 Case concerning United States Diplomatic and Consular Staff in Teheran (United States of America *v.* Iran), ICJ 1979, paras 38–9.

3 Traditionally, international law makes distinctions based on who is entitled to immunity (for example, states, international organizations, diplomatic and consular agents, heads of state, state representatives to and agents of international organizations ...), what is protected (for example, archives, property, premises of official missions, state ships ...) and to what situations immunity applies (for example, criminal or civil jurisdiction, execution, taxes).

4 Primarily, international criminal law addresses individuals and their conduct, according to the Nuremberg judgement: 'Crimes against international law are committed by men, not by abstract entities, and only by punishing individuals who commit such crimes can the provisions of international law be enforced'. Nuremberg judgement, International Military Tribunal, 1 October 1946, reproduced in *American Journal of International Law*, 1947, vol. 41, p. 221.

5 See, for example, M. Sornarajah, 'Problems in Applying the Restrictive Theory of Sovereign Immunity', *International Comparative Law Quarterly*, 1982, vol. 31, pp. 664–5. See also R.Y. Jennings, 'The Caroline and McLeod Cases', *American Journal of International Law*, 1938, vol. 32, pp. 83–99; J. Charpentier, 'L'affaire du Rainbow Warrior: le règlement interétatique', *Annuaire Français du Droit International*, 1986, pp. 873–85; Tihomir Blaskic (IT-95-14-AR 108 *bis*), Appeals Chamber, Judgement on the Request of the Republic of Croatia for Review of the Decision of Trial Chamber II of 18 July 1997, 29 October 1997.

6 H. Lauterpacht, 'The Problem of Jurisdictional Immunities of Foreign States', *British Yearbook of International Law*, 1951, vol. 28, pp. 247–50.

7 This conception leans on the *Lotus* judgement of the Permanent Court of International Justice and the principle of the residual freedom of State. Lotus Case (France *v.* Turkey), PCIJ, 7 September 1927, Serie A, No. 10, p. 19. See also H. Kelsen, 'Théorie du droit international public', *Collected Courses of the Hague Academy of International Law*, 1953, III, vol. 84, p. 121; Case concerning Military and Paramilitary Activities in and against Nicaragua (Nicaragua *v.* United States of America), ICJ 1986, para. 269; Legality of the Threat or Use of Nuclear Weapons, Advisory Opinion, ICJ 1996, Separate Opinion of Judge Guillaume, p. 291, para. 9.

8 S. Sucharitkul, 'Immunities of Foreign States before National Authorities', *Collected Courses of the Hague Academy of International Law*, 1976, I, vol. 149, p. 96; A. Watts, 'The Legal Position in International Law of Heads of States, Heads of Governments and Foreign Ministers', *Collected Courses of the Hague Academy of International Law*, 1994, vol. 247, pp. 35–7.

9 Y. Simbeye, *Immunity and International Criminal Law*, Hampshire, UK: Ashgate, 2004, pp. 109–10.

10 A. Cassese, *International Criminal Law*, 2nd edn, New York: Oxford University Press, 2008, p. 304.

11 See Taylor (SCSL-03-01-I-059), Rendering of Decision on Motion made under protest and without waiving immunity accorded to a Head of State requesting the Trial Chamber to quash the indictment and declare null and void the warrant of arrest and order for transfer of detention 23 July 2003 (Immunity motion), 31 May 2004, para. 54; Lauterpacht, 'The Problem of Jurisdictional Immunities of Foreign States', p. 221; I. Sinclair, 'The Law of Sovereign Immunity: Recent Developments', *Collected Courses of the Hague Academy of International Law*, 1980, II, vol. 167, p. 121.

12 Ben Aïad c. Gouvernement tunisien, French Court of Appeals of Alger, Decision of 22 January 1914, *Journal du Droit International*, 1914, p. 1290; Regina *v.* Bartle and the Commissioner of Police for the Metropolis and Others Ex Parte Pinochet, House of Lords, Decision of 24 March 1999, *International Legal Materials*, 1999, vol. 38, p. 644 (hereinafter *Pinochet* case).

13 The Schooner Exchange *v.* McFadden, US Supreme Court, 7 Cranch 116 (1812).

14 C. F. Gabba, 'De la compétence des tribunaux à l'égard des souverains et des États étrangers', *Journal du Droit International*, 1889, p. 547.

15 Frey and Frey, *The History of Diplomatic Immunity*, p. 351; Sucharitkul, 'Immunities of Foreign States before National Authorities', p. 119; Gladys M. Lafontant *v.* Jean-Baptiste Aristide, Eastern District of New York, 844 F. Supp. 128 (1994), reproduced in *American Journal of International Law*, 1994, vol. 88, pp. 528–32; Tachiona *v.* Mugabe, South District of New York, 169 F. Supp. 2d 259 (2001), p. 317.

16 *Pinochet* case, pp. 642, 644.

17 See, for example, Institut de Droit International, *Resolution on Immunities from Jurisdiction and Execution of Heads of State and of Government in International Law (Resolution on Immunities)*, Vancouver, 26 August 2001, Preamble, para. 3; Vienna Convention on Diplomatic Relations, 500 UNTS 95 (1961), Preamble, para. 4; Vienna Convention on Consular Relations, 596 UNTS 261 (1963), Preamble, para. 5; Convention on the Privileges and Immunities of the United Nations, 1 UNTS 15 (1946), Preamble, para. 2.

18 J. Craig Barker, *The Protection of Diplomatic Personnel*, Hampshire; UK: Ashgate, 2006, pp. 29–30.

19 Vienna Convention on Diplomatic Relations, Art. 31(1) and (2). The 1969 Convention on Special Missions provides for a similar treatment in terms of criminal immunity. See Convention on Special Missions, 1400 UNTS 231 (1969), Art. 31.

20 Y. Dinstein, *Consular Immunity from Judicial Process*, Jerusalem: Central Press, 1966, p. 89.

21 Vienna Convention on Consular Relations, Art. 43(1).

22 Ibid., Arts 43, 44.

23 H. Fox, *The Law of State Immunity*, New York: Oxford University Press, 2004, p. 459.

24 The Vienna Convention on the Representation of States in their Relations with International Organizations of a Universal Character, adopted on 14 March 1975, could be the universal instrument on this issue for states representatives, but it has not yet entered into force and would be limited to universal organisations. Vienna Convention on the Representation of States in their Relations with International Organizations of a Universal Character, UN Doc. A/CONF.67/16 (1975), reproduced in *American Journal of International Law*, 1975, vol. 69, p. 370.

25 On the issue of the existence of a customary international rule about immunity of international organisations and of their agents, see I. Scobbie, 'International Organizations and International Relations', in P. M. Dupuy (ed.), *A Handbook on International Organizations*, 2nd ed., Dordrecht/Boston/London: Martinus Nijhoff Publishers, 1998, pp. 838–40.

26 A similar Convention on Privileges and Immunities of the Specialized Agencies was adopted by GA resolution 179(II) on 21 November 1947 to address the immunities of State representatives and agents of these agencies. Convention on Privileges and Immunities of the Specialized Agencies, GA resolution 179(II), 21 November 1947, 33 UNTS 261 (1949).

27 See R. Zacklin, 'Diplomatic Relations: Status, Privileges and Immunities', in Dupuy (ed.), *A Handbook on International Organizations*, pp. 295–7.

28 Convention on the Privileges and Immunities of the United Nations, Art. 4(12).

29 Scope of Privileges and Immunities of a Permanent Observer Mission to the United Nations, Statement made by the Legal Counsel at the 92nd meeting of the Committee on Relations with the Host Country, 14 October 1982, *United Nations Juridical Yearbook*, 1982, pp. 206–7.

30 See Scobbie, 'International Organizations and International Relations', pp. 865–7.

31 See Convention on the Privileges and Immunities of the United Nations, Arts. V(18), VI(22). See, in the same vein, Protocol on the Privileges and Immunities of the European Communities (1965), OJ L 152 (1967), p. 13, Arts 12, 18.

32 Convention on the Privileges and Immunities of the United Nations, Section 19. See also European Molecular Biology Laboratory *v.* Germany, Arbitration Award of 29 June 1990, *International Law Reports*, 1997, vol. 105, pp. 55–6.

33 For further details on immunities of UN agents and State representatives to the UN, see Scobbie, 'International Organizations and International Relations', pp. 851–67.

34 See R. Siekmann, *National Contingents in UN Peace-Keeping Forces*, Dordrecht: Nijhoff, 1991, p. 139.

35 See 'The practice of the United Nations, the specialized agencies and the International Atomic Energy Agency concerning their status, privileges and immunities: Study prepared by the Secretariat', UN DOC. A/CN.4/l.118 and add. 1 and 2 (1967), *Yearbook of the International Law Commission*, 1967, Vol. II, para. 340, p. 284.

36 Fox, *The Law of State Immunity*, pp. 461–7.

37 See Geneva Convention (III) relative to the Treatment of Prisoners of War, 75 UNTS 135 (1949), Art. 82.

38 See The Schooner Exchange *v.* Mac Faddon (1812).

39 See Agreement between the Parties to the North Atlantic Treaty regarding the Status of their Forces, 199 UNTS 67(1951). See also European Union Status of Forces Agreement (EU-SOFA), 2003 OJ C321/6 (2003). See A. Sari, 'Status of Forces and Status of Mission Agreements under the ESDP: The EU's Evolving Practice', *European Journal of International Law*, 2008, vol. 19, pp. 67–100.

40 The question of knowing what is an 'act or negligence accomplished in the execution of the duty'—mentioned in Article VII(3)(a) of Agreement between the Parties to the North Atlantic Treaty regarding the Status of their Forces and in Article 17(6)(a) of EU-SOFA, which gives priority to the jurisdiction of the sending State—has been raised in several cases. See E. David, *Eléments de droit pénal international et européen*, Brussels: Bruylant, 2009, pp. 92–3. More generally on foreign armed forces, see D. Fleck (ed.), *The Handbook of The Law of Visiting Forces*, New York: Oxford University Press, 2001, p. 664.

41 Security Council, Resolution 1422, UN Doc. S/RES/1422 (2002); Resolution 1487, UN Doc. S/RES/1487 (2003). See N. Jain, 'A Separate Law for Peacekeepers: The Clash between the Security Council and the International Criminal Court', *European Journal of International Law*, 2005, vol. 16, pp. 242–53; C. Stahn, 'The Ambiguities of Security Council Resolution 1422', *European Journal of International Law*, 2003, vol. 14, pp. 85–104.

42 Security Council, Resolution 1497, UN Doc. S/RES/1497 (2003), para. 7.

43 The terminology in French-speaking related literature seems to be more precise by distinguishing 'actes de fonction' (function acts) and 'actes officiels' (official acts). See J. Salmon, 'Immunités et actes de la fonction', *Annuaire Français du Droit International*, 1992, pp. 314–57.

44 Some provisions of a few international conventions deal with the immunity of state officials, usually only addressing the issue partially or only for specific situations, and often referring to customary international law. See, for example, Vienna Convention on Diplomatic Relations, Arts 21, 31; Convention on Special Missions, Art. 21; Convention on Jurisdictional Immunities of States and their Property, UN Doc. A/59/508 (2004), Art. 3(2). National legislations were adopted to rule state immunity before domestic tribunals, but these legislations deal only partly with the immunity of State officials. See A. Dickinson, R. Lindsay, and J. P. Loonam, *State Immunity: Selected Materials and Commentary*, New York: Oxford University Press, 2004, pp. 217–522.

45 See Watts, 'The Legal Position in International Law of Heads of States, Heads of Governments and Foreign Ministers', p. 36; G. M. Danilenko, 'ICC Statute and Third States', in A. Cassese, P. Gaeta, and

J. R. W. D. Jones (eds), *The Rome Statute of International Criminal Court: A Commentary*, Oxford: Oxford University Press, 2002, p. 1885; Gladys M. Lafontant *v.* Jean-Baptiste Aristide, p. 528; Procureur général près la Cour d'appel de Paris c. Association SOS Attentats, Mlle Béatrice de Boery ep. Castelnau d'Essenault (Affaire Kadhafi), French Cour de cassation (Chambre criminelle), Decision of 13 March 2001, reproduced in *Revue Générale de Droit International Public*, 2001, No. 2, p. 474 (hereinafter *Ghaddafi* case).

46 The *Pinochet* case undoubtedly contributed to the renewal of the issue of the immunity in doctrine and its case law at the end of the 1990s, as many prosecutions were initiated against former and current foreign leaders accused of committing crimes or human rights violations. Before this case, commentators had hardly found interest in immunity of State officials for a long period, except for immunity from civil jurisdiction for former heads of State, essentially at the end of the 19th century and in the early 20th century following several cases. See M. Cosnard, *La soumission des États aux tribunaux internes. Face à la théorie des immunités des États*, Paris: Pedone, 1996, pp. 56–60. The fact that there were only a few cases on this matter, especially before criminal courts, is certainly an explanation for this lack of interest.

47 Watts, 'The Legal Position in International Law of Heads of States, Heads of Governments and Foreign Ministers', p. 52.

48 L. De Smet and F. Naert, 'Making or Breaking International Law? An International Law Analysis of Belgium's Act Concerning the Punishment of Grave Breaches of International Humanitarian Law', *Revue Belge de Droit International*, vol. 35, 2002, pp. 499–500.

49 See *Ghaddafi* case, p. 474.

50 B. S. Murty, *The International Law of Diplomacy: The Diplomatic Instrument and World Public Order*, Dordrecht/Boston/London: Martinus Nijhoff Publishers, 1989, pp. 334–5. See also Institut de Droit International, *Resolution on Immunities*, Art. 15(1).

51 Watts, 'The Legal Position in International Law of Heads of States, Heads of Governments and Foreign Ministers', p. 98.

52 See 'Report of the International Law Commission on the work of its forty-first session (2 May–21 July 1989)', UN Doc. A/44/10 (1989), *Yearbook of the International Law Commission*, 1989, vol. II, Part Two, p. 113, no. 446; Watts, 'The Legal Position in International Law of Heads of States, Heads of Governments and Foreign Ministers', pp. 107–8; *Pinochet* case, Opinion of Lord Millet, p. 644.

53 Ibid., pp. 97, 106.

54 See Saltany *v.* Reagan, US Court of Appeals, District of Columbia Circuit, 29 September 1989, *International Law Reports*, 1992, vol. 87, p. 680; H.S.A. *et al.* c. A.S. et Y.A., Belgian Cour de cassation, Decision of 12 February 2003, *International Legal Materials*, 2003, vol. 42, pp. 604–5. See also Convention on Special Missions, Art. 31.

55 The Article 15(2) of the 2001 *Resolution on Immunities* of the Institut de Droit International declares that its dispositions are 'without prejudice to such immunities to which other members of the government may be entitled on account of their official functions'. In the same way, though limited to foreign ministers, the commentary of the Article 3(2) of the ILC Draft Articles on Jurisdictional Immunities of States and their Property specifies that the draft 'articles do not prejudge the extent of immunities granted by States to [...] ministers for foreign affairs'. *Yearbook of the International Law Commission*, 1991, vol. II, Part Two, p. 22.

56 Arrest Warrant of 11 April 2000 (Democratic Republic of the Congo *v.* Belgium), Judgement, ICJ 2002, para. 54, 61.

57 Precedents concerning foreign ministers are scarce. See Chong Boon Kim *v.* Kim Yong Shik, US Hawaiian Circuit Court, 9 September 1963, *American Journal of International Law*, 1964, vol. 58, pp. 186–7; Ali Ali Reza c. Grimpel et autres, French Court of appeals of Paris, 1ère ch., Decision of 28 April 1961, *International Law Reports*, 1974, vol. 47, p. 275.

58 Congo *v.* Belgium case, Dissenting opinion of Judge Van den Wyngaert, para. 13. The use of the Chong Boon Kim *v.* Kim Yong Shik case, for example, could be debated, as the suggestion of immunity addressed to the court in this case mentioned the diplomatic status of, and not a special status recognized to, the foreign minister. Moreover, foreign ministers and heads of state or of government do not share exactly the same position in the constitutional organization of their state and on the international scene. Consequently, the analogy made by the ICJ could be questioned.

59 Simbeye, *Immunity and International Criminal Law*, pp. 125–6.

60 Gladys M. Lafontant *v.* Jean-Baptiste Aristide, p. 529; United States *v.* Noriega and others, Southern District of Florida, 8 June 1990, *International Law Reports*, 1995, vol. 99, pp. 162–3.

61 The practice of the suggestions of immunity by the United States is evidence of the political aspect of immunity. See Watts, 'The Legal Position in International Law of Heads of States, Heads of Governments and Foreign Ministers', p. 57.

62 The immunity from civil jurisdiction of heads of state and state immunities faced a similar movement. See Fox, *The Law of State Immunity*, pp. 439–41.

63 As the right to have access to a tribunal is a part of the right to a fair trial, Article 6(1) of the European Convention for the Protection of Human Rights and Fundamental Freedoms was used in several cases before the ECHR to challenge the notion of immunity. See, for example, Waite and Kennedy *v.* Germany, ECHR 1999; Beer and Regan *v.* Germany, ECHR 1999; Al-Adsani *v.* United Kingdom, ECHR 2001; Fogarty *v.* United Kingdom, ECHR 2001; McElhinney *v.* Ireland, ECHR 2001; Tsalkitzis *v.* Greece, ECHR 2006.

64 Omar Al Bashir (ICC-02/05-01/09), Warrant of Arrest for Omar Hassan Ahmad Al Bashir, 4 March 2009.

65 See, for example, D. Akande, 'International Law Immunities and the International Criminal Court', *American Journal of International Law*, 2004, vol. 98, pp. 415–19.

66 Milosevic (IT-02-54), Decision on Preliminary Motions, 8 November 2001, para. 30.

67 See Difference Relating to Immunity from Legal Process of a Special Rapporteur of the Commission on Human Rights, Advisory opinion, ICJ 1999, para. 63; Taylor (SCSL-03-01-I-059), Rendering of Decision on Immunity motion, para. 27.

68 David, *Eléments de droit pénal international et européen*, pp. 101–5; K. Kittichaisaree, *International Criminal Law*, New York: Oxford University Press, 2001, pp. 259–60.

69 Radislav Krstic (IT-98-33-A), Appeals Chamber, Decision on Application for Subpoenas, 1 July 2003, para. 26. A particular issue is raised by the Rome Statute of the ICC and the *Al-Bashir* case. Considering the conventional nature of the ICC and the *pacta tertiis* principle contained in Article 34 of the Vienna Convention on the Law of Treaties, questions arise as to whether third-party states are bound by the provisions of the Rome Statute or decisions of the ICC, and also what the consequences may be concerning immunity. See Vienna Convention on the Law of Treaties, 1155 UNTS 331 (1969), Art. 34. See Fox, *The Law of State Immunity*, pp. 432–3. See also the African Union's decision concerning the *Al-Bashir* case. Decision on the Meeting of African States Parties to the Rome Statute of the International Criminal Court (ICC), Doc. Assembly/AU/13(XIII) (2009), para. 10.

70 Congo *v.* Belgium, para. 61.

71 See C. Cissé, 'The End of Culture of Impunity in Rwanda? Prosecution of Genocide and War Crimes before Rwandan Courts and the International Criminal Tribunal for Rwanda', *Yearbook of International Humanitarian Law*, 1998, vol. 1, pp. 172–3. See also, for example, Milosevic (IT-02-54), Initial indictment ''Kosovo'', 22 May 1999; Kambanda (ICTR 97-23-A), Appeals Chamber, 19 October 2000.

72 Taylor (SCSL-03-01-I-059), Rendering of Decision on Immunity motion, para. 52.

73 Before the *Pinochet* case, most of the pleas of immunity were rejected by foreign tribunals in cases involving senior state officials. However, immunity was rejected by some tribunals but not because of the nature of the committed crimes. For example, the French Cour de cassation recognized an exception to diplomatic immunity for war crimes in the Otto Abetz case, but asserted that the accused was not accredited to the French government when he perpetrated his crimes and thus was not entitled to diplomatic immunities. Otto Abetz, French Cour de cassation (Ch. Crim.), Decision of 28 July 1950, *Revue Critique de Droit International Privé*, 1951, vol. 40, pp. 477–84. Ferdinand Marcos, former head of state of the Philippines, had his immunity waived by the new government of his State and Manuel Noriega was not recognized as the head of state of Panama. See Marcos and Marcos *v.* Federal Department of Police, Swiss Federal Tribunal, 2 November 1989, *International Law Reports*, 1996, vol. 102, pp. 203–5; United States *v.* Noriega and others, pp. 162–3. See also United States ex rel. Casanova *v.* Fitzpatrick, Southern District of New York, 16 January 1963, *International Law Reports*, 1967, vol. 34, p. 154.

74 See, for example, A. Bianchi, 'Immunity versus Human Rights: The *Pinochet* Case', *European Journal of International Law*, 1999, vol. 10, pp. 237–77.

75 *Pinochet* case, pp. 592, 641.

76 Ibid., pp. 114, 152, 166, 176–7, 190. Before this, the Nuremberg tribunal affirmed that '[t]he principle of international law, which under certain circumstances, protects the representatives of a state, cannot be applied to acts which are condemned as criminal by international law. The authors of these facts cannot shelter themselves behind their official position in order to be freed from punishment in appropriate proceedings'. Nuremberg judgement, p. 221.

77 For example, criminal proceedings were instituted against Hissene Habré, former head of state of Chad, in Senegal; Mouammar Ghaddafi, incumbent head of state of Lybia, in France; Ariel Sharon, serving head of government of Israel, and Abdulaye Yerodia Ndombasi, foreign minister of the Republic of Congo, in Belgium.

78 *Ghaddafi* case, p. 474.

79 S. Zappala, 'Do Heads of State in Office Enjoy Immunity from Jurisdiction for International Crimes? The *Ghaddafi* case before the French Cour de Cassation', *European Journal of International Law*, 2001, vol. 12, pp. 600–1.

80 Congo *v.* Belgium, paras. 54–8. See also Gladys M. Lafontant *v.* Jean-Baptiste Aristide, p. 529; C. Warbrick, 'Immunity and International Crimes in English Law', *International and Comparative Law Quarterly*, 2004, vol. 53, p. 779; J. Hartmann, 'The Gillon Affair', *International and Comparative Law Quarterly*, 2005, vol. 45, p. 745; H.S.A. *et al.* c. A.S. et Y.A., pp. 604–5.

81 Congo *v.* Belgium, para. 61. See, for example, S. Wirth, 'Immunity for Core Crimes? The ICJ's Judgement in the *Congo v. Belgium* Case', *European Journal of International Law*, 2002, vol. 13, pp 77–93.

82 A. Cassese, 'When May Senior State Officials Be Tried for International Crimes? Some Comments on The *Congo v. Belgium* case', *European Journal of International Law,* 2002, vol. 13, pp. 853–75.

83 Tihomir Blaskic (IT-95-14-AR 108 bis), para. 41.

84 *Pinochet* case, pp. 589, 649.

85 Institut de Droit International, *Resolution on Immunities,* Art. 13(2). See Cassese, *International Criminal Law*, pp. 305–14.

86 M. Ruffert, 'Pinochet Follow Up: The End of Sovereign Immunity?', *Netherlands International Law Review*, 2001, vol. 48, p. 188. However, the ECHR did not accept the *jus cogens* argument. See Al-Adsani *v.* United Kingdom, ECHR 2001, paras. 60–6.

23
Truth commissions

Eric Wiebelhaus-Brahm

More than two dozen truth commissions have been established over the past three decades as countries seek to uncover details of past human rights abuses.[1] They have been suggested as an antidote for virtually every conflict that has come to an end in recent years. Truth commissions are touted for their ability to give victims voice and to provide official acknowledgment of their suffering. Furthermore, they can provide an authoritative account of a contested period in history and, thereby, help restore society's moral underpinnings. In addition, they produce recommendations for institutional and policy reform that are designed to prevent future human rights abuses. Ultimately, the investigation hopefully contributes to the longer-term goal of reconciliation. Finally, the truth commission is seen as an ideal means of fulfilling a state's international legal obligations with respect to the right to know. Although the United Nations and others have sought to develop guidelines for truth commissions,[2] they have taken many different forms.

Yet, the truth commission is controversial. The general population, as well as activists, often expect too much from them. Critics fault the inability of truth commissions to punish perpetrators of human rights violations. In many countries, truth commissions are established as an alternative to criminal prosecution. In the best of circumstances, truth commissions recommend prosecutions and collect testimony and evidence that might contribute to them, but this has been relatively rare. Only a few truth commissions have been created in conjunction with trials. In fact, of the truth commissions that have existed, only a few are considered truly successful. Truth commission mandates and resources can limit the amount of information uncovered. Victims have highly individualized reactions to participation; some find comfort, while others feel renewed pain. Recommendations have a patchy implementation record. In fact the theoretical and empirical bases for concluding that truth commissions have the positive effects many assume have been questioned.[3]

This chapter examines the relationship between truth commissions and international criminal law in four parts. First, I trace the emergence of a right to know in international law. Second, I highlight what makes truth commissions unique among human rights bodies. Third, although each case is *sui generis*, I outline the typical course of a truth commission investigation and examine several key controversies. Finally, I evaluate how truth commissions have related to criminal prosecution.

The right to know

Treaty bodies, regional courts, and international and domestic tribunals have asserted that a right to know, or a right to truth, exists in international law. The basis of a right to know is often traced to World War II. One source is the 1949 Geneva Conventions and Additional Protocol I, which imposes an obligation on states parties to resolve cases of persons missing as a result of armed conflict. The International Committee of the Red Cross (ICRC) specifically concluded that the right is applicable in both interstate and intrastate conflicts.[4] The principle can also be found in international human rights law. Article 19 of the Universal Declaration of Human Rights includes a right to 'seek, receive and impart information'. Moreover, Article 2(3) of the International Covenant on Civil and Political Rights provides for the right to effective remedy for victims of human rights violations.

At the global level, these principles have been evolving in recent years. As early as 1995, a meeting of experts convened by the United Nations concluded that the right to truth had achieved the status of a norm of customary international law.[5] In 1996, the UN Sub-Commission on Prevention of Discrimination and Protection of Minorities provided the first detailed draft guidelines outlining the basis of a right to truth and standards for preserving evidence and managing access to information.[6] The document recommends extrajudicial commissions of inquiry, such as truth commissions, as ideal means through which states could fulfill their obligations. In 2005, the new version of the document concluded that 'victims and their families have the imprescriptible right to know the truth about the circumstances in which violations took place and, in the event of death or disappearance, the victims' fate'.[7] That same year, the UN General Assembly adopted a resolution describing the right to truth as an integral component of victims' right to remedy for human rights violations.[8] According to Principle VII of the resolution,

> Remedies for gross violations of international human rights law and serious violations of international humanitarian law include the victim's right to the following as provided for under international law: (a) Equal and effective access to justice; (b) Adequate, effective and prompt reparation for harm suffered; and (c) Access to relevant information concerning violations and reparation mechanisms.

Principle XXIV continues:

> Victims and their representatives should be entitled to seek and obtain information on the causes leading to their victimization and on the causes and conditions pertaining to the gross violations of international human rights law and serious violations of international humanitarian law and to learn the truth in regard to these violations.

Even earlier, regional bodies had begun to articulate the right. The most activity has been in the Americas. The Inter-American Commission on Human Rights (IACHR), for example, has recognized that

> the right to the truth arises as a basic and indispensable consequence for all States Parties, given that not knowing the facts related to human rights violations means that, in practice, there is no system of protection capable of guaranteeing the identification and possible punishment of those responsible.[9]

In addition, the General Assembly and Permanent Council of the Organization of American States (OAS) have passed several resolutions urging member states to provide information to relatives of victims of forced disappearance.[10] Moreover, at the 2005 MERCOSUR summit, member states adopted a declaration reaffirming the right to truth for victims and their relatives.[11] Finally, high courts within the region have recognized the right to truth.[12]

Other regions have followed suit. For example, the Council of Europe's Parliamentary Assembly has passed recommendations and resolutions regarding the right of family members to know the truth about the fate of disappeared loved ones.[13] In addition, the European Parliament has passed resolutions affirming the right to know in relation to missing persons,[14] and paramilitary disarmament and demobilization.[15] Moreover, the Council of the European Union has reached similar conclusions in relation to peace talks.[16] In Africa, the African Charter on Human and Peoples' Rights contains a 'right to receive information'.[17]

International courts and bodies have recognized that states have an obligation to investigate disappearances and inform relatives of the victim's fate.[18] The right to know the fate and whereabouts of 'disappeared' relatives, both in times of peace and in times of armed conflict, also has been confirmed by international and regional human rights bodies,[19] as well as national courts.[20] The UN Commission on Human Rights stressed the need to recognize:

> the right of victims of gross violations of human rights and serious violations of international humanitarian law, and their families, within the framework of each State's domestic legal system, to know the truth regarding such violations, including the identity of the perpetrators and the causes, facts and circumstances in which such violations took place.[21]

Several Court rulings and UN reports argue that this obligation extends to successive governments.[22] Moreover, the Inter-American Court of Human Rights has extended this right to include being kept appraised of the progress of ongoing investigations.[23]

The right to know exists at least for gross human rights violations and serious crimes under international law. The right to truth also has been cited in relation to combating impunity,[24] internally displaced persons,[25] in the context of remedies and reparation for serious human rights violations,[26] and with respect to forced disappearances.[27]

International courts and treaty bodies have found that a state's failure to provide information constitutes a human rights violation in its own right. The Human Rights Committee and supervisory bodies established under the American Convention on Human Rights have recognized that the suffering loved ones experienced due to the uncertainty surrounding a disappearance constitutes cruel, inhuman, and degrading treatment.[28] Similarly, the European Court of Human Rights has ruled that a government's failure to provide information to loved ones constitutes a breach of Article 3 of the European Convention on Human Rights and a continuing violation of a state's procedural obligation to protect the right to life under Article 2 of the convention.[29]

International bodies have also recognized a collective right to know. The Inter-American Commision on Human Rights (IACHR) has found that '[t]he right to know the truth is a collective right that ensures society access to information that is essential for the workings of democratic systems'.[30] Similarly, the Inter-American Court of Human Rights has ruled that '[s]ociety has the right to know the truth regarding atrocities of the past' 'so as to be capable of preventing them in the future'.[31] Furthermore, the Court has found that this collective knowledge can have preventive and reparatory effects.[32] The UN Commission on Human Rights also highlights a collective element to the right to truth. Specifically:

> [e]very people has the inalienable right to know the truth about past events concerning the perpetration of heinous crimes and about the circumstances and reasons that led, through

> massive or systematic violations, to the perpetration of those crimes. Full and effective exercise of the right to the truth provides a vital safeguard against the recurrence of violations.[33]

What is a truth commission?

What distinguishes truth commissions from other forms of non-judicial investigation?[34] Freeman defines a truth commission as

> An *ad hoc*, autonomous, and victim-centered commission of inquiry set up in and authorized by a state for the primary purposes of (1) investigating and reporting on the principal causes and consequences of broad and relatively recent patterns of severe violence or repression that occurred in the state during determinate periods of abusive rule or conflict, and (2) making recommendations for their redress and future prevention.[35]

Several elements of this definition are important. First, truth commissions focus on the past. The events may have occurred in the recent past, but they do not investigate contemporary violations. Second, truth commissions investigate a pattern of abuse over a set period of time. They typically examine much or all of a civil war or repressive era rather than a specific event. Truth commission mandates provide the parameters of their investigation. Third, truth commissions are temporary. Generally, they operate for one to two years, completing their work by preparing a report that documents their findings and recommendations. Fourth, truth commissions are officially authorized by the state. In theory, this provides the truth commission with greater access to information, better security, and increased assurance that its findings will be seriously considered. There is also some evidence that official acknowledgment of suffering has psychological benefits for victims.

By providing a full account of past human rights abuses and identifying their causes, the truth commission is increasingly seen as an ideal mechanism through which a state can fulfill its obligations with respect to the right to truth. The UN Commission on Human Rights recommends that:

> [s]ocieties that have experienced heinous crimes perpetrated on a massive or systematic basis may benefit in particular from the creation of a truth commission or other commission of inquiry to establish the facts surroundings those violations so that the truth may be ascertained and to prevent the disappearance of evidence.[36]

Truth commission creators may have one or several goals in mind. A recent UN report argued that

> truth commissions have the potential to be of great benefit in helping post-conflict societies establish the facts about past human rights violations, foster accountability, preserve evidence, identify perpetrators and recommend reparations and institutional reforms. They can also provide a public platform for victims to address the nation directly with their personal stories and can facilitate public debate about how to come to terms with the past.[37]

A truth commission's 'life cycle'

Although truth commissions have varied in important respects, almost all have followed a similar trajectory.

The establishment of a truth commission

Truth commissions are usually established soon after a political transition in order to maximize their impact on post-transition society. Transitional periods often provide greater opportunity for dramatic reform. Acting quickly also has practical benefits as witnesses and evidence become more difficult to find over time. The speed with which a truth commission is created depends on political circumstances, however. Moreover, it is more effective and safer to conduct investigations once the violence has truly come to an end.

Most truth commissions have been created by presidential decree, which has the advantage of speed. However, commissions established by legislatures may enjoy greater legitimacy because more parties participate in the decision. In addition, in many countries, only commissions established by legislatures have stronger investigatory powers. Still other truth commissions are the product of negotiated peace agreements. Actually establishing the commission requires the accord to hold and, often, the passage of implementing legislation. These two factors could delay a truth commission's creation. For ethical and practical reasons, the process should involve victims, human rights groups, and other civil society organizations.[38]

The mandate

A truth commission's mandate outlines the particulars of its investigation. It delineates how long the truth commission will operate. Although there are significant outliers, they have averaged between one and two years. The mandate also specifies what is to be investigated. While many have broad authority to examine all human rights violations, Chile's National Truth and Reconciliation Commission (CNVR), for example, was only permitted to investigate abuses if they resulted in the death of the victim. In addition, mandates specify the time period in which violations must have occurred in order to be eligible for investigation. Limitations on the scope of the investigation are often controversial.

Finally, the mandate delineates the powers truth commissions will possess to conduct their investigations. Commissions frequently have the ability to interview anyone, though rarely against their will. Sometimes, truth commissions have had the power to grant use immunity, through which individuals who cooperate are assured that the information they provide will not be used against them in criminal proceedings. Several truth commissions have had search and seizure and subpoena powers. However, truth commissions lack enforcement powers.

Composition of the commission

Although the mandate is important, a truth commission's course is highly dependent upon the individuals appointed to serve as commissioners. The most common approach is to appoint well-respected members of society. For example, to chair their commissions, Argentina selected widely respected author Ernesto Sabato and South Africa named Archbishop Desmond Tutu. The conventional wisdom is that commissioners should be untainted by past human rights abuses and be representative of society. This symbolic gesture can lend truth commission findings greater credibility. The UN recommends that commissioners have expertise and experience promoting and defending human rights and knowledge of international legal obligations.[39] Furthermore, it urges commissions to be gender balanced. Broad consultation in the selection process adds to their legitimacy.

In some extreme cases, governments have asked foreigners to serve as commissioners. In El Salvador, for example, the violence was so polarizing that no Salvadoran was deemed able to provide a fair assessment of what had happened. As a result, the UN Secretary-General, with the agreement of the Salvadoran government and the Farabundo Martí National Liberation Front (FMLN), selected three foreigners to serve on the Salvadoran Commission on the Truth. However, the lack of Salvadoran participation led critics to decry the commission as a foreign imposition.[40]

The operation of truth commissions

The preparatory phase

Recent truth commissions have devoted a few months to preparation before actively beginning their work. During this time, commissioners develop a strategic plan and establish procedures and policies. Staff must be recruited, including researchers, interviewers, lawyers, and forensic experts. A database must be created to manage the evidence and testimony that will soon be collected. The commission may conduct initial background research, often relying on civil society groups. Finally, commissioners frequently engage in fundraising from domestic and international donors.

Truth commissions also create public outreach campaigns to raise awareness about the upcoming investigation. A truth commission is able to begin its investigatory phase more smoothly if it creates public service announcements and pamphlets that explain the commission's goals and procedures. Spreading accurate information is important to dispel myths, encourage participation, and manage public expectations. In general, truth commissions do not devote sufficient time or resources to outreach. Civil society groups frequently fill the void and their endorsement provides legitimacy, but the workings of truth commissions are often not entirely clear to potential participants. In Sierra Leone, for example, a survey conducted after the Truth and Reconciliation Commission (TRC)'s outreach program found that 83% of respondents had a poor understanding of the commission.[41]

Investigation phase

A core activity is collecting statements from victims, witnesses, and perpetrators. Resource constraints may limit a commission's coverage. Truth commission budgets vary from less than $1 million to South Africa's $18 million per year.[42] While inexpensive by trial standards, truth commissions invariably face resource constraints. In several countries, such as Ghana,[43] civil society groups have contributed significant manpower. The Nigerian truth commission received support for outreach and training of staff from civil society groups and other private donors.[44]

Security is another major concern of the statement-taking process. Victims and witnesses may be in remote areas that are inaccessible and insecure. Statement-giving exposes the participant to reprisal and vigilante justice. South Africa's TRC was exceptional in providing a sophisticated witness protection program, including a network of safehouses. Many commissions have been permitted to take confidential statements, but they are of more limited use due to the difficulty of corroborating them.

Individuals choose to give statements for several reasons. Some hope that it may help uncover further information regarding the fate of their loved one. Others find it therapeutic. For victims, the truth commission's attention represents an official acknowledgment of their suffering. For perpetrators, it offers an opportunity to ease their conscience. Perpetrators also come forward in hopes of gaining amnesty or participating in reintegration programs. Finally, victims frequently come to a truth commission expecting that their participation will lead to reparations.[45]

Truth commissions also seek to collect physical evidence. Information from official sources may exist. Although government officials often pledge to cooperate and provide the commission with access to archives and sites where suspected abuses occurred, they do not always live up to their commitments. Records may be destroyed. Truth commissions may lack the power to subpoena documents. Events may have taken place in the distant past, which makes finding information extremely difficult. As they collect evidence, truth commissions should be careful to avoid tainting it so that it may be useful in future prosecutions.

Public hearings

Some truth commissions have conducted public proceedings. The South African TRC popularized this approach with hundreds of days of public hearings. It held victims' and amnesty hearings in venues around the country. It also conducted thematic hearings that focused on particular types of violations (e.g. against women and children), prominent events (e.g. the 1976 Soweto uprising), and institutional hearings (e.g. the role of the legal and health sector in past human rights abuses). Since the TRC, other countries, including Peru and Timor-Leste, have used public hearings with growing frequency.

There are several potential costs and benefits to conducting public hearings. Public hearings can be valuable because victims' stories and other details can be more widely known, thus limiting denials of past abuses. They may also increase the commission's credibility by making it more transparent. However, public hearings create security risks for victims and perpetrators who come forward to give testimony. Moreover, unchecked accusations may be publicly leveled. Finally, public hearings require additional time and resources to organize.

Findings: the truth commission report

A truth commission concludes by issuing a final report, which summarizes its key findings and provides recommendations for healing and prevention. Once truth commissions complete their work, they dissolve. Any follow-up, therefore, is the responsibility of other political actors. The United Nations urges states to 'disseminate, implement, and monitor implementation of, the recommendations of non-judicial mechanisms such as truth and reconciliation commissions'.[46] Legislation creating truth commissions sometimes contains clauses obliging governments to seriously consider, or even require, the implementation of truth commission recommendations. However, many are never implemented.

The question of whether to identify individual perpetrators in the final report, or to 'name names', is something many truth commissions have confronted. Truth commissions in El Salvador and Chad, for example, named individuals as perpetrators of human rights abuses. In Argentina, the National Commission for the Disappearance of Persons (CONADEP) provided a sealed list of names to the government, which was subsequently leaked to the press. Finally, in South Africa, several lawsuits were filed against the TRC by individuals who were publicly accused in hearings or in the final report. In the case of *Van Rensburg and Du Preez v. the Truth and Reconciliation Commission*, the courts sided with the TRC, but established due process restrictions.[47]

Naming names is controversial for several reasons. First, truth commissions do not provide for due process as courts do. Second, accusations may be based on weak evidence or uncorroborated testimony. Third, publicly naming individuals may make them targets of vigilante justice. As such, it is important for truth commissions to establish standards of evidence and have procedures in place that permit accused individuals to respond to allegations before they become public.

Truth commissions and criminal prosecution

Truth commissions are frequently described as alternatives to criminal prosecution in situations where trials are not feasible for political or practical reasons. Perpetrators may remain politically powerful and able to resist efforts to prosecute. *De facto* or *de jure* amnesties may be in place. In addition, perpetrators' technical expertise may be needed for the continued functioning of the state. Finally, courts may not have the capacity to prosecute or may be complicit in past abuses.

Yet, truth commissions are not substitutes for criminal prosecution. The IACHR has held that truth commissions do not fulfill a state's obligation to compensate victims and punish perpetrators.[48] In reality, the two post-conflict justice mechanisms have different goals. Trials determine the guilt and innocence of individuals against specific charges for which prosecutors have found sufficient evidence exists to bring a case. The focus is on presuming innocence and protecting the rights of the accused. Victims participate only to the extent of providing testimony relevant to determining guilt or innocence. By contrast, truth commissions tend to focus on the role of institutions as well as historical and socioeconomic factors that contributed to violations. Some argue that being in a position of power to act upon one's ideological convictions is what leads individuals to commit human rights violations.[49] Therefore, prosecution is not essential for prevention; reforming the institutional conditions that made the abuses possible is. Moreover, truth commissions are not adversarial like court proceedings; they provide an environment in which victims can tell their story on their own terms.

Truth commissions may recommend that perpetrators be tried, but, with the exception of those that 'named names', they avoid assigning individual responsibility. Nonetheless, truth commissions have possessed various powers designed to encourage the revelation of information, often with implications for criminal prosecution. Some commissions, such as Liberia's Truth and Reconciliation Commission (TRC), could recommend amnesties for individuals who cooperated with its investigation. South Africa's TRC is unique in having the power to grant amnesty to perpetrators who provided a full account of their deeds and demonstrated that their crime was politically motivated. The TRC's judgment could not be legally challenged. Although critics charged that the criteria was subjective and unverifiable, the TRC cross-checked testimony against other statements. The fact that less than one-third of the 7,000 applicants were granted amnesty suggests the process was credible. Those who did not apply for or did not receive amnesty were theoretically at risk of prosecution. However, the South African government has not actively pursued many criminal cases from the apartheid era.

Several truth commissions have offered use immunity to those who cooperate with its investigation. As described next, Timor-Leste's Commissao de Acolhimento, Verdade e Reconciliacao (CAVR) had the power to extinguish criminal and civil liability for non-serious crimes. Truth commission legislation in South Africa and Ghana explicitly forbid the use of self-incriminating evidence given to the commission in subsequent criminal prosecutions. Some commissions have adopted quasi-judicial procedures in their treatment of alleged perpetrators, such as informing them of allegations and affording them the opportunity to respond to accusations, question witnesses, and have legal representation present.

Despite pessimism about the ability of truth commissions to contribute to criminal prosecution, several examples exist. In Argentina, evidence collected by CONADEP was used by prosecutors in the trials of nine junta leaders less than two years after the commission.[50] In response to victims' requests, Peru's Truth and Reconciliation Commission (CVR) set up a Special Investigations Unit to assemble legal cases based on evidence collected by the commission. The CVR forged a formal cooperation agreement with the Attorney General's Office, which governed their interaction and facilitated the transfer of evidence. Similarly, Uganda's

Commission of Inquiry into Violations of Human Rights (CIVHR) submitted information it had accumulated to judicial authorities. Finally, in Chile, the CNVR's mandate required it to turn over evidence of criminal behavior to the courts.

Fears that truth commissions may lead to prosecution often fuel demands for a general amnesty, if one does not already exist. In El Salvador, shortly after the signing of the Chapultepec Accord that ended the country's civil war, the Legislative Assembly passed the National Reconciliation Law.[51] It provided amnesty for human rights violations committed during the war, but a compromise excluded persons identified by the upcoming truth commission as responsible for serious acts of violence. The commission interpreted its mandate to require the naming of names. To do so, it 'established three levels of evidence for its findings: "overwhelming" – conclusive or highly convincing evidence to support the Commission's finding; "substantial" – very solid evidence to support the Commission's finding; and "sufficient" – more evidence to support the Commission's finding than to contradict it'.[52] A finding required at least two corroborating sources. Before including names, the commission offered to interview individuals to give them the opportunity to respond to allegations. However, the commission did not recommend prosecution because the judicial system was complicit in past abuses.[53] The final report was swiftly condemned by the government, the military, and the Supreme Court and a blanket amnesty was passed. As a result, few perpetrators have been punished in Salvadoran courts.

In two recent cases, truth commissions have operated in concert with international tribunals. In Sierra Leone and Timor-Leste, the United Nations worked with the respective governments to establish tribunals to try those most responsible for human rights violations. Meanwhile, truth commissions provided a broad analysis of past abuses and facilitated the reintegration of low-level offenders. The remainder of this section provides a brief overview of these cases.

Sierra Leone

Initially, the architects of post-war Sierra Leone did not envision prosecuting abuses committed during the civil war. Rather, the parties agreed to the Truth and Reconciliation Commission (TRC) in the 1999 Lomé Peace Agreement. The TRC was mandated to investigate the causes, nature, and extent of violations of human rights and international humanitarian law that occurred between 1991 and 7 July 1999, when Lomé was signed, create an impartial historical record of the period, address victims' needs, promote healing and reconciliation, and prevent the repetition of such abuses.

The TRC was formally adopted by Sierra Leone's parliament in February 2000. However, when fighting resumed the following May, the government and the international community reconsidered their position on prosecution. Following Sierra Leone's request, the UN Security Council passed Resolution 1315 on 14 August 2000 authorizing the UN Secretary-General to negotiate an agreement with Sierra Leone. The result, the Special Court for Sierra Leone (SCSL), was charged with prosecuting individuals most responsible for serious violations of international humanitarian law and domestic law since 30 November 1996. Due to the renewed fighting, Sierra Leone's parliament did not approve the SCSL agreement until April 2002.

Because of the breakdown in the peace agreement, the TRC and the SCSL were created at roughly the same time. In May 2002, UN Secretary-General Annan appointed the SCSL's prosecutor and registrar. Within days, Sierra Leonean President Kabbah named the TRC's seven commissioners. In July, the TRC commissioners were sworn in and the SCSL's judges were announced. During this time, considerable effort was spent working out the relationship between the two bodies.[54] The United Nations convened several meetings of experts. International non-governmental organizations (NGOs) produced their own proposals. Despite these efforts, some issues were never formally resolved. Specifically, little attention was paid to the issue of whether incriminating evidence in TRC possession was admissible at the SCSL.[55] The TRC legislation did not provide a guarantee against self-incrimination, but did permit the TRC to take confidential statements.

A public controversy emerged regarding whether the SCSL could compel the TRC to turn over materials, including confidential evidence. The TRC favored a simple, unequivocal policy that could be easily explained, because they worried that the public would not understand the TRC's relationship with the SCSL. Moreover, they feared that giving the SCSL access to TRC records would inhibit participation. To quash these concerns, the TRC decided that all information given to it in confidence would remain confidential. In its final report, it recommended that Sierra Leone not pass legislation to give domestic or international courts access to confidential information in TRC archives. SCSL Prosecutor David Crane also sought to reassure Sierra Leoneans that the TRC was not a ruse to trap perpetrators. On numerous occasions, he emphasized that his cases would be built solely with the resources of his own office. Given the fact that the SCSL had significantly more resources than the TRC, this commitment appears unlikely to have hampered the SCSL's work.

The heart of the controversy was whether the SCSL was superior to the TRC. UN sources affirmed that the TRC and the SCSL were mutually supportive and complementary. UN Secretary-General Annan, for example, suggested a division of labor in arguing that 'relationship and cooperation arrangements would be required between the Prosecutors and the National Truth and Reconciliation Commission, including the use of the Commission as an alternative to prosecution, and the prosecution of juveniles, in particular'.[56] However, the Sierra Leonean government viewed the relationship differently. Its interpretation was that the SCSL superseded the TRC. Basing its judgment on the erroneous view that the TRC was a government body when it was, in fact, autonomous, the government concluded that

> [t]he Special Court is an international judicial body whose requests and orders require no less than full compliance by the Truth and Reconciliation Commission, as by all Sierra Leonean national institutions, in accordance to the international obligations agreed to by Sierra Leone.[57]

A confrontation was avoided because Crane and the TRC commissioners were in agreement with the UN.

Although the two bodies generally got along well, problems emerged when individuals who had been indicted by the SCSL expressed interest in appearing before the TRC. While the TRC was conducting public hearings between April and August 2003, the SCSL was simultaneously conducting investigations, issuing indictments, and making arrests. The TRC had asked permission to interview SCSL detainees in May and June 2003, but none expressed interest. However, as the TRC's public hearings concluded, three individuals, including Chief Sam Hinga Norman, requested the opportunity to testify at the TRC's public hearings. How the issue played out revealed a weakness in the post-conflict justice architecture.

When the TRC formally requested an interview with Norman, the SCSL Registrar issued a Practice Direction, which outlined a procedure in which the TRC could seek permission to interview detainees by applying to an SCSL judge and providing the questions that would be asked.[58] The Direction required the interviews to be recorded and forwarded to the Prosecutor as potential evidence. When the TRC objected, the Registrar revised the Direction so that transcripts would not be forwarded automatically to the Prosecutor. However, they would be on file with the Registrar for the use of any party in criminal proceedings. The TRC submitted a formal application on 7 October to hold a public hearing for Norman. Crane opposed the move, arguing that it was inappropriate because the Norman case was *sub judice*. He also feared that allowing Norman to testify in public could heighten tensions and frighten potential witnesses. Ultimately, SCSL Appeals Chamber President Geoffrey Robertson ruled on 28 November 2003 that the three individuals could testify before the TRC, but not in public.[59] Norman was dissatisfied with the compromise and he was never interviewed by the TRC.

Timor-Leste

In some respects, the truth commission and tribunal in Timor-Leste had a clearer division of labor. Both the CAVR and the Serious Crimes Unit were created simultaneously by the United Nations Transitional Administration in East Timor (UNTAET). The CAVR had a mandate to examine human rights abuses that occurred between Portugal's withdrawal from Timor-Leste on 25 April 1974 and UNTAET's establishment on 25 October 1999. As such, it took a longer view of violations than the Serious Crimes Unit, which looked only at abuses that occurred between 1 January 1999 and UNTAET's creation.[60] The CAVR was designed as a mechanism for lower-level offenders, while the Serious Crimes Unit was reserved for the architects of the violence.

Overall, the CAVR was crafted so as not to interfere with the Serious Crimes Unit or local courts. Witnesses were free to refuse to cooperate with the truth commission, but if they provided testimony, it could be used against them in court. The CAVR could accept confidential testimony. However, it was required to turn over such information to the Serious Crimes Unit's Office of the General Prosecutor upon request. The decision to craft the relationship between the two bodies in this way was based on the argument that any interference with potential prosecutions would go against the popular will and hamper the development of Timor-Leste's nascent judicial system.[61]

Because most perpetrators came from the same village as victims, the CAVR sponsored village-based ceremonies that were designed to facilitate the reintegration of perpetrators back into their community. The Community Reconciliation Procedures (CRPs) were a practical solution to the reality that the legal system of the newly independent country lacked the capacity to handle the volume of potential cases. Perpetrators wishing to participate gave a statement to a local CAVR representative, who forwarded it to the CAVR's central office for review. In turn, the central office passed the statement to the Serious Crime Unit's Office of the General Prosecutor with a recommendation on whether the individual should be allowed to participate in a CRP. The Prosecutor's office checked the veracity of individuals' statements and determined whether the crimes were of a level of gravity that warranted prosecution. If information of more serious crimes emerged in the course of the community ceremony, the process could be suspended while the Serious Crimes Unit reconsidered charges.

If approved, perpetrators were scheduled for a CRP. At the ceremony, they appeared before their community, confessed to their actions, faced the victims, and publicly apologized for their acts. As a symbolic punishment, perpetrators agreed to undertake community service or some other form of reconciliation. The CAVR registered the sanctions with the local court. Once punishment was fulfilled, the perpetrator gained immunity from prosecution. In the end, approximately 1,500 people participated in CRPs, far exceeding the program's goals.[62]

Conclusion

Despite some recent exceptions, many future truth commissions will operate in environments in which the prospects for criminal prosecution of past human rights abuses is uncertain at best.

Nonetheless, there are several things truth commissions can do to support such an eventuality. Truth commissions, and the governments that create them, should outline clear rules and procedures for the collection and preservation of evidence and testimony that maximize their availability and utility to prosecutors. Truth commissions should work to corroborate testimony and provide the accused with an opportunity to respond to allegations. The truth commission should be very confident in the validity of accusations before allowing them to be aired in public hearings or in final reports. Allowing truth commissions to grant use immunity or amnesty should be considered carefully and implemented in a way that is consistent with the law. Finally, truth commission archives should be constructed to secure materials from tampering or deterioration and to be available via reasonable rules of access.

The international community will also face future instances in which truth commissions and criminal proceedings operate concurrently. Post-conflict justice architects may be conscious of the importance of carefully delineating the relationship between trials and truth commissions, but problems have emerged in each case thus far. Countries considering truth commissions and criminal prosecution must consider several questions:

- Is perpetrator participation in the truth commission important enough to warrant use immunity or amnesty?
- Should prosecutors have access to any or all testimony or evidence collected by the truth commission?
- Should indicted individuals be permitted to participate in truth commissions and, if so, does participation have any bearing on criminal proceedings?

These issues have lasting significance due to the existence of the International Criminal Court (ICC). In its cases to date, the ICC has not directly dealt with the question of whether truth commissions represent adequate domestic action to address human rights abuses and, hence, forestall ICC investigation. In the long run, the ICC will need to consider how it will treat truth commission proceedings.

Notes

1 For compilations of truth commission cases, see Center for the Study of Violence and Reconciliation. Justice in Perspective. http://www.justiceinperspective.org.za/ (accessed 25 August 2009); P. B. Hayner, *Unspeakable Truths: Confronting State Terror and Atrocity*, New York: Routledge, 2001; United States Institute of Peace. Truth Commissions Digital Collection. http://www.usip.org/library/formin.html (accessed 25 August 2009).

2 UN Office for the High Commissioner for Human Rights, Rule of Law Tools for Post-Conflict States: Truth Commissions, UN Doc. HR/PUB/06/1 (2006).

3 D. Mendeloff, 'Truth-Seeking, Truth-Telling and Post-Conflict Peacebuilding: Curb the Enthusiasm?' *International Studies Review* 6, 2004, pp. 355–80.

4 Resolution II of the XXIV International Conference of the Red Cross and Red Crescent (Manila 1981); Rule 117 in ICRC, *Customary International Humanitarian Law, Volume I, Rules*, Cambridge: Cambridge University Press, 2005, p. 421.

5 UN Sub-Commission on Prevention of Discrimination and Protection of Minorities, 'The Administration of Justice and the Human Rights of Detainees: Question of Human Rights and States of Emergency, Eighth Annual Report and List of States which, since 1 January 1985, Have Proclaimed, Extended or Terminated a State of Emergency, presented by Mr. Leandro Despouy, Special Rapporteur appointed pursuant to Economic and Social Council Resolution 1985/37', UN Doc E/CN.4/Sub.2/1995/20, para. 32.

6 Set of Principles for the Protection and Promotion of Human Rights through Action to Combat Impunity, Sub-Commission on Prevention of Discrimination and Protection of Minorities, 'The

Administration of Justice and the Human Rights of Detainees Question of the Impunity of Perpetrators of Human Rights Violations (Civil and Political) Revised Final Report prepared by Mr Joinet pursuant to Sub-Commission Decision 1996/119', UN Doc. E/CN.4/Sub.2/1997/20/Rev.1 (1997), Annex II.

7 Updated Set of Principles for the Protection and Promotion of Human Rights Through Action to Combat Impunity, Report of the independent expert to update the Set of principles to combat impunity, Diane Orentlicher, UN Doc. E/CN.4/2005/102/Add.1 (2005), Principle 4. See also Study on the Right to the Truth, UN Doc. E/CN.4/2006/91 (2006).

8 Basic Principles and Guidelines on the Right to a Remedy and Reparation for Victims of Gross Violations of International Human Rights Law and Serious Violations of International Humanitarian Law, UN Doc. A/RES/60/147 (2005).

9 Parada Cea *et al.* *v.* El Salvador (case 10.480), report No. 1/99, para. 150.

10 Organization of American States, General Assembly, AG/RES. 666 (XIII-0/83), 18 November 1983, para. 5 ; AG/RES.742 (XIV-0/84), 17 November 1984, para. 5. Permanent Council, OES/Ser.G CP/ CAJP-2278/05/rev.4, 23 May 2005.

11 Comunicado conjunto de los Presidentes de les Estados partes del MERCOSUR y de los Estados asociados, Ascunción, Paraguay, 20 June 2005, para. 5.

12 The Study on the Right to the Truth, UN Doc. E/CN.4/2006/91 (2006) give several references to judgements of the Constitutional Court of Colombia (Case T-249/03, 20 January 2003 and C-228, 3 April 2002), the Constitutional Tribunal of Peru (Case 2488-2002-HC/TC, March 18, 2004) and the Federal Criminal Court of Argentina, Agreement of 1 September 2003 of the National Chamber for Federal Criminal and Correctional Matters (Case *Suárez Mason, Rol 450* and Case *Escuela Mecánica de la Armada,* Rol. 761).

13 Council of Europe, Parliamentary Assembly, Recommendation 1056 (1987); Resolution 1414 (2004), para. 3; and Resolution 1463 (2005), para. 10(2).

14 European Parliament, Resolution on missing persons in Cyprus, 11 January 1983, referred to in Study on the Right to the Truth, UN Doc. E/CN.4/2006/91 (2006) and European Parliament, Resolution on missing persons in Cyprus, RSP/2007/2533, 15 March 2007.

15 UN Doc. E/CN.4/2005/SR.48, para. 41.

16 Conclusions of the Council of the European Union on Colombia, Press release 12514/1/05 REV 1 (en, nl, da, fi), 3 October 2005, para. 4.

17 African Charter on Human and Peoples' Rights, 21 I.L.M. 58 (1982).

18 Human Rights Committee, Quinteros Almeida *v.* Uruguay, UN Doc. CCPR/C/19/D/107/1981, 21 July 1983; Inter-American Court of Human Rights, Velasquez Rodriguez, Series C, No. 4, 29 July 1988, Caballero-Delgado *v.* Colombia, Series C, No. 17, 8 December 1995, Bámaca Velásquez, vol. 70, Series C, 25 November 2000, paras 159–66.

19 Human Rights Committee, Quinteros Almeida *v.* Uruguay, UN Doc. CCPR/C/19/D/107/1981, 21 July 1983, para. 14; European Court of Human Rights, Cyprus *v.* Turkey, 10 May 2001, *Reports of Judgments and Decisions*, 2001-IV, para. 157; Inter-American Court of Human Rights, Ernest Rafael Castillo Páez *v.* Peru, 3 November 1997, para. 90, Efraín Bámaca Velásquez *v.* Guatemala, 25 November 2000, paras 200–1.

20 Human Rights Chamber for Bosnia and Herzegovina, The 'Srebrenica Cases' (49 applications) *v.* The Republika Srpska, CH/01/8365 *et al.,* Decision on admissibility and merits, 7 March 2003, available at http://www.hrc.ba/database/decisions/CH01-8365%20Selimovic%20Admissibility%20and%20 Merits%20E.pdf, paras 174–8 (accessed 20 August 2009).

21 UN Commission on Human Rights, Resolution 2005/66 (2005).

22 Inter-American Court of Human Rights, Velasquez Rodriguez *v.* Honduras, Series C, No. 4, 29 July 1988; Caballero-Delgado *v.* Colombia, Series C, No. 17, 8 December 1995. Set of Principles for the Protection and Promotion of Human Rights, UN Doc. E/CN.4/Sub.2/1997/20/Rev.1 (1997). UN Commission on Human Rights, Revised Set of Basic Principles and Guidelines on the Right to Reparation for Victims of Gross Violations of Human Rights and Humanitarian Law, UN Doc. E/CN.4/Sub.2/1996/17 (1996).

23 Inter-American Court of Human Rights, Caracazo *v.* Venezuela, vol. 95, Series C (Reparations), 29 August 2002, para. 118.

24 Updated Set of Principles, Principles 1–4.

25 Commission on Human Rights, Report of the Representative of the Secretary General, Mr. Francis M. Deng, submitted pursuant to Commission resolution 1997/39, Guiding Principles on Internal Displacement, E/CN.4/1998/53/Add.2, 11 February 1998, Principle 16 (1).

26 UN General Assembly, Resolution 60/147, 21 March 2006, Annex, Basic Principles and Guidelines on the Right to a Remedy and Reparation for Victims of Gross Violations of International Human Rights Law and Serious Violations of International Humanitarian Law, paras 11, 22(b) and 24.
27 International Convention for the Protection of All Persons from Enforced Disappearance, UN Doc. A/RES/61/177, 20 December 2006, Article 24.
28 Human Rights Committee, Quinteros Almeida *v.* Uruguay, UN Doc. CCPR/C/19/D/107/1981, 21 July 1983, American Court on Human Rights, Efraín Bámaca Velásquez *v.* Guatemala, vol. 91, Series C, 25 November 2000, paras 159–66.
29 European Court of Human Rights, Cyprus *v.* Turkey, 10 May 2001, paras 157–8.
30 Inter-American Commission on Human Rights, Ignacio Ellacuria *et al. v.* El Salvador, report No. 136/99, case 10.488, 2 December 1999, para. 224.
31 Inter-American Court of Human Rights, Efraín Bámaca Velásquez *v.* Guatemala, vol. 91, Series C, 25 November 2000, para. 77. See also Inter-American Court of Human Rights, Caracazo *v.* Venezuela, vol. 95, Series C (Reparations), 29 August 2002, para. 118. See also Inter-American Commission on Human Rights, Monsenor Oscar Arnulfo Romero and Galdamez *v.* El Salvador, report No. 37/00, case 11.481, 13 April 2000, para. 148.
32 Inter-American Court of Human Rights, Myrna Mack-Chang *v.* Guatemala, vol. 101, Series C, 23 November 2003, para. 274.
33 Updated Set of Principles, Principle 2.
34 This discussion draws primarily on M. Freeman, *Truth Commissions and Procedural Fairness*, New York: Cambridge University Press, 2006; Hayner, *Unspeakable Truths*.
35 Freeman, *Truth Commissions*, p. 18.
36 Updated Set of Principles, Principle 5.
37 The Rule of Law and Transitional Justice in Conflict and Post-Conflict Societies: Report of the Secretary-General, UN Doc. S/2004/616 (2004).
38 Study on the Right to the Truth, UN Doc. E/CN.4/2006/91 (2006) para. 16.
39 Updated Set of Principles.
40 M. L. Popkin and N. Roht-Arriaza, 'Truth as Justice: Investigatory Commissions in Latin America', *Law & Social Inquiry*, 20, 1995, p. 38.
41 B.K. Dougherty, 'Searching for Answers: Sierra Leone's Truth & Reconciliation Commission', *African Studies Quarterly*, 8(1), 2004.
42 Hayner. *Unspeakable Truths*, pp. 223–4, p. 321
43 R. Ameh, 'Uncovering Truth: Ghana's National Reconciliation Commission Excavation of Past Human Rights Abuses', *Contemporary Justice Review*, 9, 2006.
44 Human Rights Watch, *World Report 2000*, 2000, Available at http://www.hrw.org/legacy/wr2k/ (accessed 18 September 2009).
45 For example, the final report of Ghana's National Reconciliation Commission (NRC) reported that approximately 90% of statement givers cited reparations as their reason for coming before the NRC. See National Reconciliation Commission Report, 2005, available at http://www.ghana.gov.gh/ghana/national_reconciliation_commission_report.jsp_0 (accessed 18 September 2009).
46 Study on the Right to the Truth, UN Doc. E/CN.4/2006/91 (2006).
47 Du Preez and Another *v.* Truth and Reconciliation Commission (426/96) [1997] ZASCA 2; 1997 (3) SA 204 (SCA); [1997] 2 All SA 1 (A) 18 February 1997.
48 Inter-American Commission on Human Rights, Consuelo *et al. v.* Argentina, report No. 28/92, Cases 10.147, 10.181, 10.240, 10.262, 10.309, and 10.311, 2 October 1992, para. 50.
49 J. Correa Sutil, 'Dealing with Past Human Rights Violations: The Chilean Case after Dictatorship', *The Notre Dame Law Review*, 67, 1992, pp. 1457–64.
50 P. B. Hayner, 'In Pursuit of Justice and Reconciliation: Contributions of Truth Telling', in C. J. Arnson (ed.), *Comparative Peace Processes in Latin America*, Washington, DC: Woodrow Wilson Center Press, 1999, p. 367.
51 M. Popkin, 'The Salvadoran Truth Commission and the Search for Justice', *Criminal Law Forum*, 15, 2004, pp. 105–24.
52 Ibid., p. 111.
53 Commission on the Truth for El Salvador, *From Madness to Hope: The 12-Year War in El Salvador*, New York: United Nations, 1993.
54 For a broader discussion, see W. A. Schabas, 'A Synergistic Relationship: The Sierra Leone Truth and Reconciliation Commission and the Special Court for Sierra Leone', in W. A. Schabas and S. Darcy

(eds), *Truth Commissions and Courts: The Tension between Criminal Justice and the Search for Truth*, Norwell, MA: Kluwer Academic, 2004, pp. 25–29.

55 W. A. Schabas, 'The Relationship between Truth Commissions and International Courts: The Case of Sierra Leone', *Human Rights Quarterly*, 25, 2003, p. 1049.

56 Report of the Secretary-General on the establishment of a Special Court for Sierra Leone, UN Doc. S/2000/915 (2000), para. 24.

57 Office of the Attorney General and Ministry of Justice Special Court Task Force, Briefing Paper on Relationship Between the Special Court and the Truth and Reconciliation Commission, Legal Analysis and Policy Considerations of the Government of Sierra Leone for the Special Court Planning Mission, available at http://www.specialcourt.org/documents/PlanningMission/BriefingPapers/SLGovTRC_SpCt_Relationship.pdf (accessed 16 September 2009), p. 9.

58 Special Court for Sierra Leone, Registry, Practice Direction on the procedure following a request by a National Authority or Truth and Reconciliation Commission to take a statement from a person in the custody of the Special Court for Sierra Leone, 9 September 2003, available at http://www.sc-sl.org/LinkClick.aspx?fileticket=8km93ZzghVU%3D&tabid=176 (accessed 16 September 2009).

59 Special Court for Sierra Leone, Prosecutor *v.* Norman (Case No. SCSL-2003-08-PT), Decision on Appeal by the Truth and Reconciliation Commission for Sierra Leone ('TRC' or 'The Commission') and Chief Samuel Hinga Norman JP Against the Decision of His Lordship, Mr Justice Bankole Thompson Delivered on 30 October 2003 to Deny the TRC's Request to Hold a Public Hearing with Chief Samuel Hinga Norman JP, 28 November 2003.

60 The Serious Crimes Unit's mandate could be interpreted to cover earlier abuses, but time and resources led it to focus on the events precipitating international intervention.

61 P. Burgess, 'Justice and Reconciliation in East Timor: The Relationship between the Commission for Reception, Truth and Reconciliation and the Courts', *Criminal Law Forum*, 15, 2004, pp. 135–58.

62 Ibid.

24

State responsibility and international crimes

Eric Wyler and León Arturo Castellanos-Jankiewicz

Introduction

Although the concept of 'international crimes' is widely employed in academic work and in the writings of many important publicists as forming part of the regime of general international law, it has entered the realms of international and domestic practice in a rather inconsistent manner. While domestic tribunals have found legal bases in international crimes for making reparations for gross violations of humanitarian law, international jurisdictions have been much more reluctant to use these rules to attribute state responsibility for the same violations. Therefore, a body of law trumping state immunity in favor of the claimant for alleged international crimes has developed in domestic jurisdictions, standing in sharp contrast with international tribunals' reluctance to expand the scope of state obligations arising from the commission of international crimes.

Moreover, political bodies such as the Security Council have adopted measures tantamount to judicial determinations and penal sanctions for serious breaches of international law that would seem to qualify as international crimes, raising questions of competence and legitimacy.

Recent developments in international law have unveiled a series of important relationships between the law of state responsibility and international criminal law, which, if articulated appropriately, shed light on the nature of states' obligations concerning international crimes. As will be argued, practice has been divergent but the legal and factual nature of international crimes themselves gives wide room for determining the legal obligations of states. The broad values that these obligations protect are regarded as universal, and their enforcement is considered essential for the preservation of international legality and justice.

This chapter addresses state responsibility in light of recent developments concerning international crimes. The first section of this chapter offers a historical overview of the concept of state crimes, as it was addressed in the International Law Commission (hereinafter ILC) and later rejected. The second section of this chapter considers developments in judicial practice that have addressed the relationships between state responsibility and individual criminal liability for international crimes. In so doing, this section analyzes the various relationships and overlaps between the law of state responsibility for internationally wrongful acts and the regime of individual criminal liability. Equating international state responsibility to individual criminal liability has been a current tendency, resulting in theoretical and practical problems. In the view of the present authors, these legal regimes remain distinct in their respective purposes and apply their own legal standards of attribution and proof.

The crime of state

The law of state responsibility for internationally wrongful acts does not recognize the 'crime of state' as part of its regime. States cannot be held criminally liable under international law, as the law of state responsibility has remained essentially reparational and not punitive in its scope. For many years, an aggravated regime of liability for international crimes committed by states was considered as a serious option in political and doctrinal circles. However, upon completion of the Articles on State Responsibility, the ILC did not include state crimes. In this first section we consider the general aspects of the debate surrounding crimes of state (also termed 'state crimes' in this chapter), the legal consequences arising from their commission, and their eventual fate in international law.

The crime of state in the ILC

In 1976, the second Special Rapporteur on State Responsibility, Roberto Ago, presented a proposal to the ILC that would ripple across the realms of international law, generating reactions ranging from doctrine, to politics, to diplomacy, thus launching one of the most controversial debates that has touched upon the most essential aspects of contemporary international law-making and progressive development of international rules to this day.

The proposal in question concerned the introduction of Article 19[1] to the Draft Articles on State Responsibility, which sought to establish an aggravated regime of state responsibility for the violation of 'international obligations so essential for the protection of the interests of the international community as a whole, that their breach was recognized as a crime under international law'.[2]

A preliminary consideration must be underlined. The law of international state responsibility addresses the consequences arising from the breach of international obligations. Primary obligations trigger the law of state responsibility, i.e. obligations owed among states under inter-national law, whereas secondary obligations deal with the consequences arising from the breach of primary obligations. The law of international state responsibility is exclusively concerned with secondary obligations. It does not attempt to codify the entirety of international obligations owed among states, as this would be a daunting task. Therefore, only the consequences arising out of the breach of a primary obligation belong to the law of state responsibility.[3] However, Article 19 was an important exception to this rule, attempting to codify peremptory norms. The approach of defining state crimes objectively as breaches of obligations that are essential for the protection of interests of the international community was a step forward from the definition given to the character of *jus cogens* norms, which the Vienna Convention on the Law of Treaties determined not by their content but by their effect: namely, the impossibility to derogate from them by special agreement.[4] It could be argued that Ago's codification of crimes largely reflected customary international law at the time, with the probable exception of environmental obligations, which developed later in time. By defining the consequences of the breach of peremptory norms, a higher degree of legal security and certainty would have emerged, as opposed to the practical difficulties of applying the negative definition of *jus cogens* norms offered in the Vienna Convention. In sum, the main legal feature of Article 19 was to establish an 'aggravated regime'[5] of state responsibility for a serious breach of essential obligations: namely, the prohibition of aggression, the right to self-determination, the proscription of colonial domination, slavery, genocide, apartheid, and the protection of the environment.

Roberto Ago's introduction of Article 19 is circumscribed within important historical and legal developments at the time, which are properly recalled in his Fifth Report. The evolution of international law from classical bilateralism to community interest[6] had already surfaced prominently in the International Court of Justice's (hereinafter ICJ) 1970 *Barcelona Traction* judgment, which famously recognized the existence of obligations *erga omnes*, in the protection of which all states have a legal interest.[7] Ago noted that 'at least in certain circumstances, another form of responsibility could be substituted for the obligation to make reparation, and subjects of international law other than the one directly injured could be entitled to invoke the responsibility flowing from the wrongful act'.[8] This led him to conclude that, in principle, international jurisprudence supported the existence of two separate regimes of international state responsibility depending on the subject matter of the international obligation breached and consequently, that there were two different types of internationally wrongful acts of the state.[9] Grave breaches would be called international crimes, while other internationally wrongful acts not amounting to international crimes would constitute international delicts.

Moreover, the distinction between crimes and delicts was favored by those who believed that the commission of genocide, on the one hand, and the non-payment of a commercial obligation, on the other, should be treated differently by the law of state responsibility.[10] As clearly stated by Bernhard Graefrath,

> today it is not possible seriously to dispute that it makes a difference under international law whether a State is not fulfilling its obligation to pay interests for a loan or whether it launched a war against its neighbor .... Obviously, there are different categories of violations of international law which entail different legal consequences.[11]

A second development contributing to the conception of state crime was the enshrinement of the non-derogability of *jus cogens* norms in Article 53 of the 1969 Vienna Convention on the Law of Treaties,[12] according to which the content of *jus cogens* rules is so important to the international community that derogation from those rules by special agreement is prohibited.[13] This provision establishes that *jus cogens* norms require the application of superior standards for ascertaining the existence of community consensus as regards both the content and the peremptory character of the relevant rules.[14] As a corollary, Special Rapporteur Ago concluded that it was unlikely that the development concerning the inadmissibility of derogations from certain rules should not have been accompanied by a parallel development in the sphere of state responsibility. He observed that '[i]ndeed, it would seem contradictory if the same consequences continued to be applied to the breach of obligations arising out of the rules defined as "peremptory" and to the breach of obligations arising out of rules from which derogation by special agreement is permitted'.[15]

Thus, Ago's crime of state proposal relied heavily on the *erga omnes* dimension of international law, and the values-oriented approach of vesting *jus cogens* norms with a higher degree of protection and a hierarchical pre-eminence in the international legal order.

Impact of state crimes on international state responsibility

In the years that followed its introduction to the Draft Articles on State Responsibility, the concept of state crimes was widely debated in doctrine and academic works.[16] The topic eventually became controversial and highly polarized, resulting in numerous debates on the subject.[17] The following sub-sections will deal with the systemic implications of state crimes, taking this diversity of opinions into account.

Aggravated state responsibility for crimes as distinguished from domestic criminal law

The concept of crimes of state was not presented by Roberto Ago as an analogy to domestic criminal law. He did not seek criminalization of state acts in a stigmatizing sense. By introducing Article 19, he sought to establish an aggravated regime of state responsibility for breaches of the most important values in international society. As noted by Professor Georges Abi-Saab, by attaching severe consequences to the violation of these norms, Article 19 introduced a fundamental distinction between various norms of international law, as well as a certain hierarchy among them.[18]

This regime of aggravated responsibility did not have punitive consequences as a primary goal, as it aimed to guarantee international legality through pre-existing mechanisms of pressure and dispute settlement, without being analogous to domestic criminal procedure.[19]

Similarly, nowhere do we find that material damage, a common element of crimes in the domestic sphere, is indispensable to trigger international responsibility for state crimes. Whether material damage is required depends on the nature of the primary obligation breached, and there is no general rule,[20] although it is difficult to imagine crimes like genocide, slavery or apartheid being perpetrated without inflicting injury to private individuals. However, in the law of international state responsibility, 'the damage is implicitly bound up with the anti-legal nature of the act. To violate the rule is indeed always a disturbance of the interest it protects, and thus, of the subjective right of the person whose interest it is'.[21] This is especially the case for such serious violations as international crimes. As former ILC member Paul Reuter rightly noted, 'Legal terms detach themselves from their municipal moorings to acquire contours and import, more consonant with the structure and functions of international law'.[22]

Despite his important efforts, Ago left the question of the consequences arising from commission of state crimes largely open, following his nomination to the ICJ in 1979. These issues were broached in the following years by his successors, most notably Gaetano Arangio-Ruiz, Special Rapporteur on State Responsibility from 1987 to 1996.

The difficulties of harmonizing crimes of state with international normativity

While Roberto Ago got as far as establishing which wrongful acts would be considered crimes of state, Arangio-Ruiz continued the project by addressing the determination and legal attribution of state crimes. He observed that the UN Security Council, the ICJ or the UN General Assembly acting alone could not properly discharge individually 'the delicate function of determining the existence of an international crime of State and its attribution as prerequisites for the implementation of the consequences contemplated'.[23] His solution laid in making a combined use of the political and judicial elements of the UN system. Under his proposed scheme, the General Assembly or the Security Council would adopt a resolution by a qualified majority alleging that an international crime had been committed. This would pave the way for involvement of the ICJ in its advisory capacity, with a referral either by the General Assembly or the Security Council.[24] Alternatively, according to Arangio-Ruiz, the Court could be seized in its contentious function through a jurisdictional link created by a resolution of the Assembly or the Council by virtue of the envisaged Convention on State Responsibility.[25] In turn, the Court would pronounce itself on the matter, making a judicial determination on the existence of a state crime and ordering the corresponding reparations to be made, if state responsibility had been established.

Special Rapporteur Arangio-Ruiz favored the contentious approach of the ICJ over its advisory function, mainly because of the seriousness of alleged state crimes and the important legal consequences deriving from judicial attribution of state responsibility and the eventual obligation to make reparations. In his view, the findings of the Court would have carried more much weight following a pronouncement resulting from the jurisdictional confrontation between the parties, as opposed to the nature of an advisory opinion, which does not necessitate the existence of a legal dispute.[26]

The proposals described above were received with sharp criticism from states to the effect that mechanisms were already in place within the international system to deal with state crimes, as will be presented below.

Contribution of crimes of state in collective security

We now address the legal and political problems that were encountered when attempting to integrate state crimes into the international legal order of collective security. The obligations established by Article 19 largely coincided with the purposes and principles safeguarded by the Security Council, which makes the regime of collective security an ideal yardstick to evaluate the difficulties of holding states responsible for crimes.

Contrary to national legal systems, the corpus of international law is not equipped with procedures entirely appropriate for its direct execution. Many enforcement mechanisms may be envisaged that depend upon the nature of the obligation owed or contravened. The affirmation that a breached norm forms part of *jus cogens*, for example, still reveals very little about the legal effects of such an infraction.[27] The lack of centralized bodies in international law to legislate and enforce international norms as a unified system has always been a problem concerning compliance. Additionally, the multiplicity of international actors and the fragmentation of international law arising from its diversification and expansion contribute to the creation of regimes that do not apply the same legal and factual standards.[28]

For these reasons, the consequences arising out of the commission of state crimes were seriously considered by the ILC, and divergence arose between states in the General Assembly Sixth Committee concerning the practical aspects of the state crimes regime, particularly the role of the Security Council.

The authoritative work done by Marina Spinedi concerning the legislative history of state crimes offers an excellent overview of states' diverging positions concerning the consequences resulting from crimes of state:

> Italy maintained that 'the existence of an international crime could be entrusted only to a supreme international political or juridical body'. The Netherlands, Spain and Chile strongly recommended compulsory recourse to the International Court of Justice. Brazil requested that the Security Council should be made competent where all other means of settlement have failed. Against the latter suggestion, Zaire pointed out that the Security Council could be paralyzed if one of the parties to the dispute belonged to the block of one or the other super-power. Venezuela maintained that if such a power were to be given to the Security Council, the Charter would have to be amended.[29]

This wide range of views is certainly mind-boggling. Some states rightly felt that Security Council measures could not be termed forms of responsibility, as noted by France when asserting that Chapter VII was applicable even against states that hadn't committed internationally wrongful acts. Therefore, use of these measures could not constitute a special form of responsibility for international crimes, given that measures in Chapter VII of the Charter did not operate within the regime of state responsibility.[30] This view highlights the distinction between the regime of state responsibility and that of collective security.

Other proposals suggested granting complete competence to the Security Council for the observance of the state crimes. In a fitting article,[31] Special Rappoteur Arangio-Ruiz rejected this alternative by arguing for the removal of draft Article 39 from the Draft Articles on State Responsibility which was eventually discarded and reads as follows:

> Article 39
> The legal consequences of an internationally wrongful act of a State set out in the provisions of this Part [Two] are subject, as appropriate, to the provisions and procedures of the Charter of the United Nations relating to the maintenance of international peace and security.[32]

This draft article would have subjected the legal consequences of state crimes to the regime of collective security, consequently to be handled by the Security Council, a predominantly political body. In his article, Arangio-Ruiz rightly pointed out that

> The presence of a disposition like Article 39 would create a subordination of the draft Articles—and of the customary law of State responsibility that would survive those articles—not only to the UN Charter provisions, whose purpose is not to govern state responsibility, but also to the powers of a political organ that has no competence in that area of international law.[33]

He added that postponing determination of consequences arising out of internationally wrongful acts had already created a vacuum in the law of state responsibility which the Security Council would hastily fill by exercising powers in an area that was not within its sphere of competence.[34] This concern was also raised in the Sixth Committee by countries such as Japan, Australia and Spain.[35]

Some suggested that after cessation of the violation was obtained from the transgressor state, there was little difference between the consequences deriving from serious breaches and the consequences of ordinary wrongful acts,[36] while others argued that the Security Council was not able to deal with crimes of state under existing Charter provisions, in light of the Council's resolutions adopted after Iraq's invasion of Kuwait in 1991.[37]

Concerning this point, it is pertinent to address the Security Council's practice in order to determine whether the concept of state crimes contributed to the maintenance of international legality before their removal from the Draft Articles on State Responsibility in 1998. It would seem that UN Security Council Resolution 687 imposing sanctions on Iraq following its invasion of Kuwait in 1991, was tantamount to treating the actions of the Iraqi state as criminal, due to the 'punitive'[38] nature of the sanctions imposed, most importantly through the UN Compensation Commission (hereinafter UNCC). The UNCC was created for claims arising out of direct loss, damage or injury to foreign governments, nationals and corporations resulting from the unlawful invasion and occupation of Kuwait.[39] The Council also held Iraq liable for environmental damage and depletion of environmental resources—the first time such a pre-eminent body addressed environmental issues within the realm of reparations—though no mention was made of Article 19 or state crimes.

Indeed, Resolution 687 stated that Iraq was 'liable under international law'[40] for all damages caused, without categorizing the violations of international law as crimes. However, to affirm liability reveals little about causation and attribution, which are necessary to determine responsibility. No causal link was made between the damages and the obligation to make reparations, even though the Council did not hesitate to make an extra-judicial determination.

The Security Council is not empowered to make judicial determinations, nor does it enjoy the capacity to legally attribute a wrongful act to a state. As pointed out by Rosalyn Higgins, former President of the ICJ,

> [w]hether it would be wise or prudent for the Security Council to move ... into the heart of what we normally see as judicial activity—that is to say, functions that tribunals are by their training and experience and familiarity with the relevant norms very well placed to carry out—must be doubtful.[41]

Moreover, the institutional legitimacy of the UNCC has been criticized,[42] as Iraq was not represented in the proceedings, nor was it entitled to appear as a party, although it was able to present its views before the Commission's Governing Council. Nonetheless, due process of law was not observed, as the Iraqi government did not have access to the identity of the claimants or the legal briefs submitted.[43] The fact that Iraq was found to be liable 'under international law' (in the words of Resolution 687) adds to the confusion, given that no legal basis was provided to support this statement.

As it is, the UNCC is one of the largest reparations frameworks established by the international community through the Security Council. By 30 October 2008, the UN Compensation Commission had awarded compensation for a total of 1,543,619 claims, amounting to US$52,383,356,715 in awards.[44] Despite this, the Security Council did not even qualify Iraq's intervention in Kuwait as an act of aggression. It goes without saying that the Security Council never went as far as characterizing Iraq's actions as state crimes.

Another instance in which state crimes could have surfaced as a form of attributing state responsibility was during the 1998–2000 Eritrea–Ethiopia conflict, in which the Security Council only went as far as condemning the recourse to the use of force by Ethiopia and Eritrea without qualifying the conflict as a threat to the peace, a breach of the peace or an act of aggression in accordance with the UN Charter.[45] State crimes never appeared in the various Security Council resolutions addressing the conflict[46] or during the proceedings of the Eritrea–Ethiopia Claims Commission[47] and its awards.

The Eritrea–Ethiopia Commission's mandate was to decide, through binding arbitration, all claims that were related to the conflict for loss, damage or injury by the parties and their nationals, as a result of violations of international humanitarian law, including the 1949 Geneva Conventions.[48] The Commission rendered its final awards on 17 August 2009, in which the total compensation awarded to Eritrea with respect to its claims was US$161,455,000 and the amount awarded with respect to claims presented on behalf of individuals was US$2,065,865 due to Ethiopia's violation of *jus in bello*.[49] In turn, Eritrea was found to have violated *jus ad bellum* and *jus in bello*, and the Claims Commission awarded Ethiopia US$174,036,520.[50]

These examples suggest that despite the commission of wrongful acts amounting to aggression, these acts have been dealt with through different legal avenues, most importantly by ascribing liability to the responsible parties, but without addressing state crimes. Whereas the UNCC was a body established by the UN Security Council, by virtue of a quasi-judicial attribution of liability, the Eritrea–Ethiopia Claims Commission was created with the consent of the states involved and enjoyed jurisdiction to entertain the claims stemming from a common Agreement.

In conclusion, it cannot be affirmed that the aggravated responsibility regime of state crimes existed at some given moment within the competences of the Security Council. State crimes did not percolate into the regime of collective security. The question that remains open is how collective security could have functioned within the purview of state crimes, had they been adopted by the ILC as an aggravated regime of state responsibility. One could begin by considering the common ground between the regimes of collective security and state responsibility for international crimes in the UN charter. The purposes and principles of the UN Charter spell out the most essential common values of contemporary international society. From a bird's eye view, these values largely coincide with the interests protected by Article 19: the peaceful settlement of disputes and the prohibition of the use of force are enshrined in Article 2(3) and Article 2(4), respectively; the right to self-determination of people is protected by Article 1(2); and the protection of the individual and human rights are invoked in Article 1(3).

Indeed, there is a relationship between the purposes and principles of the UN and Article 19. The Security Council's main features as a collective enforcement entity are also largely spelled out in Articles 1 and 2. The functions of the Security Council, especially those conferred to it under Chapter VII concerning the use of force, are already envisaged in these dispositions. This connection was described by Roberto Ago in his Fifth Report, in which he seems to suggest that already Article 1(1) of the Charter opens the door to the collective enforcement measures under Chapter VII.[51] If not opening the door *per se*, Article 1 certainly contains the magic words to unlock it:

> The Purposes of the United Nations are
> 1. To maintain international peace and security, and to that end: to take effective collective measures for the prevention and removal of threats to the peace and for the suppression of acts of aggression or other breaches of the peace.

The opening Article of Chapter VII reads, in its first part, as follows: 'The Security Council shall determine the existence of any threat to the peace, breach of the peace, or act of aggression'.[52] Finally, according to Article 24(2) of the Charter, the Security Council shall act in accordance with the purposes and principles of the United Nations, which have been universally accepted by states.[53]

A clear distinction must be drawn between the dispute settlement mechanisms outlined in Chapter VI and peace enforcement, which is the main feature of Chapter VII. The pacific settlement of disputes contemplated in Chapter VI is outlined in Article 33(1) and comprises negotiation, enquiry, mediation, conciliation, arbitration, judicial settlement, resort to regional agencies or arrangements and any other means that states may find convenient. Action under Chapter VII is designed to take place when the pacific settlement of disputes has failed or could not have been used, as in some cases of urgency such as aggression. However, it was understood during the San Francisco Conference that the applicability of Chapter VII did not necessitate the enforcement of the settlement mechanisms contained in Chapter VI,[54] as evidenced by Article 33(2), according to which the Council 'shall' call upon the parties to a dispute to settle it by the peaceful means outlined in paragraph one 'when it deems necessary'.

These observations highlight the direct quantum leap from the purposes and principles of the UN Charter to the collective security system envisaged by the Charter's framers: the Charter aims to centralize control of the use of force within the Security Council[55] in order to safeguard the purposes and principles. But in reality, it is jumping the gun. It would seem that the system is lacking a step between Chapters VI and VII. The absence of a middle ground is manifest if one considers that there is no specific rule calling for the compulsory exhaustion of measures enlisted in Chapter VI before the Council can use Chapter VII measures. The Council is free to make its own determinations *ab initio* through Article 39. The lack of this transitional stage is painfully manifest if one considers aspects of international procedure and legality, such as those concerning the UNCC.

It is submitted here that crimes of state attempted to fill this gap by connecting the essential values of the international community to the collective security system through the assertion and protection of fundamental obligations within the law of state responsibility. Just as the collective security system asserts these values through the purposes and principles of the United Nations, state crimes would have served as the same foundation for the law of international state responsibility.

Most importantly, Article 19 would have tempered and complemented the action of the Security Council when vying for the protection of these values. Even though international responsibility and the maintenance of peace and security operate distinctly, legal attribution of responsibility has practical consequences, some of which lie within the competence of the Security Council. Similarly, the Council lacks a framework to legally attribute internationally wrongful acts.

An example of these relationships can be observed in the separate and simultaneous treatment in the ICJ and the Security Council of particular situations. This issue arose in the context of aggression in the *Nicaragua* case. Here, the United States objected that the matter was essentially one for the Council to consider, and therefore, that the Court had no jurisdiction. In response, the ICJ was of the view that 'the fact that a matter is before the Security Council should not prevent it being dealt with by the Court', and consequently, 'both proceedings could be pursued *pari passu*'.[56] The Court further noted that '[t]he argument of the United States as to the powers of the Security Council and of the Court is an attempt to transfer municipal-law concepts of separation of powers to the international plane, whereas these concepts are not applicable to the relations among international institutions for the settlement of disputes'.[57] In these passages, the Court highlighted that its decisions and those of the Security Council are not interdependent, but that each operate within different institutional frameworks. This is further confirmed in the *Diplomatic and Consular Staff* case, where the Court observed that in Resolution 461, while being actively seized of the matter concerning the diplomatic crisis in Tehran, the Security Council

> expressly took into account the Court's order of 15 December 1979 indicating provisional measures; and it does not seem to have occurred to any member of the Council that there was or could be anything irregular in the simultaneous exercise of their respective functions by the Court and the Security Council. Nor is there in this any cause for surprise.[58]

Removal from the Draft Articles on State Responsibility

In his First Report on State Responsibility, Special Rapporteur James Crawford argued for the removal of international crimes of state from the Draft Articles on State Responsibility as a concession to various state representatives in the Sixth Committee of the UN General Assembly. In doing so, he underlined the absence of procedural guarantees associated with international crimes.[59] He further noted that the Draft Articles did not describe the consequences of international crimes, nor did they lay down any procedure for determining that a crime had been committed.[60] He also warned against the risk of terminological confusion with international crimes committed by individuals.[61] Finally, one of his most persuasive arguments was that state responsibility would be relegated to a residual role when attempting to codify peremptory norms.[62] In dealing with international crimes, the ILC favored a regime of state responsibility of an objective legal nature, which would dictate the consequences of violations to obligations having an *erga omnes* character, as well as *jus cogens* norms, through rules of attribution that were laid down in Articles 40, 41, 42 and 48 of the Articles on State Responsibility, as adopted by the ILC in its 2001 Session.[63]

The desire to have a unique objective regime of international law for state responsibility was one of the main reasons for the removal of state crimes. However, Part Two of the Articles, which addresses the content of the international responsibility of a state, creates an aggravated regime for 'serious breaches of obligations under peremptory norms of general international law' by virtue of Articles 40 and 41. According to some commentators, the state crime was simply replaced by this definition,[64] hardly differing, *ratione materiae*, from Roberto Ago's proposal.[65] Articles 40 and 41 reintroduce a second category of responsibility with special legal effects. In other words, these Articles created an aggravated regime of responsibility composed of norms that are different from the general regime of non-qualified objective responsibility.[66] The commentary to the Articles identifies several 'clearly accepted' peremptory norms, which largely coincide with Ago's crimes of state: namely, the prohibitions of aggression, genocide, slavery, racial discrimination, crimes against humanity, torture and the right to self determination. Furthermore, this list is non-exhaustive.[67] Article 40 reads as follows:

1 This chapter applies to the international responsibility which is entailed by a serious breach by a State of an obligation arising under a peremptory norm of general international law.
2 A breach of such an obligation is serious if it involves a gross or systematic failure by the responsible State to fulfill the obligation.

By invoking peremptory norms, the definition relies on the notion of *jus cogens* to define serious breaches. This brings the problem back to square one, as the consequences of the breach in Article 40 are defined by the non-derogable effect of *jus cogens* norms and not by their cause or nature, as was specified previously by Article 19(2). Furthermore, 'Article 40 does not lay down any procedure for determining whether or not a breach has been committed'.[68] The commentary to the Articles adds that serious breaches are 'likely to be addressed by the competent international organizations including the Security Council and the General Assembly',[69] which does not preclude a powerful state from determining that there has been a gross or systematic breach of a peremptory norm and acting unilaterally.[70]

The ultimate elimination of state crimes from the Articles on State Responsibility has not completely removed the criminal connotations states intended to fend off. As a result of the rapid evolution of individual criminal liability through international criminal tribunals, there has been a predisposition to undertake the analysis of state responsibility for international crimes through the prism of international criminal law.[71] Moreover, several principles of individual criminal liability have been imported lock, stock and barrel to attribution and causation tests of state responsibility for international crimes by some tribunals. Finally, international tribunals have tried to articulate the relationships between individual liability and state responsibility for international crimes, and have produced important *dicta* concerning these interactions, even though many questions remain. The following section of this chapter will consider these developments.

State responsibility for international crimes

Since the Nuremberg trials, the international community has accentuated the role of individual criminal liability. Theories absorbing individual criminal liability into state responsibility have been eroded by the creation of the International Criminal Tribunal for the former Yugoslavia (hereinafter ICTY) and the International Criminal Tribunal for Rwanda (hereinafter ICTR) along with their jurisprudential development, which has culminated in the establishment of the International Criminal Court (hereinafter ICC).[72] This progress has not materialized in the law of state responsibility.[73] Therefore, the rules and instruments applying to individual criminal liability have grown in number and generally enjoy the political favor of states, which stands in contrast with governments' reluctance to adopt progressive views on state responsibility, as shown with Article 19 earlier.

Given that there is no formal recognition of the concept of 'state crimes' in international law, institutions, academicians and jurisdictions have resorted to the term 'international crimes' instead. Practice has been divergent when articulating the relationship between state responsibility and individual criminal liability for international crimes. This can be explained by the fact that, although individual criminal liability and state responsibility for international crimes may originate from the same factual complex, and both legal regimes are inspired and sustained by the same values, such as the *jus cogens* and *erga omnes* character of the norms they protect, they pursue different objectives. Indeed, state responsibility is primarily invoked to obtain reparations, while criminal liability is associated with an individual's punishment. Finally, individuals committing international crimes may do so in connection with the functions they perform as agents of the state. These common denominators make it hard to dissociate state responsibility and individual criminal liability for international crimes, and one could hastily conclude that concurrent responsibility for international crimes arises in every case. The situation gains complexity when the same primary rules address states and individuals alike. In the case of genocide, according to the interpretation of the ICJ, states and individuals can be held responsible for this international crime based on the same instrument. This leads to the application to states and individuals of similar responsibility tests and standards of proof for genocide. However, in this case, the primary norms are not formulated to address state responsibility and are more oriented towards individual criminal liability, as is shown by the subjective element of this crime[74] (*dolus specialis*), enshrined in the ICC Statute[75] and the Genocide Convention.[76]

As a result, criminal law tests have been used to determine state responsibility in order to satisfy the requirements of the relevant instruments.[77] To a certain degree, this has subjected the responsibility of the state to that of the individual. All these problems have led some observers to acknowledge that 'international law in its present form does not adequately deal with the role of systems in international crimes',[78] which can be said for the relationships between the law of state responsibility and individual criminal liability, as will be discussed below.

The core international crimes

The commission of international crimes is widely proscribed through relevant instruments that belong to the realms of general and customary international law. Aggression, genocide, crimes against humanity and war crimes all qualify as international crimes and are prohibited in international law. Most recently, torture has also been categorized as a distinct international crime which could entail individual criminal liability and state responsibility.[79] States and individuals alike have the obligation to abide by the relevant primary norms that proscribe these crimes, and both states and individuals can be held responsible for their violation. It is rather difficult to determine which crimes would entail solely individual or state responsibility. Some scholars have nonetheless tried to establish a categorization in order to identify these situations. According to Beatrice Bonafè, three main possibilities arise:

- Crimes defined in terms of pure individual conduct will result only in individual criminal liability.

- At the other end of the spectrum, certain international crimes need a preliminary determination of state conduct to proceed with the prosecution of individuals, as would be the case for aggression.
- The middle ground is the most complex and encompasses crimes whose prohibited conduct can only be carried out at a collective level, such as genocide and crimes against humanity.[80]

It is within this middle ground that the collective entity can engage the responsibility of individuals, that of a state or both. In the following sections, these problems will be highlighted and discussed, and it is submitted that a clear distinction between the regimes of international state responsibility and individual criminal liability are needed when considering these international crimes.

Aggression

The progressive outlawing of aggression in multilateral treaties, beginning with the Briand–Kellogg Pact[81] and Article 10 of the Covenant of the League of Nations in 1928 and 1929, respectively, has culminated in the prohibition of the use of force as a rule of customary international law, enshrined in Article 2(4) of the UN Charter. Furthermore, General Assembly Resolution 3314 defines and characterizes aggression as a 'crime against international peace',[82] as does the Declaration on Principles of International Law concerning Friendly Relations and Co-operation among States in accordance with the Charter of the United Nations, which asserts that state responsibility arises under international law for aggression.[83] Moreover, the ICJ qualified the prohibition of the use of force as a 'fundamental or cardinal principle' of customary international law in the *Nicaragua* case.[84] Finally, in the *Construction of a Wall* advisory opinion, the Court concluded that the illegality of territorial acquisition resulting from the threat or use of force reflected customary international law.[85] All these dispositions are addressed to states, but the ICC will be competent to deal with the crime of aggression when a definition of the term is reached by the states parties pursuant to Article 5(1)(d) of its Statute, potentially giving rise to individual and state responsibility for the same wrongful act, albeit within different regimes of international law. It should be highlighted that any definition of aggression adopted for the ICC Statute will be addressed to individuals.

Genocide

Concerning genocide, Articles II and III of the Convention on the Prevention and Punishment of the Crime of Genocide outlaw the commission of genocide, conspiracy, incitement and attempt to commit genocide, as well as complicity in genocide. The terms 'conspiracy', 'attempt' and 'complicity' in Article III, which are commonly reserved for criminal law, accentuate the responsibility of public officials and private individuals. Obligations of states are outlined in subsequent articles: Article IV calls on states parties to punish individuals responsible for genocide, and pursuant to Article V, the contracting parties undertake to enact legislation to give effect to the Convention and to provide effective penalties for persons guilty of genocide. Finally, Article VI of the Convention calls for the prosecution of persons charged with the crime of genocide. The Preamble of the Genocide Convention characterizes genocide as a 'crime' by invoking Resolution 96(I) of the General Assembly, which affirms that the commission of genocide by individuals is a crime under international law.[86] Moreover, the *ad hoc* Tribunals for Yugoslavia and Rwanda reproduce *ad pedem litterae* the dispositions established in Articles II and III of the Genocide Convention concerning the definition of genocide, its elements and the punishable acts that render individuals liable. Finally, Article 6 of the Rome Statute also transcribes Article III of the Genocide Convention when defining genocide.

At first glance, the Genocide Convention seems to be an instrument whose primary objective is to hold private individuals accountable for the commission of genocide, while obliging states to cooperate in punishing and preventing genocide. However, Article IX, the dispute settlement clause, has given way to varied interpretations. It reads as follows:

> Disputes between the Contracting Parties relating to interpretation, application or fulfillment of the present Convention, including those relating to the *responsibility of a State* for genocide or any other acts enumerated in Article III, shall be submitted to the International Court of Justice at the request of any of the parties to the dispute.[87]

During the preliminary objections phase of the Genocide case, the ICJ interpreted this disposition as widening the Convention's scope of application to states by concluding that Article IX 'does not exclude any form of State responsibility'.[88] In its judgment on the merits, the Court admitted that the states parties were not under the express obligation to refrain from committing genocide according to the actual terms of the Genocide Convention[89] but stated that

> it would be paradoxical if States were thus under an obligation to prevent … but were not forbidden to commit such acts through their own organs or persons over whom they have such firm control that their conduct is attributable to the State concerned under international law.[90]

The Court concluded that the contracting parties 'may be responsible for genocide and other acts enumerated in Article III of the Convention.[91] With this statement, the Court, willingly or not, rendered the relationship between individual criminal liability and state responsibility for the commission of genocide highly interdependent. When reading the passage, one has the impression that state responsibility for genocide has a heavy reliance on whether an individual has been found guilty of committing genocide,[92] but state responsibility for genocide is not directly dependent on findings of individual criminal liability. Inversely, when an individual is found guilty of genocide, this does not necessarily mean that there is a state plan or policy according to which the person acted, as this is not an essential component of the crime of genocide at the individual level. To be found guilty of genocide, an individual's conduct must be circumscribed within a collective organization which systematically carries out the heinous acts.[93] The question of whether this collective conduct is attributed to a state or not, and whether it amounts to state acts, is a separate one. Indeed, individual criminal responsibility has slowly dissociated itself from state responsibility, to the point that both regimes operate independently.[94] The autonomy of individual criminal liability in the case of genocide was recognized by the ILC in its 1996 Draft Code of Crimes against the Peace and Security of Mankind,[95] which deals with international crimes exclusively in terms of individual criminal liability and adopts the same definition for genocide as the Genocide Convention.

As the Court's only basis for jurisdiction, the Genocide Convention was the sole instrument upon which it was authorized to make its findings.[96] Thus, it was unable to apply customary international law, which prohibits the commission of genocide on the part of states and distinguishes itself in content from the norms primarily oriented towards establishing individual criminal liability in the Genocide Convention. This customary rule for states is evidenced by the work of the ILC[97] and the ICJ's *Armed Activities on the Territory of the Congo* judgment, in which the Court recognized that the prohibition of genocide has a *jus cogens* character.[98] Indeed, the content of these customary norms is addressed to states. By determining that states are precluded from committing genocide in light of the Genocide Convention, the Court was obligated to apply responsibility tests primarily designed for individuals, which require *mens rea* and *actus reus* to be present as elements of the international crime.

It is not contested that material acts are necessary for a state to carry out genocide, but it is highly impracticable to integrate the psychological element of *mens rea*, which the ICJ called 'specific intent' in the *Genocide* case, into a state responsibility attribution test, just as it would be erroneous to equate a state's genocidal systematic plan or policy to the criminal intent of an individual. This reasoning also follows *a contrario*, since there is no need to determine the existence of a state's genocidal plan to hold its agents responsible for genocide, as evidenced by Article II of the Genocide Convention and the Statutes of the *ad hoc* criminal Tribunals and the ICC. Despite this, the ICJ concluded that the definition of genocide in Article II of the Convention comprises mental elements such as 'deliberateness' and the 'intent to destroy in whole or in part' a protected group.[99] According to this interpretation, it is not enough to demonstrate that persons were targeted because they belong to a group to engage state responsibility. The state's intent of destroying the group in whole or in part must be proved. With the exception of the massacre in Srebrenica,[100] the Court did not find this specific intent in the numerous camps and municipalities, although it had concluded that the material element required for crimes against humanity and war crimes had been satisfied.[101] However, the Court did not enjoy jurisdiction to entertain these claims. Furthermore, in determining *dolus specialis*, the Court's methodology relied heavily on ICTY jurisprudence. In doing so, the Court analyzed factual evidence on a case-by-case basis in light of ICTY judgments that had addressed the same factual complex but which did not find individual criminal liability for genocide. In turn, the ICJ concluded that genocide had not been committed in each of these instances, with the exception of Srebrenica. International criminal tribunals do not enjoy much leeway when considering gross and systemic violations because they are designed to examine individual conduct. Their procedures and findings have relevance insofar as they address the facts and situations surrounding the alleged criminal's conduct. In other words, international criminal courts only need satisfy themselves with proof of the individual's guilt, in which case it is hard for these tribunals to consider conduct beyond that of the alleged criminal. The ICJ, on the other hand, enjoys a wider scope when considering systemic violations, but it did not fully articulate this capacity in the *Genocide* case when relying heavily on the outcomes of ICTY judgments and decisions. This methodology also sheds light upon the inherent difficulties of attempting to attribute *dolus specialis* to a state by examining the conduct of individuals.

By finding that serious violations of international law had been committed but concluding that these did not amount to genocide, and by incorporating psychological elements to state responsibility tests, the Court has placed the threshold of proof for genocide extremely high. Indeed, 'the standard of proof in interstate proceedings is different and generally lower than the standard applying in cases of individual responsibility. It is based on the balance of evidence submitted by both parties rather than on the "beyond a reasonable doubt" threshold'.[102] Moreover, the ICJ's handling of ICTY judgments seems to be an incomplete test, as these decisions should have been considered as framing the overall circumstances of the case and not in direct connection with the outcomes of individuals' trials. Once again, the responsibility of the state for genocide seems highly dependent on that of individuals according to the Court's methodology.

An alternative to applying psychological criteria as constitutive elements of the crime of genocide, as some scholars have posited, would be to prove that 'because of the overall pattern of violence, the ultimate goal of the policy of the state cannot but be that of destroying the targeted group as such'.[103] A variant of this systematic view was advanced by the Applicant of the *Genocide* case on the basis of the genocidal pattern of camp practices and their similarity throughout the territory within a specific timeframe, observing that the 'human and cultural destruction looks indeed similar from 1991 through 1999. These acts were perpetrated as the expression of one single project, which basically and effectively included the destruction in whole or in part of the non-Serb group'.[104] The Applicant was clearly distancing itself from the conduct of individual perpetrators to the organized framework reflecting the intent of higher authority.[105] The Court rejected this contention by noting that the existence of a general genocidal plan had not been demonstrated:

> specific intent to destroy the group in whole or in part, has to be convincingly shown by reference to particular circumstances, unless a general plan to that end can be convincingly demonstrated to exist; and for a pattern of conduct to be accepted as evidence of its existence, it would have to be such that it could only point to the existence of such intent.[106]

What the Court meant by 'particular circumstances' in this passage is not clear, nor does the Court develop on the nature of 'patterns' which would necessarily point to the existence of *dolus specialis*.

Be that as it may, the Court acknowledged the duality of state and individual responsibility as 'a constant feature in international law'[107] by invoking Article 25(4) of the ICC Statute, which stipulates that '[n]o provision in this Statute relating to individual criminal responsibility shall affect the responsibility of States under international law', and Article 58 of the ILC Articles on the Responsibility of States for Internationally Wrongful Acts, which asserts that the Articles are 'without prejudice to any question of the individual responsibility under international law of any person acting on behalf of a State'.

All these considerations lead to the conclusion that the primary and secondary norms addressing individuals and states concerning genocide must be distinguished. This is evidenced by the fact that individual criminal liability arises from fault and intention and seeks punishment, while state responsibility finds its origin in the wrongful act and seeks reparation by trying to attain the *status quo ante*: 'reparation must, so far as possible, wipe out all the consequences of the illegal act and re-establish the situation which would, in all probability, have existed if that act had not been committed'.[108]

War crimes and crimes against humanity

Whereas crimes against humanity may be committed in times of war or peace, war crimes may only be committed in the context of armed conflict. Concerning war crimes, Article 3 of the Hague Convention (IV) Respecting the Laws and Customs of War on Land holds belligerent parties responsible for all acts committed by persons forming part of their armed forces and liable to pay compensation for violations of its provisions. The ICJ has stated that the Hague and Geneva Conventions on humanitarian law are 'intransgressible principles of international customary law'.[109] Moreover, in the *Construction of a Wall* advisory opinion, the ICJ reiterated that the provisions of the 1907 Hague Regulations Respecting the Laws and Customs of War on Land are part of customary international law.[110] In the *Akayesu* case, the ICTR, while basing its decision on common Article 3 of the four Geneva Conventions of 1949, noted that the prohibitions stated therein apply to any conflict, even those not of an international character.[111] State responsibility for war crimes will arise if the persons committing the proscribed acts are agents of the state, as described by Article 3 of the aforementioned Hague Convention (IV). States and individuals are held separately responsible for war crimes, since the punishment of a responsible individual does not fulfill the responsibility of a state to make reparations for damages caused. The causal link between the wrongful act and state responsibility is the perpetrator's status as an agent of a state. This is spelled out in the Articles on State Responsibility for Internationally Wrongful Acts. According to Article 4, the conduct of any state organ, whether it is a person or an entity, shall be considered an act of that state, even if it exceeds its authority by acting *ultra vires*.[112] In accordance with Article 5, persons or entities that are not state organs may engage the responsibility of a state if they are empowered by the law of that state to exercise elements of governmental authority. The same rule is applicable to conduct of entities or persons directed or controlled by a state.[113]

These principles of attribution of state responsibility apply to crimes against humanity with respect to agents of the state who commit the international crimes. However, crimes against humanity need not be committed by governments or states to be punishable. They can also be instigated and perpetrated by organizations or groups.

Interestingly, national courts that are constitutionally enabled to apply customary international law within their jurisdictions have delivered judgments holding other states accountable for war crimes and crimes against humanity, basing their decisions on the intransgressible character of the principles at hand.[114] This was manifest in the *Ferrini* case,[115] in which the Italian Court of Cassation overruled a lower court's decision to dismiss an individual's plea against Germany for deportation and forced labor during World War II on the basis of state immunity. The Court of Cassation concluded that states were not entitled to jurisdictional immunity for acts performed *jure imperii* when serious violations of fundamental human rights had taken place. As a corollary, claims for damages by individuals for loss and injury arising out of the commission of international crimes should be admitted. The Court concluded that '[i]t is now obvious that the functional immunity of foreign State organs can no longer be invoked in respect of international crimes'.[116]

Whether domestic courts are the most effective jurisdictions to make these claims is doubtful. State sovereignty is still an immovable principle of international law. Even though the Italian Court of Cassation obtained jurisdiction based on the fact that the crimes had taken place in the territory of the forum state, it is difficult to envisage domestic jurisdictions passing judgment on acts of foreign states. However, if these trends are followed by substantial state practice, the law of state immunity may be subject to change over time to accommodate the need of protecting fundamental values and rights.

Conclusion

International law develops at such a pace that any prediction is difficult to be made. This seems to be especially true of the law of state responsibility for international crimes. According to the authors, the existence of different legal regime, established for different purposes within the realm of international law, accounts for the difficulty of harmonizing state and individual responsibility for international crimes.

Since the individual responsibility system has expanded faster than the law of state responsibility, the gap between the two inevitably increases. One may therefore question whether a coherent body of legal rules is likely to emerge in the future. While the pessimists would deplore this discrepancy, the optimists, among whom we are, would choose to highlight the vitality of international law and its capacity to address the societal necessities that call it into existence.

Notes

1 See R. Ago, 'Fifth Report on State Responsibility', UN Doc. A/CN.4/291 (1976), reprinted in *ILC Yearbook*, 1976, vol. II, Part Two.

2 R. Ago, 'Fifth Report on State Responsibility', p. 95. Article 19 of the Ago project reads as follows:

> 1 An act of a State which constitutes a breach of an international obligation is an internationally wrongful act, regardless of the subject-matter of the obligation breached.
>
> 2 An internationally wrongful act which results from the breach by a State of an international obligation so essential for the protection of fundamental interests of the international community that its breach is recognized as a crime by that community as a whole, constitutes an international crime.
>
> 3 Subject to paragraph 2, and on the basis of rules of international law in force, an international crime may result, *inter alia*, from:
>
> a a serious breach of an international obligation of essential importance for the maintenance of international peace and security, such as that prohibiting aggression;
>
> b a serious breach of an international obligation of essential importance for safeguarding the right to self-determination of peoples, such as that prohibiting the establishment or maintenance by force of colonial domination;
>
> c a serious breach on a widespread scale of an international obligation of essential importance for safeguarding the human being, such as those prohibiting slavery, genocide and *apartheid*;
>
> d a serious breach of an international obligation of essential importance for the safeguarding and preservation of the human environment, such as those prohibiting massive pollution of the atmosphere or of the seas.
>
> 4 Any internationally wrongful act which is not an international crime in accordance with paragraph 2, constitutes an international delict.

3 P. M. Dupuy, 'Reviewing the difficulties of codification: on Ago's classification of obligations of means and obligations of result in relation to state responsibility', *European Journal of International Law*, 1999, vol. 10, 371–85, at 373.

4 G. Abi-Saab, 'Que reste-t-il du "crime international"', in N. Angelet, O. Corten, E. David, P. Klein (eds), *Droit du Pouvoir, Pouvoir du Droit, Mélanges offerts à Jean Salmon*, Bruxelles: Bruylant, 2007, pp. 69–91.

5 G. Abi-Saab, 'The uses of article 19', *European Journal of International Law*, 1999, vol. 10, 339–51, at 351.

6 B. Simma, 'Bilateralism and community interest in the law of state responsibility', in Y. Dinstein (ed.), *International Law at a Time of Perplexity: Essays in Honour of Shabtai Rosenne*, The Netherlands: Martinus Nijhoff, 1989, pp. 821–44.

7 Barcelona Traction Case (Belgium *v.* Spain), 1970 ICJ Rep 3, para. 33.

8 R. Ago, 'Fifth Report on State Responsibility', para. 11.

9 Ibid.

10 A. Pellet, 'Le nouveau projet de la C. D. I. sur la responsabilité de l'état pour fait internationalement illicite : *requiem* pour le crime ?', in L.C. Vorah *et al.* (eds), *Man's Inhumanity to Man*, The Netherlands: Kluwer Law International, 2003, pp. 655–84, at 661.

11 B. Graefrath, 'International crimes – a specific regime of international responsibility of states and its legal consequences', in J. H. H. Weiler, A. Cassese and M. Spinedi (eds), *International Crimes of State: A Critical Analysis of the ILC's Draft Article 19 on State Responsibility*, Berlin-New York: W. de Gruyter, 1989, pp. 161–9, at 161–2.

12 Vienna Convention on the Law of Treaties, 1155 UNTS 331 (1969), Art. 53.

13 R. Ago, 'Fifth Report on State Responsibility', para. 17.

14 G. Danilenko, 'International *jus cogens*: issues of law-making', *European Journal of International Law*, 1991, vol. 2, 42–65, at 65.

15 See note 13.

16 For a complete study see Weiler, Cassese and Spinedi (eds), *International Crimes of State*.

17 For different views see A. Pellet, 'Can a state commit a crime? Definitely, yes!', *European Journal of International Law*, 1999, vol. 10, 425–34, *contra*, D. Bowett, 'Crimes of state and the 1996 report of the international law commission on state responsibility', *European Journal of International Law*, 1998, vol. 9,

163–73. See also G. Gaja, 'Should all references to international crimes disappear from the ILC draft articles on state responsibility?', *European Journal of International Law*, 1999, vol. 10, 365–70.

18 G. Abi-Saab, 'The uses of article 19', p. 340.

19 E. Wyler, 'From "state crime" to responsibility for "serious breaches of obligations under peremptory norms of general international law"', *European Journal of International Law*, 2002, vol. 13, 1147–60.

20 J. Crawford, *The International Law Commission's Articles on State Responsibility: Introduction, Texts and Commentaries*, Cambridge: Cambridge University Press, 2002, p. 84.

21 D. Anzilotti, 'La responsabilité internationale des états à raison des dommages soufferts par des étrangers', *Revue Générale de Droit International Public*, 1906, vol. 8, p. 13, quoted in Dupuy, 'Reviewing the difficulties of codification: on Ago's classification of obligations of means and obligations of result in relation to state responsibility', *European Journal of International Law*, at 372, n.3.

22 P. Reuter, 'Quelques réflexions sur le vocabulaire du droit international', in J. Basso *et al.*, *Mélanges offerts à Monsieur le Doyen Louis Trotabas*, Librairie Générale de Droit et de Jurisprudence, Paris, 1970, p. 423, quoted in Abi-Saab, 'The uses of article 19', p. 346, n. 30.

23 G. Arangio-Ruiz, 'Seventh report on state responsibility', UN Doc. A/CN.4/469 (1995), reprinted in *ILC Yearbook*, 1995, vol. II, Part One, para. 100.

24 G. Arangio-Ruiz, 'Seventh report on state responsibility', para. 101.

25 Ibid., para. 104.

26 Ibid., paras 105–9.

27 C. Tomuschat, 'L'Immunité des états en cas des violations graves des droits de l'homme', *Revue Générale de Droit International Public*, 2005, vol. 1, 51–73, at 59.

28 See 'Conclusions of the work of the study group on the fragmentation of international law: difficulties arising from the diversification and expansion of international law', UN Doc. A/CN.4/L.682/Add.1 (2006), reprinted in *ILC Yearbook*, 2006, vol. II, Part Two, hereinafter Koskenniemi Report.

29 M. Spinedi, 'International crimes of state: the legislative history', in Weiler, Cassese and Spinedi, (eds), *International Crimes of State*, pp. 77–8.

30 Ibid., pp. 65–6.

31 G. Arangio-Ruiz, 'Article 39 of the ILC first-reading draft articles on state responsibility', *Rivista di Diritto Internazionale*, vol. 83, 2000, 747–69.

32 The text of Article 39, originally proposed by Special Rappoteur Riphagen, was adopted in July 1996 amid many abstentions and with many ILC members absent.

33 G. Arangio-Ruiz, 'Article 39 of the ILC first-reading draft articles on state responsibility', p. 749.

34 Ibid., p. 768.

35 M. Spinedi, 'International crimes of state' p. 66.

36 J. Barboza, 'State crimes: a decaffeinated coffee', in L. Boisson de Chazournes and V. Gowlland-Debbas (eds), *The International Legal System in Quest of Equity and Universality, Liber Amicorum Georges Abi-Saab*, The Netherlands: Kluwer Law International, 2001, pp. 357–76, at 368.

37 D. Bowett, 'Crimes of state and the 1996 report of the international law commission on state responsibility', p. 166.

38 Ibid.

39 Security Council Resolution 687, UN Doc. S/RES/687 (1991), para. 18.

40 Ibid., para. 16.

41 R. Higgins, *Problems and Process: International Law and How We Use It*, Oxford: Oxford University Press, 1993, p. 184.

42 H. Wassgren, 'The UN Compensation Commission: lessons of legitimacy, state responsibility and war reparations', *Leiden Journal of International Law*, 1998, vol. 11, 473–92.

43 Ibid., p. 480.

44 UN Compensation Commission Web site. Available at http://www.uncc.ch/status.htm (accessed 14 October 2009).

45 Security Council Resolution 1227, UN Doc. S/RES/1227 (1999), para. 1.

46 See UN Doc. S/RES/1177 (1998); UN Doc. S/RES/1226 (1999); UN Doc. S/RES/1227 (1999); UN Doc. S/RES/1297 (2000); UN Doc. S/RES/1298 (2000); UN Doc. S/RES/1308 (2000); UN Doc. S/RES/1312 (2000); and UN Doc. S/RES/1340 (2000).

47 The Commission was established pursuant to Article 5 of the Agreement signed in Algiers on 12 December 2000 between the governments of the State of Eritrea and the Federal Democratic Republic of Ethiopia: Agreement between the Government of the State of Eritrea and the Government of the

Federal Democratic Republic of Ethiopia for the resettlement of displaced persons, as well as rehabilitation and peacebuilding in both countries, 2138 UNTS 93 (2000), Art. 5, hereinafter Algiers Agreement.

48 Algiers Agreement, Art. 5.

49 Eritrea–Ethiopia Claims Commission, Eritrea's Damages Claims, Final Award of 17 August 2009.

50 Ibid.

51 R. Ago, 'Fifth Report on State Responsibility', p. 105, para. 25.

52 UN Charter, Art. 39.

53 Koskenniemi Report, para. 40 ('The United Nations Charter has been universally accepted by States and thus a conflict between *jus cogens* norms and Charter obligations is difficult to contemplate.').

54 J. A. Frowein, 'Introduction to Chapter VII', in B. Simma (ed.), *The Charter of the United Nations*, Oxford: Oxford University Press, 2002, pp. 701–16, at 721.

55 C. Gray, *International Law and the Use of Force*, 2nd edn, Oxford: Oxford University Press, 2004, p. 195.

56 Military and Paramilitary Activities Case (Nicaragua *v.* United States of America), 1984 ICJ Rep 392, para. 93.

57 Ibid., para. 92.

58 Diplomatic and Consular Staff Case (United States of America *v.* Iran), 1980 ICJ Rep 3, para. 40.

59 J. Crawford, 'First Report on State Responsibility', UN Doc. A/CN.4/490/Add.1 (1998), reprinted in *ILC Yearbook*, A/CN.4/SER.A/1998/Add.1 (Part 1), p. 9 at para. 43.

60 Ibid., para. 48.

61 Ibid., para. 74.

62 Ibid., para. 80.

63 'Responsibility of States for Internationally Wrongful Acts', annexed to UN Doc. A/RES/56/83 (2001). The Assembly 'took note' of the Articles and commended them to the attention of governments 'without prejudice to the question of their future adoption or other appropriate action'. UN Doc. A/RES/56/83 (2001).

64 A. Pellet, 'Le nouveau projet de la C.D.I. sur la responsabilité de l'état pour le fait internationalement illicite: *requiem* pour le crime?', p. 661.

65 E. Wyler, 'From "state crime" to responsibility for "serious breaches of obligations under peremptory norms of general international law"', p. 1147.

66 G. Abi-Saab, 'Que reste-t-il du "crime international"' p. 80.

67 ILC Yearbook, 2001, vol. II, Part Two, commentary to Art. 40, p. 113 at para. 6, reproduced in UN Doc. A/CN.4/SER.A/2001/Add.1 (Part 2), commentary to Art. 26.

68 Ibid., para. 9.

69 Ibid.

70 V. D. Degan, 'Responsibility of states and individuals for genocide', in I. Buffard, J. Crawford, A. Pellet and S. Wittich (eds), *International Law between Universalism and Fragmentation,* Festschrift *in Honour of Gerhard Hafner*, The Netherlands: Koninklijke Brill NV, 2008, pp. 511–34, at 513.

71 For a pertinent analysis of this phenomenon see A. Loewenstein and S. Kostas, 'Divergent approaches to determining responsibility for genocide: the Darfur Commission of Inquiry and the ICJ's judgment in the genocide case', *Journal of International Criminal Justice*, 2007, vol. 5, 839–57.

72 A. Bianchi, 'State responsibility and criminal liability of individuals', in A. Cassese (ed.), *The Oxford Companion to International Criminal Justice*, Oxford: Oxford University Press, 2009, pp. 16–24, at 17.

73 A. Nollkaemper, 'Concurrence between individual responsibility and state responsibility in international law', *International and Comparative Law Quarterly*, 2003, vol. 52, 615–40, at 627.

74 C. Dominicé, 'La question de la double responsabilité de l'état et de son agent', in E. Yakpo and T. Boumedra (eds), *Liber Amicorum – Mohammed Bedjaoui*, The Netherlands: Kluwer Law International, 1999, pp. 143–57, at 144.

75 International Criminal Court, *Report of the Preparatory Commission for the International Criminal Court, Addendum, Part II, Finalized draft text of the Elements of Crimes*, 2 November 2000, reproduced in UN Doc. PCNICC/2000/1/Add.2, Art. 6.

76 Convention on the Prevention and Punishment of the Crime of Genocide, 77 UNTS 277 (1948), hereinafter 'Genocide Convention', Arts II, III.

77 A. Cassese, 'On the use of criminal law notions in determining state responsibility for genocide', *Journal of International Criminal Justice*, 2007, vol. 5, 875–87.

78 A. Nollkaemper, 'Introduction', in A. Nollkaemper and H. van der Wilt (eds), *System Criminality in International Law*, Cambridge: Cambridge University Press, 2009, p. 12.
79 Furundzja (ICTY-IT-95-17/1-T), Judgement, 10 December 1998, paras 139–42.
80 B. Bonafè, *The Relationship between State and Individual Responsibility for International Crimes*, Leiden–Boston: Martinus Nijhoff Publishers, 2009, pp. 251–2.
81 General Treaty for the Renunciation of War as an Instrument of National Policy, Paris, 1928.
82 UN Doc. General Assembly Resolution 3314 (XXIX) of 14 December 1974, Annex, Art. 5.
83 Declaration on Principles of International Law concerning Friendly Relations and Co-operation among States in accordance with the Charter of the United Nations, UN Doc. General Assembly Resolution 2625 (XXV) of 24 October 1970, Annex, para. 1.
84 Military and Paramilitary Activities case (Nicaragua *v.* United States of America), 1986 ICJ Rep 14, para. 190.
85 Legal Consequences of the Construction of a Wall in the Occupied Palestinian Territory, Advisory Opinion, 2004 ICJ Rep 136, para. 87.
86 UN Doc. General Assembly Resolution 96(I) of 11 December 1946.
87 Genocide Convention, Art. IX, emphasis added.
88 Case Concerning the Application of the Convention on the Prevention and Punishment of the Crime of Genocide (Bosnia and Herzegovina *v.* Serbia and Montenegro), 1996 ICJ Rep 595, para. 32, hereinafter Genocide Case. The Court found that it had jurisdiction to adjudicate upon the dispute on the basis of Article IX of the Genocide Convention by 13 votes to two.
89 Case Concerning the Application of the Convention on the Prevention and Punishment of the Crime of Genocide (Bosnia and Herzegovina *v.* Serbia and Montenegro), 2007 ICJ Rep 1, para. 166.
90 Ibid.
91 Genocide Case, para. 169.
92 P. Gaeta observes that if one takes the Court's stand, 'criminal responsibility for genocide becomes a sort of prerequisite of state responsibility'. See P. Gaeta, 'On what conditions can a state be held responsible for genocide?', *European Journal of International Law*, 2007, vol. 18, 631–48, at 644.
93 The conduct must take place in the context of a manifest pattern of similar conduct directed against a group or should be a conduct that could itself effect such destruction. See *Report of the Preparatory Commission for the International Criminal Court, Addendum, Part II, Finalized draft text of the Elements of Crimes*, 2 November 2000, reproduced in UN Doc. PCNICC/2000/1/Add.2, Art. 6.
94 See P. M. Dupuy, 'International criminal responsibility of the individual and international responsibility of the state' in A. Cassese, P. Gaeta, and R.W.D. Jones (eds), the Rome Statute of the International Criminal Court : A commentary, Vol 2, Oxford : Oxford University Press, 2002, p. 1091.
95 *ILC Yearbook*, 1996, vol. II, Part Two, p. 15, reproduced in UN Doc. A/CN.4/SER.A/1996/Add.l (Part 2).
96 Genocide Case, para. 147.
97 ILC Yearbook, 2001, vol. II, Part Two, reproduced in UN Doc. A/CN.4/SER.A/2001/Add.1 (Part 2) commentary to Art. 26.
98 Case Concerning Armed Activities on the Territory of the Congo, New Application: 2002 (Democratic Republic of the Congo *v.* Rwanda), 2006 ICJ Rep 6, para. 64. See the appended Separate Opinion of Judge *ad hoc* Dugard on the Court's invocation of *jus cogens*.
99 Genocide case, para. 187.
100 Genocide case, para. 297.
101 Genocide case, especially paras 252–6, 262–73, 307–10, 312–18.
102 A. Nollkaemper, 'Concurrence between individual responsibility and state responsibility in international law', p. 630.
103 P. Gaeta, 'On what conditions can a state be held responsible for genocide?', p. 643.
104 Genocide case, para. 370.
105 Genocide case, para. 371.
106 Genocide case, para. 373.
107 Genocide case, para. 173.
108 Factory at Chorzów, Merits, PCIJ, Series A, No. 17, 1928, p. 47.
109 Legality of the Threat or Use of Nuclear Weapons, Advisory Opinion, 1996 ICJ Rep 226, para. 79.
110 Legal Consequences of the Construction of a Wall in the Occupied Palestinian Territory, Advisory Opinion, 2004 ICJ Rep 136, para. 89.
111 Akayesu (ICTR-96-4), 2 September 1998, para. 615.

112 Articles on Responsibility of States for Internationally Wrongful Acts, Art. 7.
113 Ibid., Art. 8.
114 See Hellenic Supreme Court, Prefecture of Voiotia *v.* Federal Republic of Germany (Case No. 11/2000), 4 May 2000.
115 Italian Court of Cassation, Ferrini *v.* Federal Republic of Germany, Decision No. 5044/2004 of 11 March 2004, reprinted in *International Law Reports*, vol. 128, 2004, 659–75.
116 Ibid., para. 11. For a pertinent analysis of the Ferrini case, see A. Bianchi, 'Ferrini *v.* Federal Republic of Germany', *American Journal of International Law*, 2005, vol. 99, 242–8.

25

International criminal law and victims' rights

Carla Ferstman[1]

Introduction

International criminal law is meant to repress the worst crimes known to mankind, yet those who have suffered—the victims and affected communities—are traditionally only peripherally considered by international justice processes. The major international criminal courts and tribunals that have been established since Nuremberg have, until recently, given only sparse consideration to victims' views and concerns and limited space for their active engagement with such institutions beyond the role of prosecution witness. Similarly, these judicial bodies have been typically physically and conceptually removed from the communities most affected by the crimes, causing alienation and disillusionment and marginalising their relevance to societies in transition.

In order to address these shortcomings, the International Criminal Court (ICC) and newer specialized criminal tribunals such as the Extraordinary Chambers in the Courts of Cambodia (ECCC) have gone some distance to incorporate processes that positively affirm victims' dignity, including victims' right to be kept informed about legal proceedings, special measures of protection and support, the ability of victims to participate in legal proceedings independent from any role they may have as prosecution witnesses, and their right to claim reparations for the harm they suffered. The Statute of the International Criminal Court also establishes a specialized trust fund to both complement the ICC's reparative mandate and assist with its implementation. Such recent developments in international justice are also evidenced by standard-setting movements at the international level which have progressively recognized the importance of positively engaging and involving victims in the criminal justice process.

Despite these advances, some critics hold steadfast to the view that strengthening victims' role in criminal proceedings taints the rights of the defence, whereas others point to the procedural difficulties of such involvement, referring mainly to the potential for delays, escalation of costs and other inefficiencies. The judicial practice underscores such tensions.

This chapter outlines the evolving role of victims in international criminal law, looking in particular at victims' rights to participate in proceedings, as well as the capacity of courts to order awards for reparations to or in respect of victims. It starts by analysing the normative framework of victims' rights, then turns to a review of the judicial practice, considering in particular the emerging practice of the ICC and the ECCC. Translating legal provisions into veritable rights that can be exercized practically and effectively is, and will continue to be, a challenge in both the short and long term. The chapter concludes by offering some comments on the practice and perspectives on the way forward.

Victims' rights—what place in international criminal law?

Criminal prosecutions are an important means by which justice for victims is achieved. The public nature of criminal proceedings, the formal identification of the perpetrator and the assignation of responsibility can help meet victims' requirements of justice. Criminal trials also help to develop a public record of the wrongdoing and restore or strengthen a society based on the rule of law. Bringing perpetrators to justice might also contribute to the immediate security of victims and help to prevent future crimes; it can also help clarify the events surrounding the commission of crimes and make clear that a wrong was done.

Determining the appropriate placement of the victim in international criminal law procedure is a difficult and contentious issue, reflecting in part the differences in national procedural frameworks. Traditionally, civil law legal systems have been more advanced than common law systems when it comes to the active participation of victims in criminal trials, given their use of the 'partie civile' system, in which victims have the right to join or intervene directly in criminal proceedings as civil parties, participate as independent parties throughout the proceedings and apply for reparations at the conclusion of the criminal trial. Civil law systems typically treat such civil parties as full parties to the proceedings, with rights analogous to the prosecution and defense. In some civil law countries, victims have also the right to initiate criminal law proceedings and to act as an auxiliary or subsidiary prosecutor.[2] In contrast, in common law countries, the role of the victim has been typically restricted to the prosecution witness, with limited rights in some instances to review prosecutorial action and to provide statements on sentencing.[3]

The Statutes of the International Criminal Tribunal for the former Yugoslavia (ICTY), the International Criminal Tribunal for Rwanda (ICTR) and the Special Court for Sierra Leone (SCSL), as the international tribunals at Nuremberg and Tokyo which preceded them, took a primarily common law approach with respect to the role of victims in proceedings. Victims appeared simply as witnesses, and were not represented by independent counsel—the belief being that their interests would mirror that of the prosecutor and thus their independent voice was not solicited or required. Victims may only relay information to the judges within the questioning parameters laid down by counsel.[4] They have been exposed to indifference, insult and the dangers associated with testifying in a hostile environment against powerful defendants.[5] Although the Statutes of the *ad hoc* Tribunals make clear that victims' rights to seek compensation before domestic courts is not prejudiced, victims were not afforded the right to claim reparations before the international tribunals themselves. Even those few powers the ICTY and ICTR have to deal with reparation have been hard to invoke, and have consequently not been effective tools for victims seeking reparation.[6] Tribunal officials have criticized their lack of effectiveness.[7]

When time came to consider the provisions for the ICC Statute, there was strong resistance to calls to adopt broader, more inclusive provisions regarding victim participation and reparations, as these aspects were seen as unnecessary diversions from the ICC's core mandate of considering the criminal responsibility of individual accused persons. There was also the belief that the interests of victims and survivors mirror that of the prosecution and therefore that their voices would duplicate and potentially inflame rather than enhance proceedings.

However, the well-publicized failings of the ICTY and ICTR in respect of victims and the growing shift at the international level in the understanding of crime as not only an offence against the state but also an offence against the individual and communities eventually won out. The drafters of the ICC Statute specifically considered the text of the UN Declaration on Victims of Crime and Abuse of Power,[8] which defined crime prevention as a victims' rights issue, and sought to guarantee access to justice, fair treatment and a right to information, assistance and access to informal dispute resolution mechanisms.[9] It also had regard to the then still draft United Nations Basic Principles and Guidelines on the Right to a Remedy and Reparation for Victims of Gross Violations of International Human Rights Law and Serious Violations of International Humanitarian Law, which recognizes that victims' right to a remedy and reparations includes, *inter alia,* 'equal and effective access to justice.'[10]

The ICC provisions have influenced a host of other international treaties and standards that have subsequently been adopted, and which refer specifically to the right of victims to participate in criminal proceedings. These treaties and standards include

- The Protocol to Prevent, Suppress, and Punish Trafficking in Persons, Especially Women and Children.[11]
- The Resolution on Children as victims and perpetrators,[12] which recommends that

> States, in a manner consistent with the procedural rules of national law and the administration of justice, with regard to children, should enable children to participate, as appropriate, in criminal justice proceedings, including the investigative stage and throughout the trial and post-trial process period, to be heard and given information about their status and any proceedings that might subsequently take place.

- The Principles on the Effective Investigation and Documentation of Torture and Other Cruel, Inhuman or Degrading Treatment or Punishment.[13]
- The European Union Council Framework Decision to improve victims' standing in criminal proceedings.[14]

Victims' agency—information and participation

The United Nations Declaration of Basic Principles of Justice for Victims of Crime and Abuse of Power makes special reference to the importance of keeping victims informed in its principle 6 paragraph (a), where it is noted that states should '[i]nform[...] victims of their role and the scope, timing and progress of the proceedings and of the disposition of their cases, especially where serious crimes are involved and where they have requested such information.'

Lessons of the *ad hoc* Tribunals for the former Yugoslavia and Rwanda, international claims procedures and truth commissions suggest that victims' experiences with the procedure will be more positive if they have a clear understanding of what they will face.[15] Victims may have different objectives when coming forward to testify and it will be easy for them to develop false expectations about how the justice process will work. In most countries where the crimes occurred, victims, particularly those from rural areas, will have very little experience with national justice systems. The concept of 'international justice' will be even more remote. The ICC Statute has followed this principle by making specific reference to the obligation to inform victims and others as appropriate. For example, Article 15(6) obliges the Prosecutor to inform those that provided its office with information that he or she will not be proceeding beyond a preliminary investigation, and Article 43(6) establishes a specialized unit to assist victims and witnesses coming into contact with the Court. The Rules of Procedure and Evidence[16] (Rule 92) provide that victims participating in proceedings shall be notified in writing or other appropriate form, in a timely manner, of proceedings before the Court, including the date of hearings and any postponements, and the date of delivery of the decision, of requests, submissions, motions and other documents, and further that the Court must also give publicity to the proceedings in other ways. However, the sheer scale of the task, given the remoteness of victims and the limited budgets for community outreach and for legal representatives to liaise with clients, has hampered the effectiveness of information efforts.

With respect to victim participation, the Rome Statute allows victims whose personal interests are affected to participate in proceedings before the ICC by according them rights to be represented, to present their views and concerns 'at stages of the proceedings determined to be appropriate by the ICC and in a manner which is not prejudicial to or inconsistent with the rights of the accused and a fair and impartial trial.'[17] In contrast, before the ECCC, in order to qualify as a 'victim' entitled to civil party status, the survivor must have suffered a 'physical, material or psychological' injury and this injury must be 'the direct consequence of the offence, personal and have actually come into being.'[18]

The judges have consistently interpreted the provision on victim participation as a right of victims in the sense that victims have the 'right' to participate so long as they can show they are victims and their personal interests are affected. The timing of victim participation (when it would be appropriate for victims to participate) and the modalities of victim participation (the forms of victim participation—whether they can make an oral or written statement, and on what issues) will depend on the circumstances and what will be considered to be appropriate in light of the clear obligation for the participation not to be prejudicial to or inconsistent with the rights of the accused and a fair and impartial trial.

The ICC has specifically rejected the notion that victims' interest in participation is solely linked to obtaining an award for reparations at the end of trial. It has recognized in contrast that victims' interests 'should encompass their personal interests in an appropriately broad sense,'[19] including the need to see that 'justice is done'.[20] Despite this, participation rights are limited before the ICC. Victims are not full parties to the proceedings and do not have the same rights as the prosecution and defense. They cannot, for example, participate in the Prosecutor's investigation, and only have limited ability to access the evidence gathered by the parties and call witnesses to testify.[21] In contrast, the ECCC, based more directly on the civil law tradition, recognizes civil parties as full parties to the proceedings.[22] Not only does this mean enhanced procedural rights but also the Internal Rules make clear the role of civil parties in providing evidence.[23] Nonetheless, following the practice on victim participation before the ECCC in its first case, and in anticipation of the much larger second case in which thousands of victims had been accepted as civil parties, the judges' Rules Committee amended the Chambers' Internal Rules in February 2010 with significant restructuring of the procedure for victim participation in the trial phase and having the effect of restricting the direct access of civil party lawyers to the proceedings. In the new structure, 'Civil Party Lead Co-Lawyers', a newly established title, will operate as a bridge between the civil party lawyers and the Court. The Internal Rules provide that these Civil Party Lead Co-Lawyers are appointed to 'represent[…] the interests of a consolidated group of Civil Parties', and take 'ultimate responsibility to the court for the overall advocacy, strategy and in-court presentation of the interests of the consolidated group of Civil Parties during the trial stage and beyond'.[24]

As noted by Donat-Cattin, who traces the drafting history of Article 68(3) of the ICC Statute,

> the representative(s) of the victims is merely an optional party to the criminal process, while the defence and the prosecution are necessary parties without whom no trial could ever

> take place. Nevertheless, participation in the proceedings must be recognized as an important component towards facilitating the process of healing for victims of crimes, which is essential for rendering the ICC an institution effectively respondent to the questions of those who suffered immense pain and require that justice is done and seen to be done.[25]

In principle, victims are able to participate in ICC proceedings from the earliest investigation phases, even before the Prosecutor has narrowed down the case to specific potential accused persons and before the issuance of indictments. In its decision of 17 January 2006,[26] in response to victims' application to participate in proceedings in the investigation into crimes committed in the Democratic Republic of the Congo, the Chamber indicated that they could indeed participate, though the manner of the participation would be necessarily restricted at that early phase. This determination was controversial, particularly for the Office of the Prosecutor, as it meant that participation is not restricted to those victims affected by the crimes the prosecutor chooses to prosecute, and in this sense enables other voices to be heard. In practice, given the limited procedural rights at this stage of proceedings and the length of time it took for victims to apply to participate and for their applications to be positively considered by the Chambers, to date the right has had only minimal impact. In later jurisprudence, the general ability for victims to participate in the investigation phase has been curtailed, though in principle it remains possible for victims to participate in discrete hearings, as appropriate. The Appeals Chamber in the Situation in the Democratic Republic of Congo found, in its Judgment of 19 December 2008, that 'the decisions of the Pre-Trial Chamber acknowledging procedural status to victims, entitling them to participate generally in the investigation of a situation are ill-founded and must be set aside'.[27] It clarified that

> Article 68(3) of the Statute correlates victim participation to 'proceedings', a term denoting a judicial cause pending before a Chamber. In contrast, an investigation is not a judicial proceeding but an inquiry conducted by the Prosecutor into the commission of a crime [...]. A person has the right to participate in proceedings if a) he/she qualifies as a victim under the definition of this term provided by rule 85 of the Rules, and b) his/her personal interests are affected by the proceedings at hand; i.e. by the issues, legal or factual, raised therein.[28]

In order to participate in ICC proceedings, victims must be able to demonstrate that particular proceedings against a specific accused affect their interests. Thus, the ICC has had to determine how close a connection must exist between victim and accused, and between the victim and the particular phase of proceedings or issue under consideration by the Chamber, for victims' interests to be sufficiently affected. In this respect, the ICC has had to consider whether to enable participation of only those that suffered directly from the crimes or also family members or others.

The earliest decisions of the Court made clear that only victims who had suffered harm as a result of the specific crimes considered in the indictment could participate in proceedings.[29] So when the Prosecutor issued a narrow indictment against Lubanga relating to recruiting and enlisting child soldiers,[30] the victims who could participate in the case were the child soldiers or those who were otherwise victimized in the recruitment process by trying to protect the child soldiers. This was quite limiting for the many victims who suffered the broader repercussions of the child soldiering—the women who were raped and the villagers who were mutilated by these child soldiers. The Trial Chamber in the Lubanga case determined, in a seminal judgment, that in principle, 'a victim of any crime falling within the jurisdiction of the Court can potentially participate.'[31]

However, considering Article 68(3) of the Statute which provides that 'where the interests of the victims are affected, the Court shall permit their views and concerns to be presented and considered at stages of the proceedings determined to be appropriate', there should either be a 'real evidential link' between the victim and the evidence which the Court will be considering at trial leading to the conclusion that the victim's personal interests are affected or the victim is affected by an issue arising during the trial because his or her personal interests are in a real sense engaged by it.[32] This and several other findings of the Trial Chamber decision were appealed.[33] The Appeals Chamber has determined that while the ordinary meaning of Rule 85 does not *per se* limit the notion of victims to those directly affected by the crimes charged, Article 68(3) of the Statute, which specifically regulates the participation of victims in the proceedings, does have the effect of limiting participation in the trial phase to those victims who are linked to the charges.[34]

Before the ECCC, judicial determination of victims' participation rights have progressed differently. In Case 001 where, for the most part, neither the defence nor the prosecution challenged victim participation rights, civil party participation has proceeded with little judicial intervention, with almost all applicants accorded civil party status.[35] However, with time, judges have increasingly adopted a restrictive approach in the name of expediency and/or where it is perceived to negatively impact on the fairness of proceedings. Judges have rejected requests by victims to make submissions directly without their lawyers (other than to provide evidence) and to make submissions on sentencing.[36] Also, certain admissibility challenges were entertained at the end of the trial, potentially rendering ineligible some of the victims that had participated in earlier phases of the proceedings.[37] Cognisant of the much higher numbers of victim applicants for Case 002,[38] ECCC judges made significant changes to the rules governing civil party participation in February 2010.[39]

The complex procedures to apply to participate in proceedings, including the need to complete lengthy application forms and submit evidence difficult for many victims to obtain, together with the limited capacity of most victims owing to poor access to information and the physical and conceptual distance between themselves and the Court, have frustrated victim participation before both the ICC and ECCC. Significant backlogs in decision-making and poor correspondence with victims have left many victims puzzled and frustrated by the complexity of the process. Local civil society groups operating in the areas habited by victims have proved to be essential in assisting victims to collect information, liaising with the Court when information is missing and updating victims about the status of their claims, yet these groups have few resources and insufficient recognition by the courts that rely upon them.

Reparations to or in respect of victims

The right to a remedy and to reparation has been affirmed by a range of treaties,[40] United Nations bodies[41] and regional courts,[42] as well as in a series of declarative instruments.[43] Despite the requirement that reparation reflect and respond to the nature and gravity of the breach, it is clear that the most serious violations of human rights are by their nature irreparable and any remedy will be disproportionate to the harm suffered. Nonetheless, it is an international legal obligation that an internationally wrongful act be remedied to the fullest possible extent.[44] The aim of reparation is to eliminate, as far as possible, the consequences of the illegal act and to restore the situation that would have existed if the act had not been committed.[45] Reparation can take many forms, and the content of the right to a remedy depends on the nature of the substantive right at issue. It must be effective in practice as well as in law,[46] and must be suitable to grant appropriate relief for the legal right that is alleged to have been infringed.

Article 75 of the ICC Statute has made it possible for the ICC to order reparations to or in respect of victims, including restitution, compensation and rehabilitation. It provides that:

> the Court shall establish principles relating to reparations to, or in respect of, victims, including restitution, compensation and rehabilitation. In its decision the Court may, either upon request or on its own motion in exceptional circumstances, determine the scope and extent of any damage, loss and injury to, or in respect of, victims and will state the principles on which it is acting (Art. 75, para. 1).

The right to claim reparations was not featured in the *ad hoc* Tribunals for the former Yugoslavia or Rwanda or other international tribunals which preceded them and it was not obvious that it would be included in the ICC Statute either. The International Law Commission decided to delete from its 1994 draft statute an article on reparations (introduced in the 1993 draft) on the basis of the argument that a criminal court was not an appropriate forum in which to order reparations. It was not recognized that where national systems have, by definition, been unwilling or unable to administer criminal justice, it is unlikely that those systems will be able or willing to give effect to the victims' right to reparations.[47] In fact it is the combination of this inaccessibility of national systems for victims and the difficulty for drafters to ignore the developing normative framework at the international level that led to the incorporation of reparations into the ICC Statute.[48]

The right to claim reparations similarly did not feature in the ECCC statute, though it did make its way into its internal rules. Internal Rule 23(1) provides that the Chambers may award 'collective and moral reparation' and that such awards are to 'be borne by convicted persons.'

The challenges to afford reparations before the ICC and ECCC are immense, owing to the huge number of potential beneficiaries and their extensive pecuniary and non-pecuniary losses and the lack of resources of potential convicted persons. At the time of writing, neither court had embarked upon a reparations process, though each is expected to do so soon as both have cases nearing the end of the trial phase.

As indicated, reparations should reflect the gravity of the crimes and the harm suffered. Internationally recognized forms of reparation include restitution, compensation, rehabilitation and satisfaction and guarantees of non-repetition,[49] and in most instances some combination of these forms will be understood as adequate and appropriate in the circumstances. Under the ICC Statute, the Court may afford only some of these forms, referring specifically to restitution, compensation or rehabilitation, and its awards may be directed at individuals, collectives or both.[50] The restriction to restitution, compensation and rehabilitation is somewhat understandable, given the difficulties for an international court with a mandate to adjudicate only individual (as opposed to state or other actors') responsibility to consider more nationally transformative measures. In this context it is difficult to see how the ICC could afford specific measures aimed at satisfaction or guarantees of non-repetition, other than by ensuring the publication of the judgment, as such measures are more aptly instituted by states aiming to promote national reconciliation or restore confidence in the rule of law. The reference to both individual and collective awards will enable the judges to respond flexibly to the circumstances of the particular case and the context of victims' suffering.

The ECCC's internal rules are even more limited, referring to the possibility for the Chambers to award only collective and moral reparations, in the forms of

> a) An order to publish the judgment in any appropriate news or other media at the convicted person's expense; b) An order to fund any non-profit activity or service that is intended for the benefit of Victims; or c) Other appropriate and comparable forms of reparation.[51]

The ECCC's failure to entertain individual awards is unfortunate given the nature of the harm and the situation of victims and their families, though realistic, in light of the paucity of evidence to prove individual harm. As the ECCC is operating within a domestic context, it would also be more feasible for the ECCC, in coordination with the Cambodian Government, to develop measures of reparation which have greater national symbolic significance, and ideally Article 23(12)(c) will be interpreted to this effect.[52]

Both the ICC and ECCC have adopted an application process in which victims, or in the case of the ECCC, civil parties, may apply for reparations. Under the ICC Statute, reparations to victims may be considered by the Court on its own initiative following applications by victims. These possibilities are referred to in Article 75(1) which provides that

> [o]n this basis, in its decision the Court may, either upon request or on its own motion in exceptional circumstances, determine the scope and extent of any damage, loss and injury to, or in respect of, victims and will state the principles on which it is acting.

The ability for the Court to determine reparations *proprio motu* is important. This possibility recognizes, *inter alia*, that not all individuals who may be deserving of reparations will be in a position to apply to the Court, and that this should not prevent the Court from determining reparations in a general or specific way. It is made clear that these powers should be exercised on an exceptional basis[53] only, though the criteria for determining what may constitute such an exceptional situation are not spelt out and are likely to be considered on a case-by-case basis by the Court. Under Rule 95 of the Rules of Procedure and Evidence, should the Court decide to utilize these *proprio motu* powers, it shall request the Registrar to notify this intention to the defendant(s) [the person(s) against whom the Court is considering making a determination], and to the extent possible, to victims and other interested persons or interested States. Other interested persons might include judgment creditors who might be impacted by any decision of the Court to order reparations, and interested States might include the State in which the harm is said to have occurred and/or any other States potentially impacted by that harm, that may have an interest in an eventual reparations award.[54]

Conversely, the ECCC does not refer to *proprio motu* consideration of reparations, though few details about the reparations process have thus far been published. The Internal Rules appear to limit the right to request reparations to civil parties only, and consequently only a very limited proportion of victims will benefit, unless the rules are interpreted broadly. This is made worse by limited outreach to victims to inform them of this limitation and the fact that the Chambers has instituted very tight deadlines for victims to apply to become civil parties, currently articulated as 15 days after notification of the conclusion of the judicial investigation.[55]

Both courts have individualized reparations application processes, despite the fact that many victims may have suffered harm collectively (e.g. the incidents which gave rise to the harm may have affected communities or large groups of persons in a similar if not identical way—burning of villages, displacement, torture). The ECCC does allow victims to participate through victims' associations;[56] however, it is unclear what role such associations will have in the reparations phase, given the Internal Rules' specific reference to only civil parties as the recipients of reparations. This is also despite the fact that forms of reparations are likely to be collective before the ICC and will always be so before the ECCC. Both Courts have mechanisms to receive joint filings and submissions from affected groups, though victims seeking reparations must submit individualized applications.

In respect of both the ICC and ECCC, reparations orders are made against the convicted perpetrator who has the responsibility to comply with the award. Enforcement measures will be more straightforward at the ECCC, as it operates in a national context, though in both cases, the likelihood that perpetrators will be judgment-proof is exceedingly high. The ICC has anticipated this problem and established a trust fund for victims, which can receive voluntary contributions as well as other sources of funds.[57] The Trust Fund has a dual mandate. First, it is mandated to use its voluntary resources as necessary to provide support to victims and their families, independent of any reparations order emanating from the ICC. This possibility reflects the fact that many victims will not be able to await a Court's judgment for urgent support. Second, the Trust Fund is mandated to implement reparations orders emanated from the Court, when the Court so instructs it. The ECCC does not have a Trust Fund, though the civil parties have urged the Court to establish such a fund and to 'strongly encourage, through its reparation judgment, the Kingdom of Cambodia to take the lead in providing reparations to victims'.[58]

Conclusions

The ability of victims of the most serious international crimes to obtain justice is not obvious. International justice processes will only ever be capable of investigating and prosecuting a small proportion of the crimes. The ICC and ECCC Statutes and Rules have gone to some length to identify the procedures necessary to enable victims to engage in, and experience justice positively. It is vital that the necessary resources are set aside for this purpose and that coordination and planning amongst actors both inside these institutions and with civil society groups and other agencies assisting victims at the grassroots level are enhanced.

Reparations for the most serious international crimes will always be symbolic, as it will never be possible to fully relieve the harm caused. Whereas this should not militate against comprehensive measures of reparations, it reminds that the victims themselves should be consulted in a participatory process about what matters most. Restoring agency is central to restoring dignity. Providing victims with an active voice in all matters that concern them is therefore not only a means to a just result but also part of the result itself.

Notes

1 Director of REDRESS (www.redress.org).
2 See generally, C. Bradley, *Criminal Procedure: A Worldwide Study,* 2nd edn., Durham, NC: Carolina Academic Press, 2007, p. 45; UN Office For Drug Control & Crime Prevention, *Handbook On Justice For Victims,* New York: Centre for International Crime Prevention, 1999, p. 39.
3 M. Brienen and E. Hoegen, *Victims of Crime in 22 European Criminal Justice Systems,* Nijmegen: Wolf Publishing, 2000.
4 C. Jorda and J. de Hemptinne, 'The Status and the Role of the Victim', in A. Cassese (ed.), *The Rome Statute of the International Criminal Court: A Commentary,* Oxford: Oxford University Press, 2002, p. 1387.
5 E. Stover, *The Witnesses: War Crimes and the Promise of Justice in The Hague,* Pennsylvania: Pennsylvania Studies in Human Rights, University of Pennsylvania Press, 2005, p. 106.
6 See, Rule 105 of the Rules of Procedure and Evidence for both tribunals, which provides that the Trial Chamber may determine the matter of restitution of property taken unlawfully by the convicted person, which has yet to be applied. Rule 106 common to both Tribunals provides that judgments establishing guilt are to be binding as to the criminal responsibility of the convicted person for the purpose of an action for compensation, which might be brought by victims in national courts. Given the poor domestic legal frameworks, this provision too has failed to be useful for victims. See, C. Bassiouni and P. Manikas, *The Law of the International Criminal Tribunal for the former Yugoslavia,* Irvington-on-Hudson, New York: Transnational Publishers, 1996, p. 704.
7 See, Letter of 14 December 2000 of the UN Secretary-General, addressed to the President of the Security Council, UN Doc. S/2000/1198 (15 December 2000), and UN Doc. S/2000/1063 (3 November 2000).

Discussed in C. Ferstman, 'The Reparation Regime of the International Criminal Court: Practical Considerations' 15 *Leiden Journal of International Law* 667–86, 2002, pp. 671–74.

8 Adopted by General Assembly Resolution 40/34 of 29 November 1985.

9 Principle 4 of this Declaration provides that '[v]ictims should be treated with compassion and respect for their dignity. They are entitled to access to the mechanisms of justice and to prompt redress, as provided for by national legislation, for the harm that they have suffered.' Principle 6(B) states that the judicial process should allow 'the views and concerns of victims to be presented and considered at appropriate stages of the proceedings where their personal interests are affected, without prejudice to the accused'.

10 Adopted by General Assembly Resolution 60/147 of 16 December 2005 at para. 11(a).

11 Art. 6(2)(b) provides that victims shall be assisted in presenting their views and concerns to be considered at 'appropriate stages of criminal proceedings against offenders, in a manner not prejudicial to the rights of the defence.'

12 Adopted by the Ninth United Nations Congress on the Prevention of Crime and the Treatment of Offenders, Cairo: 29 April—8 May 1995, UN Doc. A/CONF.169/16, 12 May 1995.

13 Principles on the Effective Investigation and Documentation of Torture and Other Cruel, Inhuman, or Degrading Treatment or Punishment, G.A. Res. 9842, UN GAOR, 55th Sess., Annex, Agenda Item 114(c), UN Doc. A/RES/55/89 (2000). These prescribe that victims and their legal representatives have rights to be informed of and to have access to any hearing and to any relevant information about the investigation, including the right to present other evidence.

14 This Decision urges member states to ensure that victims have a real and appropriate role in its criminal legal system; safeguard the possibility for victims to be heard during the proceedings and to supply evidence; afford victims, who have the status of parties or witnesses, reimbursement of expenses incurred in their participation. Recommendation of the Committee of Ministers, 724th meeting of the Ministers' Deputies, Doc. No. R (2000) 19 (2000).

15 S. Kutnjak Ivkovic, 'Justice by the International Criminal Tribunal for the Former Yugoslavia,' 37 *Stanford Journal of International Law* 255–346 (2001).

16 ICC-ASP/1/3 (Part II-A), adopted and entered into force on 9 September 2002.

17 Rome Statute, A/CONF.183/9, adopted on 17 July 1998 and entered into force on 1 July 2002, Article 68(3).

18 Extraordinary Chambers in the Courts of Cambodia, Internal Rules (Rev.4) As Revised on 11 September 2009, Rule 23(2).

19 Lubanga (ICC-01/04-01/06), Decision on Victims' Participation, 18 January 2008, para. 98.

20 Lubanga (ICC-01/04-01/06 OA 8), Decision of the Appeals Chamber on the Joint Application of Victims a/0001/06 to a/0003/06 and a/0105/06 concerning the 'Directions and Decision of the Appeals Chamber of 2 February 2007', Separate Opinion of Judge Sang-Hyun Song , 13 June 2007, para. 3.

21 In a recent development, the Trial Chamber in the Lubanga case has agreed to allow three participating victims to testify in person, following the request made by their legal representative. See, Lubanga (ICC-01/04-01/06), Decision on the request by victims a/0225/06, a/0229/06 and a/0270/07 to express their views and concerns in person and to present evidence during the trial, 26 June 2009.

22 ECCC, Internal Rules, Rule 23.

23 Ibid., 23(1)(a).

24 ECCC, Internal Rules, Rule 12*ter* (5), adopted on 9 February 2010.

25 D. Donat-Cattin, 'The Role of Victims in the ICC Proceedings', in F. Lattanzi (ed.), *The International Criminal Court: Comments on the Draft Statute*, Teramo: University of Teramo, 1998, p. 266.

26 Situation in the Democratic Republic of Congo (ICC-01/04-101), Decision on the Applications for Participation in the Proceedings of VPRS 1, VPRS 2, VPRS 3, VPRS 4, VPRS 5 and VPRS 6, 17 January 2006.

27 Situation in the Democratic Republic of Congo (ICC-01/04-556), Judgment on victim participation in the investigation stage of the proceedings in the appeal of the OPCD against the decision of Pre-Trial Chamber I of 7 December 2007 and in the appeals of the OPCD and the Prosecutor against the decision of Pre-Trial Chamber I of 24 December 2007, 19 December 2008, para. 59.

28 Ibid., para. 45.

29 Lubanga (ICC-01/04-01/06-172-tEN), Decision on the Applications for Participation in the Proceedings Submitted by VPRS 1 to VPRS 6, 29 June 2006, para. 6.

30 Thomas Lubanga Dyilo—the first accused before the ICC, is charged with enlisting, conscripting and using children under the age of 15 to participate actively in hostilities [See, Lubanga (ICC-01/04-01/06), Warrant of Arrest, 10 February 2006]. Concerns have been raised about the narrowness of the indictment, given the broader reports of his involvement in murder, torture and sexual violence. The later indictments for Messrs Katanga and Ngudjolo Chui encompassed a broader range of crimes though the incidents to which they related took place in a single village [see, Katanga (ICC-01/04-01/07-1 and ICC-01/04-01/07-Anx1), Warrant of arrest, 2 July 2007 and Ngudjolo Chui (ICC-01/04-01/07-260 and ICC-01/04-01/07-260-Anx), Warrant of arrest, 2 July 2007].

31 Lubanga (ICC-01/04-01/06-1119), Decision on victims' participation, 18 January 2008, para. 95.

32 Ibid.

33 The Trial Chamber granted leave to appeal its decision of 18 January 2008 on a number of grounds, including, *inter alia*, whether the notion of victim necessarily implies the existence of personal and direct harm and whether the harm alleged by a victim and the concept of 'personal interests' under Article 68 of the Statute must be linked with the charges against the accused. See, Lubanga (ICC-01/04-01/06-1191), Decision on the Defence and Prosecution Requests for Leave to Appeal the Decision on Victims' Participation of 18 January 2008, 26 February 2008, paras 54(a) and (b).

34 See, Lubanga (ICC-01/04-01/06 OA 9 OA 10), Judgment on the appeals of The Prosecutor and The Defence against Trial Chamber I's Decision on Victims' Participation of 18 January 2008, 11 July 2008, para. 58.

35 See, S. Thomas and T. Chy, 'Including the Survivors in the Tribunal Process', in J. D. Ciorciari and A. Heindel (eds), *On Trial: The Khmer Rouge Accountability Process,* Phnom Penh: Documentation Centre of Cambodia, 2009, pp. 214–93.

36 Ibid.

37 Id.

38 Id.

39 ECCC, Internal Rules, Rule 12*ter* (5), adopted on 9 February 2010.

40 For example, the International Covenant on Civil and Political Rights (ICCPR) (1966) [Arts 2(3), 9(5) and 14(6)]; International Convention on the Elimination of All Forms of Racial Discrimination (ICERD) (1965) (Art. 6); Convention of the Rights of the Child (1989) (Art. 39); Convention against Torture and Other Cruel, Inhuman or Degrading Treatment or Punishment (UNCAT) (1984) (Art. 14); and Statute of the International Criminal Court (1998) (Art. 75). It has also figured in regional instruments, for example, European Convention for the Protection of Human Rights and Fundamental Freedoms (ECHR) [Arts 5(5), 13 and 41]; the American Convention on Human Rights (ACHR) (1969) [Arts 25, 63(1) and 68]; and the African Convention on Human and Peoples' Rights (ACHPR) (1981) [Art. 21(2)]. See also, the International Convention for the Protection of all Persons from Enforced Disappearance (ICPPED), of 2006, not yet entered into force (Art. 24). At the time of writing, the Convention has 73 signatures and four ratifications.

41 See, for example, Human Rights Committee (HRC), General Comment (GC) No. 31 [80] *Nature of the General Legal Obligation Imposed on States Parties to the Covenant* 26/05/2004, (UN Doc. No. CCPR/C/21/Rev.1/Add.13, at paras 15–17; United Nations Committee against Torture (CAT), GC No. 2, *Implementation of Article 2 by States Parties*, (UN Doc. CAT/C/GC/2/CRP. 1/Rev.4 (2007).) at para. 15.

42 See, for example, Velasquez Rodriguez Case, Inter-Am.Ct.H.R. (Ser. C) No. 4 (1988) (Judgment of 29 July 1988) at para. 174. See also Papamichalopoulos *v.* Greece (Art. 50) (1995), (Appl. no. 14556/89) ECHR Judgment (31 Oct. 1995) at para. 36.

43 Basic principles and guidelines on the right to a remedy and reparation for victims of gross violations of international human rights law and serious violations of international humanitarian law, Resolution 2005/35 [UN Doc. No. E/CN.4/RES/2005/35 (2005)] and GA Resolution 60/147 [UN Doc. No. A/RES/60/147 (2006)]. See also the UN Declaration of Basic Principles of Justice for Victims of Crime and Abuse of Power, adopted by General Assembly Resolution 40/34 of 29 Nov. 1985; and the Universal Declaration of Human Rights (UDHR) (1948) (Art. 8).

44 Chorzow Factory case, Permanent Court of International Justice, Ser. A, No. 9 at 21 (1927).

45 UN General Assembly Resolution 56/83, Annex, *Responsibility of States for Internationally Wrongful Acts*.

46 Aksoy *v.* Turkey (Applic. No. 21987/93) ECHR Judgment (18 Dec. 1996), para. 95. See also, Council of Europe, Recommendation Rec(2004)6 of the Committee of Ministers (COM) to member states on the improvement of domestic remedies (adopted by COM on 12 May 2004, at its 114th Session);

Inter-American Court on Human Rights, Judicial Guarantees in States of Emergency [Arts 27(2), 25 and 8 ACHR], Advisory Opinion OC-9/87 (8 Oct. 1987), para. 24. See also, Cordova *v.* Italy (No. 1) Applic. No. 40877/98, European Court of Human Rights (2003) at para. 58.

47 Donat-Cattin, 'The Role of Victims in the ICC Proceedings', pp. 269–70.

48 Ferstman, 'The Reparation Regime of the International Criminal Court', pp. 667–86.

49 The UN Basic Principles and Guidelines on the Right to a Remedy and Reparation.

50 Art. 75 of the ICC Statute.

51 Art. 23(12) of the Internal Rules.

52 See, Case 001, Civil Parties' Co-Lawyers Joint Submission on Reparations, 14 Sept. 2009.

53 Article 75(1) refers to 'on its own motion *in exceptional circumstances'* (emphasis added).

54 The ICC is limited by the Statute to afforded reparation 'to, or in respect of, victims' who, according to Rule 85(1) of the Rules of Procedure and Evidence, may be natural persons or legal persons, the latter being restricted to 'organizations or institutions that have sustained direct harm to any of their property which is dedicated to religion, education, art or science or charitable purposes, and to their historic monuments, hospitals and other places and objects for humanitarian purposes.' Consequently, it is not possible for the Court to award reparations to States, though they may have an interest in the proceedings which may be taken into account by the Court.

55 See, ECCC Victims' Unit, Key Message For Civil Party Applicants In Case File 002, 28 September 2009, available at http://www.eccc.gov.kh/english/cabinet/press/133/vu_statement_en.pdf.

56 Internal Rule 23(9).

57 Article 79 of the ICC Statute.

58 Case 001, Civil Parties' Co-Lawyers Joint Submission on Reparations, para. 39.

26

Amnesties

Louise Mallinder

Introduction

The end of the Cold War marked the start of a new era in global politics in which legalism and the rule of law became increasingly important in international relations and the number of international legal institutions grew.[1] In particular, international criminal law, which had largely been moribund during the previous decades, was revived with the creation of the *ad hoc* tribunals, the hybrid courts and the International Criminal Court (ICC). Human rights activists and the international legal community hailed these developments as important steps towards ending the cultures of impunity that so often prevail after mass violence.[2] Nonetheless, despite these developments, many countries continue to introduce amnesty laws to shield individuals or groups from legal sanctions, even for the most serious crimes.[3]

Although throughout history, *coups d'État*, rebellions, conflicts, and dictatorships have often resulted in amnesty laws,[4] the growth of legalism in the 1990s caused amnesties to become subject to sustained international criticism.[5] Today amnesty laws are contested both in academic research and in praxis. International actors intervene in debates on amnesty laws in countries such as Kenya, Burundi and Nepal to argue forcibly against amnesties for serious crimes. Such criticism typically locates amnesty laws and international criminal law as occupying opposing poles. Their relationships are, however, often more interwoven and complex. For example, although legislators generally enact amnesty laws to close permanently the possibility of prosecutions for specific individuals or crimes, the hybrid tribunals in Sierra Leone and Cambodia were established even though potential indictees had already been amnestied. In response to these decisions to disregard pre-existing amnesties, some commentators have voiced concerns that removing previously granted amnesties could have potentially serious repercussions for future peace initiatives both within the country concerned and internationally.[6]

In addition, where international criminal courts are established or arrest warrants are issued for crimes committed in *ongoing* conflicts, they are often criticized for endangering fragile peace negotiations by threatening the military and political leaders who must sign the agreements.[7] For example, the ICC issued arrest warrants for the leaders of the Ugandan rebel group, the Lord's Resistance Army (LRA), despite Uganda's Amnesty Act 2000. During the subsequent Juba peace talks, LRA leader Joseph Kony and the LRA negotiators frequently described the warrants as an impediment to Kony signing the final peace agreement.[8] These peace talks eventually collapsed, and although this may have occurred for multiple reasons, some commentators point to the ICC's arrest warrants as a contributing factor. However, it is too early to draw conclusions on the impact of international criminal trials or amnesties on peace initiatives as most discussions rely on anecdotal evidence and little empirical, comparative analysis has been conducted.[9] Furthermore, the growing criminological literature on international criminal justice casts doubt on the ability of international criminal courts to deter serious human rights violations, an objective that is frequently cited in arguments in favour of trials.[10]

Finally, even if international tribunals successfully prosecute human rights violators, demands for amnesty do not disappear. For example, following the Nuremberg trials, German authorities enacted broad amnesties for lower-level Nazi offenders for crimes against personal freedom, religion and even life.[11] Similarly, after the Tokyo tribunal, Japanese soldiers accused of conflict-related crimes were amnestied and many of those convicted by the international tribunal were released early.[12] More recently, persons convicted by the 'hybrid' Special Panels for Serious Crimes (SPSC) of the District Court in Dili, Timor-Leste, benefited from a clemency decree.[13] In addition, there have also been legislative initiatives to grant amnesty for serious crimes related to the Indonesian occupation and the violence in Timor-Leste in 2006.[14] The revisiting of amnesty debates in the wake of prosecutions by international tribunals and in countries that have benefited from substantial international intervention illustrates that during transitions countries rarely follow a linear path towards justice. Instead, calls for justice or forgiveness often wax and wane depending on the changing political circumstances and the salience of practical concerns such as the passage of time, the degradation of evidence and the mortality of victims, witnesses and perpetrators. As a result, amnesties remain a contentious, yet vibrant issue within international criminal law. This chapter investigates their controversial status by analysing relevant treaty provisions, customary international law and the jurisprudence of international criminal courts.

Amnesties under international criminal law

Although international criminal law has developed considerably in the past two decades, it remains 'a legal environment resembling more a patchwork than a coherent, let alone complete, system'.[15] States are subject to differing legal obligations depending on their treaty ratifications and many human rights violations are not part of international criminal law. Furthermore, several major countries that abused human rights in recent years, such as China, Russia and the United States, are not party to international criminal tribunals. Nor do these courts have jurisdiction over some notorious violators like Burma or Zimbabwe.[16] Furthermore, international criminal tribunals are restricted to investigating the offenders who are 'most responsible' for designing and ordering mass human rights violations. As a result, these courts only prosecute small numbers of offenders and the crimes of tens of thousands of perpetrators are left to domestic legal systems, which often fail to pursue trials actively and genuinely.

Despite the increased codification of international crimes, no international convention explicitly prohibits amnesty laws,[17] and indeed, 'on every occasion where an explicit amnesty prohibition or discouragement has been mooted in the context of a multilateral treaty negotiation, states have demonstrated a resolute unwillingness to agree to even the mildest discouragement'.[18] Instead, arguments that certain forms of amnesty laws are prohibited centre on obligations under treaties and customary international law to hold individuals accountable for serious crimes.

The 1948 Genocide Convention requires contracting parties to provide effective penalties for persons guilty of genocide.[19] The legal duty to prosecute genocide is undeniable and cannot be circumvented by amnesty legislation. However, many serious human rights violations do not fall within the scope of this convention as the definition of genocide is restricted to actions taken with an 'intent to destroy, in whole or in part, a national, ethnical, racial or religious group'.[20] This suggests two limitations: first, many situations of mass atrocity do not entail a specific intent to destroy a target group.[21] Second, the omission of acts directed against 'political groups'[22] means that situations such as South America's 'dirty wars' are excluded from the scope of the Genocide Convention.

Serious war crimes in *international* conflicts are also subject to individual criminal accountability. The 1949 Geneva Conventions require states to criminalize 'grave breaches' of the conventions and to prosecute or extradite perpetrators.[23] This obligation to prosecute is 'absolute', meaning 'that states parties can under no circumstances grant perpetrators immunity or amnesty from prosecution for grave breaches'.[24] Since the Second World War, such international wars are rare compared with civil conflicts and unrest, and common Article 3 of the Geneva Conventions, relating to non-international conflicts, does not contain an explicit duty to prosecute.

The duty to prosecute war crimes committed in *internal* conflicts is further complicated as the only treaty to address amnesties explicitly is the 1977 Additional Protocol II to the Geneva Conventions. Article 6(5) of this protocol encourages states parties to grant 'the broadest possible amnesty to persons who have participated' in non-international armed conflicts.[25] The Commentary on the Additional Protocol asserts that this provision is 'to encourage gestures of reconciliation which can contribute to re-establishing normal relations in the life of a nation which has been divided'.[26] Furthermore, the Plenary Meeting Notes reveal that the negotiating states rejected a proposal to exclude individuals who committed crimes against humanity from any amnesty.[27] During the 1990s, the International Committee of the Red Cross (ICRC) reinterpreted Article 6(5) to cover only 'combat immunity', under which combatants who abide by international humanitarian law are not liable for prosecution.[28] For crimes against civilians or combatants who were *hors de combat* during internal conflicts, the ICRC argued that perpetrators should be prosecuted and amnesties are not acceptable. In its 2005 study of customary international humanitarian law, the ICRC argued that its interpretation of Article 6(5) has become part of customary law. However, this ICRC study considered only a few amnesty laws[29] and a wider study undertaken by this author indicates that states continue to amnesty war crimes committed in internal conflicts. This indicates that international custom has yet to crystallize on the issue.[30]

Even if Additional Protocol II is reinterpreted to exclude amnesties for serious crimes, the protocol applies only to conflicts between government forces and 'dissident armed forces or other organized armed groups'. Many violent non-state actors do not meet the required threshold of organization required by the protocol. Furthermore, the protocol specifically excludes 'situations of internal disturbances and tensions, such as riots, isolated and sporadic acts of violence and other acts of a similar nature'.[31] As a result, such 'less intense' civil disturbances do not fall within international humanitarian law. Instead, they are regulated by international human rights law, which provides for state responsibility, rather than individual criminal accountability.[32] As a result, many human rights violations committed during 'peacetime' may be subject to 'only whatever punishment [the] state may choose—or not choose to impose'.[33]

The power of states to amnesty 'peacetime' crimes is, however, constrained by the 1984 Convention against Torture, which requires states parties to impose 'appropriate penalties' on torturers.[34] The convention's definition of torture is restricted to acts committed by persons 'acting in an official capacity'.[35] Torture committed by non-state actors would not fall within the scope of this convention. For state officials accused of torture, the convention requires states parties to investigate the facts,[36] and if appropriate, 'submit the case to its competent authorities for the purpose of prosecution'.[37] This wording is more ambiguous than the explicit obligations of the Genocide Convention. Consequently, some commentators argue that the convention allows states parties a degree of permissiveness regarding the manner in which they must carry out their duties as the convention 'does not explicitly require a prosecution to take place, let alone that punishment be imposed and served'.[38] Instead, it leaves decisions on whether to prosecute alleged torturers to the discretion of prosecutorial authorities.

The Convention on Enforced Disappearances, which has yet to enter into force, adopts similar wording to the Convention against Torture by restricting the application of the convention to persons 'acting with the authorization, support or acquiescence of the State'.[39] Where such persons are accused of enforced disappearances, the convention requires states parties to submit cases to the 'competent authorities for the purpose of prosecution'.[40] It continues that the authorities should make their decisions on whether to prosecute 'in the same manner as in the case of any ordinary offence of a serious nature' under the state's domestic law.[41] Furthermore, the convention allows for 'mitigating circumstances', including reduced penalties, for perpetrators who help to locate disappeared persons or their remains, or who identify other perpetrators.[42]

In addition to drawing on international conventions' provisions that serious crimes be prosecuted, international courts also try crimes against humanity. These crimes are not proscribed by international conventions and instead are criminalized under customary international law. Furthermore, recognizing the criminality of crimes against humanity does not automatically imply a duty to prosecute.[43] Article 38 of the International Court of Justice (ICJ) Statute requires that determinations of whether such a duty exists under customary international law must be based on state practice and *opinio juris*. This can be found in the existence or absence of relevant domestic legislation. The ICJ Statute also provides that judicial decisions and academic research can be 'subsidiary' sources of international custom. At present, some subsidiary sources strongly support the existence of a duty to prosecute crimes against humanity. However, as states continue to enact amnesty laws, or to mediate peace agreements amnestying crimes against humanity,[44] a mandatory duty to prosecute such crimes has yet to evolve into a generally recognized norm. Furthermore, for much of the period since the Nuremberg judgements, 'crimes against humanity' were understood to require a nexus to armed conflict. Although the International Criminal Tribunal for the former Yugoslavia (ICTY) moved away from this position in the *Tadić* case[45] and delegates at the Rome Conference declined to include it in the ICC Statute,[46] this nexus may still apply for many crimes against humanity committed after the Second World War.

In addition to legal disputes over definitions of crimes and the status of customary international law, interpretations of the extent of the duty to prosecute can be influenced by political perceptions of the nature of the violence. For example, during the 1992–95 conflict in Bosnia-Herzegovina, the belligerent parties and international actors held divergent views on whether the conflict was internal and being fought solely by Bosnian armed factions, or whether it was international with both Yugoslavia and Croatia participating in the violence. This dispute had significant legal implications on whether individual criminal responsibility was required under international humanitarian law. The ICTY eventually determined in the *Tadić* case that it had jurisdiction to prosecute crimes committed during internal conflicts.[47] In addition, during negotiations to establish international tribunals, political factors can affect the jurisdiction awarded to the tribunals. For example, the mandates of the International Criminal Tribunal for Rwanda (ICTR) and the SPSC in Timor-Leste were deliberately limited to 'artificial and politically convenient' periods, which excluded many serious crimes from the courts' mandates.[48]

Such political calculations have been rightly criticized as creating false hierarchies of victims and rewarding certain groups of offenders. However, states' duties to prosecute crimes under international law do not require that *every* perpetrator be prosecuted, as to impose such obligations would be unrealistic in most post-conflict situations.

Amnesties in the statutes of international criminal courts

International Criminal Court

There is no explicit reference to amnesties in the ICC Statute or the Court's Rules of Procedure and Evidence. This omission is deliberate, as the parties at the Rome Conference discussed amnesties but could not reach a consensus. During the preparatory meetings, the United States issued an informal 'non paper'[49] that suggested 'the Court should take account of domestic amnesties when deciding whether or not to exercise jurisdiction'.[50] Some participants greeted this proposition favourably. South Africa was particularly supportive, as it was concerned that the ICC would view processes like its Truth and Reconciliation Commission (TRC) as evidence of a state's unwillingness to prosecute.[51] In contrast, 'NGOs and many of the strongest state supporters of the ICC' vigorously resisted the US proposals, fearing that allowing amnesties to block the Court's jurisdiction would enable abusive governments to shield themselves.[52] The participant states' inability to reach a consensus is indicative of the incoherence of state practice on amnesties. The issue was left unresolved and the Rome Statute is arguably sufficiently ambiguous to allow the ICC to recognize certain forms of amnesty.[53]

The key provisions for amnesties are Articles 17 and 53 of the Rome Statute.[54] Article 17 outlines the principle of complementarity and provides that the ICC can only investigate or prosecute cases within its jurisdiction if the relevant state is unwilling or unable genuinely to investigate or prosecute. Although this provision would require the ICC to intervene if broad, unconditional amnesties were enacted for crimes falling within its jurisdiction, Robinson has used the example of the Amnesty Committee of the South African TRC to argue that where states undertake 'a diligent, methodical effort to gather the evidence and ascertain the facts relating to the conduct in question' before deciding whether to grant amnesty in an individual case according to strict criteria, and where prosecutions remain possible for those who do not participate or are denied amnesty, there is space for the ICC to recognize such amnesties.[55] This understanding of the ICC's complementary role was also voiced by former UN Secretary-General Kofi Annan, who argued that

> [n]o one should imagine that [the ICC's power to intervene under Article 17] would apply to a case like South Africa's, where the regime and the conflict which caused the crimes have come to an end, and the victims have inherited power. It is inconceivable that, in such a case, the Court would seek to substitute its judgement for that of a whole nation which is seeking the best way to put a traumatic past behind it and build a better future.[56]

However, critics have contended that as amnesty laws by their nature are designed to prevent prosecutions, a 'strict reading of Article 17 would not distinguish the TRC from less politically legitimate amnesties'.[57]

As the ICC's jurisdiction potentially extends to thousands of cases around the world, under Article 53 of the Rome Statute, the ICC Prosecutor has discretion in deciding whether to investigate or prosecute cases.[58] In addition to evidentiary concerns, the Statute instructs the Prosecutor to consider the following factors when deciding whether to proceed: 'the gravity of the crime', 'the interests of victims' and whether 'there are nonetheless substantial reasons to believe that an investigation would not serve the interests of justice'.[59] The meaning of the phrase 'interests of justice' has been subject to considerable scholarly debate, with some authors arguing that where indictments risk prolonging violent conflict, they cannot be considered in the 'interests of justice', and instead, preventing further crimes could be better served by amnesty processes.[60] In addition, many international non-governmental organizations (NGOs), academics and legal practitioners made submissions on the concept to the Office of the Prosecutor (OTP).

The OTP initially addressed this issue in draft regulations published in 2003, which noted that the expert opinions voiced in the consultation process leaned towards the OTP declining to investigate when an investigation or prosecution could 'exacerbate or otherwise destabilise a conflict situation' or when the start of an investigation would 'seriously endanger the successful completion of a reconciliation or peace process'.[61] This approach seems to have been reflected in the ICC Prosecutor's decision to adopt 'a "low-profile" approach' during the 2004–05 Betty Bigome peace process for the conflict in northern Uganda, which began after the OTP formally started investigating the situation in January 2004.[62] Furthermore, in his 2005 report to the UN Security Council, the ICC Prosecutor indicated that he would consider 'various national and international efforts to achieve peace and security' when deciding to proceed in a particular case.[63]

More recently, the OTP's approach seems to have shifted. In September 2007, it published its *Policy Paper on the Interests of Justice*. This paper states that the OTP's discretion to suspend an investigation or prosecution in the interests of justice is '*exceptional* in its nature and there is a *presumption* in favour of investigation or prosecution'.[64] Although the paper does not systematically explore criteria for exceptional suspensions, a few can be discerned, including that decisions must conform to the 'objects and purpose of the Statute'.[65] According to the Statute's preamble, these are to prevent serious crimes and to guarantee 'lasting respect for international justice'.[66] The paper assumes that trials will further these goals and does not engage with criminological analyses that argue that the power of international prosecutions to prevent mass atrocity is limited.[67] Furthermore, it does not consider whether during ongoing conflicts, prevention of serious crimes could be better served by amnesties to facilitate peace accords, rather than prosecutions. Indeed, in contrast to its earlier position, the OTP restricted its scope to consider peace processes by distinguishing between 'the concepts of the interests of justice, and the interests of peace' and finding that the latter 'falls within the mandate of institutions *other than* the Office of the Prosecutor'.[68] Furthermore, the paper argues that '[t]he concept of interests of justice established in the Statute, while necessarily broader than criminal justice in a narrow sense ... should not be conceived so broadly as to embrace all issues related to peace and security'.[69] The paper does, however, refer to 'other forms of justice', including 'domestic prosecutions, truth seeking, reparations programs, institutional reform and traditional justice mechanisms' as means of pursuing '*broader* justice'.[70] It 'fully endorses' the '*complementary* role' that such measures can play, particularly in 'dealing with large numbers of offenders and addressing the impunity gap' which results from the ICC's jurisdiction being limited to only the most serious crimes.[71] This recognition of other justice mechanisms seems to support the idea that ICC investigations could coexist with a range of domestic transitional justice mechanisms, which in some jurisdictions have been accompanied by amnesties to facilitate truth-recovery and institutional reform.

Special Court for Sierra Leone (SCSL)

Article IX of the 1999 Lomé Accord provided 'absolute and free pardon and reprieve to all combatants and collaborators in respect of anything done by them in pursuit of their objectives, up to the time of the signing of the present Agreement', and pledged that the government would take 'no official or judicial action' against any of the combatants, including Foday Sankoh, the leader of the rebel Revolutionary United Front (RUF).[72] This amnesty provision was intended by the parties to the conflict to cover all crimes committed during the war. However, when signing the agreement, the Special Representative of the UN Secretary-General, Francis Okelo, appended a handwritten disclaimer stating 'the UN holds the understanding that the amnesty provisions of the Agreement shall not apply to international crimes of genocide, crimes against humanity, war crimes and other serious violations of international humanitarian law'.[73]

Following the Lomé Accord, the violence in Sierra Leone continued until May 2001 and prompted the Sierra Leonean government to change its strategy. In August 2000, the president wrote to the United Nations to request assistance in establishing an international tribunal, arguing that the RUF had reneged on its promises. The United Nations responded positively to the request and, following negotiations with the government, the United Nations presented a Draft Statute in October 2000.[74] In his report on the Draft Statute, the UN Secretary-General noted that the Sierra Leonean government had

> concurred with the position of the United Nations and agreed to the inclusion of an amnesty clause which would read as follows: 'An amnesty granted to any person falling within the jurisdiction of the Special Court in respect of the crimes referred to in articles 2 to 4 of the present Statute shall not be a bar to prosecution'.[75]

The Secretary-General further noted that the 'denial of legal effect to the amnesty' enabled the Special Court to prosecute crimes committed before the signing of the Lomé Accord.[76]

In January 2002, the United Nations and the government signed a formal agreement containing the Court's Statute. The Draft Statute's amnesty provision was adopted unchanged and became Article 10 of the Statute. The SCSL has since relied upon Article 10 to deny challenges to its jurisdiction.

The SCSL only indicted 13 individuals, two of whom died. Although these indictees could not rely on the amnesty, the thousands of other perpetrators within Sierra Leone were processed by the TRC and Disarmament, Demobilization and Reintegration (DDR) programmes, rather than put on trial. To reassure these surrendering combatants, the registration form used by Sierra Leone's National Committee on DDR stated in its first term of acceptance that '[i]n accordance with the Amnesty Conditions you will be exempted from criminal prosecution, with regards to any crimes committed prior to your surrender'.[77] This illustrates how amnesties and trials before international courts can coexist and are used to distinguish between divergent levels of responsibility among offenders.

Extraordinary Chambers in the Courts of Cambodia (ECCC)

In 1994, the Cambodian government, seeking to negotiate with Khmer Rouge insurgents, granted broad amnesty to guerrillas who defected within six months, including those who had committed murder, rape, pillage, destruction of private and public property and crimes against the state.[78] The amnesty excluded the Khmer Rouge leaders.[79] Subsequently, on 14 September 1996, the King pardoned the former Deputy Prime Minister of the Khmer Rouge government, Ieng Sary, for an earlier *in absentia* death sentence and granted him amnesty for the crimes covered in the 1994 amnesty on condition that he end his insurgency and defect, together with his supporters, which he did.[80]

In June 1997, the Cambodian government asked the United Nations for assistance in prosecuting the Khmer Rouge leadership. In response, the United Nations appointed a Group of

Experts, which in February 1999 recommended that the United Nations establish an *ad hoc* tribunal.[81] During the subsequent negotiations between the United Nations and the government, amnesty was the subject of bitter wrangling. This centred on the United Nations' initial insistence that the Memorandum of Understanding (MoU) state: '[t]he Parties agree that there shall be no amnesty for the crime of genocide, war crimes and crimes against humanity. An amnesty granted to any person falling within the jurisdiction of the chambers shall not be a bar to prosecution'.[82] The government opposed revoking Ieng Sary's amnesty and in March 2000, the Head of the Cambodian delegation informed the United Nations that the Cambodian 'Draft Law (Article 40) makes a clear statement of the government's intent not to request an amnesty for any person who committed crimes relating to applicable law described in Articles 3–8 of the Draft Law.' As the 1994 law excluded the Khmer Rouge leaders who were to be the targets of the tribunal, the Cambodian delegation, referring to Ieng Sary's pardon, further stated 'there has been only one case, dated 14 September 1996, when an amnesty was granted to only one person with regard to a 1979 conviction on the charge of genocide'. Despite these objections, the United Nations' preferred wording was included in Article 9 of the October 2000 Tribunal MoU.[83]

In August 2001, the government unilaterally passed legislation to establish the hybrid court, which differed significantly from the MoU. With regard to amnesty, Article 40 of the new version stated that '[t]he Royal Government of Cambodia shall not request an amnesty or pardon for any persons who may be investigated for or convicted of crimes referred to in Articles 3, 4, 5, 6, 7 and 8 of this law'.[84] The government's unilateral actions caused the United Nations to withdraw from negotiations.[85] The deadlock lasted until both sides approved the 2003 March Agreement. In relation to amnesty, this agreement stated '[t]he Royal Government of Cambodia shall not request an amnesty or pardon for any persons who may be investigated for or convicted of crimes referred to in the present Agreement'.[86] It continued by restating the government's position that only one potential indictee had benefited from the amnesty and it provided that 'the scope of this pardon is a matter to be decided by the Extraordinary Chambers'.[87] This final version of the agreement reflects the government's approach to amnesties, but with the compromise that the ECCC will decide whether to defer to Ieng Sary's amnesty.

International criminal jurisprudence on amnesties

International criminal courts have not dealt extensively with amnesty laws, and to date, only the ICTY and the SCSL have referred directly to amnesties in their decisions. In making determinations of individual criminal culpability, international criminal courts 'can only disregard an amnesty law or issue nonbinding comments about it'.[88] These decisions are only binding in the individual case. The courts do not have the power to amend or annul amnesty laws, or to determine their constitutionality under national law. In addition, they do not have the power to order a national government to amend or repeal domestic amnesty legislation. However, decisions by international tribunals to disregard national amnesties could affect the laws' domestic impact, either by providing legal reasoning which may be relied upon by national courts and, if the amnesty is individualized, by making it less attractive to potential applicants.

Amnesties were first considered by an international criminal court in the 1998 *Furundžija* case before the ICTY. In this case, the tribunal was not faced with a pre-existing amnesty law, but rather it chose to express its views *in obiter* on a hypothetical amnesty for torture. The ICTY stated that an individual could be prosecuted for torture before an international tribunal, a foreign state and a subsequent regime even if the action in question had been amnestied. The tribunal based its judgement on its view that the prohibition of torture is a 'peremptory norm of international law'. It concluded that if according to 'the *jus cogens* value of the prohibition against torture, treaties or customary rules providing for torture would be null and void *ab initio*' then national legislation shielding torturers from prosecution must not be accorded any 'international legal recognition'.[89] In making these statements, the court did not analyse state practice or *opinio juris* to support its assertions that torture was prohibited by *jus cogens* norms, nor did it determine whether such a prohibition merely requires states to refrain from committing acts of torture, rather than prohibiting amnesties for such acts. Indeed, in the subsequent paragraph, the Trial Chamber contended that the *jus cogens* character of the prohibition of torture 'entitles' every state to investigate, prosecute, punish and extradite individuals accused of torture, but the Court did not suggest that every state was *required* to do so.[90] In evaluating the ICTY's pronouncements, Freeman argues that 'the Court's logic is seriously open to question', but he notes, however, that many commentators nonetheless cite the ICTY's opinion 'as proof of the state of international law in relation to amnesties'.[91]

The ICTY revisited its position on amnesties following the 2008 arrest of Radovan Karadžić. Karadžić's defence have alleged that in 1996 US negotiator Richard Holbrooke offered him immunity from prosecution by the ICTY in exchange for withdrawing from public life.[92] The Trial Chamber addressed this alleged immunity deal in a December 2008 decision in which it argued that '[a]ccording to customary international law, there are some acts for which immunity from prosecution cannot be invoked before international tribunals'.[93] It further stated that '[t]he Trial Chamber considers it well established that any immunity agreement in respect of an accused indicted for genocide, war crimes and/or crimes against humanity before an international tribunal would be invalid under international law'.[94] To support its conclusions, the Trial Chamber referred in a footnote to the statutes of the Nuremberg and Tokyo tribunals, the ICTR, the SCSL, the ICC and its own statute; the Draft Code of Crimes against the Peace and Security of Mankind; the decision of the International Court of Justice in the *Congo v. Belgium* case which related to official immunities rather than amnesty deals; and its own case law. According to Article 38(d) of the ICJ Statute, the declarations and judicial decisions are only 'subsidiary means for the determination of rules of law'. Furthermore, 10 of the 13 sources cited do not refer to amnesty laws.[95] The Trial Chamber did not highlight any state practice to support its position. Furthermore, many of the documents cited date from after the alleged immunity deal was made. As a result, the Trial Chamber's reasoning has been described as 'undeveloped, unsatisfying, and unpersuasive'.[96] Nonetheless, it was upheld on 12 October 2009 by the Appeals Chamber, which found that individuals accused of serious violations of international humanitarian law 'can have no legitimate expectation of immunity from prosecution'.[97] The Appeals Chamber further found that 'even if the alleged Agreement were proved, it would not limit the jurisdiction of the tribunal', as the ICTY Statute could only be amended by a UN Security Council Resolution.[98]

The legality of amnesties under customary international law has also been considered by the SCSL. First, on 13 March 2004, the SCSL Appeals Chamber heard an appeal from two former RUF members, who argued that the Lomé amnesty was binding and should be applied to them. In response to this appeal, *amici curiae* briefs submitted by international legal expert Diane Orentlicher and the NGO the Redress Trust argued that a norm of customary international law had 'crystallized' to prohibit amnesties for serious human rights violations.[99] This argument was also made by the prosecutor.

In its judgement, the Appeals Chamber did not address potential conflicts between Sierra Leone's specific treaty obligations and the Lomé amnesty, as the 'only treaty imposing an obligation on Sierra Leone to prosecute for the crimes within the Statute is the Convention against Torture', which does not apply to non-state actors.[100] Although no international treaties were applicable to the case, the Appeals Chamber, however, agreed with Orentlicher's contention that 'given the existence of a treaty obligation to prosecute or extradite an offender, the grant of amnesty' for the crimes in the SCSL's statute 'is not only incompatible with, but is in breach of an obligation of a state towards the international community as a whole'.[101] However, Schabas notes that '[t]his is a far-reaching statement that finds only limited support in treaty law or state practice'.[102]

As a result of the inapplicability of international treaties, the Appeals Chamber relied mainly on the principle of universal jurisdiction to argue that although a state is entitled to grant amnesty under the principle of state sovereignty, other states do not have to respect the amnesty if it covers crimes that are subject to universal jurisdiction.[103] The Appeals Chamber relied upon the *Eichmann* case and the *Hostage* case to support its interpretation of universal jurisdiction. However, these cases concerned crimes committed during international armed conflict, rather than internal conflicts, like Sierra Leone's.[104] Nonetheless, the Appeals Chamber found that universal jurisdiction existed for the crimes within its statute. It then argued, using the *Furundžija* case and the ICJ *Congo v. Belgium* case, that where third states have jurisdiction, international courts also have jurisdiction to prosecute crimes under international law regardless of the domestic legality of the amnesty.[105] The Appeals Chamber's presentation of broad universal jurisdiction as well-established overlooks the divergences in state practice 'as to which international crimes give rise to universal jurisdiction, and uncertainty as to the circumstances in which universal jurisdiction may be exercised'. This could mean that not all the crimes in the SCSL's statute give rise to universal jurisdiction.[106]

The Appeals Chamber then discussed the status of amnesties under customary international law. The chamber did not investigate state practice on amnesties itself, but rather relied on the *amici curiae* briefs and the writings of Antonio Cassese. It cited Cassese's assertion that 'there is not yet any general obligation for states to refrain from amnesty for' crimes against humanity and that 'if a state passes any such law, it does not breach a customary rule'.[107] However, it contended that even if the Lomé amnesty did not breach customary international law, the SCSL, like courts in third states, 'is entitled in the exercise of its discretionary power, to attribute little or no weight to the grant of amnesty that is contrary to the direction in which customary international law is developing'.[108] In evaluating this argument, Schabas notes '[c]ourts, of course, should apply the law, but should they also apply "the direction in which the law is developing"? This is an odd approach, to say the least'.[109] It is particularly odd given the continued inconsistency of state practice relating to amnesties for serious human rights violations, which makes it impossible to predict whether the rule will definitely emerge and what form it will take.[110]

The Appeals Chamber considered the Lomé amnesty again a couple of months later in *Prosecutor v. Kondewa*, and in a brief judgement it confirmed its earlier decision. In a separate opinion to this decision, SCSL President Justice Robertson explored the amnesty in greater depth and, drawing upon state practice, noted that 'the degree to which international law forbids or nullifies amnesties must be open to some question'.[111] For example, he highlighted the 'substantial body of cases, comments, rulings and remarks' from international human rights monitoring bodies and jurists, but also noted that these are only subsidiary sources of international law, and that they contrast with 'the depressing number of occasions on which they have been provoked by state practice to the contrary'. Justice Robertson then pointed to the 'hand-wringing quality about the excuses for amnesty by states which grant them' to suggest that 'state practice is changing to conform with the consistent view that blanket amnesties are, at least "in general", impermissible in international law for international crimes'.[112] This is a cautious finding as it refers only to 'blanket' amnesties, suggesting that individualized or limited amnesty processes introduced in exceptional circumstances might be acceptable. In particular, Justice

Robertson argued that international law may be evolving to prohibit amnesties for military and political leaders, whilst accepting them for 'foot-soldiers'.

In a decision issued on the same day as the *Kondewa* case, the Appeals Chamber also addressed the amnesty in *Prosecutor v. Augustine Gbao*. Here, the Chamber reiterated its findings in the *Lomé Amnesty Decision* that the principle of universal jurisdiction precluded the amnesty for crimes giving rise to universal jurisdiction.[113] However, the Chamber went beyond its earlier decision to find that, based on the *Furundžija* case, the *Barcelona Traction* case at the ICJ, which was unrelated to amnesties, and a 1980 academic monograph, that 'there is ... support for the statement that there is a *crystallized* international norm to the effect that a government cannot grant amnesty for serious crimes under international law'.[114] This finding is surprising, given that firstly it is based on such scant evidence and secondly that it seems unlikely that a norm on amnesties could have crystallised in the two months that had elapsed since the *Lomé Amnesty Decision*.

Finally, pre-existing amnesties have also been considered by the Co-Investigating Judges of the ECCC. In issuing a provisional detention order against Ieng Sary, the Co-Investigating Judges held that 'apart from an allusion to genocidal acts in its preamble', the 1994 amnesty only referred 'to a number of domestic law offences subject to prosecution in accordance with national legislation applicable at the time' and therefore it did not cover crimes within the ECCC's jurisdiction.[115] This interpretation is interesting, as the 1994 Cambodian amnesty was clearly intended to apply to the atrocities committed by the Khmer Rouge, but, like amnesties elsewhere, the government described the crimes as offences under domestic law, rather than characterizing them as crimes under international law. As noted by the Co-Investigating Judges, their 'determination is of a provisional nature and does not bind the Trial and Supreme Court Chambers'.[116]

In the small number of decisions discussed here, international criminal courts have made pronouncements on the status of amnesties under customary international law. However, 'any trend in amnesty jurisprudence, as such, bears no direct relation to the formation of custom' and, as Freeman notes, 'state practice and international jurisprudence can even move in contrary directions'.[117] This problem is particularly pronounced as the courts failed to undertake a thorough assessment of state practice, which does not reflect the courts' interpretations.[118] The lack of detailed analysis underpinning the courts' decisions is problematic, not just in the relevant cases, but also because the cases, even where the amnesties are discussed *in obiter,* are widely referred to as evidence of a prohibition for amnesties for serious human rights violations, despite state practice to the contrary.

Conclusion

This chapter has explored international criminal law relating to amnesties. It has argued that this remains patchy and, as a result, some forms of amnesty for human rights violations may be permissible. It has further reviewed international criminal jurisprudence on amnesties and found that this is limited and the reasoning on customary international law is underdeveloped. These findings do not mean that amnesties have been unaffected by the development of international criminal law, and indeed, its growth has caused amnesty laws to evolve in several ways.

First, the number of amnesties enacted, including those for crimes under international law, has increased since the early 1990s. While this may seem to undermine the growth of international criminal law, Slye has argued, instead, that it is 'less a reflection of our increased tolerance of impunity and more of an indicator of the growing force of the international human rights movement and international criminal law'.[119] According to this argument, in the past, state agents may have neglected to enact amnesties for themselves or demand them from their successors simply because there was no threat that they would ever be prosecuted. Today, the growth of international criminal law means that 'certain acts by official actors are no longer beyond the reach of legal accountability', and hence, amnesties have become more valuable for violators.[120]

Secondly, although amnesties continue to cover serious human rights violations, from the late 1980s, increasing numbers of amnesties have excluded crimes under international law, although this has yet to become coherent state practice.[121]

Thirdly, the growth of human rights and legalism has affected how amnesty laws are designed in relation to other transitional justice processes. For example, the Amnesty Committee of the South African TRC was empowered to grant amnesty to perpetrators who voluntarily confessed their crimes. This process was an innovation in amnesty practice and has provided a high-profile example of the ways in which amnesty, rather than creating impunity, can contribute to truth recovery within transitional states.[122] Furthermore, offenders who did not apply for amnesty in South Africa remained liable for prosecution, which meant that the amnesty rather than preventing trials had the potential to contribute to a prosecutorial policy in which limited prosecutorial resources are focused on individuals who refuse to engage with nation-building efforts.[123]

Similarly, as international criminal courts only try small numbers of offenders who are 'most responsible' for mass atrocities, amnesties have also been designed to acknowledge divergent levels of responsibility or culpability. For example, under the Dayton peace accords, those who had perpetrated serious human rights violations remained liable for prosecution before the ICTY or domestic courts, whereas offenders who had committed less serious crimes during the conflict were amnestied. Furthermore, in Sierra Leone and Timor-Leste, small numbers of perpetrators were prosecuted by hybrid tribunals, where as the crimes of lower-level offenders were investigated by truth commissions rather than the courts.

Finally, international criminal law has been incorporated into domestic legal systems and has been used by municipal courts to restrict the scope of amnesty laws and, in some cases, to repeal the amnesty legislation. For example, in the 2005 *Julio Simón* case, the Argentine Supreme Court relied on international criminal law, which had been granted the same status as Argentina's constitution within the domestic legal system, to find that legislation enacted in 2003 to annul earlier amnesty laws was constitutional.[124]

Notes

1 C. P. R. Romano, 'The Proliferation of International Judicial Bodies: The Pieces of the Puzzle', *NYU Journal of International Law and Politics,* 31, 1998, 709–751. See also K. McEvoy, 'Beyond Legalism: Towards a Thicker Understanding of Transitional Justice', *Journal of Law and Society*, 34, 2008, 411–40.

2 M. A. Drumbl, 'Toward a Criminology of International Crime', *Ohio State Journal on Dispute Resolution,* 19, 2003, 263–82, 267.

3 For a definition of amnesty laws, see M. Freeman, *Necessary Evils: Amnesties and the Search for Justice,* Cambridge: Cambridge University Press, 2010, p. 13.

4 See, e.g. R. Parker, 'Fighting the Siren's Song: The Problem of Amnesty in Historical and Contemporary Perspective', *Acta Juridica Hungaria,* 42, 2001, 69–89.

5 See, e.g. D. F. Orentlicher, *Rule-of-Law Tools for Post-Conflict States: Amnesties,* UN Doc HR/PUB/09/1 (OHCHR, 2009).

6 See, e.g. Truth and Reconciliation Commission of Sierra Leone, *The Final Report of the Truth and Reconciliation Commission of Sierra Leone*, 2004, para. 553; W. A. Schabas, 'Amnesty, the Sierra Leone Truth and Reconciliation Commission and the Special Court for Sierra Leone', *U.C. Davis Journal of International Law & Policy,* 11, 2004, 145–69.

7 T. Unger and M. Wierda, 'Pursuing Justice in Ongoing Conflict: A Discussion of Current Practice', in K. Ambos, J. Large and M. Wierda (eds), *Building a Future on Peace and Justice: Studies on Transitional Justice, Peace and Development,* Berlin: Springer, 2008.
8 L. Mallinder, 'Uganda at a Crossroads: Narrowing the Amnesty?', Working Paper (QUB 2009).
9 I. Tallgren, 'The Sensibility and Sense of International Criminal Law', *European Journal of International Law,* 13, 2002, 561–95, 591–2.
10 R. E. Brooks, 'The New Imperialism: Violence, Norms, and the Rule of Law', *Michigan Law Review,* 101, 2003, 2275–340, 2305–6.
11 See, e.g. Bundesgesetzblatt (BGBl) 1949. p. 37f. Gesetz über die Gewährung von Straffreiheit ('Law Granting Exemption from Punishment'); Gesetz über den Erlaß von Strafen und Geldbußen und die Niederschlagung von Strafverfahren and Bußgeldverfahren vom 17.7.1954, BGBl. I. 1954, pp. 203–9 ('Law Concerning Release from Punishment and Fines and the Cancellation of Punitive and Fining Proceedings'), 1954.
12 See, e.g. Amnesty Law (Law No. 20 promulgated 28 March 1947), reprinted in *Kanpo fukkokuban,* no. 6059 (28 March 1947), p. 185.
13 Presidential Decree No 53 (19 May 2008).
14 Draft Law No. 24/I/2 on Amnesty and Other Clemency Measures (2004); Law No. 30/I/5a on 'Truth and Measures of Clemency for Diverse Offenses'.
15 S. R. Ratner, 'The Schizophrenias of International Criminal Law', *Texas International Law Journal,* 33, 1998, 237–56, 250.
16 The ICC can exercise jurisdiction over non-state parties if the UN Security Council refers a situation to it, but for Security Council members who have not ratified the Rome Statute such referrals seem unlikely.
17 R. C. Slye, 'The Legitimacy of Amnesties under International Law and General Principles of Anglo-American Law: Is a Legitimate Amnesty Possible?' *Virginia Journal of International Law Association,* 43, 2002, 173–248, 179.
18 Freeman, *Necessary Evils,* p. 33.
19 Convention on the Prevention and Punishment of the Crime of Genocide 1948, 78 UNTS 1021, Art. 5.
20 Genocide Convention, Art. 2.
21 M. P. Scharf, 'The Letter of the Law: The Scope of the International Legal Obligation to Prosecute Human Rights Crimes', *Law and Contemporary Problems,* 59, 1996, 41–61, 45.
22 Scharf, 'The Letter of the Law', 47.
23 Common Arts 49 (Geneva I); 50 (Geneva II); 129 (Geneva III); and 146 (Geneva IV).
24 Scharf, 'The Letter of the Law', 44.
25 Protocol Additional to the Geneva Conventions of 12 August 1949, and relating to the Protection of Victims of Non-International Armed Conflicts, 1977 Art. 6(5).
26 Y. Sandoz, C. Swinarski and B. Zimmerman (eds), *Commentary on the Additional Protocols of 8 June 1977 to the Geneva Conventions of 12 August 1949,* Geneva: ICRC, 1987, para. 4618.
27 K. Gallagher, 'No Justice, No Peace: The Legalities and Realities of Amnesty in Sierra Leone', *Thomas Jefferson Law Review,* 23, 2000, 149–98, 177–8.
28 T. Pfanner, Head of the ICRC Legal Division cited in D. Cassel, 'Lessons from the Americas: Guidelines for International Response to Amnesties for Atrocities', *Law and Contemporary Problems,* 59, 1996, 197–230, 218.
29 J. M. Henckaerts and L. Doswald-Beck (eds), *Customary International Humanitarian Law,* Vol 1: Rules, Cambridge: Cambridge University Press, 2005, Rule 159. Volume Two of this study looks at 'Practice' and discusses six treaties (Additional Protocol II, plus five peace treaties), which provide for amnesty; and 17 amnesty laws from 11 states. In addition, it looks to other sources of practice including national legal provisions governing the grant of amnesty, military manuals, national and international case law and UN resolutions. However, in each case, the number of the sources employed is comparatively small.
30 L. Mallinder, *Amnesty, Human Rights and Political Transitions: Bridging the Peace and Justice Divide,* Oxford: Hart Publishing, 2008, esp. Ch. 3.
31 Additional Protocol II, Art. 1.
32 Ratner, 'The Schizophrenias of International Criminal Law', 239–40.
33 Ibid., 239–40.
34 Convention against Torture and Other Cruel, Inhuman or Degrading Treatment, 1465 UNTS 85 (CAT), Art. 4.

35 Ibid., Art. 1(1).
36 Convention against Torture, Art. 6(2).
37 Ibid., Art. 7(1).
38 D. F. Orentlicher, 'Settling Accounts: The Duty to Prosecute Human Rights Violations of a Prior Regime', *Yale Law Journal,* 100, 1991, 2537–615, 2604.
39 International Convention for the Protection of All Persons from Enforced Disappearance, UN Doc. A/61/488 (20 December 2006), Art. 2.
40 Ibid., Art. 11.
41 Ibid.
42 Ibid., Art. 7(2).
43 A. O'Shea, *Amnesty for Crime in International Law and Practice,* The Hague: Kluwer, 2002, p. 205.
44 C. P. Trumbull, 'Giving Amnesties a Second Chance', *Berkeley Journal of International Law*, 25, 2007, 283–345, 296–9.
45 Prosecutor *v.* Duško Tadić, Case No. IT-94-1-I, Opinion and Judgement (7 May 1997); Prosecutor *v.* Duško Tadić, Case No. IT-94-1-A, Judgement (15 July 1999).
46 D. Robinson, 'Defining "Crimes against Humanity" at the Rome Conference', *American Journal of International Law,* 93, 1999, 43–57, 45–6.
47 Prosecutor *v.* Duško Tadić, Case No. IT-94-1-I, Opinion and Judgement (7 May 1997); Prosecutor *v.* Duško Tadić, Case No. IT-94-1-A, Judgement (15 July 1999).
48 Drumbl, 'Toward a Criminology of International Crime', 270.
49 US Delegation to Preparatory Commission, *State Practice regarding Amnesties and Pardons*, 1997.
50 N. Roht-Arriaza, 'Amnesty and the International Criminal Court', in D. Shelton (ed.), *International Crimes, Peace and Human Rights: The Role of the International Criminal Court*, Ardsley: Transnational Publishers, 2000.
51 W. A. Schabas, *An Introduction to the International Criminal Court,* Cambridge: Cambridge University Press, 2007, p. 87.
52 K. A. Rodman, 'Is Peace in the Interests of Justice? The Case for Broad Prosecutorial Discretion at the International Criminal Court', *Leiden Journal of International Law*, 22, 2009, 99–126, 103.
53 See note 50.
54 Some commentators also highlight Article 16 that allows the UN Security Council to defer ICC investigations for renewable 12-month periods and Article 20 that relates to the principle of *non bis in idem*. However, as the arguments for amnesty recognition are weaker under these articles, they are not discussed here.
55 D. Robinson, 'Serving the Interests of Justice: Amnesties, Truth Commissions and the International Criminal Court', *European Journal of International Law*, 14, 2003, 481–505, 500.
56 Cited in C. Villa-Vicencio, 'Why Perpetrators Should Not Always Be Prosecuted: Where the International Criminal Court and Truth Commissions Meet', *Emory Law Journal,* 49, 2000, 205–22, 222.
57 Rodman, 'Is Peace in the Interests of Justice?', 103.
58 M. R. Brubacher, 'Prosecutorial Discretion within the International Criminal Court', *Journal of International Criminal Justice,* 2, 2004, 71–95, 76. In the event that the ICC OTP launches an investigation but subsequently determines that there is no reasonable basis to proceed, the Pre-Trial Chamber may review the decision to end the investigation.
59 Rome Statute, 2187 UNTS 90, Art. 53(1)(c).
60 See, e.g. T. Hethe Clark, Note, 'The Prosecutor of the International Criminal Court, Amnesties, and the "Interests of Justice": Striking a Delicate Balance', *Washington University Global Studies Law Review*, 4, 2005, 389–414; C. Gallavin, 'Article 53 of the Rome Statute of the International Criminal Court: In the Interests of Justice?', *King's College Law Journal*, 14, 2004, 179–98.
61 ICC, *Draft Regulations of the Office of the Prosecutor*, 3 June 2003, 47.
62 Unger and Wierda, 'Pursuing Justice in Ongoing Conflict', p. 270.
63 ICC, *Second Report of the Prosecutor of the International Criminal Court, Mr Luis Moreno Ocampo, to the UN Security Council pursuant to UNSC 1593 (2005)*, 13 December 2005, 6.
64 OTP, *Policy Paper on the Interests of Justice*, 2007, 1.
65 Ibid.
66 Ibid., 4.
67 See, e.g. K. A. Rodman, 'Darfur and the Limits of Legal Deterrence', *Human Rights Quarterly,* 30, 2008, 529–60; O. S. Liwerant, 'Mass Murder: Discussing Criminological Perspectives', *Journal of International Criminal Justice,* 5, 2007, 917–39; F. Neubacher, 'How Can It Happen that Horrendous State Crimes Are

Perpetrated? An Overview of Criminological Theories', *Journal of International Criminal Justice*, 4, 2006, 787–99.

68 See note 64.

69 Ibid., 8.

70 Ibid.

71 Ibid.

72 Lomé Accord, Art. IX (1999).

73 Schabas, 'Amnesty, the Sierra Leone Truth and Reconciliation Commission and the Special Court for Sierra Leone', 148–9.

74 W. A. Schabas, *The UN International Criminal Tribunals: The Former Yugoslavia, Rwanda and Sierra Leone*, Cambridge: Cambridge University Press, 2006, pp. 36–7.

75 Report of the Secretary-General on the Establishment of a Special Court for Sierra Leone, UN Doc. S/2000/915, para. 24.

76 Ibid.

77 Reproduced in UN Department of Peacekeeping Operations, *Disarmament, Demobilization and Reintegration of Ex-Combatants in a Peacekeeping Environment: Principles and Guidelines* (UN 1999) Annex 2B, 109.

78 Loi relative à la mise hors-la-loi de la clique du Kampuchea democratique, (1994) (Cambodia), Art. 5.

79 Ibid., Art. 6.

80 R. C. Slye, 'The Cambodian Amnesties: Beneficiaries and the Temporal Reach of Amnesties for Gross Violation of Human Rights', *Wisconsin International Law Journal*, 22, 2004, 99–123, 101.

81 Group of Experts for Cambodia, Report of the Group of Experts for Cambodia Established Pursuant to General Assembly Resolution 52/135, para. 219.

82 Draft Tribunal Memorandum of Understanding between the United Nations and the Royal Government of Cambodia, Art. 9.

83 S. Linton, 'New Approaches to International Justice in Cambodia and East Timor', *International Review of the Red Cross*, 84, 2002, 93–119, 98.

84 The Law on the Establishment of the Extraordinary Chambers in the Courts of Cambodia for the Prosecution of Crimes Committed During the Period of Democratic Kampuchea, 2001.

85 Linton, 'New Approaches to International Justice in Cambodia and East Timor', 97.

86 Agreement between the UN and the Royal Government of Cambodia Concerning the Prosecution Under Cambodian Law of Crimes Committed During the Period of Democratic Kampuchea, 2003, Art. 11(1).

87 Ibid.

88 Freeman, *Necessary Evils*, p. 50.

89 Ibid., para. 155.

90 R. O'Brien, 'Amnesty and International Law', *Nordic Journal of International Law*, 74, 2005, 261–78, 266.

91 Freeman, *Necessary Evils*, p. 51.

92 See Letter from Radovan Karadžić to the Pre-Trial Chamber, IT-95-5/18-I (31 July 2008) 1. Karadžić had also intermittently proclaimed that this immunity is also attributable to the ICTY itself.

93 Prosecutor *v.* Radovan Karadžić, Decision on the Accused's Second Motion for Inspection and Disclosure: Immunity Issue, Case No. IT-95-5/18-PT (17 December 2008), para. 17.

94 Ibid., para. 25.

95 B. Brockman-Hawe,' International Criminal Tribunal for the former Yugoslavia *Decision on the Accused's Second Motion for Inspection and Disclosure : Immunity Issue* Trial Chamber Decision of 17 December 2008', *International and Comparative Law Quarterly*, 58, 2009, pp. 726–40, p. 729.

96 Ibid.

97 Prosecutor *v.* Radovan Karadžić, Decision on Karadžić's Appeal of Trial Chamber's Decision on the Alleged Holbrooke Agreement, Case No. IT-95-5/18-AR.73/4 (12 October 2009), para. 52.

98 Ibid., para. 53.

99 S. Williams, 'Amnesties in International Law: The Experience of the Special Court for Sierra Leone', *Human Rights Law Review*, 5, 2005, pp. 271–309, p. 290.

100 Ibid., 292.

101 Decision on challenge to jurisdiction: Lomé Accord Amnesty in Prosecutor *v.* Morris Kallon, Brima Bazzy Kamara, SCSL-2004-15-PT-060-I, SCSL-2004-15-PT-060-II, Appeal (13 March 2004), para. 73.

102 Schabas, *The UN International Criminal Tribunals*, p. 338.
103 Decision on challenge to jurisdiction, para. 67.
104 S. M. Meisenberg, 'Legality of Amnesties in International Humanitarian Law: The Lomé Amnesty Decision of the Special Court for Sierra Leone', *International Review of the Red Cross*, 86, 2004, pp. 837–51, 845–6.
105 Decision on challenge to jurisdiction, para. 70.
106 Williams, 'Amnesties in International Law', 287–8.
107 Cited in Decision on challenge to jurisdiction, para. 71.
108 Ibid., para. 84.
109 Schabas, 'Amnesty, the Sierra Leone Truth and Reconciliation Commission and the Special Court for Sierra Leone', 162.
110 Williams, 'Amnesties in International Law', 293.
111 Separate opinion of Justice Robertson in *Prosecutor v. Allieu Kondewa*, Decision on Lack of Jurisdiction/Abuse of Process: Amnesty Provided by the Lomé Accord, filed under Case No. SCSL-2004-14-AR72(E) (25 May 2004), para. 30.
112 Ibid., para. 32.
113 *Prosecutor v. Augustine Gbao, Decision on Preliminary Motion on the Invalidity of the Agreement between the United Nations and the Government of Sierra Leone on the Establishment of the Special Court*, SCSL-04-15-PT-141 (25 May 2004), para. 8.
114 Ibid., para. 9.
115 Co-Investigating Judges of the Extraordinary Chambers in the Courts of Cambodia, *Provisional Detention Order against Ieng Sary*, Criminal Case File No 002/14-08-2006 (14 November 2007), para. 13.
116 Ibid., para. 11.
117 Freeman, *Necessary Evils*, p. 48.
118 See, e.g. Mallinder, *Amnesty, Human Rights and Political Transitions*, Ch. 3.
119 Slye, 'The Legitimacy of Amnesties under International Law and General Principles of Anglo-American Law', 175.
120 Ibid.
121 See note 118.
122 See, e.g. J. Sarkin, *Carrots and Sticks: The TRC and the South African Amnesty Process*, Antwerp: Intersentia, 2004.
123 However, following the completion of the South African TRC's work, only a few prosecutions have been pursued for individuals who did not apply for or were denied amnesty, and the introduction of amended prosecutorial guidelines in 2005 casts doubt on the extent to which the political will exists for further prosecutions.
124 S. 1767. XXXVIII. 'Simón, Julio Héctor y otros s/ privación ilegítima de la libertad, etc.—causa N° 17.768—' – CSJN – 14/06/2005 (Arg.).

27

International criminal law and human rights

Thomas Marguerritte

Introduction

International human rights law and international criminal law have developed steadily since 1945. If, as international rules, they are mainly for states' concern, they are particular branches of international law to be directed towards individuals. Indeed, international human rights law gives rights to individuals, whereas international criminal law sets rules that proscribe the commission of acts and provide for the punishment of individuals who breach these prohibitions.

International human rights law is composed of a range of texts of different legal effect and geographical application. The founding international human rights instrument is the Universal Declaration of Human Rights (UDHR) of 1948, which is not legally binding but is largely ratified and, therefore, represents the common attachment of the international community to the values it proclaims. Other fundamental sources of the development of human rights include the two covenants of 1966 and the regional Conventions,[1] as well as the case law of their respective control mechanisms.

International criminal law consists of all the crimes deemed to be international by reason of their sources and their punishment. Therefore, these sources are to be found in the statutes of the international criminal courts. The most important of these is the 1998 Rome Statute, establishing a permanent International Criminal Court (ICC). Other sources include treaty and customary law as well as the case law developed by the international criminal bodies.

Criminal law usually expresses what a given society forbids its members to do under the threat of punishment.[2] In so doing, it seeks the peaceful coexistence of human beings. Therefore, criminal law attempts to deter the commission of crime by promising punishment for offenders and to preserve social peace by organizing state justice in order to avoid private retaliation, which would perpetuate the cycle of violence.[3] The extent of the prohibitions criminal law provides depends on the values defended by society. Thus, criminal law is relative to a particular community and evolves according to its concerns. Affirming the existence of criminal law at the international level therefore assumes that common values are defended by the international community as a whole, justifying an international duty to punish offenders.[4]

Human rights law expresses humanist values and concerns for the well-being of every individual.[5] The international development of human rights gives them a universally shared dimension. Yet, the history of human rights shows a definite mistrust of the criminal justice system.[6] Indeed, many provisions in human rights instruments are devoted to the protection of individuals in criminal proceedings. Human rights and criminal law used to play a bittersweet symphony, since, on the one hand, the values set forth by human rights need criminal law to be efficiently protected and, on the other hand, human rights law remains quite suspicious towards its protector. Therefore, there are two kinds of values (those protected by the substantive criminal law and those protected by the criminal procedure) and one challenge (to find the balance between competing interests).

To describe and analyse this ambivalent relationship between international criminal law and human rights, the chapter is divided into two sections: the first section shows that international criminal law is a tool for protecting and enhancing human rights, whereas the second section discusses the question of the status of human rights in international criminal proceedings.

The role of international criminal law role in protecting and enhancing respect for human rights

The relationship between international criminal law and human rights

The Appeals Chamber of the International Criminal Tribunal for the former Yugoslavia (ICTY) noted the new trend of international law of considering people's well-being in the following words: 'A state-sovereignty-oriented approach has been gradually supplanted by a human-being-oriented approach. Gradually the maxim of Roman law *hominum causa omne jus constitutum est* (all law is created for the benefit of human beings) has gained a firm foothold in the international community as well'.[7] Although it was once proposed to directly criminalize gross violations of human rights at the international level, no international criminal courts and/or tribunals have express jurisdiction to punish human rights violations.[8] Moreover, the international criminal courts can only deal with crimes that involve the international criminal responsibility of individuals,[9] and most international human rights instruments provide only for state responsibility in the event of a violation of the rights they consecrate.[10] Therefore, international criminal law and international human rights law are not concerned with the same kind of accountability and thus seem to play two separate roles.

Nevertheless, international criminal law can and does protect human rights, to a certain extent. International criminal courts have jurisdiction over genocide, war crimes and crimes against humanity, which are referred to as the 'hard core' international crimes and usually result in gross and widespread violations of human rights.[11] It is interesting to note that the Genocide[12] and Torture[13] Conventions, which are considered human rights instruments,[14] expressly provide for the punishment of persons responsible for violation.[15] These conventions show the close linkage between human rights law and international criminal law. Cassese concluded that the common value connecting the crimes included in the ICTY Statute was 'human dignity',[16] which is without doubt also at the core of human rights. However, human rights are not absolute, and every instrument provides for derogations in case of war or emergency,[17] which are also the conditions in which international crimes are most likely to occur. However, some rights are deemed to be non-derogable.[18] They are at the top of the hierarchy of international obligations and part of the still controversial concept of *jus cogens*.[19] The comparison between the core international crimes and the core human rights clearly demonstrates that international criminal law protects values and interests common to human rights.[20]

War crimes are serious violations of international humanitarian law, which imposes obligations upon warring parties. While many consider that there are no real historical links between international humanitarian law and human rights considerations,[21] in 1872 Bluntschli expressed the opinion that 'there are natural human rights that are to be recognized in times of war as in peacetime'.[22] Though international humanitarian law should not be confused with international human rights law,[23] the International Court of Justice ruled that human rights apply to armed conflict[24] and identified three possible situations: 'some rights may be exclusively matters of international humanitarian law; others may be exclusively matters of human rights law; yet others may be matters of both these branches of international law'.[25] In addition, the Security Council stated explicitly that 'essential human and inalienable human rights should be respected even during the vicissitudes of war'.[26] Thus, in time of war, international human rights law applies concurrently with international humanitarian law, which is 'increasingly perceived as part of human rights law applicable in armed conflict'.[27]

Furthermore, international humanitarian law protects values that are common to human rights. The provisions of international humanitarian law clearly respond to human rights concerns. First, each of the four Geneva Conventions of 1949 contain an article defining 'grave breaches' of the Conventions, prohibiting wilful killing and torture or inhuman treatment and providing for individual criminal responsibility.[28] Moreover, Common Article 3 to the Geneva Conventions, which has been recognized as customary law and provides for the minimum treatment that must be afforded to protected persons in both international and non-international conflicts,[29] prohibits, among other things, 'violence to life and person, in particular murder of all kinds, mutilation, cruel treatment and torture', as well as 'the passing of sentences and the carrying out of executions without previous judgment pronounced by a regularly constituted court, affording all the judicial guarantees which are recognized as indispensable by civilized peoples'.[30] These provisions echo, in particular, the right to life, the right to be free from torture or inhuman treatment, and the right to fair trial guarantees, all of which are part of the core human rights from which no derogation is permitted under any circumstances.[31]

While crimes against humanity and war crimes were tied together and overlapped significantly at Nuremberg, the categories are now distinct, and the existence of an armed conflict is no longer a requirement for recognition of a crime against humanity.[32] While war crimes derive from international humanitarian law, crimes against humanity are rooted in international human rights law.[33] Crimes against humanity are defined as 'particularly odious offenses in that they constitute a serious attack on human dignity or a grave humiliation or degradation of one or more persons'.[34] Furthermore, these crimes, based on the dehumanization of victims, negate these victims' rights as human beings.[35] The notion of crimes against humanity itself implies that there are fundamental rights that are protected by criminal sanction at the international level.[36] As a result, the enumerated *actus reus* of crimes against humanity match the core human rights norms.[37]

Genocide, which is usually referred to as the crime of crimes, rests upon a particular legal regime derived from the 1948 Convention on the Prevention and Punishment of the Crime of Genocide.[38] This convention, which has been presented as the 'quintessential human rights treaty',[39] is a peculiar human rights instrument, as it does not provide for rights, but rather for the criminal responsibility of perpetrators and an adjudication of guilt before an international tribunal.[40] Therefore, there is no doubt that the rationale for including genocide as a separate offense in the statutes of the international criminal tribunals was to allow for the punishment of the grave violations of human rights that are involved in the commission of the crime of genocide.

However, it is clear that all violations of human rights are not international crimes. The scope of international criminal law is limited to massive human rights violations.[41] Indeed, the condition that crimes against humanity must be widespread or systematic and the very nature of the crime of genocide demonstrate that the law retains a quantitative approach. Moreover, the ICC

Statute has added a new condition for war crimes, providing that the court has jurisdiction over such crimes 'when committed as part of a plan or policy or as part of a large-scale commission of such crimes'.[42] Even if this condition does not affect the definition of the crime itself, being solely a limitation upon the court's jurisdiction,[43] it shows that the international prosecutions will be limited to the most severe violations of human rights.

Moreover, all international crimes are not violations of human rights. Human rights law limits a state's actions with respect to the people under its jurisdiction,[44] while international criminal law relates to what individuals cannot do to their fellow human beings in certain circumstances. A violation of human rights implies the commission of an act that results in the abuse of a fundamental right. However, an international crime does not necessitate the actual realization of the intended crime—mere attempt is a punishable offense.[45] Furthermore, the mere occurrence of a human rights violation does not establish that the violation constitutes a crime, as intent is also necessary for a criminal conviction.[46] Therefore, international criminal law affords protection to human rights, but only in a limited manner.

Developing international criminal courts: the enhancement of human rights protection

According to the traditional approach of international law, the task of giving effect to the provisions of international human rights law and international criminal law is primarily a duty for states.[47] On the one hand, international criminal law rests upon the principle *aut judicare aut dedere*, which imposes a duty for states to prosecute or extradite those suspected of committing international crimes.[48] On the other hand, international human rights law makes it compulsory for states to take measures to prevent human rights violations, and criminal law can or even must, be used to this end.[49] This tendency of human rights law towards using criminal law as tool to enforce human rights has led to the conclusion that modern human rights law has become 'criminalist'.[50] There is a general duty for states to prevent and punish human rights violations that occur on their territory.[51] However, failure to investigate such violations results solely in state responsibility.[52]

In addition, international crimes are usually committed on a large scale and either with state agreement or by persons the state cannot control. These crimes are rarely investigated and prosecuted at the domestic level.[53] As a result, perpetrators go unpunished, which takes away any potential deterrent effect of international criminal law and any positivity of human rights. In order to prevent the commission of massive human rights violations, it is necessary to put an end to impunity.[54] Despite some attempts to develop states' jurisdiction beyond their national borders,[55] the traditional enforcement mechanisms of international criminal law have been unable to prevent and punish gross human rights violation. The former United Nations High Commissioner for Human Rights, José Ayala Lasso, duly noted that a 'person stands a better chance of being tried and judged for killing one human being than for killing 100,000'.[56]

In 1930, Dumas wrote that it is the responsibility of national jurisdictions to determine criminal responsibility. However, he noted that to avoid denial of justice, there must be an international court to determine individual and state responsibility and to judge cases on appeal in order to harmonize the interpretation of the law.[57] While this vision is still far from the reality, the international criminal tribunals, including the ICC, are products of the human movement.[58] Indeed, the ICTY and the International Criminal Tribunal for Rwanda (ICTR) are situated in the context of the principles and goals of the United Nations, among which are the promotion and encouragement of the respect for human rights and fundamental freedoms for all.[59] The Rome Statute provides for the creation of a permanent international criminal court with the power to try and punish the perpetrators of the most serious violations of human rights when national justice fails at this task.[60] The development of human rights law has made massive violations still more intolerable for the international community and has contributed to the development of international criminal tribunals.[61] Annan, when Secretary-General of the United Nations, made the following statement about the ICC,

> In the prospect of an international criminal court lies the promise of universal justice [...] to ensure that no ruler, no state, no junta and no army anywhere can abuse human rights with impunity. Only then will the innocents of distant wars and conflicts know that they, too, may sleep under the cover of justice; that they, too, have rights, and that those who violate those rights will be punished.[62]

Such a statement makes clear that the rationale behind the creation of the ICC is to put an end to impunity for major human rights offenders and, additionally, to enhance the protection of fundamental rights. But while the *ad hoc* tribunals have primacy over national legal systems, the ICC is complementary to national courts.[63] This choice reflects the central role of the states in the prosecution of international crimes. Instituting a permanent mechanism for the prosecution of international crimes is a major step towards obtaining a real deterrent effect of international criminal law and better respect for human rights.[64] Indeed, the concern of the ICC for victims' rights brought the court one step closer to becoming a human rights court, as the court can be seen as fulfilling the effective remedy requirement set down in Article 8 of the UDHR. Some even consider that state cooperation with the ICC is a way of discharging the state's obligations under international human rights law.[65]

Human rights in international criminal procedure

Nowadays, the degree of a society's civilisation is partially assessed in regards to the degree of respect and protection afforded to human rights in its criminal proceedings.[66] The history of human rights shows their propensity for protecting defendants facing criminal punishment.[67] Many fundamental rights are directed at achieving such protection, and most people agree with the principle of criminal justice expressed by Blackstone that it is better to let 10 guilty persons walk free than to let one innocent person suffer.

However, in practice, most people are stunned by the idea of granting rights to those accused of committing the most awful crimes and violating the fundamental rights of their victims. When discussing the fate of Nazi leaders following World War II, many, including the then British Prime Minister Churchill favored the recourse to summary justice.[68] The very same Churchill who, a few years later in 1956, designated the *Magna Carta* as a law that even the King cannot break, showing the superiority of those rights over all other considerations.[69] These contradictory positions indicate the difficulty of ensuring a fair trial for defendants in international criminal trials due to the nature and consequences of the crimes in question.

The charter of the International Military Tribunal (IMT) guaranteed fair trial rights for the accused.[70] Subsequently, fundamental rights for an individual interacting with the criminal justice system were enshrined in the UDHR,[71] the International Covenant on Civil and Political Rights (ICCPR)[72] and the regional human rights instruments.

Applicability of human rights to international criminal procedure

In his report on the creation of the ICTY, the then Secretary-General of the United Nations, noted that 'it is axiomatic that the International Tribunal must fully respect internationally recognized standards regarding the right of the accused' and expressed the view that these standards are to be found in Article 14 of the ICCPR.[73] The statutes of both *ad hoc* tribunals provide similar guarantees and rights for accused persons[74]—protections derived from Article 14 of the ICCPR. However, the covenant is only binding for states parties that have signed and ratified it, and thus not for the tribunals or the United Nations. Indeed, nothing in the UN Charter limits the powers of the Security Council acting under Chapter VII, and no court has the authority to control the exercise of these powers.[75] However, the promotion of human rights is one of the goals of the United Nations.[76] Therefore, if the Security Council were using its powers to derogate from internationally recognized human rights, it would undermine the credibility of the message sent to the world and detract from one of its foundations. Thus, the United Nations should respect internationally recognized human rights when it acts.[77]

Nevertheless, as already mentioned, human rights are not absolute and can be derogated in case of war or emergency threatening the life of the nation. Interestingly, while regional instruments provide that the fair trial guarantees are not derogable, the ICCPR does not provide the same level of protection.[78] However, it would be abusive to derogate from fair trial guarantees if, while the exceptional circumstances may have existed at the time the crimes were committed, the trial itself takes place in a time of peace. Moreover, these rights are clearly included in those core human rights that must be respected in all circumstances. Indeed, Common Article 3 of the Geneva Conventions prohibits convictions and executions without 'previous judgment pronounced by a regularly constituted court, affording all the judicial guarantees which are recognized as indispensable by civilized people'[79]—guarantees that are reiterated in the two Additional Protocols of 1977.[80]

Therefore, those rights apply in proceedings before the international criminal tribunals, as they do in all criminal proceedings. Judges at the international tribunals must ensure that a fair trial is given to any accused brought before them.[81] As a result, the statutes and the rules of procedure and evidence provide for a series of rights for individuals suspected[82] or accused of committing crimes within the jurisdiction of the tribunals. However, these guarantees must be interpreted in light of the most advanced standard available. Indeed, human rights evolve rapidly and the protection afforded to a defendant at the national and regional level becomes more elaborate. Therefore, it becomes necessary to determine the legal sources that the international tribunals must apply. Unlike the ICC, the statutes of the *ad hoc* tribunals do not contain an article defining the applicable law.[83] If international treaty law does not apply to any international criminal courts according to the *res inter alios acta* principle, general international law is a source of law for the international courts. The ICTR, in interpreting the rights of the accused, determined that it had to apply the ICCPR as part of general international law, but it did not have to apply the regional treaties or the case law developed by regional human rights bodies. This case law might be useful and persuasive in the application and interpretation of the law, but it is not binding on the tribunal.[84] The ICTY, dismissing the relevance of the European Court of Human Rights (ECHR) case law to the tribunal's work, maintained that the tribunal was 'in certain respects, comparable to a military tribunal, which often has limited rights of due process and more lenient rules of evidence'.[85] Therefore, the international tribunals remain free to develop their own interpretations of the principles relative to the protection of the accused in international proceedings.

The ICC Statute, contrary to the ICTY and ICTR, provides for much more detailed rights for suspects and defendants.[86] However, it is not certain that Article 21 of the Rome Statute drastically improves the protection afforded an accused in proceedings before the Court. Indeed, it does not specifically recognize any international human rights instruments as sources of law. It states only that 'the application and interpretation of law pursuant to this article must be consistent with internationally recognized human rights'. The Rome Statute makes no reference to a particular instrument, making the situation the same as that before the other international criminal tribunals. Human rights are normally interpreted expansively using a teleological method.[87] However, in the Lubanga case, Pre-Trial Chamber I ruled that Article 21(3) mandates that the court apply and interpret law in a manner consistent with internationally recognized human rights.[88] In a subsequent decision, the same chamber ruled that the reference to minimum guarantees in Article 67(1) means that sometimes the court must go beyond the terms of Article 67.[89] In both decisions, ECHR and Inter-American Court of Human Rights precedents were used to support the ruling. Nevertheless, it remains difficult to assert that the international tribunals afford the highest standard of protection for the accused. Because the tribunals are free to pick and choose what provisions of human rights law they must apply, the protection of criminal defendants in international trials is said to be lagging behind.[90]

Application of human rights rules and principles: selected issues

Cassese compared the international criminal tribunals to giants without limbs, who need the prosthetics of national authorities to work.[91] He stated that the rules of procedure regarding the rights of the accused must be interpreted in light of the most detailed human rights rules, but also must take into account the peculiarities of international trials.[92] Therefore, the rights of the accused have been adapted to the context of international trials. Judge Shahabuddeen concluded that there are fewer guarantees for the defense at the international criminal tribunals than those afforded in domestic trials.[93] While those rights have been developed primarily with a view towards national application, some adaptations made by the international criminal courts appear disproportionate. It is beyond the scope of this chapter to detail every single right deriving from the notion of a fair trial, but the remainder of this chapter will discuss certain significant issues and refer to relevant, and more detailed, texts related to the rights of the accused in criminal proceedings.[94]

The rights of the accused derive from one basic principle of criminal law: the presumption of innocence. This principle, stated in Article 14(2) of the ICCPR, is recognized in Article 66 of the Rome Statute, Article 20(3) of the ICTR Statute, and Article 21(3) of the ICTY Statute. It imposes a duty on public authorities to refrain from 'prejudging of the outcome of a trial'.[95] The ECHR has ruled that this prohibition is directed to public officials and that 'what is excluded is a formal declaration that somebody is guilty'.[96] However, this interpretation was made bearing in mind that it would be applied at the national level. It becomes quite difficult to transpose this to the international order. One issue would be determining who qualifies as a public official in international law. Even assuming the main organs of the United Nations could be considered public officials, the next issue that arises is the consideration of a Security Council resolution affirming the responsibility of one or several persons with respect to an international crime. For example, in Resolution 1034, it 'takes note that the [ICTY] issued [...] indictments against the Bosnian Serb leaders Radovan Karadzić and Ratko Mladić for their direct and individual responsibilities for the atrocities committed against the Bosnian Muslim population of Srebrenica'.[97] This has been viewed as violating the presumption of innocence, as it did not use the term 'alleged' when dealing with the responsibility of the two Bosnian Serb Leaders.[98] It is usually hard to prevent prejudgment for these kinds of crimes. International society, the states, the victims and the press usually designate the persons responsible before any tribunal has a chance to rule on the merits of the case. Yet, at the national level, it is always possible for an accused to obtain redress for statements violating the presumption of innocence by using civil actions such as libel. However, such a remedy does not exist at the international level.

Most of the discussion related to the presumption of innocence at the international criminal tribunals has dealt with the question of provisional release and has specifically dealt with the practice of those tribunals concerning detention on remand. Indeed, all human rights instruments make clear that the accused has the right to be released pending trial as a corollary to the presumption of innocence.[99] As a result, mandatory pre-trial detention is contrary to international human rights law.[100] But the international criminal courts' Rules of Procedure and Evidence (RPE) operate on the basis of detention being the rule and release being the exception.[101] Despite the fact that some judges opposed to this practice have stated that provisional release must be the rule and detention should be maintained only in extreme cases,[102] it appears that once transferred to the international criminal courts, the accused remains in detention for the duration of the trial, provisional release being granted in only a few exceptions. As of today, at the ICTY, 38 accused are currently on trial, but only two have been granted provisional release[103] and at the ICTR, all of the 36 accused currently on trial or awaiting trial are detained.[104] At the ICC, of the five accused, only two have been granted provisional release.[105]

Provisional detention is not fundamentally contrary to human rights. Such detention can be justified in certain circumstances, such as when the accused is likely to abscond or when the accused attempts to interfere with investigations by altering evidence or pressuring witnesses.[106] The concept of provisional detention is that it must be ordered only when no other means, such as bail or restrictive measures, could ensure the same results. At the international criminal courts, the main argument against provisional release was the lack of cooperation from states and the risk that the accused would escape from trial by fleeing to a non-cooperative state.[107]

However, the basis for provisional detention evolves with the passing of time, and a justified detention might become arbitrary when its justifications cease to exist. For this reason, provisional detention must be reviewed on a regular basis.[108] Indeed, if the detention is based on the necessity to avoid any interference by the accused with investigations, pre-trial detention is no longer justified when the investigations are terminated.

Time is a core issue in international criminal proceedings. Indeed, both Articles 9(3) and 14(3)(c) of the ICCPR provide for time considerations. Even if the requirements set by the latter apply independently of those in Article 9, the expeditious trial requirement becomes even more fundamental when the accused is detained.[109] Article 14 does not state express time limits, but the overall length must be reasonable. The reasonableness is assessed on a case-by-case basis, taking into account the complexity of the case, the behavior of the accused and the authorities' diligence.[110] Even if it can legitimately be advanced that the cases dealt with at the international tribunals are particularly complex, and thus trials at the international level require more time than at the domestic level,[111] the overall length of trials at the international tribunals appears to exceed the requirement set out by international human rights law. Some delays can be attributed to the behavior of the accused, but in some cases delays are caused by the prosecutor or the tribunal itself.[112] As a result, most of the accused have spent several years in detention, and some have even died before a final judgment.[113]

The completion strategy of the international *ad hoc* tribunals does not improve the situation. Referrals of a case by the international tribunals to national jurisdictions pursuant to Article 11*bis* of the *ad hoc* tribunals' RPE increase the length of proceedings to the sole prejudice of the defendants, who remain in detention once their cases have been transferred to national courts, where the proceedings must begin anew. For example, the Mejakić and others case was referred to Bosnia and Herzegovina.[114] All of the accused had already been in custody for several years at the ICTY, but the national court refused to take into consideration the time spent in custody prior to the transfer of the case in examining the reasonableness of their provisional detention.[115] This is fundamentally contrary to human rights interpretation, which states that the period to be taken into consideration in assessing the reasonableness of the detention of the accused runs from the day of arrest.[116] Moreover, the argument of the constitutional court of Bosnia and Herzegovina based on the risk of the accused absconding[117] loses all relevance, as national courts have means to ensure the presence of the accused at trial. As a result, most of the accused spent several years in custody at the ICTY without being tried, some having surrendered voluntarily, and did not have a chance to be released once their cases transferred to national courts. Even if this amount of time is deducted from the ultimate sentence, the violation of their fundamental rights remains.

One final issue to be addressed here concerns the sentencing process, which has been called contrary to the basic fundamental rights of the accused.[118] It is a principle of criminal law that an accused should not be compelled to testify against himself.[119] However, another principle of criminal law expresses the need to ensure that the accused be given the chance to present all evidence that may exonerate or attenuate his responsibility. The fact that the adjudication of guilt and the sentencing of the accused are not separate hearings seems to violate this latter principle, as the accused is therefore unable to present evidence that would be incriminating as to his guilt but mitigating as to the sentence. Initially, separate hearings were held at the ICTY,[120] but the RPE has been modified so as to allow guilt and sentence to be determined in one single judgment.[121] The ICC Statute provides for a single judgment but allows for a separate hearing on sentencing if the defendant or the Prosecutor specially asks for it.[122] However, it is unclear that the rights of the accused include a right to separate hearings. Indeed, no consensus can be found in state practice. The choice between a single hearing or separate hearings depends mainly on the legal tradition considered. Common law countries favor separate hearings, but civil law tribunals usually rule on guilt and sentence in the same judgment. As far as international criminal tribunals are concerned, both legal traditions are relevant, even if it is assumed that the international criminal procedure is mainly accusatory. The ICC tries a new approach, combining both traditions on sentencing, but only the practice that will develop will show how sentencing hearings will be used.

Control and remedies for violations

Relationships with human rights bodies

Ensuring respect for human rights in international criminal proceedings is mainly a mission for the international criminal courts themselves. Indeed, human rights bodies clearly expressed the view that it is for national courts to apply human rights and that external control by human rights bodies must only come when domestic courts fail in that task.[123] Transposing this principle to the international level leads to the conclusion that the main bodies in charge of applying human rights to the criminal proceedings are the courts themselves. Nevertheless, the question remains whether an accused who has failed before the international criminal courts in challenging fundamental rights violations can file an application to an international human rights body.

Such recourse has been qualified as 'largely speculative'.[124] It is inconceivable for an individual to apply to one of these bodies to seek a remedy for a violation directly attributable to an international organization, as these mechanisms are directed only towards states parties to the relevant instrument.[125] The case law of the different human rights bodies makes clear that they have jurisdiction *rationae personae* over state parties only.[126]

However, some accused appearing before international tribunals have tried to petition human rights bodies against states that are parties to human rights instruments and cooperate with the international tribunals. Indeed, ECHR decided that states remained responsible for violations of the European Convention on Human Rights when they delegate or cooperate with international organizations.[127] However, every attempt to obtain redress before a human rights body for a violation of a fundamental right in international criminal proceedings has failed.

Milosević, while in custody at the UN detention facility in The Hague, filed an application against the Netherlands, arguing that, being the host state of the ICTY, it was responsible for the violations of his fundamental rights by this institution.[128] The application was dismissed on the ground that the applicant had not exhausted all local remedies before applying to the court. This procedural dismissal, applying the requirement of exhaustion of local remedies strictly, hardly conceals the difficulty and reticence of the ECHR when dealing with the question of the relations between state parties to the European Convention and the international criminal tribunals.

Another accused at the ICTY, Naletilić, tried to contest his transfer to the international tribunal. On this occasion, the ECHR recognized the distinction between the legal regime of extradition to a third state and surrender to the international tribunals. It concluded that the statute and the rules of procedure of the international tribunal were offering 'all the necessary guarantees including those of impartiality and independence'.[129] This case could be compared to the case law on the 'equivalent protection principle', which held that when an organization with which a state party is cooperating protects human rights, it is presumed that no violation occurred.[130]

A recent case, although decided in a different context, rejected the application of two applicants from Kosovo claiming that states parties to the ECHR that participated in the KFOR, the NATO force in Kosovo, should be held responsible for their actions and omissions in violation of the rights protected by the Convention. Interestingly, the ECHR did not reject the applications on the ground of a lack of jurisdiction *rationae loci*, but rather *rationae personae*, concluding as follows:

> Since operations established by UN Security Council Resolutions under Chapter VII of the UN Charter are fundamental to the mission of the UN to secure international peace and security and since they rely for their effectiveness on support from member states, the Convention cannot be interpreted in a manner which would subject the acts and omissions of Contracting Parties which are covered by UN Security Council Resolutions and occur prior to or in the course of such missions, to the scrutiny of the Court.[131]

Yet, as the ICTY and the ICTR were established by UN Security Council resolutions under Chapter VII, the general wording of this observation seems to set an exception to the principle of the survival of state party responsibility in the event of cooperation with an international organization in these circumstances and would prevent any accused from successfully petitioning the ECHR.

The question might be different concerning the ICC. Indeed, as it is established by Treaty, the traditional principle that states remain responsible for violations occurring in the course of their cooperation with an international organization would be applicable. However, the UN Security Council retains the power to refer a situation to the Court.[132] The situation would therefore be discriminatory between an accused whose case was referred by the Security Council, who would not enjoy recourse before the human rights bodies, and the other accused, who, theoretically, would have this opportunity. In this respect, as the ICC Statute and rules of procedure provide for the fair trial of the accused, the Naletilić case appears more satisfactory, as it provided for control, even if only formal control, by the ECHR of the state's obligations under the convention.

The referral of a case pursuant to Article 11*bis* of the RPE would also give the opportunity for the accused to file a petition before a human rights body to which the state to whom the case is referred is a party. For example, the above-mentioned Mejakić and others' case raises a *prima facie* violation of fundamental rights of the accused as to the length of their pre-trial detention and the overall length of their trial, and the constitutional court's final judgment opens the door to a petition before the ECHR against Bosnia.

Finally, as the international courts rely on states for the execution of sentences, the detainees being held in national prisons are therefore entitled to the protection of the international human rights instruments to which the state is party and they could also petition human rights bodies. States are free to welcome convicted persons into their territory and if no state is willing to do so, the Netherlands would automatically be in charge of assuming this role.[133] An interesting situation arose in the case of Ignace Bagilishema, who has been acquitted but has remained in custody because no state has been willing to grant asylum on its territory. The Working Group on Arbitrary Detention Report of the matter decided that 'it would remain competent, since the continued detention is attributable not to the International Criminal Tribunal, but to non-cooperation on the part of states' and that it will address the question of non-cooperation by states in the future.[134]

Remedies

All human rights instruments provide that a person whose fundamental rights have been violated is entitled to reparation.[135] Compensation usually takes the form of a sum of money, but the ECHR has ruled that the recognition of a violation might be just satisfaction to the injured party.[136] The ICCPR provides that compensation be given to a person who has been unlawfully detained or arrested[137] and further provides that conviction be reversed if it came about due to a miscarriage of justice.[138] Thus, the burden is on the defendant to prove that he is entitled to compensation.[139]

Neither the Statutes nor the RPE of the *ad hoc* tribunals address the question of compensation. The presidents of the two tribunals sent a letter to the Secretary-General of the United Nations requesting that the Security Council amend the Statutes in this respect.[140] However, no steps were taken on this issue.[141] Nevertheless, the Tribunals did not stand by and have taken the view that there exists an inherent right to reparation for persons whose rights have been violated by the tribunals.

The ICTR Appeals Chamber ruled that for the most serious violations that prevent the accused from having a fair trial, the remedy would be a release and a stay of proceedings.[142] However, for minor violations, the Court stated that the adequate remedies would be a sum of money in the event of an acquittal or a reduction of sentence in the event of conviction.[143] Barayagwiza, who has been convicted and sentenced to life imprisonment, has seen his sentence finally reduced to 32 years of imprisonment.[144] Those who have been acquitted have also sought compensation.[145] While the future of such requests has been quite uncertain because of the lack of special procedures and funding at the *ad hoc* tribunals, the Rwamakuba decision would become the framework for compensation procedures.[146] The Trial Chamber held that 'it is a fundamental principle of international human rights law that any violation of a human right entails the provision of an effective remedy'[147] and ordered the registrar to give an apology to the accused and to pay him $2,000 for the moral injury sustained as a result of the violation of his right to legal assistance.

The ICC Statute provides for compensation for persons unlawfully arrested or detained and for persons wrongfully convicted due to a miscarriage of justice and the Court is empowered to decide the merits of the claims.[148] Moreover, the RPE provides for the procedure to be followed to obtain compensation.[149] The Appeals Chamber went further and ruled that, in addition to compensation,

> where fair trial becomes impossible because of breaches of the fundamental rights of the suspect or the accused by his/her accusers, it would be a contradiction in terms to put the person on trial. [...] If a fair trial cannot be held, the object of the judicial process is frustrated and the process must be stopped.[150]

Hence, a stay of proceeding could also be granted as a remedy in the case of extreme violations of the fundamental rights of the suspect or accused.

Conclusion

Two approaches to the relationship between human rights and international criminal law can be envisaged. On the one hand, they can be seen as confronting each other, criminal law being a threat for individual rights. However, despite one strain of scholarship advocating perpetual balancing between confronting interests, human rights and international criminal law can also be seen as complementing each other. Indeed, human rights act as a shield for fundamental rights, whereas international criminal law is the sword to combat their violations.[151]

Thus, these two bodies of law can be seen as the two sides of the same coin in the search for ensuring respect for human dignity. International human rights law obliges states to give effect to human rights at both the domestic and international levels by discharging their obligations to judge international criminals and bring justice to victims. If states do not comply with this obligation, they can be, when applicable, internationally responsible before human rights bodies.[152] On the other hand, international criminal law gives horizontal effect to the core of human rights by providing for individual criminal responsibility and by establishing courts to ensure that justice is done. In so doing, international criminal courts address the question under the perspective of retribution, which human rights bodies cannot do.[153] But in so doing, international criminal trials must respect the rights of the accused to ensure that no further injustice occurs. Therefore, if 'the direct criminalization of human rights violations under international criminal law is the highest level of protection that a human right can achieve',[154] only respect for the human rights of defendants in international criminal trials can achieve the rightful aspiration of justice.

Notes

1 American Convention on Human Rights (Pact of San José), 22 November 1969, available at http://www.cidh.oas.org/Basicos/English/Basic3.American%20Convention.htm (12 March 2010); African Charter on Human and Peoples' Rights (Banjul Charter), 27 June 1981, OAU Doc. CAB/LEG/67/3 rev.5, 21 ILM 58 (1982), available at http://www.africa-union.org/root/AU/Documents/Treaties/Text/Banjul%20Charter.pdf (12 March 2010); Convention for the Protection of Human Rights and Fundamental Freedoms, 4 November 1950, available at http://www.echr.coe.int/NR/rdonlyres/D5CC24A7-DC13-4318-B457-5C9014916D7A/0/EnglishAnglais.pdf (12 March 2010).

2 K. Ambos, 'On the Rationale of Punishment at the Domestic and International Level', in M. Henzelin and R. Roth (eds), *Le droit pénal à l'épreuve de l'internationalisation*, Paris: LGDJ, 2002, p. 306.

3 S. Szureck, 'Historique: la formation du droit international pénal', in H. Ascensio, E. Decaux and A. Pellet, (eds), *Droit International Pénal*, Paris: Pedone, 2000, p. 11.

4 Ibid., p. 12.

5 J. Donnelly, *Universal Human Rights in Theory and in Practice*, Ithaca, NY: Cornell University Press, 2003, pp. 13–21.
6 W. A. Schabas, 'Droit pénal international et droit de l'homme: faux frères?', in Henzelin and Roth, (eds), *Le droit pénal à l'épreuve de l'internationalisation*, p. 165.
7 Tadić (IT-94-1-AR72), Decision on the Defence Motion for Interlocutory Appeal on Jurisdiction, 2 October 1995, para. 97.
8 O. De Frouville, 'Atteintes massives aux droits de l'homme', in Ascensio, Decaux and Pellet, (eds), *Droit International Pénal*, at 417–26 ; W. A. Schabas, *An Introduction to the International Criminal Court*, Cambridge: Cambridge University Press, 2007, p. 85.
9 According to the definition of international crimes in A. Cassese, *International Criminal Law,* Oxford Oxford: University Press, 2008, p. 11; see also G. Mettraux, 'Using Human Rights Law for the Purpose of Defining International Criminal Offences—The Practice of the International Criminal Tribunal for the former Yugoslavia', in Henzelin and Roth (eds), *Le droit pénal à l'épreuve de l'internationalisation*, pp. 189–90; Kunarać *et al.* (IT-96-23 & 23/1), 22 February 2001 para. 470 (in the field of international humanitarian law, and in particular in the context of international prosecutions, the role of the state is, when it comes to accountability, peripheral); see also, Furundžija (IT-95-17/1), 10 December 1998, para. 142;
10 Streletz, Kessler and Krenz *v.* Germany, ECHR 2001, para. 51 and paras 104–6.
11 P. Pazartzis, *La répression des crimes internationaux*, Paris: Pedone, 2008, pp. 24–6 ; L. Neel, 'La judiciarisation internationale des criminels de guerre: la solution aux violations graves du droit international humanitaire?', *Criminologie* 33, 2000, 176; on the distinction between international crimes and transnational crimes see Schabas, *An Introduction to the International Criminal Court*, p. 82.
12 Convention on the Prevention and Punishment of the Crime of Genocide, New York, 9 December 1948, available at http://www.un.org/millennium/law/iv-1.htm (30 September 2009).
13 Convention against Torture and Other Cruel, Inhuman or Degrading Treatment or Punishment, adopted and opened for signature, ratification and accession by General Assembly Resolution 39/46 of 10 December 1984, entry into force 26 June 1987, available at http://www2.ohchr.org/english/law/cat.htm (30 September 2009).
14 The preamble to the Torture Convention states as follows: 'Considering the obligation of States under the Charter, in particular Article 55, to promote universal respect for, and observance of, human rights and fundamental freedoms', ibid.; see also, D. F. Orentlicher, 'Settling Accounts: The Duty to Prosecute Human Rights Violations of a Prior Regime', *Yale Law Journal* 100, 1991, p. 2551.
15 Torture Convention, Art. 4; Genocide Convention, Art. 4, Art. 5, Art. 6.
16 A. Cassese, 'Le point de vue juridique', p. 71.
17 ICCPR Art. 4§1. ECHR Art. 15§1. AmCHR Art. 27§1.
18 ICCPR Art. 4§2. ECHR Art. 15§2. AmCHR Art. 27§2; see also Torture Convention, Art. 2(2), Genocide Convention, Art. 1.
19 F. Sudre, *Droit Européen et International des Droits de l'Homme*, Paris: PUF, 2006, p. 22 ; see also, M. J. Glennon, 'De l'absurdité du droit impératif (*jus cogens*)', *Revue Générale de Droit International Public* 110, 2006, p. 529.
20 C. C. Joyner, 'Redressing Impunity for Human Rights Violations: The Universal Declaration and the Search for Accountability', *Denver Journal of International Law & Policy* 26, 1998, p. 596.
21 C. Droege, 'Elective Affinities? Human rights and Humanitarian Law', *International Review of the Red Cross* 90, 2008, p. 503–4.
22 H. J. Heintze, 'On the Relationship between Human Rights Law Protection and International Humanitarian Law', *International Review of the Red Cross* 86, 2004, p. 790 (quoting Johann Caspar Bluntschli, *Das moderne Völkerrecht der civilisierten Staaten*, 3rd edn, Nördlingen: Beck, 1878, para. 529).
23 C. Bassiouni, 'International Recognition of Victims' Rights', *Human Rights Law Review* 6, 2006, p. 205; Mettraux, 'Using Human Rights Law for the Purpose of Defining International Criminal Offences', pp. 187–8.
24 Legality of the Threat or Use of Nuclear Weapons, Advisory Opinion, ICJ Rep. 1996, para. 25 (The Court observes that the protection of the International Covenant of Civil and Political Rights does not cease in times of war, except by operation of Article 4 of the Covenant whereby certain provisions may be derogated from in a time of national emergency); see also, Legal Consequences of the Construction of a Wall in the Occupied Palestinian Territory, Advisory Opinion, ICJ Rep. 2004, para. 106; Case concerning armed activities on the territory of the Congo (Democratic Republic of the Congo *v.* Uganda), ICJ Rep. 2005, para. 216.

25 Legal Consequences of the Construction of a Wall in the Occupied Palestinian Territory, para. 106.
26 Security Council Resolution 237, UN Doc. A/237/1967 (1967); see also, General Assembly Resolution 1312 (XIII), UN Doc. A/38/49 (1958), para. 7.
27 L. Doswald-Beck and S. Vité, 'International Humanitarian Law and Human Rights Law', *International Review of the Red Cross* 293, 1993, p. 94; see also Heintze, 'On the Relationship between Human Rights Law Protection and International Humanitarian Law', p. 791.
28 Convention (I) for the Amelioration of the Condition of the Wounded and Sick in Armed Forces in the Field, Geneva, 12 August 1949, Art. 50. Convention (II) for the Amelioration of the Condition of Wounded, Sick and Shipwrecked Members of Armed Forces at Sea, Geneva, 12 August 1949, Art. 51. Convention (III) relative to the Treatment of Prisoners of War, Geneva, 12 August 1949, Art. 130. Convention (IV) relative to the Protection of Civilian Persons in Time of War, Geneva, 12 August 1949, Art. 147.
29 Military and Paramilitary Activities on the territory of Nicaragua (Nicaragua *v.* USA), ICJ 1986, para. 218.
30 Geneva Conventions (I), (II), (III), (IV), Art. 3(1)(a), (b).
31 P. Akhavan, 'Reconciling Crimes against Humanity with the Laws of War, Human Rights, Armed Conflict, and the Limits of Progressive Jurisprudence', *Journal of International Criminal Justice* 6, 2008, 33–34; Heintze, 'On the Relationship between Human Rights Law Protection and International Humanitarian Law', p. 791.
32 P. Akhavan, 'Reconciling Crimes against Humanity with the Laws of War, Human Rights, Armed Conflict, and the Limits of Progressive Jurisprudence', p. 22 (notions of 'war crimes' and 'crimes against humanity' overlap and that most war crimes are also crimes against humanity, while many crimes against humanity are simultaneously war crimes); Tadić (IT-94-1-AR72), Decision on the Defence Motion for Interlocutory Appeal on Jurisdiction, 2 October 1995, para. 141; Tadić (IT-94-1-A), 15 July 1999, para. 251; Kordić *et al.* (IT-95-14/2-T), 26 February 2001, para. 23.
33 A. Cassese, *International Criminal Law*, pp. 98–9; see also P. Akhavan, 'Reconciling Crimes against Humanity with the Laws of War, Human Rights, Armed Conflict, and the Limits of Progressive Jurisprudence', p. 26.
34 A. Cassese, *International Criminal Law*, pp. 98–9; see also, Erdemović (IT-96-22-A), 7 October 1997, Joint Separate Opinion of Judge McDonald and Judge Vohrah, para. 21.
35 M. Delmas-Marty, 'Les crimes internationaux peuvent-ils contribuer au débat entre universalisme et relativisme des valeurs', in A. Cassese and M. Delmas-Marty (eds), *Crimes internationaux et Juridictions Internationales*, Paris: PUF, 2002, p. 67.
36 L. Neel, 'La judiciarisation internationale des criminels de guerre', p. 165.
37 Statute of the ICC, Art. 7.
38 Genocide Convention (1948).
39 Report of the International Law Commission on the work of its 49th session, UN Doc. A/52/10 (1997), para. 76; see also Kayishema and Ruzindana (ICTR-95-1-T), 21 May 1999, para. 88.
40 Genocide Conventions, Art. 4.
41 G. Werle, *Principles of International Criminal Law*, The Hague: TMC Asser Press, 2005, p. 41; J. Dugard, 'Bridging the Gap between Human Rights and Humanitarian Law: The Punishment of Offenders', *International Review of the Red Cross* 234.
42 Statute of the ICC, Art. 8.
43 W. A. Schabas, *An Introduction to the International Criminal Court*, p. 87.
44 ICCPR, Art. 2; ECHR, Art. 1; AmCHR (Pact of San José) Art. 1; African Charter on Human and Peoples Rights, Art. 2.
45 Statute of the ICC, Art. 25.
46 Kupreškić *et al.* (IT-95-16-T), 14 January 2000, para. 589.
47 S. Ratner and J. Abrams, *Accountability for Human Rights Atrocities in International Law: Beyond the Nuremberg Legacy*, Oxford: Oxford University Press, 2001, pp. 3–9.
48 J. Dugard, 'Bridging the Gap between Human Rights and Humanitarian Law', p. 445; see also C. Bassiouni and E. Wise, *Aut dedere aut judicare: A Duty to Extradite or Prosecute in International Law*, Dordrecht, 1995.
49 On the obligation for states to criminalize acts resulting in human rights violations at the domestic level, see G. Werle, *Principles of International Criminal Law*, p. 40; Orentlicher, 'Settling Accounts', p. 2571; Velasquez Rodriguez, Inter-American Court of Human Rights, Ser. C No. 4, 29 July 1988, para. 174; X and Y *v.* Netherlands (8978/80), ECtHR 26 March 1985.

50 'Pénalistes', Schabas, 'Droit pénal international et droit de l'homme: faux frères?', p. 165.
51 D. F. Orentlicher, 'Settling Accounts', p. 2551; X. Philippe, 'Sanctions for Violations of International Humanitarian Law: The Problem of the Division of Competences between National Authorities and between National and International Authorities', *International Review of the Red Cross* 90, 2008, p. 360.
52 See, for example, *Süheyla Aydin v. Turkey* (25660/94), ECtHR 24 May 2005.
53 W. A. Schabas, *An Introduction to the International Criminal Court*, p. 82; Dugard, 'Bridging the Gap between Human Rights and Humanitarian Law', p. 445.
54 W. A. Schabas, *An Introduction to the International Criminal Court*, p. 90
55 Such as universal jurisdiction, see A. Margolis, 'The Growing Dominion of Universal Jurisdiction', *International Bar News* 62, 2008, 8.
56 Available at http://untreaty.un.org/cod/icc/general/overview.htm (31 August 2009).
57 J. Dumas, *La responsabilité internationale des Etats, à raison de crimes et délits commis sur leur territoire au préjudice d'étranger*, Paris: Recueil Sirey, 1930, pp. 437–8.
58 C. C. Joyner, 'Redressing Impunity for Human Rights Violations', p. 621.
59 UN Charter, Art. 1§3 ; see also, J. P. Kot and E. Etchelar, 'Les droits de la défense devant le tribunal pénal pour l'ex-Yougoslavie: droits humanitaire contre droit de l'homme?', *Observateur des Nations Unies* 17, 2004, p. 107.
60 W. A. Schabas, *An Introduction to the International Criminal Court*, p. ix; see also L. Condorelli, 'La Répression des Crimes et la Cour Pénale Internationale: Une innovation majeure en droit international', in R. Ben Achour and S. Laghmani (eds) *Justice et Juridictions Internationales*, Paris: Pedone, 2000, p. 147;
61 A. Garapon, *Des crimes que l'on ne peut ni punir, ni pardonner*, Paris: Odile Jacob, 2002, p. 110.
62 Available at http://untreaty.un.org/cod/icc/general/overview.htm (29 August 2009).
63 Statute of the ICJ, Art. 1.
64 L. Neel, 'La judiciarisation internationale des criminels de guerre', p. 175.
65 A. L. Ciampi, 'State Cooperation with the ICC and Human Rights', in M. Politi and F. Gioia (eds), *The international Criminal Court and National Jurisdictions*, Aldershot: Ashgate Publishing Limited, 2008, p. 108.
66 J. A. Andrew, *Human Rights in Criminal Procedure: A Comparative Study*, Dordrecht: Kluwer Academic Publishers Group, 1982, p. 8.
67 W. A. Schabas, 'Droit pénal international et droit de l'homme: faux frères?', p. 171.
68 A. Kochavi, *Prelude to Nuremberg: Allied War Crimes Policy and the Question of Punishment*, Chapel Hill, NC and London: University of North Carolina Press, 1998, pp. 63–91.
69 The *Magna Carta* provides in Article 39 that no free man would be taken or imprisoned or deprived of his liberties except by legal judgment of his peers and by the law of the land, available at http://www.britannia.com/history/docs/magna2.html (12 March 2010); for the citation see: available at http://www.archives.gov/exhibits/featured_documents/magna_carta/ (12 March 2010)
70 Charter of the International Military Tribunal annexed to the agreement for the Prosecution and Punishment of the Major War Criminals of the European Axis signed in London on 8 August 1945, Art. 16. Available at http://www.icrc.org/IHL.NSF/FULL/350?OpenDocument (12 March 2010).
71 UDHR, Art. 10, Art. 1, available at http://www.un.org/en/documents/udhr/ (12 March 2010).
72 ICCPR, Art. 9, Art. 14, Art. 15, available at http://www2.ohchr.org/english/law/ccpr.htm (12 March 2009).
73 Secretary General's Report on Aspects of establishing an international tribunal for the prosecution of persons responsible for serious violations of international humanitarian law committed in the territory of the former Yugoslavia, UN DOC S/25704 (1993), para. 106.
74 Statute of the ICTY, Art. 21. Statute of the ICTR, Art. 20.
75 Legal Consequences for States of the Continued Presence of South Africa in Namibia (South West Africa) notwithstanding Security Council Resolution 276, ICJ rep. 1971, para. 89; *contra* see the interesting development in the Kadi and Yusuf case (T-306/02 and T-315/01), Court of First Instance of the European Communities, 21 September 2005 and Kadi and Yusuf (C-402/05 P), European Court of Justice, 3 September 2008.
76 UN Charter, Art. 1§3.
77 The court may also risk an adverse response and encounter difficulties in obtaining full cooperation from states and regional organizations. See, for example, the Kadi and Yussuf case, ibid.
78 ICCPR, Art. 4(2).
79 Geneva Conventions (I), (II), (III), and (IV), 12 August 1949, Common Art. 3(1)(d).

80 Protocols Additional to the Geneva Conventions of 12 August 1949, Protocol I, Art. 75 and Protocol II, Art. 6.
81 A. Cassese, 'Le point de vue juridique', p. 70.
82 Statute of the ICTY, Art. 18(3); Statute of the ICTR, Art. 17(3); Rules of Procedure and Evidence of the ICTR and of the ICTY, Art. 40, Art. 40bis.
83 Statute of the ICC, Art. 21.
84 Barayagwiza, (ICTR-97-19), Decision, 3 November 1999.
85 Tadić (IT-94-1), Decision on the Prosecutor's Motion Requesting Protective Measures forVictims and Witnesses, 10 August 1995, para. 28.
86 Statute of the ICC, Art. 55, Art. 66, Art. 67.
87 W. A. Schabas, 'Droit pénal international et droit de l'homme: faux frères?', p. 168.
88 Lubanga (ICC-01/04-01/06), 10 February 2006 para. 12.
89 Lubanga (ICC-01/04-01/06), 15 May 2006, para. 97.
90 G. S. Gordon, 'Toward an International Criminal Procedure: Due Process Aspirations and Limitations', 45 *Columbia Journal of Transnational law* 45, 2007, p. 58.
91 A. Cassese cited in G. Cohen-Jonathan, 'le Conseil de Sécurité et les droits de l'Homme', in *Le droit des organisations internationales, recueil d'études en mémoire de J. Schwob*, Bruxelles: Bruylant, 1997, p. 57.
92 A. Cassese, 'Le point de vue juridique', p. 74.
93 Kovacević (IT-97-24-AR73), separate opinion of Juge Shahabuddeen, 2 July 1998, p. 4.
94 See, for example, S. Zappalà, *Human Rights in International Criminal Proceedings*, Oxford: Oxford University Press, 2003.
95 General Comment on Article 14 ICCPR, UN Doc. A/39/40 (1984), pp. 143–7
96 Krause *v.* Switzerland, ECHR 1978, para. 37; Allenet de Ribemont *v.* France, ECHR 1995, paras 37–41.
97 Security Council Resolution 1034, UN Doc. S/1995/1034 (1995), para. 7
98 W. A. Schabas, *An Introduction to the International Criminal Court*, p. 205.
99 Concluding observations of the Human Rights Committee on Argentina, 3 November 2000, UN Doc. CCPR/CO/70/ARG, para. 10; Concluding observations of the Human Rights Committee on Italy, 24 April 2006, UN Doc. CCPR/C/ITA/CO/5, para. 14; see also, Wemhoff *v.* Germany, ECHR 1968, para. 12.
100 Ilijkov *v.* Bulgaria, ECHR 2001, paras 84–5.
101 RPE of the ICTY, Art. 65(A). RPE of the ICTR, Art. 65(A). RPE of the ICC, Art. 118.
102 Hadzihasanovic *et al.* (IT-01-47), Press release of 13 December 2001.
103 Key Figures of ICTY Cases, available at http://www.icty.org/sections/TheCases/KeyFigures#procoview (1 March 2010).
104 Liste et Situation des Détenus du TPIR available at http://www.ictr.org/FRENCH/index.htm (25 February 2010).
105 Jean-Pierre Bemba Gombo (ICC-01/05-01/08-475), Decision on the Interim Release of Jean-Pierre Bemba Gombo and Convening Hearings with the Kingdom of Belgium, the Republic of Portugal, the Republic of France, the Federal Republic of Germany, the Italian Republic, and the Republic of South Africa, 14 August 2009; Bahr Idriss Abu Garda was summoned to appear before the Court on 7 May 2009 and remained at liberty after his first appearance on 18 May 2009.
106 Michael and Brian Hill *v.* Spain (526/1993), Report of the Human Rights Committee, vol. 2, UN Doc. A/52/40, para. 12.3.
107 W. A. Schabas, *The UN International Criminal Tribunals*, Cambridge: Cambridge University Press, 2006, pp. 389–95.
108 Shafiq *v.* Australia (1324/2004), 31 October 2006, Report of the Human Right Committee, vol. 2, UN Doc. A/62/40, para. 7.2.
109 Report of the Human Rights Committee, vol. 1, UN Doc. A/62/40 (2007), para. 72.
110 Ibid.
111 R. Lawson, 'Provisional Release from Pre-trial Detention', in A. Klip and G. Sluiter (eds), *Annotated Leading Cases of International Criminal Tribunals, the ICTR 2003*, Antwerp-Oxford: Intersentia, 2007, p. 25.
112 See, for example, Barayagwiza (ICTR-97-19), Decision, 3 November 1999 para. 68. (Delay in presenting the accused to a judge due to Christmas recess.)
113 See the case against the former President of Serbia, S. Milosević, (IT-02-54); see also Schabas, *The UN International Criminal Tribunals*, pp. 521–2.

114 Mejakić *et al.* (IT-02-65-AR11bis.1), Decision on Joint Defence Appeal against Decision on Referral under Rule 11*bis*, 7 April 2006.
115 Constitutional Court of Bosnia and Herzegovina, Željko Mejakić and Dušan Fuštar (AP 2499/06), Appeal filed against the Ruling of the Court of Bosnia and Herzegovina, No. H-KRN-06/200 of 27 June 2006, and the Ruling of the Court of Bosnia and Herzegovina, No. H-KRN-06/200 of 9 June 2006, 20 October 2006;
116 Nevmerzhitsky *v*. Ukraine, ECHR 2005, para. 134.
117 Constitutional Court of Bosnia and Herzegovina, Appeal of Željko Mejakić and Dušan Fuštar (AP 2499/06), 20 October 2006, para. 19.
118 W. A. Schabas, *An Introduction to the International Criminal Court*, p. 305
119 ICCPR, Art. 14(3)(g).
120 Tadić (IT-94-1-T), 14 July 1997.
121 RPE of the ICTY, Art. 85, Art. 87. RPE of the ICTR, Art. 85, Art. 87.
122 Statute of the ICC, Art. 76(2), Art. 76(3).
123 See, for example, Bourdov *v*. Russia, ECHR 2002, para. 30.
124 W. A. Schabas, *The UN International Criminal Tribunals*, p. 542.
125 Optional Protocol to the ICCPR, Art. 1, available at http://www2.ohchr.org/english/law/ccpr-one.htm (12 March 2010). See also, European Convention on Human Rights, Art. 1.
126 Report of the Working Group on Arbitrary Detention, UN Doc. E/CN.4/2003/8 (2002), para. 60; Confédération Française Démocratique du Travail *v*. the European Communities and alternatively their member states, ECHR 1978.
127 Bosphorus Hava Yollari Tuzim Ve Ticaret AS (Bosphorus Airways) *v*. Ireland, ECHR 2005, paras 155–6.
128 Milosević *v*. The Netherlands, ECHR 2002.
129 Naletilić *v*. Croatia, ECHR 2000.
130 Bosphorus Hava Yollari Tuzim Ve Ticaret AS (Bosphorus Airways) *v*. Ireland, ECHR 2005, para. 165.
131 Behrami and Behrami *v*. France and Saramati *v*. France, Germany and Norway, ECHR 2007, para. 149.
132 Statute of the ICC, Art. 13(b).
133 W. A. Schabas, *An Introduction to the International Criminal Court*, p. 320.
134 Report of the Working Group on Arbitrary Detention, 16 December 2002, UN Doc. E/CN.4/2003/8, para. 52.
135 UDHR, Art. 8; ICCPR, Art. 2; AmDHR, Art. 10; ECHR, Art. 50.
136 See, for example, Kingsley *v*. the United Kingdom, ECHR 2002.
137 ICCPR, Art. 9(5).
138 ICCPR, Art. 14(6).
139 WBE *v*. the Netherlands, 23 October 1992, UN Doc. CCPR/C/46/D/432/1990, para. 65.
140 Letter dated 19 September 2000 from the Presidents of the International Criminal Tribunal for the former Yugoslavia, annexed to the Secretary-general Letter to the President of the Security Council of 26 September 2000, UN Doc. S/2000/904; Letter dated 26 September 2000 from the Presidents of the International Criminal Tribunal for Rwanda, annexed to the Secretary-General Letter to the President of the Security Council of 28 September 2000, UN Doc. S/2000/925.
141 S. Beresford, 'Redressing the Wrongs of the International Justice System: Compensation for Persons Erroneously Detained, Prosecuted or Convicted by the *ad hoc* Tribunals', *American Journal of International Law* 96, 2002, p. 628.
142 Barayagwiza (ICTR-97-19), Decision, 3 November 1999, paras 102–12; Barayagwiza (ICTR-97-19-AR72), Decision on the Prosecutor's Request for Review or Reconsideration, 31 March 2000, para. 74.
143 Barayagwiza (ICTR-97-19-AR72), Decision on the Prosecutor's Request for Review or Reconsideration, 31 March 2000, para. 75.
144 Nahimana, Barayagwiza, Ngeze (ICTR-99-52-T), Judgment and Sentence, 3 December 2003, paras 1106–7; Nahimana, Barayagwiza, Ngeze (ICTR-99-52-A), Appeal Judgment, 28 November 2007, para. 1097.
145 See, for example, Request by Zoran Kupreškić (IT-96-16-T), 21 December 2001.
146 Rwamakuba (ICTR-98-44C-T), Decision on Appropriate Remedy, 31 January 2007.
147 Ibid., para. 16.

148 Statute of the ICC, Art. 85.
149 RPE of the ICC, Art. 173, Art. 174, Art. 175.
150 Lubanga [ICC-01/04-01/06-772 (OA4)], 14 December 2006, para. 37.
151 C. Bassiouni, *Introduction au Droit Pénal International*, Bruxelles: Bruylant, 2002, p. 84.
152 See, for example, Khashiyev *v.* Russia, Isayeva, Yusopova and Bazayeva *v.* Russia, ECHR 2005.
153 X. Philippe, 'Sanctions for Violations of International Humanitarian Law', p. 367.
154 G. Werle, *Principles of International Criminal Law*, p. 41.

Conclusions

William A. Schabas and Nadia Bernaz

International criminal law has advanced in stages that have been punctuated by lengthy periods of inactivity. The initial stage lasted only a few years, following the First World War, and it generated meagre results. Perhaps that was to be expected, given the novelty of the idea and the potential encroachment that it suggested on state sovereignty. The second stage lasted about a decade, beginning as the Second World War drew to a close.

The third stage of international criminal law can be dated from the decision of the United Nations Security Council to establish the International Criminal Tribunal for the former Yugoslavia. The idea had been quietly reviving during the 1980s from its long hibernation, spurred on by emerging doctrines in the area of human rights about accountability and impunity. When the Yugoslavia tribunal was established, the United Nations International Law Commission had nearly completed its ambitious task of preparing the draft statute of a permanent international criminal court.

Progress in the establishment of the institutions of international criminal justice moved at a dizzying pace. Within 10 years from the creation of the International Criminal Tribunal for the former Yugoslavia, there were three *ad hoc* tribunals, consuming a huge portion of the United Nations' budget. Judges of the International Criminal Court were already on the job, and the Office of the Prosecutor was identifying potential targets for its first investigations. By 2010, as the *ad hoc* tribunals were nearing the end of their activities, the International Criminal Court was completing its first trial. Yet a fourth *ad hoc* tribunal, for Lebanon, was awaiting its first indictments.

The three *ad hoc* tribunals can be said to have fulfilled their promise. They were more expensive than ever imagined, and they lasted much longer than expected. But each of the three—for the former Yugoslavia, Rwanda and Sierra Leone—brought to justice the leading suspects. They held credible trials, in which the rights of the accused were respected. They acquitted a few of the accused, and delivered stern sentences to those who were convicted of genocide, crimes against humanity and war crimes.

But in light of the history of the discipline, dating back to 1919, is there any certainty that international criminal law will continue to grow? Is a new downturn to be expected, like those that followed the first two stages in the development of this field?

To be sure, international criminal justice is a costly business, although governments seem willing to foot the bill as long as results are delivered. Yet what are those results? The great enigma remains the relationship between justice and peace. Criminal prosecution is often said to contribute to international (and internal) peace. Accountability for atrocities is held out as a necessary ingredient in processes of democratic transition. Without it, conflict is doomed to return.

Can we be sure? Probably we will never be able to prove, to the satisfaction of sceptical social scientists, that justice promotes peace. There is much empirical proof that the threat or promise of prosecution sometimes prevents conflict. There is also some evidence to show that it can help to end wars more quickly. The only way to confirm these observations is to do more of it. To the extent that confidence is maintained in the contribution of justice from what is essentially a utilitarian perspective, any prediction of a chilling of our enthusiasm for international criminal law would seem to be premature.

Vigilance, however, is of primordial importance. Attention must be paid to the efficiency of international justice institutions. Costs must be monitored in order to ensure value for the investment. Above all, the complex purposes of international criminal law, which involve a mix of both peace and justice, must never be lost from sight.

Index

FSC
www.fsc.org
MIX
Papier | Fördert
gute Waldnutzung
FSC® C083411

Kolibri 360 GmbH
Ferdinand-Jühlke-Straße 7
99095 Erfurt, Deutschland
produktsicherheit@kolibri360.de